McDougal Littell
CLASSZONE

Visit classzone.com and get connected.

ClassZone resources provide instruction, practice and learning support for students and parents.

Geography

- Brings geography to life with interactive activities and visuals
- Provides interactive maps, charts, and graphs

Current Events

- Takes you beyond the text and keeps you up-to-date on world events
- Reflects the most recent political, economic, and social issues
- Provides weekly current events quizzes to help check comprehension

Interactive ⊕ Review

- Provides a unique way to review key concepts and events
- Includes geography games, crossword puzzles, and matching games
- Helps ensure lesson comprehension through graphic organizers, animated flipcards, and review/study notes

Research and Writing

- Includes research links chapter resources, and state-specific resources
- Provides support for your writing assignments through complete writing models, rubrics, and research guides

Access the online version of your textbook at classzone.com

Your complete text, along with animated maps, charts and infographics, is available for immediate use!

McDougal Littell
Where Great Lessons Begin

McDougal Littell

World Cultures
and
GEOGRAPHY

Sarah Bednarz

Marci Smith Deal

Inéz Miyares

Donna Ogle

Charles White

CONSULTANTS

Senior Consultants

Sarah Witham Bednarz is associate professor of geography at Texas A&M University, where she has taught since 1988. She earned a Ph.D. in Educational Curriculum and Instruction specializing in geography in 1992 from Texas A&M University and has written extensively about geography literacy and education. Dr. Bednarz was an author of *Geography for Life: National Geography Standards, 1994*. In 2005 she received the prestigious George J. Miller Award from the National Council for Geographic Education.

Marci Smith Deal is the K–12 Social Studies Curriculum Coordinator for Hurst-Euless-Bedford Independent School District in Texas. She received the 2000 Distinguished Geographer Award for the State of Texas, and was one of the honorees of the 2001 National Council for Geographic Education Distinguished Teacher Award. She has served as president for the Texas Council for Social Studies Supervisors and as vice-president for the Texas Council for Social Studies. She currently serves as a teacher consultant for National Geographic Society.

Inés M. Miyares is professor of geography at Hunter College-City University of New York. Born in Havana, Cuba, and fluent in Spanish, Dr. Miyares has focused much of her scholarship on Latin America, immigration and refugee policy, and urban ethnic geography. She holds a Ph.D. in geography from Arizona State University. In 1999 Dr. Miyares was the recipient of the Hunter College Performance Excellence Award for excellence in teaching, research, scholarly writing, and service. She has just published a co-edited book on contemporary ethnic geographies in the United States.

Copyright © 2008 McDougal Littell, a division of Houghton Mifflin Company. All rights reserved.

Maps on pages A14–A37 © Rand McNally & Company. All rights reserved.

Acknowledgments for copyrighted material are on pages R109–R116 and constitute an extension of this page.

Warning: No part of this work may be reproduced or transmitted in any form or by any means, electronic or mechanical, including photocopying and recording, or by any information storage or retrieval system without the prior written permission of McDougal Littell unless such copying is expressly permitted by federal copyright law. With the exception of not-for-profit transcription in Braille, McDougal Littell is not authorized to grant permission for further uses of copyrighted selections reprinted in this text without the permission of their owners. Permission must be obtained from the individual copyright owners as identified herein. Address inquiries to Supervisor, Rights and Permissions, McDougal Littell, P.O. Box 1667, Evanston, IL 60204.

ISBN-13: 978-0-618-92153-9 ISBN-10: 0-618-92153-2

Printed in the United States of America

01 02 03 04 05 06 07 08 09—CKI—12 11 10 09 08 07

Internet Web Site: http://www.mcdougallittell.com

Senior Consultants

Donna Ogle is professor of Reading and Language at National-Louis University in Chicago, Illinois, and is a specialist in reading in the content areas, with an interest in social studies. She is past president of the International Reading Association and a former social studies teacher. Dr. Ogle is currently directing two content literacy projects in Chicago schools and is Senior Consultant to the Striving Readers Research Project. She continues to explore applications of the K-W-L strategy she developed and is adding a Partner Reading component—PRC2 (Partner Reading and Content 2).

Charles S. White is associate professor in the School of Education at Boston University, where he teaches methods of instruction in social studies. Dr. White has written and spoken extensively on the importance of civic education, both in the United States and overseas. He has worked in Russia since 1997 on curriculum reform and teacher preparation in education for democracy. Dr. White has received numerous awards for his scholarship, including the 1995 Federal Design Achievement Award from the National Endowment for the Arts, for the Teaching with Historic Places project. In 1997, Dr. White taught his Models of Teaching doctoral course at the Universidad San Francisco de Quito, Ecuador.

Middle School Teacher Consultant

Judith K. Bock earned a B.A. in Elementary Education and an M.A. in Geography and Environmental Sciences from Northeastern Illinois University. She taught as a middle school educator in gifted education for 33 years and is currently an adjunct geography professor in college geography departments in metropolitan Chicago. Ms. Bock serves on several local, state, and national geography education committees, writes geography lesson plans and curriculum, and facilitates geography workshops and institutes. She received the Distinguished Teaching Award from NCGE and was awarded the Outstanding Geographer in Illinois–2004 from the Illinois Geographical Society.

STUDENT PANEL

The following Middle School Student Panel reviewed textbook materials and technology products for this program.

Jessica Baker
Nelly Benitez
Ameer Cannon
Katie Conley
Murad Dajani
Will DiFrancesca
Tom Foydel
Philippa Gillette
Jenny Gorelick
Michael Grassle

Danielle Jackson
DeJauna Jackson
Mark Johnson
David Lenz
Andrew Mack
Madelaine Martin
Jabari McIntyre
Victoria Meliska
Sarah Peters
Brianna Ransom

Andrés Rivera-
  Thompson
Simone Samuels
Ben Shoaf
Gabriel Siegal
Kyle Siegal
Brock Snider
Hank Strickler
Jasmine Wright
Hannah Wyler

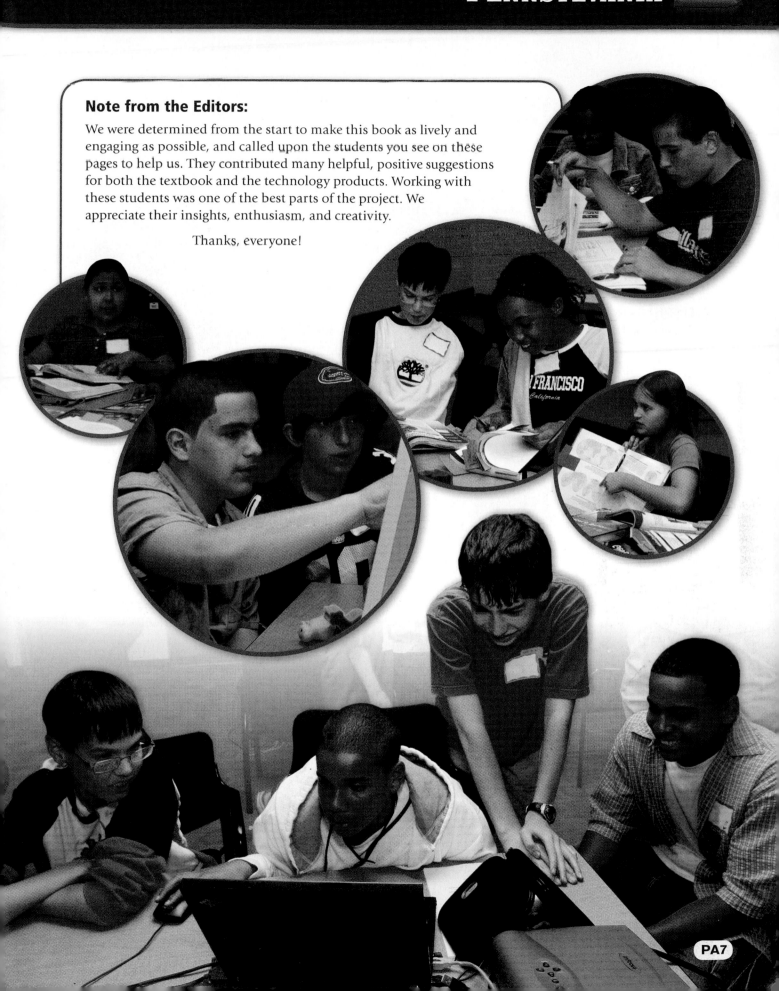

Note from the Editors:

We were determined from the start to make this book as lively and engaging as possible, and called upon the students you see on these pages to help us. They contributed many helpful, positive suggestions for both the textbook and the technology products. Working with these students was one of the best parts of the project. We appreciate their insights, enthusiasm, and creativity.

Thanks, everyone!

PENNSYLVANIA

OVERVIEW
Pennsylvania Student Edition

Independence Hall, Philadelphia, Pennsylvania © Steve Hamblin, Alamy

UNIT 1 PENNSYLVANIA

Introduction to World Geography

Online Activities
@ ClassZone.com

Animated GEOGRAPHY
Amazon Rain Forest

Explore life in a rain forest—the Yanomamo people, plants, animals, and the scientists who study them.

Interactive Review

Solve a crossword of key terms and names related to Earth's physical geography.

Online Test Practice

Review test-taking strategies and practice for your test at the end of every chapter.

UNIT 2 PENNSYLVANIA

The United States and Canada

Online Activities
@ ClassZone.com

Worldster
Kirima's Web Page

Visit Kirima's Web page to experience the sights and sounds of her world.

Interactive ‹‹ Review

Play the GeoGame to test your knowledge of the geography of the United States.

Online Test Practice

Review test-taking strategies and practice for your test at the end of every chapter.

UNIT 3 PENNSYLVANIA

Latin America

Online Activities
@ ClassZone.com

Worldster
Pedro's Web Page

Visit Pedro's Web page to experience the sights and sounds of his world.

Interactive Review

Use interactive Flip Cards to review key terms and names related to Mexico.

Online Test Practice

Review test-taking strategies and practice for your test at the end of every chapter.

UNIT 4 PENNSYLVANIA

Europe

Online Activities
@ ClassZone.com

Animated GEOGRAPHY
Victorian London

Enter the world of Victorian London and visit homes, shops, parks, and an underground railway.

Interactive Review

Play the GeoGame to test your knowledge of the geography of Western Europe.

Online Test Practice

Review test-taking strategies and practice for your test at the end of every chapter.

UNIT 5
PENNSYLVANIA

Russia and the Eurasian Republics

Online Activities
@ ClassZone.com

Zuhura's Web Page

Visit Zuhura's Web page to experience the sights and sounds of her world.

Interactive Review

Play the Name Game to test your knowledge of the Eurasian Republics.

Online Test Practice

Review test-taking strategies and practice for your test at the end of every chapter.

6
PENNSYLVANIA

Africa

Online Activities
@ ClassZone.com

Animated GEOGRAPHY
The Great Pyramid

Enter the world of ancient Egypt to see how the pyramids were built.

Interactive Review

Play the GeoGame to test your knowledge of Egypt and North Africa.

Online Test Practice

Review test-taking strategies and practice for your test at the end of every chapter.

UNIT 7 PENNSYLVANIA

Southwest Asia and South Asia

Online Activities
@ ClassZone.com

Animated GEOGRAPHY
Monsoons

Discover the life-giving and life-destroying effects of a monsoon. Hear news accounts of flooded villages.

Interactive Review

Solve a crossword of key terms and names related to Southwest Asia.

Online Test Practice

Review test-taking strategies and practice for your test at the end of every chapter.

East Asia and Southeast Asia

Online Activities
@ ClassZone.com

Worldster

Cheng's Web Page

Visit Cheng's Web page to experience the sights and sounds of his world.

Interactive Review

Play the Name Game to test your knowledge of China.

Online Test Practice

Review test-taking strategies and practice for your test at the end of every chapter.

UNIT 9 PENNSYLVANIA

Oceania and Antarctica

Online Activities
@ ClassZone.com

Animated GEOGRAPHY
The Great Barrier Reef

Dive into Australia's waters and explore life on the reef.

Interactive Review

Use interactive Flip Cards to review key terms and names related to Oceania and Antarctica.

Online Test Practice

Review test-taking strategies and practice for your test at the end of every chapter.

Animated GEOGRAPHY

CONNECT

GEOGRAPHY

HISTORY

CULTURE

ECONOMICS

Activities

FEATURES

ANALYZING Primary Sources

HISTORY MAKERS

Fun Facts!

FEATURES

COMPARING

MAPS

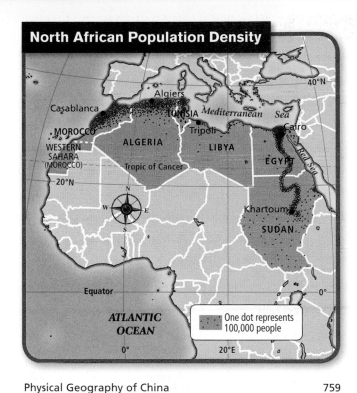

North African Population Density

One dot represents 100,000 people

GRAPHS, TABLES, AND CHARTS

GRAPHS

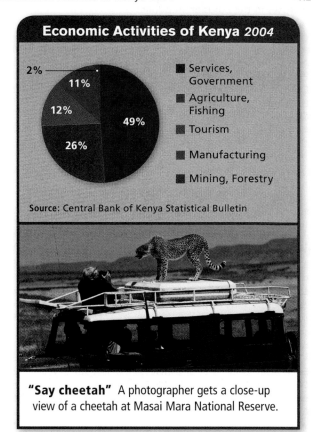

Economic Activities of Kenya 2004

- Services, Government — 49%
- Agriculture, Fishing — 26%
- Tourism — 12%
- Manufacturing — 11%
- Mining, Forestry — 2%

Source: Central Bank of Kenya Statistical Bulletin

"Say cheetah" A photographer gets a close-up view of a cheetah at Masai Mara National Reserve.

TABLES AND CHARTS

INFOGRAPHICS

Egyptian Social Roles

Pharaoh

Priests The priests cared for the temples and held religious ceremonies.

Priests and Nobles

Scribes and Government Officials

Craftspeople and Merchants

Laborers and Slaves Slaves might be prisoners of war, or people who owed debts or had committed crimes. In general, slaves were eventually freed.

Farmers

Laborers and Slaves

READING FOR UNDERSTANDING

Four Steps to Becoming a Strategic Reader

These pages explain how the *World Cultures and Geography* chapters are organized. By using the four key strategies below, you'll become a more successful reader of geography, and more knowledgeable about your state's standards.

① Set a Purpose for Reading

② Build Your Social Studies Vocabulary

③ Use Active Reading Strategies

④ Check Your Understanding

Can you find it?

Find the following items on this and the next three pages.

- **one** chapter Essential Question
- **two** places where important words are defined
- **three** online games
- **four** key strategies for reading

① Set a Purpose for Reading

Key features at the beginning of each chapter and section help you set a purpose for reading.

Ⓐ Essential Question This key question sets the main purpose for reading.

Ⓑ Connect Geography & History This feature helps you to consider the relationship between geography and history.

Ⓒ Animated Geography identifies the region or country you'll be studying.

Ⓓ Before, You Learned and **Now You Will Learn** This information helps you to connect what you've studied before to what you'll study next.

Ⓔ Key Question Each topic covered in the chapter is followed by a Key Question that sets your purpose for reading about that topic.

② Build Your Social Studies Vocabulary

The Reading for Understanding pages provide three important ways to build your vocabulary.

Ⓐ Terms & Names cover the most important events, people, places, and social studies concepts in the section.

Ⓑ Background Vocabulary lists words you need to know in order to understand the basic concepts and ideas discussed in the section.

Ⓒ Visual Vocabulary features provide visual support for some definitions.

Ⓓ Terms & Names and **Background Vocabulary** are highlighted and defined in the main text so that you'll understand them as you read.

CHAPTER 2

1 GEOGRAPHY
The Earth and Its Forces

2 GEOGRAPHY
Bodies of Water and Landforms

3 GEOGRAPHY
Climate and Vegetation

4 GEOGRAPHY

Earth's Interlocking Systems

A ⬜ **ESSENTIAL QUESTION**

How do Earth's physical systems make life on Earth possible?

B **CONNECT** Geography & History

Use the map and the time line to answer the following questions.
1. On which plate does most of the United States sit
2. Which event on the time line is supported by the

C *Animated* **GEOGRAPHY**
Earth's Tectonic Plates

✦ *Click here* to explore Earth and its systems @ ClassZone.com

Eurasian Plate

Arabian Plate

African Plate

Philippine Plate

Indo-Australian Plate

Ring

External Forces Shaping the Earth

E ▼ **KEY QUESTION** What external forces shape the Earth?

External forces also reshape the Earth's surface. The two main external forces are weathering and erosion. **Weathering** is the gradual physical and chemical breakdown of rocks near or on the Earth's surface. **Erosion** is the wearing away and movement of weathered materials from one place to another by the action of water, wind, or ice. As you can see, weathering and erosion work together to shape the Earth.

D

Weathering Weathering occurs slowly, over many years or even centuries. The two types of weathering are mechanical weathering and chemical weathering. Mechanical weathering is a process in which rocks are broken down into smaller pieces by physical means. It takes place when ice, extremes of hot and cold, or even tree roots cause rocks to split apart. It also occurs when hard objects, such as other rocks or sand, scrape or rub against a rock, and pieces of the rock break off.

Chemical weathering is caused by chemical reactions between the minerals in the rock and elements in the air or water. This process changes the make-up of the rock itself. For example, most rocks contain iron. When iron comes in contact with water, it rusts, which helps to break down the rock. Water and elements in the air can cause other minerals in rocks to dissolve.

The Grand Canyon The Grand Canyon is located on the Colorado River in Arizona. It is an example of both weathering and erosion caused by wind and water.

UNITED STATES
◉ Grand Canyon
ARIZONA
MEXICO

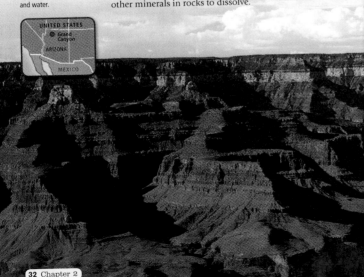

---

2 Reading for Understanding

▶ Key Ideas

D **BEFORE, YOU LEARNED**
Internal and external forces shape the surface of the Earth.

NOW YOU WILL LEARN
Interaction between landform of water makes life on Earth

▶ Vocabulary

A **TERMS & NAMES**

drainage basin the area drained by a major river

ground water water found beneath the Earth's surface

hydrologic cycle the circulation of water between the Earth, the oceans, and the atmosphere

landform a feature on the Earth's surface formed by physical force

plateau a broad, flat area of land higher than the surrounding land

relief the difference in the elevation of a landform from its lowest point to its highest point

B **continental shelf** the submer at the edge of a continent

BACKGROUND VOCABUL

atmosphere the layer of gase surround the Earth

C **Visual Vocabulary** landform

▶ Reading Strategy

Re-create the web diagram shown at right. As you read and respond to the **KEY QUESTIONS**, use the diagram to organize important details about the Earth's landforms and bodies of water.

📖 See Skillbuilder Handbook, page R4

FIND MAIN IDEAS

WATER BODIES

🔄 **GRAPHIC ORGANIZERS**
Go to Interactive Review @ ClassZ

READING FOR UNDERSTANDING

③ Use Active Reading Strategies

Active reading strategies help you note the most important information in each section.

Ⓐ Reading Strategy Each Reading for Understanding page contains a Reading Strategy diagram to help you track and organize the information you read.

Ⓑ Skillbuilder Handbook Every Reading Strategy is supported by a corresponding lesson in the Skillbuilder Handbook section at the back of this book.

Ⓒ Active Reading Strategies in the Skillbuilder Handbook will help you to read and study *World Cultures and Geography*.

drainage basin the area drained by a major river

ground water water found beneath the Earth's surface

hydrologic cycle the circulation of water between the Earth, the oceans, and the atmosphere

landform a feature on the Earth's surface formed by physical force

plateau a broad, flat area of land higher than the surrounding land

relief the difference in the elevation of a landform from its lowest point to its highest point

continental shelf the submer... at the edge of a continent

BACKGROUND VOCABULA...

atmosphere the layer of gases ... surround the Earth

Visual Vocabulary landform

▶ **Reading Strategy** Ⓐ

Re-create the web diagram shown at right. As you read and respond to the **KEY QUESTIONS**, use the diagram to organize important details about the Earth's landforms and bodies of water.

See Skillbuilder Handbook, page R4

FIND MAIN IDEAS

WATER BODIES   LA...

GRAPHIC ORGANIZERS
Go to Interactive Review @ ClassZone

Skillbuilder Handbook

Ⓒ Contents

Reading and Critical Thinking Skills

Ⓑ 1.2 Finding Main Ideas

Defining the Skill

A **main idea** is a statement that summarizes the subject of a speech, an article, a section of a book, or a paragraph. Main ideas can be stated or unstated. The main idea of a paragraph is often stated in the first or last sentence. If it is the first sentence, it is followed by sentences that support that main idea. If it is the last sentence, the details build up to the main idea. To find an unstated idea, use the details of the paragraph as clues.

Applying the Skill

The following paragraph provides reasons why Japan and Australia make such good trading partners. Use the strategies listed below to help you identify the main idea.

How to Find the Main Idea

Strategy ❶ Identify what you think may be the stated main idea. Check the first and last sentences of the paragraph to see if either could be the stated main idea.

Strategy ❷ Identify details that support the main idea. Some details explain that idea. Others give examples of what is stated in the main idea.

TRADING PARTNERS

Australia is an island. Japan is also an island, though much smaller than Australia. Australia is not as densely populated as Japan. ❷ In Japan, an average of 881 people live in each square mile. Australia averages 7 people per square mile. ❷ Australia has wide-open lands available for agriculture, ranching, and mining. ❷ Japan buys wool from Australian ranches, wheat from Australian farms, and iron ore from Australian mines. To provide jobs for its many workers, ❷ Japan developed industries. Those industries ❷ sell electronics and cars to Australia. ❶ Australia and Japan are trading partners because each has something the other needs.

Make a Chart

Making a chart can help you identify the main idea and details in a passage or paragraph. The chart below identifies the main idea and details in the paragraph you just read.

Main Idea: Australia and Japan are good trading partners because each supplies something the other needs.

Detail: Japan's population density is 881 people per square mile; Australia's is 7 per square mile.

Detail: Australia has land, natural resources, and agricultural products.

Detail: Japan buys wool, wheat, and iron ore from Australia.

Detail: Japan has many industries.

Detail: Australia buys electronics and cars from Japanese industries.

④ Check Your Understanding

One of the most important things you'll do as you study *World Cultures and Geography* is to check your understanding of events, people, places, and issues as you read.

A **Interactive Review** includes a Name Game and provides online activities to test your knowledge of the geography you just studied.

B **Section Assessment** reviews the section Terms & Names, revisits your Reading Strategy notes, and provides key questions about the section.

A **CHAPTER SUMMARY**

Key Idea 1
The Earth is composed of many layers, and its surface continually changes because of the drifting of the continents.

Key Idea 2
Interaction between landforms and bodies of water makes life on Earth possible.

Key Idea 3
The Earth's rotation and revolution influence weather, climate, and living conditions on Earth.

Key Idea 4
Human interference with physical systems causes problems with the environment.

For Review and Study Notes, go to Interactive Review @ ClassZone.com

NAME GAME

Use the Terms & Names list to complete each se on paper or online.

1. I am the hot metal center of the Earth. ____core____

2. I am a naturally formed feature on the Earth's surface. _____

3. I fall in the form of rain, snow, sleet, or hail. _____

4. I am an increase in the Earth's temperature. _____

5. I move weathered materials from one place to another._____

6. I am the trapping of the sun's heat by gases in the atmosphere. _____

7. I am a large rigid piece of the Earth's crust that is in motion._____

8. I am typical weather conditions over a period of time. _____

9. I circulate water between the Earth, oceans, and atmosphere. _____

10. I am plants that grow in a region. _____

Activities

Flip Cards

Use the online flip cards to quiz yourself on terms and names introduced in this chapter.

magma

Crossword

Complete an online crossw your knowledge of Earth's

ACROSS

1. a naturally formed fea Earth's surface

Erosion New landforms and new soil are formed by erosion. It occurs when materials loosened by weathering are moved by water, wind, or ice to new locations. Currents in streams and rivers pick up loose materials and deposit them downstream or carry them out to sea. These tiny pieces of rock, deposited by water, wind, or ice are called **sediment**. Sediment can be sand, stone, or finely ground particles called silt.

Wave action along coastlines carries rocks and sand from one place to another. Waves also pound boulders into smaller rocks. Wind erosion lifts particles from the Earth's surface and blows them great distances. The wind's actions can reshape rock Arizona's Grand Canyon is a result of both wind and water

Another type of erosion is caused by glaciers. **Glaciers** slow-moving masses of ice. They grind rocks and boulders un the ice and leave behind the rock when the ice melts. Pa central United States have been shaped by glacial erosion.

▲ **SYNTHESIZE** Explain how external forces shape the Earth surface.

ONLINE QUIZ
For test practice, go to Interactive Review @ ClassZone.com

B **Section ①⟩ Assessment**

TERMS & NAMES

1. Explain the importance of
- continent
- tectonic plate
- weathering
- erosion

USE YOUR READING NOTES

2. Categorize Use your completed chart to answer the following question:

Are external or internal forces responsible for volcanoes? Explain your answer.

INTERNAL FORCES	EXTERNAL FORCES
1.	1.
2.	2.
3.	3.
4.	4.

KEY IDEAS

3. What are the five layers that make up the Earth's interior and exterior?

4. How were the continents formed?

5. What are the two major external forces reshaping the Earth?

CRITICAL THINKING

6. Draw Conclusions How does the movement of wind, water, or ice reshape the Earth's surface?

7. Analyze Causes and Effects What is the relationship between plate movement, volcanoes, and earthquakes?

8. CONNECT to Today In which parts of the United States are external forces shaping the landscape?

9. ART Create a Puzzle Make a copy of a map of the world. Cut out the continents. Use the continents as puzzle pieces to form the continent of Pangaea. When you have finished putting the pieces together, draw an outline around the entire supercontinent.

Exploring Geography Online

World Cultures and Geography provides a variety of tools to help you explore geography online. See geography come to life in the Animation Center. Find help for your research projects in the Research and Writing Center. Review for tests with the Interactive Review, or create your own activities in the Activity Center. Go to ClassZone.com to make *World Cultures and Geography* interactive!

ClassZone.com

is your gateway to exploring geography. Explore the different **ClassZone Centers** to help you study and have fun with geography.

A **Interactive Review**
provides you with flip cards, a crossword puzzle, section quizzes, drag-and-drop map activities, and more.

B **Activity Center**
lets you explore world cultures through a **Worldster** community and participate in **WebQuests** and geography games.

C **Activity Maker**
lets you create your own activities so that you can focus on what *you* need to review.

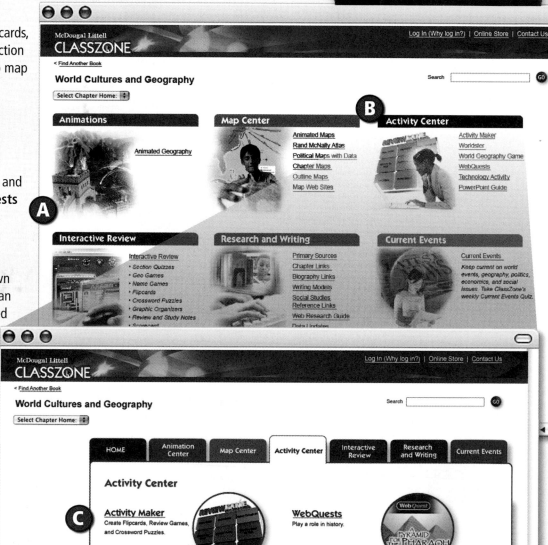

Animation Center

A rich collection of interactive features and maps on a wide variety of geographical topics at **ClassZone.com**

A **Roll-overs**
Explore the illustration by clicking on areas you'd like to know more about. This Amazon Rain Forest animation includes features about biodiversity, life in the rain forest, and more.

B **Video and Photo Gallery**
Explore the rain forest and the scientists who study it.

Review Game

- Create your own review game to study geography *your* way in the Activity Maker at **ClassZone.com**

- Select your own topics from any chapter to help you focus on specific regions, people, or events to review.

- Help your friends to explore geography online. Challenge them to play a review game that you create and modify!

PENNSYLVANIA

STEPS TO SUCCESS

Guide to Understanding
Pennsylvania's Academic Standards   PA35

- The Pennsylvania Academic Standards for Geography are grouped into four categories. Each category includes statements and descriptors.

Guide to
Test-Taking Strategies and Practice   S1

- These test-taking strategies and practice are designed to help you tackle many of the items you will find on a standardized test.

 For a complete list of the Pennsylvania Academic Standards for Geography, see page R117.

Independence Hall, Philadelphia, Pennsylvania © Steve Hamblin, Alamy

Why Study Geography?

When you study geography, you will see how the past informs your everyday life. Features like "Connecting to Your World" will tie what you are learning in your textbook to your life.

This textbook will focus and motivate you to learn more about people who have lives very different from your own.

 Explore Cultures Your textbook will transport you to cultures around the world, and show you the traditions and beliefs that made those cultures unique.

Geography allows you to view different societies to broaden your understanding of people and places. In this class, you will learn how societies have changed over time and the contributions each has made.

Improve Your Map Skills Focus on the world! Your textbook will help you appreciate how much geography affects our lives every day.

You will learn how to read all kinds of maps: time zone maps, elevation maps, and so on. You will even learn how to make a map on your own!

Become a Better Critical Thinker Many questions throughout this book will encourage you to form your own opinion.

For example, how would **your** life be different if you lived in China?

What Will I Learn?

Guide to Understanding
Pennsylvania's Academic Standards

Pennsylvania's Academic Standards for Geography are organized into four categories. Each category includes statements and descriptors.

Academic Standards for Geography
7.1 Basic Geographic Literacy
7.2 The Physical Characteristics of Places and Regions
7.3 The Human Characteristics of Places and Regions
7.4 The Interactions Between People and Places

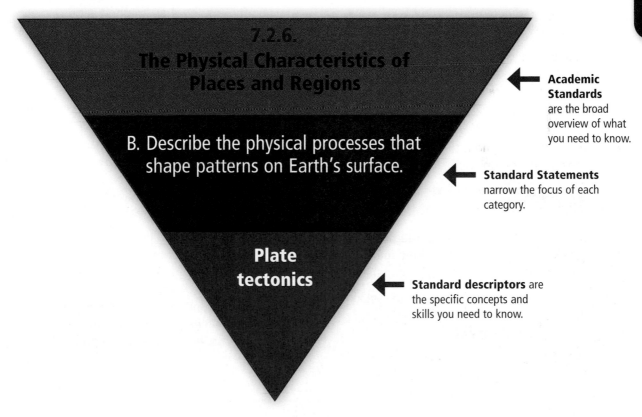

7.2.6.
The Physical Characteristics of Places and Regions

Academic Standards are the broad overview of what you need to know.

B. Describe the physical processes that shape patterns on Earth's surface.

Standard Statements narrow the focus of each category.

Plate tectonics

Standard descriptors are the specific concepts and skills you need to know.

Overview
Pennsylvania's Academic Standards

The charts that follow provide a brief overview of the standard statements and descriptors for geography. The descriptors illustrate the statements that support the standards.

 For a complete list of the Pennsylvania Academic Standards for Geography, see page R117.

7.1.6. A — Describe geographic tools and their uses.

Standard Descriptors	What It Means To *You*

• Geographic representations to display spatial information
 	
  - Absolute location
 	
  - Relative location
 	
  - Flows (e.g., goods, people, traffic)
 	
  - Topography
 	
  - Historic events
	What do you think of when you hear the word *geography*? You may think of maps and charts. Studying things that can be mapped or charted, such as the location of cities or the movement of people and goods, is an important part of geography.

7.1.9. B — Explain and locate places and regions.

Standard Descriptors	What It Means To *You*
• How regions are created to interpret Earth's complexity (i.e., the differences among formal regions, functional regions, perceptual regions) • How characteristics contribute to regional changes (e.g., economic development, accessibility, demographic change) • How culture and experience influence perceptions of places and regions	Geographers divide the world into regions to make it easier to compare places. Regions can be large or small and can be formed on the basis of physical features or cultural elements. Understanding the concept of regions will help you make sense of the geographic information you learn.

7.2.6. A

Describe the physical characteristics of places and regions.

Standard Descriptors	What It Means To *You*
• Components of Earth's physical systems (e.g., clouds, storms, relief and elevation [topography], tides, biomes, tectonic plates) • Comparison of the physical characteristics of different places and regions (e.g., soil, vegetation, climate, topography) • Climate types (e.g., marine west coast, humid continental, tropical wet and dry)	Think about your community. Is it hilly or flat? Is the soil good for agriculture? What is the weather like? The answers to these questions affect how you live and dress and the activities you enjoy. Knowing about Earth's physical systems and characteristics helps you understand why societies around the world have such richly varied cultures.

7.2.9. B

Explain the dynamics of the fundamental processes that underlie the operation of Earth's physical systems.

Standard Descriptors	What It Means To *You*
• Wind systems • Water cycle • Erosion/deposition cycle • Plate tectonics • Ocean currents • Natural hazards	Earth's physical processes affect us in many ways. Wind and ocean currents affect the weather. Erosion and the movement of soil from place to place change the physical features of our surroundings. Plate tectonics create earthquakes and volcanoes. Learning about these processes helps us appreciate the power of nature.

7.3.6. C

Describe the human characteristics of places and regions by their settlement characteristics.

Standard Descriptors	What It Means To *You*
• Current and past settlement patterns in the local area • Factors that affect the growth and decline of settlements (e.g., immigration, transportation development, depletion of natural resources, site and situation)	Where people settle and the types of communities they create are affected by geography. People settle in places that provide resources for survival and opportunities for economic activities.

7.3.9. D — Explain the human characteristics of places and regions by their economic activities.

Standard Descriptors	What It Means To *You*
• Factors that shape spatial patterns of economic activity both nationally and internationally (e.g., comparative advantage in location of economic activities; changes in resource trade; disruption of trade flows)	All human societies engage in economic activities. In the modern world, regions specialize in economic activities based on their natural and human resources. This specialization leads to trade.

7.4.6. A — Describe the impacts of physical systems on people.

Standard Descriptors	What It Means To *You*
• How people depend on, adjust to and modify physical systems on a regional scale (e.g., coastal industries, development of coastal communities, flood control) • Ways in which people adjust to life in hazard-prone areas (e.g., California and earthquakes, Florida and hurricanes, Oklahoma and tornadoes)	Every year you read or hear on the news about earthquakes, floods, wildfires, hurricanes, and tornadoes. These natural disasters affect thousands of people's lives and property. Understanding how Earth's physical systems impact people is an important part of the study of geography.

7.4.9. B — Explain the impacts of people on physical systems.

Standard Descriptors	What It Means To *You*
• Forces by which people modify the physical environment (e.g., increasing population; new agricultural techniques; industrial processes and pollution) • Spatial effects of activities in one region on another region (e.g., scrubbers on power plants to clean air, transportation systems such as Trans-Siberian Railroad, potential effects of fallout from nuclear power plant accidents)	Human history is the story of people modifying their physical environment. Some modifications, such as better agricultural techniques, improve people's quality of life. Others damage the environment and lead to long-term problems. The study of geography helps you understand the impact people have on the physical environment.

PENNSYLVANIA

Guide to
Test-Taking Strategies and Practice

The chart below provides a guide to the test-taking strategies and practice that will help prepare you for a standardized test.

- **Learn** each strategy by reviewing the numbered steps on the page listed in the column.
- **Practice** the strategy on the following page.
- **Apply** the strategies you learned at the end of each chapter.

STRATEGY	LEARN	PRACTICE	APPLY
Multiple Choice	p. S2	p. S3	p. 85, Chapter 3 p. 493, Chapter 15
Primary and Secondary Sources	p. S4	p. S5	p. 311, Chapter 10 p. 519, Chapter 16
Political Cartoons	p. S6	p. S7	p. 508, Chapter 16
Charts	p. S8	p. S9	p. 55, Chapter 2 p. 909, Chapter 29
Line and Bar Graphs	p. S10	p. S11	p. 227, Chapter 7 p. 447, Chapter 14
Pie Graphs	p. S12	p. S13	p. 251, Chapter 8
Political Maps	p. S14	p. S15	p. 23, Chapter 1 pp. 324–325, Chapter 11
Thematic Maps	p. S16	p. S17	p. 55, Chapter 2 p. 397, Chapter 12
Timelines	p. S18	p. S19	p. 166, Chapter 6 p. 405, Chapter 13
Constructed Response	p. S20	p. S21	p. 85, Chapter 3
Extended Response	p. S22	p. S23	p. 54, Chapter 2
Document-Based Questions	pp. S24–S25	pp. S26–S27	p. 12, Chapter 1 p. 515, Chapter 16

TEST-TAKING STRATEGIES AND PRACTICE

Multiple Choice

A multiple-choice question is a question or incomplete sentence and a set of choices. One of the choices correctly answers the question or completes the sentence.

1 Read the question or incomplete sentence carefully. Try to answer the question before looking at the choices.

2 Look for key words in the question. They may help you figure out the correct answer.

3 Read each choice with the question. Don't decide on your final answer until you have read all the choices.

4 Rule out any choices that you know are wrong.

5 Watch for answers with words like *all*, *never*, and *only*. These answers are often incorrect.

6 Sometimes the last choice is *all of the above*. Make sure that the other choices are all correct before you pick this answer.

7 Be careful with questions that include the word *not*.

1 **1.** The Sahara is (mostly)

choices

   A. sand, rocks, and gravel.

3 **B.** boulders and sand.

   C. cliffs and gulleys.

   D. grasses and bushes. **4**

> **2** Words like *mostly* or *partly* are key words in multiple choice. Look for answers that are mostly true or partly true about the subject.

> **4** You know that if the Sahara is a desert, **D** is incorrect. A desert cannot be mostly covered with grass and bushes.

2. Over hundreds of years, Bantu-speaking people migrated from West Africa to

   A. South and Southwest Asia.

   B. (every) continent on earth. **5**

   C. East and South Africa.

   D. (all) of North Africa and Arabia.

3. The people of West Africa passed on their history by

   A. painting pictures.

   B. telling stories.

   C. creating dances.

6 **D.** all of the above

4. Which of the following is (not) one of the nations in southern Africa?

   A. Zimbabwe

   B. Nigeria

   C. Mozambique

   D. Namibia

> **7** First rule out all the answers that name southern African countries. The answer that remains is the correct choice.

answers: 1 (A); 2 (C); 3 (D); 4 (B)

Directions: Read each question carefully. Choose the best answer from the four choices.

1. Which of the following was *not* a result of the bubonic plague?

   A. Cities worked together during the plague.

   B. Europe lost one-third of its population.

   C. The Church lost its prestige among the people.

   D. The economies of many countries were ruined.

2. Martin Luther started a reform movement when he

   A. published the New Testament in German.

   B. criticized some of the Church's practices.

   C. wrote his 95 Theses and made them public.

   D. all of the above

3. The Ottoman Empire reached its greatest size and glory under the rule of

   A. Mehmet II.

   B. Selim the Grim.

   C. Suleiman the Lawgiver.

   D. Timur the Lame.

4. During the 1700s, England controlled which of the following?

   A. the sugar trade

   B. the Atlantic slave trade

   C. the cotton trade

   D. the coconut trade

Primary and Secondary Sources

Sometimes you will need to study a document to answer a question. Documents can be either primary sources or secondary sources. Primary sources are written or created by people who either saw an event or were part of the event. A primary source can be a photograph, letter, diary, speech, or autobiography.

A secondary source is an account of events by a person who did not actually experience them. Newspaper articles and history books are some examples of secondary sources.

1 Look at the source line to learn about the document and its author. If the author is well known and has been quoted often, the information is likely true.

2 Skim the article to get an idea of what it is about.

3 Note special punctuation. For example, ellipses (. . .) indicate that words have been left out.

4 Ask yourself questions about the document as you read.

5 Review the questions to see what information you will need to find. Then reread the document.

Good Government

Chap. 2.20 Lord Ji Kang asked, "What should I do in order to make the people respectful, loyal, and zealous [hard-working]?" The Master said: "Approach them with dignity and they will be respectful. Be yourself a good son and kind father, and they will be loyal. Raise the good and train the incompetent, and they will be zealous."

2 **4** **Chap. 13.2** Ran Yong **3** . . . asked about government. The Master said: "Guide the officials. Forgive small mistakes. Promote [people] of talent." "How does one recognize that a [person] has talent and deserves to be promoted?" The Master said: "Promote those you know. Those whom you do not know will hardly remain ignored."

The *Analects* is a book of thoughts and ideas by Confucius. He was a scholar and teacher in ancient China.

1 —*The Analects of Confucius*

1. Confucius is giving advice on how to

   A. be a gentleman.

   B. be a good ruler.

   C. become wealthy.

   D. raise a good family.

2. Which sentence *best* expresses the idea of these paragraphs?

   A. The wise ruler governs people through fear.

   B. People should obey their rulers no matter what.

   C. A good ruler gives a lot of orders to people.

   D. If rulers do things well, people will follow them.

answers: 1 (B); 2 (D)

Directions: Read this passage. Use the passage and your knowledge of world cultures and geography to answer questions 1 and 2.

Before World War I

In 1892, France and Russia had become military allies. Later, Germany signed an agreement to protect Austria. If any nation attacked Austria, Germany would fight on its side. France and Russia had to support each other as well. For instance, if France got into a war with Germany, Russia had to fight Germany, too. This meant that in any war, Germany would have to fight on two fronts: France on the west and Russia on the east.

If a war broke out, what part would Great Britain play? No one knew. It might remain neutral, like Belgium. It might, if given a reason, fight against Germany.

1. If Russia and Germany went to war, which country had to help Russia?

  A. Great Britain

  B. Belgium

  C. Austria

  D. France

2. What was a result of the military alliance formed between France and Russia?

  A. Belgium would have to fight a war on the side of Germany.

  B. Great Britain would remain neutral.

  C. Germany would have to fight a war on two fronts.

  D. France and Russia would support Germany in a war.

TEST-TAKING STRATEGIES AND PRACTICE

Political Cartoons

Cartoonists who draw political cartoons use both words and art to express opinions about political issues.

1 Try to figure out what the cartoon is about. Titles and captions may give clues.

2 Use labels to help identify the people, places, and events represented in the cartoon.

3 Note when and where the cartoon was published.

4 Look for symbols—that is, people, places, or objects that stand for something else.

5 The cartoonist often exaggerates the physical features of people and objects. This technique will give you clues as to how the cartoonist feels about the subject.

6 Try to figure out the cartoonist's message and summarize it in a sentence.

1 NEXT!

4 The cartoonist uses the swastika, a symbol used during World War II.

5 The swastika looks like a huge, frightening machine. It can easily crush Poland.

2 The label "Poland" tells which country is the subject of the cartoon's title.

Daniel Fitzpatrick/ *St. Louis Post-Dispatch*, August 24, 1939.

3 The date is a clue that the cartoon refers to the beginning of World War II.

1. What does the swastika in the cartoon stand for?

    A. the Soviet Union

    B. Nazi Germany

    C. the Polish army

    D. Great Britain

6 **2.** Which sentence best summarizes the cartoonist's message?

    A. Germany will attack Poland next.

    B. Poland should stop Germany.

    C. Germany will lose this battle.

    D. Poland will fight a civil war.

answers: 1 (B); 2 (A)

Directions: Study this cartoon. Use the cartoon and your knowledge of world cultures and geography to answer questions 1 and 2.

Steve Sack, *Minneapolis Star-Tribune*, January 1, 1992.

1. How has the cartoonist drawn Saddam Hussein?

   A. as Count Dracula

   B. as Darth Vader

   C. as Frankenstein's monster

   D. as a military leader

2. Notice all the "MADE IN" labels on Saddam Hussein. The best title for the cartoon would be

   A. "A Monster Never Sleeps."

   B. "The Monster of Iraq."

   C. "They've Made a Mistake."

   D. "They've Created a Monster."

TEST-TAKING STRATEGIES AND PRACTICE

Charts

Charts present facts in a visual form. History textbooks use several different types of charts. The chart that is most often found on standardized tests is the table. A table organizes information in columns and rows.

1 Read the title of the chart to find out what information is represented.

2 Read the column and row headings. Sometimes further information on headings is provided in footnotes.

3 Notice how the information in the chart is organized.

4 Compare the information from column to column and row to row.

5 Try to draw conclusions from the information in the chart.

6 Read the questions and then study the chart again.

1 This chart is about the number of people who immigrated to different countries.

4

Immigration to Selected Countries		
Country	**Years**	**Number of Immigrants**
Argentina	1856–1932	6,405,000
Australia	1861–1932	2,913,000
Brazil	1821–1932	4,431,000
British West Indies	1836–1932	1,587,000
Canada	1821–1932	5,206,000
Cuba	1901–1932	857,000
Mexico	1911–1931	226,000
New Zealand	1851–1932	594,000
South Africa	1881–1932	852,000
United States	1821–1932	34,244,000
Uruguay	1836–1932	713,000

Source: Alfred W. Crosby, Jr. *The Columbian Exchange: Biological and Cultural Consequences of 1492*

5

3 This chart lists countries in alphabetical order. Other charts organize information by years or by numbers.

6

1. The country that received the most immigrants was

    A. Canada.

    B. the British West Indies.

    C. the United States.

    D. Brazil.

2. Different countries received immigrants in different years. According to the chart, which countries received immigrants the earliest?

    A. Argentina, New Zealand, and Canada

    B. Canada, Brazil, and the United States

    C. Mexico, United States, and British West Indies

    D. Brazil, South Africa, and Cuba

answers: 1 (C); 2 (B)

Directions: Read the chart carefully. Use the chart and your knowledge of world cultures and geography to answer questions 1 and 2.

Ancient Civilizations				
Feature	China	Egypt	Indus Valley	Mesopotamia
Location	River valley	River valley	River valley	River valley
Period	2000 B.C.–400 B.C.	3100 B.C.–332 B.C.	2500 B.C.–1500 B.C.	3500 B.C.–500 B.C.
Specialized workers	Priests; government workers, soldiers; workers in bronze, silk; farmers	Priests; government workers, scribes, soldiers; workers in pottery, stone; farmers	Priests; government officials; workers in pottery, bricks; farmers	Priests; government officials, scribes, soldiers; workers in pottery, textiles; farmers
Institutions	Walled cities; oracle-bone reading	Ruling class of priests, nobles; education system	Ruling class of priests	Ruling class of priests and nobles; education for scribes
Record keeping	Pictographic writing	Hieroglyphic writing	Pictographic writing	Cuneiform writing
Advanced technology and artifacts	Writing; making bronze and silk; irrigation systems	Papyrus; mathematics; astronomy, engineering; pyramids; mummification; medicine	Irrigation systems; indoor plumbing; seals	Wheel; plow; sailboat; bronze weapons

1. Which civilization appeared first?

   A. China

   B. Egypt

   C. Indus Valley

   D. Mesopotamia

2. The Indus Valley civilization did not have

   A. irrigation systems.

   B. walled cities.

   C. government officials.

   D. indoor plumbing.

Line and Bar Graphs

Graphs are often used to show numbers. Line graphs often show changes over time. Bar graphs make it easy to compare numbers.

1 Read the title of the graph to find out what information is represented.

2 Study the labels on the graph.

3 Look at the source line that tells where the graph is from. Decide whether you can depend on the source to provide reliable information.

4 See if you can make any generalizations about the information in the graph. Note whether the numbers change over time.

5 Read the questions carefully and then study the graph again.

1 **Exports of English Manufactured Goods, 1699–1774**

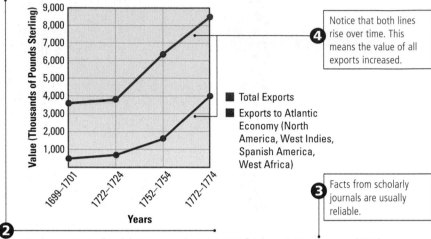

4 Notice that both lines rise over time. This means the value of all exports increased.

Total Exports
Exports to Atlantic Economy (North America, West Indies, Spanish America, West Africa)

3 Facts from scholarly journals are usually reliable.

Source: R. Davis, "English Foreign Trade, 1700–1774," *Economic History Review* (1962)

5 **1.** Which of the following is a true statement?

  A. Exports to the Atlantic economy declined over time.

  B. Total exports stayed the same over time.

  C. Total exports rose sharply after 1724.

  D. Exports to the Atlantic economy fell sharply after 1754.

1 **Nations with High Foreign Debt, 2003**

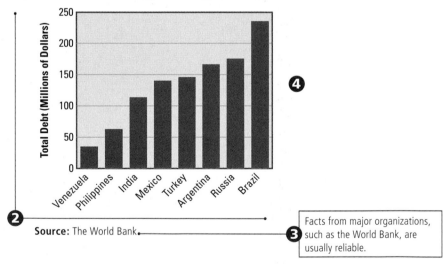

4

3 Facts from major organizations, such as the World Bank, are usually reliable.

Source: The World Bank

5 **2.** The nation with the second largest foreign debt is

  A. Brazil.

  B. Argentina.

  C. Russia.

  D. Mexico.

answers: 1 (C); 2 (C)

Directions: Study the graphs carefully. Use the graphs and your knowledge of world cultures and geography to answer questions 1 and 2.

Japan: Gross Domestic Product, 1984–2002

Source: Annual Report on National Accounts 2005, Cabinet Office of the Government of Japan

Unemployment Rates for Selected Countries, 2005

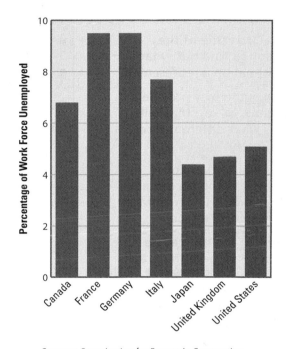

Source: Organization for Economic Cooperation and Development

1. Japan's gross domestic product increased the most between

   A. 1986 and 1990.

   B. 1990 and 1994.

   C. 1994 and 1998.

   D. 1998 and 2002.

2. Which country had the lowest unemployment rate in 2005?

   A. Japan

   B. Germany

   C. United States

   D. United Kingdom

RAND M?NALLY

World Atlas

CONTENTS

Legend

Complete Legend for Physical and Political Maps

Water Features

ATLANTIC OCEAN	Ocean or sea
	Lake
	Salt lake
	Seasonal lake
Mississippi	River
Niagara Falls	Waterfall
	Ice pack

Land Features

Mt. Mitchell 6,684 ft. △ 2,037 m.	Mountain peak
Mt. McKinley 20,320 ft. ▲ 6,194 m.	Highest mountain peak
Great Basin	Physical feature (mountain range, desert, plateau, etc.)
Nantucket Island	Island

Cultural Features

————	International boundary
————	State boundary
CANADA	Country
KANSAS	State

Population Centers

National capital	State capital	Town	Population
✪	✪	■	Over 1,000,000
✪	✪	▣	250,000 – 1,000,000
✪	✪	·	Under 250,000

Land Elevations and Ocean Depths

Land elevation

3,000 meters	9,840 feet
2,000 meters	6,560 feet
1,000 meters	3,280 feet
500 meters	1,640 feet
200 meters	656 feet
0 Sea level	0 Sea level

Water depth

0 Sea level	0 Sea level
200 meters	656 feet
2,000 meters	6,560 feet

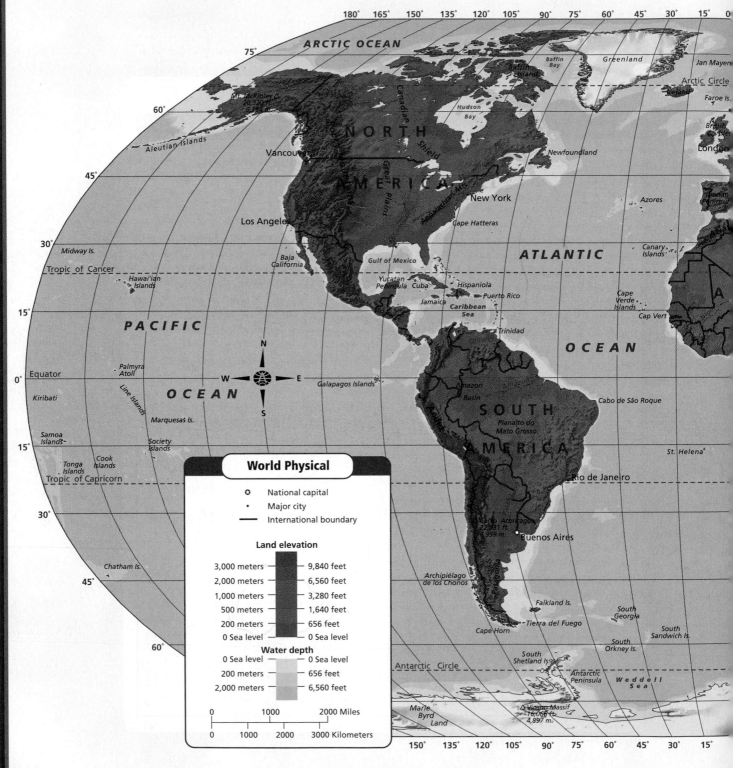

World Physical

- ⊕ National capital
- • Major city
- —— International boundary

Land elevation

3,000 meters	9,840 feet
2,000 meters	6,560 feet
1,000 meters	3,280 feet
500 meters	1,640 feet
200 meters	656 feet
0 Sea level	0 Sea level

Water depth

0 Sea level	0 Sea level
200 meters	656 feet
2,000 meters	6,560 feet

0   1000   2000 Miles
0   1000   2000   3000 Kilometers

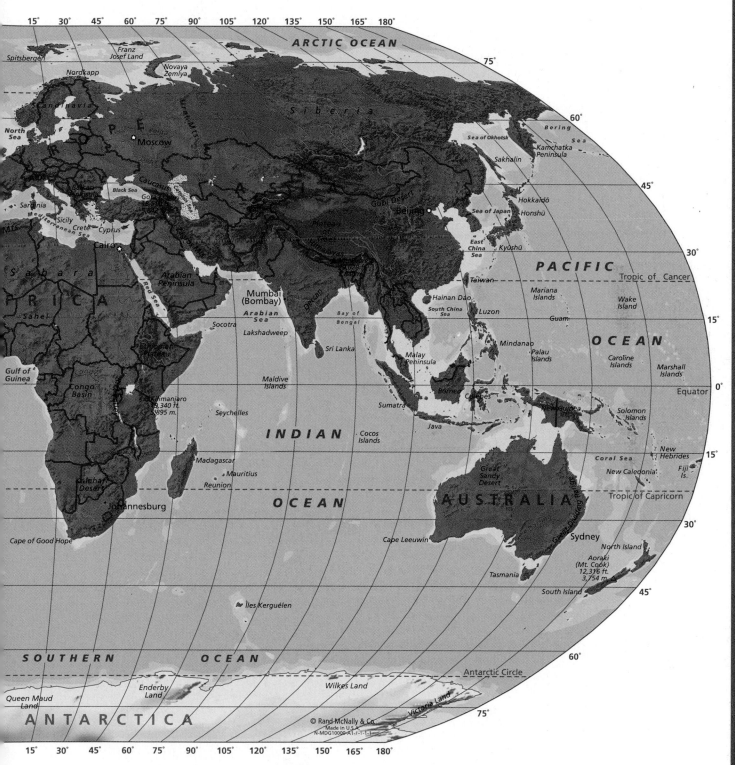

ARCTIC OCEAN

75°

Spitsbergen
Franz
Josef Land
Nordkapp
Novaya
Zemlya

Siberia

60°

Bering
Sea

Sea of Okhotsk

Kamchatka
Peninsula

Scandinavia

North
Sea

Moscow

Sakhalin

45°

Ural Mts.

Volga

Caucasus

Black Sea

Sardinia

Mediterranean

Sicily
Crete
Cyprus

Balkan

Sea

Cairo

Gobi Desert

Beijing

Hokkaidō

Honshū

Sea of Japan

PACIFIC

30°

Sahara

AFRICA

Sahel

Arabian
Peninsula

Red Sea

Plateau
of
Tibet

East
China
Sea

Kyūshū

Taiwan

Tropic of Cancer

Mumbai
(Bombay)

Deccan

Bay of
Bengal

Hainan Dao

South China
Sea

Mariana
Islands

Wake
Island

OCEAN

15°

Gulf of
Guinea

Ethiopian
Plateau

Arabian
Sea

Socotra

Lakshadweep

Sri Lanka

Luzon

Guam

Mindanao

Palau
Islands

Caroline
Islands

Marshall
Islands

Congo
Basin

Kilimanjaro
19,340 ft.
5,895 m.

Seychelles

Maldive
Islands

Malay
Peninsula

Borneo

Celebes

New Guinea

Solomon
Islands

Equator

0°

Sumatra

Java

INDIAN

Cocos
Islands

Madagascar

Mauritius

Reunion

OCEAN

Coral Sea

New
Hebrides

New Caledonia

Fiji
Is.

15°

Kalahari
Desert

Johannesburg

Great
Sandy
Desert

AUSTRALIA

Tropic of Capricorn

Cape of Good Hope

Cape Leeuwin

Sydney

North Island

30°

Aoraki
(Mt. Cook)
12,316 ft.
3,754 m

Great Dividing Range

Tasmania

South Island

45°

Îles Kerguélen

SOUTHERN

OCEAN

60°

Queen Maud
Land

Enderby
Land

Wilkes Land

Antarctic Circle

ANTARCTICA

Victoria Land

75°

© Rand McNally & Co.
Made in U.S.A.
N-MDG10000-A1-1-1-1

15° 30° 45° 60° 75° 90° 105° 120° 135° 150° 165° 180°

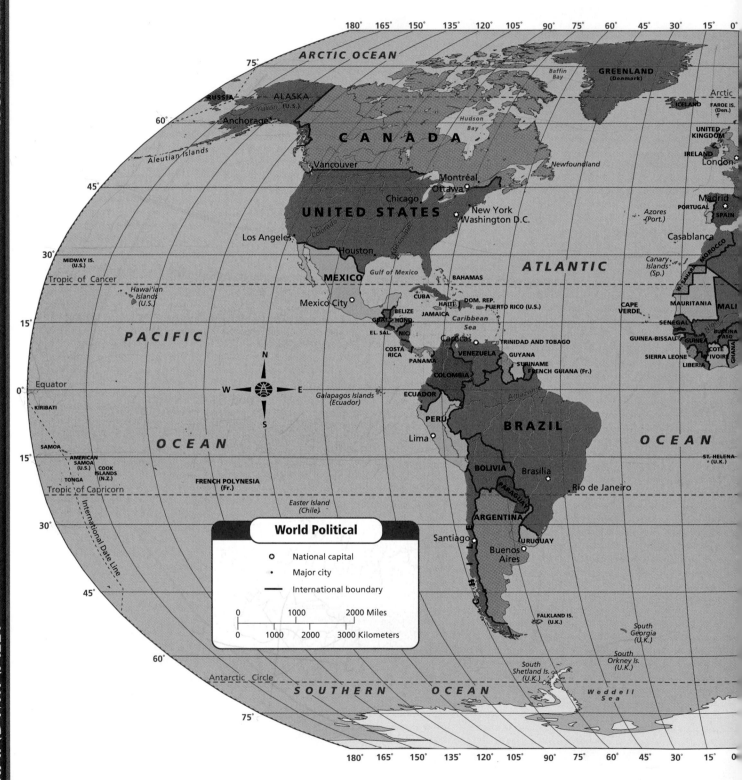

180° 165° 150° 135° 120° 105° 90° 75° 60° 45° 30° 15° 0°

ARCTIC OCEAN

75°

Baffin
Bay

GREENLAND
(Denmark)

Arctic

RUSSIA

ALASKA
(U.S.)

Yukon

ICELAND

FAROE IS.
(Den.)

60°

Anchorage

Hudson
Bay

UNITED
KINGDOM

Aleutian Islands

C A N A D A

Newfoundland

IRELAND
London

45°

Vancouver

Montréal
Ottawa

Madrid

Chicago

PORTUGAL
SPAIN

UNITED STATES

New York
Washington D.C.

Azores
(Port.)

Casablanca

30°

MIDWAY IS.
(U.S.)

Los Angeles

Colorado

A T L A N T I C

Canary
Islands
(Sp.)

MOROCCO

Tropic of Cancer

Houston

Hawai'ian
Islands
(U.S.)

MEXICO

Gulf of Mexico

BAHAMAS

W. SAHARA

MAURITANIA

MALI

15°

Mexico City

CUBA

DOM. REP.
HAITI
PUERTO RICO (U.S.)

CAPE
VERDE

BELIZE
GUAT.
HOND.
EL SAL.
NIC.
COSTA
RICA

JAMAICA

Caribbean
Sea

SENEGAL

GUINEA-BISSAU

GUINEA

BURKINA
FASO

P A C I F I C

Caracas

TRINIDAD AND TOBAGO

SIERRA LEONE

LIBERIA

CÔTE
D'IVOIRE

GHANA

PANAMA

VENEZUELA
COLOMBIA

GUYANA
SURINAME
FRENCH GUIANA (Fr.)

N

0°

Equator

W   E

Galapagos Islands
(Ecuador)

ECUADOR

Amazon

KIRIBATI

S

PERU

BRAZIL

O C E A N

SAMOA

Lima

O C E A N

15°

AMERICAN
SAMOA
(U.S.)

COOK
ISLANDS
(N.Z.)

BOLIVIA

Brasilia

ST. HELENA
(U.K.)

TONGA

FRENCH POLYNESIA
(Fr.)

Rio de Janeiro

Tropic of Capricorn

PARAGUAY

Easter Island
(Chile)

World Political

ARGENTINA

30°

International Date Line

⊕ National capital

Santiago

URUGUAY

Buenos
Aires

• Major city

—— International boundary

FALKLAND IS.
(U.K.)

South
Georgia
(U.K.)

0   1000   2000 Miles

45°

0   1000   2000   3000 Kilometers

South
Orkney Is.
(U.K.)

60°

South
Shetland Is.
(U.K.)

Weddell
Sea

Antarctic Circle

S O U T H E R N   O C E A N

75°

180° 165° 150° 135° 120° 105° 90° 75° 60° 45° 30° 15° 0°

ARCTIC OCEAN

75°

Franz Josef Land

Spitsbergen
(Nor.)

Novaya
Zemlya

60°

Bering

Circle

RUSSIA

Sea of Okhotsk

Sea

International Date Line

NORWAY   FINLAND

Moscow

Novosibirsk

45°

SWEDEN   EST.
LTH.   MONGOLIA

North
Sea   DEN.   LAT.

NETH.   GERMAN   POLAND   BELARUS

FRANCE   CZE.   UKRAINE   KAZAKHSTAN

AUS.   SLK.   HUNG.   MOLD.   Beijing

IT.   ROS.   ROM.   Black Sea   UZBEKISTAN   KYRG.   CHINA   NORTH   Sea of Japan

Rome   ALB.   BUL.   GEO.   AZER.   TURKMENISTAN   TAJ.   KOREA   JAPAN   45°

GREECE   TURKEY   ARM.   Seoul   SOUTH   Tōkyō

Mediterranean Sea   Crete   CYPRUS   LEB.   SYRIA   Tehran   KOREA   30°

TUNISIA   ISRAEL   IRAQ   IRAN   AFGHANISTAN   Shanghai   PACIFIC

JORDAN   PAKISTAN   TAIWAN   Tropic of Cancer

ALGERIA   LIBYA   EGYPT   SAUDI   KUWAIT   N E P A L   Kolkata   Hong Kong   NORTHERN   WAKE ISLAND

QATAR   Karāchi   (Calcutta)   BHU.   MARIANA ISLANDS   (U.S.)

ARABIA   U.A.E.   Mumbai   INDIA   MYANMAR   LAOS   South China   GUAM   15°

NIGER   CHAD   SUDAN   YEMEN   OMAN   (Bombay)   Arabian   Bay of   THAILAND   Sea   PHILIPPINES   (U.S.)   OCEAN

Sea   Bengal   Bangkok   VIETNAM   Manila

NIGERIA   Addis   DJIBOUTI   CAMBODIA   PALAU   FED. STATES OF   MARSHALL

Lagos   CENTRAL   Ababa   ETHIOPIA   SRI LANKA   BRUNEI   MICRONESIA   ISLANDS

CAMEROON   AFRICAN   MALAYSIA

EQUATORIAL   REPUBLIC   MALDIVES   SINGAPORE   0°

GUINEA   GABON   KENYA   SOMALIA   Borneo   New Guinea   Equator

RWANDA   SEYCHELLES   Sumatra   Jakarta   PAPUA   SOLOMON

DEM. REP.   BURUNDI   INDONESIA   NEW GUINEA   ISLANDS

OF THE CONGO   TANZANIA   Java   EAST TIMOR

ANGOLA   COMOROS   INDIAN   Coral Sea   VANUATU   15°

ZAMBIA   MADAGASCAR   NEW CALEDONIA   FIJI

NAMIBIA   ZIMBABWE   MAURITIUS   (Fr.)

BOTSWANA   MOZAMBIQUE   REUNION   Tropic of Capricorn

Johannesburg   (Fr.)   OCEAN   AUSTRALIA   Brisbane

SWAZILAND   Perth   Sydney   30°

SOUTH   LESOTHO   Melbourne   Auckland

AFRICA   NEW ZEALAND

Tasmania

Îles Kerguélen   45°
(Fr.)

SOUTHERN   OCEAN   60°

Antarctic Circle

ANTARCTICA   75°

© Rand McNally & Co.
Made in U.S.A.
N-MDG10000-PT-1-1-1-1

15° 30° 45° 60° 75° 90° 105° 120° 135° 150° 165° 180°

RAND MCNALLY

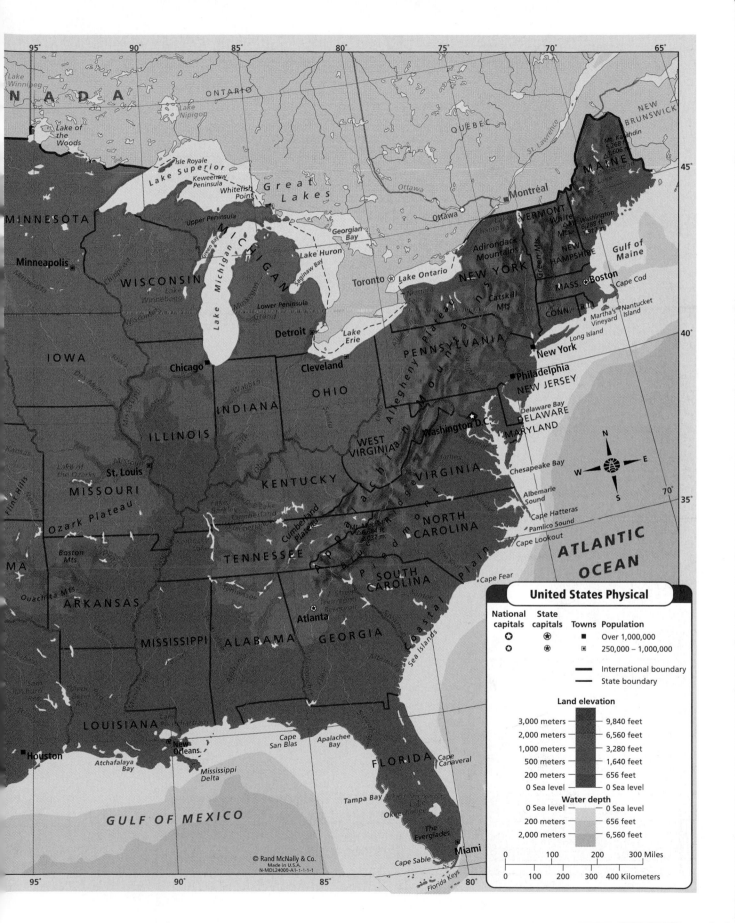

United States Physical

National capitals	State capitals	Towns	Population
✪	✪	■	Over 1,000,000
✪	✪	▣	250,000 – 1,000,000

— International boundary
— State boundary

Land elevation

3,000 meters	9,840 feet
2,000 meters	6,560 feet
1,000 meters	3,280 feet
500 meters	1,640 feet
200 meters	656 feet
0 Sea level	0 Sea level

Water depth

0 Sea level	0 Sea level
200 meters	656 feet
2,000 meters	6,560 feet

0   100   200   300 Miles

0   100   200   300   400 Kilometers

© Rand McNally & Co.
Made in U.S.A.
N-MDL24000-A1-1-1-1-1

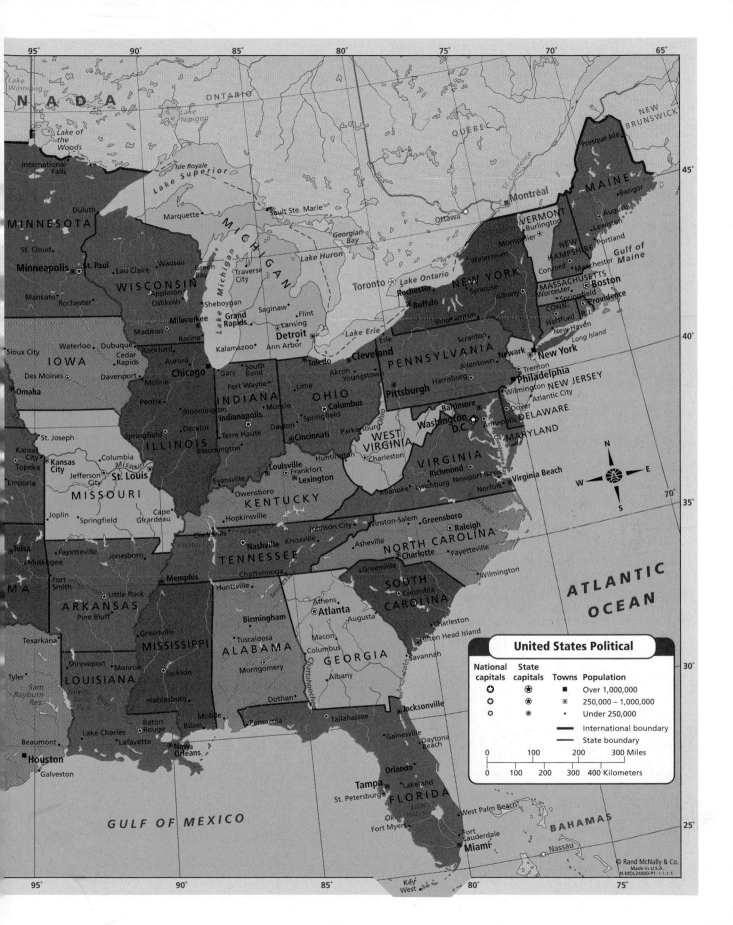

United States Political

National capitals	State capitals	Towns	Population
✪	✪	■	Over 1,000,000
✪	✪	▣	250,000 – 1,000,000
✪	✪	•	Under 250,000

International boundary

State boundary

0   100   200   300 Miles
0 100 200 300 400 Kilometers

© Rand McNally & Co.
Made in U.S.A.
N-MDL24000-P1-1-1-1-1

✦ RAND McNALLY

A21

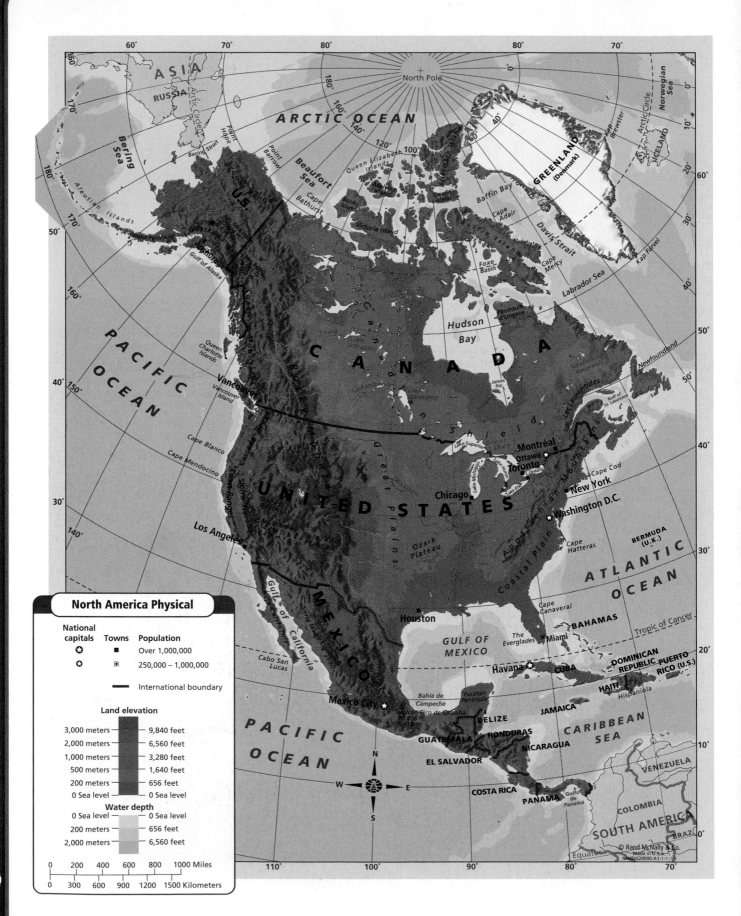

North America Physical

National capitals
⊛ Over 1,000,000
⊚ 250,000 – 1,000,000

Towns
■ Over 1,000,000
⊡ 250,000 – 1,000,000

Population

── International boundary

Land elevation

3,000 meters	9,840 feet
2,000 meters	6,560 feet
1,000 meters	3,280 feet
500 meters	1,640 feet
200 meters	656 feet
0 Sea level	0 Sea level

Water depth

0 Sea level	0 Sea level
200 meters	656 feet
2,000 meters	6,560 feet

0 200 400 600 800 1000 Miles
0 300 600 900 1200 1500 Kilometers

RAND McNALLY

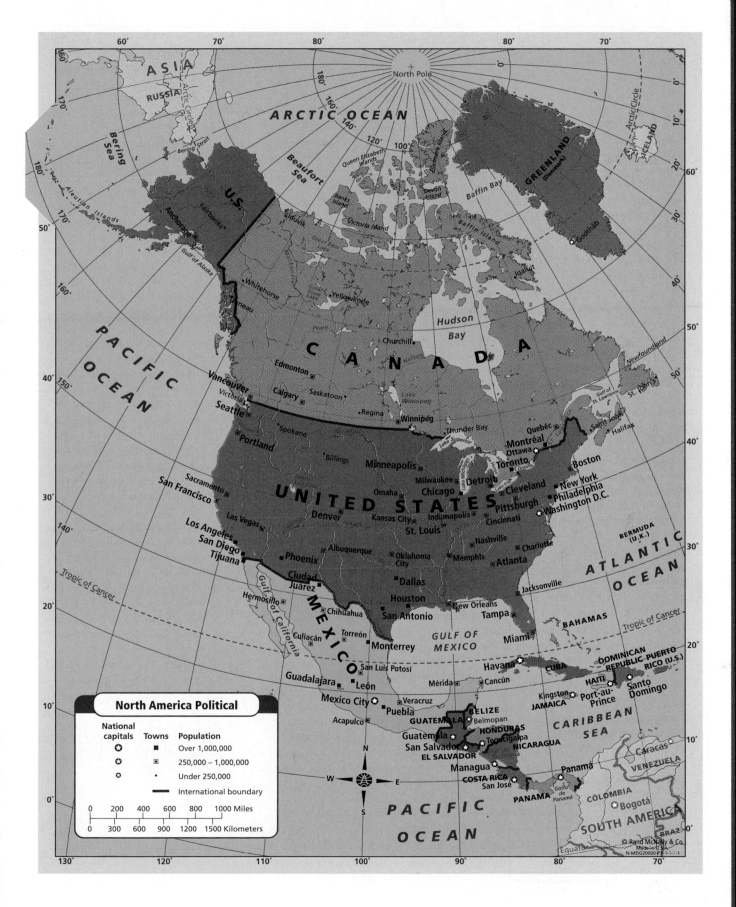

North America Political

National capitals

⊙ National capitals

Towns **Population**

■ Over 1,000,000

▣ 250,000 – 1,000,000

• Under 250,000

—— International boundary

0   200   400   600   800   1000 Miles

0   300   600   900   1200 1500 Kilometers

© Rand McNally & Co.
Made in U.S.A.
N-MDG20000-P 1-1-1-1-1

RAND MCNALLY

A23

South America Physical

National capitals
⊛ Over 1,000,000
⊙ 250,000 – 1,000,000

Towns
■ Over 1,000,000
▣ 250,000 – 1,000,000

Population

——— International boundary

Land elevation
3,000 meters	9,840 feet
2,000 meters	6,560 feet
1,000 meters	3,280 feet
500 meters	1,640 feet
200 meters	656 feet
0 Sea level	0 Sea level

Water depth
0 Sea level	0 Sea level
200 meters	656 feet
2,000 meters	6,560 feet

0   200   400   600   800   1000 Miles
0   300   600   900   1200   1500 Kilometers

© Rand McNally & Co.
Made in U.S.A.
N-MDG40000-A-1-1-1-1

RAND MᶜNALLY

South America Political

National capitals | **Towns** | **Population**
- ✪ | ■ | Over 1,000,000
- ✪ | ▣ | 250,000 – 1,000,000
- ○ | · | Under 250,000
- —— International boundary

0 200 400 600 800 1000 Miles
0 300 600 900 1200 1500 Kilometers

RAND M℠NALLY

© Rand McNally & Co.
Made in U.S.A.
N-MOG40000-P11-1-1-1

A25

GULF OF MEXICO
Havana
NORTH AMERICA
MEXICO
BELIZE
GUATEMALA
HONDURAS
EL SALVADOR
NICARAGUA
COSTA RICA
PANAMA
CUBA
JAMAICA
HAITI
DOMINICAN REPUBLIC
PUERTO RICO (U.S.)
CARIBBEAN SEA
TRINIDAD AND TOBAGO
ATLANTIC OCEAN

Barranquilla
Cartagena
Maracaibo
Caracas
Valencia
Barquisimeto
Cúcuta
Ciudad Guayana
VENEZUELA
Georgetown
GUYANA
Paramaribo
SURINAME
Cayenne
FRENCH GUIANA (Fr.)
Bucaramanga
Medellín
Manizales
Bogotá
Cali
COLOMBIA
Boa Vista
Macapá

Quito
ECUADOR
Guayaquil
Galapagos Islands (Ec.)
Equator
Iquitos
Manaus
Santarem
Belém
São Luís
Fortaleza
BRAZIL
Imperatriz
Teresina
Natal
João Pessoa
Recife
Maceió

Chiclayo
Trujillo
PERU
Lima
Huancayo
Cusco
Lago Titicaca
Arequipa
BOLIVIA
La Paz
Cochabamba
Santa Cruz
Sucre
Arica
Cuiabá
Campo Grande
Goiânia
Brasília
Montes Claros
Uberlândia
Feira de Santana
Aracaju
Salvador
Belo Horizonte
Ribeirão Preto
Campinas
Rio de Janeiro
São Paulo
Curitiba
Caxias do Sul
Porto Alegre

PACIFIC OCEAN
Antofagasta
Tropic of Capricorn
Isla San Ambrosio (Chile)
Isla San Felix (Chile)
PARAGUAY
Salta
San Miguel de Tucumán
Asunción
Resistencia
Archipiélago Juan Fernández (Chile)
Valparaíso
Santiago
Córdoba
Mendoza
Rosario
Santa Fe
URUGUAY
Buenos Aires
La Plata
Montevideo
ARGENTINA
CHILE
Concepción
Bahía Blanca
Mar del Plata
Río de la Plata

Puerto Montt
Archipiélago de los Chonos
Comodoro Rivadavia

N
W   E
S

ATLANTIC OCEAN

Río Gallegos
FALKLAND ISLANDS (U.K.)
Punta Arenas
Strait of Magellan
Tierra del Fuego

South Georgia (U.K.)

South Shetland Islands (U.K.)
South Orkney Islands (U.K.)
South Sandwich Islands (U.K.)

Drake Passage

RAND McNALLY

RAND McNALLY

70° 40° 50° 60° 70° 80°

■ Murmansk

Kola Peninsula

WHITE SEA

Timan Ridge

Gora Narodnaya
6,214 ft.
1,894 m.

FINLAND

Lake Ladoga

Ob'

Irtysh

ASIA

50°

Gulf of Finland

Severnyye Uvaly
(Hills)

70°

ESTONIA

R U S S I A

LATVIA

Valdai Hills

☆ Moscow

LITHUANIA

Central Russian Upland

Oka-Don Plain

Volga Upland

KAZAKHSTAN

Caspian Depression

Aral Sea

BELARUS

Dnieper Lowland

Donets Basin

UZBEKISTAN

Amu Darya

40°

☆ Kiev

UKRAINE

CASPIAN SEA

60°

MOLDOVA

Sea of Azov

TURKMENISTAN

ROMANIA

Crimean Peninsula

Caucasus

Gora El'brus
18,510 ft.
5,642 m.

GEORGIA

BLACK SEA

ARMENIA AZERBAIJAN

AZER.

Peninsula

IRAN

BULGARIA

İstanbul

Sea of Marmara

30°

Mt. Olympus
9,570 ft.
2,917 m.

TURKEY

SYRIA

IRAQ

Tigris

GREECE

AEGEAN SEA

LEBANON

Euphrates

© Rand McNally & Co.
Made in U.S.A.
N-MDG50000-A1-1-1-1-1

Sea of Crete

Rhodes

CYPRUS

Crete

30° 40° 50°

A27

Europe Political

National capitals	State capitals	Towns	Population
⚘	✹	■	Over 1,000,000
⚘	✹	▣	250,000 – 1,000,000
⚘	✹	•	Under 250,000

International boundary

Political subdivision boundary

0 100 200 300 400 Miles
0 200 400 600 Kilometers

ICELAND
Reykjavik

ATLANTIC OCEAN

FAROE ISLANDS (Den.)

NORWEGIAN SEA

Arctic Circle

Hammerfest

Kiruna

SWEDEN

NORWAY

Trondheim

Umeå

Tampere

Bergen

Oslo

Stockholm

Göteborg

Vänern

Vättern

Skagerrak

Kattegat

Gulf of Bothnia

BALTIC SEA

LITHUANIA

Kaliningrad

RUSSIA

Gdańsk

Szczecin

SCOTLAND

Aberdeen

Glasgow

Edinburgh

UNITED KINGDOM

NORTHERN IRELAND

Belfast

Dublin

IRELAND

Cork

Irish Sea

Liverpool

Manchester

WALES

ENGLAND

Birmingham

Cardiff

Thames

London

Plymouth

St. George's Channel

NORTH SEA

DENMARK

Copenhagen

Hamburg

Berlin

Elbe

GERMANY

POLAND

Warsaw

Łódź

Wrocław

Dresden

Katowice

Kraków

Prague

CZECH REPUBLIC

SLOVAKIA

Bratislava

English Channel

Strait of Dover

Le Havre

Brest

NETHERLANDS

Amsterdam

The Hague

Antwerp

Brussels

BELGIUM

Cologne

Essen

Bonn

Frankfurt

Lux.

LIECH.

Luxembourg

Rhine

Strasbourg

Stuttgart

Munich

Danube

Bern

SWITZERLAND

Zurich

Geneva

AUSTRIA

Vienna

Graz

SLOVENIA

Ljubljana

HUNGARY

Budapest

CROATIA

Zagreb

Paris

Nantes

FRANCE

Lyon

Bordeaux

Toulouse

Bay of Biscay

A Coruña

Gijón

Bilbao

Porto

PORTUGAL

Lisbon

Valladolid

Zaragoza

Madrid

SPAIN

Córdoba

Seville

Málaga

València

Alacant

Barcelona

ANDORRA

Marseille

Golfe du Lion

Turin

Milan

Genoa

Bologna

Nice

MONACO

Ligurian Sea

Corsica

Venice

ITALY

Florence

Rome

VATICAN CITY

Naples

Bari

Sardinia

Cagliari

TYRRHENIAN SEA

Palermo

Sicily

Messina

Catania

SAN MARINO

BOSNIA AND HERZEGOVINA

Split

Sarajevo

MONTENEGRO

Podgorica

ADRIATIC SEA

SERBIA

Belgrade

Skopje

MACEDONIA

ALBANIA

Tiranë

GREECE

Pátra

IONIAN SEA

Palma

Strait of Gibraltar

GIBRALTAR (U.K.)

Algiers

MOROCCO

AFRICA

ALGERIA

TUNISIA

MEDITERRANEAN SEA

MALTA

70° 40° 50° 60° 70° 80°

Murmansk

WHITE SEA

Oulu

FINLAND

Arkhangel'sk

RUSSIA

Syktyvkar

Ukhta

Bereznki

Petrozavodsk

Kirov

Perm'

Lake Ladoga

Helsinki

Saint Petersburg

Cherepovets

Izhevsk

Naberezhnye Chelny

Ufa

Gulf of Finland

Tallinn

ESTONIA

Yaroslavl'

Nizhniy Novgorod

Kazan'

Ivanovo

Tver

ASIA

Riga

LATVIA

Moscow

Ryazan'

Samara

Vicebsk

Penza

Vilnius

Tula

Aral Sea

Minsk

Bryansk

Lipetsk

Saratov

KAZAKHSTAN

BELARUS

Homel'

Voronezh

Ural

UZBEKISTAN

Chornobyl'

Kiev

Kharkiv

Volgograd

Atyrau

I'viv

Vinnytsia

UKRAINE

Dnipro-petrovs'k

Luhans'k

Astrakhan'

40°

Dnieper

Donets'k

Rostov-na-Donu

Dniester

Kryvyi Rih

Zaporizhzhia

Mariupol'

CASPIAN SEA

TURKMENISTAN

MOLDOVA

Iaşi

Chişinău

Krasnodar

Stavropol'

60°

Cluj-Napoca

Odesa

Sea of Azov

ROMANIA

Galaţi

Simferopol'

Vladikavkaz

Craiova

Bucharest

Sevastopol'

Constanţa

BLACK SEA

GEORGIA

T'bilisi

Baku

BULGARIA

Varna

ARMENIA

AZERBAIJAN

Sofia

Yerevan

AZER.

Plovdiv

İstanbul

Tehran

Thessaloniki

Sea of Marmara

Ankara

IRAN

AEGEAN SEA

TURKEY

Athens

Crete

SYRIA

IRAQ

Baghdad

CYPRUS

LEBANON

© Rand McNally & Co.
Made in U.S.A.
N-MDG50000-P1-1-1-1-1

30° 40° 50°

30°

40°

50°

60°

70°

80°

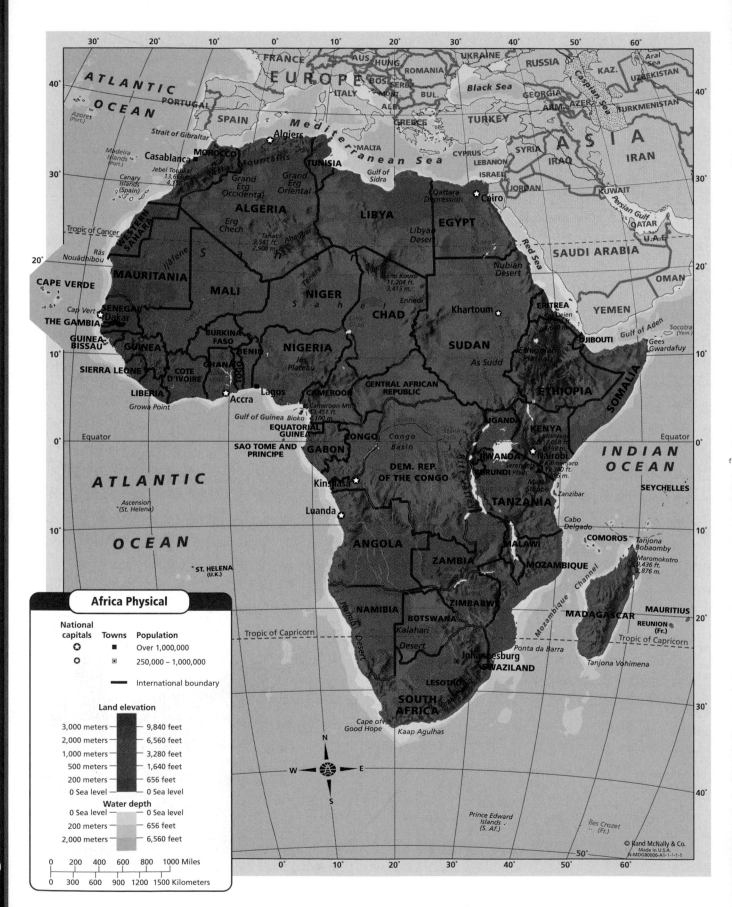

Africa Physical

National capitals
⊛ ⊙

Towns
■ ⊡

Population
Over 1,000,000
250,000 – 1,000,000

—— International boundary

Land elevation

3,000 meters	9,840 feet
2,000 meters	6,560 feet
1,000 meters	3,280 feet
500 meters	1,640 feet
200 meters	656 feet
0 Sea level	0 Sea level

Water depth

0 Sea level	0 Sea level
200 meters	656 feet
2,000 meters	6,560 feet

0   200   400   600   800   1000 Miles
0   300   600   900   1200   1500 Kilometers

RAND McNALLY

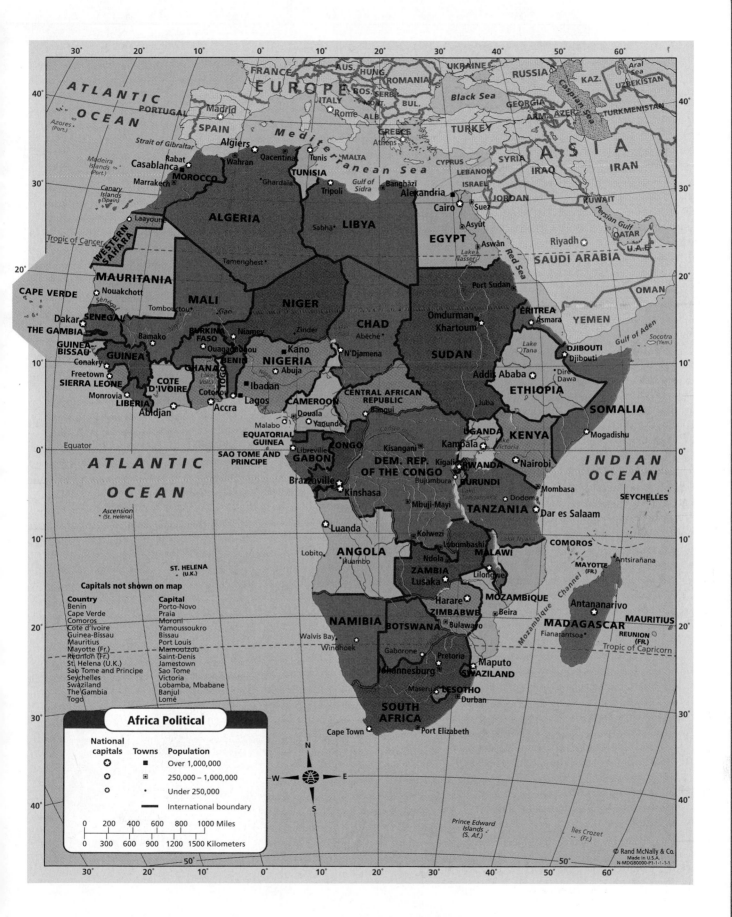

Africa Political

National capitals / **Towns** / **Population**

- National capital ◉ / Town ▪ — Over 1,000,000
- National capital ◉ / Town ▣ — 250,000 – 1,000,000
- National capital ◉ / Town • — Under 250,000
- —— International boundary

| 0 | 200 | 400 | 600 | 800 | 1000 Miles |
| 0 | 300 | 600 | 900 | 1200 | 1500 Kilometers |

Capitals not shown on map

Country	Capital
Benin	Porto-Novo
Cape Verde	Praia
Comoros	Moroni
Cote d'Ivoire	Yamoussoukro
Guinea-Bissau	Bissau
Mauritius	Port Louis
Mayotte (Fr.)	Mamoutzou
Reunion (Fr.)	Saint-Denis
St. Helena (U.K.)	Jamestown
Sao Tome and Principe	Sao Tome
Seychelles	Victoria
Swaziland	Lobamba, Mbabane
The Gambia	Banjul
Togo	Lomé

© Rand McNally & Co.
Made in U.S.A.
N-MDG80000-P1-1-1-1

Asia Physical

National capitals
⊕
✪

Towns
■
▣

Population
Over 1,000,000
250,000 – 1,000,000

—— International boundary

Land elevation

3,000 meters	9,840 feet
2,000 meters	6,560 feet
1,000 meters	3,280 feet
500 meters	1,640 feet
200 meters	656 feet
0 Sea level	0 Sea level

Water depth

0 Sea level	0 Sea level
200 meters	656 feet
2,000 meters	6,560 feet

0   200   400   600   800 Miles
0 200 400 600 800 1000 Kilometers

RUSSIA

Taymyr Peninsula
Laptev Sea
New Siberian Islands
East Siberian Sea
Bering Sea
Aleutian Islands (U.S.)

Central Siberian Uplands

Siberia

Sea of Okhotsk
Kamchatka Peninsula

Sakhalin
Tatar Strait
Kuril Islands

MONGOLIA
Gobi Desert

Hokkaido
Sea of Japan
Honshu
Tōkyō
Mt. Fuji 3,776 m
JAPAN
Shikoku
Kyushu

PACIFIC OCEAN

Tropic of Cancer

CHINA
Qinling Shandi
Qilian Shan

NORTH KOREA
SOUTH KOREA
Beijing
Yellow Sea
Shanghai
East China Sea

TAIWAN
Taiwan Strait

NORTHERN MARIANA ISLANDS (U.S.)
GUAM (U.S.)

Philippine Sea

FEDERATED STATES OF MICRONESIA

BHUTAN
MYANMAR
LAOS
THAILAND
Bangkok
CAMBODIA
VIETNAM
BNGL

Gulf of Tonkin
Hainan Island

South China Sea

Luzon Strait
Luzon
Manila
PHILIPPINES
Mindanao
Sulu Sea

PALAU

Equator

Andaman Islands (India)
Andaman Sea
Gulf of Thailand

MALAY PENINSULA

Nicobar Islands (India)

Str. of Malacca
MALAYSIA
Singapore
Sumatra

BRUNEI
MALAYSIA
Borneo

Celebes Sea
Celebes

Moluccas
Ceram

New Guinea

PAPUA NEW GUINEA

Greater Sunda Islands

Java Sea
Jakarta
Java

INDONESIA

Banda Sea
EAST TIMOR
Timor
Timor Sea

Arafura Sea

Gulf of Carpentaria

Coral Sea

AUSTRALIA

© Rand McNally & Co.
Made in U.S.A.
N-MDG60000-A1-1-1-1-1

RAND McNALLY

A33

Asia Political

National capitals
- ⊕ Over 1,000,000
- ⊕ 250,000 – 1,000,000
- ⊕ Under 250,000

State capitals
- ⊛
- ⊛
- ⊛

Towns Population
- ■ Over 1,000,000
- ▣ 250,000 – 1,000,000
- • Under 250,000
- ── International boundary

0   200   400   600   800 Miles
0 200 400 600 800 1000 Kilometers

Laptev Sea
New Siberian Islands
East Siberian Sea
Bering Sea
ALEUTIAN ISLANDS (U.S.)
Kamchatka Peninsula
Anadyr
Magadan
Sea of Okhotsk
Petropavlovsk-Kamchatskiy
Yakutsk
Sakhalin
Kuril Islands
Krasnoyarsk
Chita
Irkutsk
Qiqihar
Harbin
Vladivostok
Khabarovsk
Sapporo
Hokkaido
A S I A
Ulaanbaatar
Changchun
Shenyang
Sea of Japan
Honshu
Tokyo
Nagoya
MONGOLIA
NORTH KOREA
Beijing
Seoul
SOUTH KOREA
Osaka
JAPAN
Tianjin
Jinan
Yellow Sea
Pusan
Shikoku
Taiyuan
Kyushu
Lanzhou
Shanghai
PACIFIC
Nanjing
East China Sea
OCEAN
C H I N A
Xi'an
Wuhan
Hangzhou
Chengdu
Chongqing
Guiyang
Fuzhou
Taiwan Strait
Taipei
NORTHERN MARIANA ISLANDS (U.S.)
Lhasa
Kaohsiung
TAIWAN
Kunming
Nanning
Guangzhou
Hong Kong
GUAM (U.S.)
BHUTAN
BNGL.
Dhaka
Hainan Island
Luzon Strait
Luzon
Philippine Sea
FEDERATED STATES OF MICRONESIA
Chittagong
Hanoi
Gulf of Tonkin
MYANMAR
LAOS
Vientiane
Da Nang
South China Sea
PHILIPPINES
Manila
Cebu
Samar
PALAU
Yangon
THAILAND
VIETNAM
Mindanao
Bangkok
CAMBODIA
Phnom Penh
Ho Chi Minh City
Sulu Sea
Davao
Andaman Islands (India)
Andaman Sea
Gulf of Thailand
Celebes Sea
Manado
New Guinea
PAPUA NEW GUINEA
Nicobar Islands (India)
Bandar Seri Begawan
BRUNEI
MALAYSIA
Ceram
Medan
MALAYSIA
Kuala Lumpur
Borneo
Celebes
Coral Sea
Singapore
Sumatra
Banjarmasin
I N D O N E S I A
Banda Sea
EAST TIMOR
Arafura Sea
Gulf of Carpentaria
Palembang
Java
Jakarta
Bandung
Java Sea
Surabaya
Timor
Timor Sea
AUSTRALIA

Tropic of Cancer
Equator

80° 70° 60° 50° 40° 30°
90° 100° 110° 120° 130° 140° 150°
20° 10° 0° 10° 20°
180° 170° 160°

RAND M^cNALLY

Australia and Oceania Physical

National capitals
Towns · Population
⊕ ■ Over 1,000,000
⊕ ⊡ 250,000 – 1,000,000
── International boundary

Land elevation
9,840 feet — 3,000 meters
6,560 feet — 2,000 meters
3,280 feet — 1,000 meters
1,640 feet — 500 meters
656 feet — 200 meters
0 Sea level — 0 Sea level

Water depth
0 Sea level — 0 Sea level
656 feet — 200 meters
6,560 feet — 2,000 meters

0   200   400   600   800 Miles
0   200   400   600   800   1000 Kilometers

© Rand McNally & Co.
Made in U.S.A.
N-MJSG90000-A1-1-1-1-1

CHINA
Taipei
TAIWAN
Taiwan Strait
Luzon Strait
South China Sea
Luzon
Manila
PHILIPPINES
Mindoro
Mindanao
Philippine Sea
Sulu Sea
Celebes Sea
Celebes
Halmahera
Molucca
Banda Sea
PALAU
INDONESIA
EAST TIMOR
Timor
Timor Sea
Arafura Sea
GUAM (U.S.)
NORTHERN MARIANA ISLANDS (U.S.)
FEDERATED STATES OF MICRONESIA
MARSHALL ISLANDS
MICRONESIA
NAURU
KIRIBATI
International Date Line
Line Islands
Kiritimati
Equator
POLYNESIA
Hawaiian Islands
Hawai'i
Marquesas Is.
FRENCH POLYNESIA (Fr.)
Tuamotu Archipelago
Tahiti
Society Islands
Austral Is.
Tropic of Capricorn
PITCAIRN (U.K.)
PACIFIC OCEAN
Northern Cook Islands
COOK ISLANDS (N.Z.)
Southern Cook Islands
NIUE (N.Z.)
AMERICAN SAMOA (U.S.)
SAMOA
TOKELAU (N.Z.)
WALLIS AND FUTUNA (Fr.)
TONGA
Koro Sea
FIJI
TUVALU
MELANESIA
SOLOMON ISLANDS
Solomon Sea
Bismarck Sea
New Guinea
Mount Wilhelm 14,793 ft.
PAPUA NEW GUINEA
Port Moresby
Torres Strait
CAPE YORK PENINSULA
Gulf of Carpentaria
Great Barrier Reef
Coral Sea
VANUATU
NEW CALEDONIA (Fr.)
Kermadec Islands (N.Z.)
NORFOLK ISLAND (Austl.)
NEW ZEALAND
North Island
Wellington
Cook Strait
South Island
Chatham Islands
Brisbane
Sydney
Canberra
GREAT DIVIDING RANGE
AUSTRALIA
Great Sandy Desert
Kimberley Plateau
Gibson Desert
GREAT VICTORIA DESERT
Great Australian Bight
Melbourne
Bass Strait
Tasmania
Tasman Sea

North Pole

✪ National capital
● Town
▬ International boundary

| 0 | 200 | 400 | 600 | 800 | 1000 Miles |
| 0 | 400 | 800 | 1200 | 1600 Kilometers |

© Rand McNally & Co.
Made in U.S.A.
N-MDG10091-P1-1-1-1-1

South Pole

| 0 | 200 | 400 | 600 | 800 | 1000 Miles |
| 0 | 400 | 800 | 1200 | 1600 Kilometers |

© Rand McNally & Co.
Made in U.S.A.
N-MDG94000-P1-1-1-1-1

RAND M:NALLY

A37

UNIT 1

Introduction to World Geography

Why It Matters:

You live on a unique planet in the Sun's planetary system. It is the only planet capable of supporting a wide variety of life forms. As human beings we adapt and alter the environments on Earth.

Landsat satellite

CHAPTER 1
Understanding the Earth and Its Peoples

Fiery volcanic eruption

CHAPTER 2
Earth's Interlocking Systems

Indonesian rice fields

CHAPTER 3
Human Geography

Cave of Hands, Santa Cruz, Argentina

CHAPTER 4
People and Culture

Understanding the Earth and Its Peoples

 ESSENTIAL QUESTION

In what ways does geography help us understand our world?

CONNECT ▸ Geography & History

Use the satellite image and the time line to answer the following questions.

1. The large continent in the center of the image is Africa. How would you describe the land?

2. Which of the events listed on the time line made this image possible?

Culture
◂ **c. A.D. 1st century**
Strabo describes the world known to the Greeks and Romans in his 17-volume *Geography*.

A.D. 1

Geography
c. A.D. 2nd century
Greek geographer Ptolemy writes his 8-volume *Geography* on mapmaking.

Geography
▴ **1100** Chinese begin using the magnetic compass.

Ⓐ

Amazon Rain Forest The Amazon rain forest in South America is the largest rain forest in the world.

Ⓑ

Sahara Desert The Sahara is the largest desert in the world.

History

1730 John Hadley creates the basic design for a sextant. ▼

History

1972 First Landsat satellite is launched.

History

1960s Geographic Information Systems (GIS) development begins.

Geography

1983 The Global Positioning System (GPS) becomes operational. ▶

Today

3

Reading for Understanding

▶ Key Ideas

BEFORE YOU READ

Think about what you already know about the Earth's physical geography.

NOW YOU WILL LEARN

Geographers have specialized ways to view and interpret information about the world.

▶ Vocabulary

TERMS & NAMES

geography the study of people, places, and environments

environment the physical surroundings of a location

spatial where a place is located and its physical relationship to other places, people, or environments

location an exact position using latitude and longitude, or a description of a place in relation to places around it

place a geographical term that describes the physical and human characteristics of a location

region an area that has one or more common characteristics that unite or connect it with other areas

BACKGROUND VOCABULARY

three-dimensional an image in which there is a sense of depth and perspective

Visual Vocabulary Three-dimensional shapes

▶ Reading Strategy

Re-create the web diagram shown at right. As you read and respond to the **KEY QUESTIONS**, use the diagram to help you find main ideas about the themes and elements of geography.

 Skillbuilder Handbook, page R4

FIND MAIN IDEAS

THEMES & ELEMENTS OF GEOGRAPHY

GRAPHIC ORGANIZERS
Go to **Interactive Review** @ ClassZone.com

Themes and Elements of Geography

Connecting to Your World

Have you ever drawn a map to show someone how to get to your house? Or have you described your hometown to someone who doesn't live there? If you answered yes to these questions, you were doing what geographers do. Geographers try to answer the questions, "Where are things located?" and "Why are they there?" Basic questions like these form the framework for the subject called geography. **Geography** is the study of people, places, and environments. An **environment** is the physical surroundings of a location.

Ways of Thinking About Geography

▼ **KEY QUESTION** What are the themes and elements of geography?

Geographers study the world in **spatial** terms. This means they look at the space where a place is located and its physical relationship to other places, people, and environments. Geographers—and students of geography— use two different methods to organize geographic information: the five themes and the six essential elements of geography. The categories vary slightly, but the graphic on the next two pages will help you learn how to apply these ideas as you read this text.

Three-Dimensional Model This computer-generated model is used to study geographic conditions in the Los Angeles region.

The Five Themes of Geography

The world is a big place and studying it is a complicated task. You can make that job easier by learning five core themes of geography. These themes can help you answer geographic questions.

1 LOCATION

Where are things located?

Location means either an exact position using latitude or longitude, or a description of a place in relation to places around it.

Rio de Janeiro, Brazil

2 PLACE

What is a particular location like?

Place describes physical characteristics such as mountains or rivers, as well as human characteristics such as the people who live there.

Beijing, China

3 REGION

How are places similar or different?

Regions have physical or human characteristics that unite them and make them different from or similar to other regions.

Gobi Desert

4 MOVEMENT

How do people, goods, and ideas move from one location to another?

Movement of people, goods, and ideas changes places and regions and the people who live there.

Interstate Cloverleaf

5 HUMAN–ENVIRONMENT INTERACTION

How do people relate to the physical world?

Humans adapt to their environment and change elements of it.

Pacific Ocean Windsurfing

Six Essential Elements

Geographers use six key ideas or elements to help them understand people, places, and environments on the Earth.

1 THE WORLD IN SPATIAL TERMS

Geographers study the locations of places and distributions or patterns of features by using maps, data, and other geographic tools. Knowing about the world in spatial terms helps geographers understand physical and human patterns.

Washington, D.C.

2 PLACES AND REGIONS

Geographers look for characteristics of places and then compare their similarities and differences.

Mount Everest

Volcano Specialist

3 PHYSICAL SYSTEMS

Geographers study changes in the Earth's surface. Where and why people choose to live in certain locations may depend on Earth's surface conditions.

4 HUMAN SYSTEMS

Geographers study human settlement patterns and use of resources. This information helps explain human interactions and lifestyles.

South Asian Teapickers

5 ENVIRONMENT AND SOCIETY

Geographers study how people interact with the environment and how they use resources.

6 THE USES OF GEOGRAPHY

Geographers study patterns and processes in the world. This information helps people understand the past and plan for the future.

Surveyor

Five Themes of Geography Now that you have seen the geographic themes and elements side by side, let's look more closely at an example of one of the themes and elements as it applies to a particular place.

The theme of human-environment interaction is a good place to get an idea of how a geographer thinks. For thousands of years, people have found it valuable to settle by rivers. A river can provide food, water, transportation, and other needs of daily life. However, rivers can flood, destroying homes and villages, and taking human life. So, humans began to alter their environment by building walls called levees to protect the land from floods. Sometimes they created dams to control the flow of water and to save some water for times when they needed it. A geographer who asks the questions "Where do people choose to live?" and "Why here?" will answer that the river provides many needs for a group of people. So, people will likely be found in areas that have rivers as a resource. As it turns out, we know that early civilizations such as those in Egypt, Southwest Asia, India, and China began in river valleys.

Six Essential Elements Using the six elements helps geographers make sense both of physical processes on the Earth and of human systems devised by the people who live there.

Let's look at the element of physical systems. Geographers want to know how these systems work to reshape the Earth's surface and what impact these changes have on plants, animals, and people. Volcanoes

CONNECT to Geography

Chicago The skyline of Chicago towers over the shore of Lake Michigan. One of the largest cities in the United States, Chicago has long been the economic and cultural center of the region.

CRITICAL THINKING

Find Main Ideas Look at the image of Chicago at right. Which of the five themes and six elements of geography do the captions reflect?

High-rise buildings maximize the use of valuable land.

Chicago is a major hub for Great Lakes water transportation and a main railroad headquarters.

Chicago is located in the upper Midwest of the United States.

are an example of a physical force that changes the shape of the Earth's surface and may have a dramatic effect on human populations. A volcanic eruption may kill people, plants, and animals living in the area. Flows of lava may change the landscape, burn forests or crops, and possibly alter the course of rivers. Islands in the Pacific Ocean have been created by volcanic eruptions, and still others have disappeared between the waves when they were blown apart by eruptions. Volcanoes can also trigger earthquakes. Geographers studying physical systems point out that many volcanoes take place in certain areas of the world. Studying this pattern of volcanic action helps explain where and why people live in certain locations.

Using the five themes of geography and the six essential elements will help you to think like a geographer. The themes and elements will help you to think about particular places and the physical processes and human activities that shaped those places in the past—and continue to do so. They will also enable you to look for patterns and connections in geographic information. You will be better able to answer the two main geographic questions, "Where are things located?" and "Why are they there?" You will learn about the tools used to record and analyze geographic information in the next section.

 FIND MAIN IDEAS Identify the five themes and six essential elements of geography.

 ONLINE QUIZ
For test practice, go to
Interactive Review
@ ClassZone.com

Section ① Assessment

TERMS & NAMES

1. Explain the importance of
- geography
- environment
- spatial

USE YOUR READING NOTES

2. Find Main Ideas Use your completed web diagram to answer the following question:

What are the five themes of geography?

THEMES & ELEMENTS OF GEOGRAPHY

KEY IDEAS

3. What two questions do geographers try to answer?

4. How do geographers use the five themes?

5. What are the six elements that geographers use to look at the world?

CRITICAL THINKING

6. Summarize What does it mean to study the world in spatial terms?

7. Compare and Contrast How do you think the study of geography differs from that of history?

8. CONNECT to Today How does studying geography help you understand the world in which you live?

9. ART Make a Poster Create a poster that lists the five themes and six elements of geography. For each theme or element, include the definition and a photograph or drawing to illustrate it.

Reading for Understanding

▶ Key Ideas

BEFORE, YOU LEARNED

Geography is the study of Earth's physical features and the interaction of people with the environment and with each other.

NOW YOU WILL LEARN

Geographers use technological tools to help them understand both Earth's physical processes and the activities of people on Earth.

▶ Vocabulary

TERMS & NAMES

globe a model of the earth in the shape of a sphere

map a representation of a part of the Earth

cartographer (kahr•TAHG•ruh•fur) a geographer who creates maps

surveyor a person who measures the land

remote sensing obtaining information about a site by using an instrument that is not physically in contact with the site

Landsat a series of information-gathering satellites that orbit above Earth

Global Positioning System (GPS) a system that uses a network of earth-orbiting satellites to pinpoint location

Geographic Information Systems (GIS) a computer or Internet-based mapping technology

BACKGROUND VOCABULARY

database a collection of information that can be analyzed

debris (duh•BREE) the scattered remains of something broken or destroyed

▶ Reading Strategy

Re-create the web diagram shown at right. As you read and respond to the **KEY QUESTIONS**, use the diagram to summarize ideas about geographers' technological tools.

 Skillbuilder Handbook, page R5

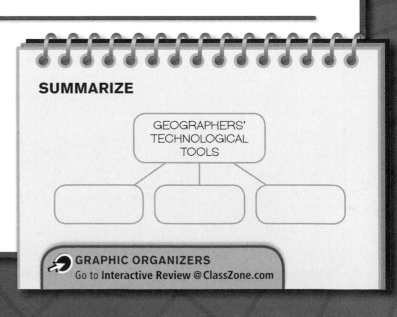

SUMMARIZE

GEOGRAPHERS' TECHNOLOGICAL TOOLS

GRAPHIC ORGANIZERS
Go to **Interactive Review @ ClassZone.com**

Technology Tools for Geographers

Connecting to Your World

When you were a much younger student, you probably used paper and pencil to do your schoolwork. Now, when you have an assignment to complete, you most likely use a computer and the Internet. Today's geographers and other scientists use high-tech instruments and advanced computer software to create maps and databases. A **database** is a collection of information that can be analyzed. Geographers use these tools and their analysis to answer geographic questions.

Gerardus Mercator
A Flemish cartographer, Mercator developed a type of map still used today.

The Science of Mapmaking

🔻 **KEY QUESTION** How has technology changed mapmaking?

In their work, geographers use photographs, graphs, globes, and maps. A **globe** is a model of the Earth in the shape of a sphere. It shows the actual shape of the Earth. But you can only see half at any one time, and it is not easy to carry around. So, geographers use maps. A **map** is a representation of a part of the Earth. Maps can help geographers see patterns in the way human or physical processes occur. **Cartographers** (kahr•TAGH•ruh•furs) are geographers who create maps.

Animated GEOGRAPHY
Landsat Satellite
This satellite provides visible and infrared views of the Earth.

Click here to see how satellites gather data @ ClassZone.com

Cartographers create maps from data collected in surveys. **Surveyors** are people who map and measure the land. They go out to a location and mark down the physical features they see, such as rivers, mountains, or towns. Today, cartographers use technologically advanced tools that provide a much more detailed and accurate picture of the world.

To create modern maps, geographers often use remote sensing equipment. **Remote sensing** means obtaining information about a site by using an instrument that is not physically in contact with the site. Generally, these instruments are cameras mounted on airplanes or Earth-orbiting satellites.

Satellites Two of the best-known satellites are Landsat and GOES. **Landsat** is actually a series of information-gathering satellites that orbit more than 100 miles above the Earth. Each has a variety of sensing devices to collect images and data. Each time a satellite makes an orbit, it gathers information from an area about 115 miles wide. Landsat can scan the entire Earth in 18 days.

GOES, or Geostationary Operational Environmental Satellite, is a weather satellite. This satellite flies in an orbit at the same speed as the

ONLINE PRIMARY SOURCE To see more works of Strabo, go to the **Research & Writing Center** @ClassZone.com

ANALYZING Primary Sources

Strabo (c. 64 B.C.–A.D. 23) was a Greek who wrote books about geography and history. His 17-volume *Geography* is the main source for information about the world known to the ancient Greeks and Romans. Strabo drew the map below for his geography book.

Strabo

DOCUMENT-BASED QUESTION
Which two continents labeled on the map were known to the ancient Greeks and Romans?

Earth's rotation. In this way it remains "stationary" above a fixed area. It gathers images of conditions that are used to forecast the weather. In 2006, there were two GOES satellites. One provided images from the eastern United States and the other from the west. You see GOES images when you watch a TV weather forecast.

Global Positioning System The U.S. Department of Defense developed technology to help American military forces know exactly where they were. The **Global Positioning System (GPS)** employs a network of Earth-orbiting satellites to collect information about the location of a receiver. The satellites beam the receiver's exact position—latitude, longitude, elevation, and time—to Earth. This information is displayed on the receiver.

A GPS receiver can be small enough to fit in your hand. It has an electronic position locator that sends a beam from where you and the device are to an orbiting satellite. The satellite measures where the GPS device is and beams back your exact position.

GPS can be used from any point on the Earth and in any type of weather. You can use its data to help you figure out "Where am I?" and "Where am I going?" GPS data can be used to determine location, aid in navigating from place to place, create maps, and track the movement of people and things. Animal biologists, for example, use GPS devices to track animals and learn about their habits.

▲ **DRAW CONCLUSIONS** Explain how technology has changed mapmaking.

COMPARING ↰ Mapping Styles: Washington, D.C.

Road Maps Road maps are created from information including aerial photographs, road surveys made with hand-held digitizers, and maps showing the positions of such features as lakes and mountains.

Satellite Images Satellite images are produced by equipment that records information in a digital format. The information is then converted to images that look like photographs.

Infrared Images Infrared images measure the radiation emitted by water bodies, vegetation, and buildings. In this type of image, the warm areas appear in light blue, areas with vegetation appear red, and water is black.

CRITICAL THINKING

Evaluate Which of these mapping styles would be the most valuable for determining where earthquake damage has occurred?

Geographic Information Systems

▼ **KEY QUESTION** How do Geographic Information Systems work?

A very technologically advanced tool geographers use is the **Geographic Information Systems (GIS)**. GIS is a computer-based mapping technology. The complete system is able to gather, store, analyze, and display spatial information about places. It combines information from a variety of sources into digital databases.

GIS can integrate geographic information, such as maps, aerial photographs, and satellite images. It can also include information such as population figures, economic statistics, or temperature readings. Someone using GIS selects the information needed to answer a geographic question. Then GIS combines layers of information to give the user a better understanding of how the data works together. It can display the information in different ways, such as on a map, design, chart, or graph. The diagram below shows how GIS works.

CONNECT — Geography & Technology

GIS GIS is a tool that allows geographers to solve problems by combining geographic information about a location from several sources.

1 A question or problem is posed. An example is, "In what general area near this town might an airport be located?" A section of land is identified for problem solving.

2 Computer databases hold geographic information about the location. The user selects layers of information that answer the question, "What geographic characteristics are important for a good airport site?"

3 A terrain map is selected to identify all areas flat enough for landing airplanes.

4 A land use map shows areas that have few homes.

5 A base map shows where roads are located so that the airport can be reached and safety concerns are addressed.

6 The layers of information are combined to create a composite map showing possible sites for the airport.

CRITICAL THINKING
Summarize What geographic information is combined in the final map?

GIS projects can range from simple, specific site questions to more complex global problems. For example, you could use GIS to determine the quickest and safest path to walk to your school. The federal government was able to use GIS to predict the location of **debris** (duh•BREE) from the space shuttle *Columbia*, which broke up upon reentry into the Earth's atmosphere in 2003. GIS can be used to plan for hurricane evacuations or to monitor the possible spread of avian flu. Urban planners use GIS to determine where to place a park or where to relocate a dangerous highway intersection. Private companies use GIS to decide where to drill for oil or even where to place a new fast-food restaurant.

GIS makes it possible for geographers to answer geographic questions quickly and accurately. They are better able to see relationships between data, to understand the past and present, and to predict future situations.

In the next section, you will learn about the many different kinds of jobs geographers perform.

 SUMMARIZE Explain how GIS works.

Fun Facts!

HOW TALL IS MT. EVEREST?

Mt. Everest is growing. In 2004, scientists used satellite images and advanced computer technology to measure Mt. Everest, the world's tallest peak. They determined that it was 29,035 feet high—7 feet taller than previously believed. It would take 20 Sears Towers to equal the height of Mt. Everest.

29,035 ft.

20 Sears Towers = 1 Mount Everest

Section 2 Assessment

ONLINE QUIZ For test practice, go to **Interactive Review** @ClassZone.com

TERMS & NAMES

1. Explain the importance of
- map
- cartographer
- Geographic Information Systems (GIS)

USE YOUR READING NOTES

2. Summarize Use your completed web diagram to answer the following question:

What are some geographers' tools besides maps and globes?

GEOGRAPHERS' TECHNOLOGICAL TOOLS

KEY IDEAS

3. What were two early means of showing the Earth's surface?

4. How did remote sensing change the way geographic data were obtained?

5. What are some ways GIS can be used?

CRITICAL THINKING

6. Make Inferences How were early geographers limited in gathering geographic information?

7. Draw Conclusions How does technology help geographers?

8. CONNECT to Today In what ways do you think that new geography technology might aid military forces in modern warfare?

9. TECHNOLOGY Make a Multimedia Presentation Use an Internet-based GIS to demonstrate the uses of this geographic tool. Give examples of the different tasks a GIS can do.

Reading for Understanding

▶ Key Ideas

BEFORE, YOU LEARNED

Geographers use technology to help them do their jobs of finding information about selected areas.

NOW YOU WILL LEARN

Geographers do many different kinds of jobs as they gather data and analyze and interpret it.

▶ Vocabulary

TERMS & NAMES

location analyst a person who studies an area to find the best location for a client

climatologist a geographer who studies climates

Visual Vocabulary Climatologist

urban planner a person who creates plans for developing and improving parts of a city

geomorphology (JEE•oh•mawr•FAHL•uh•jee) the study of how the shape of the Earth changes

REVIEW VOCABULARY

surveyor a person who maps and measures the land

Geographic Information Systems (GIS) a computer-based mapping technology

urban having to do with a city

▶ Reading Strategy

Re-create the web diagram shown at right. As you read and respond to the **KEY QUESTIONS**, use the web diagram to categorize details about careers in geography.

 Skillbuilder Handbook, page R7

CATEGORIZE

CAREERS

GRAPHIC ORGANIZERS
Go to **Interactive Review** @ ClassZone.com

Careers in Geography

Connecting to Your World

"What are you going to be when you grow up?" is a question that you may have been asked. You may not even know there are a variety of geography-related jobs. The Association of American Geographers lists nearly 150 different geography jobs. So, if you are interested in people, places, and environments, consider a job in geography. Your work will not be limited to maps—it might range from analyzing data to planning projects, or making decisions about the environment.

Modern Cartographer
A cartographer works at updating a street map.

Processing Geographic Data

▼ **KEY QUESTION** What is a geographer's main activity?

A geographer's main activity is analyzing geographic information to answer geographic questions. Jobs processing geographic data begin, of course, with collecting the information. One on-the-ground job in data collection is that of a **surveyor**. Surveyors map and measure the land directly. They may mark boundaries, study the shape of the land, or even help find sewer and water systems beneath the Earth.

Surveyor A surveyor in Dhaka, Bangladesh, gathers data for a project.

High-tech information-gathering jobs include working with **Geographic Information Systems (GIS)** data. Some examples of these jobs include remote sensing specialists and GIS analysts. Take a look back at the GIS feature in Section 2 to get an idea of what a job using GIS would be like. Data analysis jobs require the ability to think critically, high-level computer skills, and a college education.

Once data have been processed, a geographer may study the information to use in planning projects such as a new urban area, a disaster evacuation plan, or the placement of a new highway. Planners can also help determine how to make a neighborhood a better place to live. These jobs, too, require good critical thinking, writing, and computer skills, as well as a college education. Planners are valuable to the success of a community.

▲ **FIND MAIN IDEAS** Explain the main job of a geographer.

Advising Businesses and Government

▼ **KEY QUESTION** How do geographers help businesses and government?

About half of jobs using geography are in business and government. All kinds of businesses use geographic information to help build and expand their operations. A **location analyst** studies an area to find the best location for a client. The client might be a large retail store chain that wants to know which location would be best for opening a new store. The location analyst can study GIS reports on such elements as transportation networks or population in an area and give the business owners the positive and negative points about a location being considered.

In 1967, the Mexican government was looking for a location to create a new international tourist resort. They used location analysts to find an area that had good beaches and was easy to reach from the United States. The result was Cancún, today one of the world's most desirable vacation sites.

Businesses connected with natural resources such as forests also rely on geographers. Geographers help them understand the relationship between their business and the environment where their business is located. **Climatologists** are geographers who study

CONNECT **Geography & Culture**

Cancún Then and Now

In 1967, Cancún was a small, swampy island on Mexico's Caribbean coast. It had white sand beaches, many birds and mangrove trees, but few people. After it was selected as a resort site, it was quickly transformed. Today, Cancún has more than 100 hotels and 500,000 permanent residents. Many work in the tourist industry that serves the millions of visitors who come each year from all over the world.

climates. They are used by businesses that need information about climate to conduct their operations. For example, coffee-growers in Brazil must have an idea if the weather during the next year will be helpful or harmful to their crop. To determine this, a climatologist might study the long-term climate data about the region to project future weather patterns.

City governments often use an **urban planner** to create plans for improving parts of the city. Planners may help locate and design residential or business areas, or parks and recreational spaces. They may find a location for an airport, mass transit routes, or sewer and water lines.

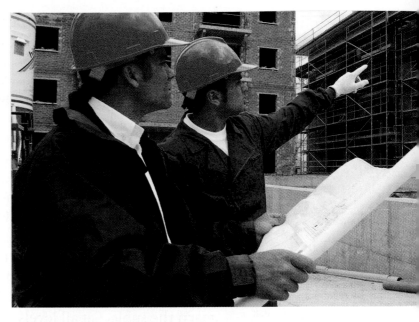

Urban Planners Planners help city governments locate projects being built in a city. **What questions might a planner ask to help a city find the right location for a project?**

▲ **FIND MAIN IDEAS** Explain how geographers help business and government.

CONNECT to Your World

Geography Competitions

Across the United States and in foreign countries, students in grades four through eight compete in geography contests. Students are quizzed on all types of geography, including physical geography—such as locations of places and land and water features—and human geography.

Students compete in Washington, D.C., for the right to represent the United States in international competition for the world championship.

CRITICAL THINKING

Journal Entry Start a page in your journal with questions you could use in a geography contest at your school.

Physical and Human Geography

▼ **KEY QUESTION** What jobs are available related to physical and human geography?

Physical geographers are sometimes called earth scientists. Some study such topics as **geomorphology** (JEE•oh•mawr•FAHL•uh•jee), that is, the study of how the shape of the Earth changes. Others study weather and climate. Still others study water, the oceans, soils, or ecology. Jobs in these fields require special scientific training.

Some geographers study social, political, and economic issues as they relate to place or region. Human geographers are usually hired by government agencies to analyze a specific problem. These geographers work closely with political scientists, economists, and sociologists. Together, they provide possible solutions to problems from many different aspects of life in an area. And, of course, geographers teach the subject at all levels of education, from elementary schools to universities.

But no matter what geography jobs people might hold, they are always trying to answer the basic geographic questions: "Where are things located?" and "Why are they there?"

Surveying the Public
Human geographers ask residents about problems in the neighborhood. **Why would geographers ask residents questions about their neighborhood?**

▲ **SUMMARIZE** Name some physical and human geography jobs.

Section ③ Assessment

ONLINE QUIZ
For test practice, go to
Interactive Review
@ ClassZone.com

TERMS & NAMES

1. Explain the importance of
 • location analyst
 • climatologist
 • urban planner

USE YOUR READING NOTES

2. Categorize Use your completed web diagram to answer the following question:

In what ways could a business use the skills of a geographer?

CAREERS

KEY IDEAS

3. What are three requirements for most careers in geography?

4. Who are the two major employers of geographers?

5. What questions do all types of geographers ask?

CRITICAL THINKING

6. Find Main Ideas How important are geographers to businesses?

7 Summarize How do you train for a geographer's job in business and government?

8. **CONNECT to Today** How do planners help governments with public projects?

9. **WRITING** **Write a Job Description** Select a specific job in the field of geography and research it on the Internet. Then write a description of the job's skill requirements and its responsibilities. If possible find a person doing that job and do an interview or have that person speak to the class.

Click here to complete these and other activities online @ ClassZone.com

CHAPTER SUMMARY

Key Idea 1
Geographers have specialized ways to view and interpret information about the world.

Key Idea 2
Geographers use technical tools to help them understand both the Earth's physical processes and the activities of people on Earth.

Key Idea 3
Geographers do many different kinds of jobs as they gather data and analyze and interpret it.

For **Review and Study Notes**, go to **Interactive Review @ ClassZone.com**

NAME GAME

Use the Terms & Names list to complete each sentence on paper or online.

1. I am a model of the Earth.
   _____ globe _____

2. I am in orbit 100 miles above the Earth.
   _____

3. I am the study of people, places, and things._____

4. I create plans for improving parts of a city.
   _____

5. I am an advanced technology tool used by geographers._____

6. I am a representation of a part of the Earth.
   _____

7. I am a person who creates maps. _____

8. I am a group of places that have something in common. _____

9. I am a description of the physical and human characteristics of a location.
   _____

10. I am a person who maps and measures the land. _____

cartographer
climatologist
environment
Geographic
   Information Systems
geography
globe
Global Positioning
   System
Landsat
location analyst
map
spatial
surveyor
place
region
urban planner

Activities

Flip Cards

Use the online flip cards to quiz yourself on terms and names introduced in this chapter.

map

Crossword Puzzle

Complete an online crossword puzzle to test your knowledge of basic geographic terms.

ACROSS
1. a model of the Earth

VOCABULARY

Explain the significance of each of the following.

1. spatial
2. remote sensing
3. environment
4. database
5. geography

Explain how the terms and names in each group are related.

6. map, globe
7. map, cartographer
8. place, region
9. remote sensing, Landsat, Global Positioning System, Geographic Information System
10. cartographer, surveyor, climatologist, urban planner

KEY IDEAS

1 Themes and Elements of Geography

11. What are the three topics you study in geography?
12. Why is geography considered both science and social studies?
13. What is the difference between location and place?
14. What forces continually change Earth's surface?

2 Technology Tools for Geographers

15. What is remote sensing?
16. How do satellites aid in mapmaking?
17. What two basic geography questions does the Global Positioning System help you answer?
18. What is an example of a technologically advanced geographer's tool?

3 Careers in Geography

19. What is the main activity of a geographer's job?
20. What does a location analyst do?
21. What does an urban planner do?
22. What types of geography are included in physical geography?

CRITICAL THINKING

23. **Categorize** Create a table that lists the five themes of geography and shows two examples of geographic information that would be included each theme's description.

FIVE THEMES	GEOGRAPHIC INFORMATION

24. **Find Main Ideas** How do people adapt to their physical world?
25. **Summarize** How does modern technology help geographers?
26. **Connect to Economics** What role do geographers play in business operations?
27. **Connect Geography & History** How does the study of geographic patterns help us to understand past events?
28. **Five Themes: Human-Environment Interaction** What can be learned about people by studying their interaction with the environment?

Answer the ESSENTIAL QUESTION

In what ways does geography help us understand our world?

Written Response Write a two- or three-paragraph response to the Essential Question. Be sure to consider the key ideas of each section as well as specific ideas about how geographers answer geographic questions. Use the rubric below to guide your thinking.

Response Rubric

A strong response will:

- discuss the two basic geographic questions
- identify and describe the five themes and six essential elements of geography

POLITICAL MAP

Use the map to answer questions 1 and 2 on your paper.

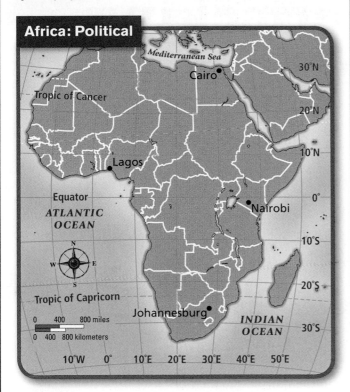

Africa: Political

Mediterranean Sea
Cairo•
Tropic of Cancer
Lagos•
Equator
ATLANTIC OCEAN
•Nairobi
Tropic of Capricorn
Johannesburg•
INDIAN OCEAN

0   400   800 miles
0 400 800 kilometers

30°N 20°N 10°N 0° 10°S 20°S 30°S

10°W 0° 10°E 20°E 30°E 40°E 50°E

1. Which of the cities shown on the map is located south of the Tropic of Capricorn?

A. Cairo
B. Johannesburg
C. Nairobi
D. Lagos

2. Which of the cities shown on the map is located at approximately 30° N and 31° E?

A. Cairo
B. Johannesburg
C. Nairobi
D. Lagos

CLIMATE GRAPH

Examine the climate graph below. Use the information in the graph to answer question 3 on your paper.

Climate: Dakar, Senegal

Temperature (°F): 100 80 60 40 20 0

Precipitation (in.): 10 8 6 4 2 0

J F M A M J J A S O N D

Source: www.worldclimate.com

3. In which months does Dakar get the most rainfall?

GeoActivity

1. INTERDISCIPLINARY ACTIVITY–TECHNOLOGY

With a small group, review new geographic technology. Choose one new tool to research further and create a museum-style display. Be sure your display shows the tool and how it works. Also, explain how the tool has changed the way geographic information is gathered.

2. WRITING FOR SOCIAL STUDIES

Imagine that you are an urban planner and have been asked to develop a plan for placement of a park in your city. Write one paragraph describing the location you chose and the reasons you selected it.

3. MENTAL MAPPING

Create an outline map of your neighborhood, city, or town and locate and label any of the following that are present in the area you map:

• physical features
• your home
• your school
• fire station
• hospital
• shopping area

Earth's Interlocking Systems

 ESSENTIAL QUESTION

How do Earth's physical systems make life on Earth possible?

CONNECT Geography & History

Use the map and the time line to answer the following questions.

1. On which plate does most of the United States sit?
2. Which event on the time line is supported by the evidence on this map?

Geography

1883 Volcanic eruption destroys two-thirds of Krakatoa Island, Indonesia.

 1500

Geography

1620 English philosopher Francis Bacon suggests the continents were once a supercontinent. ▶

Animated GEOGRAPHY
Earth's Tectonic Plates

Click here to explore Earth and its systems @ ClassZone.com

Eurasian Plate

North American Plate

Juan de Fuca Plate

Arabian Plate

African Plate

Philippine Plate

Pacific Plate

Caribbean Plate

Cocos Plate

South American Plate

Nazca Plate

Indo-Australian Plate

Scotia Plate

Antarctic Plate

0   1500   3000 miles
0   1500   3000 kilometers

Ring of Fire

The "Ring of Fire," an arc of volcanoes and earthquakes, is the result of plate movement.

Geography
1960s Scientists prove that the Earth's crust is broken into moving plates.

History
◀ **1980** Mount St. Helens erupts in Washington and causes world's largest landslide.

Today

History
1912 Continental drift theory proposed

History
2004 Indian Ocean earthquake and tsunami kill more than 280,000.

25

Reading for Understanding

▶ Key Ideas

BEFORE, YOU LEARNED

Geographers use technology to learn about physical processes on Earth.

NOW YOU WILL LEARN

The Earth is composed of many layers. Its surface continually changes because of the drifting of its plates.

▶ Vocabulary

TERMS & NAMES

magma molten rock

continent one of seven large landmasses on the Earth's surface

tectonic plate a large rigid section of the Earth's crust that is in constant motion

earthquake a sudden movement of the Earth's crust followed by a series of shocks

Ring of Fire a zone of volcanoes around the Pacific Ocean

volcano an opening in the Earth's crust from which molten rock, ash, and hot gases flow or are thrown out

weathering the gradual physical and chemical breakdown of rocks on the Earth's surface

erosion the wearing away and movement of weathered materials by water, wind, or ice

sediment pieces of rock in the form of sand, stone, or silt deposited by wind, water, or ice

glacier a large, slow-moving mass of ice

Visual Vocabulary glacier

▶ Reading Strategy

Re-create the chart shown at right. As you read and respond to the **KEY QUESTIONS**, use the chart to organize important details about the external and internal forces shaping the Earth.

 Skillbuilder Handbook, page R7

CATEGORIZE

INTERNAL FORCES	EXTERNAL FORCES
1.	1.
2.	2.
3.	3.
4.	4.

 GRAPHIC ORGANIZERS
Go to Interactive Review @ ClassZone.com

The Earth and Its Forces

Connecting to Your World

Have you ever experienced an earthquake or the eruption of a volcano? Probably not. But you may have seen these events on television. Perhaps you saw the coverage of the great earthquake in Indonesia on December 26, 2004. Hundreds of thousands of people were killed or displaced by this earthquake and the tsunami, or great wave, it caused. Earthquakes and volcanoes are just two of the many forces that change the Earth's surface.

Internal Forces Shaping the Earth

▼ **KEY QUESTION** How is the Earth's surface shaped by internal forces?

The Earth is one of eight planets that orbit the sun. It is located about 93 million miles from the sun. The Earth's circumference, or distance around, is 24,900 miles. Its diameter, or distance through the center of Earth, is about 7,900 miles. Earth is unique in the solar system—the sun and its planets—because it supports life. This is because the Earth has lots of breathable air and usable water. In fact, the Earth's surface is about three-fourths water and one-fourth land. The Earth appears to be a solid ball, but it is actually made of different layers that are like shells set inside each other.

San Francisco Earthquake The earthquake in 1989 was the worst quake since 1906.

San Francisco

CALIFORNIA

It is about 3,900 miles to the center of the Earth. The Earth has five different layers.

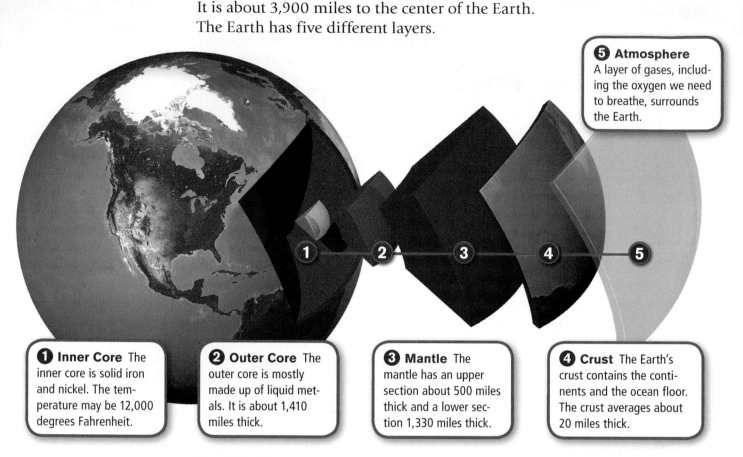

⑤ Atmosphere A layer of gases, including the oxygen we need to breathe, surrounds the Earth.

① Inner Core The inner core is solid iron and nickel. The temperature may be 12,000 degrees Fahrenheit.

② Outer Core The outer core is mostly made up of liquid metals. It is about 1,410 miles thick.

③ Mantle The mantle has an upper section about 500 miles thick and a lower section 1,330 miles thick.

④ Crust The Earth's crust contains the continents and the ocean floor. The crust averages about 20 miles thick.

Earth's Molten Interior The center of the Earth's interior is a hot metal core made up of one layer of iron and one of nickel. The inner core is solid. The outer core is liquid, because the metal has melted. Lying just above the core is the mantle. The mantle is a soft layer of hot rock, some of which is molten, or melted. It is the largest of the Earth's layers. The molten rock of the mantle is called **magma**.

The crust is the Earth's thin outer layer, or shell. It is the solid, rocky surface of the Earth that forms the ocean floors and the large landmasses called **continents**. The crust is the part of the Earth on which we live. It floats on top of the mantle. The crust is only about five miles thick under the oceans but averages about 22 miles thick under the continents. The Earth's layers are illustrated above.

Geographers have identified seven continents on the Earth's surface. The continents, in order of their size, are Asia, Africa, North America, South America, Antarctica, Europe, and Australia. Europe and Asia are actually one great landmass that is sometimes referred to as Eurasia or the Eurasian continent. Antarctica is a continent because it has a landmass beneath its icy surface. The Arctic does not, and so it is not a continent.

Tectonic Plates The surface of the Earth is constantly moving and changing, even as you read this sentence. Geographers use technological tools to observe and measure forces deep inside the Earth and on the surface that reshape the Earth's crust.

Plate movement, earthquakes, and the activity of volcanoes are all internal forces that change the landscape. The Earth's crust is divided into a number of large rigid pieces called **tectonic plates**. These plates are shown on the map at the beginning of the chapter. The continents and oceans are located on these plates, which float on the magma of the Earth's mantle. Heated magma cools as it reaches the crust and then sinks downward. This process causes the magma to act like a conveyor belt under the plates. The plates move slowly against each other, at a rate of up to four inches a year. The plate movement can cause earthquakes and volcanic eruptions. There are four types of tectonic plate movements that are shown in the diagrams below. Each of the movements causes changes in the shape of Earth's crust.

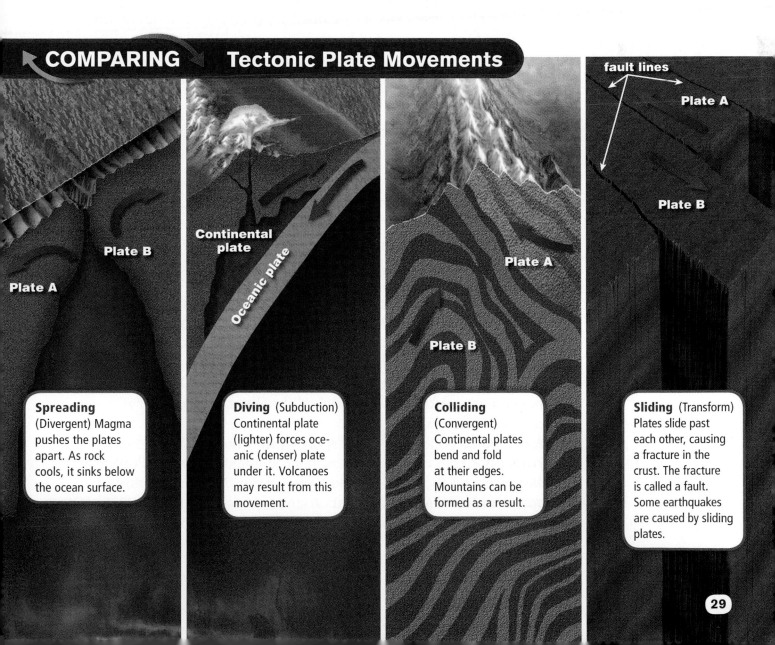

COMPARING Tectonic Plate Movements

fault lines

Plate A

Plate B

Plate B

Plate A

Continental plate

Oceanic plate

Plate A

Plate A

Plate B

Spreading (Divergent) Magma pushes the plates apart. As rock cools, it sinks below the ocean surface.

Diving (Subduction) Continental plate (lighter) forces oceanic (denser) plate under it. Volcanoes may result from this movement.

Colliding (Convergent) Continental plates bend and fold at their edges. Mountains can be formed as a result.

Sliding (Transform) Plates slide past each other, causing a fracture in the crust. The fracture is called a fault. Some earthquakes are caused by sliding plates.

① The world map at left shows the supercontinent of Pangaea about 200 million years ago as it begins to break apart.

② This world map shows the Earth about 65 million years ago. Some of the modern-day continents are visible.

CONNECT Geography & History
Draw Conclusions Which continents were connected 65 million years ago?

Continental Drift If you look at the continents, they look like giant pieces of a jigsaw puzzle waiting to be fit together. Alfred Wegener, a German meteorologist, noticed this pattern. He believed that the continents were once part of a supercontinent called Pangaea (pan•JEE•uh). He suggested that Pangaea divided and drifted apart about 200 million years ago. It contained almost all of the landmasses on Earth and was surrounded by one vast ocean. When it began to break apart, its pieces slowly moved in different directions, and some formed the continents we now know. To this day, the continents continue to move.

▲ **SUMMARIZE** Explain how internal forces shape the Earth's surface.

Extreme Events

▼ **KEY QUESTION** How are earthquakes and volcanoes connected?

Two events caused by internal forces may dramatically reshape the Earth's surface—earthquakes and volcanic eruptions. Both can be deadly, and both have powerful effects on human life.

Earthquakes An **earthquake** is a sudden movement of the Earth's crust that is followed by a series of shocks. Huge rocks along a line where faults are located slide apart and break up, causing that area of the Earth's surface to shake. The stress in the rocks builds for years. Then, energy is swiftly released outward through the ground in vibrations called shock waves.

Earthquakes occur constantly. Some we may not feel, but scientific instruments record them. Some produce slight shock waves. Other earthquakes and their aftershocks cause major disasters. Buildings collapse, cities are destroyed, and thousands of lives may be lost. Fires, floods, landslides, and avalanches can also follow earthquakes.

Earthquakes may also be triggered by the explosive action of a volcano. Most of Earth's active volcanoes are located in a zone around the rim of the Pacific Ocean called the **Ring of Fire**. A number of tectonic plates meet in this zone, and many of the largest earthquakes in the world have occurred there.

One of the biggest earthquakes ever recorded took place near the coast of Indonesia in 2004. It occurred on the floor of the Indian Ocean where two tectonic plates meet. The quake produced a giant ocean wave called a tsunami (tsu•NAH•mee). Within hours, the tsunami had devastated the coasts of 12 countries in southern Asia and eastern Africa. Whole villages were swept away, and more than 280,000 people were killed.

Volcanoes A **volcano** is an opening in the Earth's crust from which molten rock, ash, and hot gases flow. Molten rock rises from the Earth's mantle and is stored in a chamber beneath the crust. Pressure builds and forces the molten rock, or lava, to erupt onto the Earth's surface, burning or burying anything it touches. The eruption may also throw large clouds of gases and ash into the atmosphere.

Some volcanoes erupt constantly. Others are inactive, but could erupt at some future time. The most destructive eruption in recorded history happened in 1883, when two-thirds of the Indonesian island of Krakatoa (KRAK•uh•TOH•uh) was blown apart. The most active volcano in the United States is Mount St. Helens in Washington. It blew its top off in 1980. Activity occurred again in 2005.

▲ **UNDERSTAND CAUSES** Explain how earthquakes and volcanoes are connected.

CONNECT ➤ to Science

In a volcanic eruption, red-hot magma rises through cracks in the Earth's crust. Gases are released, causing a violent explosion of liquid rock, hot ash, and fiery gases into the air.

Kilauea, Hawaii

Activity
Make a Model of a Volcano
Materials
- small drink bottle (1/2 pint or 12 oz.)
- 1/4 cup of water
- a few drops of dishwashing detergent
- orange food coloring
- 1/4 cup vinegar
- 1 tablespoon baking soda
- a small square of tissue

1. Place the water, soap, food coloring, and vinegar in the bottle.

2. Wrap the baking soda in the tissue and drop the baking soda packet in the bottle. Watch the eruption.

External Forces Shaping the Earth

▼ **KEY QUESTION** What external forces shape the Earth?

External forces also reshape the Earth's surface. The two main external forces are weathering and erosion. **Weathering** is the gradual physical and chemical breakdown of rocks near or on the Earth's surface. **Erosion** is the wearing away and movement of weathered materials from one place to another by the action of water, wind, or ice. As you can see, weathering and erosion work together to shape the Earth.

Weathering Weathering occurs slowly, over many years or even centuries. The two types of weathering are mechanical weathering and chemical weathering. Mechanical weathering is a process in which rocks are broken down into smaller pieces by physical means. It takes place when ice, extremes of hot and cold, or even tree roots cause rocks to split apart. It also occurs when hard objects, such as other rocks or sand, scrape or rub against a rock, and pieces of the rock break off.

Chemical weathering is caused by chemical reactions between the minerals in the rock and elements in the air or water. This process changes the make-up of the rock itself. For example, most rocks contain iron. When iron comes in contact with water, it rusts, which helps to break down the rock. Water and elements in the air can cause other minerals in rocks to dissolve.

The Grand Canyon The Grand Canyon is located on the Colorado River in Arizona. It is an example of both weathering and erosion caused by wind and water.

Erosion New landforms and new soil are formed by erosion. It occurs when materials loosened by weathering are moved by water, wind, or ice to new locations. Currents in streams and rivers pick up loose materials and deposit them downstream or carry them out to sea. These tiny pieces of rock, deposited by water, wind, or ice are called **sediment**. Sediment can be sand, stone, or finely ground particles called silt.

Wave action along coastlines carries rocks and sand from one place to another. Waves also pound boulders into smaller rocks. Wind erosion lifts particles from the Earth's surface and blows them great distances. The wind's actions can reshape rock surfaces. Arizona's Grand Canyon is a result of both wind and water erosion.

Another type of erosion is caused by glaciers. **Glaciers** are large, slow-moving masses of ice. They grind rocks and boulders underneath the ice and leave behind the rock when the ice melts. Parts of the central United States have been shaped by glacial erosion.

Beach Erosion Ocean waves and tides eroded this section of beach in California.

 SYNTHESIZE Explain how external forces shape the Earth's surface.

Section 1 Assessment

ONLINE QUIZ For test practice, go to **Interactive Review** @ ClassZone.com

TERMS & NAMES

1. Explain the importance of
- continent
- tectonic plate
- weathering
- erosion

USE YOUR READING NOTES

2. Categorize Use your completed chart to answer the following question:

Are external or internal forces responsible for volcanoes? Explain your answer.

INTERNAL FORCES	EXTERNAL FORCES
1.	1.
2.	2.
3.	3.
4.	4.

KEY IDEAS

3. What are the five layers that make up the Earth's interior and exterior?

4. How were the continents formed?

5. What are the two major external forces reshaping the Earth?

CRITICAL THINKING

6. Draw Conclusions How does the movement of wind, water, or ice reshape the Earth's surface?

7. Analyze Causes and Effects What is the relationship between plate movement, volcanoes, and earthquakes?

8. CONNECT to Today In which parts of the United States are external forces shaping the landscape?

9. ART Create a Puzzle Make a copy of a map of the world. Cut out the continents. Use the continents as puzzle pieces to form the continent of Pangaea. When you have finished putting the pieces together, draw an outline around the entire supercontinent.

Reading for Understanding

▶ Key Ideas

BEFORE, YOU LEARNED

Internal and external forces shape the surface of the Earth.

NOW YOU WILL LEARN

Interaction between landforms and bodies of water makes life on Earth possible.

▶ Vocabulary

TERMS & NAMES

drainage basin the area drained by a major river

ground water water found beneath the Earth's surface

hydrologic cycle the circulation of water between the Earth, the oceans, and the atmosphere

landform a feature on the Earth's surface formed by physical force

plateau a broad, flat area of land higher than the surrounding land

relief the difference in the elevation of a landform from its lowest point to its highest point

continental shelf the submerged land at the edge of a continent

BACKGROUND VOCABULARY

atmosphere the layer of gases that surround the Earth

Visual Vocabulary landform

▶ Reading Strategy

Re-create the web diagram shown at right. As you read and respond to the **KEY QUESTIONS**, use the diagram to organize important details about the Earth's landforms and bodies of water.

 See Skillbuilder Handbook, page R4

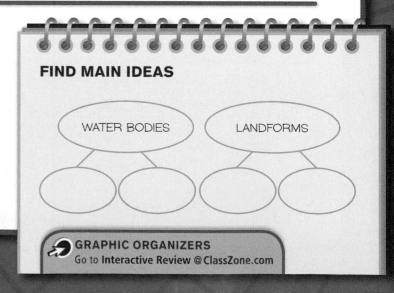

FIND MAIN IDEAS

WATER BODIES   LANDFORMS

GRAPHIC ORGANIZERS
Go to **Interactive Review** @ClassZone.com

Bodies of Water and Landforms

Connecting to Your World

How important is water to your life and to life on Earth? Without enough usable water, there would be no life. The Earth is able to support plant and animal life because of its abundance of water. It appears to be the only planet in our solar system able to do so. The Earth is sometimes called the "blue planet" because bodies of water cover so much of its surface.

The Earth from Space

Bodies of Water

▼ **KEY QUESTION** What are the two types of water supply found on Earth?

Almost three-fourths of the surface of the Earth is covered by water. Most of the water—more than 97 percent of it—is salt water. This is the water in the oceans and seas. Only about 2.5 percent of the Earth's water is fresh water—that is, water containing little or no salt.

Fresh Water Most fresh water is locked in frozen form in ice caps or glaciers. Much of the rest is found in rivers, streams, and lakes.

Iguacu Falls This series of 275 falls is located between Brazil and Argentina.

BRAZIL
Iguacu Falls
ARGENTINA

The Great Salt Lake This huge lake in northern Utah covers about 1,700 square miles. It is a remnant, or remainder, of a huge ancient fresh water lake called Lake Bonneville. That lake existed around 14,000 years ago and was about ten times as large as the Great Salt Lake. As the climate became drier and warmer over the centuries, Lake Bonneville's waters began to evaporate. But the salt it contained did not. That's why the Great Salt Lake is one of the saltiest bodies of water in the world.

CRITICAL THINKING

Summarize How did freshwater Lake Bonneville become the Great Salt Lake?

Russia's Lake Baikal, for example, is the world's largest lake and contains 20 percent of all Earth's fresh water. Rivers and streams move water downhill to or from larger bodies of water. Smaller streams and rivers that flow into a major river are called tributaries. The region drained by a river and its tributaries is called a **drainage basin**. The Amazon River system in South America is the world's largest drainage basin.

Some fresh water, called **ground water**, is found beneath the Earth's surface. This water is held in the pores and cracks of rocks and can be pumped from the ground.

Salt Water The water in the Earth's oceans and seas is called salt water because it contains a small percentage of dissolved minerals and chemical compounds called salts. Actually, all of the oceans and seas are part of the same body of water, which is divided by the continents. Geographers gave names to the different areas of the oceans.

The Earth's oceans are the Pacific, Atlantic, Indian, and Arctic, and the Southern Ocean, which is the body of water around Antarctica. The Pacific Ocean is the largest and covers almost one-third of the Earth. A body of salt water that is completely or partly enclosed by land is called a sea. An example is the Mediterranean Sea. Oceans and seas are sources of food, energy, and minerals and are used for transportation and recreation. They also help to distribute Earth's heat.

▲ **COMPARE** Compare the two types of water on the Earth.

Hydrologic Cycle

The Earth's water is renewed by a never-ending process called the hydrologic cycle, or water cycle. The **hydrologic cycle** is the circulation of water between the Earth, the oceans, and the atmosphere. Approximately 119,000 cubic miles of water evaporates into the atmosphere each year. The **atmosphere** is the layer of gases that surround the Earth.

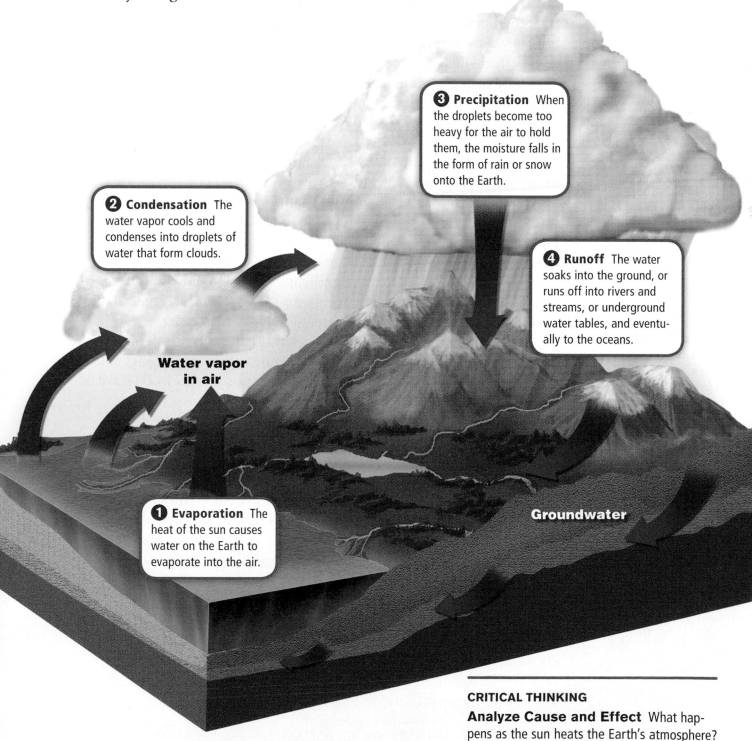

2 Condensation The water vapor cools and condenses into droplets of water that form clouds.

3 Precipitation When the droplets become too heavy for the air to hold them, the moisture falls in the form of rain or snow onto the Earth.

4 Runoff The water soaks into the ground, or runs off into rivers and streams, or underground water tables, and eventually to the oceans.

Water vapor in air

1 Evaporation The heat of the sun causes water on the Earth to evaporate into the air.

Groundwater

CRITICAL THINKING
Analyze Cause and Effect What happens as the sun heats the Earth's atmosphere?

Landforms

▼ **KEY QUESTION** How are landforms created?

Features on the Earth's surface formed by physical forces are called **landforms**. Landforms are produced by the internal and external forces that reshape the Earth. Internal forces push, move, and raise up parts of the Earth's crust. The result is the creation of new rock formations, such as mountains. External forces wear down these formations and transport the eroded materials to other locations. The eroded materials then become new landforms. These processes take a long time, but they are constantly at work. The location and size of landforms often affect where people choose to live.

Many of the same landforms found on dry land are also found under water. Those on the land are called continental landforms. Those on the sea floor are called oceanic landforms.

Continental Landforms The major continental landforms are mountains, hills, plains, and plateaus. A **plateau** is a broad area of land higher than the surrounding land. The same landforms are found on all of the continents. In fact, satellite photographs show a pattern on most continents: wide plains in the center and a narrow belt of mountains near the edge of the continent, where tectonic plates collide. For example, the landscape of the United States has the Rocky Mountains and coastal mountains in the west, the Appalachian Mountains in the east, and the Great Plains in the center.

The difference in the elevation of a landform from its lowest point to its highest point is called **relief**. Mountains show great relief compared to plains and plateaus. Many of the maps in this book have a relief indicator to show these differences in elevation.

Oceanic Landforms The landforms on the ocean floor are like an invisible landscape. Most cannot be seen from the surface of the water. But high mountains, vast plains, deep valleys, and coral reefs are present under the water's surface. Some are the result of the same tectonic forces that shape the continental landforms. The submerged

Monument Valley, Arizona In this photograph, you can see dramatic examples of relief between the floor of the valley and the tops of the landforms.

land at the edge of a continent is called the **continental shelf**. It slopes downward and then descends to the deep part of the ocean. On the deep ocean floor are volcanoes, mountain chains, plains, and trenches. These landforms are created by the movement of tectonic plates, the same forces as those on the continent.

Some of the oceanic landforms are pushed up above the water and become islands. Many islands, such as the Hawaiian Islands, are formed by volcanic action. Other islands are formed from coral reefs. However, all islands are subject to the same external forces that wear down landforms on the continent. These forces include the weathering and erosion caused by wind, water, and ice.

Indian Ocean Reef
A diver views plant and animal life on a coral reef.

▲ **SUMMARIZE** Explain how landforms are created.

Section 2 Assessment

🖱 **ONLINE QUIZ**
For test practice, go to
Interactive Review
@ ClassZone.com

TERMS & NAMES
1. Explain the importance of
• hydrologic cycle
• landform
• relief
• continental shelf

USE YOUR READING NOTES
2. Find Main Ideas Use your completed web diagram to answer the following question:

How is it possible for the oceans to have landforms?

KEY IDEAS
3. How much water on the Earth's surface is fresh water?

4. What are the four components that keep the hydrologic cycle going?

5. What are the major continental landforms?

CRITICAL THINKING
6. Find Main Ideas Why are oceans important to life on Earth?

7. Compare and Contrast How are continental and oceanic landforms the same? different?

8. CONNECT to Today In what ways does water affect your daily life?

9. TECHNOLOGY Make a Multimedia Presentation Plan a slide show about the hydrologic cycle. Sketch each step in the cycle and explain what is happening.

▶ Key Ideas

BEFORE, YOU LEARNED

The Earth's surface is covered with both continental and oceanic landforms. The hydrologic cycle circulates the water.

NOW YOU WILL LEARN

The Earth's rotation and revolution influence weather, climate, and living conditions on Earth.

▶ Vocabulary

TERMS & NAMES

solstice the time during the year when the sun reaches the farthest northern or southern point in the sky

equinox one of the two times a year when the sun's rays are over the equator and days and night around the world are equal in length

weather the condition of the Earth's atmosphere at a given time and place

climate the typical weather conditions of a region over a long period of time

precipitation falling water droplets in the form of rain, snow, sleet, or hail

vegetation region an area that has similar plants

savanna a vegetation region with a mix of grassland and scattered trees

desert a region with plants specially adapted to dry conditions

Visual Vocabulary desert

▶ Reading Strategy

Re-create the diagram shown at right. As you read and respond to the **KEY QUESTONS**, use the diagram to help you summarize information about the world's climate and vegetation.

 See Skillbuilder Handbook, page R5

SUMMARIZE

CLIMATE

VEGETATION

GRAPHIC ORGANIZERS
Go to **Interactive Review** @ ClassZone.com

Climate and Vegetation

Connecting to Your World

Every moment in the day, weather and climate are a part of your life. They affect what clothes you wear and how you get to school. You might walk or ride your bike if it is not too cold or too wet. But if it's raining or snowing you may go in a car or by bus. Some school activities, like sports, depend on weather and climate, too. In fact, weather and climate affect plant and animal life and nearly every human activity.

Inupiat Woman
The harsh climate of the Arctic makes wearing a fur parka necessary.

The Earth's Rotation and Revolution

▼ **KEY QUESTION** How does Earth's revolution affect seasons?

The Earth rotates as it revolves around the sun. Rotation is the motion of the Earth as it spins on its axis once every 24 hours. Revolution is the motion of the Earth as it circles, or makes a year-long orbit, of the sun.

Earth's Movement The Earth is tilted at a 23.5° angle. The Earth's revolution around the sun affects patterns of Earth's weather and climate. The Earth's tilt stays the same as it revolves around the sun. As a result, different parts of the Earth get direct rays from the sun for more hours of the day at certain times of the year. This causes the changing seasons.

Midnight Sun in the Arctic Multiple exposures show the position of the sun over a 24-hour period in the Arctic summer.

ARCTIC OCEAN

ARCTIC CIRCLE

ALASKA

Earth's Revolution
The seasons are related to the Earth's tilt and revolution around the sun.

CRITICAL THINKING

Compare and Contrast Which part of the Earth's surface doesn't experience seasons?

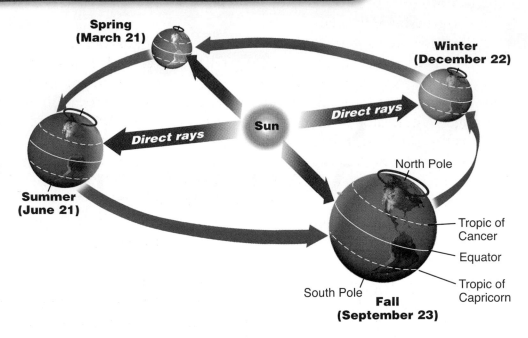

Spring (March 21)

Winter (December 22)

Direct rays

Sun

Direct rays

North Pole

Summer (June 21)

Tropic of Cancer

Equator

South Pole

Fall (September 23)

Tropic of Capricorn

Seasons The term **solstice** is used to describe the time during the year when the sun reaches the farthest northern or southern point in the sky. In the Northern Hemisphere, the summer solstice is the longest day of the year and begins summer. The winter solstice is the shortest day of the year and begins winter. These dates are reversed in the Southern Hemisphere. The beginning of spring and autumn start on the **equinox**. On these two days, the sun's rays are directly over the equator, and days and nights around the world are equal in length. The Earth's revolution brings the temperature and weather changes we call seasons to many parts of the Earth. But in some regions there is little change. The illustration above shows the position of the Earth at the start of the four seasons in the Northern Hemisphere.

▲ **SUMMARIZE** What causes seasons on Earth?

Weather and Climate

▼ **KEY QUESTION** What is the difference between weather and climate?

People often confuse weather and climate. **Weather** is the condition of the Earth's atmosphere at a given time and place. For example, today may be sunny and warm. **Climate** is the term for the typical weather conditions of a certain region over a long period of time.

Causes of Weather Several factors interact to cause weather at a particular location. They include solar energy, wind, landforms, bodies of water, water vapor, cloud cover, and elevation. The combination of all these factors varies from location to location, creating local weather conditions.

The most important weather factor is the amount of energy, in the form of heat from the sun, that a location receives. This is why, for example, the time of year influences the weather. In summer, much more solar energy is found in the atmosphere, and weather conditions change. Winds move the solar energy and moisture that air holds across the Earth. Also, land heats and cools more quickly than bodies of water do. So land located near a body of water has a different weather pattern from locations further inland.

Clouds and water vapor are connected to each other in weather patterns. Clouds hold water vapor in the atmosphere. Water vapor determines whether there will be **precipitation**, which is falling water droplets in the form of rain, snow, sleet, or hail.

Finally, as elevation above sea level rises, air becomes thinner and loses its ability to hold moisture, so it becomes cooler. The temperature drops by about 3.5°F for every 1,000-foot increase in elevation. So, you can find ice and snow on the tops of mountains even at the equator.

Causes of Climate There are many different climates around the world. A place's location on the Earth, especially its latitude, is important in determining climate. For example, climates are warmer near the equator and colder near the poles.

Wind and ocean currents help distribute the sun's heat from one part of the world to another. Ocean currents are like rivers flowing through the ocean. They move warm waters away from the equator and cold water from the poles. Air currents blowing over the ocean waters pick up heat and moisture and move them to other parts of the Earth.

▲ **COMPARE** Explain the difference between weather and climate.

Fun Facts!

IT'S RAINING FROGS!
Yes, it's true—there are recorded instances of frogs raining down on the Earth, most recently in Serbia in 2005. The most logical explanation is a strong wind that can suck light objects out of the water and later deposit them somewhere else.

In 1981, a city in southern Greece experienced a rain of frogs that landed in trees and in the streets. The species of frog was native to North Africa. That's one strong wind!

Climate and Vegetation Regions

▼ **KEY QUESTION** What are climate and vegetation regions?

To categorize climate regions, geographers divide the Earth into three general zones of latitude: tropical, middle, and high. These zones are found on both sides of the equator. Tropical latitudes are found between the equator and Tropic of Cancer and between the equator and the Tropic of Capricorn where it is usually hot. Middle latitudes extend from the tropic lines to the lines of the Arctic and Antarctic circles. High latitude refers to the cold areas around the North and South Poles.

COMPARING World Climate Regions

CONNECT Geography & Culture

1. **Region** Which type of climate is found along the equator?
2. **Place** Which climate is found in the place you live?

	TYPES	CHARACTERISTICS	VEGETATION
TROPICAL	Tropical Wet	rainy all year round	broadleaf trees
	Tropical Wet and Dry	has a rainy season	grasslands and savanna
DRY	Desert	less than 10 inches of precipitation	specially adapted plants
	Semiarid	up to 20 inches of rain	grasslands called steppe
MID-LATITUDE	Mediterranean	wet winter	plants that have adapted to a dry season in the summer
	Marine West Coast	rainy year round	mixed forests of broadleaf and needleleaf trees or only needleleaf trees
	Humid Subtropical	long, hot, humid summers	
	Humid Continental	wide range of summer and winter temperatures	grasslands and savanna
HIGH LATITUDE	Subarctic	cold dry climate	specially adapted plants
	Tundra	permanent ice and snow	specially adapted plants
	Icecap	permanent ice and snow	none
HIGHLAND	Varies with latitude, elevation, and continental location		

Climate Regions As you can see on the map on the opposite page, the Earth has five general climate regions: tropical, mid-latitude, high latitude, dry, and highland. Tropical climates are always hot and can be rainy most of the year or only during one season. The middle latitudes have the greatest variety of climates, ranging from hot and humid to cool and fairly dry. Climates along the oceans are also included in this category. High latitude climates are cool to cold all year long. Dry climates can be found in every latitude region. Highland climates are based on the elevation of a particular place. So, for example, as you go up a mountain, the climate may change from warm to cooler to cold.

Vegetation Regions The term **vegetation region** refers to an area that has similar plants. A vegetation region is named for the types of trees, grasslands, and specially adapted plants found there. The four basic types of vegetation are: forest, savanna, grasslands, and desert. Forests can be cold, tropical, or temperate. **Savanna** is a mix of grasslands and trees. Grasslands can have short or tall grasses, depending on the amount of rain. Finally, a **desert**—which can be hot or cold—has plants specially adapted to very dry conditions.

 SUMMARIZE Identify the five main climate regions.

Section 3 Assessment

ONLINE QUIZ
For test practice, go to
Interactive Review
@ ClassZone.com

TERMS & NAMES

1. Explain the importance of
- weather
- climate
- precipitation
- vegetation region

USE YOUR READING NOTES

2. Summarize Use your completed chart to answer the following question:

What are the basic causes of weather and which factor is the most important?

KEY IDEAS

3. What causes the changing seasons?

4. What are the causes of climate?

5. How are vegetation regions named?

CRITICAL THINKING

6. Analyze Causes and Effects Why are the seasons reversed in the Northern and Southern Hemispheres?

7. Draw Conclusions How does location affect climate and vegetation?

8. CONNECT to Today What weather conditions have caused problems in the United States recently?

9. WRITING Write a Description Determine what climate and vegetation region you live in. Then write a paragraph describing the climate features and types of vegetation.

AMAZON RAIN FOREST

The Amazon rain forest is one of the world's most important physical features. It acts as the "lungs of the planet" by producing oxygen, and is the home of millions of plants and animals.

⟶ **Click here** to learn more about this frog and the amazing diversity of plants and animals in the forest.

⟶ **Click here** to see Yanamamö village life in the rain forest and learn about how the Yanamamö interact with the forest.

⟶ **Click here** to see the methods scientists are using to study plants and animals in the rain forest.

The Disappearing Amazon Rain Forest

Remaining Area of Rain Forest (%)

89% 88% 86% 84% 81%

1980 1990 1995 2000 2005

Source: Brazilian National Institute of Space Research

GeoActivity

Plan a Scientific Study
With a small group, plan the scientific study of one of the plants or animals in the picture. Identify the subject you wish to study. Talk about what information you want to find. Then write questions that would help you track down that information.

Reading for Understanding

▶ Key Ideas

BEFORE, YOU LEARNED

Many different physical systems influence the way we live on Earth.

NOW YOU WILL LEARN

Human interference with physical systems can cause problems with the environment.

▶ Vocabulary

TERMS & NAMES

global warming an increase in the average temperature of the Earth's atmosphere

greenhouse effect the trapping of the sun's heat by gases in the Earth's atmosphere

greenhouse gas any gas in the atmosphere that contributes to the greenhouse effect

fossil fuels fuels such as coal, oil, and natural gas

desertification the process in which farmland becomes less productive because the land is degraded

sustainable using natural resources in a way that they exist for future generations

BACKGROUND VOCABULARY

carbon dioxide a gas composed of carbon and oxygen

emissions substances discharged into the air

degraded of lower quality

Visual Vocabulary desertification

▶ Reading Strategy

Re-create the chart shown at right. As you read and respond to the **KEY QUESTIONS**, use the chart to compare and contrast details about environmental challenges the world faces.

 Skillbuilder Handbook, page R9

COMPARE AND CONTRAST

GLOBAL WARMING	DESERTIFICATION

 GRAPHIC ORGANIZERS
Go to **Interactive Review** @ ClassZone.com

Environmental Challenges

Connecting to Your World

Have your parents or other adults ever told you that the climate seems to be changing? Maybe they said something like, "We never had hurricanes or tornados like these when I was a kid." They could be right—climates do change. Some changes take place naturally over many years, such as the build-up of ice during ice ages. But recently, scientists have noticed rapid climate changes that some believe is the result of human activity.

Global Warming

▼ **KEY QUESTION** How are global warming and the greenhouse effect related?

Global warming and desertification are two possible threats to the environment. **Global warming** is an increase in the average temperature of the Earth's atmosphere. It refers to an increase large enough to cause changes in the Earth's overall climate. The Earth's average temperature has risen between 0.9 and 1.3°F since the late 1800s. Many scientists think that temperatures may rise another 2.5 to 10.4°F by the end of the century. Some scientists believe that this warming is part of the larger cycle of warm and cold periods in the Earth's history. Others suspect that it is caused by humans.

Dori, Burkina Faso Changes in the climate have caused drought in this region, leading to fewer crops.

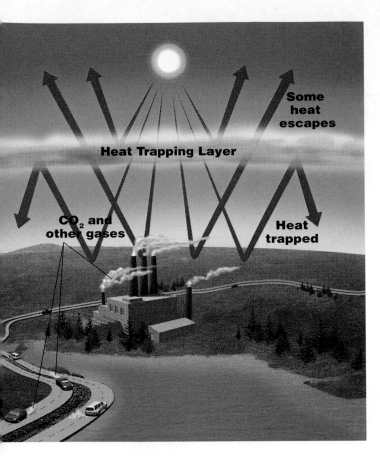

Heat Trapping Layer

Some heat escapes

CO₂ and other gases

Heat trapped

Greenhouse Effect
Trapped gases and heat combine to change the Earth's temperature. **How do humans add to the greenhouse effect?**

The Greenhouse Effect The trapping of the sun's heat by gases in the Earth's atmosphere is called the **greenhouse effect**. These gases act like the glass roof of a greenhouse. They let in solar energy, which heats up the planet, but they trap much of the heat that rises from the Earth's surface. So, the Earth becomes warmer. Some greenhouse effect is necessary. Without it, you would be living on a freezing cold planet. The temperature would be about zero degrees Fahenheit.

Any gas in the atmosphere that contributes to the greenhouse effect is called a **greenhouse gas**. Greenhouse gases include water vapor and **carbon dioxide**, a gas composed of carbon and oxygen. The burning of **fossil fuels**, such as coal, oil, and natural gas, has caused an increase in carbon dioxide in the atmosphere. As this gas builds in the atmosphere, the atmosphere becomes warmer and speeds up the heating effect.

The Impact on the Climate In theory, a more intense greenhouse effect could change the Earth's climate. Warmer temperatures could cause the ice caps and glaciers around the world to melt and sea levels to rise. Flooding could occur along coastal regions. Global land-use patterns would change. Some crops would no longer grow in certain areas. Some areas would become hotter and drier, with extreme heat waves, droughts, and more forest fires. These changes would alter the fragile relationships between living things and the environment.

Solutions Lowering the levels of greenhouse gases is a complex, worldwide goal. Some nations generate huge amounts of greenhouse gases. These gases affect not only those nations, but also the whole planet. So, humans need to take steps to reduce the levels of greenhouse gases. One solution might be to build more energy-efficient cars and factories. Another could be to use alternative energy sources such as energy produced by the sun, or the internal heat of the Earth.

In 1997, nations from around the world gathered at Kyoto, Japan, to discuss plans to reduce greenhouse gases. The result of their meeting was an agreement to cut emissions of carbon dioxide and other greenhouse gases. (**Emissions** are substances discharged into the air.) The agreement, called the Kyoto Protocol, went into effect in 2005.

▲ **SUMMARIZE** Explain how global warming takes place.

Desertification

▼ **KEY QUESTION** What causes desertification?

Desertification is the process in which farmland becomes less productive because the land is **degraded**. The land becomes more desert-like, that is, dry and unproductive. Desertification is a serious problem because it turns arid and semiarid areas into nonproductive wasteland. Each year, about 25,000 square miles of land—an area the size of West Virginia—is degraded. This process is happening in many parts of the world, including Africa, China, and the American West.

Causes and Effects In desertification, natural vegetation is removed or destroyed, and soil is exposed to wind. Without shade from the sun, the moisture in the soil evaporates more quickly. The dry top layers of soil particles then blow away. The soil becomes less able to support plant life. The loss of moisture and plants may in itself cause more desertification. But destructive practices in arid and semi-arid regions have speeded up the process. Some of these practices are

overgrazing allowing animals to graze so much that plants are unable to grow back

cultivation of marginal land planting crops on fragile soil

deforestation cutting down trees and not replanting new trees

> ➲ **ONLINE PRIMARY SOURCE** To read more of Wangari Maathai's writing, go to the **Research & Writing Center** @ClassZone.com

ANALYZING Primary Sources

Wangari Maathai (born 1940) won the 2004 Nobel Peace Prize for her work fighting deforestation in Africa. To combat desertification, she founded the Green Belt Movement, which has planted 30 million trees across Africa, including her native Kenya.

> [The Green Belt Movement] encourages women to create jobs, prevent soil loss, slow the process of desertification and [to] plant and to eat indigenous [local] food crops.
>
> Source: Speech to the 4th United Nations World Women's Conference, Beijing, China, 1995

DOCUMENT–BASED QUESTION
What is the goal of the Green Belt Movement?

Green Belt Movement

The Green Belt Movement, founded by Wangari Maathai in Kenya in 1977, is an example of a program of sustainable development. It started out as a jobs program to pay rural and urban women to plant trees. But it soon became a movement to improve the environment, slow deforestation, and halt desertification.

Solutions There are different solutions to the growing problem of desertification. Each depends on the underlying cause. Some simple solutions are to build sand fences that interrupt the wind, or to use straw mats to reduce evaporation so young plants can take root. Still another is to use solar ovens in place of open fires that require firewood. Planting tree fences and grass belts also reduces the spread of sandy areas. This practice is being used in China and Africa today.

Solutions like the ones above are examples of sustainable practices. **Sustainable** means that these practices use natural resources in such a way as to ensure that they exist for future generations. Sustainable practices work with the environment to protect the land, preserve wildlife, and repair the damage that has been done to it. The practices allow people to live a better life and ensure that resources will be available both now and in the future.

 DRAW CONCLUSIONS Explain what causes desertification.

Section 4 Assessment

ONLINE QUIZ
For test practice, go to **Interactive Review** @ClassZone.com

TERMS & NAMES

1. Explain the importance of
- global warming
- greenhouse effect
- desertification
- sustainable

USE YOUR READING NOTES

2. Compare and Contrast Use your completed chart to answer the following question:

How does the greenhouse effect contribute to global warming?

GLOBAL WARMING	DESERTIFICATION

KEY IDEAS

3. Why is global warming a problem?

4. What are greenhouse gases?

5. What are three simple solutions to controlling desertification?

CRITICAL THINKING

6. Evaluate Which environmental problem, global warming or desertification, is a greater threat to the Earth? Why?

7. Summarize How does deforestation cause desertification?

8. CONNECT to Today What might happen if more gasoline-powered motor vehicles were used around the world?

9. MATH Make a Chart Use the Internet to find information about desertification. Then make a chart that shows locations and the percentage of land that has been degraded.

Interactive ◀▶ Review

Click here to complete these and other activities online @ ClassZone.com

CHAPTER SUMMARY

Key Idea 1
The Earth is composed of many layers, and its surface continually changes because of the drifting of the continents.

Key Idea 2
Interaction between landforms and bodies of water makes life on Earth possible.

Key Idea 3
The Earth's rotation and revolution influence weather, climate, and living conditions on Earth.

Key Idea 4
Human interference with physical systems causes problems with the environment.

For **Review and Study Notes**, go to **Interactive Review** @ ClassZone.com

NAME GAME

Use the Terms & Names list to complete each sentence on paper or online.

1. I am the hot metal center of the Earth.
   _____ core 🖑 _____

2. I am a naturally formed feature on the Earth's surface. _____

3. I fall in the form of rain, snow, sleet, or hail.
   _____

4. I am an increase in the Earth's temperature.
   _____

5. I move weathered materials from one place to another. _____

6. I am the trapping of the sun's heat by gases in the atmosphere. _____

7. I am a large rigid piece of the Earth's crust that is in motion. _____

8. I am typical weather conditions over a period of time. _____

9. I circulate water between the Earth, oceans, and atmosphere. _____

10. I am plants that grow in a region. _____

climate
core
desertification
erosion
global warming
greenhouse effect
hydrologic cycle
landform
magma
precipitation
relief
sediment
tectonic plate
vegetation
weather

Activities

Flip Cards

Use the online flip cards to quiz yourself on terms and names introduced in this chapter.

magma

melted or liquid rock

Crossword Puzzle

Complete an online crosword puzzle to test your knowledge of Earth's physical systems.

ACROSS

1. **a naturally formed feature on the Earth's surface**

Asssessment

VOCABULARY

Explain the significance of each of the following.

1. tectonic plate
2. greenhouse effect
3. hydrologic cycle
4. global warming
5. desertification

Explain how the terms and names in each group are related.

6. magma, crust, and continent
7. weathering, erosion, and desertification
8. hydrologic cycle, precipitation, and atmosphere
9. greenhouse gas and global warming
10. vegetation and climate

KEY IDEAS

① The Earth and Its Forces

11. What is the continental drift theory?
12. What are the four types of tectonic plate movements?
13. How do weathering and erosion reshape the Earth's surface?

② Bodies of Water and Landforms

14. Why is the Earth sometimes called the "blue planet"?
15. What are the names of the world's five oceans?
16. What two general features do most continents have in common?

③ Climate and Vegetation

17. What are the two motions of the Earth in relation to the sun?
18. What are the four factors that influence climate?
19. What are the basic types of vegetation?

④ Environmental Challenges

20. What happens to the sun's heat in the greenhouse effect?
21. What are two alternative energy sources?
22. What are three areas of the world that have a serious problem with desertification?

CRITICAL THINKING

23. **Analyze Cause and Effect** Create a web diagram to show the effects of global warming. List at least five effects caused by a more intense greenhouse effect.

EFFECTS OF GLOBAL WARMING

24. **Summarize** Why are so many earthquakes and volcanoes found near the Ring of Fire?
25. **Draw Conclusions** Why is the surface of the Earth constantly changing?
26. **Connect to Economics** What are the economic costs of earthquakes or volcanoes?
27. **Five Themes: Human-Environment Interaction** What steps have been taken to control global warming?
28. **Connect Geography & Culture** Why might the location and size of landforms affect where people live?

Answer the
ESSENTIAL QUESTION

How do Earth's physical systems make life on Earth possible?

Written Response Write a two- or three-paragraph response to the Essential Question. Be sure to consider the key ideas of each section as well as ways in which the systems interlock. Use the rubric below to guide your thinking.

Response Rubric
A strong response will:
• discuss how the hydrologic cycle makes human occupation of the Earth possible
• describe the causes of weather and climate
• explain how the above systems affect humans

STANDARDS-BASED ASSESSMENT

✔ **Test Practice**

• Online Test Practice @ ClassZone.com
• Test-Taking Strategies and Practice at the front of this book

THEMATIC MAP

Use the map to answer questions 1 and 2 on your paper.

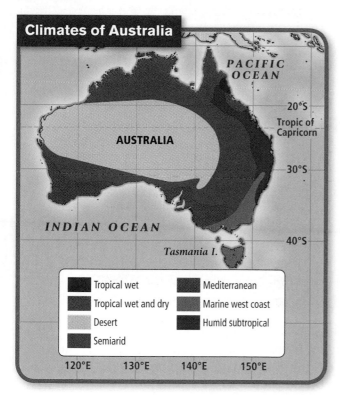

Climates of Australia

PACIFIC OCEAN

AUSTRALIA

20°S
Tropic of Capricorn

30°S

INDIAN OCEAN

40°S

Tasmania I.

Legend:
- Tropical wet
- Tropical wet and dry
- Desert
- Semiarid
- Mediterranean
- Marine west coast
- Humid subtropical

120°E   130°E   140°E   150°E

1. Which climate takes up the largest portion of Australia?

A. Desert
B. Mediterranean
C. Semiarid
D. Tropical wet and dry

2. In which part of Australia would you find a tropical wet climate?

A. northwestern   C. southwestern
B. northeastern   D. southeastern

CHART

Study the chart below. Use the information in the chart to answer questions 3 and 4.

Deadliest Earthquakes 1975 to 2005		
Country	**Year**	**Deaths**
Indonesia	2004	283,106
China	1976	255,000
Pakistan	2005	80,361
Iran	1990	40,000
Iran	2003	26,200
Armenia	1988	25,000
Guatemala	1976	23,000
India	2001	20,230
Turkey	1999	17,119
Source: USGS Earthquake Hazards Program		

3. Which country has experienced the greatest number of deadly earthquakes?

4. In what year did the single most deadly earthquake strike?

GeoActivity

1. INTERDISCIPLINARY ACTIVITY–SCIENCE

Select one of the Earth's major mountain chains and illustrate its creation on a poster. Be sure the poster shows the plates involved, the direction of the collision, and the name of the mountains that were formed.

2. WRITING FOR SOCIAL STUDIES

Review the illustration of the Earth's interior in Section 1. Write a one-paragraph description that would help a younger student understand the layers of the Earth's interior.

3. MENTAL MAPPING

Create an outline map of the world and label the following:

• the seven continents
• the five oceans

Human Geography

 ESSENTIAL QUESTION

How do natural resources affect a country's population distribution and economy?

CONNECT Geography & History

Use the satellite image and the time line to answer the following questions.

1. How much did the world's population grow between 1 A.D. and 2000?

2. How different would this image have appeared when the population of the world hit one billion?

History
◄ **1000 B.C.** Bantu migrations in Africa

1000 B.C.

Geography
1 A.D. Total world population hits 300 million.

History
180 Roman Empire at its peak ►

Animated **GEOGRAPHY**

Earth at Night

Click here to explore human geography @ **ClassZone.com**

The gold color indicates a concentration of lights.

The blue color indicates areas where little or no vegetation is found.

Geography
1804 Total population hits 1 billion.

Economics
◄ **1993** European Union established

Today

Government
◄ **1788** United States Constitution is ratified.
(Independence Hall)

Geography
1999 Total population hits 6 billion.

Population density is an average figure for a specific area. However, it does not account for the distribution of population in an area. Notice in these two examples how the pattern of population density varies even within a country.

Australia

Australia is ranked 54th in the world for total population, but 191st in population density. This is because Australia has a great deal of land but a small population. It has a lot of open space sometimes called the Outback, shown below. The heaviest population is found in the coastal cities.

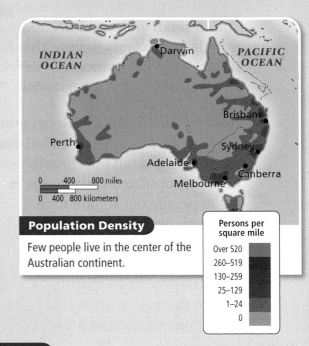

Population Density

Few people live in the center of the Australian continent.

	Persons per square mile
	Over 520
	260–519
	130–259
	25–129
	1–24
	0

Work

Australia's wide open spaces makes cattle ranching one of the biggest businesses.

Transportation

A lone vehicle travels a dusty Outback road.

Population Density

The islands of Indonesia have a greater population density than Australia.

Persons per square mile

- Over 520
- 260–519
- 130–259
- 25–129
- 1–24
- 0

Transportation

Thousands of buses and cars are needed to move Jakarta's population.

Indonesia

Indonesia is ranked 4th in the world for total population, but 60th in population density. This is because two Indonesian islands, Bali and Java, and the capital, Jakarta, are heavily populated. Other parts of the island nation are not as densely populated. Jakarta is pictured below.

Work

Manufacturing takes place in the larger cities of Indonesia.

CRITICAL THINKING

1. **Compare and Contrast** How are the patterns of density different in the two countries?

2. **Draw Conclusions** In what ways do the images illustrate how density may affect ways of living in the two countries?

Reading for Understanding

▶ Key Ideas

BEFORE, YOU LEARNED

Population patterns differ by place and region and may change over time.

NOW YOU WILL LEARN

People move from one place to another to meet their needs.

▶ Vocabulary

TERMS & NAMES

migration the process of relocating to a new region

immigrant a person who leaves one area to settle in another

push factor a reason that causes people to leave an area

pull factor a reason that attracts people to another area

culture the shared attitudes, knowledge, and behaviors of a group

diversity having many different ways to think or to do something, or a variety of people

discrimination actions that might be hurtful to an individual or a group

BACKGROUND VOCABULARY

refugee a person who flees a place to find safety

persecution cruel treatment on the basis of religion, race, ethnic group, nationality, political views, gender, or class

Visual Vocabulary diversity

▶ Reading Strategy

Re-create the chart shown at right. As you read and respond to the **KEY QUESTIONS**, use the chart to compare and contrast important details about the reasons people move.

 See Skillbuilder Handbook, page R9

COMPARE AND CONTRAST

PUSH FACTORS	PULL FACTORS
1.	1.
2.	2.

 GRAPHIC ORGANIZERS
Go to **Interactive Review @ ClassZone.com**

Why People Move

Connecting to Your World

Have you ever moved from one part of the city or town where you live to another? Maybe you moved to be closer to your school or to where a parent works. It may be that one of your parents took a job in a different city. Perhaps your family had to move to a different climate for health reasons. Whatever the reason, moving to a new, unfamiliar area could change your life in many ways.

Moving Day About 112 million Americans relocate every year.

Causes of Migration

▼ **KEY QUESTION** Why do people move from place to place?

From earliest times, people have moved to new locations. This process of relocating to a new region is called **migration**. A person who leaves one country to settle in another is called an **immigrant**. Population geographers often talk about push-pull factors when they study migration. The **push factors** are the reasons that cause people to leave an area. **Pull factors** are the reasons that attract people to another area. For example, a group may decide to move to a better location after their crops fail for several years. The crop failure is the "push" factor, and the better location is the "pull" factor. Together, they give the group a reason for migrating. Generally, the causes of migration are environmental, economic, cultural, or political.

Ellis Island, New York Millions of people entered the United States here between 1892 and 1954.

NEW YORK
Ellis Island
ATLANTIC OCEAN

Push Factors In early times, a change in environment was a major cause of migration. For example, climate changes thousands of years ago brought on an ice age. People in northern Europe moved south in order to survive. Sometimes, an environment is unable to support growing numbers of people. So some part of the group needs to move to a place that would better support them.

Political actions may push a person or group to migrate to a new area. **Refugees** might flee a place to find safety from war. For example, beginning in 2003, an ethnic war in the Darfur region of Sudan caused about 2 million people to flee to refugee camps. Governments can force people to relocate even if they do not want to go. Cruel treatment, or **persecution**, of a particular group could also cause people to leave. People have sometimes been persecuted for their religion, race, nationality, political views, or membership in an ethnic group.

Pull Factors The desire for land has pulled people to new regions for thousands of years. During the 1800s, millions immigrated to the United States in search of land to farm or ranch. Economic opportunities are still a major reason for migration. Today, people move to find a job or to get a better job.

Sometimes people move for cultural reasons. For example, they may want to return to an area they consider the homeland of their people. Another pull factor may be that the land or the region has religious significance. Israel is an example of both reasons. Jews from all over the world immigrate to Israel because they consider it their homeland, and because it also contains many Jewish holy sites.

▲ **SUMMARIZE** What are the push-pull factors of migration?

COMPARING Migration Factors

PUSH FACTORS	PULL FACTORS
Environmental • lack of resources to support an entire group • change in climate or vegetation	**Economic** • availability of land • job opportunities
Political • escape from war or persecution • forced removal	**Cultural** • return to a homeland • desire to live near a holy site

CRITICAL THINKING

Make Inferences Which factor do you think is most often the cause of migration?

Where People Migrate

▼ **KEY QUESTION** What are the two kinds of migration?

Geographers identify two different types of migration. Internal migration occurs when people move within a country. Moving across a continent or even to another continent is called external migration.

Internal Migration Internal migration happens when people move from one place to another but stay within the same country. Someone who does this is called a migrant. If you move from Pennsylvania to California, you have moved a very long distance, but you have stayed within the United States, so you are an internal migrant. Two of the most common forms of internal migration are moving from rural areas or small towns to cities, and from cities to suburbs.

The world is becoming more urban. In many countries, more than 70 percent of the population lives in urban areas. Pull factors attract people to cities. If migrants can't find affordable housing in the city, they often build houses on the outskirts. This kind of growth on the outskirts of a city is sometimes called urban sprawl. In developed countries such as the United States, sprawl happens as new suburbs are built around the edges of a city.

External Migration Migration across parts of a continent may take place quickly, but sometimes it takes hundreds or even thousands of years. For example, Bantu-speaking people of Africa slowly spread across the southern half of the continent from 1000 B.C. to A.D. 1100. The push factor was environmental. The numbers of Bantu people were increasing, and they needed more land for farming and herding.

Migration also takes place from one continent to another continent. The countries of the Western Hemisphere as well as Australia and New Zealand, are filled with immigrants from Europe, Africa, and Asia.

▲ **COMPARE** Explain the difference between internal and external migration.

Kuba Mask The Kuba are a Bantu-speaking people.

Animated GEOGRAPHY

Bantu Migrations

🔗 *Click here* to learn more about the migrations of Bantu people @ ClassZone.com

- ■ Bantu homeland
- ← Earliest migrations to A.D. 1
- ← Later migrations

CONNECT Geography & Culture
Movement Toward which body of water did the eastern branch of the early migrations move?

The Effects of Migration

▼ **KEY QUESTION** How does migration affect people and lands?

People bring the customs and traditions of their culture with them when they relocate. **Culture** is the shared attitudes, knowledge, and behaviors of a group. As a result of migration, the cultures of both the immigrants and the people living in an area may change. Migration also has economic and political effects, both positive and negative.

Cultural Effects When different groups in an area interact, they learn about each other—what they eat, wear, and believe. If people accept these different ideas and behaviors, it adds to the diversity of the group. **Diversity** means having many different ways to think about or to do something, or it may refer to a variety of people. Many people believe that having diversity in a group makes it stronger.

Earlier you learned about the Bantu-speaking people and how they spread across southern Africa. Wherever they settled, the Bantu brought their language and iron-making skills to the people in the region. Even if the Bantu moved on, their language and iron-working techniques remained. So migration changed the existing culture in several ways.

Migration does not always benefit the people who move. This is especially true if a group did not want to move. For example, refugees who flee war may be forced into overcrowded camps with little hope of returning home. Another possible result of migration is **discrimination**, actions that might be hurtful to an individual or group. For example, the group discriminated against may not be able to get jobs or housing.

CONNECT ▶ **Geography & Culture**

Bantu Languages

The Bantu spread their languages when they migrated across Africa. Today, about 240 million Africans speak one of the hundreds of Bantu languages as their first language. Some 50 million of them in central and east Africa speak Swahili (swah•HEE•lee), also known as Kiswahili (KEY•swah•HEE•lee).

Economic Effects The arrival of a new group can help or hurt a region's economy. If more workers are needed or the new workers have special talents, the region's economy may be improved. This was the case with the Bantu who brought iron-making skills with them.

The arrival of large numbers of people sometimes strains a region's resources. This occurs when, for example, war refugees with limited resources crowd into refugee camps. The living conditions may be very poor and the additional numbers make life in the camps miserable. In 2005, many thousands of people fled their homes as warfare swept Sudan in Africa. The refugees found little shelter, water, or firewood in the camps. In fact, violence often broke out over the available water. Security and protection for the people in the camps can also become a problem. Governments may not be able to adequately provide for the refugees or may need to ask other nations to help care for the people.

Political Effects The policies of a country or region can be affected by the arrival of immigrants. Sometimes immigrants may be viewed as unwanted or dangerous. The government of a country might then support actions to remove the immigrants or allow them to be treated badly in hopes that they will leave. The immigrants may worry about their personal safety and ability to provide for themselves and their families.

In the best of times, the new immigrants make contributions to the country and are viewed as assets. For example, many immigrant groups brought valuable skills to the United States and were given the opportunity to become citizens.

Water Cans at a Refugee Camp Water is scarce in this African refugee camp. Each day people line up in hopes of getting a supply of water.

 DRAW CONCLUSIONS Identify positive and negative effects of migration.

ONLINE QUIZ For test practice, go to **Interactive Review** @ ClassZone.com

Section ❷ Assessment

TERMS & NAMES

1. Explain the importance of
- migration
- push factor
- pull factor
- culture

USE YOUR READING NOTES

2. Compare and Contrast Use your completed chart to answer the following question:

Which factors do you think are more powerful in encouraging migration?

PUSH FACTORS	PULL FACTORS
1.	1.
2.	2.

KEY IDEAS

3. What has been a major push factor in migration since earliest times?

4. Which form of internal migration has affected most countries?

5. What are the three ways that migration affects people and lands?

CRITICAL THINKING

6. Analyze Causes and Effects How do push-pull factors work together?

7. Summarize How is a culture affected by migration?

8. CONNECT to Today What are the pull factors that would attract people to move to your community?

9. HISTORY Create a Push-Pull Poster Choose two immigrant groups that came to the United States at any time in its history. Create a poster with images to show where they came from, what pushed them from their homeland, and what pulled them to the United States.

Human Geography **71**

Reading for Understanding

▶ Key Ideas

BEFORE, YOU LEARNED

Migration changes places and regions by introducing new people and cultures.

NOW YOU WILL LEARN

Economic activities in an area depend on the presence of natural resources.

▶ Vocabulary

TERMS & NAMES

natural resource something that is found in nature that is necessary or useful to humans

economy a system for producing and exchanging goods and services among a group of people

economic system a way people use resources to make and exchange goods

command economy an economic system in which the production of goods and services is decided by a central government

market economy an economic system in which the production of goods and services is decided by supply and the demand of consumers

Gross Domestic Product (GDP) the total value of all the goods and services produced in a country in a year

export a product or resource sold to another country

import a product or resource that comes into a country

specialization a focus on producing a limited number of a specific products

BACKGROUND VOCABULARY

raw material an unprocessed natural resource that will be converted to a finished product

▶ Reading Strategy

Re-create the chart shown at right. As you read and respond to the **KEY QUESTIONS**, use the chart to categorize important details about types of economic systems.

 Skillbuilder Handbook, page R7

CATEGORIZE

ECONOMIC SYSTEMS			
Traditional	Market	Command	Mixed
1.	1.	1.	1.
2.	2.	2.	2.
3.	3.	3.	3.

 GRAPHIC ORGANIZERS
Go to **Interactive Review** @ ClassZone.com

Resources and Economics

Connecting to Your World

What natural resources are found in your area? A **natural resource** is something found in nature that is necessary or useful to humans. Forests, mineral deposits, and fresh water are examples of natural resources. Often, the presence of natural resources attracts people to a particular area. Think about how important natural resources are to your life, to your community, and to your country. How are they being used, and how long will they last?

Natural Resources

▼ **KEY QUESTION** What are the different types of natural resources?

Natural resources are essential for economic development, but resources are not equally distributed around the world. People learn to use the resources in their own areas to their best advantage. However, just because a natural resource is present does not mean it can or will be used. People in some countries may not have the technology to take the resource and turn it into usable products. For example, iron ore is useless until technology turns it into iron and steel products. Technology changes over time, making the value of resources change as well.

Copper Mine
This copper mine in Spain has been producing copper since Roman times.

SPAIN

Geographers divide natural resources into three main categories: renewable, non-renewable, and unlimited. Renewable resources are those that nature can replace, such as trees or plants. Unlimited resources are things such as sunlight and wind—these never run out and often are used to produce energy. Non-renewable resources can't be easily replaced, so when they are used up, there aren't additional resources. Minerals and fuels like coal and oil fall into this category.

▲ **CATEGORIZE** Identify three basic types of resources.

CONNECT Geography & Economics

Natural Resources The map below shows the location of some major non-renewable resources. When supplies of these resources are gone, countries relying on them for their economies will have to change their economic focus.

Energy Resources
- Coal
- Natural gas
- Petroleum
- Uranium

Minerals
- Bauxite
- Copper
- Gold
- Iron ore
- Silver

Types of Resources		
Renewable	**Non-Renewable**	**Unlimited**
• Can be replaced through natural processes • Examples are trees, animals, and other living things. • Can be lost if they are used faster than they can be replaced	• Can't be replaced once they have been removed from the ground • Examples are metals, such as gold and iron, and fossil fuels, such as oil and coal. • Once they are used up, these resources are gone forever.	• Resources used to produce energy • Examples are sunlight, geothermal heat, winds, and tides. • Always available no matter what amount is used

CRITICAL THINKING

Draw Conclusions Which of the three categories of natural resources are likely to be most desirable?

Economic Systems

▼ **KEY QUESTION** What are the four basic economic systems?

An **economy** consists of the production and exchange of goods and services among a group of people. Economies exist at the local, regional, national, and international levels. **Economic systems** are different ways that people use resources to make and exchange goods and services.

Four basic economic systems are traditional, command, market, and mixed.

Traditional economy Goods and services are traded, but money is rarely exchanged. This process is called "barter" and is the oldest economic system. It is not used much today.

Command economy A **command economy** is one in which production of goods and services is decided by a central government. The government usually owns most of the resources and businesses that make the products or provide the services. This type of economy is also called a planned economy.

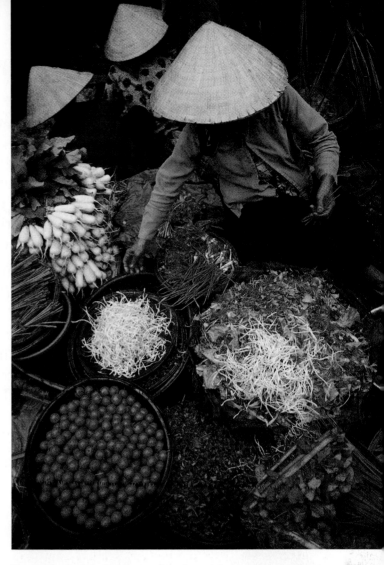

Food Market in Vietnam Supply and demand help determine which products will be sold. **How is this market different from most food markets in the United States?**

Market economy When the production of goods and services is determined by the supply and the demand of consumers it is called a **market economy**. It is also known as a demand economy, or capitalism. This is the type of economy found in the United States.

Mixed economy In this economy, a combination of command and market economies provides goods and services.

Economic activities are all the different ways that people make a living under these economic systems, including manufacturing, agriculture, fishing, and providing services. Some countries have a wide mix of economic activities while others may have only one or two main economic activities.

▲ **SUMMARIZE** Name the four basic types of economic systems.

Measuring Economic Development

▼ **KEY QUESTION** How is economic development measured?

To measure economic development, geographers may look at such figures as literacy, health information, life expectancy, or the value of a country's economy. One of the most important measures used is Gross Domestic Product (GDP). The **Gross Domestic Product (GDP)** measures the total value of all the goods and services produced in a country in a year. Countries are divided into two categories based on economic development: developing or developed nations.

Developing Nations These nations have low GDP and few economic activities. Many people raise food or animals to survive and have little or no machinery or advanced technology to do the work.

Developed Nations These nations have high GDP and many economic activities, especially business and information processing, and a lot of high-level technology. Food is grown on commercial farms, and most people work in offices and factories.

▲ **COMPARE** Identify information used to measure development.

COMPARING ▶ Economic Development

Geographers use many different measurements to look at the development level of a country's economy. Here is a comparison of some developing nations and some developed nations.

◀ *Brazilian coffee bean worker*

	Status	GDP	GDP/Person In US Dollars*	Infant Mortality (1000 Live Births)	Life Expectancy (At Birth)	Literacy Rate (Percent)
Burkina Faso	developing	5.4 billion	1,300	91.4	48.9	26.6
India	developing	719.8 billion	3,400	54.6	64.7	59.5
Uruguay	developing	13.2 billion	9,600	11.6	76.3	98.0
Germany	developed	2.8 trillion	30,400	4.1	78.8	99.0
Japan	developed	4.9 trillion	31,500	3.2	81.3	99.0
United States	developed	12.5 trillion	42,000	6.4	77.9	99.0

* official exchange rate   Source: *CIA World Factbook, 2006*

CRITICAL THINKING

Compare and Contrast How can you tell Uruguay has developed more than Burkina Faso?

World Trade

 KEY QUESTION Why do countries trade with one another?

Early trade networks started because people who did not have certain resources, such as salt, wanted them. For trade to happen, nations usually have to give up some of their resources in exchange. Products or resources sold to other countries are called **exports**. Products or resources that come into a country are called **imports**. For example, U.S.-made mining equipment sold to Brazil is an export of the United States. Brazilian coffee sold to the United States is a U.S. import.

A country may choose to focus on producing only one or two products or resources and exclude other economic activities. This practice is called **specialization**. Countries specialize because it allows them to trade for products they can't produce themselves. For example, a country may sell cocoa beans or wheat or iron ore in exchange for machinery, or chemicals, or electronic goods. In general, developing nations specialize in **raw materials** or low-cost items, while developed nations sell high-level technology goods or services. This focus leads to interdependence between countries. When countries produce the same trade items, competition results.

 FIND MAIN IDEAS Explain why nations trade.

Section 3 Assessment

TERMS & NAMES

1. Explain the importance of
- economic system
- Gross Domestic Product (GDP)
- export
- import

USE YOUR READING NOTES

2. Categorize Use your completed chart to answer the following question:

In which economic system are the production of goods and services determined by consumer demand?

ECONOMIC SYSTEMS			
Traditional	Market	Command	Mixed
1.	1.	1.	1.
2.	2.	2.	2.
3.	3.	3.	3.

KEY IDEAS

3. What is a natural resource?

4. What are the four basic economic systems?

5. What is the difference between an export and an import?

CRITICAL THINKING

6. Summarize How do geographers divide countries into developed and developing nations?

7. Compare and Contrast How are command and market economic systems different?

8. CONNECT to Today What natural resources are located in your area and how are they used?

9. TECHNOLOGY Create a Multimedia Presentation Use the Internet to study the imports and exports of the United States or another country. Plan a slide show about major exports and what countries buy them and major imports and what countries sell them.

Reading for Understanding

▶ Key Ideas

BEFORE, YOU LEARNED

People have different ways to use and trade the Earth's natural resources.

NOW YOU WILL LEARN

The world is divided into many political regions and organizations.

▶ Vocabulary

TERMS & NAMES

government an organization set up to make and enforce rules for a society

citizen a person who owes loyalty to a country and receives its protection

representative democracy a type of government in which citizens hold political power through elected representatives

monarchy a type of government in which a ruling family headed by a king or queen holds political power

oligarchy (AHL•ih•GAHR•kee) a type of government in which a small group of people holds power

dictatorship a type of government in which an individual holds complete political power

communism a type of government in which the Communist Party holds all political power and controls the economy

Visual Vocabulary monarchy (The queen of Denmark)

▶ Reading Strategy

Re-create the chart shown at right. As you read and respond to the **KEY QUESTIONS**, use the chart to categorize important details about types of government.

 See Skillbuilder Handbook, page R7

CATEGORIZE

	RULER	BASIS OF RULE
Democracy		
Monarchy		
Dictatorship		
Oligarchy		
Communism		

 GRAPHIC ORGANIZERS
Go to **Interactive Review** @ ClassZone.com

Why We Need Government

Connecting to Your World

You live in one of nearly 200 countries in the world. Some countries are tiny when compared to the United States; others are larger in physical size or in population. All countries have one thing in common—a government. A **government** is an organization set up to make and enforce rules for a group of people. It has authority over the land within its boundaries.

Passport An official document that allows a person to travel abroad.

Types of Government

▼ **KEY QUESTION** What types of government operate around the world?

Government is needed to provide security, make and enforce the laws, furnish the services that keep a country running, and protect the rights of citizens. A **citizen** is a person who owes loyalty to a country and receives its protection. The government also acts on behalf of the people in the country when it deals with other countries. As you have read, all countries have some type of government. The types differ mainly over how much power the people have. Some countries are ruled by a single person, others by a small group, and still others are ruled by many people.

U.S. Capitol Building This is the official seat of government for the country.

Washington, D.C.
UNITED STATES

② Reading for Understanding

▶ Key Ideas

BEFORE, YOU LEARNED

People belong to specific groups that share a common culture.

NOW YOU WILL LEARN

Cultures do not remain the same but change over time.

▶ Vocabulary

TERMS & NAMES

agricultural revolution the shift from gathering food to raising food

innovation something new that is introduced for the first time

technology people's application of knowledge, tools, and inventions to meet their needs

diffusion the spread of ideas, inventions, and patterns of behavior from one group to another

cultural hearth an area where a culture originated and spread to other areas

BACKGROUND VOCABULARY

domestication the raising and tending of a plant or animal to be of use to humans

nomad a person who has no set home but moves from place to place in search of food for animals

Visual Vocabulary nomad group

▶ Reading Strategy

Re-create the diagram at right. As you read and respond to the **KEY QUESTIONS**, use the diagram to analyze the causes and effects of cultural change.

 Skillbuilder Handbook, page R8

ANALYZE CAUSE AND EFFECT

Innovation	Diffusion
1. _____	1. _____
2. _____	2. _____

CULTURAL CHANGE

🔊 **GRAPHIC ORGANIZERS**
Go to **Interactive Review** @ ClassZone.com

How Does Culture Change?

Connecting to Your World

Think about all the information and communication tools you have in your daily life. Did you include cell phones, mp3 players, DVDs, digital cameras, or laptop computers? When your parents were your age, none of these devices were available to them. These improvements in technology have changed the ways many people live their lives—and this change has taken place in only one generation. Cultural change happens much more rapidly now than it did in the past.

Zulu Girl, South Africa, with Cell Phone

Culture Change and Exchange

▼ **KEY QUESTION** How does culture change?

Culture changes over time. The changes may be very slow or quite rapid. Some changes are simple, such as changes in clothing styles. Other changes are more complex, such as the agricultural revolution. In the **agricultural revolution**, which happened thousands of years ago, humans shifted from gathering food to raising food. Because the food source was more reliable, fewer people were needed for raising food, and ways of life changed. Two ways that culture changes are through innovation and diffusion.

Camels Go to Pasture Traditional ways are replaced by modern ones.

Assessment

VOCABULARY

Explain the significance of each of the following.

1. culture
2. ethnic group
3. religion
4. language
5. technology

Explain how the terms and names in each group are related.

6. culture, religion, and language
7. innovation, diffusion, and cultural hearth
8. domestication and agricultural revolution

KEY IDEAS

1 **What Is Culture?**

9. Why are there different cultures?
10. How do people learn about their culture?
11. What are two of the most important elements of culture?
12. What are the three types of religious beliefs?
13. Why is language important to a culture?
14. How does language change?

2 **How Does Culture Change?**

15. How does innovation change culture?
16. How does diffusion change culture?
17. What is a cultural hearth?
18. Why was culture change a slow process in earlier times?
19. Why might a people accept a cultural change?
20. In what way is cultural change forced upon a people?

CRITICAL THINKING

21. **Categorize** Create a table to list the factors that have helped or limited cultural change over the years.

HELP	LIMIT

22. **Make Generalizations** What makes each culture unique?
23. **Make Inferences** Why are families important in a culture?
24. **Connect to Economics** Why was the agricultural revolution such a dramatic cultural change?
25. **Five Themes: Movement** How have aspects of culture been spread throughout history?
26. **Connect Geography & Culture** How important is culture to a person's sense of identity?

Answer the
ESSENTIAL QUESTION

How does culture develop, and how does it shape our lives?

Written Response Write a two- or three-paragraph response to the Essential Question. Be sure to consider the key ideas of each section and the fact that all human beings are a part of a culture.

Response Rubric
A strong response will:
- explain the nature of culture and its elements
- discuss how culture shapes the lives of individuals

STANDARDS-BASED ASSESSMENT

 Test Practice

- Online Test Practice @ ClassZone.com
- Test-Taking Strategies and Practice at the front of this book

THEMATIC MAP

Use the map and your knowledge of geography to answer questions 1 and 2 on your paper.

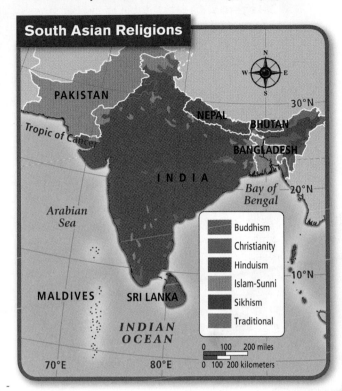

South Asian Religions

Legend:
- Buddhism
- Christianity
- Hinduism
- Islam-Sunni
- Sikhism
- Traditional

0 100 200 miles
0 100 200 kilometers

1. Which of the following countries has a large Buddhist population?

A. India
B. Sri Lanka
C. Bangladesh
D. Nepal

2. Which of the following countries has a large population of Muslims?

A. Bhutan
B. Sri Lanka
C. Bangladesh
D. India

CHART

Study the chart below. Use the information in the chart to answer questions 3 and 4.

Languages of Europe	
Country	**Languages Spoken**
Austria	German, Slovene, Croatian, Hungarian
Belgium	Flemish, French, German
France	French
Germany	German
Netherlands	Dutch, Frisian
Switzerland	German, French, Italian, Romansch

Source: *Infoplease database 2006*

3. In which countries is a single language spoken?

4. If you only spoke German, in which countries would you need a translator?

GeoActivity

1. INTERDISCIPLINARY ACTIVITY–MATHEMATICS

With a small group, research world religions on the Internet. Use a computer program to create a database and a graph showing the three countries with the largest number of members for each of the major religions, and the total population of those countries.

2. WRITING FOR SOCIAL STUDIES

Reread the paragraphs on the elements of culture. Then write a paragraph describing the culture of your community. Discuss such elements as religion, language, government, and economic activities.

3. MENTAL MAPPING

Create a map of your town or neighborhood showing schools and places of worship. Be sure to include

- elementary, middle, and high schools, public and private
- any places of worship

UNIT 2

The United States and Canada

Why It Matters:

The United States and Canada are two of the largest countries in the world. Because both nations have vast land areas, abundant resources, and well-educated populations, they have become two of the wealthiest countries in the world.

Statue of Liberty in New York

CHAPTER 5

The United States

Chateau Frontenac in Quebec

CHAPTER 6

Canada

Meet Kirima

In this unit, you will meet Kirima, a middle-school girl from Nunavut, Canada. Learn more about her on Worldster @ ClassZone.com

The United States and Canada occupy the central and northern four-fifths of the continent of North America. The two countries are bound together not only by physical geography and cultural heritage but also by strong economic and political ties. As you study the maps, notice geographic patterns and specific details about the region. Answer the questions on each map in your notebook.

As you study the graphs on this page, compare the landmass, population, rivers, and mountains of Canada with those of the United States (and in a few cases other regions). Then jot down the answers to the following questions in your notebook.

Comparing Data

1. How does Canada compare in size to the United States?

2. Approximately how many times larger is the population of the United States than that of Canada?

3. Which U.S. rivers are more than twice as long as the Mackenzie River in Canada?

4. What is the difference in height between the tallest peak in the United States and the tallest peak in Canada?

Comparing Data

Landmass

Canada
3,855,103 sq. mi.

Continental United States
3,165,630 sq. mi.

Population

Canada
32,270,500

United States
296,410,404

| 0 | 50 | 100 | 150 | 200 | 250 | 300 |

Population (in millions)

Rivers

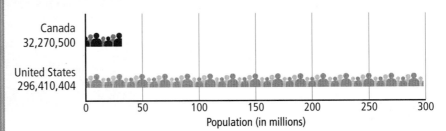

Mackenzie (Canada)
1,120 mi.

Rio Grande
1,885 mi.

Mississippi
2,357 mi.

Missouri
2,466 mi.

Nile (Egypt)
4,160 mi. — World's Longest

| 0 | 1000 | 2000 | 3000 | 4000 |

Length (in miles)

Mountains

World's Tallest
Mt. Everest
Nepal-Tibet
29,035 ft.

U.S. Tallest
Mt. McKinley
United States
20,320 ft.

Mt. Logan
Canada
19,524 ft.

Mt. St. Elias
U.S.-Canada
18,008 ft.

Mt. Foraker
United States
17,400 ft.

Population Density

ARCTIC OCEAN

Baffin Bay

Arctic Circle

60°N

Hudson Bay

Persons per square mile

Over 520
260–519
130–259
25–129
1–24
0

Toronto

40°N
60°W

Chicago

New York
Philadelphia

PACIFIC OCEAN

ATLANTIC OCEAN

Los Angeles

0   250   500 miles
0   250   500 kilometers

Dallas

Tropic of Cancer

Gulf of Mexico

Miami

20°N

PACIFIC OCEAN
22°N

20°N

0   75   150 miles
0   75   150 kilometers

160°W   158°W   156°W

THINK LIKE A GEOGRAPHER

1. **Human-Environment Interaction** Where are the areas of greatest population density?

2. **Region** Which color represents the most widespread population density level in the United States?

120°W   100°W

ARCTIC OCEAN

ALASKA
(U.S.)

Baffin
Bay

Arctic Circle

60°N

40°W

Hudson
Bay

CANADA

40°N

60°W

Tropical
Tropical wet
Tropical wet and dry

Dry
Desert
Semiarid

Mid-Latitude
Mediterranean
Marine west coast
Humid subtropical
Humid continental

High Latitude
Subarctic
Tundra
Icecap

Highland

UNITED
STATES

ATLANTIC
OCEAN

PACIFIC
OCEAN

N
W   E
S

Tropic of Cancer

| 0 | 250 | 500 miles |
| 0 | 250 | 500 kilometers |

Gulf of Mexico

20°N

PACIFIC OCEAN

22°N

HAWAII
(U.S.)

| 0 | 75 | 150 miles |
| 0 | 75 | 150 kilometers |

20°N

160°W   158°W   156°W

THINK LIKE A GEOGRAPHER

1. **Region** Why might most of the population of Canada be clustered along the border with the United States?

2. **Place** What climate is found throughout most of Canada?

120°W   100°W

Economic Activity

Land use
- Commercial agriculture
- Livestock raising
- Dairying
- Forestland
- Limited agriculture

Major resources
- Coal
- Fish
- Gold
- Iron ore
- Natural gas
- Oil
- Silver
- Timber
- Uranium
- Other minerals
- Manufacturing center

ARCTIC OCEAN

ALASKA (U.S.)

Baffin Bay

Arctic Circle

60°N

40°W

CANADA

Hudson Bay

Montréal

Toronto

Boston

Detroit

New York City

Chicago

Philadelphia

UNITED STATES

ATLANTIC OCEAN

St. Louis

San Francisco/ San Jose

Los Angeles

PACIFIC OCEAN

Tropic of Cancer

Houston

MEXICO

Gulf of Mexico

40°N

60°W

20°N

0   250   500 miles
0   250   500 kilometers

PACIFIC OCEAN

HAWAII (U.S.)

22°N

20°N

0   75   150 miles
0   75   150 kilometers

160°W   158°W   156°W

120°W   100°W

THINK LIKE A GEOGRAPHER

1. **Human-Environment Interaction** What is the main land use in Canada?

2. **Location** Near what bodies of water might American or Canadian fishermen be likely to live?

The United States and Canada

The United States and Canada occupy the central and northern four-fifths of the continent of North America. The chapters in this unit provide information about the geography, history, culture, government, and economics of the United States and Canada.

GEOGRAPHY

The United States and Canada extend from the Atlantic to the Pacific oceans and north to the Arctic ocean. The United States also reaches to the Gulf of Mexico. In total area, each country ranks among the largest in the world—Canada ranks second and the United States is fourth. In addition to their huge landmass, both countries are rich in natural resources.

HISTORY

Both the United States and Canada have been settled by immigrants from all over the world, beginning with the first settlers who probably migrated from Asia after the last Ice Age. The geographic richness of North America's resources has attracted immigrants from around the world and has enabled both the United States and Canada to develop into global economic powers. This continuing immigration is a recurring theme in the history of both countries; so is the constant migration of people within each country.

CULTURE

As you know, culture involves the following factors: food and shelter, religion, language, education, and political and social organization. In Canada, there are two official languages— English and French—because France played an important early role in the history and development of the country. In the United States, English is the predominant language. Both countries have highly diverse populations that have come from around the world to live within their borders.

Samuel de Champlain
Champlain founded Quebec, the first permanent French settlement in North America.

GOVERNMENT

Both Canada and the United States are representative democracies. In such a system of government, citizens hold political power through elected representatives. Canada and the United States are also federal republics. In a federal republic, power is divided between the national government and various state, territorial, or provincial governments. The personal freedoms guaranteed by the Canadian and U.S. governments have drawn millions to their shores.

Mount Rushmore Massive likenesses of four American presidents were carved on Mount Rushmore in the Black Hills of South Dakota.

ECONOMICS

The United States and Canada both have market economies. This is an economy in which the production of goods and services is determined by the demand from consumers. This kind of economy is also called a demand economy, or capitalism. Migration across the continent, combined with industrialization and urbanization, stimulated economic development in the United States and Canada. The economies of these two nations have been transformed by technology and by the movement toward globalization.

Toronto People skate outdoors in Toronto, one of Canada's booming economic centers.

Click here to compare the most recent data on countries @ ClassZone.com

Unit Writing Project

News Broadcast
As you read this unit, think of an issue to present in a television news broadcast. You might choose an issue like immigration, poverty, or outsourcing of jobs. Pretend you are a TV news reporter and gather information as you read each chapter.

Think About:

- how you will organize your script
- five things to be sure to tell the viewer: who, what, where, when, and why

United States

The United States is made up of 50 states, the District of Columbia, and 4 territories. Alaska, Hawaii, and the territories are separated from the 48 mainland states.

United States

GEOGRAPHY
Capital: Washington, D.C.
Total Area: 3,718,711 sq. mi.
Population: 296,410,404

ECONOMY
Imports: cars; oil; televisions; clothes
Exports: food; computers; machinery

CULTURE
Language: No official language
Religion: Christian 85%; Jewish 2%; Muslim 2%

District of Columbia

Total Area: 68 sq. mi.
Population: 550,521

Alabama

Capital: Montgomery
Total Area: 52,419 sq. mi.
Population: 4,557,808

Alaska

Capital: Juneau
Total Area: 663,267 sq. mi.
Population: 663,661

Arizona

Capital: Phoenix
Total Area: 113,998 sq. mi.
Population: 5,939,292

Arkansas

Capital: Little Rock
Total Area: 53,179 sq. mi.
Population: 2,779,154

California

Capital: Sacramento
Total Area: 163,696 sq. mi.
Population: 36,132,147

Colorado

Capital: Denver
Total Area: 104,094 sq. mi.
Population: 4,665,177

Connecticut

Capital: Hartford
Total Area: 5,543 sq. mi.
Population: 3,510,297

Delaware

Capital: Dover
Total Area: 2,489 sq. mi.
Population: 843,524

Florida

Capital: Tallahassee
Total Area: 65,755 sq. mi.
Population: 17,789,864

Georgia

Capital: Atlanta
Total Area: 59,425 sq. mi.
Population: 9,072,576

Hawaii

Capital: Honolulu
Total Area: 10,931 sq. mi.
Population: 1,275,194

Idaho

Capital: Boise
Total Area: 83,570 sq. mi.
Population: 1,429,096

Illinois

Capital: Springfield
Total Area: 57,914 sq. mi.
Population: 12,763,371

Indiana

Capital: Indianapolis
Total Area: 36,418 sq. mi.
Population: 6,271,973

Corn Harvest A combine harvests corn in Indiana.

Iowa

Capital: Des Moines
Total Area: 56,272 sq. mi.
Population: 2,966,334

Kansas

Capital: Topeka
Total Area: 82,277 sq. mi.
Population: 2,744,687

Kentucky

Capital: Frankfort
Total Area: 40,409 sq. mi.
Population: 4,173,405

Louisiana

Capital: Baton Rouge
Total Area: 51,840 sq. mi.
Population: 4,523,628

Maine

Capital: Augusta
Total Area: 35,385 sq. mi.
Population: 1,321,505

Maryland

Capital: Annapolis
Total Area: 12,407 sq. mi.
Population: 5,600,388

Massachusetts

Capital: Boston
Total Area: 10,555 sq. mi.
Population: 6,398,743

Michigan

Capital: Lansing
Total Area: 96,716 sq. mi.
Population: 10,120,860

Gray Wolf A gray wolf lopes through the snow in Minnesota.

Minnesota

Capital: St. Paul
Total Area: 86,939 sq. mi.
Population: 5,132,799

Mississippi

Capital: Jackson
Total Area: 48,430 sq. mi.
Population: 2,921,088

Lizard A mountain short-horned lizard near Santa Fe, New Mexico

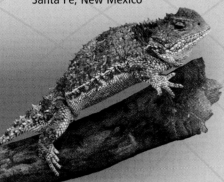

Missouri

Capital: Jefferson City
Total Area: 69,704 sq. mi.
Population: 5,800,310

Montana

Capital: Helena
Total Area: 147,042 sq. mi.
Population: 935,670

Nebraska

Capital: Lincoln
Total Area: 77,354 sq. mi.
Population: 1,758,787

Nevada

Capital: Carson City
Total Area: 110,561 sq. mi.
Population: 2,414,807

New Hampshire

Capital: Concord
Total Area: 9,350 sq. mi.
Population: 1,309,940

New Jersey

Capital: Trenton
Total Area: 8,721 sq. mi.
Population: 8,717,925

New Mexico

Capital: Santa Fe
Total Area: 121,590 sq. mi.
Population: 1,928,384

New York

Capital: Albany
Total Area: 54,556 sq. mi.
Population: 19,254,630

North Carolina

Capital: Raleigh
Total Area: 53,819 sq. mi.
Population: 8,683,242

North Dakota

Capital: Bismarck
Total Area: 70,700 sq. mi.
Population: 636,677

Ohio

Capital: Columbus
Total Area: 44,825 sq. mi.
Population: 11,464,042

Heron A heron takes flight.

Oklahoma

Capital: Oklahoma City
Total Area: 69,898 sq. mi.
Population: 3,547,884

Oregon

Capital: Salem
Total Area: 98,381 sq. mi.
Population: 3,641,056

Pennsylvania

Capital: Harrisburg
Total Area: 46,055 sq. mi.
Population: 12,429,616

Rhode Island

Capital: Providence
Total Area: 1,545 sq. mi.
Population: 1,076,189

South Carolina

Capital: Columbia
Total Area: 32,020 sq. mi.
Population: 4,255,083

South Dakota

Capital: Pierre
Total Area: 77,117 sq. mi.
Population: 775,933

Tennessee

Capital: Nashville
Total Area: 42,143 sq. mi.
Population: 5,962,959

Texas

Capital: Austin
Total Area: 268,581 sq. mi.
Population: 22,859,968

Utah

Capital: Salt Lake City
Total Area: 84,899 sq. mi.
Population: 2,469,585

Vermont

Capital: Montpelier
Total Area: 9,614 sq. mi.
Population: 623,050

Virginia

Capital: Richmond
Total Area: 42,774 sq. mi.
Population: 7,567,465

Washington

Capital: Olympia
Total Area: 71,300 sq. mi.
Population: 6,287,759

West Virginia

Capital: Charleston
Total Area: 24,230 sq. mi.
Population: 1,816,856

Wisconsin

Capital: Madison
Total Area: 65,498 sq. mi.
Population: 5,536,201

Wyoming

Capital: Cheyenne
Total Area: 97,814 sq. mi.
Population: 509,294

Rocky Mountain Bighorn Sheep Bighorn sheep are found in many Rocky Mountain states, including Wyoming.

U.S. Territories

American Samoa

Capital: Pago Pago
Total Area: 84 sq. mi.
Population: 62,700 (2004)

Guam

Capital: Agana
Total Area: 209 sq. mi.
Population: 165,000 (2004)

U.S. Virgin Islands

Capital: Charlotte Amalie
Total Area: 136 sq. mi.
Population: 109,000 (2004)

Puerto Rico

Capital: San Juan
Total Area: 3,515 sq. mi.
Population: 898,000 (2004)

Click here to compare the most recent data on countries @ ClassZone.com

Puffins Atlantic puffins on Machias Seal Island in Canada

Canada

Canada is made up of 10 provinces and 3 territories. The 3 territories are sparsely populated but make up about 41 percent of the country's landmass.

Canada

GEOGRAPHY
Capital: Ottawa
Total Area: 3,855,103 sq. mi.
Population: 32,270,500

ECONOMY
Imports: machinery; chemicals; oil
Exports: food; natural gas; wood

CULTURE
Language: English; French
Religion: Christian 77%; Muslim 2%; Jewish 1%

Alberta
Capital: Edmonton
Total Area: 255,541 sq. mi.
Population: 3,256,800

British Columbia
Capital: Victoria
Total Area: 364,764 sq. mi.
Population: 4,254,500

Manitoba
Capital: Winnipeg
Total Area: 250,116 sq. mi.
Population: 1,177,600

New Brunswick
Capital: Fredericton
Total Area: 28,150 sq. mi.
Population: 752,000

Newfoundland and Labrador
Capital: St. John's
Total Area: 156,453 sq. mi.
Population: 516,000

Northwest Territories
Capital: Yellowknife
Total Area: 519,734 sq. mi.
Population: 43,000

Nova Scotia

Capital: Halifax
Total Area: 21,345 sq. mi.
Population: 937,900

Nunavut

Capital: Iqaluit
Total Area: 808,185 sq. mi.
Population: 30,000

Ontario

Capital: Toronto
Total Area: 415,598 sq. mi.
Population: 12,541,400

Prince Edward Island

Capital: Charlottetown
Total Area: 2,185 sq. mi.
Population: 138,100

Quebec

Capital: Quebec City
Total Area: 595,391 sq. mi.
Population: 7,598,100

Saskatchewan

Capital: Regina
Total Area: 251,366 sq. mi.
Population: 994,100

Yukon Territory

Capital: Whitehorse
Total Area: 186,272 sq. mi.
Population: 31,000

Polar Bear A polar bear in a field of tundra fireweed near Hudson Bay

The United States

 ESSENTIAL QUESTION

How did a developing nation grow into a world power?

CONNECT > **Geography & History**

Use the map and the time line to answer the following questions.

1. Which of the Great Lakes is located entirely within the United States?

2. In what year did Hurricane Katrina occur and how did the location of New Orleans contribute to the damage caused by it?

History

1565 Pedro Menéndes de Avilés founds the city of St. Augustine in Florida for Spain. ▶

1492

Government

1787 The Constitution of the United States is written in Philadelphia.

History

1775 American Revolution begins with the battles of Lexington and Concord. ▶

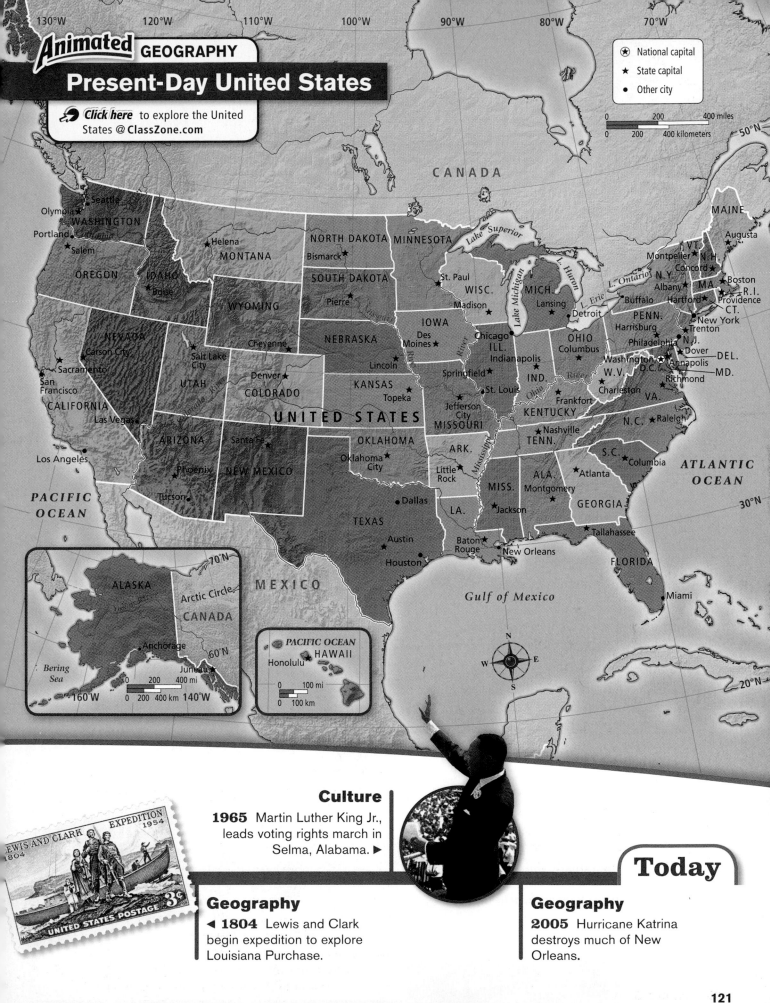

Present-Day United States

Click here to explore the United States @ ClassZone.com

Legend:
- ★ National capital
- ★ State capital
- • Other city

200   400 miles
200   400 kilometers

CANADA

CANADA

MEXICO

PACIFIC OCEAN

ATLANTIC OCEAN

Gulf of Mexico

WASHINGTON — Olympia, Seattle, Portland, Salem
OREGON
IDAHO — Boise, Helena
MONTANA
NORTH DAKOTA — Bismarck
MINNESOTA — St. Paul
SOUTH DAKOTA — Pierre
WYOMING — Cheyenne
NEVADA — Carson City
CALIFORNIA — Sacramento, San Francisco, Las Vegas, Los Angeles
UTAH — Salt Lake City
COLORADO — Denver
NEBRASKA — Lincoln
IOWA — Des Moines
WISC. — Madison
MICH. — Lansing, Detroit
ILL. — Chicago, Springfield
IND. — Indianapolis
OHIO — Columbus
KANSAS — Topeka
MISSOURI — Jefferson City, St. Louis
KENTUCKY — Frankfort
ARIZONA — Phoenix, Tucson
NEW MEXICO — Santa Fe
OKLAHOMA — Oklahoma City
ARK. — Little Rock
TENN. — Nashville
TEXAS — Dallas, Austin, Houston
LA. — Baton Rouge, New Orleans
MISS. — Jackson
ALA. — Montgomery
GEORGIA — Atlanta
S.C. — Columbia
N.C. — Raleigh
VA. — Richmond, Charleston
W.V.
PENN. — Harrisburg, Philadelphia, Pittsburgh
N.Y. — Albany, Buffalo, New York
MAINE — Augusta
VT. — Montpelier
N.H. — Concord
MA — Boston
R.I. — Providence
CT. — Hartford
N.J. — Trenton
DEL. — Dover
MD. — Annapolis
Washington, D.C.
FLORIDA — Tallahassee, Miami

UNITED STATES

Lake Superior, Lake Michigan, Lake Huron, L. Erie, L. Ontario
Missouri River, Mississippi River, Ohio River, Columbia R., Colorado R.

ALASKA — Anchorage, Juneau
Arctic Circle, Bering Sea, CANADA
70°N, 60°N, 160°W, 140°W
0 200 400 mi
0 200 400 km

HAWAII — Honolulu
PACIFIC OCEAN
0 100 mi
0 100 km

N E S W

Culture

1965 Martin Luther King Jr., leads voting rights march in Selma, Alabama. ▶

Geography

◀ **1804** Lewis and Clark begin expedition to explore Louisiana Purchase.

LEWIS AND CLARK EXPEDITION 1804 1954
UNITED STATES POSTAGE 3¢

Today

Geography

2005 Hurricane Katrina destroys much of New Orleans.

Reading for Understanding

▶ Key Ideas

BEFORE, YOU LEARNED

Our planet has a great variety of landforms and bodies of water, as well as great variety in its climate and vegetation.

NOW YOU WILL LEARN

The physical geography of the United States varies greatly from coast to coast.

▶ Vocabulary

TERMS & NAMES

Appalachian (AP•uh•LAY•chee•uhn) **Mountains** a mountain chain in the eastern United States, running parallel to the Atlantic Ocean

Great Lakes five lakes forming the largest group of freshwater lakes in the world

Mississippi River the largest river and chief waterway of the United States

Great Plains a vast grassland in central North America

Gulf of Mexico an arm of the Atlantic Ocean that lies south of the United States

Piedmont (PEED•MAHNT) a hilly, upland region between the Appalachian Mountains and the coastal plain of the South

Everglades huge wetlands of southern Florida

Rocky Mountains a mountain range that extends about 3,000 miles from New Mexico to Alaska

Continental Divide a high ridge line in the Rocky Mountains that divides east-flowing from west-flowing rivers

Mt. McKinley (also called Denali) the tallest mountain of North America, located in Alaska

Grand Canyon a deep gorge cut through northern Arizona by the Colorado River

REVIEW

continent one of seven large landmasses on the surface of the earth

▶ Reading Strategy

Re-create the chart that is shown at right. As you read and respond to the **KEY QUESTIONS**, use the chart to organize important details about the physical geography of the United States.

 Skillbuilder Handbook, page R7

CATEGORIZE

	LANDFORMS	CLIMATE	VEGETATION
Northeast			
Midwest			
South			
West			

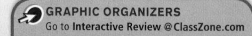 **GRAPHIC ORGANIZERS**
Go to **Interactive Review** @ ClassZone.com

From Coast to Coast

Connecting to Your World

What outdoor activities do you enjoy? Sports such as surfing and scuba diving are popular in Hawaii. Many people go skiing and snowboarding in the snowy mountains of Colorado. The United States is a large country with nearly every type of landscape and climate. One thing that helps to define the major U.S. regions is the type of activities common to the area.

Northeast

🔻 **KEY QUESTION** What are the geographic advantages and disadvantages of the Northeast?

The United States stretches across the North American **continent**, or large landmass. The country can be divided into four regions: Northeast, Midwest, South, and West. The features that set the regions apart are their landforms, climates, plants, animals, and ways of life. The Northeast includes the New England states of Maine, New Hampshire, Vermont, Massachusetts, Rhode Island, and Connecticut, as well as New York, Pennsylvania, and New Jersey.

Surfing and Skiing
These are two activities that can be enjoyed in the varied U.S. landscapes.

Appalachian Mountains These mountains extend for almost 2,000 miles in the eastern United States and Canada.

Landforms, Climate, and Vegetation The two most important physical features of the Northeast are the Atlantic Ocean **Ⓐ** (shown on the map on the next page) and the **Appalachian** (AP•uh•LAY•chee•uhn) **Mountains Ⓑ**. The Atlantic coastline, which forms the region's eastern border, has deep-water harbors that support trade. The Appalachians are a mountain chain that runs parallel to the Atlantic Coast.

In much of the Northeast, especially in New England, the terrain is too hilly and rocky to make good farmland. Most of the region lacks mineral wealth, but Pennsylvania has coal and iron ore deposits.

Summers are warm and humid. Winters are cold and snowy, with the most snow falling in the northernmost states. Despite the effects of the logging industry, forests still stretch over much of the region.

Life in the Northeast The Northeast was one of the first areas of North America to be heavily settled by Europeans. Because of the area's rocky land and good harbors, fishing and shipping became more profitable than farming. Textile mills built in the Northeast in Lowell, Massachusetts, were among the first U.S. factories.

The Northeast is still the most densely populated and industrialized region of the United States. The coast is crowded with cities. Shipping and manufacturing are major parts of the economy, but service industries also play a large part. New York City, the largest city in the country, is a world center of finance, trade, and culture.

▲ COMPARE AND CONTRAST Describe the geographic advantages and disadvantages of the Northeast.

Midwest

▼ KEY QUESTION What are the most important features of the Midwest's geography?

The central and northern part of North America has one of the largest areas of lowlands on the planet. Those plains make up most of the Midwest. The region stretches from Ohio west to the Dakotas and from Canada south to the Ohio River, Missouri, and Kansas.

Mississippi River
Minneapolis, Minnesota is located on the Mississippi River. **Why might important cities be located along a major river?**

Minneapolis

Mississippi River

Gulf of Mexico

Physical Geography of the United States

CANADA

C Great Lakes

COAST RANGES
CASCADE RANGE
ROCKY MOUNTAINS
SIERRA NEVADA
COAST RANGES
GREAT BASIN
GREAT PLAINS

Mississippi R.
Missouri R.

D

UNITED STATES

A

ATLANTIC OCEAN

B

Ohio R.

APPALACHIAN MOUNTAINS

COASTAL PLAIN

Mississippi R.

PACIFIC OCEAN

Rio Grande

MEXICO

Gulf of Mexico

E

40°N

30°N

0   250   500 miles
0   250   500 kilometers

Elevation
13,100 ft. (4,000 m)
6,600 ft. (2,000 m)
3,280 ft. (1,000 m)
650 ft. (200 m)
0 ft. (0 m)
Below sea level

▲ Mountain peak

BROOKS RANGE
Mt. McKinley 20,320 ft.
ALASKA RANGE
Gulf of Alaska
0   300 mi
0   300 km
120°W

Kauai
Niihau Oahu Molokai
PACIFIC OCEAN Lanai Maui
Kahoolawe
Hawaii
0   100 mi
0   100 km
100°W

CONNECT
Geography & Culture
READING A PHYSICAL MAP

Physical geography maps show landforms and bodies of water.

• Use the key to identify elevation.

• Use the scale to estimate distance.

1. **Movement** What landform might have restricted movement westward from the east coast?

2. **Location** Which rivers flow into the Pacific Ocean?

Landforms, Climate, and Vegetation The Great Lakes C make up the world's largest group of freshwater lakes. Four of the lakes—Ontario, Erie, Huron, and Superior—form part of the U.S.-Canada border. The Mississippi River D is the largest river and most important trade waterway in the United States. West of the Mississippi lies the vast, mostly treeless Great Plains. Its native plants are prairie grasses and wildflowers. Huge herds of bison once roamed the plains. The Midwest has a harsh climate, with hot summers and cold winters.

Life in the Midwest The Midwest is the major farming region of the United States, with corn, wheat, and dairy among its important products. The Midwest also contains major manufacturing areas, such as Detroit, Michigan, home of the automobile industry. The Midwest's largest city is Chicago, a port and transportation hub along Lake Michigan. The St. Lawrence Seaway connects Chicago to the Atlantic, and canals and rivers connect the city to the Gulf of Mexico E.

▲ **EVALUATE** Describe geographic features of the Midwest.

South

▼ **KEY QUESTION** What is the climate of most of the South?

The South stretches from the Atlantic Ocean to Texas; it contains 16 states. On a map, its most noticeable feature is the giant peninsula of Florida.

Landforms, Climate, and Vegetation The South shares two features with other regions. The Appalachians extend into the South, and the Mississippi River runs through it. A broad plain stretches along the coasts of the Atlantic Ocean and Gulf of Mexico. Between the Atlantic Coastal Plain and the Appalachians lies the **Piedmont** (PEED•MAHNT), which is a hilly, upland region.

Most of the South has hot, rainy summers and mild winters. The southern tip of Florida is the only part of the continental United States to lie in the tropics. Florida is also home to the **Everglades**, a wetland filled with grasses and mangrove trees.

Life in the South The South was first a farming region. Then in the 20th century, industries moved there because of the mild climate, newly invented air conditioning, and lower wages for workers. Now the South has many booming cities. In addition, Kentucky and West Virginia mine for coal, and many of the Gulf States drill for oil. Deadly hurricanes sometimes hit places on the South's long coastline. In 2005, Hurricane Katrina struck the Gulf Coast, including New Orleans, Louisiana. Most of the city was flooded. Rebuilding New Orleans is a challenge that will take years to complete.

▲ **FIND MAIN IDEAS** Describe the climate of the South.

Everglades National Park A cluster of dwarf cypresses grows in this park in Florida. **What wildlife might thrive in a subtropical wetland such as the Everglades?**

West

▼ **KEY QUESTION** What are the climates found in the West?

A huge region of dramatic scenery, the West includes all the states from the Great Plains to the Pacific, plus Alaska and Hawaii.

Landforms, Climate, and Vegetation The West's most visible feature is the **Rocky Mountains**, which extend 3,000 miles from Alaska to New Mexico. The **Continental Divide**, a high ridge line that separates the east-flowing and west-flowing rivers of the continent, runs through the mountains. The tallest mountain in North America is **Mt. McKinley** (also called Denali) in Alaska.

The West has varied climates, plants, and animals. Much of the region has an arid or desert climate, but the Northwest coast is rainy. Hawaii has a tropical climate; most of Alaska is cold. Cacti such as the many-armed saguaro (suh•GWAHR•oh) grow in the deserts, while the redwoods, tallest of all trees, grow along the Pacific coast. Wildlife includes snakes, lizards, wild cats, wolves, and the massive grizzly bear.

Life in the West Ranching, mining, and logging are important industries in the region. Parts of California and Hawaii are devoted to agriculture, while oil drilling is a major industry in Alaska. Recently, high-tech industries have clustered in California and Washington.

Some areas, such as southern California, are very urban, but most Western states are sparsely populated. The West has many national parks to preserve its landscapes. One is at the **Grand Canyon**, a deep, colorful gorge that the Colorado River cut through northern Arizona over many millions of years.

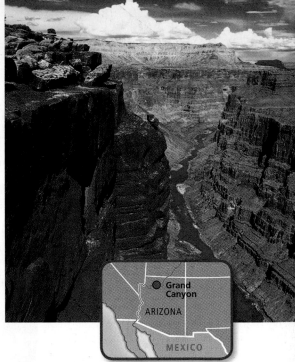

The Grand Canyon The Grand Canyon in Arizona was created by erosion caused by the Colorado River.

 SUMMARIZE Describe the climates of the West.

Section ① Assessment

ONLINE QUIZ
For test practice, go to
Interactive Review
@ ClassZone.com

TERMS & NAMES

1. Explain the importance of
- Great Lakes
- Mississippi River
- Great Plains
- Rocky Mountains

USE YOUR READING NOTES

2. Categorize Use your completed chart to answer the following question:

Which of the four regions have mountains? Name the mountains found in each region.

	LANDFORMS	CLIMATE	VEGETATION
Northeast			
Midwest			
South			
West			

KEY IDEAS

3. How did the geography of the Northeast affect its economic development?

4. In what way does the Mississippi River provide an economic link between the Midwest and South?

5. Why are there many national parks in the West?

CRITICAL THINKING

6. Draw Conclusions Why is the Northeast coast so crowded with cities?

7. Analyze Causes Why is the South in more danger from hurricanes than the Midwest or the Northeast?

8. CONNECT to Today In 2005, the U.S. government debated whether to allow companies to drill for oil in a part of Alaska that had been protected for wildlife. What arguments might be made for banning or allowing drilling?

9. SCIENCE Create a Poster Learn about the Grand Canyon in an encyclopedia or educational Web site. Then create a poster explaining how it was formed.

The United States is divided into four main regions. They are distinguished from one another by their landforms, bodies of water, climates, and economies.

WEST

The West has a great variety of scenery (see Wyoming's Grand Tetons below), climate, and economic activities.

Landforms: Rocky Mountains
Bodies of Water: Pacific Ocean
Climate: varied—arid; rainy and mild; cold; tropical
Economy: ranching, mining, logging, farming, high-tech industries

Bears are found throughout the West.

Bald eagles thrive in the Alaskan wilderness

Alaska

Hawaii

MIDWEST

The Midwest has extremes in weather and ways of life, ranging from farming (see Kansas alfalfa farm below) to manufacturing.

Landforms: Great Plains
Bodies of Water: Great Lakes, Mississippi River
Climate: hot summers, cold winters
Economy: farming, manufacturing, transportation, trade

Prairie dogs are common on the Great Plains.

NORTHEAST

The Northeast was the first area of North America to be heavily settled by Europeans. It is still the most densely populated region.

Landforms: Appalachian Mountains and Coastal Plain
Bodies of Water: Atlantic Ocean (see Maine lighthouse on Atlantic coast above)
Climate: warm, humid summers; cold, snowy winters
Economy: trade, manufacturing, service industries

Seagulls are common along the Atlantic coast.

SOUTH

The South has attracted industries and people in part because of the warm climate.

Landforms: Appalachian Mountains, Everglades (see above)
Bodies of Water: Gulf of Mexico, Mississippi River, Atlantic Ocean
Climate: hot rainy summers and mild winters
Economy: farming, manufacturing, coal mining, oil drilling

Alligators thrive in the Everglades.

CRITICAL THINKING

1. **Compare and Contrast** Which region does not have mountains as one of its basic landforms?

2. **Compare and Contrast** In which region does farming not play a major role in the economy?

▶ Key Ideas

BEFORE, YOU LEARNED

The United States spans the North American continent from the Atlantic to the Pacific oceans.

NOW YOU WILL LEARN

Native Americans and peoples from other continents all came together to build a nation.

▶ Vocabulary

TERMS & NAMES

land bridge dry land that appeared between Asia and Alaska during the Ice Age

immigrant a person who moves to one country from another

colony a group of people who settle a distant land but are ruled by their homeland

Constitution the document that is the basis for the U.S. government

Louisiana Purchase the action by which President Thomas Jefferson bought the Louisiana Territory from France

Lewis and Clark Expedition a journey made by Lewis and Clark to explore the Louisiana Terrritory

manifest destiny the idea that the United States should own all the land between, and even beyond, the Atlantic and Pacific oceans

Civil War (1861–1865) a conflict between North and South over the issues of states' rights and slavery

transcontinental railroad a railroad that crosses a continent

Great Depression a period of severe economic decline from 1929 into the early 1940s

Dust Bowl a region of the Great Plains that suffered drought and suffocating dust storms

▶ Reading Strategy

Re-create the diagram shown at right. As you read and respond to the **KEY QUESTIONS**, use the outer ovals to note important details.

 Skillbuilder Handbook, page R4

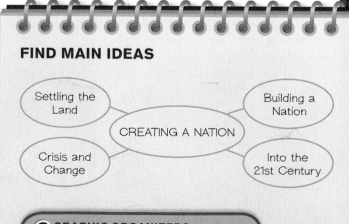

FIND MAIN IDEAS

Settling the Land

Building a Nation

CREATING A NATION

Crisis and Change

Into the 21st Century

GRAPHIC ORGANIZERS
Go to **Interactive Review** @ClassZone.com

Creating a Nation

Connecting to Your World

What do you think of when someone mentions U.S. history? Do you picture Native Americans hunting bison? Maybe you think of Pilgrims landing in New England or of the Liberty Bell. No matter what image comes to mind, it is probably connected in some way to geography. The ways that people chose to live on the land, the movement of people, and the interaction of cultures all have played a crucial role in shaping the past.

Settling the Land

▼ **KEY QUESTION** Who were the first groups to settle the land that became the United States?

The history of the United States involves many different cultures, including Native Americans, Europeans, Asians, and Africans. Sometimes various groups such as Native Americans and European settlers fought, but more often, they learned from each other and helped to create a new, American culture. For example, the music of African slaves blended with that of Irish and Scottish settlers to form a new American music. The history of the United States is also the story of how a developing nation on the Atlantic coast grew to span a continent.

The Liberty Bell
The Liberty Bell was rung to announce the first public reading of the Declaration of Independence in Philadelphia on July 8, 1776.

Bison Hunt Huge herds of bison once roamed the Great Plains.

A Land Bridge

Today, Alaska and Siberia are separated by the Bering Strait, a strip of sea only 55 miles wide. During the last ice age, glaciers moved south from the North Pole, freezing up the waters of the Bering Strait and exposing more land. This formed the Beringia land bridge, over which the earliest Americans may have migrated from Asia.

Native Americans Scientists believe that the first inhabitants of North America came from Asia. According to one theory, the Ice Age glaciers held so much frozen water that ocean levels fell. The drop in sea level uncovered a **land bridge**, a stretch of dry land between Asia and Alaska. Many thousands of years ago, Asians hunting for food crossed into North America. Other people dispute the land bridge theory. Some scientists believe that people came from Asia on boats.

No matter how humans arrived, people eventually spread to all parts of the Americas. Those who settled North America are split into two main groups: the Inuit, who live in the far north, and Native Americans, who are divided into many smaller groups. By the year 1500, hundreds of cultural groups lived in North America. They spoke different languages. Some lived by hunting and fishing, while others farmed. Most lived in close-knit societies organized by clans.

The First Colonies In the 1500s, Europeans began to come to North America. This began a pattern of immigrants coming to the United States from around the world. An **immigrant** is a person who moves to one country from another. Some Europeans came looking for gold or land. Others came to find religious freedom. Many Africans were brought to the colonies by force to work as slaves.

Over time, Europeans started many American colonies. A **colony** is a group of people who settle a distant land but are ruled by their homeland. The Spanish founded St. Augustine, Florida, one of the oldest U.S. settlements. They also built missions in the Southwest. English settlements include Jamestown, Virginia, and Plymouth Colony in Massachusetts. The French colony, New France, included eastern Canada and lands near the Great Lakes and Mississippi River.

▲ **SUMMARIZE** Describe the first groups that settled the United States.

Building a Nation

▼ **KEY QUESTION** How did the United States gain new territory?

In 1763, Great Britain defeated France in the French and Indian War and took over New France. To pay off the war debt, Britain's rulers imposed new taxes on the American colonists.

Thomas Jefferson (1743–1826) was the third president of the United States. He was proud of having written the Declaration of Independence. Here is the most famous quotation from it.

> We hold these truths to be self-evident [obvious], that all men are created equal, that they are endowed [provided] by their Creator with certain unalienable [not able to be taken away] Rights, that among these are Life, Liberty and the pursuit of Happiness.
>
> Source: *The Declaration of Independence,* by Thomas Jefferson

DOCUMENT–BASED QUESTION

Why might it be more accurate to say that people have a right to pursue happiness instead of the right to be happy?

Benjamin Franklin reads Jefferson's Declaration. ▶

ONLINE PRIMARY SOURCE To read more of Thomas Jefferson's writing, go to the **Research & Writing Center** @ ClassZone.com

Britain also passed laws to control the colonies. The colonists objected to the new laws because they had no representatives in the British lawmaking body to speak for their interests and concerns.

The Revolution and Constitution In 1775, the Revolutionary War began, and in 1776, the colonies proclaimed their freedom in the Declaration of Independence, written by Thomas Jefferson. By 1783, the United States had won the war against Great Britain and become a new nation.

Americans feared abuses of power, so they set up a weak national government. But leaders soon realized that the government was too weak to run the country well. In 1787, leaders from 12 states met to create a new government. They wrote the **Constitution** of the United States, the document that is the basis for the U.S. government.

The Constitution set up a federal government—a union of states with a central authority—divided into three equal branches.

1. The legislative branch, Congress, makes the laws. It consists of two houses—the Senate and the House of Representatives.

2. The executive branch is led by the president, the head of the government. George Washington, who won the 1788 presidential election, was the first president of the United States.

3. The judicial branch settles disputes about laws and includes all the courts in the country, including the Supreme Court.

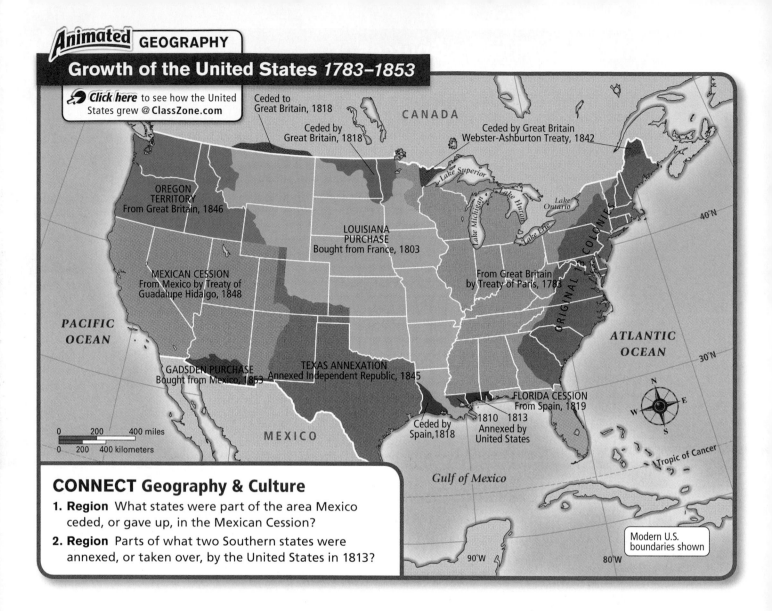

Animated GEOGRAPHY

Growth of the United States *1783–1853*

Click here to see how the United States grew @ ClassZone.com

Ceded to Great Britain, 1818

Ceded by Great Britain, 1818

CANADA

Ceded by Great Britain Webster-Ashburton Treaty, 1842

OREGON TERRITORY
From Great Britain, 1846

LOUISIANA PURCHASE
Bought from France, 1803

MEXICAN CESSION
From Mexico by Treaty of Guadalupe Hidalgo, 1848

From Great Britain by Treaty of Paris, 1783

ORIGINAL 13 COLONIES

PACIFIC OCEAN

ATLANTIC OCEAN

GADSDEN PURCHASE
Bought from Mexico, 1853

TEXAS ANNEXATION
Annexed Independent Republic, 1845

FLORIDA CESSION
From Spain, 1819

1810 1813
Annexed by United States

Ceded by Spain, 1818

MEXICO

Gulf of Mexico

Tropic of Cancer

Modern U.S. boundaries shown

0   200   400 miles
0   200   400 kilometers

CONNECT Geography & Culture

1. **Region** What states were part of the area Mexico ceded, or gave up, in the Mexican Cession?

2. **Region** Parts of what two Southern states were annexed, or taken over, by the United States in 1813?

The Nation Grows Even before the war, Americans had begun to move west to new lands. After the war, the United States gained all of Britain's territory south of Canada and west to the Mississippi. In 1803, President Thomas Jefferson bought Louisiana, a large territory between the Mississippi River and the Rocky Mountains, from France. The **Louisiana Purchase** doubled the size of the United States. Jefferson sent Meriwether Lewis and William Clark to explore the region. The **Lewis and Clark Expedition** gained valuable knowledge of the West.

During the 1800s, many Americans believed in **manifest destiny**, the idea that the United States should own all the land between, and even some beyond, the oceans. The United States gained that territory piece by piece. Texas declared itself free from Mexico in 1836 and became a state in 1845. Then the United States and Mexico fought the Mexican War (1846–1848). The United States gained a huge region stretching from Texas west to the Pacific and north to Oregon.

▲ **FIND MAIN IDEAS** Describe how the United States acquired new territory.

Crisis and Change

▼ **KEY QUESTION** How did regional differences help to cause and end the Civil War?

The Northeast became the first manufacturing region. In contrast, large farms called plantations were common in the South. Plantations needed a lot of workers, and the South became a region that relied on African slave labor.

Growing Pains and Civil War From the nation's beginning, some Americans wanted to end slavery. In time, the country split into opposing sides: Northern free states and Southern slave states. The South came to believe that states had the right to reject federal laws and even to secede, or withdraw, from the Union.

In 1860, Abraham Lincoln, a Northerner who hated slavery, was elected president. In response, 11 Southern states seceded from the Union, forming the Confederate States of America. Fighting broke out over secession, and the **Civil War** began in 1861.

At first, the South won more battles. But the North had a larger population and factories to make the supplies the army needed, and so the North defeated the South in 1865. After the war, North and South were reunited.

Expansion In 1867, the U.S. government purchased Alaska from Russia. In 1898, the United States won the Spanish-American War and gained Puerto Rico, Guam, and the Philippines.

The economy also grew, especially in the Northeast. Immigrants poured into U.S. cities. A larger population needed more food, clothing, and housing. Factories replaced hand manufacturing with machines that made goods more quickly. In 1869, workers completed the first **transcontinental railroad** that crossed the continent from coast to coast. The United States continued to build railroads, making it easier to ship goods to market.

▲ **COMPARE AND CONTRAST** Explain how regional differences helped to cause and end the Civil War.

HISTORY MAKERS

Abraham Lincoln (1809–1865)

Born in a log cabin, Abraham Lincoln was a self-educated man. When he ran for president in 1860, his critics said he lacked experience. They mocked his rough appearance. Yet Lincoln became president and led the nation through its worst crisis.

During the Civil War, he helped plan the North's war strategy. His Gettysburg Address inspired the nation. Above all, he never forgot his main goal—to save the union. Lincoln achieved that goal but paid a terrible price. Days after the war ended, a Southerner killed him.

 ONLINE BIOGRAPHY
For more on the life of Abraham Lincoln, go to the **Research & Writing Center @ ClassZone.com**

The Dust Bowl

During World War I, farmers plowed up the Great Plains to plant crops. When drought hit in the 1930s, crops died. Wind storms blew away the soil, which no longer had the deep roots of prairie plants to hold it. Dust damaged farms across a 25,000-square-mile region called the Dust Bowl. Dust clouds are shown rolling in over Lamar, Colorado, in 1934.

Into the 21st Century

🔻 **KEY QUESTION** What changes did the United States experience during the 1900s?

During much of the 1700s and 1800s, Americans were more concerned with challenges that their own country faced than with events around the world. During the 1900s, however, the U.S. role in the world changed.

Turmoil and Change When World War I started in Europe in 1914, most Americans wanted to stay out of the fighting. Then Germany sank a number of ships, killing U.S. civilians. The United States joined the war in 1917 and help the Allies to win it.

After the war, the 1920s seemed to be an era of wealth and progress. For example, the affordable automobile was built and more people than ever owned stocks. But problems lurked behind the good times. In 1929, stock prices plunged, and many people lost their money. That began the **Great Depression**, a period of severe economic decline (1929–early 1940s) in the United States. Businesses failed, and millions were out of work. Life was hard in the **Dust Bowl**, a large area in the Great Plains that suffered drought and dust storms.

By the late 1930s, war was again raging in Europe and Asia, and again the United States wanted to avoid fighting. Then in 1941, Japan attacked Pearl Harbor, Hawaii, and the United States went to war. The fighting lasted for four more years until the war ended in 1945.

Fun Facts!

SEABISCUIT

During the dark days of the Depression, the story of Seabiscuit (at far right) lifted people's spirits. He was an unlikely looking race horse who managed to defeat some of the great racing champions of the day, such as War Admiral. Seabiscuit stood for the underdog overcoming adversity.

Nation and World U.S. life was transformed in the 20th century. The civil rights and women's liberation movements brought more equality. Rapid technological change was spurred by space exploration, including the moon flights and the space shuttle program.

After World War II, the United States became a world leader. For decades, it competed with the Communist Soviet Union to be the strongest political and military power. When the Soviet Union fell apart in 1991, the United States was the richest and most powerful nation in the world.

In the 21st century, the United States confronted the danger of terrorism, which is the use of violence for political purposes. On September 11, 2001, terrorists flew airplanes into the World Trade Center in New York City and into the Pentagon. Approximately 3,000 people died. The U.S. government responded by launching a war against terrorism.

The United States also tries to be a leader in helping people. For example, when a deadly tsunami struck South Asia in December 2004, Americans gave more than $1 billion to relief efforts. Americans also serve in agencies that improve life in developing countries.

Moon Landing Apollo 15 moon base, established between July 30 and August 7, 1971

▲ **FIND MAIN IDEAS** Describe U.S. changes during the 1900s.

Section 2 Assessment

TERMS & NAMES

1. Explain the importance of
- land bridge
- Louisiana Purchase
- manifest destiny
- Dust Bowl

USE YOUR READING NOTES

2. Find Main Ideas Use your completed diagram to answer the following question:

How did the U.S. role in the world change during the 1900s?

Settling the Land

Building a Nation

CREATING A NATION

Crisis and Change

Into the 21st Century

KEY IDEAS

3. Which three events added the largest amounts of land to the United States?

4. How did physical geography make human suffering during the Great Depression worse?

5. In what ways is the United States a world leader?

CRITICAL THINKING

6. Compare How was the U.S. response to the September 11 attacks similar to its response to the Pearl Harbor attack?

7. Evaluate Review the physical geography you studied in Section 1. What do you think was the biggest obstacle to building the transcontinental railroad?

8. CONNECT to Today Does technology make it more or less likely that the United States will return to its old policy of not taking part in world affairs? Explain.

9. WRITING Write a Personal Response Find one of Lincoln's Civil War speeches. Write a paragraph analyzing why that speech inspired people.

Reading for Understanding

▶ Key Ideas

BEFORE, YOU LEARNED

From the nation's beginnings until the present time, people from many countries have moved to the United States.

NOW YOU WILL LEARN

The United States is one of the most diverse nations in the world, and it has a rich culture blended from many world cultures.

▶ Vocabulary

TERMS & NAMES

public education schooling that is paid for by the government

literacy the ability to read and write

cultural blending something new created from combining the elements of two or more cultures

jazz a type of music that developed from a blending of African rhythms, American band music, and the musical styles of African Americans and Europeans

blues a type of music with lyrics that express sorrow, usually about problems in love or the hardships of life

BACKGROUND VOCABULARY

official language a language that by law must be used for government, business, and education

REVIEW

culture the behavior patterns, arts, and beliefs of a group of people

Visual Vocabulary Jazz in New Orleans

▶ Reading Strategy

Re-create the chart shown at right. As you read and respond to the **KEY QUESTIONS**, use the chart to organize important details about the diverse culture of the United States.

 Skillbuilder Handbook, page R7

CATEGORIZE

RELIGION	LANGUAGE	ETHNICITY	ARTS & CULTURE
1.	1.	1.	1.
2.	2.	2.	2.
3.	3.	3.	3.

 GRAPHIC ORGANIZERS
Go to **Interactive Review** @ ClassZone.com

A Diverse Culture

Connecting to Your World

Think about some of the most popular foods in the United States. Many of them are versions of food that came from another country. Many recreational activities, too, came from overseas. Martial arts developed in East Asia, yoga originated in India, skiing first began in Norway, and baseball grew out of an English game. The **cultures**—behavior, arts, beliefs—of countless immigrants have made American culture what it is today.

Cultural Diversity

▼ **KEY QUESTION** What are some ways that immigrants have made U.S. culture more diverse?

People have come to the United States from all over the world. As you learned in Section 2, the earliest colonists were Spanish, English, and French. In addition, hundreds of thousands of Africans were brought to America as slaves. In the mid 1800s, millions of Northern Europeans came, mainly from Ireland, Germany, and the United Kingdom. After 1900, immigrants came largely from Italy, as well as from Russia and other Eastern European countries. In recent years, most immigrants have come from Mexico, other Latin American nations, and Asia.

Martial Arts Students practice karate, a Japanese martial art.

New York City A crowd strolls in the middle of Fifth Avenue in New York during a street festival.

ET

The

nic

ma

lati

cor

of

up

4 p

CRI

1. C

2. M

co

Challenges of Diversity Immigrants have added much richness to American culture. But living in such a diverse country also has its difficulties. For example, immigrants tend to settle in cities where they can find other people from their homeland. As a result, some cities end up with high percentages of immigrants, many of whom don't speak English. These people face limited employment options and are more likely to live in poverty.

Diversity also affects education. Most immigrant children learn to speak and read English, but that learning doesn't happen overnight. In some places, such as California, teachers have classes in which students speak several different languages. Teaching such a group English—or any other subject—can be a tough job.

Finally, diversity sometimes leads to debate. Many people say that the United States is a melting pot. By that, they mean that over time, people who come to the United States adopt a uniform American culture. In recent times, some people have objected to that idea. They believe that a person does not have to give up his or her language or customs to be an American. Instead, they like to describe the United States as a quilt or a mosaic, in which many individual pieces make up the whole but still remain unique.

▲ **MAKE INFERENCES** Explain how immigrants have made U.S. culture more diverse.

CONNECT to Math

From 1892 to 1924, Ellis Island (shown below) in New York harbor was the main entry point for immigrants. An estimated 17 million immigrants passed through its facilities. After immigration services moved to New York City, Ellis Island served as a detention center for both aliens and deportees.

U.S. Immigration *1820–2004*

Country of Origin	Number of Immigrants (to the nearest thousand)
Germany	7,238,000
Mexico	6,849,000
Italy	5,446,000
United Kingdom	5,337,000
Ireland	4,788,000
Other	40,211,000
Total	69,869,000

Sources: Office of Immigration Statistics, Department of Homeland Security

Activity

Make a Pie Graph

1. Calculate the percentage of immigrants from each country on the chart. First divide the number of immigrants from a country by the total. Then multiply the answer by 100. For example:

   $7,238,000 \div 69,869,000 = .104$

   $.104 \times 100 = 10.4 \text{ percent}$

   That is the percentage of immigrants who came from Germany.

2. Draw a circle on a piece of paper. Draw a wedge on the circle that represents 10.4 percent of its total. Add wedges for each of the other countries and for Other.

3. Color each wedge a different color. Label the wedges with the country names. Add the numbers beneath the names.

The Arts and Popular Culture

▼ **KEY QUESTION** How has cultural blending affected U.S. arts?

Cultural diversity has had a huge impact on American arts. This impact can clearly be seen in literature and music.

Literature Many writers have produced novels about immigrants and their children. For example, Amy Tan wrote *The Joy Luck Club* about Chinese mothers and their Chinese-American daughters. Much American literature deals with American history or American experiences. For example, *The Great Gatsby* by F. Scott Fitzgerald portrays a man chasing the American dream during the 1920s.

Jazz, Blues, Country, and Rock American music has also been affected by cultural blending. One example of this is jazz. **Jazz** is a type of music that African Americans developed from a blending of African rhythms, American band music, and the musical styles of African Americans and Europeans. Another distinctive type of music related to jazz is the blues. **Blues** features lyrics that express sorrow, usually about problems in love or the hardships of life.

Two other types of American music developed from the blending of different styles. Country music grew out of folk music, the blues, and religious music. Great artists of country music include Hank Williams and Patsy Cline. Rock music evolved from elements of the blues, country music, and American popular songs. Chuck Berry and Elvis Presley were important names in the early history of rock music.

CONNECT → Geography & Culture

The Blues and the Mississippi Delta
The blues developed in the South. One region closely associated with the music is the Delta, a broad, flat area in northwestern Mississippi. Many people there worked as sharecroppers, farming someone else's land for little reward. The blues were the perfect way for people in the Delta to express their troubles. Great blues artists include Robert Johnson (at right), Bessie Smith, and Muddy Waters.

DRAW CONCLUSIONS
What do you think some of the topics of Mississippi Delta blues might be?

Today's American Music Scene Chances are that you and your friends listen to a wide range of music without even realizing it. Some of the most popular songs on the radio today echo the earlier blues and rock of your parents' generation, or even classical music. And there's a growing internationalism, with music from all parts of the world showing up in the CD racks. One of the most popular musical trends is hip-hop.

Hip-hop music developed in the South Bronx section of New York City in the 1970s. One technique involved in hip-hop is rapping, a form of chanted street poetry set to rhythmic music. Another technique is sampling, in which an existing song provides an underlying rhythm or melody and other sounds are superimposed over it—such as music made by scratching on a turntable or "beatboxing," creating beats and sound effects using the mouth. By the 1990s, hip-hop was a regular on the music charts and had begun to spread world-wide.

However, the biggest story in American music today has nothing to do with the kinds of music people are listening to—it's all about how we are listening. Access to music of all kinds and in huge numbers is higher than ever, thanks to the Internet. Online music services offer databases of inexpensive downloadable music from all genres with a click of the mouse. And all those songs can now be loaded right onto a player that easily fits into the palm of your hand. There's no predicting what the next change in music technology will be, but the evidence is clear: more people will be "wired" to a broad range of music that increases every day.

Play Ball Fans cheer during a Seattle Mariners baseball game at Safeco Field in Seattle.

Sports, Entertainment, and Leisure Americans are avid sports fans. Many people take part in team sports and individual activities such as in-line skating or golf. In addition, millions follow team sports such as baseball, basketball, and football—both at stadiums and on television. In fact, the national football championship, the Super Bowl, is one of the most highly watched television programs each year.

Americans spend a lot of time on leisure activities and entertainment. Leisure is time that is free from work or other duties. One reason Americans have so much leisure time is that the United States is a prosperous nation. Perhaps the two most popular forms of entertainment are movies and television. A film or TV program can have an audience of millions. These two forms of entertainment have created experiences that the majority of Americans share. They help to unify the culture.

Other common pastimes in the United States include a wide variety of hobbies. Some of the most popular are playing computer games, camping, raising pets, gardening, and collecting things such as baseball cards, stamps, or autographs.

Finally, many Americans use part of their free time to improve their society. For example, some people cook meals at shelters for homeless people. Others volunteer to pick up litter along highways. Often, people find that helping others not only makes them feel better about themselves, but it makes their communities better too.

Skateboarding An 11-year-old boy skateboards in New York City.

 ANALYZE CAUSES AND EFFECTS Explain how cultural blending has affected the arts in the United States.

Section 3 Assessment

ONLINE QUIZ
For test practice, go to
Interactive Review
@ ClassZone.com

TERMS & NAMES

1. Explain the importance of
- public education
- literacy
- cultural blending
- jazz

USE YOUR READING NOTES

2. Categorize Use your completed chart to answer the following question:

What are some elements and examples of the diversity that makes up the culture of the United States?

RELIGION	LANGUAGE	ETHNICITY	ARTS & CULTURE
1.	1.	1.	1.
2.	2.	2.	2.
3.	3.	3.	3.

KEY IDEAS

3. Why do people come to the United States?

4. In what way is American English an example of cultural blending?

5. How has the physical geography of the United States affected its literature?

CRITICAL THINKING

6. Draw Conclusions How does public education help immigrants adapt to living in the United States?

7. Analyze Effects How did the development of the blues lead to additional cultural blending in music?

8. CONNECT to Today Do you think that the United States today is more like a melting pot or a mosaic? Use evidence to support your answer.

9. TECHNOLOGY Plan a Web Page Look for more examples of cultural blending in U.S. culture. Plan a Web page that would explain what cultural blending is and give examples from categories such as food, fashion, literature, music, and recreational activities.

Reading for Understanding

▶ Key Ideas

BEFORE, YOU LEARNED

The United States is a country of great diversity that continues to draw immigrants from around the world.

NOW YOU WILL LEARN

The United States purchases goods from and sells goods to many countries around the world.

▶ Vocabulary

TERMS & NAMES

amendment a written change to the U.S. Constitution that must go through an approval process

representative democracy a type of government in which citizens hold political power through elected representatives

republic another term for representative democracy

federal system a government system in which powers are divided between the national and state governments

free enterprise an economic system in which businesses are free to operate without much government involvement

market economy an economic system in which the production of goods and services is decided by supply and the demand of consumers

Interstate Highway System a network of more than 45,000 miles of roads that links every major U.S. city

global economy economy in which buying and selling occurs across national borders

multinational corporation a company that operates in more than one country

REVIEW

import to bring something from one country into another

export to send something from one country to another

▶ Reading Strategy

Re-create the chart shown at right. As you read and respond to the **KEY QUESTIONS**, use the chart to note the main ideas about the government and economy of the United States.

 Skillbuilder Handbook, page R7

CATEGORIZE

GOVERNMENT	ECONOMY
1.	1.
2.	2.
3.	3.

 GRAPHIC ORGANIZERS
Go to **Interactive Review** @ ClassZone.com

Democracy and Free Enterprise

Connecting to Your World

Have you ever had an election in your classroom? The candidate gives a speech and asks you and your classmates for their support and their votes. At national political conventions you may have seen on television, music is played, and balloons are dropped from the ceiling. People wave signs and cheer. Why do people become so excited? They hope that they have just chosen the person who will be elected the nation's next leader. In the United States, citizens play a role in selecting their own government. Not all countries recognize the people's right to choose their leaders.

The U.S. Government

▼ **KEY QUESTION** What are the three branches of the U.S. government?

As Section 2 explained, the U.S. government is based on a written constitution. This document has changed since it was first written in 1787. Changes are added through **amendments**, written additions that must go through an approval process. There have been 27 amendments.

Political Action
A crowd waves American flags at a political convention. **What issues are most important to you and your classmates?**

COMPARING Branches of the U.S. Government

LEGISLATIVE	EXECUTIVE	JUDICIAL
• U.S. Congress creates, abolishes, and changes laws	• President either signs laws or vetoes [rejects] them	• U.S. Supreme Court interprets laws
• approves appointments and treaties	• enforces laws	• overturns laws that conflict with the Constitution
• imposes taxes	• appoints judges and other officials	• hears certain cases involving federal law or treaties
• declares war	• commands the military forces	• reviews cases on appeal
• impeaches and tries officials for misconduct	• directs foreign and national security affairs	

CRITICAL THINKING

Draw Conclusions What is the main way in which the president acts as a check on the Congress?

A Federal Republic The U.S. government is a **representative democracy**. A democracy is a government in which the people govern. The United States is much too large for every citizen to take part in making laws and policies, so U.S. citizens elect officials to represent them. Another term for a representative democracy is a **republic**.

The Constitution also created a **federal system** in which power is divided between the national and state governments. As you learned in Section 2, the national government is further divided into three branches: legislative, executive, and judicial.

Checks and Balances Recall that Americans fought for independence because they believed that Britain had ruled them unfairly. As a result, they tried to prevent future abuses of power. They wrote a Constitution that gives each branch of government the ability to act as a check, or limit, upon the other two. Those limits keep power in balance by spreading it across the branches. That's why people say our government is a system of checks and balances.

For example, Congress makes the laws, but the president must sign them before they go into effect. And the Supreme Court has the power to say that a law is not valid. These are just some of the ways that the branches of government act as checks on each other.

▲ **CATEGORIZE** Describe the three branches of the U.S. government.

The U.S. Economy

▼ **KEY QUESTION** Who controls the U.S. economy?

The U.S. economy is based on **free enterprise**—businesses are free to operate without much government involvement. Individuals and companies own most of the resources, equipment, and factories.

A Market Economy The United States has a **market economy**, in which individuals and businesses can make their own choices about what to buy and sell. The freedom people have to try to make money has enriched the country as a whole. The U.S. economy produces goods and services worth more than the output of any other country.

Service industries—businesses that provide services, not products—account for 78 percent of the money earned by the U.S. economy. Service industries include banks, insurance companies, hotels, restaurants, and repair shops. Manufacturing accounts for 21 percent and agriculture accounts for 1 percent.

Agriculture and Industry of the United States

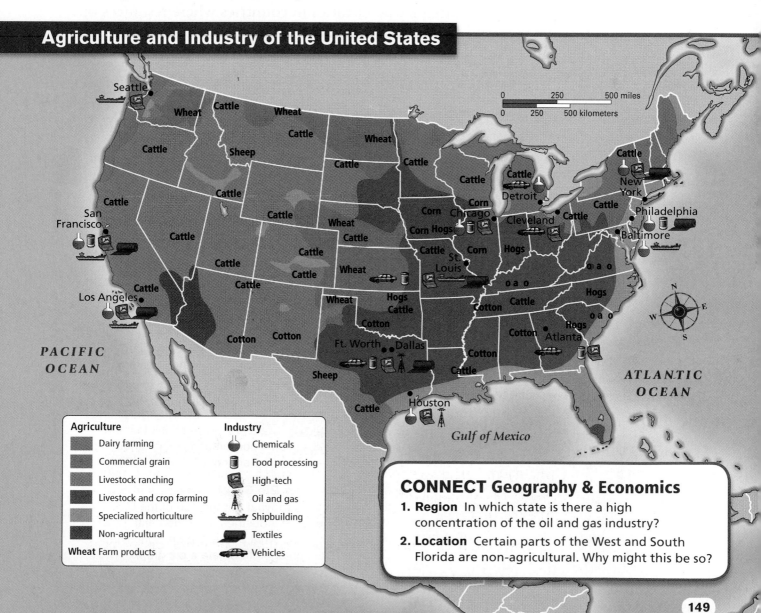

Agriculture
- Dairy farming
- Commercial grain
- Livestock ranching
- Livestock and crop farming
- Specialized horticulture
- Non-agricultural

Wheat Farm products

Industry
- Chemicals
- Food processing
- High-tech
- Oil and gas
- Shipbuilding
- Textiles
- Vehicles

CONNECT Geography & Economics
1. **Region** In which state is there a high concentration of the oil and gas industry?
2. **Location** Certain parts of the West and South Florida are non-agricultural. Why might this be so?

The U.S. government does not run the economy, but it plays an important role. It promotes safety, fights unfair business actions, and builds structures to help economic growth. For example, the government paid to construct the **Interstate Highway System**, a network of more than 45,000 miles of roads that links major U.S. cities. The highways improved the transport of goods and people.

Globalization and a Changing Economy One of the biggest changes in recent times is the rise of a **global economy**, in which much buying and selling occurs across international borders. Technologies such as the Internet have linked businesses around the world.

The United States trades with many other countries. It **imports** goods such as automobiles, clothing, and petroleum. It **exports** goods such as airplanes, computers, and plastics. Canada, Mexico, Japan, and China are among the biggest U.S. trading partners.

The creation of **multinational corporations**, or companies that operate in more than one country, has added to the global economy. Such corporations often locate factories in countries where resources or labor are cheap. Many multinational corporations have their headquarters in the United States.

Highway System The Los Angeles freeways help to unify a widespread city. **How might a highway system link a region?**

 FIND MAIN IDEAS Explain who controls the U.S. economy.

Section 4 Assessment

ONLINE QUIZ
For test practice, go to
Interactive Review
@ ClassZone.com

TERMS & NAMES

1. Explain the importance of
- federal system
- free enterprise
- market economy
- multinational corporation

USE YOUR READING NOTES

2. Categorize Use your completed chart to answer the following question:

What are some duties of government that might affect the economy?

GOVERNMENT	ECONOMY
1.	1.
2.	2.
3.	3.

KEY IDEAS

3. How did the Constitution create a system of checks and balances in the government?

4. How did the Interstate Highway System affect the U.S. economy?

5. Which countries are the main U.S. trading partners?

CRITICAL THINKING

6. Contrast What are differences between the roles that individuals and government play in the economy?

7. Draw Conclusions Why might Canada and Mexico be major trading partners of the United States?

8. CONNECT to Today How do you think that the growth of multinational corporations might affect the government's role in the economy?

9. MATH Create a Pie Graph Look back through this section to learn what percentage of the U.S. economy is service industries, what percentage is manufacturing, and what percentage is agriculture. Use those percentages to create a pie graph.

Interactive Review

Click here to complete these and other activities online @ ClassZone.com

CHAPTER SUMMARY

Key Idea 1
The physical geography of the United States varies greatly from coast to coast.

Key Idea 2
Native Americans and peoples from other continents all came together to build a nation.

Key Idea 3
The United States is one of the most diverse nations in the world, and it has a rich culture blended from many world cultures.

Key Idea 4
The United States purchases goods from and sells goods to many countries around the world.

For **Review and Study Notes**, go to **Interactive Review** @ ClassZone.com

NAME GAME

Use the Terms & Names list to complete each sentence on paper or online.

1. I am a swampy region located in southern Florida. **Everglades**

2. I am vast grassland in north-central North America. _____

3. I am a mountain chain that runs from Alaska to New Mexico. _____

4. I am a mountain chain that runs parallel to the Atlantic coast from the Northeast to the South. _____

5. I cut through a plateau in Arizona. _____

6. Most of me lies on the U.S.–Canada border, although one part of me lies entirely inside the United States. _____

7. I run along the high ridge line of the Rocky Mountains. _____

8. I am located in Alaska. _____

9. I lie to the south of the United States. _____

10. I stretch across the United States and link every major city. _____

Appalachian Mountains
continental divide
Dust Bowl
Everglades
Grand Canyon
Great Lakes
Great Plains
Gulf of Mexico
Interstate Highway System
land bridge
Mississippi River
Mt. McKinley
Piedmont
Rocky Mountains

Activities

GeoGame

Use this online map to show what you know about the physical geography of the United States. Drag and drop each place name to its location on the map.

Appalachian Mountains
Great Lakes
Great Plains
Mississippi River
Rocky Mountains

To play the complete game, go to **Interactive Review** @ ClassZone.com

Crossword Puzzle

Complete the online crossword puzzle to test your knowledge of how the United States became a nation.

ACROSS
1. president during the Civil War

VOCABULARY

Explain the significance of each of the following.

1. Lewis and Clark Expedition
2. Great Lakes
3. Civil War
4. Great Depression
5. literacy
6. cultural blending
7. republic
8. free enterprise

Explain how the first term in each group relates to the terms that follow.

9. immigrant: land bridge, colony
10. Constitution: amendment, federal system

KEY IDEAS

1 From Coast to Coast

11. What are three major geographic features that run from north to south?
12. What is the nation's largest agricultural region, and what are its main crops?
13. Which region has the most mountainous terrain?

2 Creating a Nation

14. How did the French and Indian War help lead to the Revolutionary War?
15. What was the purpose of Lewis and Clark's journey?
16. Which neighboring country lost large amounts of land to the United States?

3 A Diverse Culture

17. Which immigrant groups came to the United States in large numbers during the mid-1800s?
18. How have African Americans contributed to culture?
19. Why might some immigrants object to the concept of the United States as a melting pot?

4 Democracy and Free Enterprise

20. Why is the U.S. government considered a representative democracy?
21. What is a federal system?
22. What economic change was spurred by technology?

CRITICAL THINKING

23. **Compare and Contrast** Create a table to compare and contrast the transcontinental railroad and the Interstate Highway System.

RAILROAD	HIGHWAY SYSTEM

24. **Distinguish Fact from Opinion** The Declaration of Independence lists several complaints about the British king, including "imposing Taxes on us without our Consent." Is that complaint fact or opinion? Explain.

25. **Draw Conclusions** When you consider the part farming plays in the overall economy, do you think most Americans live in urban or rural areas? Why?

26. **Five Themes: Location** In 1941, Japan bombed the U.S. naval base at Pearl Harbor, Hawaii. Why would the Japanese view Pearl Harbor as a big military threat?

27. **Connect Geography & Culture** The number of Spanish speakers is growing. How might U.S. culture change as a result?

Answer the ESSENTIAL QUESTION

How did a developing nation grow into a world power?

Written Response Write a two paragraph response to the Essential Question. Be sure to consider the key ideas of each section as well as specific ideas about how the United States grew. Use the rubric below to guide your thinking.

Response Rubric
A strong response will:
- explain the steps by which U.S. territory grew
- discuss the influences that created U.S. diversity
- analyze the elements of the U.S. economy

STANDARDS-BASED ASSESSMENT

✓ **Test Practice**

• Online Test Practice @ClassZone.com
• Test-Taking Strategies and Practice
  at the front of this book

ELEVATION GRAPH

Use the elevation graph to answer questions 1 and 2 on your paper about the elevation of the western United States at 38° north latitude.

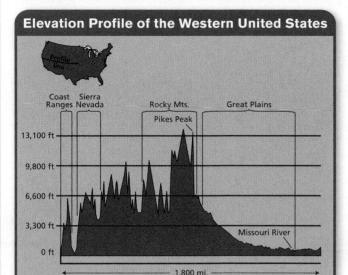

Elevation Profile of the Western United States

Coast Ranges — Sierra Nevada — Rocky Mts. — Pikes Peak — Great Plains

13,100 ft
9,800 ft
6,600 ft
3,300 ft
0 ft

Missouri River

1,800 mi.

1. Which of the following has the highest general elevation?

A. Coast Ranges
B. Sierra Nevada
C. Rocky Mountains
D. Great Plains

2. Which has the lowest elevation?

A. between Sierra Nevada and Rocky Mountains
B. between Rocky Mountains and Great Plains
C. between Coast Ranges and Sierra Nevada
D. in the Coast Ranges

ANALYZING PRIMARY SOURCES

Examine the Great Seal of the United States shown below. Use the seal to answer questions 3 and 4 on your own paper.

3. Why might the motto *E Pluribus Unum* (one from many) be on the Great Seal of the United States?

4. Why might the eagle on the seal clutch an olive branch in one claw and arrows in the other claw?

GeoActivity

1. INTERDISCIPLINARY ACTIVITY–MUSIC

Working in a small group, find three or four examples of jazz that you like. Concentrate on instrumental music, not songs with lyrics. In a group discussion, compare and contrast the pieces. Then play the music and present your findings in class.

2. WRITING FOR SOCIAL STUDIES

Research to find out more about the American bison–including how large it is, how long it lives, what it eats, what its habits are, and where it still can be found. Create a booklet about the bison to teach younger students about this American animal.

3. MENTAL MAPPING

Create an outline map of the United States and label the following:

• Appalachian Mountains
• Rocky Mountains
• Atlantic Ocean
• Pacific Ocean
• Gulf of Mexico
• Mississippi River
• Great Lakes
• Great Plains

CHAPTER 6

Canada

ESSENTIAL QUESTION

How is Canada managing its resources in the 21st century?

CONNECT Geography & History

Use the map and the time line to answer the following questions.

1. When was the city of Quebec founded?
2. On what body of water are both Quebec and Montreal located?

Geography

1608 Samuel de Champlain founds Quebec City. ▶

1600

Geography

1791 Great Britain creates Upper and Lower Canada.

Culture

1763 Great Britain takes over New France, causing Canada to have two major languages. ▶

TOUJOURS
ALWAYS

Animated GEOGRAPHY
Present-Day Canada

Click here to explore
Canada @ ClassZone.com

ARCTIC OCEAN

ALASKA (U.S.)

Beaufort Sea

Banks Island

Queen Elizabeth Islands

Ellesmere I.

GREENLAND (Denmark)

Arctic Circle

60°N

Victoria Island

Baffin Bay

Baffin Island

Davis Strait

YUKON TERRITORY

Great Bear Lake

★ Whitehorse

NORTHWEST TERRITORIES

★ Yellowknife

Great Slave Lake

NUNAVUT

Igaluit

Labrador Sea

50°N

C A N A D A

Hudson Bay

NEWFOUNDLAND AND LABRADOR

BRITISH COLUMBIA

ALBERTA

Edmonton ★

SASKATCHEWAN

MANITOBA

Lake Winnipeg

Saskatchewan R.

QUEBEC

St. John's
Newfoundland

Gulf of St. Lawrence

PRINCE EDWARD ISLAND

• Saskatoon

★ Regina

ONTARIO

NEW BRUNSWICK

★ Charlottetown

• Calgary

• Vancouver

Victoria ★

Winnipeg ★

Thunder Bay •

Quebec ★

Fredericton ★

NOVA SCOTIA

Halifax ★

Montreal •

L. Superior

L. Huron

St. Lawrence R.

Ottawa ★

40°N

★ National capital
★ Provincial capital
• Other city

U N I T E D
S T A T E S

L. Michigan

★ Toronto

L. Ontario

L. Erie

ATLANTIC OCEAN

0   250   500 miles
0 250   500 kilometers

Windsor •

110°W   100°W   90°W   80°W   70°W

History
1867 Canada becomes a dominion in the British Empire.

Government
1931 Canada becomes self-governing. (Parliament building in Ottawa) ▶

Today

Culture
1908 Lucy Maud Montgomery publishes *Anne of Green Gables.*

Economics
1992 NAFTA (North American Free Trade Agreement) unites Canada, the United States, and Mexico in a free-trade zone.

Reading for Understanding

▶ Key Ideas

BEFORE, YOU LEARNED

The United States has a great number of landforms and bodies of water, as well as great variety in its climate and vegetation.

NOW YOU WILL LEARN

The physical geography of Canada shares many landforms and bodies of water with the United States.

▶ Vocabulary

TERMS & NAMES

province a Canadian political unit, similar to a U.S. state

territory a Canadian political unit that doesn't have enough people to be a province

Canadian Shield a horseshoe-shaped, rocky plateau that covers much of eastern central Canada

Hudson Bay a large inland sea to the north of the province of Ontario

St. Lawrence Seaway a waterway made up of the St. Lawrence River, the Great Lakes, and several canals

hydroelectric having to do with electricity created by water-powered engines

Nunavut (NOO•nuh•VOOT) a territory created in 1999 from the eastern part of the Northwest Territories and home to many Inuit

REVIEW

Great Lakes five lakes forming the largest group of freshwater lakes in the world

tundra a cold, dry climate and vegetation adapted to the climate in the Arctic Circle

Visual Vocabulary tundra

▶ Reading Strategy

Re-create the chart that is shown at right. As you read and respond to the **KEY QUESTIONS**, use the chart to organize important details about the physical geography of Canada.

 Skillbuilder Handbook, page R7

CATEGORIZE

	LANDFORMS & WATER	CLIMATE	RESOURCES
Atlantic Provinces			
Core Provinces			
Prairie Provinces			
British Columbia & Territories			

 GRAPHIC ORGANIZERS
Go to **Interactive Review** @ ClassZone.com

Mountains, Prairies, and Coastlands

Connecting to Your World

The United States has long coastlines on its eastern and western borders. It also has vast plains in the center and towering mountains in the west. What you may not know is that Canada, located north of the United States, shares many of the same geographic features. In this section, you will learn more about the landscape of Canada, the second largest country in the world. You will also learn how its northern location affects its climate.

Landforms and Bodies of Water

▼ **KEY QUESTION** What are the four regions of Canada?

You have learned that the United States can be divided into four regions, and that each region contains many states. Canada can also be divided into regions. It has political units called **provinces**, which are similar to states. It also has **territories**, political units that don't have enough people to become provinces. Canada's 13 provinces and territories are often divided into four geographic regions: the Atlantic Provinces, the Core Provinces, the Prairie Provinces, and British Columbia and Territories.

Niagara Falls
Niagara Falls forms a natural boundary between Canada and the United States.

Map: CANADA — Lake Ontario, Niagara Falls, Lake Erie, U.S.

Atlantic Provinces This region includes Newfoundland, Nova Scotia, New Brunswick, and Prince Edward Island. (See map opposite.) The Appalachian Mountains **Ⓐ** extend into the region. In most places, the soil is poor for farming. Because the Atlantic coast has good harbors, the Atlantic Provinces became a region of seafarers instead.

The western edge of the region lies on the **Canadian Shield Ⓑ**, a horseshoe-shaped plateau that covers much of east-central Canada. During the Ice Age, glaciers scraped the soil from the shield, leaving exposed rock. Much of the Canadian Shield is too barren to settle.

Core Provinces Bodies of water border the Core Provinces of Quebec and Ontario. **Hudson Bay Ⓒ** is a large inland sea to the north, and the St. Lawrence River **Ⓓ** and **Great Lakes** lie to the south. That river, those lakes, and several canals form the **St. Lawrence Seaway**, a waterway linking the Atlantic Ocean to the heart of North America.

Quebec and Ontario are the most densely populated provinces, even though most of their lands lie on the barren Canadian Shield. People have crowded into a narrow region of fertile land along the Great Lakes and St. Lawrence River. Many rivers flow from the Canadian Shield into this area. Canadians have built **hydroelectric** plants on the rivers, to create electricity from water-powered engines.

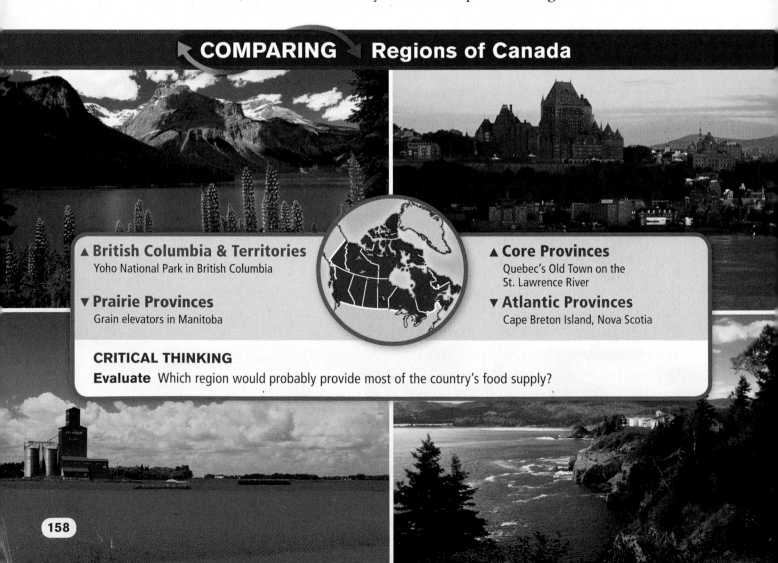

COMPARING ◄ Regions of Canada

▲ **British Columbia & Territories**
Yoho National Park in British Columbia

▼ **Prairie Provinces**
Grain elevators in Manitoba

▲ **Core Provinces**
Quebec's Old Town on the St. Lawrence River

▼ **Atlantic Provinces**
Cape Breton Island, Nova Scotia

CRITICAL THINKING

Evaluate Which region would probably provide most of the country's food supply?

Physical Geography of Canada

13,100 ft. (4,000 m)
6,600 ft. (2,000 m)
3,280 ft. (1,000 m)
650 ft. (200 m)
0 ft. (0 m)
Below sea level

Glacier
▲ Mountain peak

CONNECT Geography & Culture

1. **Region** What landform is south of Hudson Bay and north of the Great Lakes?
2. **Location** What is one of the main functions of the St. Lawrence River?

Prairie Provinces The Great Plains, which you studied in an earlier chapter, extend northward into the Prairie Provinces—Manitoba, Saskatchewan (sa•SKACH•uh•WAHN), and Alberta. To the west, this region is bordered by the Canadian Rockies **E**. The Prairie Provinces are mostly flat grasslands and are one of Canada's major farming regions. Evergreen forests are found in the north.

British Columbia and Territories British Columbia is bounded by the Pacific Ocean to the west and the Canadian Rockies to the east. British Columbia has a scenic coast and jagged coastal mountains.

Canada's three territories are the Yukon, the Northwest Territories, and **Nunavut** (NOO•nuh•VOOT), created in 1999 from the eastern part of the Northwest Territories. Nunavut is home to many native peoples. It has a rocky mainland and thousands of Arctic Islands.

The Northwest Territories contain two of Canada's largest lakes, the Great Bear and Great Slave lakes. The Mackenzie River **F**, Canada's longest, runs from the Great Slave Lake to the Arctic Ocean.

▲ **SUMMARIZE** Name the four regions of Canada.

Midnight Sun Under the midnight sun, snowmobiles pull sleds loaded with supplies back to camp across the Arctic ice in Nunavut, Canada. **What other means of transportation might people use on the Arctic ice?**

Climates of Canada

▼ **KEY QUESTION** What are some influences on Canada's climates?

Think of the coldest states that you know of within the United States. Canada is located even farther north than those states—so far north that it reaches into the Arctic Circle.

A Northern Land Canadians think of themselves as a people of the far north, but in reality the northernmost lands are thinly populated. Since the northern part of Canada lies much closer to the North Pole than to the equator, its climate is very cold. Some places remain frozen all year, and most of the region is **tundra**, flat treeless land near the Arctic Circle. Also, places that are far from the equator have a great variation in the hours of sunlight they receive during the year. Winter days are very short, and the long period of darkness increases the cold. Because life in the far north is so harsh, about 90 percent of all Canadians live within about 200 miles of the U.S. border.

Mild and Harsh Climates Bodies of water also influence Canada's climate. The Atlantic and Pacific oceans have a moderating effect on the coasts; winters are warmer and summers cooler there. Similarly, the Great Lakes make the climates of southern Ontario and Quebec milder. In contrast, the Prairie Provinces, located far from the oceans, have very cold winters and warm to hot summers.

The oceans and lakes make nearby lands humid, while the Prairie Provinces are drier. Mountains also play a role in causing this difference. Winds blowing in from the Pacific pass over the coastal mountains. As they rise, they drop moisture, causing high rainfalls in parts of British Columbia. The lands east of the mountains are arid.

▲ **FIND MAIN IDEAS** Describe influences on Canada's climate.

Resources of the Regions

▼ **KEY QUESTION** What are the main resources of each region?

Canada has many natural resources, which have helped it to develop a strong economy. Each region has its own distinct set of resources.

- The Atlantic Provinces have an abundance of timber and mineral wealth, especially coal. The Gulf of St. Lawrence and coastal waters supply plentiful stocks of seafood for export.

- The Core Provinces have a flat fertile plain in the south, plus a mild, humid climate that is good for farming. The St. Lawrence Seaway is a resource that aids transportation and economic growth. Other rivers are used to create hydroelectric power.

- The fertile plains of the southern Prairie Provinces are used to raise grain. Oil and natural gas are found in the region, especially in Alberta.

- British Columbia has forests, minerals, hydroelectric power, ocean fishing, and some fertile lands and valleys. The territories also have resources, such as oil, natural gas, and lead, that have not been developed because they are located far from markets.

▲ **CATEGORIZE** Describe the resources of each of Canada's regions.

Fun Facts!

BEARS ON ICE!
Churchill, Manitoba, is called the polar bear capital of the world. Polar bears live on sea ice and hunt seals. But in the southwestern Hudson Bay, the ice pack melts in summer, forcing the bears onto land. Every year in late fall, polar bears gather near Churchill waiting for the bay to freeze so they can return to the ice.

Section 1 Assessment

⚡ **ONLINE QUIZ** For test practice, go to **Interactive Review @ ClassZone.com**

TERMS & NAMES

1. Explain the importance of
- province
- territory
- Hudson Bay
- Nunavut

USE YOUR READING NOTES

2. Categorize Use your completed chart to answer the following question:

What mountain chain separates the Prairie Provinces and British Columbia?

	LANDFORMS & WATER	CLIMATE	RESOURCES
Atlantic Provinces			
Core Provinces			
Prairie Provinces			
British Columbia & Territories			

KEY IDEAS

3. Which two regions are the biggest farming areas of Canada?

4. Which two regions have ocean fishing as a major part of their economies?

5. Why haven't Canadians developed the mineral resources of the territories?

CRITICAL THINKING

6. Analyze Effects Give one economic advantage and one disadvantage of the Canadian Shield.

7. Contrast How is the climate of the center of the country different from the climates of the coasts?

8. CONNECT to Today What technologies might make it possible to use the mineral wealth of the territories?

9. SCIENCE **Sketch a Map** Learn about the Ice Age glaciers in an encyclopedia, a science book, or an educational Web site. Then sketch a map showing which parts of North America were covered by glaciers.

Animated GEOGRAPHY
The St. Lawrence Seaway

 Click here to enter the St. Lawrence Seaway
@ ClassZone.com

SHIPS INTO THE HEARTLAND

The St. Lawrence Seaway connects the Great Lakes to the Atlantic Ocean by way of the St. Lawrence River and a system of canals and locks. The seaway enables ships to sail into the heart of the continent. It was completed in the 1950s as a joint project of the United States and Canada.

Click here to see how ships are raised and lowered 600 feet by a series of locks.

A A seaway lock is a watertight chamber with gates at either end that allows a ship to be lifted or lowered from one level to another. Here the lock gates open to allow a ship to enter.

B When all gates are shut, water is let into the lock through a sluice (small channel) to raise or lower the water level.

C Once the water in the chamber is level with the canal ahead, the second gate opens and the ship moves on.

Click here to see how millions of tons of goods are shipped on the seaway each year. Most of the freight, consisting of bulk cargo such as grains and minerals, travels from North America to Europe.

The Andes

Route of the St. Lawrence Seaway

MINN.
Duluth • Lake Superior
0   100   200 miles
0   100   200 kilometers

CANADA

QUEBEC
Quebec •

St. Lawrence
Seaway

WISCONSIN

Lake Michigan

Lake Huron

ONTARIO

St. Lawrence River

Montreal •

MAINE

U.S.

MICHIGAN

Toronto •

VT.

N.H.

ATLANTIC
OCEAN

Chicago •

Detroit •

Lake Erie

Buffalo •

Lake Ontario

N.Y.

MASS.

ILLINOIS

IND.

OHIO

Cleveland •

PENN.

Ⓒ

Ⓐ

GeoActivity

Build a Lock Use a cardboard
shoebox to make a lock. If you
have two or more shoeboxes, you
might show ships moving in two
directions. Use small plastic boats
and trucks to show how the
boats move in the seaway. Cargo
trucks and other vehicles might
be positioned along the docks.

Mexico Mexico's landforms include mountains, **plateaus**, and plains. You can see these on the map opposite. Two major mountain ranges are the **Sierra Madre Occidental** Ⓐ, located in western Mexico, and the **Sierra Madre Oriental** Ⓑ, located in eastern Mexico. Mexico sits on three large **tectonic plates**, and the movement of these plates causes earthquakes and volcanic activity.

Between the two mountain ranges lies the vast Mexican Plateau, making up about 40 percent of Mexico's land regions. Most of Mexico's people live in this area. The plateau rises about 4,000 feet above sea level in the northern part to about 8,000 feet in the southern part. Several volcanoes frame the southern edge of the plateau. East and west of the plateau, along the Gulf of Mexico and the Pacific Ocean, lie the coastal plains.

Mexico has few major rivers. Most of the rivers are not deep enough or wide enough for large boats to move through. Mexico's largest river is the Rio Grande, which is the northern border with Texas.

Sea Turtles These hawksbill sea turtles are swimming over reefs in the Caribbean Sea off the coast of the Cayman Islands.

Central America South of Mexico are the countries of Central America. Central America is an **isthmus**, a strip of land that connects two large landmasses. It connects the North and South American continents.

Highlands, the hilly sections of a country, make up most of Central America. Like Mexico, Central America lies at the edge of tectonic plates, so earthquakes occur often. A string of volcanoes, some of which are active, lines the Pacific Coast. Plains lie along both the Pacific and Caribbean coasts.

The Caribbean Islands East of Central America lie the Caribbean Islands. The islands are made up of three main parts. The Bahamas are an **archipelago**, a chain of nearly 700 islands. The **Greater Antilles** Ⓒ include the largest islands of Cuba, Jamaica, Hispaniola (which includes Haiti and the Dominican Republic), and Puerto Rico. The **Lesser Antilles** Ⓓ include the remaining smaller islands. Many of the Caribbean Islands are actually the exposed tops of underwater mountains. Mountains and highlands make up the interior of most Caribbean Islands, and plains circle the highlands.

🔺 **COMPARE AND CONTRAST** Describe how the geography of Mexico, Central America, and the Caribbean Islands is alike.

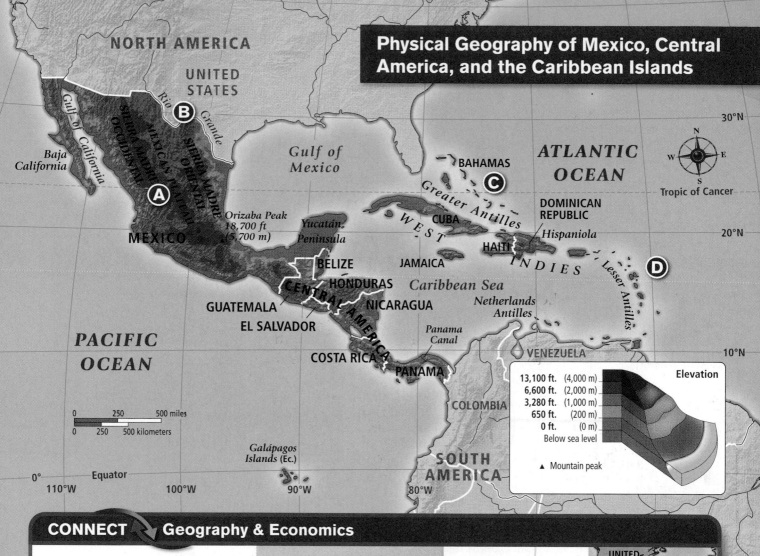

Physical Geography of Mexico, Central America, and the Caribbean Islands

NORTH AMERICA

UNITED STATES

Ⓑ

Rio Grande

Baja California

Gulf of California

SIERRA MADRE OCCIDENTAL

MEXICAN PLATEAU

SIERRA MADRE ORIENTAL

Ⓐ

MEXICO

Orizaba Peak 18,700 ft (5,700 m)

Yucatán Peninsula

Gulf of Mexico

BAHAMAS

Ⓒ

ATLANTIC OCEAN

Greater Antilles

CUBA

WEST

DOMINICAN REPUBLIC

Hispaniola

HAITI

JAMAICA

INDIES

Lesser Antilles

Ⓓ

BELIZE

CENTRAL AMERICA

HONDURAS

Caribbean Sea

GUATEMALA

NICARAGUA

Netherlands Antilles

EL SALVADOR

Panama Canal

PACIFIC OCEAN

COSTA RICA

PANAMA

VENEZUELA

COLOMBIA

Tropic of Cancer

30°N

20°N

10°N

0 250 500 miles
0 250 500 kilometers

Galápagos Islands (Ec.)

SOUTH AMERICA

Elevation

13,100 ft. (4,000 m)
6,600 ft. (2,000 m)
3,280 ft. (1,000 m)
650 ft. (200 m)
0 ft. (0 m)
Below sea level

▲ Mountain peak

0° Equator

110°W   100°W   90°W   80°W

CONNECT ▸ Geography & Economics

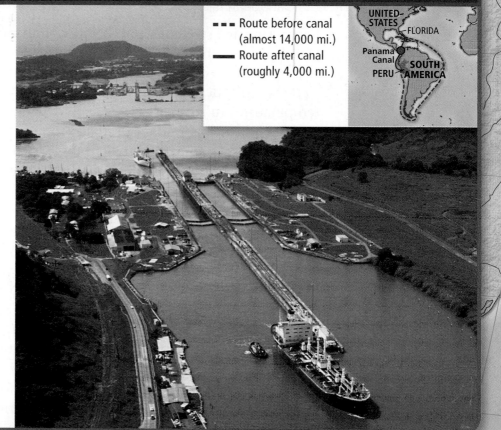

Route before canal (almost 14,000 mi.)

Route after canal (roughly 4,000 mi.)

UNITED STATES

FLORIDA

Panama Canal

PERU

SOUTH AMERICA

Panama Canal The Panama Canal was built by cutting through the Central American land bridge, which connected the Atlantic and Pacific oceans. Before the canal was opened in 1914, a ship bringing copper from Peru to Florida had to sail south around South America and then north. Using the canal shortened the distance and time.

CRITICAL THINKING

1. **Movement** By how many miles did the canal shorten a ship's journey?

2. **Make Inferences** Why was Panama a good choice for building a canal?

201

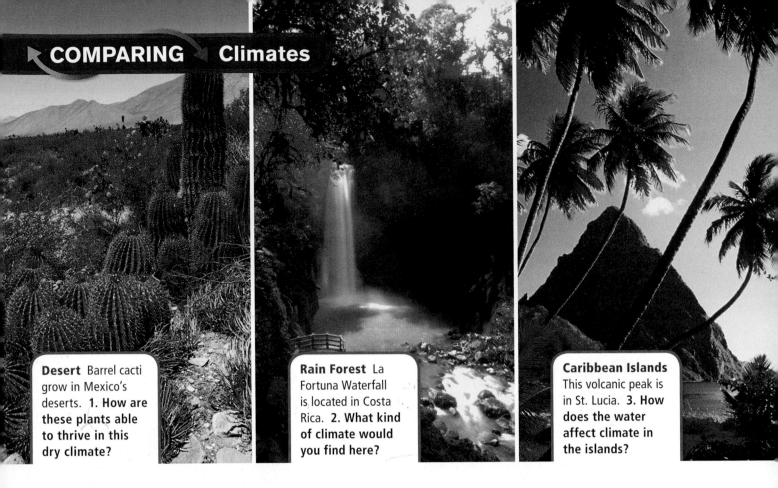

COMPARING Climates

Desert Barrel cacti grow in Mexico's deserts. **1. How are these plants able to thrive in this dry climate?**

Rain Forest La Fortuna Waterfall is located in Costa Rica. **2. What kind of climate would you find here?**

Caribbean Islands This volcanic peak is in St. Lucia. **3. How does the water affect climate in the islands?**

Climate and Vegetation

▼ **KEY QUESTION** What is a major influence on the climate of the Caribbean Islands?

Latin America stretches across more than one-half of the Western Hemisphere. It has a wide variety of climates and vegetation.

Mexico About half of Mexico lies south of the tropic of Cancer. The temperatures in this part of Mexico are generally warm and constant year-round, with abundant rainfall. Tropical rain forests thrive here.

A greater variation in temperatures exists in places located north of the tropic of Cancer. The driest areas are in the deserts of northwestern Mexico, as well as in the northern part of the Mexican Plateau. Desert shrubs grow in this climate. In Mexico's mountains and highlands, average temperatures vary with increases in elevation. The vegetation here consists mostly of coniferous and deciduous forests.

Central America All of Central America is located in the tropical zone, so temperatures are generally warm year-round. The plains along the Caribbean coast receive the greatest amount of precipitation. The climate is perfect for the lush rain forests that grow there.

As in Mexico, places at higher elevations in Central America experience cooler average temperatures than those at lower elevations. Winds that blow inland from the warm Caribbean Sea bring heavy rains on the eastern side of the mountains. Places on the westward side and in the interior highlands receive the least amount of precipitation. Forests of oak and pine grow at higher elevations, while desert shrubs grow in the drier areas on the Pacific side.

The Caribbean Islands Winds play a big role in the climate of the Caribbean Islands. The waters in the Caribbean Sea stay warm most of the year and heat the air over them. Warm winds blow across the islands, keeping the temperatures warm and constant year-round. The Lesser Antilles are divided into islands that face the wind and those that are protected from the wind. Those protected from the wind receive less rain than those facing the wind.

As in Mexico and Central America, elevation influences climate in the islands' mountains. The islands' climates allow diverse vegetation, including rain forests, deciduous forests, and desert shrubs, to grow there.

 SUMMARIZE Describe the major influence on the climate of the Caribbean Islands.

Tree Frog A red-eyed tree frog, a unique animal found in Costa Rica's rain forest, hops a ride on a caiman, an alligator-like reptile.

Section ❶ Assessment

ONLINE QUIZ
For test practice, go to
Interactive Review
@ ClassZone.com

TERMS & NAMES

1. Explain the importance of
- isthmus
- archipelago
- Greater Antilles
- Lesser Antilles

USE YOUR READING NOTES

2. Categorize Use your completed chart to answer the following question:

How does climate influence the location of rain forests in Central America?

LANDFORMS	INFLUENCES ON CLIMATE	VEGETATION
1.	1.	1.
2.	2.	2.
3.	3.	3.

KEY IDEAS

3. How did Latin America get its name?

4. Where do most people in Mexico live?

5. What affects climate in the mountains and highlands of Mexico and Central America?

CRITICAL THINKING

6. Analyze Causes and Effects How did the Panama Canal help trade in Latin America?

7. Make Generalizations What generalization can you make about climate in Mexico, Central America, and the Caribbean Islands?

8. CONNECT to Today In 1999, the United States gave control of the Panama Canal to Panama. How do you think the country of Panama will benefit from the canal?

9. WRITING Create a Poster Choose a country in Central America or one of the Caribbean Islands and prepare a captioned poster for a geography fair. Include information about the country's land, climate, and vegetation.

Reading for Understanding

▶ Key Ideas

BEFORE, YOU LEARNED

The physical geography of much of Mexico, Central America, and the Caribbean Islands consists of mountains and highlands.

NOW YOU WILL LEARN

The physical geography of South America consists of a wide variety of landforms and climates.

▶ Vocabulary

TERMS & NAMES

Andes Mountains a mountain range located on South America's west coast and extending the full length of the continent

altiplano a high plateau

llanos (YAH•nohs) grasslands of western Venezuela and northeastern Colombia

Pampas grassy plains in south-central South America

Amazon River South America's longest river (about 4,000 miles, or 6,400 kilometers) and the second-longest river in the world

REVIEW

highlands mountainous or hilly sections of a country

rain forest a broadleaf tree region in a tropical climate

Visual Vocabulary *altiplano*

▶ Reading Strategy

Re-create the diagram shown at right. As you read and respond to the **KEY QUESTIONS**, use the diagram to summarize each of the main parts of Section 2.

📖 **See Skillbuilder Handbook, page R5**

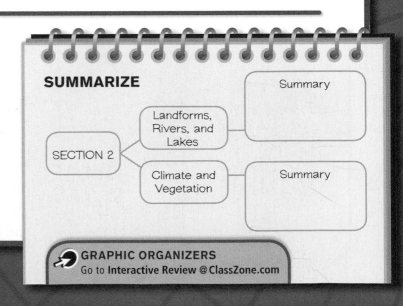

SUMMARIZE

SECTION 2 → Landforms, Rivers, and Lakes → Summary

SECTION 2 → Climate and Vegetation → Summary

GRAPHIC ORGANIZERS
Go to **Interactive Review @ ClassZone.com**

Physical Geography of South America

Connecting to Your World

Look carefully at a map of South America, and you will see many physical features similar to those that define North America, particularly the United States. Just as the Rocky Mountains rise in western North America, the Andes Mountains stretch the entire length of western South America. Great river systems drain both continents, and large plains are central to both North and South America. Of course, as you will soon learn, there are important differences as well.

Landforms, Rivers, and Lakes

▼ **KEY QUESTION** What are the main features of South America's landscape?

South America has nearly every type of physical feature, including mountains, grasslands, plains, and **highlands**. The continent has few large lakes but is drained by five major river systems, including the Amazon River, one of the largest rivers in the world.

Patagonia Deserts, plateaus, and highlands make up this area.

The Andes As the map on the opposite page shows, the **Andes Mountains** Ⓐ stretch along western South America for a distance of about 5,500 miles. Longer than any other mountain range above sea level, the Andes are the world's second-highest range. Only the Himalayas in Asia are higher. The tallest Andean peak, Mount Aconcagua, is the Western Hemisphere's tallest mountain. People living in the Andes grow crops on terraces cut into the mountains.

The Andes region also includes valleys and the *altiplano*, or "high plateau," shared by Peru and Bolivia. Made up of a series of basins between mountains, the *altiplano* is one of the world's highest inhabited regions. Its southern half contains important deposits of copper, silver, tungsten, and tin.

Plains and Highlands The Central Plains extend eastward from the Andes and cover about three-fifths of South America. The *llanos*, Gran Chaco, Amazon rain forest, and Pampas make up the Central Plains. The *llanos* (YAH•nohs) are wide grasslands that stretch across northeastern Colombia and western Venezuela. There, cattle ranches and small farms are common.

A tropical **rain forest** in the Amazon Basin Ⓑ covers about 40 percent of Brazil. The Gran Chaco is a largely uninhabited area consisting of subtropical grasslands and low forests. Nearly half of this region is located in Argentina. The remainder extends into Paraguay and Bolivia. Just south of the Gran Chaco lies a large grassy plain called the **Pampas**, Argentina's most populated area.

The Eastern Highlands are two separate regions. The Guiana Highlands Ⓒ to the north of the Amazon Basin consist of tropical forests and grasslands. The Brazilian Highlands Ⓓ to the south cover about one-fourth of South America and consist mostly of hills and plateaus.

3,000 ft.
2,000 ft.
1,000 ft.

3,212 ft.
1,450 ft.
176 ft.

Niagara Falls
Sears Tower
Angel Falls

Physical Geography of South America

Caribbean Sea
Netherlands Antilles
CENTRAL AMERICA
VENEZUELA
Orinoco River
Llanos
COLOMBIA
GUYANA
SURINAME
FRENCH GUIANA
GUIANA HIGHLANDS
ECUADOR
Negro River
AMAZON
Amazon River
BASIN
PERU
Amazon River
Madeira River
ANDES
Lake Titicaca
Mato Grosso Plateau
BOLIVIA
Altiplano
Atacama Desert
Gran Chaco
PARAGUAY
Paraguay River
ANDES
Mount Aconcagua 22,834 ft (6,960 m)
Pampas
Paraná River
Uruguay River
URUGUAY
Rio de la Plata
CHILE
ARGENTINA
Patagonia
Falkland Islands
Tierra del Fuego
Cape Horn
Drake Passage

ATLANTIC OCEAN
Equator
SOUTH AMERICA
BRAZIL
Araguaia River
BRAZILIAN HIGHLANDS
Tropic of Capricorn
ATLANTIC OCEAN

PACIFIC OCEAN

Elevation

13,100 ft.	(4,000 m)
6,600 ft.	(2,000 m)
3,280 ft.	(500 m)
650 ft.	(200 m)
0 ft.	(0 m)
Below sea level	

▲ Mountain peak

A B C D

N
W E
S

0°
10°S
20°S
30°S

90°W 80°W 70°W 60°W 50°W 40°W 30°W 20°W

0   250   500 miles
0   250   500 kilometers

CONNECT Geography & History
READING A PHYSICAL MAP

Use the key in this physical map to identify the elevations of Patagonia and the Amazon Basin.

1. **Place** What two oceans border South America?
2. **Region** Where are large areas of highlands found in South America?

50°S

Rivers and Lakes South America has five large river systems. The largest is the Amazon river system, which carries about one-fifth of the Earth's river water. The **Amazon River** flows from the Andes to the Atlantic Ocean and is about 4,000 miles long. The river and its tributaries drain much of Brazil and Peru, as well as parts of Colombia, Ecuador, Bolivia, and Venezuela. South America's other river systems are the Rio de la Plata, the Magdalena-Cauca, the Orinoco, and the São Francisco.

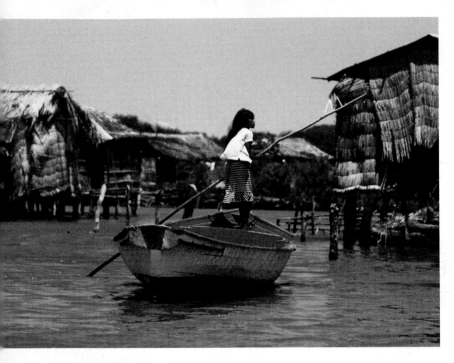

South America has few large natural lakes. The largest, Lake Maracaibo in northwestern Venezuela, covers an area of more than 5,000 square miles. About two-thirds of Venezuela's total petroleum output comes from the Lake Maracaibo region. Lake Titicaca is the second largest lake in South America. Located in the altiplano at an elevation of 12,500 feet, Lake Titicaca is the world's highest navigable lake.

▲ **SUMMARIZE** List the main geographic features of South America.

Lake Maracaibo A girl uses a pole to move her boat between houses on Lake Maracaibo. **How have people living on Lake Maracaibo adapted to their environment?**

Climate and Vegetation

▼ **KEY QUESTION** What kinds of vegetation are found in the tropical and desert climates of South America?

South America has a wide range of climates—from the steamy rain forest of the Amazon Basin to the icy cold of the upper Andes. Because climate largely determines the vegetation of a region, South America has a great variety of plant life as well.

Mountain Climates The climate of the Andes Mountains changes with elevation. For example, near the equator, the climate at the lowest elevations is tropical. However, if you were to climb midway up the mountains, you would most likely find a more temperate, or mild, climate. At an elevation of more than 15,000 feet, you would encounter extremely low temperatures and icy winds. The only vegetation would be a sparse assortment of mosses, lichens, and dwarf shrubs. Climate zones at various elevations in the Andes are compared on the opposite page.

Ⓐ Guanaco (a kind of llama) in the Chilean Andes

Ⓑ Potato fields in Peru

Ⓐ **Tierra Helada (Frozen Land)**
- Above 10,000 feet
- Livestock: llamas, sheep

Ⓒ **Tierra Templada (Temperate Land)**
- 3,000–6,000 feet
- Crops: corn, cotton, coffee, citrus fruits

Ⓑ **Tierra Fría (Cold Land)**
- 6,000–10,000 feet
- Crops: wheat, apples, potatoes, barley

Ⓓ **Tierra Caliente (Hot Land)**
- Sea level–3,000 feet
- Crops: bananas, cacao, sugar cane, rice

CRITICAL THINKING
Draw Conclusions What zones are most productive for growing crops?

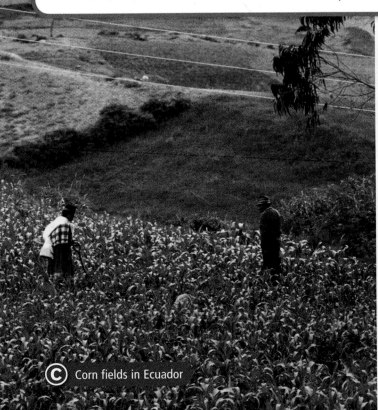

Ⓒ Corn fields in Ecuador

Ⓓ Sugar cane fields in Colombia

The Olmec, a Cultural Hearth The Olmec were traders and skilled farmers. As farming began to thrive, the Olmec could count on a steady food supply. Having enough food led to a larger population and allowed the Olmec to focus on tasks other than farming. An adequate food supply also led to the growth of cities.

Olmec cities included plazas, housing areas, and ceremonial centers. Their oldest known city is San Lorenzo. The Olmec are known for their huge stone sculptures of heads. Some sculptures show a half-human, half-animal **jaguar**, the Olmec's chief god.

The Olmec began to abandon their cities beginning around 600 B.C. for unknown reasons. However, historians consider the Olmec civilization a **cultural hearth**, the place of origin of a major **culture**. The Olmec culture shaped other cultures in the region, particularly the Maya.

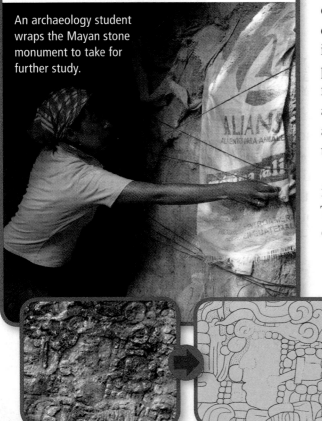

CONNECT History to Today

A Recent Maya Discovery

In 2005, archaeologists working in Guatemala at the site of an ancient Mayan city made an exciting discovery—a stone monument with the carving of a woman's face. The carving dates back to around the A.D. 500s, making it the earliest known likeness of a woman that the Maya carved in stone. This is significant because it suggests that women had important leadership roles in Mayan society early on in Mayan history.

An archaeology student wraps the Mayan stone monument to take for further study.

The Maya, Masters of the City The Maya lived in villages in southern Mexico and northern Central America as early as 1500 B.C. At the height of their civilization, around A.D. 250, the Maya built impressive cities with stone temples, pyramids, plazas, palaces, and ball courts. They were farmers and traders. Corn, beans, and squash were important crops. The Maya also traded salt, chocolate, and cotton with other cultures.

The Maya were advanced in their knowledge of science and technology. They created a 365-day calendar by watching the stars. The calendar identified events throughout the year, such as planting times and holidays. The Maya used a mathematical system based on the number 20 and were the first people to use the zero. They also developed **glyph** writing, carved symbols that stood for a syllable or a word.

In about A.D. 900, the Maya started abandoning their cities, like the Olmec had done earlier. The reasons remain unclear. However, descendants of the Maya still live in the region today.

▲ **COMPARE AND CONTRAST**
Explain how the Olmec and Mayan civilizations were alike and different.

Stone Carving
The drawing (right) helps to more clearly see what is carved in part of the stone monument.

Olmec, Maya, Aztec, and Inca

Click here to explore these ancient civilizations @ ClassZone.com

ATLANTIC OCEAN

Tropic of Cancer

Gulf of Mexico

• Chichén Itzá

Tenochtitlán •

YUCATÁN PENINSULA

• San Lorenzo • Tikal

Caribbean Sea

20°N

Inca road in Bolivia

10°N

Pyramid of the Sun, Mexico

ANDES

0°

PACIFIC OCEAN

• Cuzco

☐	Olmec 1200 B.C.–600 B.C.
▨	Maya A.D. 250–A.D. 900
▨	Aztec A.D. 1200–A.D. 1521
▧	Inca A.D. 1438–A.D. 1533

0   500   1,000 miles
0   500   1,000 kilometers

20°S

ANDES

Tropic of Capricorn

CONNECT Geography & History
READING A THEMATIC MAP

Thematic maps focus on specific types of information. When reading this thematic map, use

• the title to find out what civilizations are featured in the map

• the key to identify what civilization the colors and symbols stand for

Place What civilization occupied the Yucatán Peninsula?

30°S

100°W   90°W   80°W   70°W   60°W

215

The Aztec and the Inca

▼ **KEY QUESTION** How did the Aztec and the Inca use their environments to develop their empires?

Two great civilizations, the Aztec and the Inca, developed vast **empires**, political systems in which people or lands are controlled by one ruler. Both civilizations were very powerful in their regions until the Spanish conquered them in the 1500s.

The Aztec, a Military Culture The **Aztec** moved from northern Mexico into the Valley of Mexico and what is now Mexico City in about the A.D. 1300s. They took control of the valley in about 1428 and ruled their empire until 1521. The Aztec built a strong military empire through warfare and by collecting tribute—money, goods, or crops—from the people they defeated.

The Aztec built Tenochtitlán (teh•NOHCH•tee•TLAHN), their capital city, on an island in Lake Texcoco. The city included houses and causeways, or roads made of earth. At its height, the population reached around 300,000. A great pyramid dedicated to Huitzilopochtli, the sun and war god, stood in the center of the city. The Aztec used the watery environment around Tenochtitlán to create **chinampas**, or island gardens, to grow food and flowers.

ONLINE PRIMARY SOURCE To read more legends of the Aztec and Inca, go to **Research & Writing Center @ ClassZone.com**

ANALYZING Primary Sources

The Eagle on the Prickly Pear Why would the Aztec build a city in the middle of a swampy lake? According to legend, one of their gods predicted that they would see a prickly pear cactus with an eagle sitting on top of it. The Aztec wandered until they saw this sign. There they built Tenochtitlán, which is now Mexico City.

> [A]s they passed through the reeds, there in front of them was the prickly pear with the eagle perched on top, . . . his claws punching holes in his prey. When he saw the Mexicans in the distance, he bowed to them. . . . The . . . spirit said, 'Mexicans, this is the place.' And with that they all wept. 'We are favored,' they said. 'We are blessed. We have seen where our city will be. Now let us go rest.'
>
> Source: *The Eagle on the Prickly Pear*, retold by John Bierhorst

DOCUMENT-BASED QUESTION
How did the Aztec know where to stop to build their capital city?

Inca, Mountain Empire The **Inca** lived in the Andes Mountains in what is now Peru. They controlled a large empire from the early 1400s until 1533. The empire centered around Cuzco (KOOZ•koh), the Inca's mountain capital city. By 1500, the empire extended about 2,500 miles along the west coast of South America. The Inca built complex cities such as Machu Picchu. To farm the steep land, they cut terraces into the mountainsides, where they grew corn and potatoes. They built aqueducts, or canals, to irrigate the land. On higher areas, the Inca grazed llamas.

The Inca adapted to difficult conditions. They built 14,000 miles of roads on which runners carried messages. To keep records, they used *quipus* (KEE•poos), counting tools of knotted cords. Today's descendants of the Inca, the Quechua (KEHCH•wuh), make up about 45 percent of Peru's population. They still use terraces and aqueducts, raise corn and potatoes, and graze llamas.

 SYNTHESIZE Describe how the Inca changed their environment to develop an empire.

Machu Picchu Flowers grow on the slopes of Machu Picchu today.

 ONLINE QUIZ
For test practice, go to
Interactive Review
@ ClassZone.com

Section 3 Assessment

TERMS & NAMES

1. Explain the importance of
- Olmec
- Maya
- Aztec
- Inca

USE YOUR READING NOTES

2. Compare and Contrast Use your completed Venn diagram to answer the following question:

How were the ways the Aztec and Inca modified their environments similar?

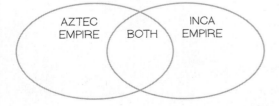

AZTEC EMPIRE — BOTH — INCA EMPIRE

KEY IDEAS

3. What are the earliest known civilizations in what is now southern Mexico?

4. How did the Aztec build their large empire?

5. How were the Inca able to communicate throughout their large empire?

CRITICAL THINKING

6. Compare and Contrast How was the decline of the Mayan and Olmec civilizations different from the decline of the Aztec and Inca civilizations?

7. Identify Problems and Solutions What problems might an empire have in ruling millions of people?

8. CONNECT to Today Each year, around 300,000 people visit Machu Picchu. What problems do you think this presents for this archaeological site? Explain.

9. WRITING Write a Newspaper Article Imagine that you are a reporter visiting a city in one of the early Latin American civilizations. Write a short article that describes the city's architecture.

Animated GEOGRAPHY
Chinampas

 Click here to enter the *chinampas*
@ ClassZone.com

ISLAND GARDENS

Much of the land around Tenochtitlán, where the Aztec settled, was swampy, posing a challenge for farming. The Aztec were resourceful at adapting to their environment. They built *chinampas*, human-made islands created for planting. The rich soil allowed the Aztec to grow crops and flowers.

Click here to see how the Aztec built the *chinampas*. Learn how the Aztec used woven mats and mud from the lake to build the chinampas.

Click here to see how the Aztec lived on the *chinampas*. Learn where they lived, what they wore, and what they ate.

Click here to see how *chinampas* are used today and the problems they face.

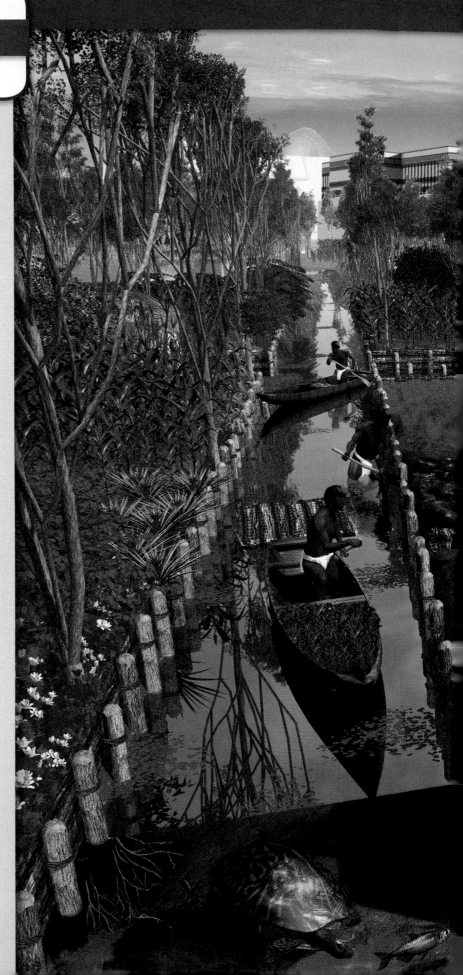

Tenochtitlán

MEXICO
Tenochtitlán

Valley
of
Mexico

Lake
Texcoco

Tenochtitlán

—— Causeways
▇ Chinampas

GeoActivity

Make a Model Work with a partner to create a small model of a *chinampa*. Apply what you have learned about how the Aztec built *chinampas* to make a model using materials similar to those the Aztec used.

Reading for Understanding

▶ Key Ideas

BEFORE, YOU LEARNED

Powerful civilizations arose in Latin America but eventually fell to conquerors.

NOW YOU WILL LEARN

Life under the conquerors was hard, as the people of Latin America struggled to gain their independence.

▶ Vocabulary

TERMS & NAMES

Columbian Exchange the movement of plants and animals between Latin America and Europe after Columbus' voyage to the Americas in A.D. 1492

conquistador (kahn•KWIHS•tuh•DAWR) Spanish word for "conqueror"

colony overseas territory ruled by a nation

mestizo (mehs•TEE•zoh) person with mixed European and Indian ancestry

Father Hidalgo father of Mexican independence

Simón Bolívar leader for independence in northern South America

José de San Martín leader for independence in southern South America

REVIEW

empire a political system in which people or lands are controlled by one ruler

Visual Vocabulary *conquistador*

▶ Reading Strategy

Re-create the time line shown at right. As you read and respond to the **KEY QUESTIONS**, use the time line to show the events that led to independence in Mexico and countries in South America.

 See Skillbuilder Handbook, page R6

SEQUENCE EVENTS

A.D. 1521   A.D. 1826

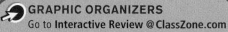

GRAPHIC ORGANIZERS
Go to **Interactive Review** @ ClassZone.com

From Colonization to Independence

Connecting to Your World

If you had lived in Europe before Christopher Columbus arrived in the Americas, you would have never enjoyed chocolate, corn, turkey, peppers, potatoes, or tomatoes. And if you had lived in the Americas, you would never have eaten oranges, bananas, beef, or pork. After the Spanish came to America, plants and animals were exchanged, or traded, between America and Europe. This came to be known as the **Columbian Exchange**.

Conquered Lands

▼ **KEY QUESTION** How did Spanish rule affect life in Latin America?

After Columbus arrived in 1492, life for the Indians changed dramatically. In 1521, a Spanish **conquistador** (kahn•KWIHS•tuh•DAWR), or conqueror, Hernán Cortés, defeated the Aztec. And in 1533 Francisco Pizarro, another Spanish *conquistador*, defeated the Inca.

The Exchange
The graphic shows the goods and diseases transferred between the two hemispheres. **What vegetables did Europeans bring to the Americas?**

Columbian Exchange

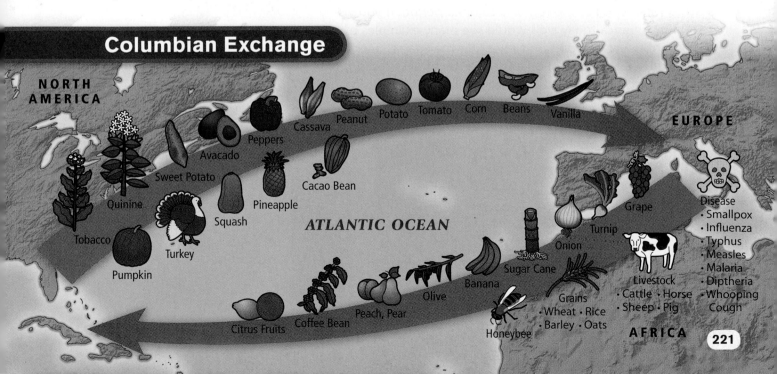

NORTH AMERICA

EUROPE

ATLANTIC OCEAN

AFRICA

Quinine, Avacado, Peppers, Cassava, Peanut, Potato, Tomato, Corn, Beans, Vanilla, Sweet Potato, Cacao Bean, Pineapple, Squash, Tobacco, Turkey, Pumpkin, Grape, Turnip, Onion, Sugar Cane, Banana, Olive, Livestock · Cattle · Horse · Sheep · Pig, Grains · Wheat · Rice · Barley · Oats, Honeybee, Peach, Pear, Coffee Bean, Citrus Fruits

Disease
· Smallpox
· Influenza
· Typhus
· Measles
· Malaria
· Diptheria
· Whooping Cough

Colonial Rule By the mid-1500s, the Spanish had set up **colonies**, or overseas territories ruled by a nation, in various parts of Latin America. Spain's goal was to take advantage of the resources and vast lands in its new **empire**.

To rule the empire, Spain set up a class society. At the top were the *peninsulares* (peh•neen•soo•LAHR•ehs), people born in Spain. They held the high government positions. Below them were the *criollos* (kree•OH•lohs), Spaniards born in Latin America. They were often wealthy, but could not hold high government offices. These two groups controlled land, wealth, and power in the colonies.

Below the *criollos* were the **mestizos** (mehs•TEE•zohs), people of Spanish and Indian ancestry. They had little power. Finally, African enslaved persons and Indians were at the bottom and had no power.

Colonial Economy One of Spain's main purposes in creating colonies was to make Spain wealthy. To do so, Spain set up a system known as *encomienda* (ehn•koh•mee•EHN•duh). Under this system, Indians mined, ranched, and farmed for Spanish landlords. The Indians lived in poverty and hardship, essentially enslaved.

Spain, however, grew wealthy. The Spanish established huge ranches to raise cattle and sheep and large plantations to grow sugar cane, coffee, and cacao in various parts of Latin America. Spain made huge profits from the gold and silver extracted from Mexican mines.

▲ **SYNTHESIZE** Explain how life changed for people in Latin America under Spanish rule.

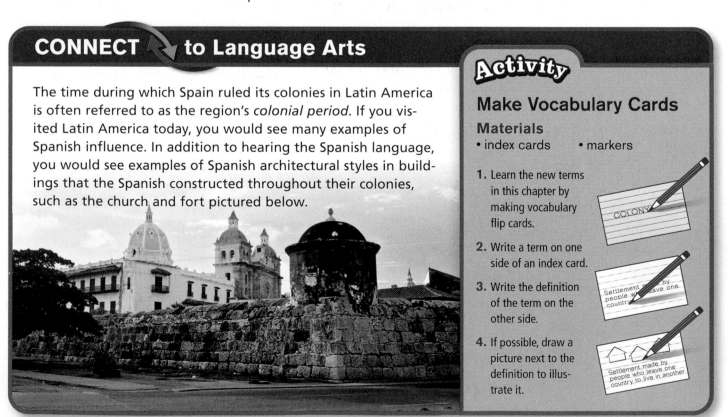

CONNECT to Language Arts

The time during which Spain ruled its colonies in Latin America is often referred to as the region's *colonial period*. If you visited Latin America today, you would see many examples of Spanish influence. In addition to hearing the Spanish language, you would see examples of Spanish architectural styles in buildings that the Spanish constructed throughout their colonies, such as the church and fort pictured below.

Activity

Make Vocabulary Cards

Materials
• index cards   • markers

1. Learn the new terms in this chapter by making vocabulary flip cards.

2. Write a term on one side of an index card.

3. Write the definition of the term on the other side.

4. If possible, draw a picture next to the definition to illustrate it.

Independence from the Spanish

▼ **KEY QUESTION** What events led to independence in Mexico and South America?

In the 1800s, Spain began paying less attention to its Latin American colonies because it was fighting a war in Europe against Napoleon. Various groups in Latin America saw a chance to gain their freedom. The *criollos* and *mestizos* began to organize an independence movement. They called upon the Indians and enslaved persons to join their rebellion. By 1826, all of Latin America, except Cuba and Puerto Rico, became independent.

Mexico's Path to Independence In the late 1700s and early 1800s, freedom was in the air. The people of Mexico had heard about the American Revolution of 1776 and the French Revolution of 1789. The rights of all people were being talked about around the world. Many people in Mexico became excited by these ideas. They wanted their independence from Spain.

The first step toward independence happened in 1810 in a small village in north central Mexico. **Father Hidalgo**, a priest in the village, called on the people to rebel against Spain. The rebellion failed, however, and Father Hidalgo was captured and executed by the Spanish.

A new leader took Father Hidalgo's place. José María Morelos y Pavón also organized an army to fight the Spanish. He and other revolutionaries declared Mexico's independence in 1813. However, the Spanish defeated Morelos, and he was executed in 1815.

In 1821, the revolutionaries made a plan to win the support of all the groups in Mexico. The plan guaranteed independence, freedom of religion, and equality. Spain then declared Mexico independent with the Treaty of Cordoba in August 1821.

Mexico's struggle for independence lasted 11 years. But Mexico still had hard times ahead. You will learn more about Mexico's struggle toward democracy in the next chapter.

HISTORY MAKERS

Father Miguel Hidalgo
1753–1811

Father Hidalgo, a priest in the village of Dolores, sympathized with the Indians and *mestizos* and joined a secret society to work for Mexican independence. On September 16, 1810, Father Hidalgo rang the church bell in Dolores and urged his parishioners to fight for freedom. Thousands joined his army, but with clubs and farm tools as weapons, they were no match against the Spanish soldiers.

Today, Father Hidalgo is known as the father of Mexican independence. To honor him, Mexican Independence Day is celebrated on September 16.

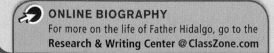 **ONLINE BIOGRAPHY**
For more on the life of Father Hidalgo, go to the **Research & Writing Center @ ClassZone.com**

Independence for South America Just as they did in Mexico, the American and French revolutions had inspired dreams of freedom among people throughout South America. Beginning in 1810, two leaders led the fight for independence from Spain.

Simón Bolívar, a Venezuelan general, led the fight in the northern part of South America. To honor his efforts, South Americans call him "the Liberator." **José de San Martín**, an Argentine general, led the fight for independence in the southern part of South America. By 1825, nearly all of South America was free from Spanish rule.

Brazil, a Portuguese colony, also gained independence at this time. When Brazilians demanded independence in 1822, Dom Pedro, the son of the Portuguese king, declared Brazil independent and made himself emperor. You will read more about Brazil in a later chapter.

 SUMMARIZE Discuss the events that led to independence in Mexico and South America.

CONNECT ▸ History & Economics

Coffee

Coffee was first grown in Africa. European colonists brought coffee trees, like those shown in the illustration below, to the Americas in the Columbian Exchange. Brazil and Colombia, along with the rest of Latin America, produce two-thirds of the world's coffee.

Section ❹ Assessment

ONLINE QUIZ
For test practice, go to
Interactive Review
@ ClassZone.com

TERMS & NAMES

1. **Explain the importance of**
   - Columbian Exchange
   - *conquistador*
   - colony
   - *mestizo*

USE YOUR READING NOTES

2. **Sequence Events** Use your time line to answer the following question:

   How long was much of Latin America under Spanish rule?

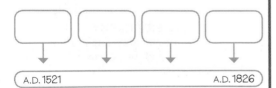

A.D. 1521   A.D. 1826

KEY IDEAS

3. Why were the *mestizos* important in Mexico's fight for independence?

4. Who was Father Hidalgo and why was he important?

5. How did most of South America gain its independence?

CRITICAL THINKING

6. **Analyze Causes and Effects** Why did Mexicans decide to fight for independence from Spain?

7. **Evaluate** What geographical challenges did South Americans have in their fight for independence?

8. **CONNECT to Today** What problems from the colonial days might still affect people in Latin America today?

9. **TECHNOLOGY** **Write a Biography** Use the Internet to find more information about one of the leaders for independence in Latin America discussed in this section. Then use a word processor to write a brief biography of that individual.

Interactive ←Review

Click here to complete these and other activities online @ ClassZone.com

CHAPTER SUMMARY

Key Idea 1
The geography of Mexico, Central America, and the Caribbean Islands contains mountains, highlands, and plains.

Key Idea 2
The physical geography of South America consists of a wide variety of landforms and climates.

Key Idea 3
People adapted to these challenging geographic and climatic conditions and developed great civilizations.

Key Idea 4
Life under the conquerors was hard, as the people of Latin America struggled to gain their independence.

For **Review and Study Notes**, go to **Interactive Review @ ClassZone.com**

NAME GAME

Use the Terms & Names list to complete each sentence on paper or online.

1. I am built to make farming on mountainsides easier. ____terrace____

2. I am the civilization that built a vast empire in Peru. _____

3. I am a large plain in Argentina. _____

4. I am the civilization that is considered the cultural hearth of southern Mexico. _____

5. I am the father of Mexican independence. _____

6. I am a large region that includes Mexico, Central and South America, and the Caribbean Islands. _____

7. I allowed plants, animals, and ideas to be traded between Europe and the Americas. _____

8. I am the large islands in the Caribbean Sea. _____

9. I am a landform on which the Panama Canal is located. _____

10. I am the place on which the Aztec grew food and flowers. _____

chinampas
Columbian Exchange
Father Hidalgo
Greater Antilles
Inca
isthmus
Latin America
Lesser Antilles
Olmec
Pampas
Simón Bolívar
terrace

Activities

GeoGame

Use this online map to show what you know about present-day Latin America. Click and drag each place name to its location on the map.

Brazil

Mexico

Caribbean Sea

Gulf of Mexico

Amazon River

To play the complete game, go to **Interactive Review** @ ClassZone.com

Crossword Puzzle

Complete an online crossword puzzle to test your knowledge of the geography and history of Latin America.

ACROSS
1. Mayan writing—a carved symbol that stands for a syllable or word

VOCABULARY

Explain the significance of each of the following.

1. Latin America
2. isthmus
3. Andes Mountains
4. Pampas
5. Amazon River
6. Aztec
7. Inca
8. *chinampas*
9. *mestizo*
10. Simón Bolívar

Explain how the terms and names in each group are related.

11. Olmec, Maya, and Aztec
12. Pampas, Andes Mountains, and Amazon River

KEY IDEAS

1 Physical Geography of Mexico, Central America, and the Caribbean

13. Why are Mexico, Central and South America, and the Caribbean Islands called Latin America?
14. What are two mountain ranges in Mexico?
15. Why is Central America's climate warm year-round?

2 Physical Geography of South America

16. Where is the world's largest tropical rain forest?
17. What is the largest river system in South America?
18. What affects climate in the Andes Mountains?

3 Ancient Civilizations

19. Where was the Mayan civilization located?
20. What features did Tenochtitlán have?
21. How did the Inca keep records?

4 From Colonization to Independence

22. Who defeated the Aztec and Inca empires?
23. Who were the *mestizos* and why are they important?
24. How did most South American countries become independent?

CRITICAL THINKING

25. **Compare and Contrast** Create a table to compare and contrast the landforms, farming methods, and building methods in the Aztec and Inca empires.

AZTEC	INCA

26. **Analyze Causes and Effects** How did the lives of Indians change after the Spanish conquered them?
27. **Identify Problems and Solutions** How might the Spanish have prevented rebellion?
28. **Connect to Economics** How did the *encomienda* system prevent the Mexican economy from being open to all people?
29. **Five Themes: Human-Environment Interaction** How did the Aztec and Inca use technology to change the environment?
30. **Make Inferences** What problems did Latin Americans likely face after independence?

Answer the ESSENTIAL QUESTION

How have Latin America's geography and resources helped shape its history?

Written response Write a two- or three-paragraph response to the Essential Question. Be sure to consider the key ideas of each section as well as specific details about how geography affected ancient civilizations. Use the rubric to guide your thinking.

Response Rubric

A strong response will:
- discuss the geographic features in one region
- summarize how the geography affected the history of the region's people

SECONDARY SOURCE

Use context clues in the paragraph below to answer questions 1 and 2.

> The full knowledge of the Maya calendar must have been guarded . . . by the ruling elite, since it was undoubtedly a source of great power. . . . One might assume, however, that even the poorest farmer had some knowledge of the basic system, by which to guide his family's daily life.
>
> Source: The Ancient Maya, by Robert J. Sharer

1. What is the most likely reason that the ruling elite guarded knowledge of the calendar?

A. They did not want the farmers to be confused.

B. They wanted to stop other people from stealing the calendar.

C. They believed the knowledge gave them power over others.

D. They didn't want others to use the knowledge against them.

2. What statement does the paragraph support?

A. The Maya did not know about the calendar.

B. Most Maya had some knowledge of the calendar.

C. Most Maya did not care about the calendar.

D. The ruling elite wanted everyone to know about the calendar.

LINE GRAPH

Use the line graph below to answer questions 3 and 4 on your paper.

Aztec and Incan Population Decline After 1520

Source: *The Population of Latin America: A History*

3. Between what years did the Aztec population show the sharpest decline?

4. What was the Inca population in 1520? In 1620?

1. INTERDISCIPLINARY ACTIVITY–DRAMA

With a small group, find another legend from the ancient civilizations of Latin America, such as the Aztec legend about the volcano Popocatépetl. Create a skit of the legend to present to the class.

2. WRITING FOR SOCIAL STUDIES

Reread the part of Section 2 about Tenochtitlán. Imagine that you are visiting the city. Write a letter to a friend telling about your visit. Describe the features of the city and give your impression of it.

3. MENTAL MAPPING

Create an outline map of Latin America and label the following:

• Mexico
• Mexico City
• Central America
• Panama Canal
• Greater Antilles

• Lesser Antilles
• South America
• Amazon River

Mexico

 ESSENTIAL QUESTION

How does Mexico reflect both ancient traditions and the challenges of the modern world?

CONNECT **Geography & History**

Use the map and the time line to answer the following questions.

1. What Mexican states are located on a peninsula on the Pacific Coast?

2. What was one result of the Mexican Revolution?

History

◄ **1864** Napoleon appoints Maximilian as Emperor of Mexico. (Maximilian)

1848

Geography
1848 Mexico signs treaty of Guadalupe Hidalgo and loses territory to the United States.

Economics
1917 New constitution redistributes land more equally among the people.

History
◄ **1910** Mexican Revolution begins.

UNITED STATES

Tijuana

BAJA CALIFORNIA

Ciudad Juárez

SONORA

Gulf of California (Sea of Cortez)

CHIHUAHUA

COAHUILA

BAJA CALIFORNIA SUR

NUEVO LEÓN
Monterrey

Gulf of Mexico

DURANGO

SINALOA

TAMAULIPAS

Tropic of Cancer

ZACATECAS

SAN LUIS POTOSÍ

AGUASCALIENTES

QUERÉTARO

TLAXCALA

YUCATÁN

NAYARIT

León

GUANAJUATO

HIDALGO

QUINTANA ROO

Guadalajara

JALISCO

Mexico City
MÉXICO

VERACRUZ

Bay of Campeche

CAMPECHE

COLIMA

Puebla
PUEBLA

TABASCO

BELIZE

National capital

Other city

PACIFIC OCEAN

MICHOACÁN

DISTRITO FEDERAL

MORELOS

GUERRERO

OAXACA

CHIAPAS

GUATEMALA

Gulf of Tehuantepec

HONDURAS

N W E S

Río Grande

0   150   300 miles
0   150   300 kilometers

Government

▲ **1929** The Institutional Revolutionary Party (Partido Revolucionario Institucional, or PRI) comes to power.

Culture

1990 Octavio Paz wins Nobel Prize for Literature.

Economics

1992 Mexico signs the North American Free Trade Agreement (NAFTA).

Today

Government

◄ **2000** Vicente Fox is elected president of Mexico.

Reading for Understanding

▶ Key Ideas

BEFORE, YOU LEARNED

Mexico rebelled against colonial rule and gained its independence from Spain in 1821.

NOW YOU WILL LEARN

Mexico had to overcome many obstacles as the country moved toward establishing a democracy.

▶ Vocabulary

TERMS & NAMES

Antonio López de Santa Anna (1794–1876) Mexican general, president, and leader of Mexican independence from Spain

Republic of Texas constitutional government of Texas after independence from Mexico

annex to add to an existing territory

cession surrendered territory

Benito Juárez (1806–1872) Indian who became president and a Mexican national hero

Mexican Revolution a fight for reforms in Mexico from 1910 to 1920

Constitution of 1917 Mexican constitution written during the revolution that is still in effect today

Vicente Fox Mexican president from the National Action Party who was elected in 2000

REVIEW

constitution a formal plan of government

revolution the overthrow of a ruler or government; a major change in ideas

▶ Reading Strategy

Re-create the chart shown at right. As you read and respond to the **KEY QUESTIONS**, look for the effects of the causes that are listed.

 See Skillbuilder Handbook, page R8

ANALYZE CAUSES AND EFFECTS

CAUSES	EFFECTS
Mexico and the United States could not agree on the border of Texas.	
Benito Juárez instituted a new constitution in 1857.	
Huge gap existed between rich and poor; most Mexicans did not own land.	
The Constitution of 1917 was created.	

 GRAPHIC ORGANIZERS
Go to **Interactive Review** @ ClassZone.com

A Struggle Toward Democracy

Connecting to Your World

Think what an important part George Washington played in the U.S. fight for independence from Britain. In Mexican history, General **Antonio López de Santa Anna** played a key role in Mexico's fight for independence from Spain. He served as both a soldier and a president. As president, however, Santa Anna was not able to establish a secure government. Several factors made it difficult for the Mexican people to create a stable government.

War and Reform

▼ **KEY QUESTION** What challenges did Mexico have in establishing a stable government?

During Spanish rule, Mexicans had little control over their lives. Spain made many decisions for Mexico. As a result, after gaining independence in 1821, Mexico had trouble establishing a stable government. The Mexican people had no experience in governing themselves, and the nation had a weak economy. Invasion by foreign countries also prevented Mexico from establishing a strong government.

Santa Anna

Reform Demands
Protests, pictured in this mural by David Siquieros, led to the Mexican Revolution.

Mexican culture is a blend of both Indian and Spanish traditions. The influences of both cultures are evident in Mexico today.

Indian Traditions

Before the Spanish conquest in 1521, Mexico's Indian groups had well-established, unique cultures. Indian groups created cities with huge structures. They held celebrations, such as festivals to remember those who died. Crops such as corn, chilies, and tomatoes contributed to their flavorful diet.

Food

Tortillas, a popular Mexican food made from corn, date back to the ancient Aztecs.

Clothing

These girls wear handmade, colorful dresses.

Festivals

Mexican children of Indian ancestry dressed in traditional clothing participate in a local festival.

▲ *Ruins of Mayan temple at Palenque, Mexico*

Spanish Traditions

The Spanish conquest brought European customs and traditions to the region. The Spanish built their traditional square cities that surrounded plazas and included government buildings and churches. They honored their dead on All Saints' Day and All Souls' Day in November. They introduced foods such as oranges, wheat, beef, pork, sugar cane, coffee, and onions to the Mexican diet.

Food

Mexican sweet breads are made from wheat, which the Spaniards brought to Mexico.

Clothing

These dancers are dressed in traditional Spanish clothing from the colonial period.

Festivals

Mexican children participate in a procession celebrating Easter, a Roman Catholic holiday.

▲ *Spanish colonial church in Taxco, Mexico*

CRITICAL THINKING

1. **Evaluate** Why are Mexican traditions today a blend of Native American and Spanish traditions?

2. **Compare and Contrast** Based on the large photos, how do Native American and Spanish architecture compare?

Tropical and mountain climates are both found in Middle America and Spanish-speaking South America. Each climate supports its own unique vegetation and animal life.

Tropical

The climate in tropical regions is hot year-round, with abundant rainfall. This climate produces the thick, green rain forests and the many exotic plants and animals that live in them. Farmers plant crops, such as sugar cane and bananas, that thrive in the tropical conditions.

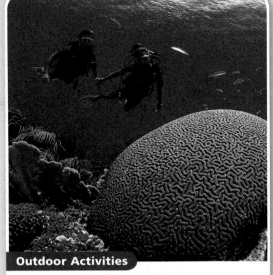

Outdoor Activities

Scuba divers explore the coral reefs off the coast of Bonaire, one of the Caribbean islands.

Nevis Peak and Botanical Gardens on the Caribbean island of Nevis ▼

Agriculture

A farmer harvests sugar cane on the island nation of Barbados.

Wildlife

Sloths, such as this one hanging upside down from a branch, live in the tropical forests of Central America and South America and spend most of their lives in trees.

Mountain

Unlike the fairly constant climate of the tropical areas, the highland climate of the Andes Mountains varies with changes in elevation. Temperatures range from warm in the lower elevations to freezing in the highest elevations. Farming is difficult in this climate, but several crops, such as potatoes, barley, and wheat, grow well there. Various species of plants and animals have adapted to the mountain conditions.

Outdoor Activities

Ice climbers make their way up Huayna Potosi, a mountain in Bolivia popular among mountain climbers.

Sacsayhuamán, an ancient Inca fortress, overlooks the city of Cuzco, Peru. ▼

Agriculture

These Ecuadorian farmers are harvesting barley.

Wildlife

The spectacled bear makes its home in the Andes Mountains. It gets its name from the markings around its eyes.

CRITICAL THINKING

1. **Compare and Contrast** What differences can be seen between tropical and mountain climate regions?

2. **Form an Opinion** Which climate region is more appealing to you? Why?

São Paulo

Tresópolis

Urban and Rural Populations 1950–2000

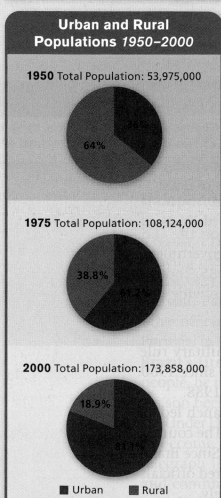

1950 Total Population: 53,975,000

36%

64%

1975 Total Population: 108,124,000

38.8%

61.2%

2000 Total Population: 173,858,000

18.9%

81.1%

■ Urban ■ Rural

Population Density of Brazilian States

RORAIMA

AMAPÁ

Equator 0°

AMAZONAS

PARÁ

MARANHÃO

CEARÁ

RIO GRANDE DO NORTE

ACRE

PIAUÍ

PARAÍBA

PERNAMBUCO ● Recife

RONDÔNIA

TOCANTINS

ALAGOAS 10°S

MATO GROSSO

BAHIA

SERGIPE

GOIÁS

DISTRITO FEDERAL

MINAS GERAIS

MATO GROSSO DO SUL

SÃO PAULO

● Belo Horizonte

ESPÍRITO SANTO

Tropic of Capricorn

RIO DE JANEIRO 20°S

PARANÁ

Rio de Janeiro

São Paulo

SANTA CATARINA

ATLANTIC OCEAN

RIO GRANDE DO SUL

● Pôrto Alegre

0   200   400 miles

0   200   400 kilometers

70°W   60°W   50°W   40°W

Persons per square mile

Over 250

60–250

0–60

Source: Population Division of the Department of Economic and Social Affairs of the United Nations Secretariat, *World Population Prospects: The 2004 Revision* and *World Urbanization Prospects: The 2003 Revision*

CRITICAL THINKING

1. **Draw Conclusions** What is the population density in most of Brazil?
2. **Evaluate** About how many people lived in urban areas in Brazil in 2000?

Many poor Brazilians who moved from rural areas work at low-income jobs or are unemployed. Most live in neighborhoods called **favelas**, located on the outskirts of cities. In 1960 the Brazilian government moved the capital city from **Rio de Janeiro** (REE•oh day zhuh•NAYR•oh) to **Brasília**, about 600 miles inland. The Brazilian government has encouraged people to move inland, even offering land to people who are willing to move to the nation's interior.

Favela This *favela* is located outside of Rio de Janeiro. **Why might it be located there?**

Bridging the Gap Between Rich and Poor Today, Brazil has one of the largest economies in the world. However, one of the major challenges facing Brazil is how to bridge the large gap between the rich and poor. A small number of Brazilians live comfortably or in luxury, but most Brazilians are poor. Brazil has one of the most uneven distributions of land in the world. Two percent of landowners own most of the land, while more than half of Brazil's farmers work on less than three percent of the land. To help narrow the income gap, Brazil will have to create more jobs for the nation's poor.

▲ **SUMMARIZE** Discuss some of the challenges facing Brazil today.

Section 1 Assessment

ONLINE QUIZ
For test practice, go to
Interactive Review
@ ClassZone.com

TERMS & NAMES
1. Explain the importance of
• Pedro Álvares Cabral
• *favela*
• Rio de Janeiro
• Brasília

USE YOUR READING NOTES
2. Sequence Events Use your time line to answer the following question:

How long after becoming a republic did military rule end in Brazil?

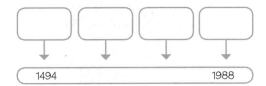

1494   1988

KEY IDEAS
3. What European nation developed Brazil as its colony?
4. Where do most people in Brazil live today?
5. Why did the Brazilian government offer land to people to move to the nation's interior?

CRITICAL THINKING
6. Make Inferences How has uneven land distribution contributed to poverty in Brazil?
7. Analyze Causes and Effects Why has urbanization resulted in the creation of *favelas* in Brazil's cities?
8. CONNECT to Today What is one action Brazil's government hopes to take to narrow the income gap between its rich and poor?
9. WRITING Write a Newspaper Article Research information about Brazil's government. Find out who is the current president, how the legislative branch is organized, and the term of office for both. Present your findings in the form of a newspaper article.

Reading for Understanding

▶ Key Ideas

BEFORE, YOU LEARNED

Brazil's government is dealing with problems resulting from urbanization.

NOW YOU WILL LEARN

Several cultures have influenced Brazil's unique culture.

▶ Vocabulary

TERMS & NAMES

Candomblé (kahn•duhm•BLEH) African religious practices that are mixed with Roman Catholic beliefs to produce a unique belief

quilombos (kih•LOHM•buhs) communities created by escaped African slaves

samba (SAM•buh) music and dance, with roots in African rhythms; the most famous form of Brazilian music worldwide

cuíca (kwee•kuh) a friction drum used in the samba

bossa nova (BAHS•uh NOH•vuh) a jazz version of the samba

capoeira (KAP•oh•AY•ruh) a Brazilian dance combined with martial arts

REVIEW

immigrant a person who leaves one area to settle in another

mural a wall painting

Visual Vocabulary *capoeira*

▶ Reading Strategy

Re-create the chart shown at right. As you read and respond to the **KEY QUESTIONS**, use the chart to organize important details about Brazil's people and culture.

 See Skillbuilder Handbook, page R7

CATEGORIZE

ART AND ARCHITECTURE	MUSIC	ENTERTAINMENT
1.	1.	1.
2.	2.	2.
3.	3.	3.

 GRAPHIC ORGANIZERS
Go to **Interactive Review** @ ClassZone.com

A Multicultural Society

Connecting to Your World

Think about some of the foods you eat. Think about the music that you and your family enjoy. Chances are that many of the foods you enjoy and the music you listen to have their roots in a variety of cultures. If you visited Brazil, you would see how a variety of cultures has also influenced the foods, music, and other aspects of Brazilian culture today.

A Blend of Many Cultures

▼ **KEY QUESTION** What cultures have most influenced Brazil?

Brazilian culture includes European, African, Asian, and Indian influences. Portuguese is the official language. Most Brazilians are Roman Catholic. At the same time, Brazilians of African ancestry mix *Candomblé* (kahn•duhm•BLEH), West African religious practices, with Catholicism to create a unique Brazilian blend.

Brazilian Diversity
These Brazilian girls are getting ready to participate in Carnival in Rio de Janeiro.

Daniel Munduruku is a Munduruku Indian. He has written several books about his culture. Here he describes learning the ancient myths of his people.

> When I was a . . . boy, my grandfather would . . . tell the stories that explained the origins of our people and the vision of the universe. . . . Now . . . I realize that those ancient myths say what cannot be said. They are pure poetry, and through them I see how an identity can be created in the oral tradition.
>
> Source: *Tales of the Amazon, How the Munduruku Indians Live*

CRITICAL THINKING

Summarize How is storytelling important in the Munduruku culture?

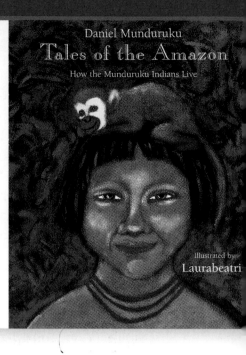

Daniel Munduruku
Tales of the Amazon
How the Munduruku Indians Live

Illustrated by
Laurabeatri

Native Brazilians Up to 6 million Indians lived in Brazil before the Portuguese arrived. Tens of thousands died from diseases brought by the European colonists. Today, only about 700,000 Indians live in Brazil, mostly in the Amazon rain forest. They make up less than one percent of Brazil's population. The Tupi and Guarani make up the largest groups. Other tribes, such as the Yanomami and Bororo, still follow traditional ways of hunting and farming.

The Brazilian government has set up reservations to protect these cultures. But even isolated groups now have contact with outsiders, such as miners, loggers, and researchers, who move into the area to study native cultures. This increased contact threatens the groups' traditional ways of life, arts, crafts, and languages.

Yanomami Woman A Yanomami woman poses with her child. **How might being photographed threaten the Yanomami's traditional way of life?**

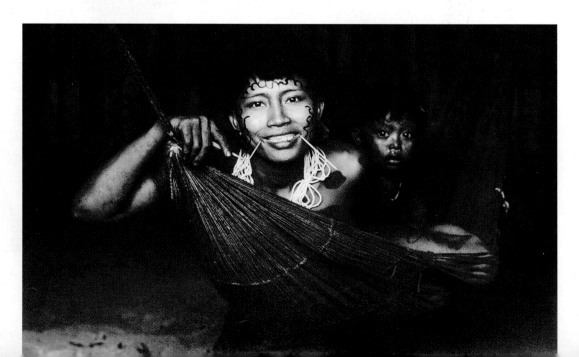

Africans Today, most Brazilians with African ancestry live in the nation's northern and coastal regions and make up about 6 percent of the population. The Portuguese brought Africans to Brazil between the 1500s and 1800s to work on the sugar plantations. In fact, of all the slaves brought to North and South America, more than a third were brought to Brazil.

Some of these slaves escaped to freedom in Brazil's inland northern region, where they established communities that were similar to their African homes. They called the settlements **quilombos** (kih•LOHM•buhs), an African word for "housing." By the end of the 1600s, as many as 25,000 Africans may have lived in these communities. *Quilombos* can still be found in parts of Brazil today, particularly in the northern part, where people continue their traditional way of life. Today most Brazilians of African ancestry live in the northeastern state of Bahia. Its capital, Salvador, was the center of the Portuguese empire, sugar industry, and slave trade.

African influences are evident in various parts of Brazilian culture. African slaves created Brazil's national food, *feijoada* (fayh•zhoo•AH•duh), a bean stew. African rhythms play an important role in Brazilian music. Brazil's art and literature also reflect an African influence.

Europeans and Asians In the 1700s, Europeans viewed Brazil as a place to acquire wealth. With the discovery of gold and diamonds, many immigrated to Brazil to make their fortunes. After Brazil declared its independence, many Europeans, including Italians, Spanish, Portuguese, and Germans, came to work in Brazil, mostly in the coffee industry. Today, people of European ancestry make up about half of Brazil's population. Most live in the southern part of the country.

Japanese **immigrants** first began arriving in Brazil in the early 1900s. Most came to work on coffee or tea farms. More Japanese arrived after World War II. Today Brazil has the largest Japanese population outside of Japan, with most making their homes in the state of São Paulo. In recent years, Asians from China and Korea have also immigrated to Brazil.

▲ **EVALUATE** Explain how Brazil's culture is a blend of several cultures.

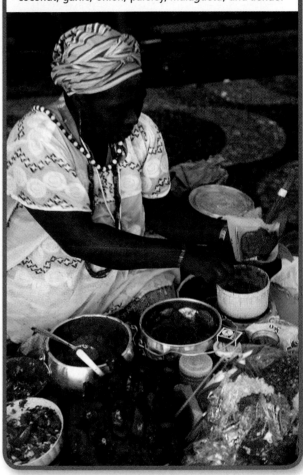

CONNECT **History & Culture**

African Influence on Brazilian Food

Since most slaves brought to Brazil arrived from West Africa, West African cooking has had a strong influence on Brazilian food. Palm oil, called *dendê*, and chili peppers, called *malagueta*, are basic West African cooking ingredients. Today, Bahian cooks make *moqueca*, a popular stew. It is made with seafood, coconut, garlic, onion, parsley, *malagueta*, and *dendê*.

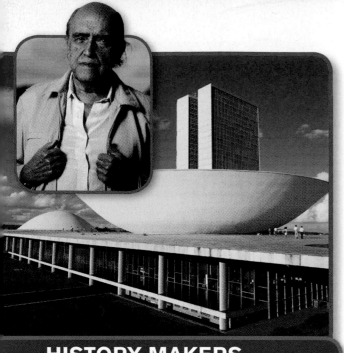

Arts and Entertainment

▼ **KEY QUESTION** What are some ways Brazilians enjoy holidays and leisure time?

Brazil's art, literature, music, and celebrations reflect the nation's blend of cultural traditions. Brazil's Carnival, in particular, highlights Brazil's cultural diversity.

Architecture and Art Brazil's earliest art included the crafts made by Brazil's Indian groups. Their work included such items as pottery, baskets, and jewelry. Native American groups today continue to make these handicrafts, many of which are sold to tourists in Brazilian markets.

António Francisco Lisboa, known as Aleijadinho, is a well known sculptor of the colonial period. He created religious sculptures for many churches in the mid- to late 1700s. Today, Mario Cravo Junior is an important sculptor who creates statues made with concrete.

Cândido Portinari is a famous Brazilian painter and muralist. His six largest **murals** are found in New York's United Nations building and in Washington's Library of Congress. Much of his art reflects rural life and social concerns.

Brazil is the home of Oscar Niemeyer, one of the world's most famous architects. He is best known for designing several buildings in Brasília, Brazil's capital. Niemeyer has also designed a variety of buildings in several countries throughout the world, including France, Ghana, Israel, and Lebanon. More recently, Niemeyer created a unique design for an art museum near the city of Rio de Janeiro.

Music and Dance Brazilian music is a blend of African, European, and Indian cultures. Brazilians enjoy dancing to the **samba** (SAM•buh), the most famous form of Brazilian music. The samba developed in the early 1900s and has its roots in African rhythms. The samba has many forms, but the most popular is the street samba danced during the celebrations of Carnival, a Brazilian holiday. The drum plays a major role in Brazilian music. Brazilian drums come in many shapes and sizes, each producing its own sound and rhythm. Drummers play the surdo, a bass drum, and the **cuíca** (kwee•kuh), a friction drum, to create samba rhythms.

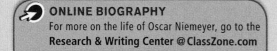

A Day in Pedro's Life

 To learn more about Pedro and his world, go to the **Activity Center @ ClassZone.com**

Hi! My name is Pedro. I am 13 years old and live in São Paulo, the largest city in Brazil and the third largest city in the world in population. I attend a public school, a short walk from my apartment. Many of my friends live in the same apartment building, so there's always someone to do things with. Let me tell you about my day.

This is how to say "Hello, my name is Pedro" in Portuguese:

"Oi, meu nome é Pedro."

6 A.M. My family and I have breakfast before my parents go to work and my sister and I go to school. Today we're having cereal and papaya.

7 A.M.–noon My school day begins early. Because of overcrowded schools, many students go to school in two shifts. I like having the morning shift. My school year runs from March to December.

1 P.M. My family and I get together for the main meal of the day. Today I'm looking forward to *feijoada*, which is a dish made with black beans and beef.

6 P.M. After I finish my homework and have a small snack, I'm off to the local park to play soccer. Next to playing the game, my favorite thing to do is to watch our city's professional team play soccer.

CONNECT to Your Life

Journal Entry Think about your typical daily schedule. How are the meals you eat and the time you eat the same as and different from Pedro's? Record your ideas in your journal.

The *cuíca* and other percussion instruments create the energetic sounds of the samba during Carnival celebrations (shown below). The *cuíca* is an African friction drum made by attaching a stick to the center of a drum skin. The drummer holds the drum in one hand and puts the other arm inside the drum. The sound is made by rubbing the stick with a wet piece of cloth or leather. When the stick is rubbed, the drum skin vibrates, producing a distinctive sound.

▲ *The inside of a* cuíca

Make a *Cuíca*

Materials
- plastic cup or strong food container
- nail
- waxed dental floss

1. With a nail, make two holes, about an inch apart , in the bottom of the cup or container.

2. Push a three-foot piece of dental floss through both holes and make sure the two ends of the floss are the same length.

3. Tie the two ends into a knot as close to the hole inside the cup as possible so the string doesn't slip out.

4. Hold the cup in one hand and slide your fingers along the string with the other to make your own *cuíca* music.

Another popular form of Brazilian music and dance is the **bossa nova** (BAHS•uh NOH•vuh). It mixes the samba beat with the sounds of jazz. Brazilian jazz musicians popularized the bossa nova in the rest of the world. Brazilian samba-reggae is a popular form of music based on African drum traditions. **Capoeira** (kap•oh•AY•ruh) combines dance and the martial arts. It developed in Brazil from African origins. During Portuguese rule, the Portuguese forbade the African slaves to fight. So the Africans created fight dances, which developed into *capoeira*.

Festivals Brazilians are known for Carnival, celebrated every year for four days before the beginning of the Christian season of Lent. The holiday combines a Roman Catholic festival with African celebrations and includes parades and street parties. The world's most famous Carnival takes place in Rio de Janeiro. Thousands of spectators line the streets to watch costumed people ride elaborately decorated floats. In clubs and other places, thousands of dancers, who have been practicing for months, participate in samba dance competitions.

Recreation Brazil's thousands of miles of coastline provide extensive sandy beaches. On weekends, thousands of Brazilian families flock to the beaches to swim and enjoy picnics. Copacabana Beach in Rio de Janeiro attracts millions of tourists every year.

Brazil's most famous sport is football (soccer). It is played everywhere—in cities, beaches, and rural areas. People of all ages play it for fun. Professional football teams draw huge crowds of enthusiastic fans in football stadiums in many Brazilian cities. Maracana Stadium in Rio de Janeiro, one of the world's largest stadiums, holds more than 150,000 people. Brazil's teams have produced some of the world's top football players, such as Pelé and Ronaldo. Brazil's national football team has won 5 of the 17 World Cups ever awarded, the most for any football team. The World Cup is a trophy awarded to a nation's football team for winning the world championship.

Beach in Recife, Brazil
Children enjoy playing in the waters of Boa Viagem beach, a popular beach in Recife.

 SUMMARIZE Describe the ways Brazilians enjoy holidays and their leisure time.

Section 2 Assessment

 ONLINE QUIZ
For test practice, go to
Interactive Review
@ ClassZone.com

TERMS & NAMES

1. Explain the importance of
- *Candomblé*
- *quilombos*
- *cuíca*
- *capoeira*

USE YOUR READING NOTES

2. Categorize Use your completed chart to answer the following question.

What contributions has Oscar Niemeyer made to Brazilian culture?

ART AND ARCHITECTURE	MUSIC	ENTERTAINMENT
1.	1.	1.
2.	2.	2.
3.	3.	3.

KEY IDEAS

3. What four cultures have contributed to modern Brazilian culture?

4. Where do most Brazilians of African ancestry live?

5. What type of music and dance is identified worldwide as Brazilian?

CRITICAL THINKING

6. Make Inferences Why are the traditional ways of life of some Indian groups in Brazil threatened?

7. Draw Conclusions How have Africans contributed to Brazilian culture?

8. CONNECT to Today Why do you think the Brazilian government has set up reservations to protect traditional Indian cultures?

9. ART Make a Collage Create a collage that illustrates ways people enjoy themselves in Brazil. Use the information in the section as well as in other sources. Then make a collage that features the various sources of entertainment in Brazil.

Reading for Understanding

▶ Key Ideas

BEFORE, YOU LEARNED

The culture of Brazil today is a blend of many cultures.

NOW YOU WILL LEARN

An abundance of natural resources helps make Brazil a major industrial nation.

▶ Vocabulary

TERMS & NAMES

hydroelectricity electric power generated by water

ethanol (EHTH•uh•NAWL) a liquid made by using a chemical process to convert sugar cane to a kind of alcohol that can be used for fuel

deforestation the cutting and clearing away of trees

boycott to stop buying and using products from certain sources as a way of protest

REVIEW

economy a system for producing and exchanging goods and services among a group of people

export a product or resource sold to another country

rain forest a broadleaf-tree region in a tropical climate

global warming an increase in the average temperature of the Earth's atmosphere

BACKGROUND VOCABULARY

mechanized equipped with machinery

self-sufficient able to provide for one's own needs without outside help

▶ Reading Strategy

Re-create the web diagram shown at right. As you read and respond to the **KEY QUESTIONS**, use the diagram to organize main ideas and details about Brazil's economy.

 See Skillbuilder Handbook, page R4

FIND MAIN IDEAS

ECONOMY

GRAPHIC ORGANIZERS
Go to **Interactive Review** @ ClassZone.com

Developing an Abundant Land

Connecting to Your World

In the early 1900s, Henry Ford invented a way to manufacture cars that would make them affordable for most people. His invention sparked the U.S. automobile industry and made the United States a major producer of automobiles. Today Brazil has become a leading maker of automobiles in the world and one of the most industrialized countries in South America.

Creating an Economic Giant

▼ **KEY QUESTION** What factors have helped Brazil become an important industrial nation?

Brazil's **economy** is the largest in South America and one of the largest in the world. Brazil's climate makes it possible for the nation to grow a wide range of crops. The abundance of natural resources, used to develop a variety of industries and manufactured goods, has helped to make Brazil a growing economic power. **Hydroelectricity**, or electric power generated by water, is provided by power plants along the Amazon River and many other rivers flowing through Brazil. Hydroelectricity supplies most of the energy needed to run these industries.

Itaipu Dam The dam, built on the Paraná River, provides about 25 percent of Brazil's power.

Agriculture About one-fifth of Brazil's workers are employed in agriculture. Most farming and livestock grazing takes place in the southern and southeastern parts of Brazil, which have the nation's best soil and climate for agriculture. Farms and ranches in this part of Brazil are generally large and **mechanized**. Farms in the northern part of Brazil, however, are smaller and generally depend on manual labor to produce crops.

Brazil is one of the world's leading exporters of agricultural products, second only to the United States. Brazil is the world's largest producer of sugar cane and coffee. It is a major producer of soybeans (the nation's primary farm **export**), oranges, wheat, corn, and beef, as well as a world leader in the raising of cattle, hogs, and poultry.

Industries Brazil is rich in minerals, and a major producer of the world's gold and diamonds. Brazil has large deposits of iron, manganese, and bauxite, which are important raw materials used in manufacturing. Most large manufacturing plants are located in Brazil's southeastern section. In recent years, Brazil has invested in high-tech equipment to run its manufacturing industries, which employ about 10 percent of its workers. Brazil has one of the largest steel plants in Latin America and is a world leader in automobile production.

CONNECT Geography & Economics

Deforestation More than half of the Amazon rain forest is located in Brazil. As Brazil's economy developed, many people moved to the Amazon region to develop its resources. Several economic activities have contributed to deforestation, including:

- logging by the timber industry to export woods such as mahogany
- clearing the forests for raising crops and livestock and for housing
- mining minerals for export and as raw materials

CRITICAL THINKING

Make Inferences How might the opportunity to make money contribute to deforestation?

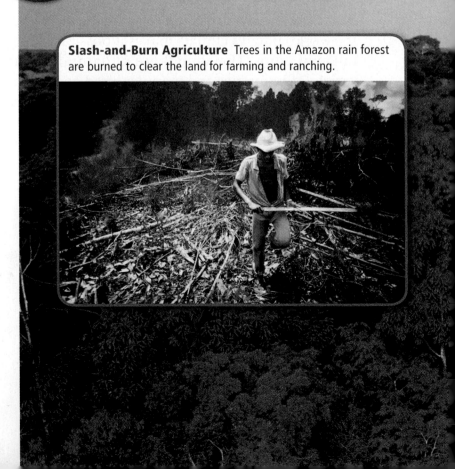

Slash-and-Burn Agriculture Trees in the Amazon rain forest are burned to clear the land for farming and ranching.

Service industries employ about half of Brazil's workers. Many Brazilians work for government agencies, hotels and restaurants, and stores.

Brazil is leading the way in becoming energy **self-sufficient**. Hydroelectric power from Brazil's major rivers provide most of the nation's energy needs. In fact, Brazil expects to become energy-independent in the near future.

▲ **ANALYZE CAUSES AND EFFECTS** Explain why Brazil has become an important industrial nation.

Preserving the Rain Forest

▼ **KEY QUESTION** Why is preserving the rain forest important?

The Amazon **rain forest**, the world's largest rain forest, covers one-third of South America. In the past, rain forests covered about 14 percent of the Earth's surface. Today, because of **deforestation**, the cutting down and clearing away of trees, rain forests cover only 6 percent of the Earth's surface.

Sloth The sloth makes its home in the treetops of the rain forest. **How might deforestation affect this animal?**

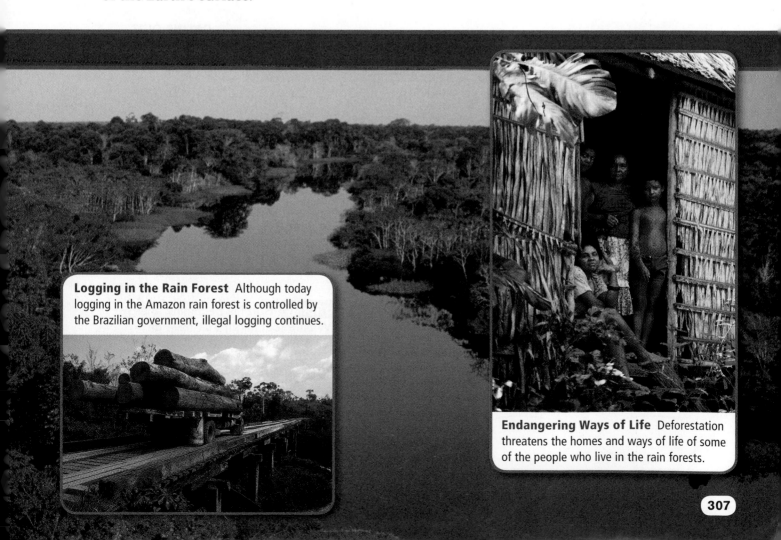

Logging in the Rain Forest Although today logging in the Amazon rain forest is controlled by the Brazilian government, illegal logging continues.

Endangering Ways of Life Deforestation threatens the homes and ways of life of some of the people who live in the rain forests.

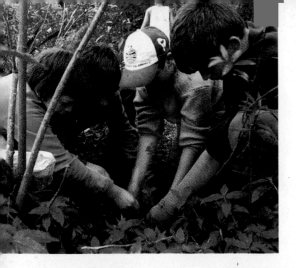

Why Save It? You read earlier in this book that the rain forest is an important resource. Rain forests help to regulate the world's climate by absorbing carbon dioxide and producing oxygen. As trees are cut down, less carbon dioxide is absorbed, which contributes to **global warming**. Rain forests are home to millions of species of plants and animals, more than half of the world's species. Many medicines are made from rain-forest plants. Destroying rain forests endangers the traditional ways of life of some of the people who live there.

Preserving the Brazilian Rain Forest These children are planting trees to reverse the effects of deforestation.

What Is Being Done? Many governments, groups, and individuals are working to preserve the rain forests. Recently, Brazil's government presented plans to declare about 193,000 square miles of the Amazon rain forest a protected area. Some groups raise money to buy land to create large rain forest reserves. Some organize protests against plans that might result in deforestation. Others organize boycotts of products that destroy the forests. To **boycott** is to stop buying or using certain products as a form of protest. Still others work to educate people about the importance of rain forests to the world.

 SUMMARIZE Explain why preserving rain forests is important.

ONLINE QUIZ
For test practice, go to
Interactive Review
@ ClassZone.com

Section ❸ Assessment

TERMS & NAMES

1. Explain the importance of
- hydroelectricity
- ethanol
- deforestation
- boycott

USE YOUR READING NOTES

2. Find Main Ideas Use your web diagram to answer the following question:

What industry employs half of Brazilian workers?

ECONOMY

KEY IDEAS

3. What is Brazil's major export crop?

4. Where does most farming take place in Brazil?

5. How is Brazil becoming energy self-sufficient?

CRITICAL THINKING

6. Analyze Causes and Effects What effect has rain-forest deforestation had on the world's climate?

7. Identify Problems and Solutions What do you think is the best solution for curbing the deforestation of rain forests?

8. **CONNECT to Today** Brazil is becoming energy-independent. What effect might that have on Brazil's economy?

9. **LANGUAGE ARTS** **Write a Slogan** Imagine that you are working for an organization dedicated to preserving the rain forest. Write a slogan for the organization to use to educate people about the reasons that preserving rain forests is important.

Interactive ← Review

Click here to complete these and other activities online @ ClassZone.com

CHAPTER SUMMARY

Key Idea 1
Brazil's government is dealing with the problems resulting from urbanization.

Key Idea 2
Several cultures have influenced Brazil's unique culture.

Key Idea 3
An abundance of natural resources helps make Brazil a major industrial nation.

For **Review and Study Notes**, go to Interactive Review @ ClassZone.com

NAME GAME

Use the Terms & Names list to complete each sentence on paper or online.

1. I am the capital of Brazil. __Brasília__

2. I am a community created by escaped African slaves. _____

3. I am the first emperor of Brazil.
   _____

4. I am a government official who helped abolish slavery in Brazil. _____

5. I am the city famous for Carnival.
   _____

6. I am the music of Brazil that is best known worldwide. _____

7. I am a neighborhood located in areas surrounding big cities.
   _____

8. I am a cleaner, renewable fuel for cars.
   _____

9. I am a religious practice brought from Africa to Brazil. _____

10. I destroy millions of acres of forest.
    _____

Brasília
Candomblé
capoeira
cuíca
deforestation
Dom Pedro I
Dom Pedro II
ethanol
favela
quilombo
Rio de Janeiro
samba

Activities

Flip Cards

Use the online flip cards to quiz yourself on the terms and names introduced in this chapter.

Pedro Álvares Cabral

Portuguese explorer who claimed Brazil for Portugal

Crossword Puzzle

Complete an online puzzle to test your knowledge of Brazil's history, economy, and culture.

ACROSS
1. friction drum used in the samba

VOCABULARY

Explain the significance of each of the following.

1. Treaty of Tordesillas
2. Pedro Álvares Cabral
3. Dom Pedro I
4. Dom Pedro II
5. Brasília
6. Rio de Janeiro
7. hydroelectricity
8. ethanol
9. deforestation
10. boycott

Explain how the terms and names in each group are related.

11. *Candomblé, cuíca,* and *quilombos*
12. samba and *capoeira*

KEY IDEAS

① From Portuguese Colony to Modern Giant

13. What explorer claimed Brazil for Portugal?
14. How did Brazil become independent?
15. What is Brazil's biggest economic challenge?
16. How has Brazil's urban population changed in the last half of the 20th century?

② A Multicultural Society

17. What Portuguese influences are seen in Brazil today?
18. Where does the largest Japanese population live in Brazil today?
19. How have Africans influenced Brazilian culture?
20. Why is Carnival considered a blend of European and African traditions?

③ Developing an Abundant Land

21. How has having an abundance of natural resources benefited Brazil?
22. Why does most farming and ranching in Brazil take place in the southern and southeastern parts?
23. What provides most of Brazil's energy needs?
24. What actions are people taking today to help preserve the rain forest?

CRITICAL THINKING

25. **Analyze Causes and Effects** Create a diagram to explain the causes of deforestation of the Amazon rain forest.

26. **Evaluate** How did the introduction of coffee plants in Brazil affect its economy?
27. **Summarize** What did Brazil's government do to try to relieve overcrowding in its cities?
28. **Five Themes: Human-Environment Interaction** How might deforestation affect the Indians of the Amazon rain forest?
29. **Connect to Economics** Why is narrowing the income gap important for Brazil's government to address?
30. **Connect Geography & History** What historical events have contributed to Brazil's cultural diversity?

Answer the ESSENTIAL QUESTION

How have Brazil's people used the country's abundant natural resources to make Brazil an economic giant?

Written response Write a two- or three-paragraph response to the Essential Question. Be sure to consider the key ideas of each section. Use the rubric below to guide your thinking.

Response Rubric
A strong response will:
• include how Brazil's natural resources have contributed to the growth of industries
• explain how Brazilian Indians, Africans, and European and Asian immigrants have helped make Brazil an economic power

✓ Test Practice

• Online Test Practice @ ClassZone.com

• Test-Taking Strategies and Practice
  at the front of this book

PRIMARY SOURCE

Use the primary source below to answer
questions 1 and 2.

> It is not just those who depend directly
> on the tropical forests who suffer from
> deforestation, but the entire population of
> tropical forest countries. The forests assist
> in the regulation of local climate patterns,
> protecting watersheds, preventing floods,
> guaranteeing and controlling huge flows
> of life-giving water. Strip away the forests
> and there is, first, too much water . . .
> and then too little.
>
> Source: Charles, Prince of Wales, from a
> speech given on February 6, 1990

1. What observation does the passage support?

A. Deforestation hurts no one.

B. Deforestation prevents flooding.

C. Rain forests help to prevent floods.

D. Rain forests affect only a few people.

2. What is the best title for this passage?

A. Prince Charles Helps the Rain Forests

B. Where Are the Rain Forests?

C. Deforestation—Is It Serious?

D. The Rain Forest and Water Supply

LINE GRAPH

Use the graph below to answer questions
3 and 4.

Population in São Paulo and Rio de Janeiro 1970–2000

Source: United Nations Department of Economic and
Social Affairs/Population Division, *World Urbanization
Prospects: The 2003 Revision*

**3. What was the population of Rio de Janeiro
in 2000?**

**4. Between what years did São Paulo's
population increase the most?**

GeoActivity

1. INTERDISCIPLINARY ACTIVITY–SCIENCE

Research the four layers of a
tropical rain forest. Find out the
differences in the four layers, the
kinds of plants that grow there,
and the kinds of animals that live
in each layer. Include a diagram to
illustrate the four layers.

2. WRITING FOR SOCIAL STUDIES

Unit Writing Project Decide
on the place from your
journal that you found most
interesting, and find more
information about it. Then write
an article for a travel magazine
describing the place and giving
reasons for people to visit it.

3. MENTAL MAPPING

Create an outline map of Brazil
and label the following:

• Bahia
• Salvador
• São Paulo
• Brasília
• Rio de Janeiro
• The Amazon River

UNIT 4

Europe

Why It Matters:

In the past, Europeans used the oceans and seas to make voyages for trade and to build empires. Their culture spread around the world. Today, Europeans still play a large part in world affairs.

The Alps

CHAPTER 11 Europe: Physical Geography and History

Notre Dame Cathedral

CHAPTER 12 Western Europe

London Street Scene

CHAPTER 13 United Kingdom

Prague, Czech Republic

CHAPTER 14 Eastern Europe

The cultures of ancient Greece and Rome shaped the people who came after them. The influence of both cultures can still be seen today.

Greece

The Greeks developed new ideas about architecture and the gods. They created a new art form—the Greek drama. Other cultures, including ancient Rome, picked up many of these ideas. We can still see ancient Greece in ruins like the Acropolis, shown below, and reflected in our own culture.

Religion

Poseidon is the Greek god of the sea. The Greeks often showed their gods as looking like human beings, but with divine powers.

Daily Life

Greek pottery provides a good record of daily life. This pot shows women collecting water from a public fountain.

Entertainment

Many Greek plays were performed during religious festivals, in large amphitheaters.

Rome

Roman culture was based on values of strength and loyalty. The Romans picked up some Greek ideas about the gods and architecture. They transformed these ideas into styles that were uniquely Roman, as seen in the Forum, shown below.

Religion

The Romans called the god of the sea Neptune. Roman depictions of their gods and goddesses frequently seem more realistic and three-dimensional than those of the Greeks.

Daily Life

Agriculture and trade formed the basis of the Roman economy. Shops occupied the ground story of many ancient buildings.

Entertainment

Chariot races, which took place in oval arenas called circuses, drew huge crowds.

CRITICAL THINKING

1. **Compare and Contrast** What do their forms of entertainment suggest about the differences between Greek and Roman culture?

2. **Make Inferences** Why might these cultures have saved their classical buildings?

Italy can be roughly divided into three regions: northern, central, and southern. While northern and southern Italy share aspects of Italian culture, they are also different.

Northern Italy

The craggy Alps of northern Italy are dotted with villages, such as St. Magdalena, shown below. Tourists often come to hike or ski in the mountains. The northern region is also highly industrialized, however, with major metropolitan areas such as Milan and Turin. Many of Italy's cities with populations of 100,000 or greater are in the north.

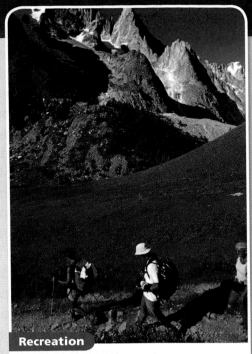

Recreation

Like these hikers, many people enjoy the rugged trails winding through the Italian Alps.

Work

Northern Italy has more factories than farms defining the region's major cities. Workers at this factory in Bologna manufacture Ducati motorcycles.

Southern Italy

Southern Italy also has mountains, but it benefits more from the coastline along the Mediterranean and Adriatic seas than does northern Italy. Many of the tourists visiting southern Italy come to relax on sandy beaches in towns such as Minori, shown below.

The south is also much less industrialized than the north. Southern Italy has fewer big cities and more people are employed in agriculture, such as growing and harvesting grapes and olives.

Recreation

Sunbathers lounge on the beach in Sorrento, enjoying its warm Mediterranean climate.

Work

These men are gathering olives to make olive oil in an orchard in Bisceglie. It is located in the southern region of Puglia, where the arid climate is particularly suited to growing olives.

CRITICAL THINKING

1. **Compare and Contrast** What geographic features are characteristic of each region?

2. **Make Inferences** Which region do you think is wealthier and why?

369

Reading for Understanding

SECTION 2

▶ Key Ideas

BEFORE, YOU LEARNED

After the division and fall of the Roman Empire, Greece and Italy developed into different nations.

NOW YOU WILL LEARN

Like Greece and Italy, Spain and Portugal were ruled by foreigners. After gaining independence, both developed overseas empires to fuel their economies.

▶ Vocabulary

TERMS & NAMES

Moors the group of Muslims from North Africa who conquered Spain in the eighth century

Reconquista the successful effort by the Spanish to drive the Moors out of Spain

Christopher Columbus Italian navigator and explorer who sailed for Spain and explored the Caribbean and the coast of Central and South America

Basque (bask) an ethnic group living in the western Pyrenees and along the Bay of Biscay in Spain and France; also the name of their language

BACKGROUND VOCABULARY

separatist a person who wants a region to break away from the nation it is a part of

Visual Vocabulary Christopher Columbus reaches the New World.

▶ Reading Strategy

Re-create the Venn diagram shown at right. As you read and respond to the **KEY QUESTIONS**, use the diagram to help you compare and contrast Spain and Portugal.

 Skillbuilder Handbook, page R9

COMPARE AND CONTRAST

SPAIN   BOTH   PORTUGAL

GRAPHIC ORGANIZERS
Go to **Interactive Review** @ClassZone.com

②
FOCUS ON

Spain and Portugal

Connecting to Your World

Without ever visiting Spain, most Americans know more about Spanish culture than they think. For over 300 years, Spain had an empire in what is today Mexico and the southwestern United States. In places where Spain once ruled, the impact of Spanish culture is easy to see. Many southwestern cities have Spanish names and buildings influenced by Spanish architecture. Throughout the United States, many people speak Spanish and eat Spanish food. Spanish culture itself was the product of influences from many other cultures.

Spain

▼ **KEY QUESTION** What regional differences affect Spain's culture?

For centuries, Spain was part of the Roman Empire. When the empire fell, a Germanic tribe conquered the peninsula and established a Christian kingdom. It lasted until the early A.D. 700s, when the **Moors**, Muslim peoples from North Africa, took control of southern Spain. Spain's Moorish rulers brought a more advanced culture to medieval Europe. Muslim scholars made new discoveries in medicine, mathematics, and other fields. They remained there for almost eight centuries, when groups of Christians still living in northern Spain succeeded in driving them out of the region.

Spanish Food
Spanish food—including small appetizers called *tapas*, such as this squid dish—has become popular in the United States.

The Alhambra
Located in Granada, Spain, the Alhambra was a Moorish palace and fortress.

SPAIN

● Granada

Click here to enter Victorian London @ ClassZone.com

LONDON AROUND 1890

London grew rapidly during the 19th century. By 1901, over 6.5 million people lived there. All these people required services, such as transportation and law enforcement. Rapid growth also affected London society as different social classes interacted.

 Click here to experience what daily life in Victorian London would have been like. Learn more about the different social classes that shared the city, such as the upper-class residents shown above. See some of the public services needed to keep the city running, including electricity and the London Underground.

 Click here to learn more about the economic activities that might have taken place in this important commercial center. Connected to the world by the Thames River, the city attracted all types of businesses, from street stalls to major factories.

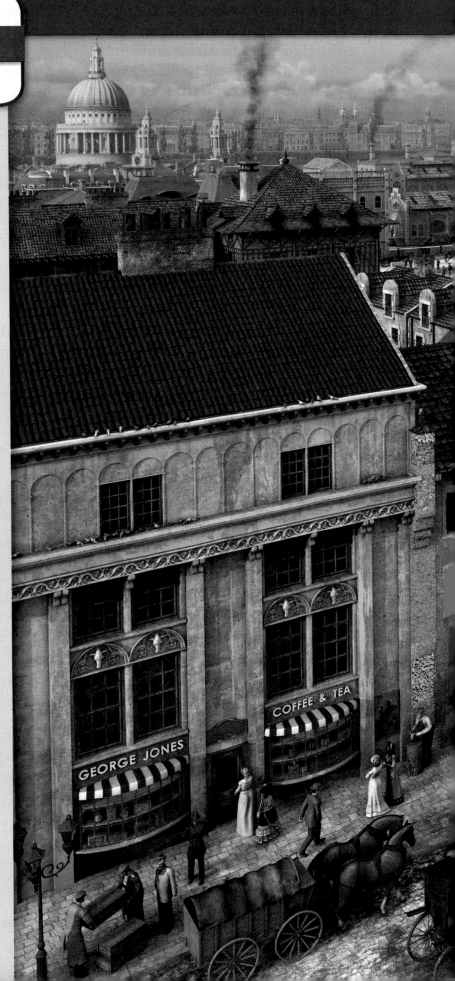

Growth of London

London, 1700
Growth to 1800
Growth to 1900
Greater London, 2007

0 2.5 5 miles
0 2.5 5 kilometers

N

Thames River

GeoActivity

A Victorian Talk Show
Break into groups of four. One person will pretend to be someone from this London street who is appearing on a talk show. The rest of the group will interview him or her. Choose the best question and answer from your group and share it with the class.

Reading for Understanding

▶ Key Ideas

BEFORE, YOU LEARNED

Great Britain became an industrial leader with a worldwide empire. Today, it no longer has a great empire, but it remains a respected European power.

NOW YOU WILL LEARN

Britain's history as an industrial and colonial power has shaped its culture. Britain's increasingly diverse population continues to enrich its cultural life.

▶ Vocabulary

TERMS & NAMES

Briton a British person

Gaelic any of the Celtic family of languages spoken in Ireland or Scotland

multicultural relating to or including many different cultures

Church of England the official church of England headed by the Archbishop of Canterbury

William Shakespeare an English playwright and poet during the late 16th and early 17th centuries

REVIEW

immigrant a person who leaves one area to settle in another

Visual Vocabulary William Shakespeare

▶ Reading Strategy

Re-create the web diagram shown at right. As you read and respond to the **KEY QUESTIONS**, use the diagram to help you find main ideas about British culture.

 Skillbuilder Handbook, page R4

FIND MAIN IDEAS

- Literature
- Multi-culturalism
- Leisure Time
- BRITISH CULTURE
- Bustling Cities
- Music

GRAPHIC ORGANIZERS
Go to **Interactive Review @ ClassZone.com**

From Shakespeare to J. K. Rowling

Connecting to Your World

Have you ever read a Harry Potter book? One day in 1990, an idea for a book popped into the head of J. K. Rowling, a British author. She wanted to write about a young boy named Harry who could do magic. Today, millions of people around the world know about this boy. Rowling's Harry Potter books have made publishing history, selling out at bookstores hours after they are put on the shelves. Rowling is just one part of Great Britain's rich cultural heritage.

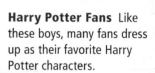

Harry Potter Fans Like these boys, many fans dress up as their favorite Harry Potter characters.

Life in the United Kingdom

▼ **KEY QUESTION** What influences have made British culture more diverse in recent years?

Before World War II, most British people shared the same ethnicity and religious beliefs. Today, people of many different faiths and customs make their home in the United Kingdom. Many of them have immigrated from the former colonies of the British empire. The influence of these newcomers can be seen throughout Britain. Although some changes have caused tensions, the mix of old and new traditions is making many British cities lively places to live.

Tower Bridge The Tower Bridge, built in 1894, spans the Thames River near London's modern City Hall, the round building at right.

Reading for Understanding

▶ Key Ideas

BEFORE, YOU LEARNED

European nations experienced many changes after World War II.

NOW YOU WILL LEARN

Poland, Ukraine, and the Baltic States faced many challenges after shaking off Communist rule.

▶ Vocabulary

TERMS & NAMES

Baltic States Latvia, Lithuania, and Estonia, three countries that border the Baltic Sea

Lech Walesa (lehk wah•LEHN•suh) Polish leader who cofounded Solidarity and served as president of Poland from 1990 to 1995

Solidarity Poland's first independent labor union, cofounded by Lech Walesa

Russification the effort to make countries occupied by the Soviet Union more Russian by replacing local languages and customs

bread basket an abundant grain-producing region

deport to expel from a country

BACKGROUND VOCABULARY

brain drain the loss of skilled workers who move in search of better opportunities

REVIEW

communism a type of government in which the Communist Party holds all political power and controls the economy

command economy an economic system in which the production of goods and services is decided by a central government

market economy an economic system in which the production of goods and services is decided by the supply of goods and the demand of consumers

▶ Reading Strategy

Re-create the chart shown at right. As you read and respond to the **KEY QUESTIONS**, use the chart to help you categorize information about the Eastern European nations in this chapter.

 Skillbuilder Handbook, page R7

CATEGORIZE

	LANGUAGE	GOVERNMENT	ECONOMY
Poland			
Ukraine			
Latvia			
Lithuania			
Estonia			

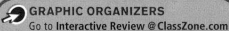 **GRAPHIC ORGANIZERS**
Go to **Interactive Review** @ClassZone.com

Poland, Ukraine, and the Baltic States

Connecting to Your World

After the American Revolution, Americans quickly learned that building a strong independent nation was not easy. It took time to create a stable government and prosperous economy. In this section, you will read about Poland, Ukraine, and the three **Baltic States**, Latvia, Lithuania, and Estonia. Along with the rest of Eastern Europe, they gained independence from **communism** in the 1990s. Like the United States, they faced difficult choices. Many countries found the new freedom challenging.

Poland

▼ **KEY QUESTION** What actions did government leaders take to prepare Poland for a market economy?

Poland's name comes from the Slavic word *Polanie*, which means plain or field. The Northern European Plain covers much of Poland. Its flat, fertile land began attracting Slavic settlers as early as 2000 B.C. During the Middle Ages, Poland ruled an empire that covered much of central and eastern Europe. By the late 18th century, however, Poland was conquered by its neighbors. It did not regain its independence until after World War I.

Polish Countryside
Freshly plowed fields cover these gently rolling hills in the Roztocze region of southeast Poland.

POLAND

Roztocze

History During World War II, both Germany and the Soviet Union, a union of Communist republics led by Russia, invaded Poland. At the end of the war, Soviet troops drove the Germans out of Poland and supported Communists in gaining control of the government. By the 1950s, Communist rule was firmly established in Poland and throughout Eastern Europe. Communist leaders took over the economy and limited the rights of citizens.

During the 1970s, Poland faced food shortages and rising prices. As economic conditions worsened, people questioned Communist rule. In 1980, thousands of Polish workers went on strike, led by **Lech Walesa** (lehk wah•LEHN•suh). They demanded better pay, greater political freedom, and recognition of **Solidarity**, the nation's first independent labor union. Communist leaders saw public support for Solidarity growing. In 1989, they reached an agreement with Solidarity that led to government reform. Poland held its first free elections. The new government lifted many restrictions on Polish citizens.

Culture Before World War II, Poland was a diverse nation, with Germans, Jews, Ukrainians, and other ethnic groups. However, the war caused many groups to migrate and shifted Poland's borders. Almost all of the 3 million Jews living in Poland were killed during the Holocaust. Today, most people in Poland are Poles. Their ancestors belonged to the Slavic tribes that settled in Poland long ago. Polish, a Slavic language, is spoken throughout the country.

Catholic Mourners
People gather in Pilsudski Square in Warsaw, Poland, to mourn the death of Pope John Paul II.

Most Poles are Roman Catholics, which unites the Polish people. During Communist rule, when religious practice was restricted, many continued to practice the Catholic faith. In 1978, Cardinal Karol Wojtyla (voy•TIH•wah) became the world's first Polish pope, Pope John Paul II. He made Catholic Poles very proud. In visits to Poland, he encouraged efforts to gain greater freedom.

Poland has a rich cultural tradition, with a strong emphasis on education. Many outstanding scientists, such as Nicolaus Copernicus and Marie Curie, were Polish. Like other nations, Poland has to work hard to preserve its folk culture in the face of mass media and urbanization.

Government and Economics In 1990, Lech Walesa became Poland's first president. He helped Poland shift to democracy. In 1997, Poland adopted a new constitution to reflect its democratic government. Today, Poland is a republic. Voters elect the nation's president and legislature. The prime minister runs the government.

In the 1990s, Poland's leaders enacted a series of economic reforms to pave the way from a **command economy** to a **market economy**. Polish leaders sold government-owned industries to private companies. They shut down many old and inefficient factories and invited foreign companies to invest in Poland. Today, the country's major industries include production of coal, iron, steel, and machinery. Poland also has a large shipbuilding industry. Poland joined the European Union in 2004. Membership gave it new markets for such farm products as potatoes and rye and for manufactured goods.

Although Poland's transition to a market economy was more successful than that of many Eastern European nations, it still faces many economic challenges. High unemployment remains a serious problem. Factory closings have left many workers without jobs. Lack of good jobs for skilled workers has caused a serious **brain drain**, as many of Poland's bright young people leave the country in search of better job opportunities in Western Europe or the United States.

🔺 **SUMMARIZE** Explain how Poland became a market economy.

↪ **ONLINE PRIMARY SOURCE** To read the rest of Walesa's speech, go to the **Research & Writing Center** @ ClassZone.com

ANALYZING Primary Sources

Lech Walesa (born 1943) led the struggle to form Solidarity. His peaceful resistance helped end Communist rule in Poland.

> We respect the dignity and the rights of every man and every nation. The path to a brighter future of the world leads through honest reconciliation [resolution] of the conflicting interests and not through hatred and bloodshed.
>
> Source: Lech Walesa, Nobel Peace Prize acceptance speech, 1983

DOCUMENT–BASED QUESTION
How does Walesa suggest conflicts among nations should be settled?

Solidarność REG. PIŁA

UKRAINE

Ukraine

▼ **KEY QUESTION** How did Soviet control affect the economy and culture of Ukraine?

For Ukraine, once a part of the Soviet Union, independence has not been easy. Nearby Russia still plays a part in its political and economic life. Ukraine faces many challenges as it seeks ties with the West while maintaining good relations with Russia.

History In the 800s, the town of Kiev in Ukraine was the center of the first eastern Slavic state, Kievan Rus. After 400 years as a powerful state, invading nomads conquered the territory. Ukraine came under foreign rule for centuries. By the late 1700s, it was part of the Russian Empire. In 1922, Ukraine became one of the first Soviet republics.

Soviet policies caused great hardships for the nation. In the 1930s, the Soviets took land from Ukrainian farmers to form huge, government-run farms called collectives. They required almost all crops to be sent to cities to feed the workers there. Millions of farm families starved. On April 26, 1986, the world's worst nuclear power accident occurred in Ukraine at the Chernobyl power plant. Radiation from Chernobyl has affected an estimated 7 million people in and around Ukraine.

Ukrainians had been protesting Soviet rule since the 1960s. When the Soviet Union collapsed in 1991, Ukraine finally gained its independence and began to rebuild.

CONNECT to Science

The Chernobyl explosion put large amounts of radiation into the atmosphere. The chart below shows the radiation released by a form of radioactive iodine during the week after the accident. The petabecquerel, or PBq, is a measure of radioactivity. For reference, a household smoke detector, which is very safe, emits 0.00000000003 PBq of radiation.

◄ *radiation inspectors*

Date of Release	Amount (in PBq)
April 26	704
April 27	204
April 28	150
April 29	102
April 30	69
May 1	62
May 2	102

Source: Nuclear Energy Agency, "Chernobyl: Assessment of Radiological and Health Impacts"

Activity

Make a Line Graph

Materials
- Graph paper
- Markers

1. Draw two lines for your graph. Label the vertical axis "Level of Radiation" and the horizontal axis "Date of Radiation Release."

2. Divide the horizontal axis into ten segments and label each. Divide the vertical axis into units of 100. Put a dot on the graph that represents the radiation measured for each date. Connect the dots. Title your line graph.

Culture About three-fourths of Ukraine's population is ethnic Ukrainian. Russians are the largest ethnic minority, at about one-fifth of the population. Under Soviet rule, the government imposed a **Russification** policy on the country. The Russian language replaced Ukrainian in schools, newspapers, and the government. After decades of speaking Russian, many Ukrainians knew it better than their native language. In 1991, Ukrainian became the official language, but Russian is still widely spoken.

About two-thirds of Ukrainians live in Kiev and other cities. Western Ukraine is heavily rural. Most people in rural areas live in large villages. They are employed in farming or in making small handicrafts, such as the traditional decorated eggs known as *pysanky*.

Government and Economics In 1990, Ukraine held its first free, multiparty election. Today, Ukraine is a democracy with a president, prime minister, and legislature. Ukrainians are committed to free elections. In 2004, tens of thousands of them took part in the Orange Revolution, a peaceful protest against fraud in the presidential election.

Ukrainians remain divided on plans for reform. Some favor closer ties to Russia. Others hope for EU membership and trade with Western Europe. Ukraine maintains good relations with Russia, whom it depends on for oil and natural gas. Ukraine belongs to the Commonwealth of Independent States (CIS), a group of former Soviet republics that cooperate on political and economic matters.

Ukraine is rich in natural resources and fertile soil. Most heavy industries are in eastern Ukraine near the nation's coal deposits. Ukraine's rich soil has made it the **bread basket**, or major grain-producing region, of Europe. However, Ukraine has lagged behind many former Communist countries in converting to private ownership. Many farms and factories also lack modern equipment.

▲ ANALYZE EFFECTS
Identify how Soviet control affected Ukraine's economy and culture.

Pysanky

Beautifully decorated Easter eggs known as *pysanky* are among the most famous Ukrainian crafts. The word *pysanky* means "written egg." Artists create intricate and colorful designs by drawing patterns on the eggs with wax and then dipping them in different-colored dyes. The wax prevents parts of the egg from picking up color. Many of the images and colors on the egg have special meaning. Designs are often passed down within a family for generations. The eggs are given as gifts during the Easter holiday.

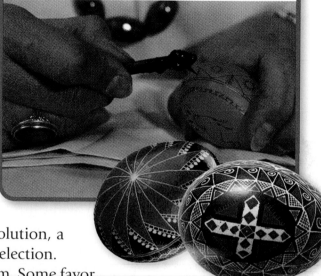

Ukrainian Farm
Farmers harvest wheat on a collective farm near Lvov, Ukraine. **How does equipment affect farm production?**

ESTONIA
LATVIA
LITHUANIA

The Baltic States

▼ **KEY QUESTION** How are the Baltic States alike and different from each other?

The Baltic States—Estonia, Latvia, and Lithuania—share a coastline on the Baltic Sea. They also share the challenge of becoming part of prosperous, modern Europe.

Striving for Independence The Baltic States have a long history of foreign rule. At different times, Danes, Swedes, Poles, and Germans have controlled them. By the late 1700s, they belonged to the vast Russian Empire. They remained a part of it until it ended in 1918. In 1940, the Soviet Union occupied the Baltic States and forced them to join it. In all three countries, the Soviets decided to **deport**, or expel, the thousands of people who resisted their rule. The Soviets brought in Russian workers to replace them. In 1990, the Baltic States became the first Soviet republics to declare independence. The Soviet Union formally recognized their claims in September 1991.

Culture Although they share a common history, each Baltic state has its own language and customs. In Lithuania, most people speak Lithuanian and are Roman Catholics. The people of Latvia speak Latvian, while Estonians speak Estonian, a language related to Finnish. Most Estonians and Latvians are Lutheran Protestants.

Throughout the Baltic States, the Soviet policy of Russification brought population changes. For instance, before Soviet rule, Latvians made up three-fourths of that country's population. Now they make up just over half. In each country, Russians are the largest minority. During the Soviet era, many people left farms and villages to work in urban factories. Today, two-thirds of the people in the Baltic States live in cities. The people of Latvia, Lithuania, and Estonia have had to work to preserve their own languages, customs, and traditions.

Song Festival These girls are dressed up to participate in the All-Estonian Song Festival, held every five years in the capital city of Tallinn.

Government and Economics The Baltic States are republics with an elected president and legislature. A prime minister heads the government and carries out government operations.

The Baltic States are now successful market economies. Most industries and farms are privately owned. In 2004 all became EU members. Germany has become a key trade partner, while trade with Russia is decreasing. Estonia's major industries are electronics, wood products, and textiles. Latvia's factories make vehicles, farm machinery, and fertilizers. Lithuania produces machine tools, appliances, and electric motors.

During decades of Communist rule, government leaders ignored many serious environmental problems. Old and faulty wastewater-treatment plants, leaking sewers, and fertilizer, oil, and chemical run-off from factories and farms have polluted the Baltic Sea. All Baltic countries are now involved in the cleanup.

Independence Rally
Many Eastern European nations held rallies to protest Communist rule, such as this one in Kaunas in southern Lithuania in 1989.

 COMPARE AND CONTRAST Explain how the Baltic States are similar to and different from each other.

Section 1 Assessment

ONLINE QUIZ
For test practice, go to
Interactive Review
@ ClassZone.com

TERMS & NAMES

1. Explain the importance of
- Baltic States
- Solidarity
- Russification
- deport

USE YOUR READING NOTES

2. Categorize Use your completed chart to answer the following question:

What kind of government does Poland have?

	LANGUAGE	GOVERNMENT	ECONOMY
Poland			
Ukraine			
Latvia			
Lithuania			
Estonia			

KEY IDEAS

3. What were the goals of Solidarity in Poland?

4. How did the Soviet Union carry out its Russification policy in the Ukraine?

5. What environmental issue do the Baltic States face today?

CRITICAL THINKING

6. Form and Support Opinions Why do many Eastern European countries want to join the European Union?

7. Analyze Causes and Effects Why are many people in the Baltic States concerned about each country's national identity?

8. CONNECT to Today Why might Polish leaders want to encourage young people to stay in Poland?

9. ART Give a Presentation Do research to learn more about one of the folk arts of the countries in this section. Give a short presentation on where and how this craft is made, how it is used, and any customs associated with it. Show pictures of the craft.

Reading for Understanding

▶ Key Ideas

BEFORE, YOU LEARNED

Independence brought political and economic changes and new challenges for Poland, Ukraine, and the Baltic States.

NOW YOU WILL LEARN

After decades of Communist rule, Hungary and the Czech Republic made economic and political reforms.

▶ Vocabulary

TERMS & NAMES

Magyar an ethnic Hungarian person or the Hungarian language

Czechoslovakia (CHEHK•uh•sluh•VAH•kee•uh) former country in Eastern Europe that existed from 1918 until 1993, when it split into the Czech Republic and Slovakia

Velvet Revolution the peaceful protest by the Czech people that led to the smooth end of communism in Czechoslovakia

BACKGROUND VOCABULARY

strategic relating to a plan of action designed to achieve a specific goal

standard of living an economic measure relating to the quality and amount of goods available to a group of people and how those goods are distributed across the group

eclectic made up of parts from a variety of sources

Visual Vocabulary Velvet Revolution

▶ Reading Strategy

Re-create the Venn diagram shown at right. As you read and respond to the **KEY QUESTIONS**, use the diagram to help you compare and contrast Hungary and the Czech Republic.

 Skillbuilder Handbook, page R9

COMPARE AND CONTRAST

HUNGARY   BOTH   CZECH REPUBLIC

GRAPHIC ORGANIZERS
Go to **Interactive Review @ ClassZone.com**

Hungary and the Czech Republic

Connecting to Your World

Have you ever played chess or checkers? In these games, the player who controls the middle of the board can have a **strategic** advantage. That player can move in many different directions. Hungary sits right between the eastern and western regions of Europe and shares borders with seven other countries. It can choose which neighbors to befriend. Unlike good chess players, however, Hungary did not always have a choice about which way it moved.

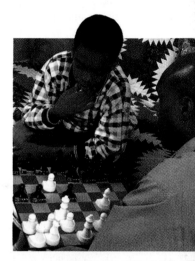

Playing Chess A boy learns to play chess from his father.

Hungary

▼ **KEY QUESTION** How is Hungary's location an advantage in rebuilding its economy?

Hungary's central location attracted many groups. Hungary's earliest settlers were the **Magyar**, or ethnic Hungarian, people. In the late tenth century, Magyar leaders created a stable and prosperous kingdom. Then, in 1526, the Ottoman Turks and Austria conquered and divided Hungary's territory. Eventually, Austria drove out the Ottomans and took over. Hungary fought for independence from Austria's harsh rule.

Budapest The Széchenyi Chain Bridge was the first to cross the Danube River in Budapest.

Budapest
HUNGARY

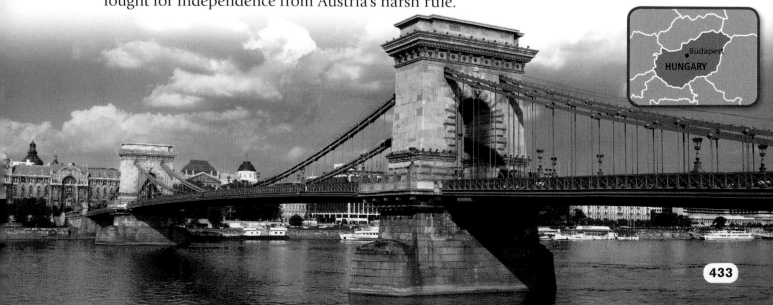

History By 1867, Austria had been weakened by many costly wars, and it was forced to share power with Hungary. Together they ruled an empire known as Austria-Hungary. During World War I, Austria-Hungary fought on the losing side. After its defeat, its territory was divided up. Hungary was independent but lost much of its land.

During World War II, Soviet troops invaded Hungary. They were followed by Communist Party agents, who wanted to make sure the Communists gained control of the government. Many Hungarians opposed Communist rule. They resented the loss of their freedom. In 1956, thousands of protesters flooded the streets of Budapest, the nation's capital, demanding that Soviet troops leave. The Soviet Union responded by sending more troops and tanks to crush the uprising. Thousands of protesters died in the fighting.

In later decades, Communist Party officials gave Hungarians greater economic freedom, allowing some private ownership of business. In 1989, as the Soviet government began to fall apart, the Hungarian government agreed to allow other political parties. A year later, Hungarian reformers removed the Communists from power in the country's first free elections.

Culture Most Hungarians are Magyars, descendants of Hungary's early settlers. Hungarians speak Hungarian, also called Magyar, a language related to Finnish and Estonian. As you can see from the map at right, Hungarian is different from the languages spoken in surrounding countries. About two-thirds of Hungarians are Roman Catholics. One-fourth are Protestants. Other ethnic groups include Croats, Roma (also called Gypsies), Romanians, and Slovaks.

During the Communist era, many Hungarians moved from farms to cities. Everyday life changed as a result. In cities today, modern influences like blue jeans and pop music clash with traditional dress and folk songs. Budapest is a good example of Hungary's mix of old and new. It is actually two cities divided by the Danube River. Medieval Buda sits on the western bank and Pest, which underwent a surge of development in the 18th century, sits on the eastern bank.

Fun Facts!

PAPRIKA AND VITAMIN C

Paprika is a very popular spice in Hungarian food. It comes from a pepper that flavors food and also fights the common cold. When a cold starts, many people drink orange juice for extra vitamin C. In 1932, Hungarian scientist Albert Szent-Gyorgyi found that a paprika pepper contains five to six times more vitamin C than an orange.

Traditional and Modern
(left) Teenagers perform at a Hungarian folk dance. (right) The crowd enjoys the show at the Sziget Music Festival in Budapest.

Languages of Eastern Europe

Indo-European Branches
- Baltic
- Slavic
- Romance
- Illyrian

Uralic Branch
- Finno-Ugric

Polish Spoken language

North Sea

Baltic Sea

Estonian

Latvian

Lithuanian

Belarusian

Polish

Czech

Slovak

Ukrainian

Hungarian

Moldovan

Slovene

Adriatic Sea

Serbo-Croatian

Romanian

Bulgarian

Albanian Macedonian

CONNECT Geography & Culture

1. **Place** What language branch does Albanian belong to?
2. **Region** Which branch is most common in Eastern Europe?

Government and Economics Hungary is a parliamentary democracy. Voters elect the members of parliament, called the National Assembly, to serve four-year terms. The National Assembly elects the president and the prime minister. The president—who serves a five-year term—is the commander in chief of the armed forces, but has little power. The prime minister is the head of government.

Before World War II, most Hungarians were farmers living in rural villages. Under Communist rule, officials worked hard to expand industry. As industry increased, many Hungarians moved to cities to work in government-run factories. By the 1990s, employment in agriculture decreased from over half to one-eighth of the population.

In the decades after the failed Hungarian revolt in 1956, the government began to allow some private businesses to operate. After the Communists lost the 1990 elections, Hungary's new leaders lifted many government controls on business and sold most remaining state-owned businesses and farms. The country moved rapidly toward a market economy. Today, it has one of the highest **standards of living** in Eastern Europe. Hungary joined the EU in 2004. The nation's central location and the Danube River help boost trade. EU members Germany, Austria, France, and Italy are its main trade partners.

▲ **FIND MAIN IDEAS** Explain how Hungary's location is helpful in rebuilding its economy.

CZECH REPUBLIC SLOVAKIA

The Czech Republic

▼ **KEY QUESTION** How did freedom from Communist rule change the Czech Republic?

Like Hungary, the Czech Republic was once part of Austria-Hungary. It also spent many decades controlled by a Communist government. Today, it is one of the most prosperous countries in Eastern Europe.

History In the 900s, Slavic peoples established the kingdom of Bohemia alongside two other regions, Moravia and Slovakia. The Czech regions of Bohemia and Moravia maintained close ties throughout their histories. Both became part of the Austrian empire in 1526. Slovakia, a region of Slovaks, became part of Hungary. In 1918, after Austria-Hungary's defeat in World War I, Europe's leaders made the lands that had been Bohemia, Moravia, and Slovakia into the nation of **Czechoslovakia** (CHEHK•uh•sluh•VAH•kee•uh). Czechs and Slovaks were thrown together within the new borders.

Czechoslovakia lasted only a few decades as an independent nation. In 1948, Communists took over the country. In 1968, the Soviet Union crushed efforts by Czech Communist leaders to give citizens greater freedom. Fearing their own people might demand more freedom, the Soviets sent troops and tanks to end protests.

In 1989, thousands of protesters filled the streets of Prague calling for an end to Communist rule. Massive protests convinced Communist leaders to resign. The end of Communist rule took place so smoothly, that this protest became known as the **Velvet Revolution**. In 1990, voters elected protest leader Václav Havel president. Three years later, Czech and Slovak leaders agreed to divide the country into the Czech Republic and Slovakia. Some call this friendly split the "Velvet Divorce."

Culture Most people in the Czech Republic are Czechs. They speak Czech, a Slavic language. The country has many smaller ethnic groups including Slovaks, Germans, Roma (Gypsies), Hungarians, and Poles. Before World War II, Czechoslovakia had a large Jewish population. Almost all the nation's Jews were killed during the Holocaust. Roman Catholics are the largest religious group in the Czech Republic.

HISTORY MAKERS

Václav Havel (born 1936)

Václav Havel's (VAHT-slahv HAH-vuhl) admirers call him a hero for his role in leading the Velvet Revolution. During Czechoslovakia's years of Communist rule, the country's leaders called him a danger to society. A well-known playwright, he spent several years in prison for openly opposing Communist rule. After the end of communism, grateful citizens chose Havel as Czechoslovakia's first president. He later served as the first president of the new Czech Republic.

 ONLINE BIOGRAPHY
For more on the life of Václav Havel, go to the
Research & Writing Center @ ClassZone.com

The Czech Republic has a tradition of fine art. Composer Antonin Dvorák (DVAWR•zhahk) wrote music inspired by the Czech landscape and folk music. Famous Czech writers include Franz Kafka and Milan Kundera, whose books explore the human condition. For centuries, Czech artists have crafted beautiful glassware. Glittering Czech crystal chandeliers hang in opera houses, palaces, and mansions around the world today.

Prague Residents and tourists alike use the Charles Bridge to cross the Vltava River and get around Prague.

The culture of the Czech Republic is a vibrant mix of old and new. Prague is the nation's capital and largest city. In the 1300s, it became a center of art and learning in Europe. The city has many beautiful Renaissance buildings. It is known as the "City of a Hundred Spires" because of the churches that dot its streets. Contemporary influences are making their marks on Prague. Young people dance to modern pop music in clubs that have opened in basements in the historic sections of town. Each year, millions of tourists add to the **eclectic** atmosphere of the Czech Republic.

CONNECT Geography & Culture

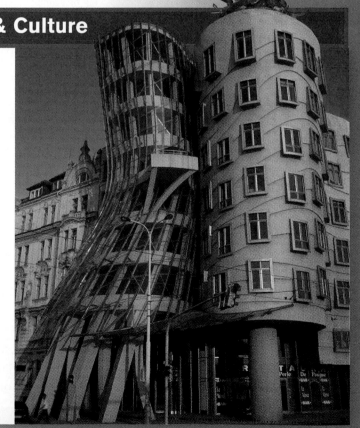

The Dancing House Prague is known for its architecture. A popular stop on any tour of Prague is the Rasin Building, nicknamed the Dancing House. Although it is made of concrete, steel, and glass, it seems to swirl and twist, like a couple dancing.

Not everyone is a fan of the building, built by American architect Frank Gehry and Czech architect Vlado Milunic in 1996. Some feel it clashes with the older historic buildings that surround it. However, supporters find it lively and exciting, a symbol of the new Czech Republic.

CRITICAL THINKING
Make Inferences Why might some Prague residents want the city to build more new buildings like the Dancing House?

To learn more about Radek and his world, go to the **Activity Center @ ClassZone.com**

To introduce himself, Radek says:

"Dobrý den. Jmenuju se Radek."

Hello! My name is Radek. I am 14 years old and live in Brno in the southeastern part of the Czech Republic. With almost 400,000 people, it is the second largest city after Prague. We live in a small apartment. On weekends, I like to read, listen to music, or watch television. Sometimes my family takes the train to Prague. Here's my day.

7 A.M. My sister and I eat breakfast with our parents. They both have to go to work and we go to school. I have rye bread or a roll with butter and jam and a glass of milk. Sometimes we have slices of cheese or salami, too.

8 A.M.–4 P.M. I have to work hard at school, especially in my English class. Everyone has to take courses in at least one foreign language. My school has many after-school activities. I joined the gymnastics club. I'm looking forward to our first competition!

6 P.M. In the evening, my family eats dinner. Sometimes, my grandmother comes over and helps my mother make roast duck with *knedlíky*, or potato dumplings, and cabbage. It's one of my favorite meals.

7 P.M. Today is my name day. In the Czech Republic, each day of the year has a different name assigned to it. It's traditional to celebrate your birthday and your name day. Some of my friends and I are going out for ice cream sundaes to celebrate.

CONNECT to Your Life

Journal Entry Think about your own birthday. How do you celebrate it? Do you have other special occasions, like Radek, that you celebrate with your family? Record your ideas in your journal.

Government and Economics The Czech Republic is a parliamentary democracy. Voters elect members of parliament. The parliament elects the president, who serves as the head of state. The president appoints a prime minister to oversee the daily operations of government.

Before Communist rule, the Czech economy was diverse and balanced. Under communism, however, the government shifted the economy toward heavy industry. After Communist control ended, the country's new leaders had to regain the balance that it once had. This has led to some unemployment as factory jobs decline.

On the whole, however, the Czech Republic's transition from a command to a market economy has been a smooth one. Most farms and factories have been sold to private owners. The Czech Republic joined the EU in 2004. Foreign investment and exports of Czech products, especially to Germany, have helped the economy continue growing. It has been among the most successful economies of the former Communist nations in Eastern Europe.

Škoda Auto This Czech company has been manufacturing cars for over 100 years. When Communist rule ended, the industry privatized and Volkswagen took over the company.

 SUMMARIZE Explain how the Czech Republic changed after gaining freedom from Communist rule.

Section 2 Assessment

ONLINE QUIZ For test practice, go to **Interactive Review** @ClassZone.com

TERMS & NAMES

1. Explain the importance of
- Magyar
- Czechoslovakia
- Velvet Revolution

USE YOUR READING NOTES

2. Compare and Contrast Use your completed chart to answer the following question:

How did Hungary's fight for independence differ from the Czech Republic's and how were they similar?

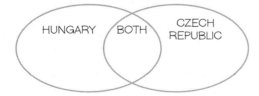

KEY IDEAS

3. What ethnic group do many Hungarians belong to?

4. How was Czechoslovakia formed?

5. How did the Velvet Revolution change Czechoslovakia?

CRITICAL THINKING

6. Analyze Causes and Effects How do you think the failure of the 1956 Hungarian revolt affected other Eastern European nations?

7. Find Main Ideas How did Václav Havel influence Czechoslovakia?

8. CONNECT to Today Why do you think the Czech Republic recently built new expressways and rail links to Germany?

9. WRITING Express an Opinion The young people who led the Hungarian revolt in 1956 were called freedom fighters by some and lawbreakers and traitors by others. Write a paragraph telling how you think they should be remembered.

Reading for Understanding

▶ Key Ideas

BEFORE, YOU LEARNED

The Czech Republic and Slovakia became independent countries without conflict or bloodshed.

NOW YOU WILL LEARN

In the 1990s the breakup of Yugoslavia was violent. Ethnic divisions and economic and political issues led to war.

▶ Vocabulary

TERMS & NAMES

Yugoslavia a country on the Balkan Peninsula from 1918 to 1991

Josip Broz Tito the Communist leader of Yugoslavia from 1953 to 1980

ethnic cleansing removing an ethnic or religious group from an area by force or the mass killing of members of such a group

Kosovo a self-governing province within Serbia

Slobodan Milosevic president of Serbia from 1989 to 1997 and of Yugoslavia from 1997 to 2000; a key figure in the ethnic conflicts in the Balkans in the 1990s

BACKGROUND VOCABULARY

Bosniac an ethnic Muslim from Bosnia and Herzegovina

refugee a person who flees a place to find safety

Visual Vocabulary Josip Broz Tito

▶ Reading Strategy

Re-create the web diagram shown at right. As you read and respond to the **KEY QUESTIONS**, use the diagram to help you find main ideas about the Balkans.

 Skillbuilder Handbook, page R4

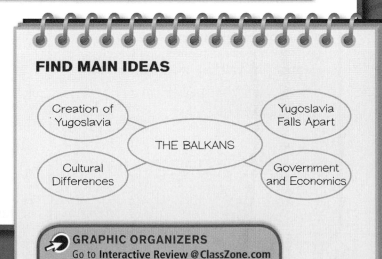

FIND MAIN IDEAS

- Creation of Yugoslavia
- Cultural Differences
- THE BALKANS
- Yugoslavia Falls Apart
- Government and Economics

⤵ **GRAPHIC ORGANIZERS**
Go to **Interactive Review @ ClassZone.com**

The Balkans

Connecting to Your World

At the opening ceremonies of the Olympic Games, athletes from around the globe proudly display their national flags as they march around a packed stadium. The games demonstrate that people of different religions, languages, and beliefs can come together without conflict. In 1984, the Winter Olympic Games took place in Sarajevo, a city in what was then Yugoslavia on the Balkan Peninsula. In the 1990s, wars caused by ethnic conflict destroyed much of the city, including the Olympic facilities. Sarajevo has been rebuilt, but memories of the violence that destroyed it remain.

Sarajevo The flame is lit (above) at the 1984 Winter Olympics opening ceremonies. This Muslim cemetery (below) is in Sarajevo.

History and Culture

▼ **KEY QUESTION** What caused the breakup of Yugoslavia?

In the 500s, various groups of Slavic peoples settled the Balkan Peninsula. Centuries of foreign rule created differences in the religion, language, and customs of these Slavic groups. When these groups joined together in one nation in the 20th century, their ethnic differences became a time bomb waiting to explode.

441

Creation of Yugoslavia After World War I, Slavic groups formed a country on the Balkan Peninsula called the Kingdom of Croats, Serbs, and Slovenes. It was renamed **Yugoslavia** in 1929. When World War II ended, **Josip Broz Tito** took over Yugoslavia. It became a Communist state consisting of six republics: Bosnia-Herzegovina, Croatia, Macedonia, Montenegro, Serbia, and Slovenia. Within each republic, the majority of people belonged to the same ethnic group. Tito's tight control brought political stability and helped unite Yugoslavia.

Yugoslavia Falls Apart After Tito died in 1980, Yugoslavia faced many economic and political problems. The other republics felt Serbia was trying to take control. In 1991, Slovenia, Macedonia, Croatia, and Bosnia-Herzegovina each declared independence. War broke out in Bosnia, as Serbs clashed with **Bosniacs** and Croats. Serbian troops occupied parts of Bosnia, using force to drive all non-Serbs out. This tactic, known as **ethnic cleansing**, left thousands dead or homeless. A 1995 peace plan gave most of Bosnia to the Bosniacs and Croats and the rest to the Bosnian Serbs. In 1998, rebels in the Serbian province of **Kosovo** began fighting for independence. Violence between Serb forces and the Albanian majority in Kosovo lasted until late 1999. In 2002, Serbian leader **Slobodan Milosevic** was tried for war crimes related to ethnic cleansing in Bosnia and Kosovo. He died in prison before his trial ended. By 2003, Yugoslavia no longer existed.

Cultural Differences Five new nations resulted from the breakup of Yugoslavia: Bosnia and Herzegovina, Croatia, Macedonia, Serbia and Montenegro, and Slovenia. As the map on the next page suggests, most of the former Yugoslav republics are dominated by one ethnic group. Most Balkan peoples speak Slavic languages. The biggest difference among ethnic groups is in religion. These countries have had to find ways to accept their differences. They have also had to work to return their cities to the cultural centers they once were.

▲ **ANALYZE CAUSES** Explain why Yugoslavia collapsed.

Dubrovnik, Croatia
Dubrovnik is known for its terra cotta roofs, some of which were damaged in the ethnic conflict in the 1990s and needed to be repaired.

COMPARING Ethnic Distribution in the Balkans

Similarities and Differences Yugoslavia brought many ethnic groups together in one nation. In the 1990s, differences in language, religion, and culture overwhelmed similarities, until the region erupted in conflict. Today, these groups must find ways to live together.

A Slovenia Most residents of Slovenia are Slovenes. They speak Slovenian and are mostly Roman Catholic. Slovenia has much in common with its Western European neighbors.

B Montenegro Following the breakup of Yugoslavia, Montenegro and Serbia were joined as one country. Montenegro declared independence in 2006. Montenegrins speak Serbo-Croatian. Most of them are Orthodox Christians.

C Serbia Serbia includes a mix of ethnic groups. Like Croats, Serbs speak Serbo-Croatian, but they use the Cyrillic alphabet. They are mostly Orthodox Christians. The province of Kosovo has a large Albanian population. They speak Albanian—which is not related to any surrounding language—and are mostly Muslim.

F Croatia The majority population in Croatia is Croat. They speak a language called Serbo-Croatian, which is written in the Roman alphabet. Most are Roman Catholics.

E Bosnia and Herzegovina This republic is one of the most ethnically diverse of the former Yugoslav republics. It is made up of Croats, Bosniacs, and Serbs. Bosniacs are Muslims, and they speak Serbo-Croatian.

D Macedonia For the most part, Macedonians and Albanians live here. Macedonians speak Macedonian and are mostly Orthodox Christians.

Legend:
- Albanian
- Croat
- Hungarian
- Macedonian
- Montenegrin
- Muslim
- Serb
- Slovene
- No clear majority
- Former Yugoslavia, 1992
- Current Border

Source: CIA Reference Map Series, 1993, 1995; Yugoslavian Census of 1991

CRITICAL THINKING

1. **Make Inferences** Given the distribution of ethnic groups, which region do you think experienced the most conflict?

2. **Compare and Contrast** What are the main differences between Serbs, Croats, and Bosniacs?

Government and Economics

▼ **KEY QUESTION** What governmental and economic problems do many former Yugoslav republics face?

Today, the remaining ethnic tensions have made it difficult for the former Yugoslav republics to form stable governments. One concern is protecting the rights of all ethnic groups to prevent future conflicts. In Bosnia and Herzegovina, the people elect the legislature and a three-member presidency—one Bosniac, one Croat, and one Serb—to represent the country's ethnic majorities. Serbia and Montenegro are two republics that formed one country in 2003. In 2006, however, a majority of Montenegrins voted to become an independent nation.

Wartime destruction and the movement of **refugees** between nations have forced the Balkan countries to rebuild their economies. Market economies have been slow to develop. Macedonia and Bosnia and Herzegovina are the poorest. Like Serbia, they suffer from high unemployment. Slovenia is the most prosperous nation, as a result of stable government and less involvement in the 1990s conflict. It is the only EU member. Croatia was another wealthy republic. Today, it is slowly recovering from billions of dollars worth of war damage.

▲ **ANALYZE EFFECTS** Explain the governmental and economic problems faced by the former Yugoslav republics.

Ljubljana, Slovenia
Visitors enjoy the sights on this street in Slovenia's capital. **Why is tourism important to the former Yugoslav republics' economies?**

Section ❸ Assessment

🔗 **ONLINE QUIZ**
For test practice, go to
Interactive Review
@ ClassZone.com

TERMS & NAMES

1. Explain the importance of
- Yugoslavia
- Josip Broz Tito
- ethnic cleansing
- Kosovo

USE YOUR READING NOTES

2. Find Main Ideas Use your completed chart to answer the following question:

How did Tito's death affect Yugoslavia?

KEY IDEAS

3. What kind of economic system did Yugoslavia have under Tito?

4. Why did much of the ethnic fighting occur in Bosnia and Kosovo?

5. What economic problem is shared by many of the former Yugoslav republics?

CRITICAL THINKING

6. Analyze Causes and Effects How did ethnic diversity make it harder to unite Yugoslavia?

7. Identify Problems and Solutions How might Balkan nations protect the rights of all ethnic groups equally in order to prevent future conflicts?

8. **CONNECT to Today** What might be the benefits of EU membership for Slovenia?

9. **GOVERNMENT** **Draft a Bill of Rights** Draft a Bill of Rights for the ethnic groups living in the Balkans. List ten rights these groups should have. Consider the rights of ethnic minorities in these countries.

Interactive ← Review

Click here to complete these and other activities online @ ClassZone.com

CHAPTER SUMMARY

Key Idea 1
Poland, Ukraine, and the Baltic states faced challenges after shaking off Communist rule.

Key Idea 2
After decades of Communist rule, Hungary and the Czech Republic made economic and political reforms.

Key Idea 3
In the 1990s the breakup of Yugoslavia was violent. Ethnic divisions and economic and political issues led to war.

For **Review and Study Notes**, go to **Interactive Review @ ClassZone.com**

NAME GAME

Use the Terms & Names list to complete each sentence on paper or online.

1. I am a self-governing province within Serbia and Montenegro. **Kosovo**

2. I am the Communist leader who kept Yugoslavia from splitting apart for over 40 years. _____

3. I am a region where grain production thrives. _____

4. I am the policy practiced by the Soviet Union in an effort to make occupied countries more Russian._____

5. I am another name for the countries of Latvia, Lithuania, and Estonia. _____

6. I am another term for ethnic Hungarians. _____

7. I mean to expel someone from a country. _____

8. I am the leader who helped start Poland's first independent trade union. _____

9. I am the Serbian leader who was charged with war crimes. _____

10. I am the Balkan country that split into six nations._____

Baltic States
bread basket
crossroads
Czechoslovakia
deport
ethnic cleansing
Josip Broz Tito
Kosovo
Lech Walesa
Magyar
Russification
Slobodan Milosevic
Solidarity
Václav Havel
Yugoslavia

Activities

GeoGame

Use this online map to reinforce your understanding of Eastern Europe. Drag and drop each place name in the list to its location on the map.

Geo GAME
Poland
Kiev
Budapest
Czech Republic
Ukraine

To play the complete game, go to **Interactive Review @ ClassZone.com**

Crossword Puzzle

Complete an online crossword puzzle to test your knowledge of Eastern Europe.

ACROSS
1. Communist leader of Yugoslavia from 1953 to 1980

VOCABULARY

Explain the significance of each of the following.

1. Lech Walesa
2. bread basket
3. Magyar
4. Velvet Revolution
5. ethnic cleansing
6. Kosovo

Explain how the terms and names in each group are related.

7. Baltic States and Russification
8. Yugoslavia and Czechoslovakia
9. Josip Broz Tito and Slobodan Milosevic

KEY IDEAS

1 Poland, Ukraine, and the Baltic States

10. Which Eastern European countries were part of the Soviet Union before it collapsed?
11. What effect did Solidarity have on Polish resistance to Communist rule in the 1980s?
12. How did the ownership of farms and factories in Poland, Ukraine, and the Baltic States change after the collapse of communism?
13. How did the Soviet policy of Russification affect Ukraine and the Baltic States?

2 Hungary and the Czech Republic

14. Why did the 1956 Hungarian revolt fail?
15. How has industrial growth affected where people in Hungary and the Czech Republic live?
16. What is the Czech Republic's capital and largest city?
17. How was the Czech Republic able to move peacefully from Communist rule to democratic government?

3 The Balkans

18. How did Yugoslavia change during Tito's rule?
19. What led to the violence in Kosovo?
20. In what way are many of the languages spoken in the Balkans similar?
21. What helped Slovenia make a smooth transition to a market economy?

CRITICAL THINKING

22. **Compare and Contrast** How have Poland, Hungary, and the Czech Republic changed from command to market economies?

COMMAND ECONOMY	MARKET ECONOMY

23. **Form and Support Opinions** Why have many former Communist countries wanted closer ties with Western Europe?
24. **Compare and Contrast** How were the roles of Lech Walesa and Václav Havel in their nations' history similar?
25. **Connect Geography & Government** What effect did the collapse of Communist governments have on Eastern Europe?
26. **Connect Geography & History** How do the new governments of the former Yugoslav republics reflect their recent history?
27. **Five Themes: Place** How were the breakups of Czechoslovakia and Yugoslavia different?

Answer the ESSENTIAL QUESTION

In what ways has Eastern Europe changed since the end of World War II?

Written Response Write a two- or three-paragraph response to the Essential Question. Consider the key ideas of each section as well as specific ideas about Eastern Europe. Use the rubric below to guide your thinking.

Response Rubric
A strong response will:
- discuss changes in government and civil rights
- discuss changes in economies
- discuss the impact of Communist rule on language and national identity

STANDARDS-BASED ASSESSMENT

✓ Test Practice
- Online Test Practice @ ClassZone.com
- Test-Taking Strategies and Practice at the front of this book

HISTORICAL MAP

Use the map to answer questions 1 and 2 on your paper.

Division of Poland 1795

1. **What three countries divided Poland among them?**

   A. Russia, Prussia, and Austria

   B. Sweden, Prussia, and Hungary

   C. Sweden, Russia, and Prussia

   D. Russia, Hungary, and the Ottoman Empire

2. **Which country gained the majority of Polish territory?**

   A. Austria   C. Prussia

   B. Russia   D. Sweden

BAR GRAPH

Examine the graph below. Use the graph to answer questions 3 and 4 on your paper.

Selected Eastern European GDPs

*Constant 1990 prices in U.S. dollars

Source: UN Statistics Division National Accounts Database

3. **Which country's GDP dropped between 1985 and 1995?**

4. **During which time period did all three nations see the biggest increase in GDP?**

GeoActivity

1. INTERDISCIPLINARY ACTIVITY—MATHEMATICS

With a small group, pick a country in this section. Find information on the religious makeup of the country, the percentage of people who live in urban and rural areas, and the percentage of people who can read. Use the information to create three pie graphs.

2. WRITING FOR SOCIAL STUDIES

Unit Writing Project Review your presentation about the European country you want to visit. Write a journal entry that describes how you spent your favorite day there, after your class decided to make the trip.

3. MENTAL MAPPING

Create an outline map of Eastern Europe and label the following:

- Hungary
- Poland
- Czech Republic
- Ukraine
- Latvia
- Lithuania
- Estonia
- Prague
- Chernobyl

UNIT 5

Russia and the Eurasian Republics

Why It Matters:

Since gaining their independence, Russia and the Eurasian republics have worked to stabilize their governments and economies. Achieving these goals will help ensure peace in the region and strengthen Russia's position as a world leader.

Moscow's Red Square

CHAPTER 15 Russia

Registan Square in Uzbekistan

CHAPTER 16 The Eurasian Republics

Meet Zuhura

In this unit, you will meet Zuhura, a middle-school girl from Uzbekistan. Learn more about her on **Worldster** @ClassZone.com

Climate, Vegetation, and Resources

▼ **KEY QUESTION** What types of natural resources are found in Russia?

Although Russia has many climates, it is mainly a cold-weather country. One Siberian town has recorded temperatures as low as –96°F. Such cold can burst tires and crack steel.

Extreme Climate All of Siberia has frigid weather during the winter. Temperatures remain so low in some areas that they are covered by a layer of permanently frozen ground called **permafrost**. However, the region can also have temperatures of nearly 100°F during the summer. These extreme temperature ranges are caused by two factors: Russia's northern latitude and its distance from any ocean. Much of the country lies many miles away from the oceans, which help moderate temperatures.

The climate is milder in European Russia. As a result, this region is more densely populated. However, even here the climate can be challenging. For example, the area around Moscow has snow on the ground for about five months of the year.

CONNECT to Math

Siberian winters are very cold. As you can see in the photo below, boiling water tossed into the region's wintry air can explode into a shower of ice crystals. Find out just how cold the winter is in Siberia. Follow the steps shown here to calculate the average temperature for each season in the Siberian town of Yakutsk.

Activity

Calculate Averages

1. Study the graph below.

2. Add the temperatures for the months in each season. For winter, you would add together: 18 + 40 + 45 + 33 + 8. Place a negative sign before the sum of these numbers.

3. Divide by the number of months in each season. For winter, you would divide by 5. Place the negative sign before the result. This is the average winter temperature in Yakutsk.

Average Temperatures in Yakutsk

Source: *Gateway to Russia*

A Reindeer in the tundra

B Autumn in the taiga

A **Tundra** The **tundra** in far northern Russia is a flat, treeless plain with long, harsh winters and short summers.

C **Steppe** The **steppe** is the grassland plain that stretches south of the taiga. Rich, fertile soil covers much of the steppe.

B **Taiga** The **taiga** (TY•guh) is a vast forest that lies south of the tundra. It is the largest forestland in the world.

D **Semidesert & Mountain** This area in the far southwest of Russia has dry lowlands around the Caspian Sea and rich vegetation near the Caucasus Mountains.

CRITICAL THINKING

Evaluate Which region probably provides the best farmland?

C Steppe in south-central Siberia

D Wildflowers in the central Caucasus Mountains

Islam, **Buddhism**, **Judaism**, and other forms of Christianity are also practiced. In fact, over 15 percent of the population practices Islam. However, many Jews left Russia for the United States and Israel because they were persecuted for practicing their religion.

Food Russians generally eat a hearty diet that uses a lot of root vegetables, such as beets, carrots, onions, and potatoes. These vegetables grow well in the cool Russian climate. They are also warm and filling foods for the cold Russian winters.

Traditional Russian dishes are eaten throughout the world. They include thin pancakes, served with smoked salmon and sour cream, called *blinis* (BLEE•neez), and beet soup called *borscht* (bawrsht). Tea is a traditional beverage, which Russians enjoy piping hot and strong.

Sports Not surprisingly, winter sports, such as hockey, ice skating, and skiing, are popular in Russia. However, the most popular sport is soccer. Tennis has also soared in popularity. In fact, in 2006, five of the top 15 women tennis players in the world were Russian, including tennis star Maria Sharapova. Russian athletes also compete seriously in the Olympics.

FIND MAIN IDEAS Identify some of the elements that shape the daily lives of the Russian people.

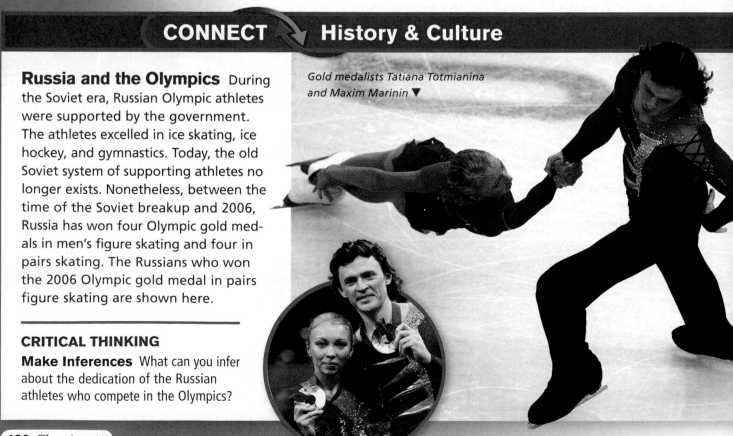

CONNECT History & Culture

Russia and the Olympics During the Soviet era, Russian Olympic athletes were supported by the government. The athletes excelled in ice skating, ice hockey, and gymnastics. Today, the old Soviet system of supporting athletes no longer exists. Nonetheless, between the time of the Soviet breakup and 2006, Russia has won four Olympic gold medals in men's figure skating and four in pairs skating. The Russians who won the 2006 Olympic gold medal in pairs figure skating are shown here.

Gold medalists Tatiana Totmianina and Maxim Marinin ▼

CRITICAL THINKING

Make Inferences What can you infer about the dedication of the Russian athletes who compete in the Olympics?

Cultural Heritage

▼ **KEY QUESTION** Who are some of the great Russian writers, artists, and composers of the 1800s and 1900s?

As you have learned, rulers such as Peter the Great and Catherine the Great encouraged the Russian people to adopt European customs. As a result, European culture gradually influenced Russian culture. Eventually, Russian literature and music that blended European and traditional styles began to emerge during the early 1800s. Soon Russia began to produce important works of literature, music, and art that are still highly regarded today.

Literature **Leo Tolstoy** (TOHL•stoy) is one of Russia's greatest novelists. In novels such as *War and Peace* (1869), Tolstoy showed deep concern for moral issues and for the welfare of the Russian people. In fact, the writer influenced Indian leader Mohandas Gandhi and his nonviolent independence movement. In turn, Gandhi inspired the nonviolent activism of civil rights leader Martin Luther King Jr.

Russia also boasted one of the best playwrights of the early 1900s. Anton Chekhov (CHEHK•awf) wrote insightful plays, including *The Three Sisters* (1901) and *The Cherry Orchard* (1904). Later in the century, Alexander Solzhenitsyn (SOHL•zhuh•NEET•sihn) described life in a Soviet labor camp under Stalin's rule in his short novel, *One Day in the Life of Ivan Denisovich* (1962). This novel led the Soviet Union to increase censorship.

ANALYZING Primary Sources

Alexander Solzhenitsyn (born 1918) is a Russian novelist who was arrested in 1945 for criticizing Stalin and spent eight years in prisons and labor camps like the one shown here. In this essay, Solzhenitsyn writes about what freedom means to him.

> This, I believe, is the single most precious freedom that prison takes away from us: the freedom to breathe freely, as I now can. No food on earth . . . is sweeter to me than this air steeped in the fragrance of flowers, of moisture and freshness.
>
> Source: "Freedom to Breathe," essay by Alexander Solzhenitsyn

DOCUMENT–BASED QUESTION
What do you think Solzhenitsyn means by "the freedom to breathe freely"?

Throughout its history, Russia has adopted cultural influences from the West. That cultural exchange continues today. But even as Russia changes, it maintains its character. As these pictures show, the country mixes Western styles with a definite Russian flavor.

Traditional Russia

For hundreds of years, Russians have retreated to their country houses, or dachas, to work in their vegetable gardens. They might also boil water for their tea in a samovar or listen to music played on a balalaika (BAL•uh•LY•kuh). Who knows? The house might even be decorated with nesting Matryoshka (MA•tree•OHSH•kuh) dolls.

Matryoshka Dolls

Traditional dolls nestle one inside the other and depict a round-faced peasant girl.

Beverages

Since the mid-1700s, beautifully decorated samovars have been used in Russia to prepare tea.

◀ *A traditional dacha in western Russia*

Music

This triangular folk guitar comes in many sizes, including the bass balalaika shown here.

Modern Russia

Many people in Russian cities live in high-rise apartment buildings built during the Soviet era. Further Western influence can be seen in the vending machines and music clubs that dot the cities. Even some traditional Matryoshka dolls now have a Western twist.

Matryoshka Dolls

Today, Matryoshka dolls can depict anyone, including George W. Bush and Vladimir Putin.

Soviet-style apartment blocks in a suburb of Moscow ▼

Beverages

Russians enjoy American-style soft drinks, but the machines dispense the soda into real glasses.

Music

Russian rock musicians often play unusual instruments, such as the cello seen here, in addition to electric guitars and drums.

CRITICAL THINKING

1. **Compare and Contrast** What different lifestyles do the dacha and apartment building suggest?

2. **Draw Conclusions** Which pictures best represent a blend of traditional and modern Russia?

CHAPTER

16

The Eurasian Republics

1
GEOGRAPHY

Center of a Landmass

2
HISTORY & CULTURE

Historic Crossroads

3
GOVERNMENT & ECONOMICS

The Challenge of Independence

ESSENTIAL QUESTION

How can the Eurasian republics meet the challenges of independence?

CONNECT — **Geography & History**

Use the map and the time line to answer the following questions.

1. When did the Mongols conquer Central Asia?
2. What body of water lies between Azerbaijan and Turkmenistan?

Culture

◄ **600s** Arabs spread Islam to Transcaucasia and Central Asia.
(Muslim prayer rug)

600

Culture

700s Turkish peoples migrate to Central Asia.

History

1200s Mongols conquer Central Asia and stabilize trade along Silk Roads.
(Mongol conqueror Timur the Lame) ►

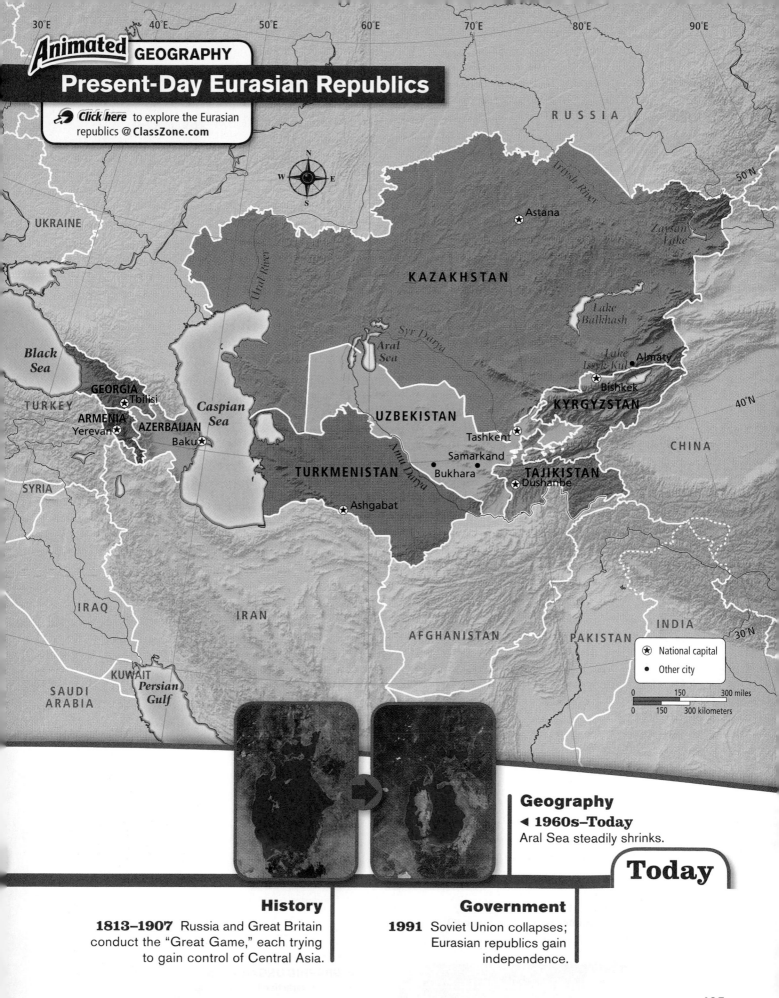

RUSSIA

UKRAINE

50°N

Irtysh River

Astana

KAZAKHSTAN

Zaysan Lake

Lake Balkhash

Black Sea

Aral River

Syr Darya

Aral Sea

Lake Issyk-Kul

Almaty

GEORGIA

Tbilisi

Caspian Sea

UZBEKISTAN

Bishkek

KYRGYZSTAN

TURKEY

ARMENIA

AZERBAIJAN

Yerevan

Baku

Tashkent

40°N

CHINA

Amu Darya

Samarkand

SYRIA

TURKMENISTAN

Bukhara

TAJIKISTAN

Dushanbe

IRAQ

Ashgabat

IRAN

AFGHANISTAN

PAKISTAN

INDIA

30°N

KUWAIT

Persian Gulf

SAUDI ARABIA

Legend

⊛ National capital

• Other city

0 150 300 miles
0 150 300 kilometers

Geography
◄ **1960s–Today**
Aral Sea steadily shrinks.

Today

History
1813–1907 Russia and Great Britain conduct the "Great Game," each trying to gain control of Central Asia.

Government
1991 Soviet Union collapses; Eurasian republics gain independence.

Reading for Understanding

▶ Key Ideas

BEFORE, YOU LEARNED

Russia's vast geography and variety of climates form a land of great diversity.

NOW YOU WILL LEARN

The geography and climate of the Eurasian republics pose challenges, but the countries are rich in natural resources.

▶ Vocabulary

TERMS & NAMES

Transcaucasia (TRANS•kaw•KAY•zhuh) a region between the Black and Caspian seas that contains the republics of Armenia, Azerbaijan (AZ•uhr•by•JAHN), and Georgia

Central Asia a region that contains the republics of Kazakhstan (KAH•zahk•STAN), Kyrgyzstan (KEER•gee•STAN), Tajikistan (tah•JIHK•ih•STAN), Turkmenistan (TURK•mehn•ih•STAN), and Uzbekistan (uz•BEHK•ih•STAN)

Caucasus (KAW•kuh•suhs) **Mountains** a mountain range that runs between the Black Sea and the Caspian Sea

landlocked completely surrounded by land

Tian Shan (TYAHN SHAHN) a mountain range that runs across Kyrgyzstan and Tajikistan

Kara Kum a huge desert that covers most of Turkmenistan

Aral Sea an inland body of water in Central Asia that has been steadily shrinking

Lake Balkhash a lake in eastern Kazakhstan

REVIEW

Eurasia a term used to refer to a single continent that is made up of Europe and Asia

Caspian Sea a sea situated between Transcaucasia and Central Asia; the largest inland body of water in the world

▶ Reading Strategy

Re-create the Venn diagram shown at right. As you read and respond to the **KEY QUESTIONS**, use the diagram to compare and contrast the landforms, climates, and resources of Transcaucasia and Central Asia.

 See Skillbuilder Handbook, page R9

COMPARE AND CONTRAST

TRANSCAUCASIA   BOTH   CENTRAL ASIA

GRAPHIC ORGANIZERS
Go to **Interactive Review** @ ClassZone.com

Center of a Landmass

Connecting to Your World

You have already learned that the Soviet Union was a Communist country that consisted of Russia and the surrounding republics. Remember that some geographers place this enormous nation in a region they call **Eurasia**, a landmass made up of both Europe and Asia. When the Soviet Union broke apart in 1991, 15 independent republics were formed. Three of these republics are located between the Black and Caspian seas in a region called Transcaucasia. Five more independent republics lie in Central Asia, a region east of the Caspian Sea.

Landforms and Bodies of Water

▼ **KEY QUESTION** What are the major landforms and bodies of water in Transcaucasia and Central Asia?

Transcaucasia consists of the republics of Armenia, Azerbaijan, and Georgia. **Central Asia** contains the republics of Kazakhstan, Kyrgyzstan, Tajikistan, Turkmenistan, and Uzbekistan. Both regions are very mountainous and boast some of the largest lakes in the world.

Tian Shan The Tian Shan, which is Chinese for "Heavenly Mountains," stretch for nearly 1,500 miles.

TIAN SHAN

Human-Environment Interaction

▼ **KEY QUESTION** What has led to some of the environmental problems in Central Asia?

For decades the Soviet Union attempted to overcome its geographic limits by trying to increase its farmable land. The government also took advantage of some of its vast, uninhabited areas by carrying out experimental projects in them. Unfortunately, these projects sometimes had unintended negative results, particularly in Central Asia.

Aral Sea In the 1960s, the Soviet Union began using river water from the Syr Darya and Amu Darya for an irrigation project. This project was part of a plan to convert areas of Central Asian desert into thriving cotton farms. Indeed, the production of cotton soon soared. However, since the Aral Sea received most of its water from the two rivers, the irrigation caused the sea to drastically shrink. The sea even split into two, the small Aral and the large Aral. Recent efforts have helped raise the level of the small Aral. As a result, fish, jobs, and people have begun to return to the area. But the Soviet plan caused one of Earth's greatest environmental disasters.

CONNECT ↷ to Science

By the end of the 20th century, irrigation and evaporation had caused the Aral Sea to shrink about 75 percent. The retreating waters left behind dry beds filled with salt, fertilizers, and pesticides. These chemicals had washed into the sea from the cotton farms. Windstorms then blew the chemicals into the surrounding area. As a result, the rates of cancer and other diseases greatly increased in the nearby population.

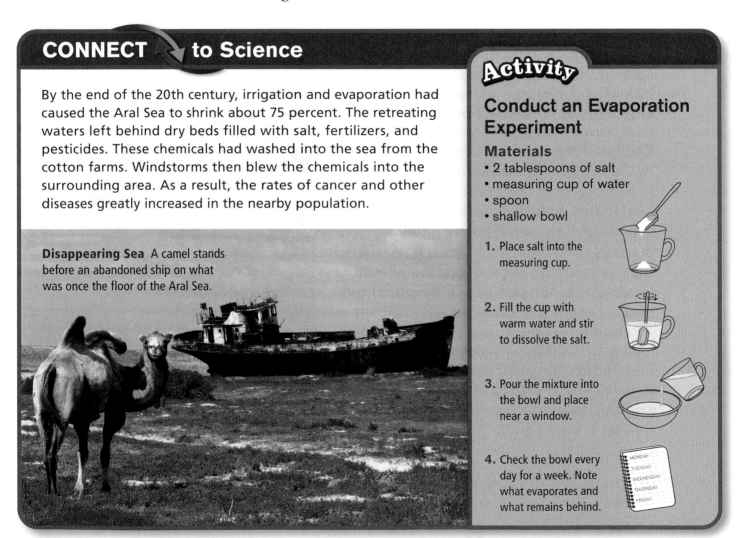

Disappearing Sea A camel stands before an abandoned ship on what was once the floor of the Aral Sea.

Activity

Conduct an Evaporation Experiment

Materials
• 2 tablespoons of salt
• measuring cup of water
• spoon
• shallow bowl

1. Place salt into the measuring cup.

2. Fill the cup with warm water and stir to dissolve the salt.

3. Pour the mixture into the bowl and place near a window.

4. Check the bowl every day for a week. Note what evaporates and what remains behind.

Nuclear Testing Other Soviet programs have caused problems in Central Asia. As you may recall, the Soviet Union and the United States engaged in a weapons race during the Cold War. Between 1949 and 1990, the Soviet government used part of the vast steppes in northern Kazakhstan to test their nuclear weapons. Unfortunately, radiation from this testing poisoned the soil, food, and water over about a 7,000-square-mile area. The radiation caused dramatic increases in the rates of leukemia, birth defects, and mental illness in the area.

Recently, the nations of Central Asia have taken steps to avoid more environmental problems. For example, Kazakhstan has started to develop more light industry to prevent an over-dependence on heavy industries. This measure should help decrease the region's air and water pollution problems.

Nuclear Blast The Soviets conducted about 715 nuclear tests. In this picture, a test site is destroyed in Kazakhstan in 2000.

 ANALYZE CAUSES Explain what led to some of the environmental problems in Central Asia.

Section 1 Assessment

ONLINE QUIZ
For test practice, go to
Interactive Review
@ ClassZone.com

TERMS & NAMES

1. Explain the importance of
- Transcaucasia
- Central Asia
- Kara Kum
- Aral Sea

USE YOUR READING NOTES

2. Compare and Contrast Use your completed Venn diagram to answer the following question:

What element of their physical geography offers great promise for the futures of both Transcaucasia and Central Asia?

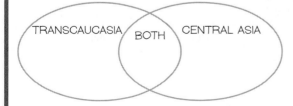

TRANSCAUCASIA   BOTH   CENTRAL ASIA

KEY IDEAS

3. What types of landforms are found in Kazakhstan?

4. Why does Central Asia have a harsh climate?

5. What areas of Transcaucasia have rich soil?

CRITICAL THINKING

6. Make Inferences Which region do you think is more densely populated, Transcaucasia or Central Asia? Explain your answer.

7. Compare and Contrast How are the landforms and bodies of water of Georgia and Armenia similar and different?

8. CONNECT to Today What lessons can be learned today from the Aral Sea environmental disaster?

9. WRITING Prepare an Environmental Report Do further research about the causes and effects of pollution in Central Asia. Also find out about possible solutions for these problems. Then write an environmental report that summarizes your research.

Reading for Understanding

▶ Key Ideas

BEFORE, YOU LEARNED

The Eurasian republics are largely mountainous and desert regions with harsh climates.

NOW YOU WILL LEARN

The geographic location of the Eurasian republics has attracted many different cultures, ideas, and conquerors.

▶ Vocabulary

TERMS & NAMES

nomad member of a group who makes a living by herding animals and moving from place to place as the seasons change

Islam a religion that is based on the teachings of the prophet Muhammad

Muslim a follower of Islam

Silk Roads major trade routes that ran from China to the rest of East Asia, through Central Asia, and into Europe

Russification the process of making a culture more Russian

yurt a portable, tentlike structure used by the nomads of Central Asia

REVIEW

ethnic group a group of people who share language, customs, and a common heritage

Visual Vocabulary Russification

▶ Reading Strategy

Re-create the web diagram shown at right. As you read and respond to the **KEY QUESTIONS**, use the diagram to record main ideas about the history and culture of the Eurasian republics. Add ovals as needed.

 See Skillbuilder Handbook, page R4

FIND MAIN IDEAS

Influenced by many ethnic groups

HISTORY AND CULTURE IN EURASIAN REPUBLICS

 GRAPHIC ORGANIZERS
Go to **Interactive Review** @ ClassZone.com

Historic Crossroads

Connecting to Your World

Imagine that you had to move every few months. In the summer, you might live in New England. Then in the fall, you would move to the Midwest. Finally, in the winter, you would go to the Southwest. In the spring, you would start the cycle all over again. This way of life probably sounds very different from your own, but it is similar to the way thousands of nomads live. **Nomads** are people who make a living by herding animals and moving from place to place as the seasons change. The people who first lived in Transcaucasia and Central Asia led a nomadic way of life.

Nomadic Man This man's weather-beaten face reflects a life lived largely out of doors.

Regions of Exchange

▼ **KEY QUESTION** How have various groups of people and trade influenced Transcaucasia and Central Asia?

For centuries, many groups of people moved through Transcaucasia and Central Asia. Some of them settled in these regions and had a major influence on culture. Three main reasons for this movement were military conquest, migration, and trade.

Nomadic Home Nomads live in yurts, portable tents that usually consist of several layers of felt stretched around a wooden frame.

Africa is the world's second-largest continent in terms of both landmass and population. The equator runs across the middle of the continent. The vast Sahara Desert dominates Africa's northern half. As you study the maps, notice geographic patterns and details about the region. Answer the questions on each map in your notebook.

As you study the graphs on this page, compare the landmass, population, rivers, and deserts of Africa with those of the United States. Then jot down the answers to the following questions in your notebook.

Comparing Data

1. Compare Africa's landmass to that of the United States. About how much larger is Africa than the United States?

2. Of the rivers listed, which two are closest in length?

Comparing Data

Landmass

Africa
11,618,197 sq. mi.

Continental United States
3,165,630 sq. mi.

Population

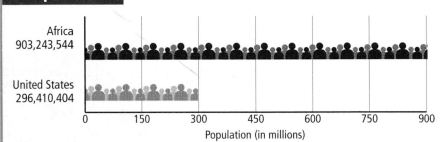

Africa
903,243,544

United States
296,410,404

Population (in millions)
0   150   300   450   600   750   900

Rivers

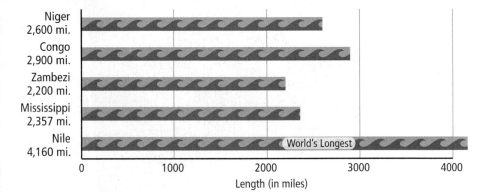

Niger 2,600 mi.
Congo 2,900 mi.
Zambezi 2,200 mi.
Mississippi 2,357 mi.
Nile 4,160 mi.   World's Longest

Length (in miles)
0   1000   2000   3000   4000

Deserts

World's Largest
Sahara
Africa
3,500,000 sq. mi.

U.S. Largest
Mojave
United States
25,000 sq. mi.

Namib
Africa
102,248 sq. mi.

Kalahari
Africa
about 100,000 sq. mi.

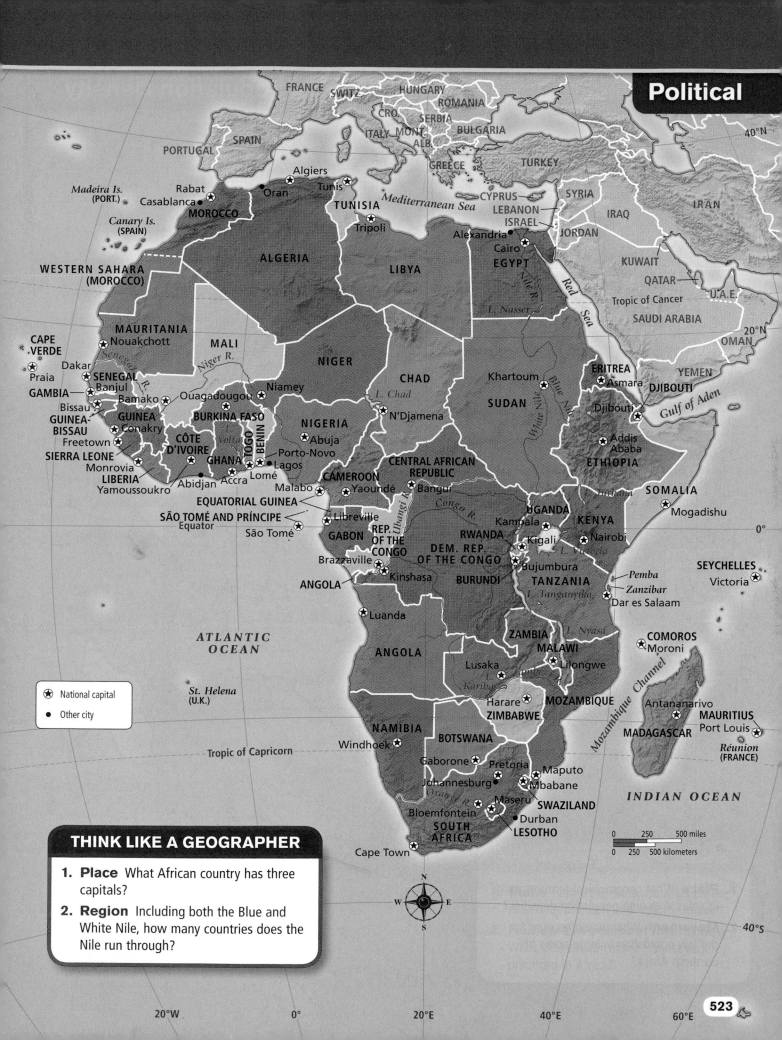

FRANCE SWITZ HUNGARY
ROMANIA
CRO. SERBIA
ITALY MONT. BULGARIA
ALB.
GREECE
SPAIN
PORTUGAL
Madeira Is. (PORT.)
Algiers
Rabat ● Oran Tunis
Casablanca ● MOROCCO
Canary Is. (SPAIN)
WESTERN SAHARA (MOROCCO)
TUNISIA Mediterranean Sea
Tripoli
TURKEY
CYPRUS
LEBANON
ISRAEL
Alexandria ●
Cairo ●
EGYPT
JORDAN
IRAQ
SYRIA
IRAN
KUWAIT
QATAR
Tropic of Cancer
U.A.E.
SAUDI ARABIA
OMAN

ALGERIA LIBYA
Nile R.
L. Nasser
Red Sea

MAURITANIA
Nouakchott
MALI
CAPE VERDE
Dakar ● Senegal R.
Praia SENEGAL
GAMBIA Banjul
Bamako ●
Bissau Niger R.
GUINEA-BISSAU GUINEA
Conakry
Freetown
SIERRA LEONE
Monrovia
LIBERIA
Yamoussoukro
Abidjan ●
CÔTE D'IVOIRE
Volta R.
Niamey
Ouagadougou
BURKINA FASO
TOGO BENIN
GHANA
Lomé
Accra ●
NIGER
NIGERIA
Abuja
Porto-Novo
Lagos ●
CHAD
L. Chad
N'Djamena
Khartoum ●
SUDAN
White Nile Blue Nile
ERITREA
Asmara ●
DJIBOUTI
Djibouti
Gulf of Aden
YEMEN

ADDIS
Ababa
ETHIOPIA
SOMALIA
Mogadishu

CAMEROON
Yaoundé
Malabo
EQUATORIAL GUINEA
SÃO TOMÉ AND PRÍNCIPE
Equator
São Tomé
Libreville
GABON
REP. OF THE CONGO
Brazzaville
Kinshasa
ANGOLA
Luanda
CENTRAL AFRICAN REPUBLIC
Bangui
Ubangi R. Congo R.
DEM. REP. OF THE CONGO
UGANDA
Kampala
RWANDA
Kigali
Bujumbura
BURUNDI
TANZANIA
L. Tanganyika
Dar es Salaam
Pemba
Zanzibar
L. Turkana
KENYA
Nairobi
L. Victoria
SEYCHELLES
Victoria

ATLANTIC OCEAN

St. Helena (U.K.)

ANGOLA
ZAMBIA
Lusaka
L. Nyasa
MALAWI
Lilongwe
COMOROS
Moroni

Kariba
Harare
ZIMBABWE
MOZAMBIQUE
Mozambique Channel
Antananarivo
MADAGASCAR
MAURITIUS
Port Louis
Réunion (FRANCE)

NAMIBIA
Windhoek
Tropic of Capricorn

★ National capital
● Other city

BOTSWANA
Gaborone
Pretoria
Johannesburg ●
Maputo
Mbabane
Orange R.
Bloemfontein
Maseru
SWAZILAND
Durban ●
LESOTHO
SOUTH AFRICA
Cape Town
INDIAN OCEAN

250 500 miles
0
0 250 500 kilometers

N
W E
S

THINK LIKE A GEOGRAPHER

1. **Place** What African country has three capitals?

2. **Region** Including both the Blue and White Nile, how many countries does the Nile run through?

20°W   0°   20°E   40°E   60°E

40°N
20°N
0°
20°S
40°S

Africa

The country cards on these pages present information about the 53 nations in Africa.

Algeria

GEOGRAPHY
Capital: Algiers
Total Area: 919,595 sq. mi.
Population: 32,854,000

ECONOMY
Imports: industrial equipment; food; consumer goods
Exports: petroleum; natural gas

CULTURE
Language: Arabic; Tamazight
Religion: Sunni Muslim 99%

Angola

GEOGRAPHY
Capital: Luanda
Total Area: 481,354 sq. mi.
Population: 15,941,000

ECONOMY
Imports: consumer and capital goods
Exports: petroleum; diamonds; coffee

CULTURE
Language: Portuguese
Religion: Catholic 62%; Protestant 15%; traditional beliefs 5%

Benin

GEOGRAPHY
Capital: Porto-Novo
Total Area: 43,483 sq. mi.
Population: 8,439,000

ECONOMY
Imports: food; petroleum
Exports: cotton yarn

CULTURE
Language: French
Religion: traditional beliefs 35%; Catholic 26%; Muslim 21%

Botswana

GEOGRAPHY
Capital: Gaborone
Total Area: 231,804 sq. mi.
Population: 1,765,000

ECONOMY
Imports: machinery; food; tobacco; wood
Exports: diamonds; textiles; meat

CULTURE
Language: English; Tswana
Religion: traditional beliefs 39%; African Christian 31%; Protestant 11%

Burkina Faso

GEOGRAPHY
Capital: Ouagadougou
Total Area: 105,869 sq. mi.
Population: 13,228,000

ECONOMY
Imports: petroleum; food
Exports: cotton; shea nuts; gold

CULTURE
Language: French
Religion: Muslim 49%; traditional beliefs 34%; Christian 17%

Burundi

GEOGRAPHY
Capital: Bujumbura
Total Area: 10,745 sq. mi.
Population: 7,548,000

ECONOMY
Imports: consumer and capital goods
Exports: coffee; tea

CULTURE
Language: Rundi; French
Religion: Catholic 57%; Protestant 20%; traditional beliefs 7%

Cameroon

GEOGRAPHY
Capital: Yaoundé
Total Area: 183,568 sq. mi.
Population: 16,322,000

ECONOMY
Imports: minerals; industrial equipment
Exports: petroleum; lumber; cocoa beans

CULTURE
Language: French; English
Religion: Christian 47%; traditional beliefs 24%; Muslim 21%

Cape Verde

GEOGRAPHY
Capital: Praia
Total Area: 1,557 sq. mi.
Population: 507,000

ECONOMY
Imports: food; machinery; metals
Exports: shoes; clothing; fish

CULTURE
Language: Portuguese
Religion: Catholic 91%; Muslim 3%

Yellow-billed hornbill
found in southern Africa

Central African Republic

GEOGRAPHY
Capital: Bangui
Total Area: 240,535 sq. mi.
Population: 4,038,000

ECONOMY
Imports: road vehicles; raw cotton; food
Exports: wood; diamonds; cotton; coffee

CULTURE
Language: French; Sango
Religion: Catholic 18%; Muslim 16%; Protestant 14%; other Christian 35%

Chad

GEOGRAPHY
Capital: N'Djamena
Total Area: 495,755 sq. mi.
Population: 9,749,000

ECONOMY
Imports: petroleum
Exports: cattle, sheep, and goats; cotton

CULTURE
Language: Arabic; French
Religion: Muslim 54%; Catholic 20%; Protestant 14%

Comoros

GEOGRAPHY
Capital: Moroni
Total Area: 838 sq. mi.
Population: 798,000

ECONOMY
Imports: rice; meat and fish; vehicles
Exports: vanilla; cloves; ylang-ylang

CULTURE
Language: Comorian; Arabic; French
Religion: Sunni Muslim 98%

Democratic Republic of Congo

GEOGRAPHY
Capital: Kinshasa
Total Area: 905,568 sq. mi.
Population: 57,549,000

ECONOMY
Imports: petroleum products
Exports: diamonds; cobalt; copper; gold

CULTURE
Language: French; English
Religion: Catholic 41%; Protestant 32%

Republic of Congo

GEOGRAPHY
Capital: Brazzaville
Total Area: 132,047 sq. mi.
Population: 3,999,000

ECONOMY
Imports: petroleum products
Exports: wood; sugar

CULTURE
Language: French; Lingala; Monokutuba
Religion: Catholic 49%; Protestant 17%; African Christian 13%

Côte d'Ivoire

GEOGRAPHY
Capital: Yamoussoukro
Total Area: 124,503 sq. mi.
Population: 18,154,000

ECONOMY
Imports: petroleum; food products
Exports: cocoa beans; wood; coffee beans

CULTURE
Language: French
Religion: Muslim 39%; Christian 30%; nonreligious 17%; animist 12%

Djibouti

GEOGRAPHY
Capital: Djibouti
Total Area: 8,880 sq. mi.
Population: 793,000

ECONOMY
Imports: food; transport equipment
Exports: hides and skins; leather

CULTURE
Language: Arabic; French
Religion: Sunni Muslim 97%; Christian 3%

Egypt

GEOGRAPHY
Capital: Cairo
Total Area: 386,662 sq. mi.
Population: 74,033,000

ECONOMY
Imports: machinery; food; iron and steel
Exports: petroleum; food; raw cotton

CULTURE
Language: Arabic
Religion: Muslim 84%; Christian 15%

Equatorial Guinea

GEOGRAPHY
Capital: Malabo
Total Area: 10,831 sq. mi.
Population: 504,000

ECONOMY
Imports: petroleum products; machinery
Exports: methanol; wood; cocoa beans

CULTURE
Language: Spanish; French
Religion: Catholic 80%; Muslim 4%; African Christian 4%

Eritrea

GEOGRAPHY
Capital: Asmara
Total Area: 46,842 sq. mi.
Population: 4,401,000

ECONOMY
Imports: live animals; cereals; iron
Exports: raw sugar; vegetables and fruits; fish; sesame seeds

CULTURE
Language: Afar; Arabic; Tigre; Kunama
Religion: Christian 51%; Muslim 45%

Ethiopia

GEOGRAPHY
Capital: Addis Ababa
Total Area: 435,186 sq. mi.
Population: 77,431,000

ECONOMY
Imports: machinery; road vehicles; iron
Exports: coffee; leather; sesame seeds

CULTURE
Language: Amharic
Religion: Ethiopian Orthodox 50%; Muslim 33%; Protestant 10%

Gabon

GEOGRAPHY
Capital: Libreville
Total Area: 103,347 sq. mi.
Population: 1,384,000

ECONOMY
Imports: petroleum products
Exports: wood; manganese

CULTURE
Language: French
Religion: Catholic 57%; Protestant 18%; Muslim 3%

The Gambia

GEOGRAPHY
Capital: Banjul
Total Area: 4,363 sq. mi.
Population: 1,517,000

ECONOMY
Imports: food; machinery; petroleum
Exports: peanuts; fruits and vegetables

CULTURE
Language: English
Religion: Muslim 95%; Christian 4%

Ghana

GEOGRAPHY
Capital: Accra
Total Area: 92,456 sq. mi.
Population: 22,113,000

ECONOMY
Imports: petroleum; machinery; food
Exports: gold; cocoa beans; aluminum

CULTURE
Language: English
Religion: traditional beliefs 24%; Muslim 20%; Protestant 17%; African Christian 14%

Guinea

GEOGRAPHY
Capital: Conakry
Total Area: 94,926 sq. mi.
Population: 9,402,000

ECONOMY
Imports: refined petroleum; food
Exports: bauxite; gold; diamonds; fish

CULTURE
Language: French
Religion: Muslim 85%; Christian 10%

Guinea-Bissau

GEOGRAPHY
Capital: Bissau
Total Area: 13,946 sq. mi.
Population: 1,586,000

ECONOMY
Imports: food; transport equipment
Exports: cashews; cotton; logs

CULTURE
Language: Portuguese
Religion: traditional beliefs 45%; Muslim 40%; Christian 13%

Kenya

GEOGRAPHY
Capital: Nairobi
Total Area: 224,962 sq. mi.
Population: 34,256,000

ECONOMY
Imports: petroleum; machinery; chemicals
Exports: horticultural products; coffee

CULTURE
Language: Swahili; English
Religion: Catholic 22%; African Christian 21%; Protestant 20%

Lesotho

GEOGRAPHY
Capital: Maseru
Total Area: 11,720 sq. mi.
Population: 1,795,000

ECONOMY
Imports: food products; commodities
Exports: clothing; machinery

CULTURE
Language: Sotho; English
Religion: Catholic 38%; Protestant 13%; African Christian 12%

Liberia

GEOGRAPHY
Capital: Monrovia
Total Area: 43,000 sq. mi.
Population: 3,283,000

ECONOMY
Imports: food and live animals; petroleum
Exports: logs and timber; rubber

CULTURE
Language: English
Religion: traditional beliefs 63%; Muslim 16%; Protestant 14%

Libya

GEOGRAPHY
Capital: Tripoli
Total Area: 679,362 sq. mi.
Population: 5,853,000

ECONOMY
Imports: machinery; food; road vehicles
Exports: crude and refined petroleum; natural gas

CULTURE
Language: Arabic
Religion: Sunni Muslim 96%

Madagascar

GEOGRAPHY
Capital: Antananarivo
Total Area: 226,657 sq. mi.
Population: 18,606,000

ECONOMY
Imports: petroleum; machinery
Exports: textiles; vanilla; cloves; shellfish

CULTURE
Language: Malagasy; French
Religion: traditional beliefs 48%; Protestant 23%; Catholic 20%

Malawi

GEOGRAPHY
Capital: Lilongwe
Total Area: 45,745 sq. mi.
Population: 12,884,000

ECONOMY
Imports: food; machinery; chemicals
Exports: tobacco; sugar; tea; clothing

CULTURE
Language: Chichewa
Religion: Protestant 39%; Catholic 25%; Muslim 15%

Mali

GEOGRAPHY
Capital: Bamako
Total Area: 478,767 sq. mi.
Population: 13,518,000

ECONOMY
Imports: machinery; petroleum products
Exports: gold; raw cotton; live animals

CULTURE
Language: French
Religion: Muslim 82%; traditional beliefs 16%

Mauritania

GEOGRAPHY
Capital: Nouakchott
Total Area: 397,955 sq. mi.
Population: 3,069,000

ECONOMY
Imports: food products; vehicles
Exports: iron ore; fish

CULTURE
Language: Arabic; Fulani; Soninke; Wolof
Religion: Sunni Muslim 99%

Mauritius

GEOGRAPHY
Capital: Port Louis
Total Area: 788 sq. mi.
Population: 1,245,000

ECONOMY
Imports: fabrics; yarn; food; live animals
Exports: sugar; fabric; ships' stores

CULTURE
Language: English
Religion: Hindu 50%; Christian 32%; Muslim 17%

Morocco

GEOGRAPHY
Capital: Rabat
Total Area: 172,414 sq. mi.
Population: 31,478,000

ECONOMY
Imports: food; tobacco; cotton fabric
Exports: knitwear; phosphoric acid

CULTURE
Language: Arabic
Religion: Muslim 98%

Mozambique

GEOGRAPHY
Capital: Maputo
Total Area: 309,496 sq. mi.
Population: 19,792,000

ECONOMY
Imports: machinery; refined petroleum
Exports: aluminum; electricity; cotton

CULTURE
Language: Portuguese
Religion: traditional beliefs 50%; Catholic 16%; Muslim 11%

Meerkats Meerkats, like this family in South Africa, live in groups of between 3 and 25.

Namibia

GEOGRAPHY
Capital: Windhoek
Total Area: 318,696 sq. mi.
Population: 2,031,000

ECONOMY
Imports: food; machinery; metals
Exports: diamonds; metals; fish; meat

CULTURE
Language: English
Religion: Protestant 48%; Catholic 18%; African Christian 11%

Niger

GEOGRAPHY
Capital: Niamey
Total Area: 489,191 sq. mi.
Population: 13,957,000

ECONOMY
Imports: food; capital goods
Exports: uranium; cattle; onions; cowpeas

CULTURE
Language: French
Religion: Sunni Muslim 91%

Nigeria

GEOGRAPHY
Capital: Abuja
Total Area: 356,669 sq. mi.
Population: 131,530,000

ECONOMY
Imports: machinery; chemicals; food
Exports: crude petroleum

CULTURE
Language: English
Religion: Muslim 44%; independent Christian 15%; African indigenous 10%

Rwanda

GEOGRAPHY
Capital: Kigali
Total Area: 10,169 sq. mi.
Population: 9,038,000

ECONOMY
Imports: capital goods; food
Exports: niobium and tantalum; tea; coffee

CULTURE
Language: Rwanda; French; English
Religion: Catholic 51%; Protestant 29%; traditional beliefs 9%

São Tomé and Príncipe

GEOGRAPHY
Capital: São Tomé
Total Area: 386 sq. mi.
Population: 157,000

ECONOMY
Imports: investment goods; agricultural products; petroleum
Exports: cocoa beans; copra; coffee

CULTURE
Language: Portuguese
Religion: Catholic 90%

Senegal

GEOGRAPHY
Capital: Dakar
Total Area: 75,749 sq. mi.
Population: 11,658,000

ECONOMY
Imports: food and live animals
Exports: petroleum; fresh crustaceans

CULTURE
Language: French
Religion: Muslim 88%; traditional beliefs 6%; Christian 6%

Seychelles

GEOGRAPHY
Capital: Victoria
Total Area: 176 sq. mi.
Population: 81,188

ECONOMY
Imports: food; mineral fuels; machinery
Exports: canned tuna; fresh and frozen fish; petroleum

CULTURE
Language: Creole; English; French
Religion: Catholic 90%; Anglican 7%

Sierra Leone

GEOGRAPHY
Capital: Freetown
Total Area: 27,699 sq. mi.
Population: 5,525,000

ECONOMY
Imports: food and live animals; fuels
Exports: diamonds; cacao; rutile

CULTURE
Language: English
Religion: Sunni Muslim 46%; traditional beliefs 40%; Christian 11%

Somalia

GEOGRAPHY
Capital: Mogadishu
Total Area: 246,201 sq. mi.
Population: 8,228,000

ECONOMY
Imports: raw sugar; cereals
Exports: goats; sheep; bovines; camels

CULTURE
Language: Somali; Arabic
Religion: Sunni Muslim 99%

South Africa

GEOGRAPHY
Capital: Pretoria/Cape Town/Bloemfontein
Total Area: 471,011 sq. mi.
Population: 47,432,000

ECONOMY
Imports: machinery; petroleum; chemicals
Exports: diamonds; gold; iron and steel

CULTURE
Language: Afrikaans; English; Xhosa; Zulu
Religion: independent churches 39%; Protestant 32%; traditional beliefs 8%

Sudan

GEOGRAPHY
Capital: Khartoum
Total Area: 967,499 sq. mi.
Population: 36,233,000

ECONOMY
Imports: machinery; food; chemicals
Exports: petroleum; sesame seeds; gold

CULTURE
Language: Arabic; English
Religion: Sunni Muslim 70%; traditional beliefs 12%; Catholic 8%

Swaziland

GEOGRAPHY
Capital: Mbabane
Total Area: 6,704 sq. mi.
Population: 1,032,000

ECONOMY
Imports: food; machinery; chemicals
Exports: soft drink concentrates; sugar

CULTURE
Language: Swati; English
Religion: African indigenous Christian 46%; Protestant 15%

Tanzania

GEOGRAPHY
Capital: Dodoma
Total Area: 364,900 sq. mi.
Population: 36,766,356

ECONOMY
Imports: food; machinery
Exports: gold; diamonds; gemstones; cashews; coffee; tea

CULTURE
Language: Swahili; English
Religion: Christian 47%; Muslim 32%

Togo

GEOGRAPHY
Capital: Lomé
Total Area: 21,925 sq. mi.
Population: 6,145,000

ECONOMY
Imports: food; petroleum; cement
Exports: cement; phosphates; cotton

CULTURE
Language: French
Religion: traditional beliefs 38%; Catholic 24%; Muslim 19%

Tunisia

GEOGRAPHY
Capital: Tunis
Total Area: 63,170 sq. mi.
Population: 10,102,000

ECONOMY
Imports: fabric; food; machinery
Exports: clothing; knitwear; phosphates

CULTURE
Language: Arabic
Religion: Sunni Muslim 99%

Uganda

GEOGRAPHY
Capital: Kampala
Total Area: 91,136 sq. mi.
Population: 28,816,000

ECONOMY
Imports: machinery; food
Exports: fish products; tea; cereal; cotton

CULTURE
Language: English
Religion: Catholic 33%; Protestant 33%; traditional beliefs 18%; Muslim 16%

Zambia

GEOGRAPHY
Capital: Lusaka
Total Area: 290,586 sq. mi.
Population: 11,668,000

ECONOMY
Imports: machinery; printed matter; cereals
Exports: refined copper; base metals; food

CULTURE
Language: English
Religion: traditional beliefs 27%; Protestant 23%; Catholic 17%

Zimbabwe

GEOGRAPHY
Capital: Harare
Total Area: 150,804 sq. mi.
Population: 13,010,000

ECONOMY
Imports: machinery; chemicals; food
Exports: tobacco; ferroalloys; cotton lint

CULTURE
Language: English
Religion: animist 41%; Protestant 24%; African indigenous Christian 14%

Hippopotamuses Once common across the continent, hippos are now found mostly in East and Central Africa.

CHAPTER 17

Africa
Physical Geography and Early History

1 GEOGRAPHY

Africa's Geographic Extremes

2 HISTORY

Human Beginnings in Africa

 ESSENTIAL QUESTION

How do humans interact with the extreme African environment?

CONNECT ➤ **Geography & History**

Use the map and the time line to answer the following questions.

1. The highest mountain in Africa is closest to what coast?

2. From what locations might it have been easiest for *Homo erectus* to migrate out of Africa?

History
6–7 Million Years Ago
First hominids appear. ▶

8,000,000 B.C.

History
1.8 Million Years Ago
Homo erectus begins to migrate out of Africa.

Culture
2.5 Million Years Ago
Hominids develop first tools, beginning the Stone Age. ▶

10°W 0° 10°E 20°E 30°E 40°E 50°E 60°E

EUROPE

ASIA

40°N

30°N

Mediterranean Sea Suez Canal

Gulf of Sidra

ATLAS MOUNTAINS

Canary Islands

Tropic of Cancer

AHAGGAR MOUNTAINS

LIBYAN DESERT

Red Sea

Nasser

Nubian Desert

20°N

S A H A R A

Tibesti Mountains

S A H E L

Senegal R.

L. Chad

10°N

Gulf of Aden

Niger R.

Benue R.

ETHIOPIAN PLATEAU

HORN OF AFRICA

Mt. Cameroon 13,451 ft. (4,100 m)

Gulf of Guinea

Ubangi R.

Congo R.

C O N G O   B A S I N

White Nile *Blue Nile*

GREAT RIFT VALLEY

Mt. Kenya 17,058 ft. (5,199 m)

Equator 0°

Mt. Kilimanjaro 19,341 ft. (5,895 m)

Pemba I.

Zanzibar I.

ATLANTIC OCEAN

0 400 800 miles
0 400 800 kilometers

Katanga Plateau

Victoria Falls

10°S

.St. Helena

Mozambique Channel

Réunion

Elevation	
13,100 ft. (4,000 m)	
6,600 ft. (2,000 m)	
1,600 ft. (500 m)	
650 ft. (200 m)	
0 ft. (0 m)	
Below sea level	

▲ Mountain peak
— Rift valleys

NAMIB DESERT

KALAHARI DESERT

20°S

Tropic of Capricorn

INDIAN OCEAN

30°S

Cape of Good Hope

History
195,000 Years Ago
Earliest known *Homo sapiens* appears in Ethiopia.

Geography
3100 B.C. Upper Egypt and Lower Egypt are united. ▶

2000 B.C.

Culture
◀ **4000 B.C.** Early sickle blades are used for farming in Egypt.

Reading for Understanding

▶ Key Ideas

BEFORE, YOU LEARNED

Landforms in the Earth's tropical zones have warm climates.

NOW YOU WILL LEARN

Africa, the world's second largest continent, lies almost entirely in the tropics.

▶ Vocabulary

TERMS & NAMES

basin a region drained by a river system

escarpment a steep slope separating two flat areas of different heights

Mount Kilimanjaro the highest mountain in Africa, in northeast Tanzania (TAN•zuh•NEE•uh)

Sahara the world's largest desert

Victoria Falls a 355-foot waterfall on the Zambezi River in South Central Africa

Nile River the longest river in the world, which empties into the Mediterranean Sea in northeast Egypt

canopy the highest layer in a forest, formed by the treetops

Sahel (suh•HAYL) a semiarid region just south of the Sahara

desertification the change of fertile land to desert

REVIEW

tectonic plates a large rigid section of the Earth's crust that is in constant motion

savanna a grassland in the tropics or subtropics

Visual Vocabulary Sahara

▶ Reading Strategy

Re-create the chart shown at right. As you read and respond to the **KEY QUESTIONS**, use the chart to summarize information about the physical geography of Africa.

 Skillbuilder Handbook, page R5

SUMMARIZE

	AFRICA'S CLIMATE	AFRICA'S VEGETATION
Along Equator		
Tropical Zones		
Outside Tropics		

 GRAPHIC ORGANIZERS
Go to **Interactive Review** @ ClassZone.com

Africa's Geographic Extremes

Connecting to Your World

Africa, the world's second largest continent, is a land of geographic extremes. Parts of the vast Sahara may not see a drop of rain for years. In contrast, areas in Africa's rain forest region may receive more than five feet of rain a year. On Africa's savanna, herds of zebras, gazelles, and elephants graze, hunted by lions and leopards. They are just a few of Africa's thousands of animal and plant species.

The Plateau Continent

▼ **KEY QUESTION** What are some of Africa's geographic features?

Most of Africa is a plateau, a high and flat landform. The African plateau overlooks a thin strip of coastline. Several places on the plateau contain bowl-shaped areas called **basins**. The Niger River flows through the Niger Basin, the Sudan River flows through the Sudan Basin, and the Congo River flows through the Congo Basin. In the Chad Basin in West Central Africa, water collected to form Africa's fourth largest lake, Lake Chad.

Lion Most African lions, like this one in Kenya, now live in protected wildlife reserves.

Africa's Serengeti Wildebeests and zebras graze on the Serengeti Plain in Tanzania.

KENYA
Lake Victoria
Serengeti Plain
TANZANIA

Distinctive Landforms Slow, dramatic forces shaped Africa. Erosion gradually molded southern Africa's **Great Escarpment**, a slope separating the high plateau of the interior from the narrow eastern coast.

Earlier you learned that **tectonic plates** move inside the earth. In eastern Africa, sections of the African Plate are slowly pulling apart. This change, called divergence, opened the Great Rift, a series of valleys running 4,000 miles down most of the continent. Long, deep lakes formed in the Great Rift, including Lake Nyasa and Lake Tanganyika. However, Lake Victoria, Africa's largest lake, lies in a shallow basin between two rift valleys. The Earth's plates pushing together produced Africa's volcanic mountains. These include Mount Kenya, Mount Cameroon, and Africa's highest mountain, **Mount Kilimanjaro**.

The **Sahara**, the world's largest desert, stretches across North Africa. Sahara is the Arabic word for "desert." Its total area is roughly equal to that of the continental United States. Other African deserts include the Kalahari and Namib, both located in southern Africa.

Rivers of Africa Most of Africa's rivers have rapids and waterfalls, making them hard to navigate. The Congo River winds through Central Africa. Many tributaries feed into the Congo, making the Congo river system the largest in Africa. While much of the upper Congo is navigable, 32 high waterfalls dot the river near its mouth. People who live near **Victoria Falls**, a 355-foot waterfall on southern Africa's Zambezi River, call it Mosi-oa-Tunya (MOH•see•oh•ah•TOON•yah), "the smoke that thunders," because of its roaring mist.

Congo River This satellite photo shows Kinshasa and Brazzaville, two capital cities on opposite banks of the Congo River. The city areas are the lighter areas in the photo. **What might the dark green areas represent?**

Congo River from Space

REP. OF THE CONGO
Brazzaville
DEM. REP. OF THE CONGO
Kinshasa

Brazzaville

Kinshasa

Congo River

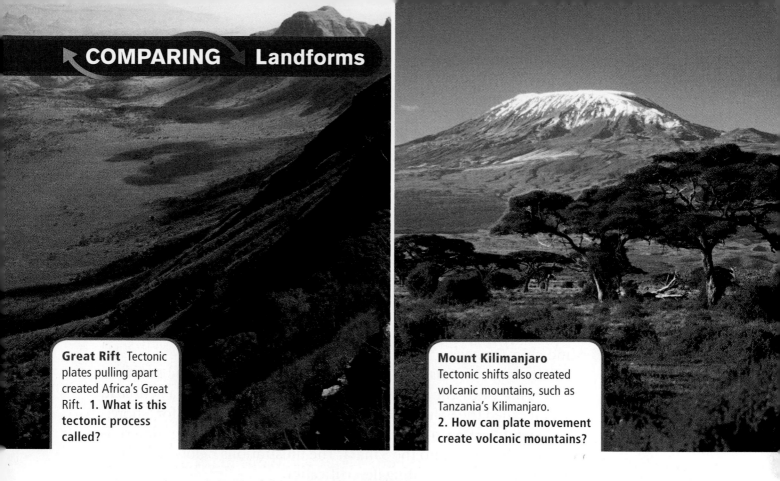

Great Rift Tectonic plates pulling apart created Africa's Great Rift. **1. What is this tectonic process called?**

Mount Kilimanjaro Tectonic shifts also created volcanic mountains, such as Tanzania's Kilimanjaro. **2. How can plate movement create volcanic mountains?**

The world's longest river, the **Nile**, flows north through northeast Africa for more than 4,000 miles. For thousands of years, people have depended on the Nile's annual floods to enrich their soil for farming. But for most of that time, no one knew where the river began. The ancient Greek geographer Ptolemy guessed the Nile's source was in a snowy area he called the "Mountains of the Moon." In the 1870s explorers found that Lake Victoria was the main source of the Nile.

▲ **SUMMARIZE** Describe the key geographic features in Africa.

Climate, Plants, and Animals

▼ **KEY QUESTION** How does Africa's location shape its climate?

The Equator divides the Earth into two hemispheres, and also runs right through Africa's midpoint. Turn the page to see climate and vegetation maps of Africa.

A Warm Continent Along the Equator, the climate is tropical wetland. Bands of tropical wet and dry climate border these wetlands. Next come strips of semiarid climate, and then deserts. In the southeast part of the continent lies a small area of humid subtropical and marine west coast climates. Areas of higher elevation have a highland climate, with rainy winters, dry summers, and typically cooler temperatures than tropical and semiarid climates.

EXTREME INSECTS

The Goliath Beetle, found in Africa's rain forest, is one of the heaviest insects in the world. It is about five inches long and can weigh up to 100 grams, or 3.5 ounces. Goliath beetles are harmless to humans, feeding on dead plant matter, other insects, and animal waste.

Africa's vegetation mirrors the climate, with rain forests **A** (on the map, opposite) along the Equator. Areas of grasslands and woodlands, called **savannas** **B**, are in the wet, dry, and semiarid regions. Scattered shrubs and some grasses grow in the desert **C**. The plants most able to survive in the desert have long root systems that can reach underground water sources. Mediterranean vegetation grows along Africa's northern coast and southern tip. In those areas, native plants include shrubs, small trees, and grasses.

Animal and Plant Life Ferns and mosses make up the rain forest's ground floor, below a middle story of trees and palms. The top layer, towering to about 150 feet, is called the **canopy**. There, leaf-filled branches sprout dazzling orchids. The canopy is also home to fruit-eating parrots and pigeons, seed-eating beetles, and gorillas and chimpanzees.

Grazing animals feed on the grasses and trees of the savanna. Bordering both the savanna and the Sahara Desert is a semiarid region called the **Sahel** (suh•HAYL), from the Arabic word for "shore." But **desertification**, a process in which fertile land becomes desert, is turning the Sahel into the Sahara. The illustrations below show how human activity is speeding desertification.

▲ **DRAW CONCLUSIONS** Describe how Africa's location affects its vegetation.

CONNECT ↪ Geography & Science

Desertification Climate change expanded the Sahara in ancient times. Today, human activity is speeding up the process.

1. The Sahel receives very little rainfall. The vegetation lives in a fragile state.

2. Farming, overgrazing by livestock, and the collection of wood for fuel can erode and expose soil.

3. Vegetation gradually disappears. The remaining plants do not cover the soil as well as the grass did.

4. With less vegetation covering the fertile topsoil, the soil eventually dries up and blows away.

CRITICAL THINKING

Draw Conclusions What impact might desertification have on people living in the affected areas?

Vegetation Regions of Africa

Click here to see regions of Africa @ ClassZone.com

Legend:
- Tropical rain forest
- Tropical grassland
- Desert and dry shrub
- Temperate grassland
- Mediterranean shrub

Scale: 500 / 1,000 miles — 500 / 1,000 kilometers

Map labels: Mediterranean Sea, Nile River, Red Sea, Tropic of Cancer, 40°N, 30°N, 20°N, Gulf of Aden, 10°N, Lake Chad, Shari River, Logone R., Gulf of Guinea, ATLANTIC OCEAN, Ubangi R., Congo River, Lake Victoria, Equator, 0°, Lake Tanganyika, Lake Nyasa, Zambezi R., Mozambique Channel, INDIAN OCEAN, 10°S, 20°S, Tropic of Capricorn, Orange River, 20°E, 40°E, 60°E

Letters on map: C, B, A, C

Climates of Africa

Map labels: Mediterranean Sea, Red Sea, Tropic of Cancer, 20°N, Chad, Gulf of Guinea, Equator, 0°, Victoria, Tanganyika, Nyasa, Mozambique Channel, ATLANTIC OCEAN, Tropic of Capricorn, 20°S, INDIAN OCEAN, 40°S, 60°S, 40°W, 20°W, 0°, 20°E, 40°E, 60°E, 80°E

Legend:

Tropical
- Tropical wet
- Tropical wet and dry

Dry
- Desert
- Semiarid

Mid-Latitude
- Mediterranean
- Marine west coast
- Humid subtropical

Highland

CONNECT Geography & Culture
READING A VEGETATION MAP

Africa's vegetation regions closely mirror the continent's climate zones. As you study Africa's vegetation,

- compare the two maps shown
- note how the climate and vegetation bands are similar
- think about how these vegetation zones affect human activity

1. **Location** What type of vegetation zone lies between Africa's northern coast and the rest of the continent?

2. **Human-Environment Interaction** Which vegetation zones would best support livestock?

541

Africa's Population

▼ **KEY QUESTION** What challenges does Africa's growing population face?

Population distribution in Africa varies dramatically. Large areas of the Sahara, for example, have no people at all. But more than 95 percent of Egypt's population live along the Nile Valley, making it one of the most densely populated places on Earth. The most densely populated areas in Africa are along rivers, lakes, and coastlines. Although most Africans live in rural areas, African cities are growing steadily.

Africa's population is the second-largest, but fastest-growing, in the world. This rapid growth sometimes causes problems. Most countries have few doctors to care for the sick. In addition, the United Nations estimates that about 40 million children south of the Sahara do not attend primary school. African nations and the UN are working to improve education by training more teachers and making school more affordable.

More than 1,500 languages are spoken in Africa. The Democratic Republic of the Congo, in Central Africa, has more than 200 languages and dialects just within its own borders. Many Africans also use a second language to ease communication. For example, French is a language commonly spoken in some West and Central African countries. The language remains in Africa from the years when France held colonies in the region.

▲ **FIND MAIN IDEAS** Describe some of the challenges for Africa's growing population.

Schoolgirl in Ghana
Although school is free for children under 16 in Ghana, nearly 25 percent of children in the country have never attended school.

Africa's Resources

▼ **KEY QUESTION** What are some of Africa's natural resources?

Africa's savannas once teemed with wildlife. But hunters and poachers killed animals for game, and farmers have turned grassland habitats into farmland. To halt this decline, many African countries have established national parks. There, protected animals live in their natural habitats, tourists can take pictures of the animals, and scientists can study their behavior.

Energy and Other Mineral Resources Oil is one of Africa's most valuable resources. Oil-producing countries include Algeria, Kenya, Libya, Egypt, Angola, and Nigeria. Africa also produces about 40 percent of the world's diamonds and more than half of its gold. South Africa has abundant gold, diamonds, and platinum. Other diamond-producing countries include Ghana and Namibia. Zambia produces copper and cobalt, while Zimbabwe mines chromium.

Are Resources Enough? Even the richest mineral resources do not guarantee economic success. For example, the oil that enriches Nigeria has also led to conflicts between ethnic groups over who profits from the resources. Oil production also brings natural gas deposits to the surface, which are often burned off. This "gas flaring" wastes an energy source and harms the environment. Oil companies are now looking for ways to better use natural gas resources. In Angola, rebel groups have mined diamonds, possibly using slave labor, and have sold them to fund civil wars. The United Nations and other groups are working to keep these "conflict diamonds" off the world market.

African countries that export farm crops usually concentrate on one or two crops, a practice put in place during Africa's colonial era. For example, Ethiopia and Uganda export coffee, while Chad exports cotton. But, as with oil wealth, relying on any single crop puts a country at risk when prices fall or resources run out. Many countries are working to make their economies more diverse.

Drying Food These Nigerian women are using the heat from gas flares to dry food on round trays. However, the flaring releases pollutants into the air.

▲ **SUMMARIZE** Identify some of Africa's key resources.

ONLINE QUIZ For test practice, go to **Interactive Review** @ ClassZone.com

Section ❶ Assessment

TERMS & NAMES

1. Explain the importance of
- basin
- savanna
- Sahel
- desertification

USE YOUR READING NOTES

2. Summarize Use your completed chart to answer the following question:

How does Africa's vegetation reflect the climate it grows in?

	AFRICA'S CLIMATE	AFRICA'S VEGETATION
Along Equator		
Tropical Zones		
Outside Tropics		

KEY IDEAS

3. The Nile is the world's longest river, but the Congo river system is Africa's longest. How is this difference possible?

4. What process formed the Great Escarpment?

5. What have been some of the problems associated with Africa's oil resources?

CRITICAL THINKING

6. Analyze Causes and Effects How have plate tectonics shaped Africa's landscape?

7. Identify Problems and Solutions Why is it risky for a country to depend on a single resource?

8. CONNECT to Today How might increasing oil consumption in the United States affect African oil-exporting countries?

9. ART Tourism Brochure Create a brochure for an African national park. Include information on the animals and habitats people will see, and explain how the park will protect those animals and habitats.

Africa: Physical Geography and Early History **543**

Reading for Understanding

▶ Key Ideas

BEFORE, YOU LEARNED

Africa is home to thousands of plant and animal species, and has a wealth of natural resources.

NOW YOU WILL LEARN

Human life first emerged on this warm continent.

▶ Vocabulary

TERMS & NAMES

hominid a human primate; an early human

bipedal walking on two feet

Stone Age the earliest period of human culture, in which people used stone tools

animism the belief that spirits exist in animals, plants, natural forces, and ancestors

griot (gree•OH) a West African storyteller

stateless societies groups that have no single authority, but make decisions based on compromise

lineage descent from an ancestor

REVIEW

fossil remains of early life preserved in the ground

culture the shared attitudes, knowledge, and behaviors of a group

BACKGROUND VOCABULARY

ancestor an early relative

domesticate to adapt or train plants or animals for human use

patrilineal descent from father to father

▶ Reading Strategy

Re-create the web diagram shown at right. As you read and respond to the **KEY QUESTIONS**, use the diagram to record the main ideas about African societies.

Skillbuilder Handbook, page R4

FIND MAIN IDEAS

Values
1._____
2._____

AFRICAN SOCIETIES

Stateless Societies
1._____
2._____

Lineage
1._____
2._____

GRAPHIC ORGANIZERS
Go to **Interactive Review** @ ClassZone.com

Human Beginnings in Africa

Connecting to Your World

Have you ever made an exciting discovery? Perhaps you found a treasure on the street or learned something that made you decide to become a drummer, dancer, hockey player, or scientist.

If you're really lucky, you may make a find that changes the way people think. Anthropologist Donald Johanson had that kind of luck in Ethiopia in 1974 when he and his assistants took a new route back to their vehicle. They stumbled on the bones of a **fossil**, which they named Lucy after a popular song. Lucy was an early human, called a **hominid**. She lived about 3.2 million years ago.

Lucy This early human is the most-studied fossil to date.

Human Ancestors

▼ **KEY QUESTION** What were some of the important hominid finds in Africa?

Lucy, an adult female, probably stood about three and a half feet tall and weighed a little over 60 pounds. She and other hominids were **bipedal**, meaning they walked on two feet. If early hominids used tools, the tools have since disappeared. The first tools that scientists have found—stones to cut meat—date back a mere 2.5 million years.

Animated GEOGRAPHY

Archaeological Dig in East Africa
Scientists continue to look to Africa for clues about early human development.

Click here to see fossils found in East Africa @ ClassZone.com

Chad Skull A reconstruction of the 6.5-million-year-old skull found in Chad in 2001

Important Discoveries Older hominids have been found since Lucy's discovery. Scientists unearthed a six- to seven-million-year-old skull in Chad in 2001. It resembles both a human skull and an ape skull. Scientists wonder whether this and other finds could be early human **ancestors**. Other important discoveries include:

Australopithecines (aw•STRAY•loh•PIHTH•uh•seenz) Like Lucy, these hominids first walked upright in eastern, southern, and central Africa about 4 million years ago.

Homo habilis (HOH•moh–HAB•uh•luhs) Tool-using hominids appeared between 1.5 and 2 million years ago in Africa. In 1960, Mary and Louis Leakey found the skull of a creature they named *Homo habilis*, or "handy man," near chipped pebble tools.

Homo erectus (HOH•moh–ih•REHK•tus) In 1984, scientists found the skeleton of "Turkana Boy" in Kenya. This pre-teen lived about 1.6 million years ago. *Homo erectus* fossils have also been discovered in Asia. They were the first hominids to leave Africa.

Homo sapiens (HOH•moh–SAY•pee•EHNZ) People identical to modern humans first appeared about 150,000 years ago.

Stone Age The **Stone Age**, during which hominids first began using stone tools, began 2.5 million years ago. During this important period, people also learned how to control fire and use language.

▲ **SUMMARIZE** Describe the key hominid finds in Africa.

ONLINE PRIMARY SOURCE To read accounts of important discoveries, go to the **Research & Writing Center @ ClassZone.com**

ANALYZING Primary Sources

Oldest human footprints Mary Leakey and the footprints she discovered in 1978

Mary Leakey (1913–1996), as a young girl, was determined to study the Stone Age. Her most famous discovery was a set of hominid footprints, preserved in dried lava in Tanzania. In a 1978 letter, she wrote:

> We have found magnificent hominid footprints this year, in a dual trail 23 metres [75 feet] long! (confidential) It is a most important find and demonstrates that 3½ m.y. [million years] ago the fully bipedal, striding gait had been completely developed.
>
> Mary Leakey, letter to paleontologist Dick Hooijer

DOCUMENT-BASED QUESTION:
Why were these footprints so important?

The Stone Age in Africa is divided into two periods. The Paleolithic period lasted from 2.5 million years ago to 8000 B.C. During this period, hominids hunted and gathered food. Early humans also chopped meat with sharpened stone tools. Later, they tamed fire, used harpoons and needles, and developed language. The Neolithic period lasted from 8000 B.C. to 3500 B.C. People living at this time polished stone tools and made pottery. They began to grow crops, **domesticate** animals, and live in villages. Around 3500 B.C. they developed writing.

Hand axes These stone tools from the Paleolithic period were found in Tanzania.

Activity

Create a Time Line

Materials
• paper
• pencil
• ruler

1. Reread this chapter and add the dates for the sequence of hominid discoveries in Africa.

2. Look for specific dates in the text. Make sure to match the correct events and dates.

Characteristics of African Societies

▼ **KEY QUESTION** What is the nature of an extended family in African society?

In the previous section, you learned that hundreds of separate languages may be spoken in a single African country. Still, many African **cultures** share certain traits.

Beliefs and Values A typical African family probably wouldn't fit around your dinner table. The extended family of Africa consists of as many as five generations of relatives and spouses who all obey a single leader. This large family works together, protects its members from outsiders, and cares for its weakest members.

Today many Africans are Muslims or Christians. But Africans may also practice traditional religions. Traditional African religions maintain that an all-powerful God created everything. They also believe that spirits exist in animals, plants, natural forces, and ancestors, an idea called **animism**.

One generation of Africans passes information to the next by telling stories. West Africans call their storytellers **griots** (gree•OHZ). You need a good memory to be a griot because some of the best stories about ancestors and other heroes go on for hours or even days. Griots usually accompany their stories with music. Today many popular griots perform on television and record their stories on CDs.

Elders in African Societies
Elders often fill teaching roles, like this Masai elder in Kenya.

Stateless Societies Traditional African cultures didn't organize themselves into states, with one person at the top. Instead they formed stateless societies. In a **stateless society**, two or more equal groups would cooperate.

The extended families that made up these groups were based on lineage. **Lineage** means descent from one parent back several generations to a single ancestor. For example, your own **patrilineal** descent goes back from your father, to his father, and so on.

In traditional African stateless societies, lineages with equal power would share authority. If members clashed, elders from the warring lineage groups would meet to make peace.

To create relationships with people in other lineages, a stateless society uses a system of age sets. Your age set would be the boys or girls born around the same time as you. If you were a boy in the Nandi tribe of Kenya, for example, you would go through military training with your age set. The warrior set, responsible for fighting and governing the tribe, would stay in power for about 15 years. Then it would become a set of elders, and the next younger age set would move up.

 FIND MAIN IDEAS Describe the structure of an African extended family.

ONLINE QUIZ
For test practice, go to
Interactive Review
@ ClassZone.com

Section ② Assessment

TERMS & NAMES

1. Explain the importance of
- hominid
- animism
- stateless societies
- lineage

USE YOUR READING NOTES

2. Find Main Ideas Use your completed diagram to answer the following question:

What are the roles of elders in traditional African societies?

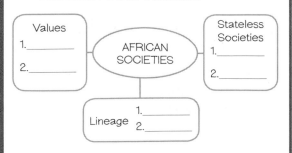

KEY IDEAS

3. Who is Lucy, and how old is she?

4. Which was the first human to leave Africa?

5. How would warring lineage groups make peace?

CRITICAL THINKING

6. Summarize What major human advances took place during the Stone Age?

7. Compare and Contrast What similarities do African cultures share?

8. CONNECT to Today What systems of age sets exist in the United States?

9. MATH **Draw a Scale Time Line** Find a way to demonstrate how long ago Lucy lived. You might start by making a scale with 100 years equal to 1 inch. How many inches, feet, or yards would it take to show 1,000 or 1 million years? How about 3.5 million years?

Interactive ◄Review

Click here to complete these and other activities online @ **ClassZone.com**

CHAPTER SUMMARY

Key Idea 1
Africa, the world's second largest continent, lies almost entirely in the tropics.

Key Idea 2
Human life first emerged on this warm continent.

For **Review and Study Notes**, go to **Interactive Review @ ClassZone.com**

NAME GAME

Use the Terms & Names list to complete each sentence on paper or online.

1. I am the longest river in the world. _____ _____ Nile River _____

2. I am a process that changes grasslands and semi-arid regions into deserts. _____

3. I am a landform some Africans call Mosi-oa-Tunya, "the smoke that thunders." _____

4. I am the top layer of the rain forest. _____

5. I am Africa's grasslands, where antelopes, giraffes, and elephants graze. _____

6. We are the slowly shifting blocks that make up the Earth's surface layer. _____

7. I can tell stories that last for many hours or even days._____

8. I am the belief that trees, animals, and ancestors have living spirits. _____

9. We do not have a single leader, but resolve problems by having our elders meet and talk until they agree. _____

10. I am the earliest period of human history. _____

animism
canopy
desertification
griot
hominid
Mount Kilimanjaro
Nile River
Sahel
savanna
stateless societies
Stone Age
tectonic plates
Victoria Falls

Activities

Flip Cards

Use the online flip cards to quiz yourself on the terms and names introduced in this chapter.

Hominid

Crossword Puzzle

Complete an online crossword puzzle to test your knowledge of Africa's geography and early history.

ACROSS
1. the world's largest desert

VOCABULARY

Explain the significance of each of the following.

1. Mount Kilimanjaro
2. Nile River
3. savanna
4. Sahel
5. desertification
6. hominid
7. bipedal
8. animism
9. stateless societies
10. lineage

Explain how the terms and names in each group are related.

11. Sahel, desertification, savanna
12. stateless societies, culture, lineage

KEY IDEAS

① Africa's Geographic Extremes

13. What geographic process formed Africa's Great Rift Valley?
14. What makes many African rivers hard to navigate?
15. How do many Africans communicate with people who don't speak their language?
16. What minerals make South Africa a wealthy country?

② Human Beginnings in Africa

17. Why was Lucy such an important discovery?
18. What does a griot do?
19. How are African extended families structured?
20. How do stateless societies create relationships between people of different lineages?

Goliath Beetle

CRITICAL THINKING

21. **Analyze Causes and Effects** Create a table to show some of the effects of human settlement on rain forests and grasslands.

CAUSES	EFFECTS
cut down rain forests for farmland	
cut trees for firewood and use grass for grazing	

22. **Summarize** What events led to the formation of game parks in Africa?
23. **Compare and Contrast** How are traditional African religions similar to and different from Christianity and Islam?
24. **Five Themes: Movement** How might family members moving to a city affect a traditional extended family structure?
25. **Connect Geography & Science** Why can't scientists say for sure whether *Australopithecines* like Lucy used tools?

Answer the ESSENTIAL QUESTION

How do humans interact with the extreme African environment?

Written Response Write a two- or three-paragraph response to the Essential Question. Be sure to consider the key ideas of each section. Use the rubric below to guide your thinking.

Response Rubric
A strong response will:
- describe Africa's landforms, climate, and vegetation
- explain how climate and terrain have influenced African population density
- identify the resources available in Africa

STANDARDS-BASED ASSESSMENT

LINE GRAPH

Use the line graph and your knowledge of Africa to answer questions 1 and 2.

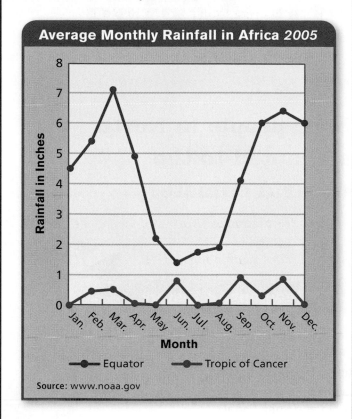

Average Monthly Rainfall in Africa 2005

Source: www.noaa.gov

1. When is the "dry season" along the Equator?

A. September through December

B. January through March

C. March through May

D. June through August

2. In what month did the most rain fall along the Tropic of Cancer?

A. March

B. June

C. September

D. November

ELEVATION PROFILE

Use the elevation profile at the Equator to answer questions 3 and 4 on your own paper.

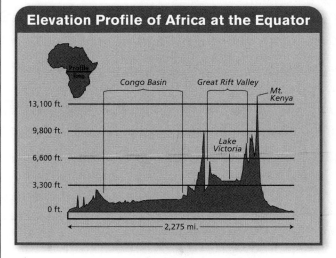

Elevation Profile of Africa at the Equator

3. At what elevation is Mount Kenya?

4. Based on this elevation profile, why might Africa be called the "plateau continent"?

GeoActivity

1. INTERDISCIPLINARY ACTIVITY–SCIENCE

With a small group, choose one of Africa's native animals to research. Find out where the animal lives, what it eats, whether it has predators, and if its habitat has been threatened by hunting or farming. Present your findings to the class.

2. WRITING FOR SOCIAL STUDIES

Reread the description of griots in Section 2. Write a story, poem, or rap about one of your ancestors or an American folk hero. Memorize your story and present it to your class without using notes.

3. MENTAL MAPPING

Create an outline map of Africa and label the following:

- Lake Victoria
- Lake Chad
- Nile River
- Great Rift
- Great Escarpment
- Sahara Desert
- Sahel

Egypt and North Africa

 ESSENTIAL QUESTION

How have people in North Africa adapted to the region's arid climate?

CONNECT ➤ **Geography & History**

Use the map and time line to answer the following questions.

1. Which country receives the most rainfall?

2. About how many years separate the building of the Great Pyramid and Suez Canal?

Culture
◀ **2600 B.C.–2500 B.C.**
Great Pyramid built

History
1516 Selim I rules
the Ottoman Empire
at the time of
Egypt's conquest. ▶

3100 B.C.

History
3100 B.C. Upper and
Lower Egypt united

History
A.D. 642 Muslim invaders
spread Islam to North Africa.

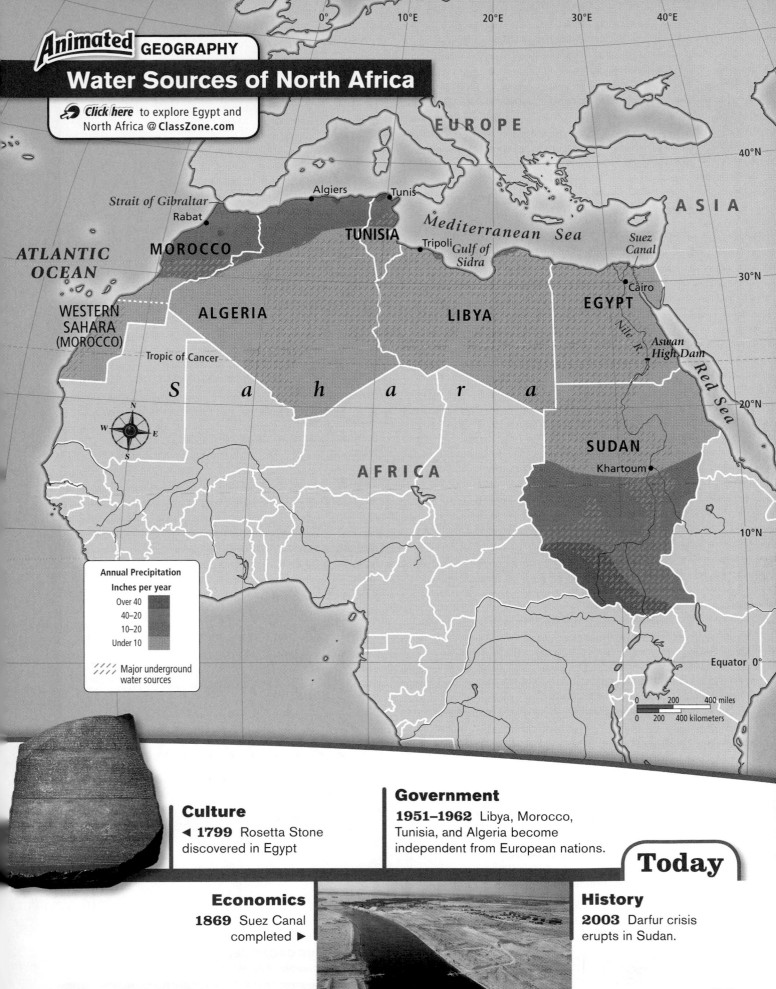

EUROPE

ASIA

ATLANTIC
OCEAN

Strait of Gibraltar
Rabat

Algiers

Tunis

Mediterranean Sea

Tripoli *Gulf of
Sidra*

Suez
Canal

MOROCCO

TUNISIA

WESTERN
SAHARA
(MOROCCO)

ALGERIA

LIBYA

EGYPT

Cairo

Nile R.

Aswan
High Dam

Red Sea

Tropic of Cancer

S   a   h   a   r   a

SUDAN

Khartoum

N
W   E
S

AFRICA

Annual Precipitation

Inches per year

Over 40
40–20
10–20
Under 10

//// Major underground
water sources

40°N

30°N

20°N

10°N

Equator 0°

0   200   400 miles
0   200   400 kilometers

Culture

◄ **1799** Rosetta Stone
discovered in Egypt

Government

1951–1962 Libya, Morocco,
Tunisia, and Algeria become
independent from European nations.

Today

Economics

1869 Suez Canal
completed ►

History

2003 Darfur crisis
erupts in Sudan.

Reading for Understanding

SECTION 1

▶ Key Ideas

BEFORE, YOU LEARNED

The Nile, the world's longest river, runs through Egypt.

NOW YOU WILL LEARN

The Nile made the great civilizations of ancient Egypt possible.

▶ Vocabulary

TERMS & NAMES

silt fertile soil deposited by a river

delta the triangle-shaped deposit of rich soil at a river's mouth

Aswan High Dam a structure to control the floodwaters of the Nile River and provide electricity

cataract a high waterfall or rapids

dynasty a family or group that rules for several generations

pharaoh a ruler of ancient Egypt

pyramid an ancient Egyptian structure, built over or around a tomb

Nubia in ancient times, the Nile River valley of southern Egypt and northern Sudan

Kush an ancient Nubian kingdom in northern Sudan

hieroglyphics an Egyptian writing system in which picture symbols stand for meanings or sounds

papyrus a paperlike material made from the stems of the papyrus reed

BACKGROUND VOCABULARY

mummy a body prepared for burial according to ancient Egyptian practice

REVIEW

Nile River the longest river in the world, which empties into the Mediterranean Sea in northeast Egypt

▶ Reading Strategy

Re-create the chart shown at right. As you read and respond to the **KEY QUESTIONS**, use the chart to analyze causes and effects related to the Nile River's annual floods.

 See Skillbuilder Handbook, page R8

ANALYZE CAUSE AND EFFECT

CAUSE	EFFECT
1.	1.
2.	2.
3.	3.

GRAPHIC ORGANIZERS
Go to **Interactive Review @ ClassZone.com**

Ancient Egypt: Pyramids and Pharaohs

Connecting to Your World

In 1993, the Mississippi River overflowed after heavy rains. Levees broke, submerging farms, towns, and roads under the muddy water. About 50 people died, and thousands more had to leave their homes. The Mississippi River flood of 1993 was a disaster. But in ancient Egypt, annual river floods were seen as a good thing.

Egypt's Lifeline

▼ **KEY QUESTION** Why is the Nile called Egypt's lifeline?

Egypt, in Africa's northeast corner, receives little rainfall. As a result, the country has relied on the **Nile River** for its economy. Each year, the Nile flooded due to upstream rain, depositing rich black soil called **silt** along its banks. The silt at the river's mouth formed a triangular shape, called a **delta**. Most of Egypt's population clustered in the Nile's river valley and delta. The Nile's yearly floods made these regions so fertile that ancient Egyptians called their country Kemet, or the Black Land.

Animated GEOGRAPHY

The Nile Valley
The world's longest river creates a ribbon of fertile soil, cutting through the desert.

↪ *Click here* to take a journey down the ancient Nile @ ClassZone.com

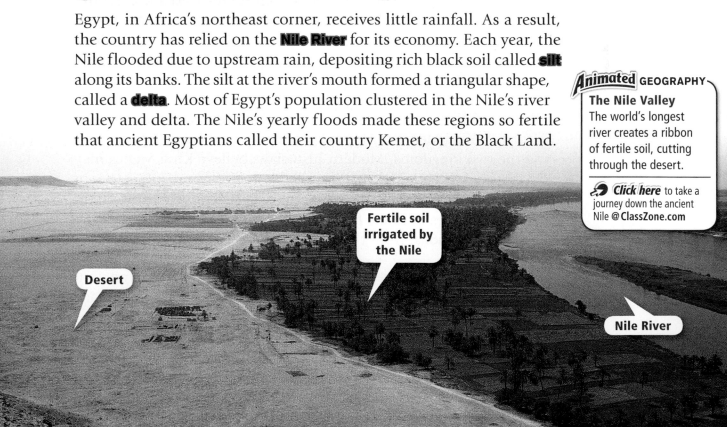

Desert

Fertile soil irrigated by the Nile

Nile River

Aswan High Dam

The Aswan High Dam contains the Nile floodwaters in a reservoir called Lake Nasser. In addition to increasing irrigated land, the dam provides electricity for factories and farm villages. But with little silt reaching the Nile's mouth and flood plain, farmers must now use costly chemical fertilizers, and the Nile delta is actually decreasing in size.

Aswan High Dam
Lake Nasser

The Nile Then and Now In ancient Egypt, the Nile Valley provided various grasses and reeds used for huts, sandals, baskets, simple boats, and other products. Ancient Egyptians also dug canals to irrigate their fields and channel the Nile's water. Each June, floods would leave behind silt in a narrow strip along the flood plain and at the delta. Today the **Aswan High Dam** controls the Nile's flooding and provides year-round irrigation. Since the Aswan High Dam opened in 1970, Egypt has doubled its agricultural production.

🔺 **FIND MAIN IDEAS** Describe how the Nile has acted as Egypt's lifeline.

History of Ancient Egypt

🔻 **KEY QUESTION** What other civilizations competed with ancient Egypt for power?

Ancient Egypt, one of the world's first great civilizations, arose along the banks of the Nile. For centuries, geography kept Egypt isolated. Six **cataracts**, or high waterfalls and rapids, make the Nile hard to navigate in the south. Deserts surround the Nile in the west and east, and the Mediterranean Sea borders Egypt to the north. People created farming villages along the Nile by about 4000 B.C. Eventually these villages became two kingdoms, Upper Egypt in the south and Lower Egypt at the Nile delta.

Uniting Upper and Lower Egypt Tradition says that around 3100 B.C., King Menes of Upper Egypt conquered Lower Egypt, uniting the two kingdoms. Modern historians believe King Menes may have been a legend, and that it probably took several rulers to join the kingdoms. King Menes is said to have founded the first Egyptian **dynasty**, or series of rulers from one family. These rulers came to be known as **pharaohs**, from the Egyptian words for "great house."

Old, Middle, and New Kingdoms Historians divide ancient Egyptian history into three periods. During the Old Kingdom, a strong central government supervised the construction of gigantic tombs called **pyramids**. Farmers and laborers built these structures when the Nile's floodwaters covered their fields. During the Middle Kingdom, Egypt conquered its southern neighbor, **Nubia**. Nubia provided Egypt with slaves, soldiers, and gold. Instead of pyramids, Middle Kingdom pharaohs built tombs in the desert sands. During the New Kingdom, Egypt became the strongest power in the world. A powerful pharaoh named Queen Hatshepsut led armies, sent off trade expeditions, and built splendid temples. Egypt's power peaked under the 66-year reign of Ramses II. He regained Asian territories that earlier pharaohs had lost. Statues of Ramses II still stand all over Egypt.

Conquest by Foreigners After Ramses' death in 1213 B.C., Egypt began to decline. Eventually, it fell to foreign invaders, including the **Kush** kingdom of Nubia. After an Assyrian invasion ended Kushite rule of Egypt, the Kush civilization withdrew south. In 332 B.C., Alexander the Great of Macedonia conquered Egypt. After Alexander's death, one of his generals, Ptolemy (TAHL•uh•mee), became king of Egypt, starting a dynasty that lasted nearly 300 years. One of the last Ptolemies, Queen Cleopatra, married the co-ruler of Rome, Mark Antony. Antony and Cleopatra's attempt to seize power from Antony's co-ruler failed in 31 B.C. The next year, Egypt became a Roman territory.

Animated GEOGRAPHY

Egyptian and Kush Kingdoms

Click here to learn more about Queen Hatshepsut and the New Kingdom @ ClassZone.com

Legend:
- Old Kingdom (2575–2130 B.C.)
- Additional area of Middle Kingdom (1938–1630 B.C.)
- Egyptian Empire during New Kingdom (1539–1075 B.C.)
- Kingdom of Kush, 700 B.C.
- Cataract

CONNECT Geography & History

Movement Which kingdom extended farthest north?

▲ **SUMMARIZE** List the civilizations that interacted with ancient Egypt.

CONNECT to History

Egyptians decorated pyramid walls with elaborate paintings. They honored pharaohs by giving them "perfect" features, no matter how they really looked. Scenes might show pharaohs' accomplishments in life, or show them enjoying the afterlife.

Activity

Make a Pyramid

Materials
- construction paper
- ruler
- scissors
- tape
- markers

1. Research Egyptian pyramids and art.

2. Draw and cut out a six-inch square and four six-inch equilateral triangles (triangles whose sides are of equal length).

3. Decorate one side of each triangle with hieroglyphics and Egyptian paintings.

4. Tape the four sides together so that their top points meet. Then tape three of the bottom sides to the square base.

5. Leave one of the triangles unattached to the square so you can see inside.

Culture of Ancient Egypt

🔻 **KEY QUESTION** What were some of the accomplishments of ancient Egyptian culture?

Ancient Egyptians built great cities, where architects, doctors, artisans, and engineers worked. They also invented a form of paper. But their most lasting achievement is probably the pyramids. These giant structures served as both monuments and tombs for the pharaohs.

Social Systems Ancient Egyptian social classes formed a kind of pyramid, as shown below. At the top was the pharoah, then a small upper class. Skilled or educated workers made up the middle classes. The largest groups, farmers, laborers and slaves, were at the pyramid's base.

Most boys followed their fathers' occupations, and girls usually became wives and mothers. Women could own, buy, sell, and inherit property, and divorce their husbands.

Egypt's Gods and the Afterlife Egyptians worshiped several deities, and considered their pharaohs to be earthly versions of them. One New Kingdom pharaoh, Akhenaton, promoted the worship of only one deity, the sun god Aton. When Akhenaton died, the new king, Tutankhamen, brought back worship of the old gods.

Tutankhamen "King Tut" was nine years old when he became pharaoh, and he ruled with the help of advisors.

Animated GEOGRAPHY
Egyptian Social Roles

🦅 **Click here** to hear from each level of Egyptian society @ ClassZone.com

Social Systems Egyptian society was arranged with the largest group at the bottom and a small ruling class on top.

CRITICAL THINKING
What levels of the pyramid would require the most education?

Pharaoh Egyptians considered their pharaohs to be gods.

Priests The priests cared for the temples and held religious ceremonies.

Scribes The scribes were trained in the art of writing and record keeping.

Laborers and Slaves Slaves might be prisoners of war, or people who owed debts or had committed crimes. In general, slaves were eventually freed.

Pharaoh

Priests and Nobles

Scribes and Government Officials

Craftspeople and Merchants

Farmers

Laborers and Slaves

Egyptians believed in an afterlife that resembled life on Earth. To preserve a person's body for the next life, they embalmed and dried it, and wrapped it in linen bandages, making a **mummy**. Egyptians also mummified pets, such as cats and monkeys. They packed their family members' tombs with items they thought they would need in the afterlife: clothes, food, makeup, and jewelry. Egyptian rulers had the fanciest tombs of all. The pharaohs' burial chambers were full of items such as sparkling gold treasures and statues of servants to care for them in the afterlife.

Ancient Egyptian Contributions Ancient Egypt made advances in language, science, and mathematics. Egyptians invented a form of picture writing called **hieroglyphics** which was used in temples, tombs, and on monuments. A different script was used on scrolls of **papyrus**, a paperlike material made from papyrus grass. The Egyptian calendar was based on the Nile farming cycle of flooding, planting, and harvesting. Doctors in ancient Egypt understood that a person's pulse was connected to the heart, and knew how to set broken bones. Egyptians used geometry to set land borders and design buildings.

 SUMMARIZE Name some of the advancements of ancient Egypt.

Hieroglyphics The word hieroglyphics comes from the Greek word for "sacred carving." **Why might the Greeks have called hiero-glyphics "sacred"?**

Section 1 Assessment

ONLINE QUIZ
For test practice, go to
Interactive Review
@ ClassZone.com

TERMS & NAMES

1. Explain the importance of
- Nile River
- delta
- Kush
- hieroglyphics

USE YOUR READING NOTES

2. Analyze Cause and Effect Use your completed chart to answer the following question:

What were the results of the Nile's annual floods?

CAUSE	EFFECT
1.	1.
2.	2.
3.	3.

KEY IDEAS

3. Why did ancient Egyptians cluster around the valley and delta of the Nile River?

4. What three periods make up ancient Egyptian history?

5. What was the largest social class in ancient Egypt?

CRITICAL THINKING

6. Summarize What are some positive and negative effects of the Aswan High Dam?

7. Evaluate What rights did women have in ancient Egypt?

8. CONNECT to Today What are the risks and benefits of living near a great river?

9. SCIENCE Create a Multimedia Presentation Using the library or Internet, research mummification and create a slide show to demonstrate the process. Show all the steps from removal of organs and embalming to drying and wrapping.

Click here to enter the Great Pyramid
@ ClassZone.com

PYRAMIDS

The Great Pyramid of Khufu is Egypt's largest pyramid, originally standing 481 feet high. For more than 4,000 years it stood as the world's tallest building.

Click here to visit the pyramids of Egypt today. Learn about the rulers of ancient Egypt and their belief in the afterlife.

Click here to see how a pyramid was built. Learn about the materials and methods and the people who built them.

Click here to explore the passageways and chambers of the Great Pyramid's interior.

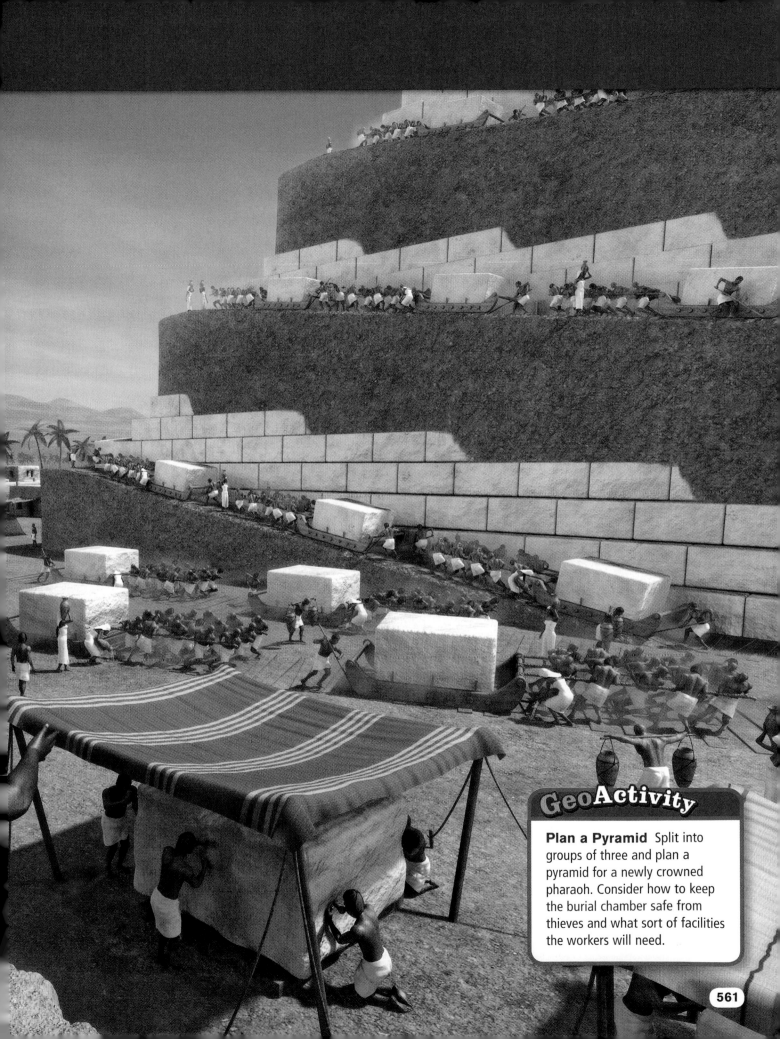

Reading for Understanding

▶ Key Ideas

BEFORE, YOU LEARNED

Ancient Egyptians built a great civilization, but were conquered by foreign powers.

NOW YOU WILL LEARN

A blending of cultures has made Egypt a leader for North Africa, as well as for Southwest Asia.

▶ Vocabulary

TERMS & NAMES

Rosetta Stone an ancient Egyptian stone that provided a key to decipher hieroglyphics

Islam a religion believing in one god, called Allah, and his prophet on Earth, Muhammad

Muslim a follower of Islam

Suez Canal a waterway linking the Red Sea with the Mediterranean Sea

protectorate a weaker country or area controlled by a stronger country

Anwar el-Sadat president of Egypt from 1970 to 1981

Camp David Accords peace treaty between Egypt and Israel, signed in 1979

Sudan a country of northeast Africa, located south of Egypt

BACKGROUND VOCABULARY

modernize to accept modern ways or ideas

Visual Vocabulary Suez Canal

▶ Reading Strategy

Re-create the time line shown at right. As you read and respond to the **KEY QUESTIONS**, use the time line to order important events in Egypt and Sudan.

 See Skillbuilder Handbook, page R6

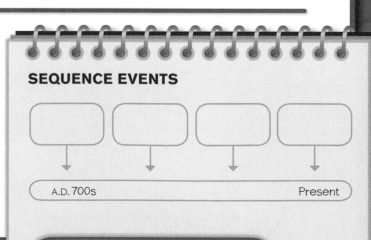

SEQUENCE EVENTS

A.D. 700s   Present

↪ **GRAPHIC ORGANIZERS**
Go to **Interactive Review** @ ClassZone.com

Modern Egypt and Sudan

Connecting to Your World

Have you ever created a secret code? Typically, one set of letters stands for letters you already know. Hieroglyphics were like a mysterious code until the 1799 discovery of a carved stone called the **Rosetta Stone**. It contained the same text in ancient Greek, Egyptian script, and hieroglyphics. Since scholars knew the first two scripts, they were able to crack the code of hieroglyphics. But no one in the world today knows how ancient Egyptian was spoken.

From Ancient to Modern Times

▼ **KEY QUESTION** What foreign powers ruled Egypt?

The Arabic language became the dominant language in Egypt and North Africa because of a culture shift in the 600s and 700s. Around that time, Arabs from Southwest Asia introduced a new religion called Islam.

Rosetta Stone
This discovery was the key to decoding Egyptian hieroglyphics.

Temple of Luxor A white mosque stands amid the ruins of this ancient temple.

Luxor

EGYPT

Influence of Islam **Islam** is the belief in one god, called Allah, and his prophet on Earth, Muhammad. Followers of Islam are called **Muslims**. (You will learn more about the spread of Islam in the next unit.) Arab Muslims invaded Egypt in A.D. 639. Afterward, Egyptians began to speak Arabic, and many adopted the Muslim faith. Islamic empires ruled Egypt for more than 1,000 years. The Ottoman Empire took control in 1517, but other groups contended for power.

During Napoleon Bonaparte's rule, France briefly occupied Egypt, beginning in 1798. The Ottomans regained control in 1801 under a military leader, Muhammad Ali. He tried to **modernize** Egypt. Though Muhammad Ali's efforts failed, his son Said (sa•EED) made a more lasting change. Under Said's reign, in 1859, workers began to dig the **Suez Canal**, a waterway linking the Red Sea with the Mediterranean. The canal continues to be a key trade route for Egypt, Europe, and Southwest Asia.

Becoming Independent The valuable trade route created by the Suez Canal led more foreign powers to try to control Egypt. Britain invaded Egypt in 1882. During World War I, Britain declared Egypt a **protectorate**, or country controlled by a stronger nation.

After the war, Egyptians began to call for independence. Britain granted independence in 1922, but kept troops in Egypt to guard the Suez Canal. During World War II, Egypt and other Arab nations formed the Arab League, which opposed the formation of Israel in 1948. Egypt lost four wars with Israel between 1948 and 1973. In 1977, Egyptian President **Anwar el-Sadat** traveled to Israel. In 1979, Egypt and Israel signed the **Camp David Accords**, the first peace treaty between Israel and an Arab state. The Arab League expelled Egypt for signing the treaty, but readmitted Egypt in 1989.

Egypt remains a leader in North Africa and the Arab world. Its capital, Cairo, is Africa's biggest city. In Africa, only Nigeria has more people. Although Egypt is not a big oil producer, Saudi Arabia is the only Middle Eastern country with a stronger economy.

▲ **SEQUENCE EVENTS** Identify the foreign powers that ruled Egypt.

HISTORY MAKERS

Muhammad Ali Pasha 1769–1849

As an officer in the Ottoman army, Muhammad Ali helped rid Egypt of French invaders. In 1805, he became Egypt's governor, or Pasha. During his 44-year reign, he attempted to transform Egypt into a modern country. Muhammad Ali brought European advisors and teachers to Egypt and sent Egyptians to study in Europe. He also tried to bring industry to this agricultural land. Muhammad Ali's descendants ruled under British control, but his family held power in Egypt until 1953.

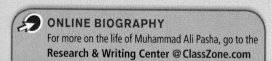

ONLINE BIOGRAPHY
For more on the life of Muhammad Ali Pasha, go to the
Research & Writing Center @ ClassZone.com

Life in Egypt Today

▼ **KEY QUESTION** How do most Egyptians live?

Egyptian city life is hectic and noisy. Huge slums adjoin wealthy residential areas, and the streets teem with traffic and overcrowded streetcars. People might wear Western clothes or traditional Egyptian clothing: a shirt and pants for men and a long, colorful flowing gown for women. Culturally, most Egyptians consider themselves Arabs and practice Islam.

More than half of Egyptians live in the countryside. Most villagers tend small farms on land often owned by wealthier landowners. Electric power is common in rural areas. Poor city dwellers and villagers alike eat a diet of bread, beans, and vegetable stew. Sweetened coffee or tea are popular drinks.

National Government Egypt's president serves a six-year term and may be re-elected indefinitely. The powerful president also leads the armed forces, appoints a prime minister and cabinet, and even appoints some members of the parliament. In 2005, Egypt allowed multiple candidates to run for president. Previously, parliament had selected single candidates for citizens to vote on.

Economic Structure and Activities Despite its role as a regional leader, Egypt is still a developing nation, struggling with unemployment and with how to feed its growing population. Agriculture employs more than one-third of Egyptian workers, but accounts for only one-sixth of the economy.

Cairo The Nile winds through Egypt's capital city. **If you are traveling south along the Nile, are you headed upstream or downstream?**

Service industries, such as banking, education, and trade, employ half of Egypt's workers and account for more than half of the economy. Thanks to Egypt's high-grade cotton, textile production provides one-third of the economy. In this socialist country, the government owns most major industries. But change is under way. To stimulate Egypt's economy, the government tries to attract foreign investment in Egypt's energy and tourism industries. Tourists, lured by ancient temples and pyramids, provide the largest share of Egypt's foreign funds.

▲ **SUMMARIZE** Describe daily life in Egypt.

Sudan: Egypt's Neighbor

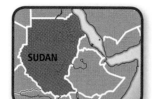

▼ **KEY QUESTION** What cultural differences are behind the conflicts in Sudan?

You already learned that ancient Egypt controlled Nubia, or northern Sudan. After ancient Egypt lost control, Nubia's Kush kingdom endured until its collapse around A.D. 350. Modern **Sudan**, Egypt's southern neighbor, is Africa's largest nation in area. Part of Sudan extends into central Africa, with its savannas and rain forests. Northern Sudan is covered by desert.

Culture: Regional Differences Most people who live in the northern two-thirds of Sudan speak Arabic, the country's official language, and follow Islam. In the southern third of Sudan, various African groups practice traditional animist religions. A few are Christians.

Most Sudanese people live on subsistence farms or herd animals in the desert. Three out of ten Sudanese live in cities and towns. Sudan's main urban center—the area surrounding the capital, Khartoum—is home to more than six million people. Near the capital, two million more Sudanese live in refugee camps, displaced by civil wars.

Modern History of Sudan In the 1800s, Sudan again came under Egyptian control. But in 1881, a Sudanese Muslim teacher led a four-year revolt, overturning Egyptian rule. In 1898, Britain and Egypt joined forces to conquer Sudan. Britain ruled Sudan until 1956.

Between independence and 1998, military governments ruled Sudan. Conflicts between Sudan's Arab Muslim north and non-Muslim,

CONNECT · History & Culture

Lost Boys of Sudan

The Lost Boys were orphans of Sudan's civil war. These children and young adults banded together to make a harrowing journey from Sudan to Ethiopia, back to Sudan, and then to refugee camps in Kenya. In 2001, the United States took in 3,600 Lost Boys across the country, primarily in Texas, Michigan, and Arizona. Now mostly adults, many Lost Boys work one or two jobs while attending high school or college classes.

non-Arab south led to two civil wars during the 20th century. Millions of people lost their lives. A separate conflict in a western region of Sudan called Darfur erupted in 2003. This war pitted Arab herders, aided by government militias, against non-Muslim ethnic groups. Tens of thousands of civilians died, and roughly two million farmers were forced from their homes.

Herding Sudan's government donated these goats to people in refugee camps.

Government and Economy Drought and famine periodically plague Sudan, which remains mired in the Darfur conflict. Under Sudan's 1998 constitution, the president serves a five-year term and appoints a cabinet. Voters elect most members of the legislature, who serve terms of four years.

This developing economy depends heavily on agriculture. Sudanese factories, which employ about four percent of the population, manufacture cement, food products, food, and textiles. In 1999, Sudan began producing oil, currently the country's leading export. But most of Sudan's roads remain unpaved, and four out of ten people live in poverty.

▲ **FIND MAIN IDEAS** Describe the cultural differences leading to Sudan's civil wars and conflicts.

ONLINE QUIZ
For test practice, go to **Interactive Review** @ ClassZone.com

Section 2 Assessment

TERMS & NAMES

1. Explain the importance of
- Rosetta Stone
- Suez Canal
- protectorate
- modernize

USE YOUR READING NOTES

2. Sequence Events Use your completed time line to answer the following question:

What was the last foreign power to control Egypt?

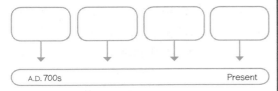

A.D. 700s   Present

KEY IDEAS

3. Why were the Camp David Accords important?

4. With which culture and religion do most Egyptians identify?

5. What natural and political problems have plagued Sudan?

CRITICAL THINKING

6. Draw Conclusions Why do you think the Suez Canal has been so important to Egypt?

7. Make Inferences Why has the Sudanese government's attempt to enforce Islamic law caused problems in this mostly Muslim country?

8. CONNECT to Today Terrorist bombings at popular Egyptian tourist sites took place in 2004 and 2005. Why do such attacks threaten Egypt's economy?

9. MATH Make a Graph Make a bar graph showing Egypt's major industries. Your graph should clearly show which industries employ most people and which industries are most profitable.

Reading for Understanding

▶ Key Ideas

BEFORE, YOU LEARNED

Egypt's modern culture was shaped by many outside forces, including the spread of Islam and conquest by the Ottoman Empire.

NOW YOU WILL LEARN

The Ottomans and Islam also influenced other North African nations, as did European and colonizing powers.

▶ Vocabulary

TERMS & NAMES

Berbers (BUR•buhrz) the original inhabitants of North Africa and the Sahara

Carthage (KAR•thihj) an ancient North African city-state

Punic Wars (PYOO•nik) wars fought between Rome and Carthage during the 3rd and 2nd centuries B.C.

Maghrib (MUHG•ruhb) the Arab name for North Africa, which means "the West"

Atlas Mountains series of mountain ranges stretching from Morocco to Tunisia

souk (sook) open-air market

jellaba a traditional Berber garment; a robe with full sleeves

dictatorship a state or government ruled by a leader with absolute power

Visual Vocabulary souk

▶ Reading Strategy

Re-create the web diagram shown at right. As you read and respond to the **KEY QUESTIONS**, use the diagram to compare and contrast important information about Morocco, Algeria, and Libya.

 See Skillbuilder Handbook, page R9

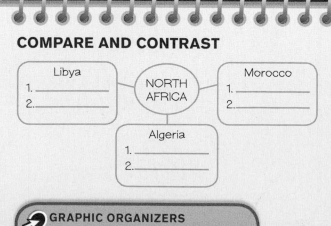

COMPARE AND CONTRAST

Libya
1. _____
2. _____

NORTH AFRICA

Morocco
1. _____
2. _____

Algeria
1. _____
2. _____

🔊 **GRAPHIC ORGANIZERS**
Go to **Interactive Review** @ ClassZone.com

Other Nations of North Africa

Connecting to Your World

What happens in your home town on July 4? More than 200 years after declaring independence from Britain in 1776, U.S. citizens still celebrate the 4th of July with picnics, parades, concerts, and fireworks. By contrast, Libya celebrated its first Independence Day in 1951. Algeria won its freedom in 1962. Like many African nations, these North African countries have enjoyed less than 100 years of independence.

A Muslim Region

🔻 **KEY QUESTION** What cultures have most influenced North Africa?

Hazardous desert trade routes connected ancient North Africa to the sub-Saharan bulk of the continent. In contrast, just eight miles separate Europe from North Africa at the Strait of Gibraltar. As a result, ancient North Africans looked to Europe for trade and cultural contacts.

Ramadan Ramadan is a holy month of fasting in the Muslim faith. Here, men pray in the streets of Algiers.

Reading for Understanding

▶ Key Ideas

BEFORE, YOU LEARNED

Europeans traveled to other lands, such as the Americas, establishing colonies to build wealth.

NOW YOU WILL LEARN

Colonizers also traveled to West Africa, dividing up land once held by great trading empires.

▶ Vocabulary

TERMS & NAMES

Ghana a West African kingdom between the A.D. 700s and the A.D. 1000s in what is now Mauritania and Mali; a modern country in West Africa

trans-Saharan across the Sahara

Mali a West African empire between the A.D. 1200s and the A.D. 1500s; a modern West African country

Mansa Musa (MAHN•sah moo•SAH) leader of the Mali empire from 1312 to about 1337

Songhai (sawng•hy) an ancient West African empire, which was most powerful about A.D. 1500

imperialism the practice of one country controlling the government and economy of another country or territory

Pan-Africanism a movement calling for the unity of all people of African descent

BACKGROUND VOCABULARY

camel a humped mammal used in the desert as a pack animal and provider of meat, milk, and wool

self-rule independent government

▶ Reading Strategy

Re-create the diagram shown at right. As you read and respond to the **KEY QUESTIONS**, use the diagram to organize important details about West Africa.

 Skillbuilder Handbook, page R4

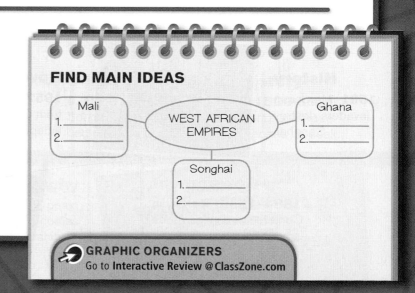

FIND MAIN IDEAS

Mali
1. _____
2. _____

WEST AFRICAN EMPIRES

Ghana
1. _____
2. _____

Songhai
1. _____
2. _____

GRAPHIC ORGANIZERS
Go to **Interactive Review** @ ClassZone.com

Three Trading Empires

Connecting to Your World

What makes a country strong? Is it the size of a nation or population? The United States' strength results partly from its size, population, and military power, but also from trade. Trade helps a nation build wealth, which makes it strong. Trade with other peoples allowed early West African cultures to build empires in Africa.

Three Trading Empires

▼ **KEY QUESTION** How did West African trading empires become wealthy?

Crossing the Sahara was always difficult, but it became easier around 2,000 years ago. That's when southwest Asian traders introduced camels to the region. **Camels** are perfectly adapted to the desert. Their feet can navigate soft sand, and they can survive without food or water for weeks. For centuries, camel caravans crossed the Sahara along established trade routes. These routes gave rise to three great empires.

Camel Caravan
Nomadic Tuareg people lead their camels across the Sahara.

CONNECT Geography & History

1. **Movement** Which ancient empire might have had the easiest time trading with other peoples?
2. **Location** Which ancient empire covered the most area?

Ghana The Soninke people of **Ghana** founded the first West African empire around A.D. 700. Ancient Ghana began as a trading center for grains, cattle, and metals. Camel caravans from the Arabic world arrived at Ghana's markets, introducing Islam to the region and establishing a **trans-Saharan** trade. *Trans-Sahara* means "across the Sahara." Caravans brought books, salt, cloth, and tools from Arabia to Ghana, and carried back slaves, ivory, and gold. Taxing the gold trade enriched Ghana's rulers. In 1076, Moroccan Berbers conquered Ghana's major city. More defeats followed, and Ghana collapsed around 1200.

Mali As Ghana declined, several small states competed to control the empire. Between 1235 and 1240, a king named Sundiata conquered the other states to found a new empire east of Ghana. This empire, **Mali**, thrived because it controlled a large new gold field at the center of the trans-Saharan trade.

Sundiata's great-nephew **Mansa Musa** (MAHN•sah moo•SAH) ruled Mali from 1312 to about 1337, spreading Islam throughout the empire. Mosques, courts, and schools in Timbuktu, the capital of Mali's trading empire, made the city a major center of Muslim learning. After 1400, Mali gave way to a stronger empire.

Songhai The Songhai empire developed from large towns near the present-day border between Mali and Niger. Songhai's strength came from its control of the trans-Saharan trade. Sunni Ali, a great military leader, ruled Songhai from 1464 to 1492. In 1493, Askia Muhammad became king, eventually enlarging Songhai to its greatest extent. Askia, known as Askia the Great, promoted the spread of both Islam and trade. The last of West Africa's three great empires declined after Moroccan fighters defeated Songhai in 1591.

▲ **SUMMARIZE** Describe how the three empires of West Africa gained wealth.

European Imperialism

▼ **KEY QUESTION** Why did Europeans come to Africa?

In the 1500s, Portuguese traders made their way to Africa. Soon Holland and other European powers also vied for the rich trade in slaves, gold, and ivory.

The Slave Trade Shortly after the Portuguese arrived in West Africa, they started enslaving Africans and shipping them to Europe. Before this time, African powers had sent some slaves to Asia and Europe. But the Atlantic slave trade exceeded anything that had come earlier. Scholars say it was history's single largest forced movement of people. African merchants and rulers sold enslaved Africans to Europeans, who sent the slaves to the Americas. The slave trade devastated Africa. Between the late 1400s and the middle 1800s, 10 to 12 million enslaved persons came to the Americas. Slave raiding and warfare emptied towns and villages, destroying ancient patterns of culture, work, and trade.

Europeans Carve Up Africa Even after the slave trade ended, Europeans continued to raid Africa for cheap labor, natural resources, and markets. European **imperialism**, or control of weaker nations, grew with the European industrialization of the late 19th century. Railroads, steamships, and the repeating rifle helped Europeans control much of Africa. In the 1880s, European powers carved Africa into a colonial map for European convenience. The new colonial boundaries ignored traditional ethnic boundaries. In many cases, this grouped long-standing enemies together in colonies.

HISTORY MAKERS

Askia Muhammad 1441?–1538

Askia (AS•kee•uh) Muhammad, shown here in an artist's rendering, ruled the West African Songhai empire at its most powerful. He became king by overthrowing the son of Sunni Ali, an earlier ruler. Askia enlarged Songhai by seizing big chunks of Mali. He also conquered several states ruled by the Hausa people, and colonized Berber towns. In 1528, Askia Muhammad's son took power.

 ONLINE BIOGRAPHY
For more on the rulers of West Africa, go to the **Research & Writing Center @ ClassZone.com**

Impact of Imperialism By 1914, only Liberia, founded by former U.S. slaves, and Ethiopia were free of European control. Africans resisted colonization, but superior weapons helped Europeans hold power. Different colonial powers had different styles of control, as shown in the chart below. The British ruled indirectly, letting Africans take over some parts of government. France refused to share any power, considering its colonies part of a global French nation.

The scars of imperialism still mark Africa. Colonizers discouraged industrial development, keeping colonies dependent. Wars of conquest and resistance cost many lives. So did the brutal demands of plantation work. Colonial boundaries remained after independence and still cut across ethnic lines.

▲ **ANALYZE POINTS OF VIEW** Describe why Europeans wanted to colonize Africa.

African Colonies Gain Independence

▼ **KEY QUESTION** How did African colonies win independence?

In the early 1900s, some colonies sent African students overseas to universities. These well-educated Africans began to dream of freedom for their own people. They joined with former slaves and descendents of slaves in the Americas in calling for freedom and unity for all people of African descent. Their movement became known as **Pan-Africanism**. African soldiers fought alongside Allied forces in World War I and World War II. After the wars, Africans began to demand independence for their own countries. Some Europeans also

COMPARING ◀ Forms of Colonial Rule

	INDIRECT RULE of African Colonies	**DIRECT RULE** of African Colonies
Methods	• Local governments used • Limited self-rule • Goal: to develop future leaders • Government based on European styles, but may have local influences	• Foreign officials brought in to rule • No self-rule • Goal: to get colonies to adopt European culture • Government based only on European styles
Examples	British colonies such as Nigeria	French colonies such as French West Africa

CRITICAL THINKING

Draw Conclusions Which form of rule do you think would be the best long-term method, and why?

began to question whether it was right to maintain colonies. Britain's indirect control of its colonies helped prepare African leaders for eventual **self-rule**. More tightly controlled colonial governments left newly independent nations to struggle on their own.

Methods of Attaining Independence The first West African colony to win independence was the Gold Coast. In 1957, it peacefully separated from Great Britain and reclaimed the ancient name of Ghana. Nigeria won independence in 1960. Independence for some other West African countries came only after years of guerrilla warfare. For example, war erupted in the Portuguese colony of Guinea-Bissau in the early 1960s. The conflict dragged on until 1974. By the end of 1975, Portugal had given up the last of its African claims.

 COMPARE Describe the paths different colonies took toward independence.

Independence Guinea-Bissau citizens celebrate the end of Portuguese colonization in 1974.

Section 1 Assessment

TERMS & NAMES

1. Explain the importance of
- Ghana
- Mansa Musa
- Songhai
- Pan-Africanism

USE YOUR READING NOTES

2. Find Main Ideas Use your completed diagram to answer the following question:

What did the ancient West African empires have in common?

Mali
1. _____
2. _____

WEST AFRICAN EMPIRES

Ghana
1. _____
2. _____

Songhai
1. _____
2. _____

KEY IDEAS

3. What were the names of West Africa's great empires?

4. How did industrialization promote European imperialism in Africa?

5. How did West African countries win independence from their colonizers?

CRITICAL THINKING

6. Evaluate How did World Wars I and II lead some Europeans to question colonialism?

7. Make Inferences Why do you think the modern nation of Ghana chose the name of an ancient empire in a different location?

8. CONNECT to Today In 1994 in Rwanda, 800,000 people were killed in ethnic fighting. How has Africa's colonial past promoted such conflicts?

9. TECHNOLOGY Create a Multimedia Presentation Create a slide show about historical Timbuktu. Focus on Timbuktu's history as a prominent center of trade and Islamic learning.

Reading for Understanding

▶ Key Ideas

BEFORE, YOU LEARNED

Colonizers traveled to West Africa, dividing up land once held by great trading empires.

NOW YOU WILL LEARN

Nigeria and Ghana have struggled to maintain stable governments and productive economies.

▶ Vocabulary

TERMS & NAMES

Hausa (HOW•suh) a people of northern Nigeria and southern Niger

Yoruba (YAWR•uh•buh) a people of south-western Nigeria, parts of Benin, and Togo

Igbo (IHG•bo) a people of southeastern Nigeria

coup (koo) military takeover

Biafra (bee•AF•ruh) a largely Igbo region of Nigeria that declared its independence in 1967, but surrendered after losing a civil war in 1970

Kwame Nkrumah (KWAHM•eh uhn•KROO•muh) modern Ghana's first president

Kente cloth a brightly colored, woven cloth made by the Ashanti and Ewe peoples

BACKGROUND VOCABULARY

stability durability; resistance to change

subsistence farming farming that produces just enough to feed the farmer's family

Ashanti (uh•SHAN•tee) a people of Ghana

Visual Vocabulary kente cloth

▶ Reading Strategy

Re-create the chart shown at right. As you read and respond to the **KEY QUESTIONS**, use the chart to summarize information about Nigeria and Ghana.

 Skillbuilder Handbook, page R5

SUMMARIZE

NIGERIA	GHANA
1.	1.
2.	2.
3.	3.
4.	4.

 GRAPHIC ORGANIZERS
Go to **Interactive Review** @ClassZone.com

Nigeria and Ghana

Connecting to Your World

How does your family make important decisions, such as where to take a vacation or whether to move to a new apartment? In some families, a parent or both parents make the decisions. Some families seek out the advice of an older relative. However your family makes decisions, you're probably used to your own system. Like your family, West African societies had their own familiar ways of ruling themselves and solving conflicts. But when a familiar system disappears, things get confusing.

NIGERIA

Nigeria

▼ **KEY QUESTION** How have Nigeria's main ethnic groups gotten along since independence?

When European powers colonized Africa, they didn't recognize the systems of governing the Africans used. Instead, they imposed European-style centralized governments to replace African stateless systems. Most ruling officials were Europeans. When African nations gained freedom in the mid-1900s, few Africans knew how to run a European-style government. As a result, many African governments lacked **stability**.

River Port The Niger River remains an important West African transportation route. **Why might the Niger River be important to international trade?**

History Since Independence In Section 1, you learned that colonial powers drew Africa's borders without considering the culture or history of African peoples. Nigeria is just one of the African countries where conflict has grown from cultural divisions.

The three largest groups in Nigeria are the **Hausa**, who live in the north; the **Yoruba**, who live in the southwest; and the **Igbo** (IHG•bo), who live in the east. After independence in 1960, Nigeria's major ethnic groups clashed. The Igbo and other southern groups resented the Hausa's greater political power.

Ethnic conflict between the groups fueled an Igbo-led **coup**, or military takeover, in 1966. In 1967, the Igbo broke away from Nigeria to create their own state, called **Biafra**. A three-year civil war followed, causing many deaths from fighting and starvation. Biafra surrendered and rejoined Nigeria in 1970. Military leaders ruled Nigeria from 1966 to 1979, and again from 1983 until 1999. A new constitution and democratic elections restored a civilian government in 1999. But ethnic and religious tensions still simmer.

Ethnic Groups of Nigeria

NIGER

Niger R.

Lake Chad

Kano
Hausa

Kaduna

BENIN

NIGERIA

Abuja

JOS PLATEAU

TOGO

Benue

Yoruba
•Ibadan

CAMEROON

Benin City
Lagos   *Igbo*

N

0   100   200 miles
0   100   200 kilometers

Igbo Ethnic group
★ Capital city
Oil field

Bioko

ATLANTIC OCEAN

EQUATORIAL GUINEA

CONNECT Geography & History

Place Abuja, Nigeria's capital, was a planned city. Why might Nigeria want its capital in the center of the country?

Nigerian Culture and Daily Life More than 250 ethnic groups, who speak many different languages, live in Nigeria, whose official language is English. Nigeria's 132 million people make it Africa's most populous nation, and one of the world's largest. About half of Nigerians are Muslim, while 40 percent are Christian. Many people also practice traditional animist religions or mix them with Islam or Christianity.

At least two-thirds of Nigerians survive on less than one dollar a day. Most are poor farmers who live in grass, mud, or wood homes in clusters called compounds. In rural areas, people wear long, loose robes. Wealthy city dwellers live in modern houses or apartments and often wear Western clothes. Poor Nigerians, who have flooded the cities since the 1960s, often crowd into slums.

Nigerian authors Chinua Achebe (CHIHN•wah ah•CHAY•bay) and Wole Soyinka (WOH•lay shaw•YING•kuh) wrote their most famous works in English. In 1986, Soyinka became the first African to win the Nobel Prize for Literature. Nigerian music pulses with drums, xylophones, and string and wind instruments. The Yoruba are famous for their wood carvings. Nigerian art, especially sculptures, have inspired Western artists.

Ken Saro-Wiwa was a Nigerian activist fighting for the rights of his Ogoni people. He and eight others were arrested and hanged in 1995 by Nigeria's military government. Many around the world believed Saro-Wiwa was convicted on false charges. Shortly before his death, Saro-Wiwa smuggled writings out of prison.

> It is also very important that we have chosen the path of non-violent struggle. Our opponents are given to violence and we cannot meet them on their turf, even if we wanted to. Non-violent struggle offers weak people the strength which they otherwise would not have. The spirit becomes important, and no gun can silence that.
>
> Source: Ken Saro-Wiwa, A Month and a Day: A Detention Diary

DOCUMENT–BASED QUESTION
What does "we cannot meet them on their turf" mean?

 ONLINE PRIMARY SOURCE To read more of Saro-Wiwa's works, go to the **Research & Writing Center** @ClassZone.com

Government and Economics An elected president and vice president head Nigeria's government. They're assisted by an appointed cabinet and a two-house National Assembly.

Nigerians depend largely on agriculture for their livelihood. Two out of three Nigerian workers are farmers, who produce much of the world's cocoa, peanuts, and rubber. But most of Nigeria's farmers practice **subsistence farming**. Their food crops include maize, beans, and other vegetables and fruits. While manufacturing industries are developing, mining and petroleum produce the majority of the nation's wealth. In addition to producing coal, gold, iron ore, and natural gas, Nigeria is also one of the world's biggest oil exporters. Oil has contributed to Nigeria's wealth—and to its problems. In the 1970s, oil profits funded government programs to improve the standard of living. But relying too heavily on oil exports slowed development of Nigeria's other industries. Oil spills have also polluted certain areas, ruining farmland and poisoning fish.

▼ **SUMMARIZE** Summarize Nigeria's ethnic conflicts since independence.

Elections A new Nigerian constitution and free elections in 1999 ended nearly 30 years of military rule.

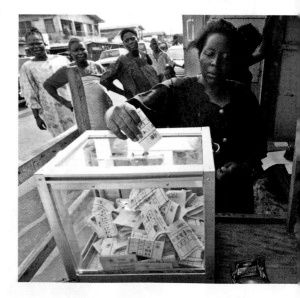

While most West African countries have some sort of coastline, the Sahara still dominates countries such as Mauritania, Mali, and Niger.

Desert Life

Desert settlements, like this one in Mali, form near water sources. Mud-brick structures can provide insulation from the desert heat. Still, many African desert-dwellers live nomadically, moving from place to place.

Desert village near Mopti, Mali ▼

Work

Cattle herders move their livestock from one place to another.

Transportation

For centuries, camels have been the traditional means of crossing the Sahara.

Traditional mud-brick houses ▶

Coastal Life

West African coastal villages, like this one in Côte d'Ivoire, rely heavily on fishing for food. Commercial fishing further out to sea can jeopardize fish stocks. Countries such as Mauritania are banning some foreign fishing boats from fishing off their coasts.

Fishing village near Fresco, Côte d'Ivoire ▼

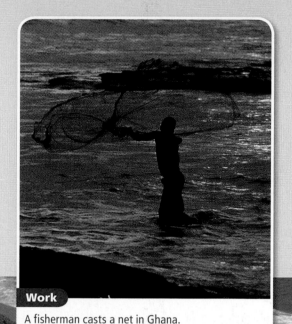

Work

A fisherman casts a net in Ghana.

Transportation

Fishing boat in Ghana

◄ *Coastal housing*

CRITICAL THINKING

1. **Compare and Contrast** How do people in these regions adapt their living arrangements to their surroundings?

2. **Make Inferences** Why would cattle herders need to move from place to place?

Reading for Understanding

▶ Key Ideas

BEFORE, YOU LEARNED

Nigeria and Ghana have struggled to maintain stable governments and productive economies.

NOW YOU WILL LEARN

Mali and Côte d'Ivoire are developing countries with lively cultural traditions.

▶ Vocabulary

TERMS & NAMES

federation colonies, states, or countries that have joined together

inflation a price increase or a fall in the purchasing power of money

infrastructure basic services a community needs, such as roads, railroads, water and power lines, schools, and post offices

millet a grain raised in West Africa, often made into porridge

BACKGROUND VOCABULARY

rig to influence or fix the results of an election

REVIEW

drought a long period of little or no rainfall

famine a severe food shortage

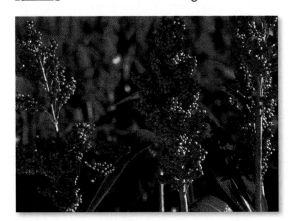

Visual Vocabulary millet

▶ Reading Strategy

Re-create the Venn diagram shown at right. As you read and respond to the **KEY QUESTIONS**, use the diagram to compare and contrast information about Mali and Côte d'Ivoire.

 Skillbuilder Handbook, page R9

COMPARE AND CONTRAST

CÔTE D'IVOIRE   BOTH   MALI

⊙ GRAPHIC ORGANIZERS
Go to **Interactive Review** @ ClassZone.com

Mali and Côte d'Ivoire

Connecting to Your World

Have you ever worked hard on something, only to feel like you got none of the benefit or credit? Mali produces more gold than any other African country except South Africa and Ghana. But despite Mali's natural wealth, local mining communities keep little of the wealth that their mines produce.

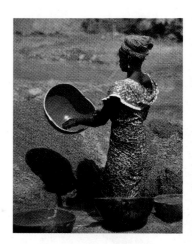

Panning for Gold
Gold helped build the West African trading empires and is a key resource in modern Mali.

Mali

MALI

▼ **KEY QUESTION** What does Mali's economy rely on?

Mali, located where three powerful African empires once reigned, remains one of the world's poorest countries. Nearly two-thirds of Mali's people live in poverty. Residents of Mali cluster in the basin of the Niger River because most of the country is located within the Sahara.

After overcoming fierce resistance from Africans, France seized a huge territory in West Africa in 1895. This territory included present-day Mali, then called French Sudan. French Sudan joined the Federation of West Africa in 1904. A **federation** is a group of colonies or states with a single government. In 1958, French Sudan won the right to govern itself within the larger French community. In 1960, the Republic of Mali gained full independence from France.

Mud-Brick Mosque
Rebuilt in 1907, the mud-brick Great Mosque dominates the ancient trading town of Djenné.

COCOA

Cocoa is one of Côte d'Ivoire's biggest exports. Cocoa beans are the seeds of the cacao tree. Large pods grow on the trees, ranging from yellow to purple in color. These pods contain 20 to 60 seeds inside a sticky white pulp. The seeds are gathered and processed as cocoa beans.

Our Lady of Peace This cathedral in Côte d'Ivoire's capital is the world's largest Christian church.

Côte d'Ivoire

▼ **KEY QUESTION** How has Côte d'Ivoire's economy suffered in recent years?

Côte d'Ivoire (KOHT dee•vwahr) lies west of Ghana and east of Liberia on Africa's west coast. Like Mali, its northern neighbor, Côte d'Ivoire was once part of French West Africa. In the early 1700s, the French established coastal trading posts in present-day Côte d'Ivoire, exchanging European goods for ivory and slaves. Later, French colonizers forced West Africans to build roads and railroads, and to toil on cocoa, coffee, and logging plantations. These thriving plantations made Côte d'Ivoire West Africa's wealthiest French colony. The colony won independence from France in 1960, 14 years after the French ended forced labor.

History Since Independence Félix Houphouët-Boigny (OOF•WAY BWAH•nyuh), an African doctor, led the independence movement of French West African colonies. He became Côte d'Ivoire's first president in 1960, and held office until he died in 1993. After Houphouët-Boigny's death, political instability hurt Côte d'Ivoire's economy. The military took over the government in 1999. In 2000, a **rigged**, or fixed, election caused mass protest, leading to a three-year civil war. In 2003, a power-sharing government came to office, but occasional violence continued. In 2005, South Africa hosted talks between the Ivoirian government and rebel leaders. Although the war formally ended, rebels still control the northern half of the country.

Government President Houphouët-Boigny spent millions transforming his hometown, Yamoussoukro (YAH•moo•SOO•kroh), into Côte d'Ivoire's capital. But most business still takes place in Abidjan, the nation's largest city. Under Côte d'Ivoire's constitution, the president is elected by popular vote for a five-year term. He appoints a prime minister, who governs with the aid of a one-house National Assembly. Until 1990, Côte d'Ivoire had a single-party government.

Economics Two out of three Ivoirians are farmers, and the country is one of the world's biggest exporters of coffee, cocoa, and palm oil. But Côte d'Ivoire's dependence on a few products means the economy rises or falls with shifting worldwide prices. Continuing warfare threatens profits too. Côte d'Ivoire has offshore oil reserves, which may feed this developing nation's growth. The country's infrastructure is well-developed, with more than 4,000 miles of paved roads, cell phone access, and some Internet availability. Abidjan's seaport is one of the most modern in West Africa.

World Cup Côte d'Ivoire's national soccer team earned its first World Cup trip in 2006.

Ivoirian Culture and Daily Life Our Lady of Peace, the world's largest Christian church, dominates the skyline of Côte d'Ivoire's capital. But Christians in the southern regions of the country are outnumbered by Muslims and people following traditional African religions, especially in rural regions and the north. Most Ivoirians belong to the Akan, Kru, Mandes, or Voltaic peoples. Soccer is popular in Côte d'Ivoire. The Elephants, Côte d'Ivoire's national team, surprised the world by qualifying for their first-ever World Cup in 2006. About 25 percent of the population are immigrants, mostly from poorer neighboring countries. French is the country's official language, but most people speak ethnic languages or a common tongue, Dioula. Côte d'Ivoire's literacy rate—over 50 percent—is among the highest in West Africa.

Nearly half of Ivoirians live in cities, and many urban areas have French and Southwest Asian communities. However, the recent civil war led many Europeans to leave the country. There is a large divide in the cities between the poor and wealthier people. Crime has risen because of recent fighting. Côte d'Ivoire had more than 215,000 homeless children in 2004, including 50,000 in Abidjan.

Villagers live with extended families in compounds. The compounds are usually dried clay structures with thatched or metal roofs. Ethnic groups govern their villages in different ways; some with councils of elders, some with single chiefs. Trading, herding, and farming are the main activities. Important crops in the region are yams, root vegetables similar to sweet potatoes; and **millet**, a grain often made into porridge.

Ivoirian arts include music, storytelling by griots, and mask-making. The Dan people use masks to symbolize a chief's authority. The popular Festival of Masks is held in Côte d'Ivoire's forest region each November. Other mask ceremonies celebrate harvests. Alpha Blondy, a world-famous Ivoirian musician, blends African and Caribbean sounds in a style called "Afro-reggae." Zouglou is a musical style originating in Abidjan. Sung in French slang and local languages, it is similar to American hip-hop.

Mask Festival Yacouba people celebrate the Festival of Ignames, or yams.

▲ **SEQUENCE EVENTS** Explain what led to Côte d'Ivoire's economic struggles.

Section ❸ Assessment

ONLINE QUIZ
For test practice, go to
Interactive Review
@ ClassZone.com

TERMS & NAMES

1. **Explain the importance of**
   • inflation
   • infrastructure
   • drought
   • famine

USE YOUR READING NOTES

2. **Draw Conclusions** Use your completed diagram to answer the following question:

   Why is Côte d'Ivoire's economy more successful than Mali's?

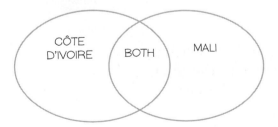

KEY IDEAS

3. In what year did both Mali and Côte d'Ivoire win their independence from France?

4. What are Mali's main exports?

5. What natural resource may improve Côte d'Ivoire's economy?

CRITICAL THINKING

6. **Compare and Contrast** How did Mali's taking the name of an ancient empire differ from Ghana's?

7. **Analyze Cause and Effect** What happened to spark Côte d'Ivoire's civil war?

8. **CONNECT to Today** Tensions remain high between Côte d'Ivoire's government and opposition leaders. What do you think might happen if French and West African peacekeeping troops leave the country?

9. **ART** **Draw a Mask** Research Bambara masks on the Internet. Copy a picture of your favorite mask and label it to describe its key elements and their symbolic meanings.

CHAPTER SUMMARY

Key Idea 1
Colonizers traveled to West Africa, dividing up land once held by great trading empires.

Key Idea 2
Nigeria and Ghana have struggled to maintain stable governments and productive economies.

Key Idea 3
Mali and Côte d'Ivoire have a wealth of natural resources, but are two of Africa's poorest countries.

For **Review and Study Notes**, go to **Interactive Review @ ClassZone.com**

NAME GAME

Use the Terms & Names list to complete each sentence on paper or online.

1. I am an ancient empire as well as a modern country that used to be known as the Gold Coast. _____Ghana_____

2. I led the Mali Empire in the 14th century. _____

3. I am perfectly equipped for desert travel. _____

4. I am an ancient empire, whose main city was Timbuktu, as well as a modern West African country. _____

5. I am a region of Nigeria that broke away in a civil war in 1967. _____

6. I was modern Ghana's first president. _____

7. I am used by the Ashanti people to make clothing for religious ceremonies. _____

8. I am a nation's roads, bridges, schools, and post offices. _____

9. I am rising prices or a fall in the value of money.

10. I am a collection of states, colonies, or countries. _____

Biafra
camel
federation
Ghana
Igbo
imperialism
inflation
infrastructure
Kente cloth
Mali
Mansa Musa
Kwame Nkrumah
Songhai
subsistence
trans-Saharan
Yoruba

Activities

GeoGame

Use this map to reinforce your knowledge of West African geography. Drag and drop each name in the list to its location on the map.

Ghana
Mali
Côte d'Ivoire
Bamako
Abuja

To play the complete game, go to **Interactive Review @ClassZone.com**

Crossword Puzzle

Complete an online crossword puzzle to test your knowledge of the region.

ACROSS
1. a woven ceremonial fabric from Ghana

VOCABULARY

Explain the significance of each of the following.

1. Songhai
2. federation
3. infrastructure
4. imperialism
5. Ghana
6. Kente cloth
7. coup
8. Kwame Nkrumah

Explain how the terms and names in each group are related.

9. trans-Saharan, Ghana, and Mali
10. coup, Igbo, and Biafra

KEY IDEAS

① Three Trading Empires

11. Why is Askia Muhammad known as Askia the Great?
12. Which European countries first explored Africa?
13. Which West African country remained free in the era of European imperialism?
14. What effect did World War II have on the African struggle for independence?

② Nigeria and Ghana

15. What is the official language of Nigeria and Ghana?
16. Which African nation is the continent's most populous country?
17. What Nigerian art form inspired Western painters?
18. Why did the Gold Coast choose the ancient name of Ghana?

③ Mali and Côte d'Ivoire

19. What difficulties has Mali faced since independence?
20. In what year did Mali get its first democratic government?
21. What made Côte d'Ivoire the wealthiest colony in French West Africa?
22. What are Côte d'Ivoire's main exports?

CRITICAL THINKING

23. **Compare and Contrast** Create a chart to compare and contrast Ghana and Mali. Show their dates of independence, major products or industries, and chief challenges.

	GHANA	MALI
challenges		

24. **Make Predictions** What factors could affect Côte d'Ivoire's economy in the future?
25. **Connect to Economics** Which West African country would you predict will have the greatest economic success in the coming years? Why?
26. **Five Themes: Region** In Nigeria and Côte d'Ivoire, why does Islam dominate in northern regions, while Christianity and African religions prevail in the south or along the coast?
27. **Connect Geography & Culture** What makes Mali a cultural crossroads?

Answer the ESSENTIAL QUESTION

How have centuries of colonialism affected West Africa?

Written Response Write a two- or three-paragraph response to the Essential Question. Be sure to consider the key ideas of each section. Use the rubric below to guide your thinking.

Response Rubric
A strong response will:
• summarize colonialism in West Africa
• note colonialism's lingering effects on industry, ethnic conflict, and government corruption
• explain how concentration on a single crop or resource benefited colonizers, not Africans

STANDARDS-BASED ASSESSMENT

 Test Practice

• Online Test Practice @ ClassZone.com

• Test-Taking Strategies and Practice
at the front of this book

BAR GRAPH

Use the bar graph and your knowledge of geography to answer questions 1 and 2.

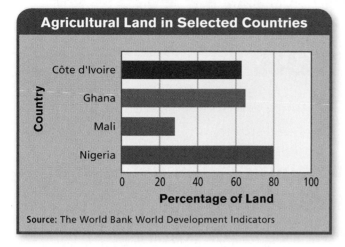

Agricultural Land in Selected Countries

Source: The World Bank World Development Indicators

1. Which nation has the highest percentage of agricultural land?

A. Côte d'Ivoire

B. Ghana

C. Mali

D. Nigeria

2. Why might Mali have such a low percentage of agricultural land?

A. because Mali is landlocked

B. because Mali's economy is more focused on industry

C. because the northern part of Mali is in the Sahara

D. because Mali has no rivers for irrigation

PRIMARY SOURCE

Nigerian author Chinua Achebe gained fame for *Things Fall Apart*, his novel about Nigeria under colonial rule. In this passage, he discusses why his book is read worldwide. Use the passage to answer questions 3 and 4.

> I knew I had a story, but how it fit into the story of the world—I really had no sense of that. Its meaning for my Igbo people was clear to me, but I didn't know how other people elsewhere would respond to it. Did it have any meaning or resonance for them? I realized it did when . . . the whole class of a girls' college in South Korea wrote to me and each one expressed an opinion about the book. And then I learned something, which was that they had a history that was similar to the story of *Things Fall Apart*—the history of colonization.

Source: Chinua Achebe, interview in *Atlantic Monthly*, August 2, 2000

3. Why might people from other countries relate to Achebe's novel?

4. What can you infer about Achebe's reaction to the book's success?

GeoActivity

1. INTERDISCIPLINARY ACTIVITY–SCIENCE

With a small group, research malaria and the waterborne illnesses that plague much of West Africa. Make a brief oral presentation to your class, describing preventive measures.

2. WRITING FOR SOCIAL STUDIES

Research the beginnings of Pan-Africanism. Write a short essay on how the movement for freedom in Africa was related to the struggle for African-American civil rights.

3. MENTAL MAPPING

Create an outline map of West Africa and label the following:

• Atlantic Ocean
• Ghana
• Accra
• Nigeria
• Abuja

• Lagos
• Côte d'Ivoire
• Yamoussoukro
• Mali
• Bamako

East, Central, and Southern Africa

 ESSENTIAL QUESTION

How do boundaries set during colonial times affect stability in these regions today?

CONNECT Geography & History

Use the map and the time line to answer the following questions.

1. What nation is surrounded completely by the country of South Africa?

2. What sea route would Portuguese explorers have had to take to reach Kenya's coast in 1498?

Geography
1000 Great Zimbabwe is built. ▶

A.D. 50

History
50 Aksum begins to emerge. (Obelisk of Aksum) ▶

Culture
330 King Ezana establishes Christianity as Aksum's state religion.

Geography
1498 Vasco da Gama of Portugal reaches Kenya's coast.

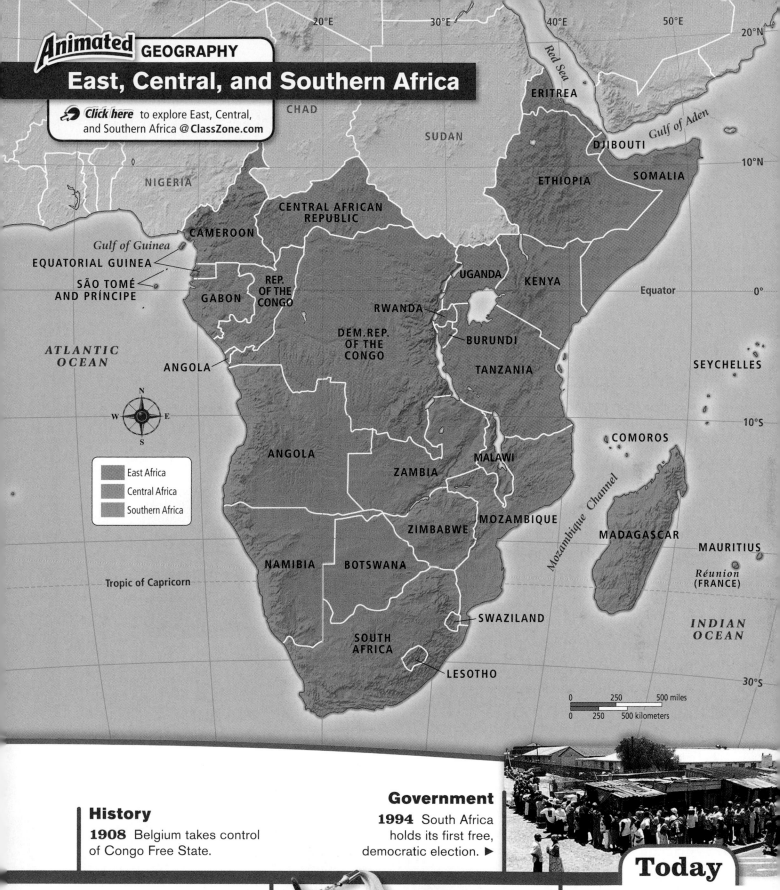

20°E 30°E 40°E 50°E 20°N

CHAD

SUDAN

NIGERIA

ERITREA

Red Sea

Gulf of Aden

DJIBOUTI 10°N

ETHIOPIA SOMALIA

CENTRAL AFRICAN REPUBLIC

CAMEROON

Gulf of Guinea

EQUATORIAL GUINEA

SÃO TOMÉ AND PRÍNCIPE

GABON

REP. OF THE CONGO

UGANDA KENYA

Equator 0°

RWANDA

DEM. REP. OF THE CONGO

BURUNDI

ANGOLA

TANZANIA

ATLANTIC OCEAN

SEYCHELLES

10°S

N W E S

COMOROS

ANGOLA

MALAWI

ZAMBIA

Mozambique Channel

MADAGASCAR

MAURITIUS

ZIMBABWE

MOZAMBIQUE

Réunion (FRANCE)

East Africa
Central Africa
Southern Africa

NAMIBIA BOTSWANA

INDIAN OCEAN

Tropic of Capricorn

SWAZILAND

SOUTH AFRICA

LESOTHO

30°S

0 250 500 miles
0 250 500 kilometers

History
1908 Belgium takes control of Congo Free State.

Government
1994 South Africa holds its first free, democratic election. ▶

Today

History
1963 Kenya wins independence. (Jomo Kenyatta) ▶

Government
2006 Angola and Congo (Kinshasa) hold long-awaited national elections.

605

Reading for Understanding

1

▶ Key Ideas

BEFORE, YOU LEARNED

Colonial powers took over many regions in Africa.

NOW YOU WILL LEARN

Ethiopia remained an independent nation throughout most of its history.

▶ Vocabulary

TERMS & NAMES

Aksum an empire that controlled much of northern Ethiopia from the first to the eighth century A.D.

obelisk a pillar-shaped stone monument

Haile Selassie (HY•lee suh•LAS•ee) emperor of Ethiopia from 1930 to 1974

Eritrea a former region of Ethiopia that became an independent country in 1993

BACKGROUND VOCABULARY

Horn of Africa a horn-shaped extension of land on the east coast of Africa

modernize to accept new ways or ideas

Red Sea a narrow sea that divides northeast Africa from the Arabian Peninsula

REVIEW

Kush an ancient Nubian kingdom in northern Sudan

dynasty a family or group that rules for several generations

Visual Vocabulary Red Sea

▶ Reading Strategy

Re-create the web diagram shown at right. As you read and respond to the **KEY QUESTIONS**, use the diagram to organize important ideas about Ethiopia.

 Skillbuilder Handbook, page R4

FIND MAIN IDEAS

History

Culture

ETHIOPIA

Government

Economy

GRAPHIC ORGANIZERS
Go to **Interactive Review** @ ClassZone.com

Ethiopia

Connecting to Your World

Hundreds of workers took more than six years to create 60-foot carvings of four presidents at Mount Rushmore, South Dakota. Ethiopia's mountains contain an even more amazing monument. Eight hundred years ago, using nothing but hand tools, workers carved 11 Christian churches out of solid rock.

Rock Church One of 11 churches carved out of solid rock in Lalibela, Ethiopia.

A History of Independence

▼ **KEY QUESTION** How did ancient Aksum's location make it a powerful trading empire?

Ethiopia is one of the longest-settled regions in the world. **Aksum**, the first major state to develop in Ethiopia, became important about A.D. 100. This kingdom achieved its greatest strength between the 300s and 600s.

Ancient Aksum Aksum was located near the **Horn of Africa** and expanded into parts of southwest Arabia. This major trade center exported spices, ivory, ebony, animal skins, and tortoiseshell. Trading partners included Arabia, India, and perhaps China. Aksumites built more than 100 carved stone pillars, called **obelisks**, in their capital. Some stood as monuments over rulers' tombs.

A Rugged Country Ethiopia's landforms include rift valleys and highlands.

ETHIOPIA

Rift Valley

Ancient Aksum A.D. 300–700

← Trade Routes

Mediterranean Sea
Jerusalem
Memphis Petra
EGYPT
SAHARA
Thebes
Berenice
Mecca
ARABIAN PENINSULA
NUBIA (KUSH)
Meroë
Red Sea
Aksum Adulis
AKSUM
Roha
Aden
Malao
HORN OF AFRICA
Blue Nile River
0 400 800 miles
0 400 800 kilometers
30°E 40°E 50°E
20°N
10°N

CONNECT Geography & History

1. **Movement** Aksum had trade access to what areas outside of Africa?
2. **Location** Traveling by land, what was Aksum's closest trading partner?

During the 300s, Aksum's King Ezana conquered **Kush** and made Christianity Aksum's state religion. But Muslim conquests in North Africa in the 600s hurt Aksum's trading power by taking over sea routes. The kingdom shifted to the south and moved its capital to Roha, the city that would become Lalibela. As Aksum declined, a new **dynasty**, the Zagwe, rose beginning in 1137. During the Zagwe reign, workers created 11 Christian churches from the rock at Lalibela.

Remaining Independent The Zagwe dynasty lasted less than 100 years, replaced by a line of emperors said to descend from the biblical King Solomon. These emperors had the backing of the Ethiopian Christian church and built a national identity. Menelik II became emperor of Ethiopia in 1889 and defeated Italy's 1896 invasion attempt.

Ethiopia's next important leader, **Haile Selassie**, took power in 1930. Haile Selassie's attempts to **modernize** Ethiopia included ending legal slavery and giving the country its first constitution. Ethiopia briefly fell to Italy during World War II but regained independence afterwards. In the later years of Haile Selassie's rule, Ethiopia fought a civil war in a region called **Eritrea**, along the **Red Sea**. In 1974, a coup removed Haile Selassie from power.

Recent Ethiopian History Ethiopia has suffered many setbacks in recent years. The coup that removed Haile Selassie brought a brutal military dictator named Mengistu to power. The state took control of land, industry, and banking. Mengistu waged war with neighboring Somalia and continued the conflict with Eritrea. The Mengistu government also badly mishandled a famine in 1984. A rebel group defeated Mengistu in 1991 and agreed to Eritrea's independence. But fighting along this tense border continued during 2005. More droughts in the 1990s and early 2000s resulted in millions of deaths. Ethiopia adopted a new constitution in 1994 and held multiparty elections the following year. But in November 2005, election violence led to scores of shootings.

▲ **DRAW CONCLUSIONS** Describe how location helped Aksum dominate trade.

Government and Economics

▼ **KEY QUESTION** What problems have hurt Ethiopia's economy?

Ethiopia is the oldest independent country in Africa, and one of the oldest in the world. Yet its first multiparty elections weren't held until 1995. The party that won in 1995 repeated its victories in 2000 and 2005. But some Ethiopians believed the 2005 election was dishonest, and they disputed the results in violent protests.

Structure of the Government and Economy Ethiopia has many political parties. The party with the most members in the legislature chooses the prime minister, who runs the executive branch and chooses the cabinet ministers. Ethiopia's legislature has two houses. The members of one house are elected directly by the voters, while representatives of the other house of the legislature are selected by state councils.

Despite its fertile soil and plentiful highland rainfall, Ethiopia remains poor. It has suffered from bad government; conflicts, such as the wars with Eritrea; natural disasters, including droughts; and limited use of its resources. The government owns all the land. A few farmers grow cash crops, but most Ethiopians are subsistence farmers. Overgrazing and deforestation have eroded the soil, destroying productive land while leaving fertile ground uncultivated. This landlocked country has no commercial fishing, and little mining and industry. Political instability has discouraged foreign investment in Ethiopia's economy. Most of the roads are unpaved, and only one railroad operates.

Like many other developing countries, Ethiopia has inadequate educational and health systems. Since schooling isn't required, the country's literacy rate hovers at just about 40 percent. Malaria, typhoid, and other diseases pose serious health risks.

What the Economy Produces Ethiopia's factories produce textiles, cement, food products, and shoes for domestic use. The country's top export is coffee. Other exports include animal skins and hides, oilseed, and sugarcane.

Like coffee, the cereal product teff is native to Ethiopia. Teff is the world's smallest grain. Its name comes from the Amharic word for "lost." Teff is well adapted to Ethiopia's highland soil, high in nutrients, and easily digested by people who can't eat wheat and other grains. Sorghum, another major grain product, is favored for its ability to grow in very dry conditions.

▲ **ANALYZE CAUSES** Identify causes of Ethiopia's economic troubles.

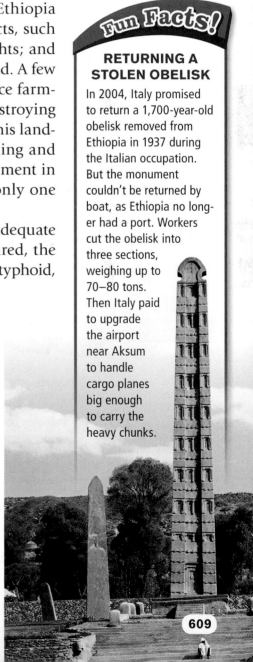

Fun Facts!

RETURNING A STOLEN OBELISK

In 2004, Italy promised to return a 1,700-year-old obelisk removed from Ethiopia in 1937 during the Italian occupation. But the monument couldn't be returned by boat, as Ethiopia no longer had a port. Workers cut the obelisk into three sections, weighing up to 70–80 tons. Then Italy paid to upgrade the airport near Aksum to handle cargo planes big enough to carry the heavy chunks.

Ethiopian Culture and Life

▼ **KEY QUESTION** What effects has religion had on Ethiopian culture?

When ancient Aksum moved south, its Christian population was separated from other Christian states. This led Ethiopian Orthodox Christianity to develop apart from other types of Christianity. For one thing, Ethiopian Orthodox Christians observe the Jewish laws of diet. They also pray in their ancient language of Ge'ez (gee•EHZ).

Daily Life Most Ethiopians live in rural areas, where they farm or herd cattle, goats, or sheep. Using wooden plows and oxen, subsistence farmers depend on rain to grow their cereal crops, such as teff, corn, wheat, or sorghum. Herders, like the Borana in the arid south, often must migrate to find water for their animals.

Ethiopian city dwellers live in Western-style houses, work in tall office buildings, and wear Western clothing. In rural regions, some people live in round mud and wood houses with thatched or tin roofs, while others live in rectangular stone houses. Many adults wear a white cotton cloth called a *shamma* over their shirts or dresses.

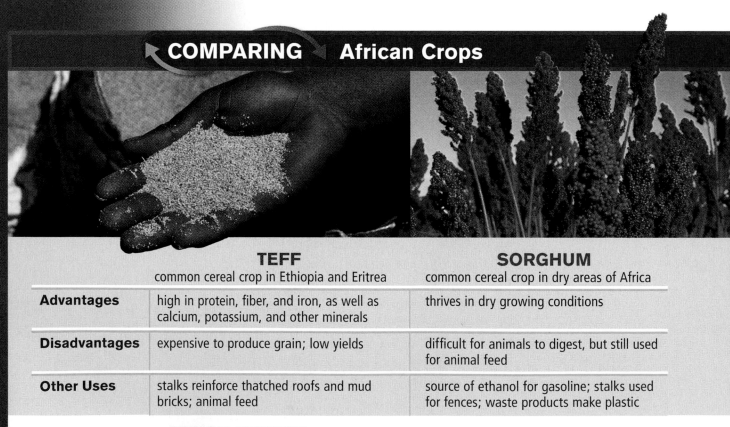

◄ COMPARING ► African Crops

	TEFF common cereal crop in Ethiopia and Eritrea	**SORGHUM** common cereal crop in dry areas of Africa
Advantages	high in protein, fiber, and iron, as well as calcium, potassium, and other minerals	thrives in dry growing conditions
Disadvantages	expensive to produce grain; low yields	difficult for animals to digest, but still used for animal feed
Other Uses	stalks reinforce thatched roofs and mud bricks; animal feed	source of ethanol for gasoline; stalks used for fences; waste products make plastic

CRITICAL THINKING

1. **Evaluate** Which grain would you grow for animal feed, and why?

2. **Make Inferences** Which grain might be useful in reducing dependence on oil, and why?

Ethiopians eat spicy meat or vegetable stews called *wat*, scooped up by hand with *injera* (ihn•JEER•uh), a flat sour bread made from fermented teff. Soccer and volleyball are popular sports. A game called *genna*, which resembles field hockey, is traditionally played at Christmas.

Cultural Traits Until 1974, Christianity was the official religion of the country's rulers, and it inspired much of Ethiopia's art and literature. In today's Ethiopia, however, Muslims slightly outnumber Christians. About nine out of ten Ethiopians are Muslim or Christian, while the rest follow traditional African religions.

Ethiopians of all faiths place a high value on moral behavior, hospitality, politeness, respect for elders, and the pursuit of wisdom. Some of Ethiopia's hundred languages are related to Arabic and Hebrew. Others are African.

The Arts Traditional Ethiopian arts include obelisks, the rock churches of Lalibela, church walls covered with paintings called frescoes, and lavishly illustrated Bibles. Modern artists and musicians continue to draw on their Ethiopian Orthodox faith for artistic inspiration. Today's Ethiopian writers write in modern Ethiopian languages, including Amharic.

Injera A woman pours injera batter onto a hot griddle. **How does injera appear to differ from sandwich bread?**

▲ **SUMMARIZE** Explain how religion has influenced Ethiopian culture.

ONLINE QUIZ For test practice, go to **Interactive Review** @ ClassZone.com

Section 1 Assessment

TERMS & NAMES

1. Explain the importance of
- Aksum
- Horn of Africa
- Haile Selassie
- Red Sea

USE YOUR READING NOTES

2. Find Main Ideas Use your completed diagram to answer the following question:

What is Ethiopia's main export?

KEY IDEAS

3. What major accomplishment occurred during the Zagwe dynasty?

4. What features differentiate Ethiopian Orthodox Christianity from other Christian sects?

5. Why is there little commercial fishing in Ethiopia?

CRITICAL THINKING

6. Make Inferences Why do you think Menelik II is a national hero in Ethiopia?

7. Identify Solutions What changes could improve conditions in Ethiopia? Explain your answer.

8. CONNECT to Today In 2006, Ethiopia announced that its economy had grown due to a shift away from its concentration on agriculture. How could diversifying Ethiopia's products improve its economy?

9. WRITING Create a Menu Design a menu for an Ethiopian restaurant, including simple illustrations. Research the Ethiopian dishes *injera* and *wat*, so that you can describe their ingredients.

Reading for Understanding

▶ Key Ideas

BEFORE, YOU LEARNED

West African kingdoms built vast trading empires.

NOW YOU WILL LEARN

Trade was also important in East Africa, particularly in what is now Kenya.

▶ Vocabulary

TERMS & NAMES

safari an overland expedition for exploring, hunting, or photography

monsoon a seasonal wind bringing heavy rainfall

Swahili an African language, commonly spoken in East Africa

Mau Mau a Kenyan independence movement that began in the 1940s

Jomo Kenyatta independent Kenya's first president

BACKGROUND VOCABULARY

porridge a soft food made by boiling cereal grain in milk or water

Visual Vocabulary safari

▶ Reading Strategy

Re-create the chart shown at right. As you read and respond to the **KEY QUESTIONS**, use the chart to make inferences about Kenya's government, history, and culture.

Skillbuilder Handbook, page R11

MAKE INFERENCES

FACTS	INFERENCES
1.	1.
2.	2.
3.	3.
4.	4.

GRAPHIC ORGANIZERS
Go to **Interactive Review** @ ClassZone.com

Kenya

Connecting to Your World

One hundred years ago, Europeans and Americans traveled to Africa on hunting or exploring expeditions called **safaris**. This year, thousands of people will go on safari to Kenya's Masai Mara, famous for lions, or Amboseli National Reserve, noted for elephants. But the only shooting tourists will do is with their cameras. Safaris bring Kenya millions of tourist dollars each year.

History of a Trading Region

▼ **KEY QUESTION** How did the Swahili language develop?

The ancient kingdom of Aksum controlled trade to Arabia. After the 600s, that trade fell into the hands of Muslim invaders. Now you'll learn how Muslim trading cities spread down the East African coast, affecting inland African populations.

Elephants Elephants graze at Amboseli National Reserve.

Mombasa Arches representing elephant tusks welcome visitors to Kenya's main port city.

Inland Villages, Coastal Cities Earlier you learned that the Bantu-speaking people of Africa migrated across the southern part of the continent between 1000 B.C. and A.D. 1100. Bantu speakers, seeking land for their farms and herds, eventually reached Africa's east coast. Their iron-working skills helped them produce farming tools.

KENYA

Mombasa

	EAST AFRICAN TRADING CITIES	TRADING CITIES OF RENAISSANCE ITALY
Goods Traded	Exported gold, iron, ivory, beads, tortoiseshell, and slaves. Imported cotton and luxury goods, such as porcelain	Exported salt, wool, olive oil, grain. Imported silk, precious stones, pepper and other spices
Trading Partners	Persian Gulf states, India, China	northern and western Europe, Persia, India, and China
Trade winds/ patterns enabling trade	seasonal winds of the western half of the Indian Ocean that blow between West India and East Africa	overland trade with Europe, sailing routes across the Mediterranean, and overland to the Far East along the Silk Roads

CRITICAL THINKING

1. Analyze Effects Why did East African trading cities depend on trade winds?

2. Make Inferences How did merchants become wealthy?

Along this same coast, traders from Arabia had established several dozen thriving trading cities by the 1400s, including Mombasa and Malindi in today's Kenya. **Monsoons**, seasonal rain-bearing winds, propelled Arab trade ships to India. These ships carried gold, leopard skins, beads, copper, and ivory, brought to the coast by inland African traders. Other than trade, the inland villagers—farmers and herders who practiced African religions—had little to do with the Muslim city dwellers. But their trade contacts produced one important cultural effect. By the 1400s, most townspeople spoke a blend of Bantu and Arabic, an ancestor of today's African language **Swahili**.

European Domination By the early 1500s, Portugal controlled the wealthy East African cities. The Portuguese traded small numbers of slaves. In the late 1800s, Europe began the scramble for African colonies you learned about in the last chapter. After Germany and Britain divided East Africa, the territory that would become Kenya was called British East Africa. The British encouraged Europeans to settle in British East Africa and establish huge farms.

Independence and Afterward During the 1940s, East Africans began uniting to oppose British rule. Britain's refusal to consider their demands triggered a revolution in 1952. A resistance group called the **Mau Mau** led this revolt. The British imprisoned thousands of rebels, including **Jomo Kenyatta**, a Kenyan political leader. Kenyatta spent seven years in prison, despite denying Mau Mau involvement.

By the late 1950s, Britain agreed to national elections. Kenya won independence in 1963, and the following year Jomo Kenyatta became the nation's first **president**. Kenyatta's attempts to modernize Kenya included expanding educational opportunities and limiting property ownership to Kenyans. Kenyatta died in 1978 and was succeeded by his vice president, Daniel Moi, who led until 2002. For most of its recent history, Kenya has been a one-party state, despite a 1991 amendment establishing a multiparty system. In 2002, the head of a multi-ethnic party won a peaceful democratic presidential election.

▲ **SUMMARIZE** Describe how East African trade created Swahili.

Life in Kenya

▼ **KEY QUESTION** What interests do many Kenyans share?

Since independence, the Kenyan government has tried to promote national pride. That's difficult in a country where some 40 ethnic groups struggle to get along and no single culture dominates.

Daily Life and Activities Kenya's largest ethnic group is the Kikuyu, followed by the **Luhya** (LOO•yah), Kalenjin (KAL•uhn•jihn), Luo, and Kamba. Most groups have their own language, but many Kenyans also know Swahili and English, the country's official languages. At least two-thirds of Kenyans are Christian. About 10 percent follow traditional African religions. Another 10 percent are Muslim, living mostly along the coast.

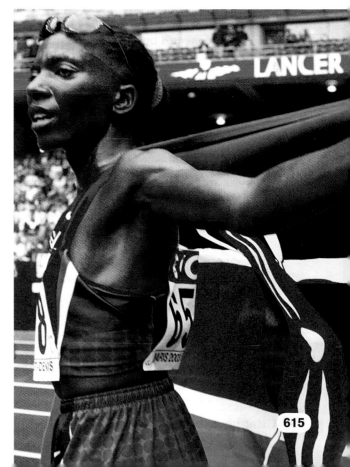

Kenyan Runners
Catherine Ndereba celebrates her marathon victory at the 2003 world track and field championships.
What is Ndereba holding behind herself?

One of Kenya's most famous writers, Ngugi wa Thiong'o, wrote novels in English and in his native Kikuyu. Most Kenyans enjoy dancing and dance performances and follow their favorite soccer teams. Several Kenyan runners have won Olympic medals for track and field. Kenyan runners also regularly win the yearly Boston Marathon.

About three out of four Kenyans live in rural areas. A farming family typically occupies a small house with a thatched roof, mud walls, and dirt floors. A few Kenyans, like the Masai, are nomadic herders. Every day, most Kenyans eat maize, or corn, which they grind and cook as **porridge**, then mix with other vegetables to make a stew.

▲ **SUMMARIZE** Identify the common interests of many Kenyans.

615

Iraq

GEOGRAPHY
Capital: Baghdad
Total Area: 168,754 sq. mi.
Population: 28,807,000

ECONOMY
Imports: consumer goods
Exports: petroleum; food

CULTURE
Language: Arabic; Kurdish
Religion: Shiite Muslim 62%; Sunni Muslim 34%; Christian 3%

 Israel

GEOGRAPHY
Capital: Jerusalem
Total Area: 8,019 sq. mi.
Population: 6,725,000

ECONOMY
Imports: machinery; diamonds; chemicals
Exports: diamonds; chemicals; electronics

CULTURE
Language: Hebrew; Arabic
Religion: Jewish 76%; Muslim 16%; Christian 2%

Jordan

GEOGRAPHY
Capital: Amman
Total Area: 35,637 sq. mi.
Population: 5,703,000

ECONOMY
Imports: food; machinery; petroleum
Exports: clothing; chemicals; potash

CULTURE
Language: Arabic
Religion: Sunni Muslim 94%; Christian 4%

 Kuwait

GEOGRAPHY
Capital: Kuwait
Total Area: 6,880 sq. mi.
Population: 2,687,000

ECONOMY
Imports: machinery; food; chemicals
Exports: petroleum; ethylene

CULTURE
Language: Arabic
Religion: Muslim 85%

Lebanon

GEOGRAPHY
Capital: Beirut
Total Area: 4,015 sq. mi.
Population: 3,577,000

ECONOMY
Imports: machinery; food; chemicals
Exports: jewelry; machinery; chemicals

CULTURE
Language: Arabic
Religion: Christian 38%; Shiite Muslim 34%; Sunni Muslim 21%; Druze 7%

 Maldives

GEOGRAPHY
Capital: Male
Total Area: 116 sq. mi.
Population: 329,000

ECONOMY
Imports: food; oil; constuction goods
Exports: clothing; tropical fish; jet fuel

CULTURE
Language: Divehi
Religion: Sunni Muslim 100%

 Nepal

GEOGRAPHY
Capital: Kathmandu
Total Area: 54,363 sq. mi.
Population: 27,133,000

ECONOMY
Imports: machinery; fabrics; fuels
Exports: clothing; carpets; shawls

CULTURE
Language: Nepali
Religion: Hindu 81%; Buddhist 11%; Muslim 4%; Kirat 4%

 Oman

GEOGRAPHY
Capital: Muscat
Total Area: 82,031 sq. mi.
Population: 2,567,000

ECONOMY
Imports: machinery; cars; food; chemicals
Exports: petroleum; natural gas

CULTURE
Language: Arabic
Religion: Ibadiyah Muslim 75%; Hindu 6%; Christian 5%; Buddhist 1%

Pakistan

GEOGRAPHY
Capital: Islamabad
Total Area: 310,403 sq. mi.
Population: 157,935,000

ECONOMY
Imports: machinery; petroleum; chemicals
Exports: textiles; leather; rice; carpets

CULTURE
Language: Urdu
Religion: Sunni Muslim 79%; Shiite Muslim 17%; Christian 3%; Hindu 1%

Qatar

GEOGRAPHY
Capital: Doha
Total Area: 4,416 sq. mi.
Population: 813,000

ECONOMY
Imports: machinery; cars; food; chemicals
Exports: natural gas; petroleum; iron; steel

CULTURE
Language: Arabic
Religion: Muslim 83%; Christian 10%; Hindu 3%

Saudi Arabia

GEOGRAPHY
Capital: Riyadh
Total Area: 756,985 sq. mi.
Population: 24,573,000

ECONOMY
Imports: cars; machinery; food; chemicals
Exports: petroleum; chemicals

CULTURE
Language: Arabic
Religion: Sunni Muslim 84%; Shiite Muslim 10%; Christian 4%

Sri Lanka

GEOGRAPHY
Capital: Colombo
Total Area: 25,332 sq. mi.
Population: 20,743,000

ECONOMY
Imports: textiles; petroleum; food
Exports: clothing; tea; precious stones

CULTURE
Language: Sinhala, Tamil
Religion: Buddhist 77%; Muslim 9%; Hindu 8%; Christian 7%

Syria

GEOGRAPHY
Capital: Damascus
Total Area: 71,498 sq. mi.
Population: 19,043,000

ECONOMY
Imports: food; chemicals; machinery; iron
Exports: petroleum; cotton; vegetables

CULTURE
Language: Arabic
Religion: Sunni Muslim 74%; Shiite Muslim 12%; Christian 6%; Druze 3%

Turkey

GEOGRAPHY
Capital: Ankara
Total Area: 301,384 sq. mi.
Population: 73,193,000

ECONOMY
Imports: chemicals; machinery; petroleum
Exports: textiles; cars; machinery; iron

CULTURE
Language: Turkish
Religion: Sunni Muslim 67%; Shiite Muslim 30%; Christian 1%

United Arab Emirates
the Burj Al Arab Hotel in Dubai in the United Arab Emirates

United Arab Emirates

GEOGRAPHY
Capital: Abu Dhabi
Total Area: 32,000 sq. mi.
Population: 4,496,000

ECONOMY
Imports: machinery; food; textiles
Exports: petroleum; natural gas; gold

CULTURE
Language: Arabic
Religion: Sunni Muslim 80%; Shiite Muslim 16%

Yemen

GEOGRAPHY
Capital: San'a
Total Area: 203,850 sq. mi.
Population: 20,975,000

ECONOMY
Imports: food; machinery; petroleum
Exports: petroleum; fish; fruits

CULTURE
Language: Arabic
Religion: Sunni Muslim 60%; Shiite Muslim 40%

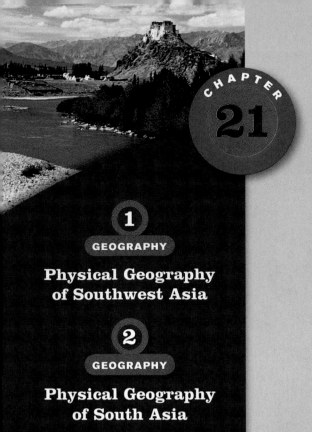

CHAPTER 21

Southwest Asia and South Asia

Physical Geography and History

 ESSENTIAL QUESTION

How have physical geography and history interacted in Southwest and South Asia?

CONNECT → Geography & History

Use the map and the time line to answer the following questions.

1. When did cities appear in the Indus River valley?
2. In ancient times, people of the Indus Valley traded with people on the Tigris and Euphrates rivers. What water route would they take between the regions?

Culture
◀ **c. 3000 B.C.** Cotton cloth is woven in South Asia (and is still being woven today, as the photo shows).

Culture
c. 2400 B.C. Sumerians use the cuneiform writing system. ▼

3000 B.C.

Geography
c. 2500 B.C. Cities develop in the Indus River valley of South Asia.

Animated GEOGRAPHY

Present-Day Southwest Asia and South Asia

Click here to explore Southwest and South Asia @ ClassZone.com

MONGOLIA

RUSSIA

GEORGIA

ARMENIA

AZERBAIJAN

TURKMENISTAN

TAJIKISTAN

CHINA

Istanbul

Ankara ✪

TURKEY

Black Sea

Caspian Sea

Mediterranean Sea

Nicosia ✪ SYRIA

CYPRUS Beirut

LEBANON Damascus ●

ISRAEL

Tel Aviv-Yafo ●Amman

●Jerusalem

JORDAN

Tigris R.

Euphrates R.

Tehran ✪

IRAN

Kabul ✪

AFGHANISTAN

Islamabad ✪

Lahore ●

Disputed Border

Disputed Border

30°N

●Baghdad

IRAQ

Basra●

Kuwait✪

KUWAIT

EGYPT

Medina ●

Manama

BAHRAIN

Riyadh ✪

QATAR ●Doha

SAUDI ARABIA

Persian Gulf

●Abu Dhabi

UNITED ARAB EMIRATES

Disputed Border

Muscat ✪

Jiddah ●

●Mecca

Red Sea

SUDAN

ERITREA

ETHIOPIA

PAKISTAN

Karachi ●

Tropic of Cancer

Delhi ●

New Delhi ✪

Kathmandu ✪

NEPAL

INDIA

Ahmadabad ●

Narmada River

Godavari River

Mumbai ●

Krishna River

Hyderabad ●

Bangalore ●

BHUTAN

Thimphu ✪

Ganges River

Brahmaputra R.

Dhaka ✪

BANGLADESH

Kolkata ●

20°N

MYANMAR

Bay of Bengal

Chennai ●

Andaman Islands (INDIA)

OMAN

Sanaa ✪

YEMEN

Gulf of Aden

Socotra (YEMEN)

Arabian Sea

Lakshadweep Islands (INDIA)

SRI LANKA

Colombo ●

INDIAN OCEAN

Nicobar Islands (INDIA)

10°N

Equator

Male ✪ MALDIVES

Inset map

30°E

CYPRUS

Nicosia ✪

Mediterranean Sea

Beirut ●

LEBANON

Tel Aviv-Yafo ●

ISRAEL

Gaza Strip

EGYPT

TURKEY

SYRIA

Damascus ✪

West Bank

●Jerusalem

✪Amman

JORDAN

SAUDI ARABIA

IRAQ

30°N

40°E

0	250 500 miles
0	250 500 kilometers

✪ National capital

● Other city

Geography

c. 1900 B.C. The Sarasvati River of South Asia disappears, perhaps because of earthquakes.

History

▲ **c. 2200 B.C.** Ziggurats are first built in Sumerian cities.

1500 B.C.

Government

◀ **c. 1750 B.C.** Hammurabi of Babylon compiles a law code.

Reading for Understanding

Key Ideas

BEFORE, YOU LEARNED

Africa has variety in its physical geography, including savannas, mountains, and deserts.

NOW YOU WILL LEARN

Southwest Asia has vast deserts and extensive mountain ranges that are similar to those in certain parts of Africa.

Vocabulary

TERMS & NAMES

Arabian Peninsula peninsula of Southwest Asia between the Red Sea and Persian Gulf

Anatolian peninsula in Southwest Asia between the Black Sea and Mediterranean

Plateau of Iran a high plateau in central and eastern Iran, surrounded by mountains

Tigris River a river of Southwest Asia that flows from a plateau on the Anatolian peninsula to the Persian Gulf

Euphrates (yoo•FRAY•teez) **River** a river of Southwest Asia that flows from a plateau on the Anatolian peninsula to the Persian Gulf

oasis fertile or green spot in desert created by underground water coming to the surface

REVIEW

plateau a high area of flat land

Visual Vocabulary Women carry water from an oasis near Khimsar, Rajasthan, India.

Reading Strategy

Re-create the diagram shown at right. As you read and respond to the **KEY QUESTIONS**, use the outer ovals to note important details about the region's physical features, water shortage, and earthquake threats.

 See Skillbuilder Handbook, page R4

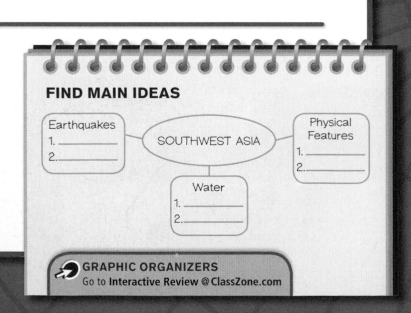

FIND MAIN IDEAS

Earthquakes
1. _____
2. _____

SOUTHWEST ASIA

Physical Features
1. _____
2. _____

Water
1. _____
2. _____

GRAPHIC ORGANIZERS
Go to **Interactive Review** @ClassZone.com

Physical Geography of Southwest Asia

Connecting to Your World

Have you ever seen pictures of the moon's surface? Many of NASA's moon photographs show plains of powdery grey dust with mountains looming in the background. The moon is a very dry place with no water or plants. Although Earth has water, did you know that some regions on Earth look almost as desolate? Southwest Asia has harsh deserts and tall mountains. Yet Southwest Asia also has livable areas, small watered regions where millions of people live.

Physical Features

▼ **KEY QUESTION** What are the three subregions of Southwest Asia?

Perhaps you have heard the name *Middle East* on the news. That term is often used for the region of Southwest Asia. If you look at the map in this section, you will see that Southwest Asia is located where three continents—Africa, Asia, and Europe—meet. As a result, it has historically been a crossroads, a place where roads meet and a place through which many travelers journey.

Mt. Damavand
Snow-capped Mount Damavand is located in Iran.

Rub al-Khali
Deserts such as the Rub al-Khali cover most of the Arabian Peninsula.

SAUDI ARABIA

Rub al-Khali

Peninsulas and Plateaus Southwest Asia can be divided into three subregions, which are listed below. (See map on opposite page.)

1. The **Arabian Peninsula** Ⓐ is bordered by the Red Sea, Arabian Sea, and Persian Gulf. A peninsula is a piece of land linked to a larger landmass but nearly surrounded by water. Deserts cover most of the Arabian Peninsula. The Rub al-Khali is the largest.

2. The **Anatolian peninsula** Ⓑ, or Anatolia (also called Asia Minor), is home to most of Turkey. This peninsula is bounded by the Black Sea to the north and the Mediterranean to the south.

3. Extending east from Anatolia is the **Plateau of Iran** Ⓒ. A **plateau** is a high area of uplifted, then eroded land. The Persian Gulf lies to the southwest and the Caspian Sea to the north.

Deserts, Mountains, and Rivers Southwest Asia is an arid region with many deserts. The dry climate is partially caused by the terrain. For example, mountains lining the Mediterranean and Black Sea coasts of Anatolia prevent rain from reaching inland areas.

Mountains also affect the climate of the Plateau of Iran. The Elburz Mountains stop moist winds blowing from the Caspian Sea, and the Zagros Mountains block winds from the Persian Gulf.

Rivers are the major freshwater sources in the region. The **Tigris River** and the **Euphrates River** both flow from the Anatolian peninsula to the Persian Gulf. The land between these rivers is a farming region. To the southwest, the Jordan River borders parts of Syria, Jordan, the West Bank, and Israel. The river flows into a lake that is called the Dead Sea because it is so salty that almost nothing can live in it.

▲ **SUMMARIZE** Identify the three subregions of Southwest Asia.

Providing Water

▼ **KEY QUESTION** What methods have people used to provide water to arid Southwest Asia?

Living in an arid region can be challenging because people need water for drinking, bathing, and farming. Most people in Southwest Asia are crowded into coastal areas that receive rain or places with sources of water, such as river valleys and oases. An **oasis** is a fertile or green spot in the desert where underground water comes to the surface.

Ancient Techniques Residents of Southwest Asia have found ways to get the water they need to live in dryer areas. About 2,500 years ago, the people living in what is now Iran developed a technology called the qanat (KA•naht). A qanat Ⓓ, a type of underground water supply system, is illustrated on the next page.

THE DEAD SEA

The Dead Sea is a land-locked salt lake, so salty that almost nothing can live in the water. It is so salty that you cannot sink. Salt concentration in the Dead Sea is around 31.5 percent, about nine times higher than in the world's oceans. The evaporation rate of the water is more than 55 inches per year. This keeps the water very salty.

Physical Geography of Southwest Asia

EUROPE
Black Sea
GREECE
GEORGIA
ASIA
B ARMENIA
TURKEY
Anatolian Peninsula
AZERBAIJAN
TURKMENISTAN
TAURUS MOUNTAINS
Caspian Sea
CYPRUS
ELBURZ MOUNTAINS
Mt. Damavand
18,386 ft.
(5,604 m)
SYRIA
Mediterranean Sea
LEBANON
Plateau of Iran
ISRAEL
ZAGROS MOUNTAINS
IRAN
AFRICA
SYRIAN DESERT
IRAQ
C
JORDAN
EGYPT
KUWAIT
PAKISTAN
Persian Gulf
Strait of Hormuz
SAUDI ARABIA
BAHRAIN
UNITED ARAB EMIRATES
Gulf of Oman
Tropic of Cancer
20°N
QATAR
A
Disputed Border
INDIA
Red Sea
ARABIAN PENINSULA
OMAN
Arabian Sea
RUB' AL-KHALI
ERITREA
YEMEN
Socotra (YEMEN)
10°N
Gulf of Aden
40°E
50°E
60°E
70°E

Elevation

13,100 ft.	(4,000 m)
6,600 ft.	(2,000 m)
3,280 ft.	(1,000 m)
650 ft.	(200 m)
0 ft.	(0 m)
Below sea level	

▲ Mountain peak

0   200   400 miles
0   200   400 kilometers

Animated GEOGRAPHY

Qanats: An Ancient Irrigation Technology

Click here to see how a qanat works @ ClassZone.com

The ancient Iranians dug 30- to 100-foot shafts at the foot of mountains to tap into the water table. They built underground tunnels that followed the slope of the land. These qanats collect water that seeps into the ground from melting snow and rivers and streams. They can carry water to villages as much as 50 miles away for drinking and irrigating fields. They can supply most of a village's water.

CRITICAL THINKING

1. **Make Inferences** What basic fact about the physical geography of the region has created a need for qanats?

2. **Draw Conclusions** What advantages do qanats have over canals that are located on the surface?

1 People first had to locate an underground source of water that was higher than the place where they needed water.

2 Someone who was skilled in building qanats would dig a series of narrow vertical shafts.

D

3 By connecting the shafts horizontally, the builder made an underground tunnel for water.

4 The tunnel sloped down to the village or fields that needed the water; gravity made the water flow.

655

In ancient times, the knowledge of how to make qanats spread from Iran to many other places. People living along rivers such as the Tigris and the Euphrates relied on surface water to grow their crops. They irrigated by building large canals to carry water from the river to their villages. Smaller canals carried water to the fields. In some arid regions such as Iran and Afghanistan, people still use qanats.

Modern Techniques Many nations in Southwest Asia have taken on huge projects to bring water to dry areas. Such water projects can make it possible to live on and farm previously unusable land. But sometimes the projects cause tension and even conflict.

In the 1950s, Israel began to build a giant system of canals, pipelines, and tunnels. Its purpose was to carry water from the Jordan River and Sea of Galilee to the Negev Desert. The project caused tensions with Syria and Jordan, who share those two water sources and worried that Israel would use too much water. Water and oil are two resources in the region that cause competition over scarce supplies.

Turkey has been working on its own large water project. Both the Tigris and Euphrates rivers begin in Turkey on the Anatolian peninsula. Turkey has been building a system of dams to create hydroelectric power and to divert water from the rivers to some of its farmlands. Syria and Iraq are located farther down the Tigris and Euphrates rivers. Both countries fear that if Turkey uses too much water for irrigation, they won't receive enough to meet their needs.

▲ **FIND MAIN IDEAS** Describe the methods people have used to provide water in Southwest Asia.

CONNECT to Math

One definition of a desert is a region that receives less than 10 inches of precipitation a year. By that definition, many cities of Southwest Asia are built in deserts. One such city is Damascus, Syria, which receives approximately seven inches of rain a year (see chart). One way to learn more details about the climate of a place is to create a graph in which the bars show average monthly rainfall.

Average Monthly Rainfall (Damascus, Syria)	
Month	**Rainfall** (inches)
January	1.5
February	1.3
March	0.9
April	0.5
May	0.2
June	0.0
July	0.0
August	0.0
September	0.0
October	0.4
November	1.0
December	1.7

Source: www.worldclimate.com

Activity

Make a Rainfall Graph

Materials

- graph paper
- pencil
- ruler
- colored pencils

1. On a piece of paper, draw the horizontal axis and the vertical axis. On the vertical axis, place 20 marks, evenly spaced. Mark them 0.1, 0.2, 0.3, 0.4, etc., on up to 2.0.

2. Below the horizontal axis, write the names of all 12 months. You may abbreviate them. Space them evenly.

3. For each month, draw a bar whose height indicates the average amount of rainfall. Color all of the bars the same color.

The Threat of Earthquakes

▼ **KEY QUESTION** Why does Southwest Asia have many earthquakes?

Southwest Asia has long been a crossroads where people meet, but it is also a place where several of the great plates that make up Earth's crust meet in a kind of continental collision zone. As a result, Southwest Asia is prone to deadly earthquakes. In August 1999, a major earthquake hit Izmit, Turkey. More than 17,000 people were killed, many of them crushed when buildings collapsed on them. Thousands more lost their homes. In December 2003, the city of Bam, Iran, experienced an earthquake that killed about 26,000 people. Sometimes, faulty building construction, rather than the strength of the earthquakes, causes many of these deaths.

▲ **SUMMARIZE** Explain why Southwest Asia has many earthquakes.

Earthquake Damage People walk past rubble from collapsed buildings in western Turkey after the 1999 earthquake.

Section 1 Assessment

ONLINE QUIZ For test practice, go to **Interactive Review** @ ClassZone.com

TERMS & NAMES

1. Explain the importance of
- Arabian Peninsula
- Plateau of Iran
- Euphrates River
- oasis

USE YOUR READING NOTES

2. Find Main Ideas Use your completed chart to answer the following question:

What are some possible solutions to the problems caused by living in such an arid region?

KEY IDEAS

3. How do the mountains of Southwest Asia affect its climate?

4. How did people in ancient times move water from the Tigris and Euphrates rivers to their crops?

5. What might be done to limit earthquake damage in the region?

CRITICAL THINKING

6. Make Inferences When two countries rely on the same river, what issues might arise?

7. Compare and Contrast How is a qanat different from a surface irrigation system?

8. CONNECT to Today What might be some problems with building dams in a region prone to earthquakes?

9. SCIENCE Create an Informative Poster Working with a partner, research in the library or on the Internet to learn about the Richter scale, which is used to measure earthquakes. Then create a poster listing how much damage happens at each level on the scale.

Reading for Understanding

▶ Key Ideas

BEFORE, YOU LEARNED

The physical geography of Southwest Asia is made up of deserts and mountains, and the region is mostly arid.

NOW YOU WILL LEARN

The physical geography of South Asia is made up of mountains, plateaus, and plains, and there are wet and dry seasons.

▶ Vocabulary

TERMS & NAMES

subcontinent a large landmass that is part of a continent but is considered a separate region

Himalayas (HIHM•uh•LAY•uhz) the highest mountains in the world, which stretch along northern India, separating it from the rest of Asia

Mount Everest the world's tallest mountain, located in the Himalayas

Deccan (DEHK•uhn) **Plateau** a high area of land at the center of the Indian subcontinent

Indus River a river in South Asia that flows from the Himalayas to the Arabian Sea

Ganges (GAN•JEEZ) **River** a river of South Asia that flows southeast from the Himalayas to the Bay of Bengal

monsoon a seasonal wind system that produces a wet or dry period in a region

cyclone a violent storm with fierce winds that rotate in a circular pattern like a hurricane

tsunami (tsu•NAH•mee) a series of giant, destructive ocean waves caused by underwater earthquakes, volcanoes, or landslides

BACKGROUND VOCABULARY

famine a severe shortage of food that causes widespread hunger

▶ Reading Strategy

Re-create the chart shown at right. As you read and respond to the **KEY QUESTIONS**, use the chart to compare and contrast the physical geography of South Asia with that of Southwest Asia.

 See Skillbuilder Handbook, page R9

COMPARE AND CONTRAST

	SOUTH ASIA	SOUTHWEST ASIA
Physical Features		
Climate		

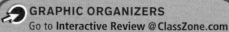
GRAPHIC ORGANIZERS
Go to **Interactive Review** @ ClassZone.com

Physical Geography of South Asia

Connecting to Your World

In many places, just five inches of rain can cause floods. In Mumbai (also known as Bombay), India, 37 inches of rain fell on July 26, 2005. Streets flooded and landslides buried neighborhoods. India has a climate with separate dry and wet seasons, but even during the wet season, 37 inches of rain in one day is rare.

Mumbai, India Man buying vegetables from a street vendor during the 2005 monsoon

Physical Features of the Peninsula

🔻 **KEY QUESTION** What are the three main rivers of the Indian subcontinent?

Millions of years ago, a huge supercontinent, Pangaea, broke apart into separate continents. Scientists believe that when that happened, India became a separate landmass. Over time, it inched north until it hit Asia. The collision pushed up high mountains where the two landmasses met. Those mountains form the northern boundary of the kite-shaped Indian subcontinent. A **subcontinent** is a large landmass that is part of a continent, yet is considered a separate region or entity.

Indian Subcontinent Scientists predict that as the two tectonic plates that formed the Himalayas continue to push against each other, India will become one huge mountain range.

Formation of the Himalayas

INDIA

Ganges River

Himalayas

Indian Ocean

Collision Zone

Indian Plate

Eurasian Plate

Mountains and Plateaus The mountains of South Asia include the Hindu Kush in the northwest. The **Himalayas** (HIHM•uh•LAY•uhz) extend east of the Hindu Kush. **Mount Everest Ⓐ**, the world's tallest peak, is located in the Himalayas. (See map on opposite page.)

Mountains called the Western Ghats and Eastern Ghats run along India's two coastlines, which form a "V" in the south. Between them stretches an area of high land called the **Deccan Plateau Ⓑ**. It is a largely arid region. One of the world's largest deserts, the Thar Desert, lies northwest of the Deccan.

Bodies of Water and Islands The Arabian Sea borders India's west coast and the Bay of Bengal borders the east. Both are part of the Indian Ocean, which lies to the south. Several rivers water the subcontinent. In the west, the **Indus River Ⓒ** runs from the Himalayas to the Arabian Sea. The **Ganges** (GAN•jeez) **River Ⓓ**—one of the largest, most important rivers of India—flows from the Himalayas to the Bay of Bengal. The Brahmaputra (BRAH•muh•POO•truh) River Ⓔ also starts in the Himalayas, but it joins the Ganges before reaching the bay. Together, the rivers have deposited silt and created an immense fertile delta in what is now Bangladesh (BAHN•gluh•DEHSH).

COMPARING River Systems

Indus River, Stakna Ldakh, India

Ganges River, Varanasi, India

	INDUS RIVER	**GANGES RIVER**
Source	the Himalayas	the Himalayas
Route	mostly south through Pakistan	mostly southeast through India
Length	1,800 miles	1,560 miles
Destination	Arabian Sea	Bay of Bengal

CRITICAL THINKING

Compare What do the two rivers have in common?

Physical Geography of South Asia

40°N

TURKMENISTAN   TAJIKISTAN

HINDU KUSH

Khyber Pass

Disputed border

CHINA

Disputed border

AFGHANISTAN

30°N

PAKISTAN

Indus

Thar Desert

©C

H I M A L A Y A S

Mt. Everest
29,035 ft.
(8,850 m.)

NEPAL   Ⓐ   BHUTAN

INDO-GANGETIC PLAIN

Ⓓ   Ganges   River

Brahmaputra River

Ⓔ

Tropic of Cancer

BANGLADESH

Narmada River

Ganges
Delta

MYANMAR

20°N

INDIA

Godavari River

Arabian
Sea

Ⓑ   DECCAN
PLATEAU

THAILAND

GHATS

Bay of
Bengal

WESTERN GHATS

EASTERN

N
W   E
S

10°N

INDIAN
OCEAN

SRI
LANKA

| 0 | 150 | 300 miles |
| 0 | 150 | 300 kilometers |

MALDIVES

0° Equator

70°E   80°E   90°E

Elevation

13,100 ft.	(4,000 m)
6,600 ft.	(2,000 m)
1,600 ft.	(500 m)
650 ft.	(200 m)
0 ft.	(0 m)
Below sea level	

▲ Mountain peak

CONNECT
Geography & Culture
READING A PHYSICAL MAP

Physical geography maps show landforms and bodies of water. When reading a physical map, use

- the scale to estimate distance across India at its widest point
- the legend to identify elevation of regions and major mountain peaks in the Himalayas

1. **Location** Into what body of water does the Indus River flow?

2. **Movement** What barriers restrict movement into the Indian subcontinent?

Two island nations lie off India's coast. To the southeast is Sri Lanka, a tropical island with some mountains. To the southwest is a group of islands called the Maldives, flung over 500 miles of ocean. The Maldives are made of reefs, ridges of coral formed on the slopes of undersea volcanoes. They barely rise above the water's surface.

▲ **SUMMARIZE** List the three main rivers of the Indian subcontinent.

Extreme Weather and Natural Disasters

▼ **KEY QUESTION** What are some natural disasters in South Asia?

Floods are common in South Asia. Even though the climate has wet and dry seasons, no one can predict yearly rainfall. The variable rainfall sometimes causes problems.

Monsoons India's climate is affected by monsoons. A **monsoon** is a seasonal wind system that produces wet and dry seasons. In India, winter winds blow from the northeast and cross vast stretches of land and high mountains before reaching India. As a result, the winter monsoon is dry. Summer winds blow from the southwest and cross the Indian Ocean, so they pick up moisture and bring rain.

If the summer monsoon brings too much rain, floods occur. But that is not the only danger. A drought can result if the monsoon has failed to bring normal levels of moisture. Drought can lead to **famine**, a severe shortage of food that causes widespread hunger.

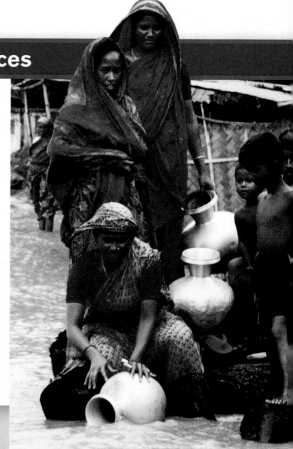

ANALYZING Primary Sources

Associated Press Newspapers cover disasters as they are happening. This story tells of monsoon flooding in India.

August 16, 2002 Monsoon rains have sent India's Brahmaputra River surging from its channel, swallowing up villages, drowning hundreds of people and leaving millions homeless. . . . Annual monsoon flooding has wreaked havoc across South Asia, killing more than 900 people in India, Bangladesh, and Nepal since June and displacing or trapping about 25 million more.

Source: *The Associated Press*

DOCUMENT-BASED QUESTION
Why might rain in the Himalayas contribute to flooding in Bangladesh?

Another kind of weather that causes hardship and destruction is a **cyclone**, a violent storm with fierce, rotating winds, similar to a hurricane. Cyclones can form in the ocean and then blow ashore. In 1970, a severe cyclone hit Bangladesh, and about 300,000 people were killed.

Natural Disasters India became part of Asia when one great landmass collided with another. Those two plates of Earth's crust are still pushing against each other, which makes South Asia prone to earthquakes. In October 2005, an earthquake that measured 7.6 on the Richter scale rocked Kashmir. Many buildings collapsed or were buried by landslides. About 75,000 people died.

Earthquakes in the ocean floor can lift part of Earth's crust, shifting a huge amount of seawater. The result is a **tsunami**, a series of giant ocean waves that wash over coastal areas. In December 2004, a powerful undersea earthquake occurred in the Indian Ocean near Indonesia. This triggered a tsunami that raced west across the ocean and caused damage in 12 nations, including a number in South Asia. The waves left destroyed villages, ruined fields, and dead bodies. An estimated 300,000 people died.

2004 Tsunami Aerial photo shows damage caused by 2004 tsunami to seaside town in Sri Lanka.

▲ **CATEGORIZE** List some natural disasters in South Asia.

Section 2 Assessment

ONLINE QUIZ
For test practice, go to **Interactive Review** @ ClassZone.com

TERMS & NAMES
1. Explain the importance of
- Himalayas
- Ganges River
- cyclone
- tsunami

USE YOUR READING NOTES
2. Compare and Contrast Use your completed chart to answer the following question:

What are some of the differences between South and Southwest Asia in terms of physical features and climate?

	SOUTH ASIA	SOUTHWEST ASIA
Physical Features		
Climate		

KEY IDEAS
3. Why is India considered a subcontinent?

4. Why is the winter monsoon dry and the summer monsoon wet?

5. Why is South Asia so prone to earthquakes?

CRITICAL THINKING
6. Make Inferences How might farmers in a monsoon climate plan their work around the seasons?

7. Evaluate What might be some advantages and disadvantages of living in Bangladesh?

8. CONNECT to Today Many scientists claim that the global climate is getting warmer and polar icecaps might melt, raising the level of the oceans. Predict how that might affect the Maldives and Bangladesh.

9. WRITING Write an Appeal Review the descriptions of the disasters in this section. Choose one disaster, and imagine that you work for a relief agency such as UNICEF. Write an appeal or advertisement asking for aid for the victims.

Monsoons

 Click here to explore the effects of monsoons @ ClassZone.com

LIVING WITH EXTREME WEATHER

Monsoons shape the lives of people in South Asia. If the summer monsoons bring the right amount of rain, then crops grow and there is a good harvest. If monsoons bring too much rain, then crops are flooded and the harvest is spoiled. The illustration at right shows both positive (near right) and negative (far right) effects of summer monsoons.

Click here to see how Asia benefits from summer monsoons. Learn how monsoons provide relief from months of scorching heat. Rain helps crops to grow (as shown above in a rice field), nourishes the rain forest, and produces floodwaters that deposit sediment to replenish the soil. **A**

Click here to witness the harmful effects of summer monsoons. See how too much monsoon rain causes floods that ruin crops and lives. **B**

Summer Monsoons   Winter Monsoons

The summer and winter monsoons of South Asia blow from different directions. The summer monsoons blow from the southwest and the winter monsoons from the northeast.
- The summer monsoons are wet winds.
- The summer monsoons pick up water from the ocean.
- The winter monsoons are dry winds.
- The winter monsoons blow dry and cool because they cross the Himalayas.

Ⓑ

GeoActivity

Make a Poster Working with a partner, use the Internet to research summer monsoons. Create a poster showing ways of coping with flooding from monsoon rains, such as disaster shelters. Add a map showing the extent of monsoons in South Asia. Write a paragraph explaining how summer monsoons affect the people of the region.

Reading for Understanding

▶ Key Ideas

BEFORE, YOU LEARNED

The physical geography of both Southwest Asia and South Asia is rich and varied.

NOW YOU WILL LEARN

In both regions, civilizations developed first in river valleys where there was an abundant supply of water.

▶ Vocabulary

TERMS & NAMES

Mesopotamia the land between the Tigris and Euphrates rivers

silt the fine soil carried by rivers and deposited on nearby lands

civilization an advanced form of culture that developed in cities

Sumer a region of city-states in Mesopotamia that was home to the first civilization

city-state a political unit made up of a city and its surrounding lands

ziggurat a temple built atop a series of increasingly smaller platforms

polytheistic believing in many gods

cuneiform the first-known writing system, which used wedge-shaped symbols and was developed in Sumer

Fertile Crescent a region stretching from the Persian Gulf northwest up the Tigris and Euphrates rivers and west over to the Mediterranean Sea

Hammurabi's Code one of the world's first law codes, compiled by the ruler Hammurabi

Harappan civilization an ancient civilization that developed along the Indus River

BACKGROUND VOCABULARY

grid a network of horizontal and vertical lines that create squares or rectangles

▶ Reading Strategy

Re-create the chart shown at right. As you read and respond to the **KEY QUESTIONS**, use the chart to note the main achievements of the civilizations discussed in this section.

 See Skillbuilder Handbook, page R5

SUMMARIZE

SUMERIAN	HARAPPAN

 GRAPHIC ORGANIZERS
Go to **Interactive Review** @ ClassZone.com

River Valley Civilizations

Connecting to Your World

How would you get to sporting events or to the mall if the wheel had never been invented? How would you keep track of important information if you had no way to write it down? Think about what life would be like if your home didn't have indoor toilets, or if you couldn't wear cotton T-shirts or jeans. The people of ancient river valley civilizations invented many things that we rely on every day, including the wheel, writing, indoor plumbing, and cotton cloth.

Wheel The two-wheeled chariot was invented by the Sumerians in Mesopotamia around 3000 B.C.

Mesopotamia and the Fertile Crescent

▼ **KEY QUESTION** What are the main characteristics of civilization?

In Section 1, you learned that the Tigris and the Euphrates rivers flow from Anatolia to the Persian Gulf. What you didn't learn is that the land between the two has its own name—**Mesopotamia**, which means "land between the rivers." In the spring, rain and melting snow in the Anatolian highlands fed the Tigris and Euphrates. As the swollen rivers rushed downhill, they picked up soil. When the rivers reached the flat region of Mesopotamia, they overflowed and spread over a wide area. The fine soil in the water, called **silt**, settled on the land. Silt is very fertile and makes good soil for farming.

Animated GEOGRAPHY

Mesopotamia This floating village is located in the marshes of southern Iraq near the eastern end of Mesopotamia.

Click here to learn more about Mesopotamia @ClassZone.com

Civilization Arises The earliest humans lived by hunting animals and by gathering nuts, fruits, and seeds. Over time, they learned to save and plant some seeds to ensure they would have a food supply. That was the start of agriculture. When people began to irrigate their fields, their ability to grow crops improved and they had extra food.

Farming changed human life. Instead of wandering to find food, people settled in one place. In time, villages grew into cities. City dwellers had to figure out how to defend their city and how to do jobs such as building irrigation canals. To solve such problems, societies developed a more complex way of life. The advanced form of culture that arose in cities is called **civilization**. Civilization has five traits:

Advanced Cities Cities arose as places where farmers could store and trade their extra food.

Specialized Workers When a society has extra food, not everyone has to farm. Some can build houses or make pottery.

Complex Institutions A civilization has institutions such as an army, schools, a government, and a temple for worship.

Record Keeping People in cities needed to record information such as how much food they had stored. So civilizations developed record keeping, which involved writing.

Advanced Technology Early civilizations developed new technologies such as irrigation and bronze tools.

CONNECT Geography & Culture

Cuneiform

For writing supplies, Sumerians used a material they had a lot of—tablets made of clay from the riverbeds. At first, Sumerians drew pictures that stood for words. Later, they used a sharpened reed to make wedge-shaped marks in soft clay. The marks were combined into symbols that became the writing system called cuneiform. When the clay dried, it hardened, making a permanent record.

Sumerian Civilization The first civilization of Mesopotamia arose in **Sumer**, which was a land of many city-states. A **city-state** was made up of a city and nearby farmlands.

Walls surrounded the cities of Sumer. Buildings were made of dried mud because few trees grew in Mesopotamia. In many Sumerian cities, one building towered over all the others. It was the **ziggurat**, a temple built on a series of increasingly smaller platforms that made the ziggurat peak like a mountain. The Sumerian people were **polytheistic**, which means they believed in many gods.

The Sumerians invented many things we still use today, including the wheel and the plow. The Sumerians also developed the first writing system, which is called **cuneiform**.

▲ **FIND MAIN IDEAS** Give the main characteristics of civilization.

City-States and Empires

▼ **KEY QUESTION** Who were two rulers of Mesopotamian empires?

The first rulers of city-states were priests, because people believed priests communicated with the gods. However, cities often came under attack because they stored extra food and wealth that outsiders wanted. In wartime, military leaders gained power. Eventually, those leaders became permanent rulers called kings, chosen with the approval of the priests.

The First Empire In 2334 B.C., a ruler named Sargon came to power. He conquered many cities and became the first king to rule all of Mesopotamia. His empire stretched from the Persian Gulf up the two great rivers and over to the Mediterranean Sea, a region called the **Fertile Crescent**. Sargon built a wealthy capital city called Akkad. During his grandson's rule, invaders broke up the empire.

Hammurabi About 500 years after Sargon, another great empire rose in Mesopotamia. A king of Babylon named Hammurabi conquered other city-states and built a vast and powerful empire. Because of his conquests, Hammurabi was the ruler of many peoples with different customs. He wanted a consistent way to govern his subjects, so he compiled a set of laws that applied to everyone under his rule. **Hammurabi's Code** was one of the earliest law codes in the world. His concept of justice—that punishment should fit the crime—has continued to evolve.

▲ **SUMMARIZE** Identify two rulers of Mesopotamian empires.

HISTORY MAKERS

Hammurabi (died about 1750 B.C.)

When Hammurabi became king, Babylon was a small state. Hammurabi led Babylon in conquering surrounding lands. One tactic he used was to dam main waterways to deprive his enemies of water.

During his reign, Hammurabi oversaw the creation of one of the world's oldest set of laws. He made Babylon so magnificent that for centuries after his death, it remained one of the most important cities of the ancient world.

 ONLINE BIOGRAPHY
For more on the life of Hammurabi, go to the **Research & Writing Center @ ClassZone.com**

Indus River Valley Civilization

▼ **KEY QUESTION** What were some of the accomplishments of the Harappan civilization?

An ancient civilization also developed on the Indus River in what is now Pakistan. As you know, monsoons cause South Asia to have a rainy season and a dry season. During the rainy season, the Indus River often flooded and deposited fertile silt on the land. Farming villages sprang up, and some gradually grew into cities.

Mohenjo-Daro Ruins of the ancient city of Mohenjo-Daro, located in present-day Pakistan

Ruins of more than 100 settlements have been found spread across a vast area of South Asia. The two greatest cities of this civilization are called Mohenjo-Daro and Harappa, and the culture is called the **Harappan civilization**. It is also known as the Indus Valley civilization. The ruins of those cities show that the Harappan people had advanced technology and a system of measurement. The cities were laid out on a **grid** with straight streets that crossed at right angles. Houses had indoor plumbing, and there was a sewer system. The Harappan civilization used a system of weights and bricks that were a standard size. The Harappan people engaged in trade with Afghanistan, Persia, and Mesopotamia. The Harappans developed their own writing system to keep records. Around 2000 to 1500 B.C., the Harappan civilization declined, and people left the cities. No one knows why, but possible causes include earthquakes, a shift in the river's course, and attacking invaders. The Harappan people might simply have exceeded the environment's ability to support the population.

▲ **SUMMARIZE** Describe accomplishments of Harappan civilization.

Section 3 Assessment

ONLINE QUIZ
For test practice, go to
Interactive Review
@ ClassZone.com

TERMS & NAMES
1. Explain the importance of
- Mesopotamia
- civilization
- Sumer
- Harappan civilization

USE YOUR READING NOTES
2. Summarize Use your completed chart to answer the following question:

What were some achievements of the civilizations mentioned in this section?

SUMERIAN	HARAPPAN

KEY IDEAS
3. What were examples of complex institutions in Sumer?

4. What was Sargon's important achievement?

5. What are some possible causes for the decline of the Harappan civilization?

CRITICAL THINKING
6. Make Inferences Which developed first, specialized workers or complex institutions? Explain.

7. Compare How were the Sumerian and Harappan civilizations similar?

8. CONNECT to Today In Southwest Asia, farmers dig up objects from ancient ruins and sell them. Do you think historic objects should be kept in museums or owned by individuals? Explain.

9. TECHNOLOGY Plan a Multimedia Presentation Choose either the Sumerian or Harappan civilization and use books, the Internet, or a field trip to a museum to learn more about it. Plan a multimedia presentation showing its art, geography, and technology.

Interactive ⬅Review

Click here to complete these and other activities online @ ClassZone.com

CHAPTER SUMMARY

Key Idea 1
Southwest Asia has vast deserts and extensive mountain ranges that are similar to those in certain parts of Africa.

Key Idea 2
The physical geography of South Asia is made up of mountains, plateaus, and fertile plains, and the climate has wet and dry seasons.

Key Idea 3
In both regions, civilizations developed first in river valleys where there was an abundant supply of water.

For **Review and Study Notes**, go to **Interactive Review @ ClassZone.com**

NAME GAME

Use the Terms & Names list to complete each sentence on paper or online.

1. I am a mountain range running between the Indian subcontinent and Asia. __Himalayas__

2. I am the region that lies between the Tigris and Euphrates rivers. _____

3. I am a landform covered mostly by desert. _____

4. I flow from the Himalayas to the Bay of Bengal. _____

5. I lie in the center of the Indian subcontinent. _____

6. I am home to most of Turkey in Asia. _____

7. I am the tallest of my kind in the world. _____

8. I flow from the Himalayas to the Arabian Sea. _____

9. I flow from Anatolia to the Persian Gulf not far from the Euphrates. _____

10. I stretch from the Persian Gulf up two rivers and over to the Mediterranean Sea. _____

Anatolian peninsula
Arabian Peninsula
Deccan Plateau
Euphrates River
Fertile Crescent
Ganges River
Himalayas
Indus River
Plateau of Iran
Mesopotamia
Mount Everest
Sumer
Tigris River

Activities

Flip Cards

Use the online flip cards to quiz yourself on the terms and names introduced in this chapter.

ziggurat

Crossword Puzzle

Complete an online crossword puzzle to test your knowledge of Southwest Asia and South Asia.

ACROSS
1. Sumerian writing system that used clay tablets

VOCABULARY

Explain the significance of each of the following.

1. Arabian Peninsula
2. Anatolian peninsula
3. Plateau of Iran
4. Tigris River
5. subcontinent
6. Indus River
7. monsoon
8. Mesopotamia
9. ziggurat
10. Fertile Crescent

Explain how the first term in each group relates to the terms that follow.

11. civilization: city-state, cuneiform, ziggurat
12. subcontinent: Himalayas, Deccan Plateau

KEY IDEAS

1 Physical Geography of Southwest Asia

13. Where are the three subregions of Southwest Asia located in relationship to each other?
14. What is a qanat, and how does it work?
15. What is the main climate on the Arabian Peninsula?
16. Why does Turkey's water project worry its neighbors?

2 Physical Geography of South Asia

17. How were the Himalayas formed?
18. How were the Maldives formed?
19. What happens when the summer monsoon brings either too much or too little rain?
20. What are the dangers associated with cyclones?

3 River Valley Civilizations

21. What is one positive result of having rivers that overflow their banks during spring floods?
22. How did humans change from hunting and gathering to farming?
23. How did the leadership of city-states in Sumer change from priests to kings?
24. What were Harappan cities like?

CRITICAL THINKING

25. **Compare and Contrast** Create a table to compare and contrast the physical geography of Southwest Asia and South Asia.

SOUTHWEST ASIA	SOUTH ASIA

26. **Draw Conclusions** How did Sumerian priests retain some power under kings?
27. **Compare** What do the Indus, Ganges, and Brahmaputra rivers all have in common?
28. **Connect to Language Arts** An ancient Sumerian proverb says, "Whoever has walked with truth generates life." What do you think that means?
29. **Five Themes: Human-Environment Interaction** Cities with the gridlike design of Harappan culture were found across South Asia. How might that have happened?

Answer the
ESSENTIAL QUESTION

How have physical geography and history interacted in Southwest and South Asia?

Written Response Write a two- or three-paragraph response to the Essential Question. Be sure to consider the key ideas of each section about the rise of civilization in the region. Use the rubric below to guide your thinking.

Response Rubric
A written response will
• discuss the physical geography of each region
• relate physical geography to Sumerian civilization
• relate the physical geography of South Asia to the Harappan civilization

STANDARDS-BASED ASSESSMENT

☑ **Test Practice**
- Online Test Practice @ ClassZone.com
- Test-Taking Strategies and Practice at the front of this book

BAR GRAPH

Use the bar graph and your knowledge of Southwest Asia to answer questions 1 and 2 on your paper.

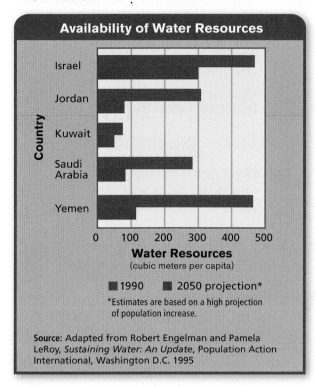

Availability of Water Resources

Country — Water Resources (cubic meters per capita)

■ 1990 ■ 2050 projection*

*Estimates are based on a high projection of population increase.

Source: Adapted from Robert Engelman and Pamela LeRoy, *Sustaining Water: An Update*, Population Action International, Washington D.C. 1995

1. Which country is projected to have the greatest supply of water by 2050?

A. Yemen
B. Israel
C. Kuwait
D. Jordan

2. Which country is projected to have the smallest supply of water by 2050?

A. Kuwait
B. Jordan
C. Saudi Arabia
D. Yemen

INFOGRAPHIC

Use this Indian farming calendar to answer questions 3 and 4 on your paper.

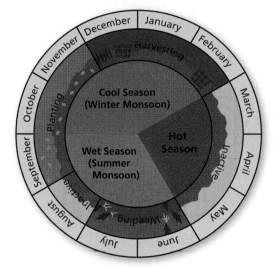

Source: India Country Studies

3. Which season is the most productive?

4. Which season is the least productive?

GeoActivity

1. INTERDISCIPLINARY ACTIVITY–ART

Working in a small group, find photographs of the statues and jewelry created by the ancient Sumerian and Harappan civilizations. Choose three from each region, and plan a multimedia presentation that will show and compare the art of the two regions.

2. WRITING FOR SOCIAL STUDIES

Research to learn what some of the laws in Hammurabi's code were. Write a review of those laws, quoting two or three examples and then explaining what you think their effect on society was and whether they were fair.

3. MENTAL MAPPING

Create an outline map of South Asia and label the following:

- Himalayas
- Deccan Plateau
- Indus River
- Ganges River
- Brahmaputra River
- Arabian Sea
- Bay of Bengal
- Indian Ocean
- Sri Lanka

Southwest Asia

 ESSENTIAL QUESTION

How might changes in political culture affect the stability of the region?

CONNECT Geography & History

Use the map and the time line to answer the following questions.

1. Which country in the region has the world's largest oil reserves?

2. What body of water is surrounded by oil-producing nations?

History

◄ **c. 960s B.C.**
Solomon, king of Israel,
builds a temple.

Culture

about 4 B.C. Jesus
of Nazareth is born.

1000 B.C.

Geography

c. 330 B.C. Alexander the Great
(at right) conquers Palestine. ►

Animated GEOGRAPHY

Economic Activity of Southwest Asia

Click here to explore Southwest Asia @ ClassZone.com

Black Sea

Istanbul

TURKEY

CYPRUS

Mediterranean Sea

Caspian Sea

Tehran

SYRIA

LEBANON
ISRAEL
WEST BANK
GAZA STRIP
Tel Aviv

JORDAN

IRAQ

IRAN

KUWAIT

Persian Gulf

SAUDI ARABIA

BAHRAIN

QATAR

OMAN

Gulf of Oman

UNITED ARAB EMIRATES

Abu Dhabi

Tropic of Cancer

Arabian Sea

Red Sea

OMAN

YEMEN

Gulf of Aden

INDIAN OCEAN

Predominant land use

- Commercial agriculture
- Nomadic herding
- Limited agriculture

Major resources

- Coal
- Copper
- Lead
- Natural gas
- Oil
- Other minerals

0   125   250 miles
0   125   250 kilometers

History

◄ **1520** Suleyman I becomes sultan of the Ottoman Empire.

Today

Culture

about A.D. 570 The prophet Muhammad is born.

Economics

▲ **2006** Saudi Arabia has the world's largest oil reserves.

Reading for Understanding

▶ Key Ideas

BEFORE, YOU LEARNED

The physical geography of Southwest Asia is harsh, with mountains, deserts, and a severe climate.

NOW YOU WILL LEARN

The physical geography of the region has influenced the history and culture of many countries.

▶ Vocabulary

TERMS & NAMES

Bedouin an Arabic-speaking, traditionally nomadic people of Southwest Asia

Muhammad (also spelled Mohammed) the founder and major prophet of Islam

monotheism a belief in one god

Islam a monotheistic religion based on the teachings of Muhammad and the writings of the Qur'an, the Muslim holy book

Muslim a believer in the religion of Islam who accepts Allah as the only god

Ottoman Empire a Muslim empire based in Turkey that lasted from the 1300s to 1922

OPEC Organization of Petroleum Exporting Countries, founded in 1960

Kurd a member of an ethnic group that does not have its own country but whose homeland lies in parts of Turkey, Iraq, and Iran

Persia a historic region of Southwest Asia located mostly in what is now Iran

shah title for the king of Persia or Iran

theocracy a government run by religious leaders

Visual Vocabulary
Shah of Persia (Iran)

▶ Reading Strategy

Re-create the chart shown at right. As you read and respond to the **KEY QUESTIONS**, use the chart to note the main ideas about the region's history, government, culture, and economics.

 Skillbuilder Handbook, page R4

FIND MAIN IDEAS

	SAUDI ARABIA	IRAQ	IRAN
History			
Government			
Culture			
Economics			

GRAPHIC ORGANIZERS
Go to **Interactive Review @ ClassZone.com**

Saudi Arabia, Iraq, and Iran

Connecting to Your World

Have you ever heard people say that they can't wake up until they've had their morning cup of coffee? Drinking coffee is just one of many things that our culture gained from Southwest Asia. The people of Southwest Asia (along with people in Egypt) invented algebra, recorded many observations about the stars, and discovered medicines that we still use today. Southwest Asia was also the birthplace of three major religions—Judaism, Christianity, and Islam. You will learn about Islam in this section.

Saudi Arabia

🔻 **KEY QUESTION** How did the Arabian Peninsula become a Muslim region?

Saudi Arabia occupies more than three-fourths of the Arabian Peninsula. As you learned earlier, deserts such as the Rub al-Khali cover most of the peninsula. Hardly anyone lives in the deserts; in fact, the name *Rub al-Khali* means "empty quarter." Lack of water is one of Saudi Arabia's biggest problems. No permanent rivers exist, and the country is using up its supplies of underground water.

Saudi Arabia Sand dunes are common in the deserts of the Arabian Peninsula, with an occasional water source such as the springs shown here. **How might scarcity of water affect settlement in the Arabian Peninsula?**

Reading for Understanding

▶ Key Ideas

BEFORE, YOU LEARNED

Various countries in the region are struggling with how to preserve past legacies as they organize their societies to move into the future.

NOW YOU WILL LEARN

Turkey, Syria, and Lebanon are all struggling with similar issues of how to reconcile representative government with their traditions.

▶ Vocabulary

TERMS & NAMES

Istanbul the largest city of Turkey, formerly called Constantinople (capital of the Byzantine, or Eastern Roman, Empire) and originally called Byzantium in ancient times

European Union an organization of European nations whose members cooperate on economic, social, and political issues

Golan Heights a region that was formerly part of southwest Syria that Israel has occupied since the 1967 war

peacekeeping referring to military forces whose purpose is to prevent or end war

extended family the family unit that contains more relatives than just parents and children, including grandparents and other close family

Beirut capital of Lebanon and a center of banking and finance

REVIEW

Ottoman Empire a Muslim empire based in Turkey that lasted from the 1300s to 1922

Palestine Liberation Organization (PLO) a political group that claims to represent all Palestinians and to be working toward gaining an independent Palestinian nation

▶ Reading Strategy

Re-create the chart shown at right. As you read and respond to the **KEY QUESTIONS**, use the chart to organize important facts about Turkey, Syria, and Lebanon.

 Skillbuilder Handbook, page R7

CATEGORIZE

	TURKEY	SYRIA	LEBANON
History			
Culture			
Government			
Economics			

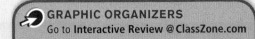

GRAPHIC ORGANIZERS
Go to **Interactive Review @ ClassZone.com**

Turkey, Syria, and Lebanon

Connecting to Your World

Think about the other students who were in your class last year. Even if you come from very different backgrounds or families, you have something in common. You know what that teacher was like and what the classroom rules were. And you share some of the same memories. The countries of Turkey, Syria, and Lebanon have a similar link. Their people have very different ethnic heritages, but they were all part of the Ottoman Empire that you read about in Section 1.

Istanbul

Turkey

🔻 **KEY QUESTION** What steps did Mustafa Kemal take to modernize Turkey?

The **Ottoman Empire** began in the 1300s when a group of Turkish people took over most of Anatolia and parts of the Balkan Peninsula in Europe. During the next two centuries, the empire expanded to include more of Europe and most of Southwest Asia and North Africa. But over time, the empire grew weak because of losses in wars and revolts within the empire. After being defeated in World War I, the empire came to an end. In its place, the much-smaller nation of Turkey was founded in 1923 on the Anatolian Peninsula.

Istanbul Shown is the Galata Bridge in Istanbul, Turkey. The western part of the city is in Europe and the eastern part is in Asia. **Why might Istanbul be a good location for trade?**

India is one of the oldest cultures in the world. It continues to observe many of its traditions in terms of beliefs, clothing, diet, and work. At the same time, it is rushing in the 21st century to embrace the modern world and improve the standard of living of its people.

Traditional India

Traditional India is a land of the Taj Mahal, Hindu temples, beautiful saris, and rickshaws careening down narrow village streets. Although much of the developing middle class is modernizing, millions continue to follow the traditional ways in clothing, food, work, and daily life.

The village of Gulmarg, a former hill station to which the British retreated to escape the heat of the plains, sits on a hillside beneath the Himalayas. ▼

Architecture

Carvings cover this Hindu temple in Chennai.

Transportation

Even in cities, tradition still plays a part, as shown by bicycle rickshaws in Varanasi.

Jobs

A potter throws pots on wheel in the village of Gunupur.

Modern India

Modern India is racing to become a center of high-tech jobs and widespread prosperity. India's growing middle class is increasingly willing to abandon the sari for jeans, the railway for jet flights across the country, and the farming village for high-tech centers such as Bangalore.

Architecture

The Mumbai Stock Exchange is an example of contemporary architecture in the city of Mumbai.

Transportation

Traffic jams the street in front of the Capitol movie theater in Mumbai.

Jobs

Call-center workers in Bangalore serve customers in the United States and Britain.

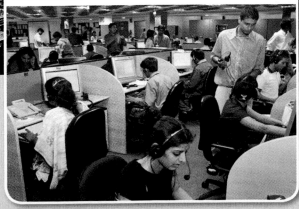

▲ *Aerial view of Mumbai, India*

CRITICAL THINKING

1. **Compare and Contrast** What differences can be seen in the kinds of jobs that are available in the city and in the village?

2. **Make Inferences** How would a person's life change in moving from village to city?

UNIT 8

East Asia and Southeast Asia

Why It Matters:

East Asia is home to several countries that are important members of the world economy. The nations of Southeast Asia are working hard to strengthen their economies. In the coming decades, both regions are expected to have a strong voice in world affairs.

Forbidden City in Beijing

CHAPTER 25 China

Blend of old and new in Seoul, South Korea

CHAPTER 26 The Korean Peninsula

Floating Shinto gate near Hiroshima

CHAPTER 27 Japan

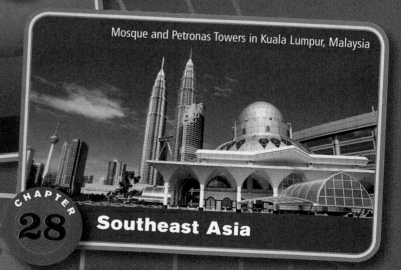

Mosque and Petronas Towers in Kuala Lumpur, Malaysia

CHAPTER 28 Southeast Asia

CHAPTER 25

China

 ESSENTIAL QUESTION

How is China's traditional way of life changing in response to global trends?

1 GEOGRAPHY
Land of Three Rivers

2 HISTORY
Middle Kingdom to Communist Power

3 CULTURE
Changing Chinese Culture

4 GOVERNMENT & ECONOMICS
A Rising Power

CONNECT → **Geography & History**

Use the map and the time line to answer the following questions.

1. What is the capital of China?
2. On what river is the Three Gorges Dam?

Culture
479 B.C. Confucius, China's greatest teacher, dies. ▶

Culture
A.D. 65 Buddhism begins to travel to China from India.

500 B.C.

History
221 B.C. Shi Huangdi unifies China into an empire. ▶

80°E   100°E   120°E   60°N   140°E   50°N

R U S S I A

KAZAKHSTAN

MONGOLIA

MANCHURIA

Harbin •

Changchun •

Shenyang •   40°N

Ürümqi •

NORTH
KOREA   Sea of
Japan
(East Sea)

KYRGYZSTAN

TAJIKISTAN

AFGHANISTAN

Beijing ✪

Huang He (Yellow R.)   Dalian •   SOUTH
KOREA   JAPAN

Tianjin •

Disputed Border   • Jinan   Yellow
Sea

PAKISTAN   C H I N A   • Xi'an   Nanjing •   • Shanghai   30°N

TIBET   Chengdu •   Wuhan •   Grand Canal   Hangzhou •

Lhasa •   Chongqing •   Chang Jiang (Yangtze R.)   East
China
Sea

NEPAL   Three
Gorges
Dam

BHUTAN

I N D I A   BANGLADESH   Xi Jiang (West R.)   TAIWAN   20°N

Guangzhou •   Tropic of Cancer

MYANMAR   Hong Kong •   PACIFIC
OCEAN

VIETNAM   PHILIPPINES

LAOS   Hainan

✪ National capital   South China
Sea   10°N

• Other city   N
W   E
S

THAILAND   250   500 miles

CAMBODIA   250   500 kilometers

Geography

◄ **1421** Beijing becomes
the capital of China.
(Forbidden City)

Today

Geography

609 The Grand Canal links the
Huang He and Chang Jiang rivers.

Government

◄ **1949** The Communists
win the civil war; Mao Zedong
becomes head of government.

Reading for Understanding

▶ Key Ideas

BEFORE, YOU LEARNED

South Asia contains mountains, plateaus, and plains. Its wet and dry seasons can cause floods and drought.

NOW YOU WILL LEARN

China has varied landforms, ranging from high mountains to river valleys. It has diverse climates, plants, and animals.

▶ Vocabulary

TERMS & NAMES

Three Gorges Dam a barrier built on the Chang Jiang to control floods

hydroelectric power electricity made by water-powered engines

Himalayas (HIHM•uh•LAY•uhz) a mountain range that divides China from India

Taklimakan (TAH•kluh•muh•KAHN) **Desert** the second largest sand desert in the world

Gobi (GOH•bee) **Desert** a high desert in China and Mongolia

Huang He (hwahng huh) a river that flows from the Kunlun Mountains to the Yellow Sea

Chang Jiang (chahng jyahng) the longest river in Asia, flowing through eastern China

Xi (she) **Jiang** a river in southeast China

seismic (SYZ•mihk) having to do with earthquakes

REVIEW

plateau a high area of flat land

Visual Vocabulary plateau

▶ Reading Strategy

Re-create the chart shown at right. As you read and respond to the **KEY QUESTIONS**, use the chart to organize important details about the physical geography of China.

 See Skillbuilder Handbook, page R7

CATEGORIZE

	WESTERN CHINA	EASTERN CHINA
Geographic Features		
Climate		
Plants and Animals		
Types of Agriculture		
Natural Disasters		

 GRAPHIC ORGANIZERS
Go to **Interactive Review** @ ClassZone.com

Land of Three Rivers

Connecting to Your World

Much like the Mississippi in the United States, the Chang Jiang (chahng jyahng) River in eastern China has been both China's best friend and worst enemy. The fertile farmland and the transportation that the river provides help China feed its enormous population. But seasonal floods take a terrible toll on the million or so people who live near the river's banks. The **Three Gorges Dam** should prevent the floods. The dam will also generate **hydroelectric power**, electricity from water-powered engines. The dam was completed in 2006 but is not projected to begin operating until 2009.

China's Geographic Features

▼ **KEY QUESTION** What are the main geographic features of western China and eastern China?

Everything about the People's Republic of China is on a big scale. China is the third largest country in area and has a population of 1.3 billion—the largest in the world. Western China contains some of the world's harshest geographic features, while eastern China is one of the world's most densely populated places.

Animated GEOGRAPHY

Lake to be created by the dam — Three Gorges Dam

Chang Jiang (Yangtze R.)

Chongqing · Wuhan · Shanghai

CHINA

Three Gorges Dam Officials say the dam will relieve flooding on the Chang Jiang and produce more energy. Some people disagree. **What problems do you think the dam could cause?**

Click here to see more of the Three Gorges Dam project @ ClassZone.com

China's Varied Climate and Resources

▼ **KEY QUESTION** How are the climate and resources of western and eastern China different?

Western and eastern China have very different climates and natural resources. Because of its climate differences, China also has a variety of plants and animals.

Life in Western China You've learned that western China is thinly populated because it is mostly mountains and deserts. The highest mountains are cold year-round. At lower elevations, summers are cool but sunny. Animals such as wild sheep and mountain antelope roam the highlands. Forests grow at elevations of around 12,000 feet and provide a home for wildcats.

As you might guess, almost nothing survives in the Gobi and Taklimakan deserts. They get little rain and have very sparse vegetation. Temperatures dip below 0°F in winter and rise to higher than 120°F in summer.

Many highlanders are nomadic herders of horses and of grazing animals, such as yaks, sheep, and goats. Because vegetation is scarce—mostly mosses and short shrubs—grazing herds must keep moving to find new sources of food.

Western China's main resources are petroleum, natural gas, and lead. Pipelines carry both oil and natural gas to the east.

Life in Eastern China Eastern China has a milder climate than western China. Northeastern China has a climate like the Northeast and Midwest of the United States, with cold winters, warm summers, and enough rain for farming. Mixed and broadleaf forests provide homes for leopards, deer, and more than 265 kinds of birds. In contrast, southeastern China has mild winters and hot, rainy summers. The region has mixed forests of wild tea and citrus trees, oaks, cypresses, and pines. Alligators, giant salamanders, monkeys, and pangolins—scaly animals that look like anteaters—live inland.

Wherever rain falls in China, bamboo grows. Bamboo is important to Chinese culture. Its long, woody stems are used to make chopsticks, among other things. Bamboo is also a vital food for the giant panda, China's most treasured animal. The panda, an endangered species, spends about 12 hours a day eating—and it eats mainly bamboo.

Most of China's farmland is in eastern China. Many people think that all Chinese farmers grow rice, but in northern China they grow wheat, soybeans, and millet. These crops need less water than rice. Rice is grown in the rainy southeast, where the climate is so mild and the soil is so rich that farmers grow two or three crops a year.

Chinese farmers use traditional methods that are centuries old. They don't have the huge tractors or other large farm equipment that U.S. farmers use. The use of farm machinery, such as small hand-held tractors, has been on the rise since the 1990s, but China still relies on long hours of human labor in the fields.

Eastern China has abundant natural resources, such as tin and iron. In 2003, China produced about 35 percent of the world's coal, but at a deadly cost; 80 percent of all deaths in coal mines worldwide occur in China. The government is using clean coal technologies and modernizing equipment to improve safety.

▲ **COMPARE AND CONTRAST** Compare the climate and resources of western and eastern China.

COMPARING   Western and Eastern China

	WESTERN	EASTERN
Population	thinly populated	heavily populated
Geographic Features	an arid climate and little usable farmland	important rivers, plentiful rain, rich farmland
Land Use	used mostly for grazing animals	used for agriculture
Resources	supplies of petroleum, natural gas, and lead	rich with coal and other resources

CRITICAL THINKING

1. **Analyze Effects** How is land use in each part of China affected by its geographic features?
2. **Make Inferences** Which part of China would most likely contribute more to the country's overall economy?

The Rise of Communism

▼ **KEY QUESTION** What impact did communism have on China?

A new dynasty called the Qing (chihng) took over China in 1644. During the 1800s, European nations wanted to trade with China. When the Qing rulers refused, the Europeans defeated China in a series of wars. The Europeans forced the Qing to open China and let them trade in several port cities. The United States and Japan were also given the right to trade in China.

China's population had grown rapidly, but food production did not increase at the same rate. People became angry about the widespread hunger and also about China's defeat at the hands of foreigners. As a result, many rebellions against the Qing took place.

In 1912, a group called the Nationalist Party defeated the Qing and set up a republic. The Nationalists then had to fight many warlords. By 1928, they had united China.

Communist Revolution In 1921, a group of students and others formed the Chinese Communist Party. **Communism** is a system in which the government holds nearly all political power and the means of production in the name of the people. The Communists wanted to take over China. They set up bases in the countryside and gave land to peasants, many of whom joined them.

By 1930, civil war had broken out between the Nationalists and Communists. In 1934, the Nationalist army surrounded the Communists. To escape, the Communists fled on the Long March, walking for 6,000 miles.

Japan invaded China in 1937. The Nationalists and Communists stopped fighting and worked together to fight Japan. After Japan was defeated at the end of World War II, the civil war began again. In 1949, the Communists won and formed the People's Republic of China. The Nationalists fled to Taiwan (TY•wahn), an island off of China's southeast coast.

The Long March *1934–1935*

0   200   400 miles
0   200   400 kilometers

Huang He (Yellow R.) • Beijing
40°N
• Yan'an
LUPAN MTS.
Nanjing
GREAT SNOWY MTS.   **C H I N A**   Shanghai
Chang Jiang (Yangtze R.)
• Luding
• Zunyi
• Ruijin
Taiwan
Xi Jiang (West R.)
20°N

⊛ National capital
← Route of march
▨ Communist base, 1934
▨ Communist base, 1935

110°E   120°E

CONNECT Geography & History

1. **Movement** What direction or directions did the Communists travel during their Long March?
2. **Place** What advantage did they gain by moving to a new base in the mountains? Explain how this would affect their ability to defend themselves.

Chairman Mao In 1949, **Mao Zedong** (MOW dzuh•dahng) became chairman, or head, of China's Communist government. He seized farmland from large landholders and divided it among the peasants. The government also took over all industry and business. It even controlled the personal lives of the Chinese people.

In 1958, Mao started an economic plan called the Great Leap Forward. He believed in using the hard work of peasants instead of modern technology to increase food production. Thousands of peasants were sent to work on huge, government-owned farms. Mao's program failed to increase food production, so in 1961 it was stopped. The Great Leap Forward resulted in over 20 million deaths from starvation. Some leaders began to talk about reversing Mao's policies.

In 1966, Mao called for a Cultural Revolution to stop those plans. He urged millions of high school and college students to form groups called Red Guards. They attacked educated people and criticized leaders who wanted change. The Red Guards closed schools and factories. They caused so much chaos that Mao finally had to send the army to stop them. After Mao died in 1976, the leaders who wanted change took over China.

Mao Zedong For 27 years, Mao Zedong was the most powerful man in China. This portrait still hangs outside the old palace of the emperors. **Why do you think Mao's portrait hangs outside a palace?**

 DRAW CONCLUSIONS Explain the impact of communism on China.

ONLINE QUIZ For test practice, go to **Interactive Review** @ ClassZone.com

Section 2 Assessment

TERMS & NAMES

1. Explain the importance of
- Shi Huangdi
- dynastic cycle
- Confucianism
- Mao Zedong

USE YOUR READING NOTES

2. Identify Problems and Solutions

Use your completed problem-solution chart to answer the following question:

How successful was Mao Zedong at solving the two problems of keeping order and feeding people? Explain.

PROBLEMS	SOLUTIONS
Gaining Power	
Keeping Order	
Feeding a Large Population	

KEY IDEAS

3. Why did China's emperors think it was a good idea to employ scholar-officials who had studied Confucianism?

4. How did the iron plow and the horse collar help to feed China's large population?

5. How did the inventions of paper and block printing make record-keeping easier?

CRITICAL THINKING

6. Draw Conclusions How was the Mandate of Heaven connected to the dynastic cycle?

7. Analyze Effects In what ways did the Communists promote change, and in what ways did they oppose it?

8. CONNECT to Today Why do you think the Chinese people still honor Mao?

9. TECHNOLOGY Create a Multimedia Presentation Create a slide show about a group of inventions that changed farming, government, education, or trade. Show how the inventions work and explain why they made a difference.

Animated GEOGRAPHY
The Great Wall of China

 Click here to enter the Great Wall of China @ ClassZone.com

DEFENDING CHINA

Many barriers protect China: mountains to the west and south, an ocean to the east. But in the north, nomads were able to invade China, so the Chinese built a barrier—the Great Wall—to try to stop them.

 Click here to see the Great Wall as it snakes across mountains, plains, and deserts. Learn about the challenges of building and maintaining about 4,000 miles of walls.

 Click here to see the weapons used in a Great Wall battle. Learn about watchtowers, lookout soldiers, and the signals used to warn of an attack.

crenellation

Ming Wall

paved road

parapet

stone or brick wall

interior of earth, stones, and rubble

quarried stone base

 Click here to see inside the Great Wall. The construction methods were so sound that the Wall has lasted for centuries.

The Great Wall of China Over Time

GOBI DESERT

Beijing

C H I N A

Huang He (Yellow R.)

Yellow Sea

Xi'an

Luoyang

N

| 0 | 150 | 300 miles |
| 0 | 150 | 300 kilometers |

The Great Wall of China was built over many years.

- During the Warring States period (403 to 221 B.C.), rival kingdoms built separate walls.
- After Shi Huangdi united China (221 B.C.), a more connected wall was built.
- Ming Dynasty (A.D. 1368 to 1644) rulers repaired and added new sections to the wall.

GeoActivity

Sketch a Battle Plan You have received word that a group of invading nomads are bearing down on the part of the Great Wall that you defend. Sketch a battle plan to defeat the nomads, and use the surrounding terrain in your strategy.

Reading for Understanding

▶ Key Ideas

BEFORE, YOU LEARNED

China has a very long history. The people lived a traditional life during much of that history—until the Communist Revolution.

NOW YOU WILL LEARN

Some aspects of traditional life survive in China, while new ways of life have been developed.

▶ Vocabulary

TERMS & NAMES

Daoism (DOW•IHZ•uhm) a Chinese belief system based on the idea of natural order in the world

Dao (DOW) according to the belief system of Daoism, a force that guides the whole universe

Silk Roads trade routes used between China and Southwest Asia

Buddhism a religion that is based on the teaching of Siddhartha Gautama

Siddhartha Gautama (sihd•DAHR•tuh GAW•tuh•muh) the founder of Buddhism also known as the Buddha, or "enlightened one"

Buddha the founder of Buddhism who taught that people could end their suffering by stopping their desire for wordly goods

BACKGROUND VOCABULARY

ritual a set of regularly followed ceremonies

communal shared ownership of property

REVIEW

Confucianism a Chinese belief system based on the teachings of Confucius

▶ Reading Strategy

Re-create the web diagram shown at right. As you read and respond to the **KEY QUESTIONS**, use the outer ovals to record main ideas about changes in Chinese culture. Add ovals as needed.

 See Skillbuilder Handbook, page R4

FIND MAIN IDEAS

Influence of western nations

CHANGES IN CHINESE CULTURE

GRAPHIC ORGANIZERS
Go to **Interactive Review @ ClassZone.com**

Changing Chinese Culture

Connecting to Your World

Have you ever asked your grandparents what life was like when they were your age? Cultural change can happen at any place and time. For example, Mei (may) Ling's grandmother, who lives in the country, talks of the village school she attended. Mei Ling's parents moved to Shanghai in search of better jobs. As a result, Mei Ling attends a big urban school instead of a village school. The move from the farm to the city is just one type of change in China. In this section, you'll learn how traditional Chinese culture is affected by these changes.

Chinese Family Like Mei Ling, this Chinese girl has a strong relationship with her grandmother.

Traditional Chinese Culture

🔻 **KEY QUESTION** What are some aspects of traditional Chinese culture?

Chinese culture is thousands of years old. Though life has changed in modern China, traditional values—such as close family ties and respect for one's parents and ancestors—remain strong.

Martial Arts Chinese students practice traditional martial arts.

Family and Village Life In traditional Chinese culture, family was very important. Older men made all the major decisions for the family. Men were taught to perform **rituals** honoring their ancestors. Women were taught that it was their duty to marry, have children, and care for their husbands' parents. Children were expected to respect their parents and care for them in old age.

For thousands of years, most Chinese people were farmers. Each day the villagers would go out to the fields to work. Nearly all Chinese lived in small rural villages of about 200 people. Houses in the village were crowded closely together. Most had a courtyard where chickens and pigs wandered in search of food. Small vegetable gardens provided food for the family meals. The villagers shared a well and bought some goods at local markets.

Beliefs Three different belief systems—Confucianism, Daoism, and Buddhism—have influenced Chinese life. **Confucianism** is the belief system based on the teachings of Confucius, whom you learned about in Section 2. In Confucianism, the person who is older or has more power has a responsibility to be kind to others. The younger or less powerful person is expected to be respectful and obedient. Confucianism also teaches that people can help to better themselves through education.

The second Chinese belief system, **Daoism** (DOW•IHZ•uhm), is based on the ideas of a teacher named Laozi. He taught that the world has a natural order and that a force called the **Dao** (DOW), meaning "the Way," guides all things. Laozi taught that people should observe nature and use those observations to find a way to peace and harmony.

Confucius' Birthday Celebration Dancers in traditional costumes celebrate the birth of Confucius in 551 B.C. **Why do the Chinese still honor Confucius?**

CONFUCIANISM

- Social order and good government should be based on strong family relationships.
- Respect for parents and elders helps to create order in society.
- Education helps to improve both individuals and society.

DAOISM

- The natural order—or the relationship among all living things in the universe—matters more than the social order.
- A universal force called the Dao (meaning "the Way") guides all things.
- Humans should learn to live simply and in harmony with nature.

BUDDHISM

- People suffer because of emotional attachments and their desire for worldly goods.
- People can stop suffering and achieve peace (or nirvana) by not wanting.
- To achieve nirvana, people should follow the Eightfold Path: right views, goals, speech, actions, job, effort, concentration, and meditation.

CRITICAL THINKING

Compare and Contrast How are the three belief systems similar? How are they different?

Missionaries who traveled the **Silk Roads**, the trade routes used between China and Southwest Asia, brought **Buddhism** to China. Buddhism is a religion based on the teachings of **Siddhartha Gautama** (sihd•DAHR•tuh GAW•tuh•muh), also known as the **Buddha**, or "enlightened one." Buddha taught that people suffer because their minds are not at ease. This suffering comes from wanting life to be different. The Buddha said people could stop the suffering by accepting life as it is and following the Eightfold Path, detailed above.

Written Language The development of a written Chinese language allowed the government to communicate with people in all parts of the empire, no matter what language they spoke. Chinese characters do not represent sounds, as Western letters do. They represent ideas or words. People who spoke differently could still read each other's letters because they used the same characters to write.

The Arts Some of traditional China's greatest achievements in the arts were in bronze casting, jade carving, and dance. Bronze objects such as bells and containers featured geometric designs and were decorated with tigers, snakes, birds, and oxen. Jade was used to make jewelry, containers, and statues. There were two kinds of traditional Chinese dance: one based on proper behavior as taught by Confucius, and one based on Chinese warrior exercises, which we call martial arts.

▲ **SUMMARIZE** Discuss some of the aspects of traditional Chinese culture.

Chinese Character This character stands for the Dao, which means "the way."

Persons per square mile

Over 520
260–519
130–259
25–129
1–24
0

CONNECT Geography & Culture

1. **Place** Which color represents the densest population?
2. **Region** Which part of China has the densest population?

Changes in Chinese Life

▼ **KEY QUESTION** How did life change in China after the Communists took over?

The traditional Chinese way of life changed dramatically with the rise of communism. Family farms ceased to exist, and farms were reorganized into **communal** farms where ownership was shared. The farms were strictly controlled by the government. Every family had a registration booklet listing its members. Families needed the booklet to get food, medical services, housing, schooling, and jobs.

Moving to Cities As a part of the new way of life under the Communists, people had to get government permission to move. But little movement was allowed until after 1978, when economic reforms were made. These reforms brought new industry to the cities. As a result, workers were allowed to move from farms into towns or cities to fill jobs there. Workers also moved into cities on the east coast where the booming economy required many construction workers. Industry even began to emerge in rural areas.

Beijing China's capital is a crowded, rapidly modernizing city. Today, China has about 1.3 billion people, compared with about 298 million in the United States.

Population in China

1950

12.5%

87.5%

2005

40.5%

59.5%

■ Urban   ■ Rural

Source: *China Statistical Yearbook 2004* and *Globalis*

CRITICAL THINKING

Compare and Contrast
By how much did the urban population increase between 1950 and 2005?

The shift in population to the cities was a major change in Chinese society. Today, about 60 percent of Chinese people live in rural areas, compared to almost 88 percent in 1950. Part of the reason for this spectacular urban growth is due to the expanded industrial sites in smaller towns, especially in eastern China. China has 34 cities with over a million people. In comparison, the United States has 9 cities of that size. China's two largest cities, Beijing and Shanghai, are huge. At the end of 2004, Beijing had 14.9 million residents and Shanghai, China's largest city, had 17.4 million. The population of these two cities is about equal to that of the state of California.

Jobs and Education After the economic reforms of 1978, China's new leaders set very high standards for education. Today, students are expected to study many hours; they have little time for extracurricular activities. The law calls for school attendance through ninth grade. More rural children now complete nine years of schooling. Students must then do well on national exams to be able to go on to trade school, high school, or college. However, education is not free. Parents must pay fees and buy textbooks.

Cities have more educational opportunities than rural areas. Many city teenagers go on to high school. However, in the past, only a very small percentage of students went to college. Today, China's goal is to have 20 percent of its students in college by 2010.

▲ **EVALUATE** Explain how life changed in China after the Communists took over.

Worldster
A Day in Cheng's Life

To learn more about Cheng and his world, go to the **Activity Center @ ClassZone.com**

In Chinese, Cheng's name looks like this:

Hi! My name is Cheng. I am 14 years old and live in Yihuang, a rural town of about 20,000 in eastern China. Studying is very important to me. But I don't study all the time! On weekends, my friends and I play table tennis, basketball, or use the computers at the community center. Let me tell you about my day.

8 A.M.–5:30 P.M. I have a long school day. We begin by saluting the flag and exercising. During the day, I have classes in Chinese, math, science, and history.

7 A.M. I have breakfast with my parents before they go to work and I leave for school. Today we're having eggs, peanuts, and steamed buns for breakfast.

6 P.M. I'm meeting my parents and other family members at my grandparents' house for dinner. Tonight we're having one of my favorites, Four Happiness Pork along with rice and vegetables.

7 P.M. I have a basketball game tonight. I play on my school team. We're pretty good! After-school activities for other kids in my class are sports like gymnastics or music lessons. When I get home, I'll have homework to do.

CONNECT to Your Life

Journal Entry Think about your own daily schedule. What do you spend most of your day doing? How is your life different from Cheng's life? Record your ideas in your journal.

Clashes Over Popular Culture

▼ **KEY QUESTION** How has the government tried to control popular culture?

Life in modern China is a blend of old and new ways. Many people still live in rural areas and lead a more traditional life. But even that way of life is changing now that they have more access to television, computers, and cell phones. The Chinese government attempts to control the content available to people through technology.

Recently, the Communists began tighter control of foreign television programs. The government is taking this action because it is worried about the spread of democratic ideas. Television programs are forbidden to use the English language or show violence.

People in cities and even in many small towns have access to e-mail and the Internet. However, they cannot visit Web sites the government does not approve of or send messages that criticize their leaders.

In the past, the government demanded that art spread Communist ideas. Now theaters and art galleries show plays and works about a variety of subjects in the artists' own styles. Writers are beginning to discuss social issues but are not allowed to criticize the government.

▲ **DRAW CONCLUSIONS** Draw conclusions about how the Chinese government controls popular culture.

ONLINE QUIZ
For test practice, go to
Interactive Review
@ ClassZone.com

Section 3 Assessment

TERMS & NAMES

1. Explain the importance of
- Daoism
- Silk Roads
- Buddhism

USE YOUR READING NOTES

2. Find Main Ideas Use your completed web to answer the following question:

How have Chinese society and culture changed since dynastic times?

KEY IDEAS

3. What are the most important traditional Chinese values?

4. Which three belief systems influenced Chinese society?

5. How has the distribution of population in China changed since the 1950s?

CRITICAL THINKING

6. Draw Conclusions Why do you think the Chinese government is encouraging more students to go to college?

7. Summarize In what ways has life in China changed since the new leadership took over after 1978?

8. (**CONNECT to Today**) Which Confucian idea continues to influence Chinese society?

9. (**ART**) **Sketch a Design** Use the Internet or art books to find examples of Chinese bronze vessels. Create and sketch a design that could be used to create a bronze vessel.

Until the 1970s, many more Chinese lived in the countryside than in cities. Then people began moving into the cities in record numbers. Today more than 40 percent of all Chinese live in the cities.

Traditional Countryside

Market day in small towns and villages is an important day for rural Chinese to do their shopping or to sell goods. Most of the goods are produced in the area near the marketplace. Market day is also a time to see friends and relatives who live in the area.

Outdoor vegetable market in eastern China ▼

Jobs

A young boy feeds his water buffalo. Water buffalo still provide power for farm work.

Production

Peasants gather tomatoes for sale at the local market.

Transportation

A farmer transports geese and chickens to market.

Jobs

China's economic boom has triggered many construction projects, especially in cities.

Booming Cities

Life in bustling, noisy cities like Shanghai and Beijing is very different from the less hectic life of the rural areas. Many people work in factories, as street vendors, at office jobs, or at their own businesses. Shopping takes place in Western-style malls or in stores in city neighborhoods.

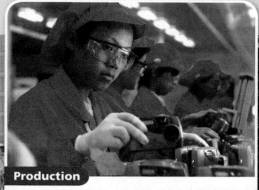

Production

High-tech assembly plants like this digital camera plant have popped up in many Chinese cities.

Transportation

With a top speed of 267 miles per hour, Shanghai's maglev (magnetic levitation) train is the fastest in the world.

▲ *Crowded, busy street in Shanghai*

CRITICAL THINKING

1. **Compare and Contrast** What differences can be seen in the way goods are sold in the city and in the country?

2. **Make Inferences** In what ways would a person's life change if he or she moved from the country to the city?

Reading for Understanding

SECTION 4

▶ Key Ideas

BEFORE, YOU LEARNED

Although some traditional ways of life are still practiced, life has changed in China. More people are living in cities.

NOW YOU WILL LEARN

Small changes in the Chinese government and big changes in the Chinese economy are taking place.

▶ Vocabulary

TERMS & NAMES

province a governmental division like a state

National People's Congress (NPC) China's national law-making body

demonstration a public gathering to protest a policy or action

Tiananmen (tyahn•ahn•mehn) **Square** the location of a huge demonstration for democratic rights that occurred in 1989

command economy an economy in which the government owns all land, factories, and businesses, and decides what will be produced

free enterprise an economy in which business is privately owned

reform action to improve social or economic conditions

Visual Vocabulary Tiananmen Square

▶ Reading Strategy

Re-create the chart shown at right. As you read and respond to the **KEY QUESTIONS**, use the chart to summarize information about China's government and economy.

 See Skillbuilder Handbook, page R5

SUMMARIZE

GOVERNMENT	ECONOMY	ISSUES AND TRENDS

 GRAPHIC ORGANIZERS
Go to **Interactive Review** @ ClassZone.com

A Rising Power

Connecting to Your World

Take a look at the labels in your clothing or shoes, or on a small electronic device such as an inexpensive calculator. Many goods that Americans use every day are made in China. This is a big change from the days of Mao when most products produced in China stayed there. Chinese people had little contact with foreigners or their businesses. Today, China, a rising power in Asia and the world, welcomes foreigners and foreign companies.

A Strong Central Government

▼ **KEY QUESTION** Who controls China's central government?

For centuries, China has had a strong national government. It controlled **provinces**, state-like governmental units, and local areas. Today, the national government makes decisions that the provinces and local governments must carry out. The Chinese national law-making body is called the **National People's Congress**, or **NPC**. Local and provincial People's Congresses elect members of this body. However, in reality, the Communist Party sets the country's policies by selecting candidates for elections and controlling the NPC.

2008 Summer Olympics
When China hosts the Summer Olympics in 2008, thousands of foreigners will have an opportunity to see how much more modern China has become.

Shanghai Harbor Shanghai's harbor is one of the largest ports in the world.

Government and the Communist Party As you can see in the diagram below, the NPC chooses the president and the State Council, or cabinet. The president chooses a prime minister to run the government. The NPC also selects judges for the courts. However, every government office is watched over by Communist Party officials. They make sure the government follows the Party's plans.

Political Trends You learned that the government keeps tight control of people's lives. Beginning in April 1989, **demonstrations** against corruption and for more democratic freedoms took place at Beijing's **Tiananmen** (tyahn•ahn•mehn) **Square**. In early June, the government brutally cracked down on the demonstrators. But the event reflected increasing citizen pressure for reforms in China.

Today, people are a little freer to protest against government policies. But the government still limits many basic rights. Demonstrations are often broken up by force. Protestors are beaten or jailed if they continue to speak out against the government.

▲ **FIND MAIN IDEAS** Tell who controls China's central government.

◄ COMPARING ► Chinese and U.S. Governments

CHINESE GOVERNMENT

Chinese citizens elect members of their local People's Congress. After that election they have no more input into government.

LOCAL PEOPLE'S CONGRESSES

▼ select ▼

NATIONAL PEOPLE'S CONGRESS

▼ select ▼ select ▼ select ▼

PRESIDENT   JUDICIARY

MILITARY COMMISSION   STATE COUNCIL

U.S. GOVERNMENT

U.S. citizens elect representatives and the President for the national government.

CITIZENS

◄ elect ►

CONGRESS   PRESIDENT

approve ◄   ► appoint

SUPREME COURT

CRITICAL THINKING

1. **Compare and Contrast** How is the selection of a president in China different from the selection of a president in the United States?
2. **Evaluate** How does division of power in the U.S. government differ from China's?

Economic Reforms

▼ **KEY QUESTION** How did economic reforms bring Western influences to China?

Under Mao, China had a **command economy**. That means the central government owned all the land, materials, and factories. It decided what goods would be produced. However, in 1978, leader Deng Xiaoping (duhng show•pihng) began to allow elements of **free enterprise**. In this type of economy, people can own a business and sell their products for a profit. The government invited foreign companies to invest in big projects and build factories in China.

International Trade The **reforms**, or improvements, described above dramatically changed China's economy. Today, China makes more low-cost goods than any other country and is a big player in international trade. Most of China's trade is with the United States, Taiwan, and Japan. As you can see in the graph below, in 15 years China's exports and imports skyrocketed.

Industries of China

Imports and Exports *1989–2004*

Sources: *China Statistical Yearbook 2004* and *Globalis*

PACIFIC OCEAN

Chemicals
Electronics
Machinery
Steel
Textiles
Vehicles

CONNECT Geography & Economics

1. **Location** Which two industries are found in every city shown on the map?

2. **Evaluate** How much did exports increase between 1989 and 2004?

More Economic Opportunities The Chinese government still owns part of most large Chinese firms, but now there are also many privately owned Chinese companies. In a move to attract foreign businesses, Chinese cities give companies tax breaks. They have also built airports, hotels, malls, and public transportation. Many foreign companies build factories in China. Some sell their products in China, and others buy products made by Chinese companies. As a result, many new jobs have been created.

Now the government is starting to develop western China. It is building roads and railways to the area and drilling there for oil and natural gas. Foreign companies are opening offices, factories, and stores in western Chinese cities.

Western Influences Economic changes have brought more Chinese people into contact with Europeans and Americans. Some of these people are students, scientists, and business people who travel to the West. Others work with Westerners in China. As a result, these groups have become more comfortable with Western ideas.

American and European chains opened stores in China—some in large, new malls like the one shown below. The Chinese now eat at many well-known Western fast-food restaurants. Water parks, miniature golf, and ski resorts are now all part of Chinese life.

Western companies also influence the treatment of Chinese workers. Many demand safe, clean, and comfortable factories for workers and limit the number of hours people can work.

▲ **ANALYZE EFFECTS** Detail the Western influences that economic reforms brought to China.

CONNECT ➤ Economics & Culture

Chinese Malls Shopping in malls is a new experience for most Chinese. In recent years, the Chinese have constructed some of the world's largest malls. In fact, China is projected to have 7 of the 10 largest malls in the world by 2010.

The South China Mall, currently the world's largest, is about three times the size of the Mall of America in the United States. Luchu Commercial City, the mall shown here, is located in Gangzhou.

CRITICAL THINKING
Make Inferences How do Chinese malls reflect Western influences?

Current Issues and Trends

▼ **KEY QUESTION** What challenges does China face in the 21st century?

With a population of over a billion, China needs to make sure its economy continues to grow. That growth is needed to supply enough jobs for its workers. The transportation and communication systems need to be expanded, and the country also needs to generate more electricity. As you learned in Section 1, the Three Gorges Dam will help produce more electricity. China has plans for 46 additional dams. However, this expansion does not come without problems. Huge projects like the dams or the creation of immense farms in western China often have negative effects on the environment.

Environment China faces serious air and water pollution problems. The country has 16 of the 20 most polluted cities in the world. China ranks behind only the United States in the creation of greenhouse gases. Because most industries use coal for fuel, China also creates large amounts of sulphur dioxide, a gas that contributes to acid rain. Agricultural projects in the northwestern regions of China have turned some farms into dust bowls. Each year, dust blowing out of China sweeps into Korea, Japan, and the United States.

Many rivers and lakes are polluted with wastes from manufacturing processes and raw sewage. Overall, about 700 million people only have contaminated water to use for drinking, cooking, and bathing. The Chinese government has begun to actively enforce environmental protection laws.

Air Pollution Getting to work in Chinese cities often requires masks to filter out harmful pollution. Lung-related diseases are on the rise in polluted cities. **Why has pollution increased so much in Chinese cities?**

Expanding Freedoms In part, the Chinese government began to work on environmental issues as a result of pressure from groups within the country. Changes in China's government have made some environmental protests possible.

Though Chinese society is changing, concerns about basic personal freedoms remain. For example, many workers are forced to work long hours in unhealthy conditions. Some religious groups are not allowed to worship as they wish. As a result, newly formed civic organizations are looking for ways to gain democratic freedoms for the Chinese people.

Chinese Space Program Two years after its first manned space flight, China put two more astronauts in space. They spent five days performing experiments and testing equipment. **What does having a space program tell you about the nation?**

Space Program As China develops, it has tried to show the world that it is a modern nation. Its space program, which China began in the 1950s, is one of those efforts. By 1970, it had sent a satellite into orbit. China's spacecraft are launched and returned to China's space center located in Inner Mongolia.

Only three nations in the world—China, the United States, and Russia—have a manned space program. In 2003, the spacecraft Shenzhou V (shen•joh five) carried a Chinese taikonaut, or astronaut, into space. The name of the spacecraft means "Divine Vessel." In 2005, millions of Chinese watched on television as two men were sent into space in Shenzhou VI. China's space program has a goal of reaching the moon with an unmanned probe by the year 2010. Eventually, China will launch a space station. The Chinese government hopes their space program will build Chinese pride and show the rest of the world how far China has advanced in science and technology.

▲ **CATEGORIZE** Discuss the challenges that China faces in the future.

Section ④ Assessment

ONLINE QUIZ
For test practice, go to
Interactive Review
@ ClassZone.com

TERMS & NAMES

1. Explain the importance of
- NPC
- Tiananmen Square
- command economy
- free enterprise

USE YOUR READING NOTES

2. Summarize Use your completed chart to answer the following question:

What economic challenges does China face?

GOVERNMENT	ECONOMY	ISSUES AND TRENDS

KEY IDEAS

3. What role does the Chinese Communist Party play in the government of China?

4. How has China's economy changed since the death of Mao?

5. Why are some Chinese concerned about basic personal freedoms?

CRITICAL THINKING

6. Synthesize In what way is the Communist Party more powerful than the Chinese government?

7. Draw Conclusions How might the presence of Western companies in China change working conditions?

8. CONNECT to Today How could environmental problems hold back the growth of China's economy?

9. MATHEMATICS Create a Graph Review the chart on exports and imports. Create a line graph with one line showing China's exports and one line showing its imports.

Interactive ⟵Review

Click here to complete these and other activities online @ ClassZone.com

CHAPTER SUMMARY

Key Idea 1
China has varied landforms, ranging from high mountains to river valleys. It has diverse climates, plants, and animals.

Key Idea 2
Throughout history, China's rulers have struggled with the problem of feeding so many people.

Key Idea 3
Some aspects of traditional life survive in China, while new ways of life have been introduced.

Key Idea 4
Small changes in the Chinese government and big changes in the Chinese economy are taking place.

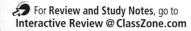
For **Review and Study Notes**, go to **Interactive Review @ ClassZone.com**

NAME GAME

Use the Terms & Names list to complete each sentence on paper or online.

1. I am also known as the Yellow River or "China's Sorrow." _____ **Huang He** 🖑 _____

2. I am China's longest river and the Three Gorges Dam was built to control my floods. _____

3. I am the highest mountain range in the world and divide China from India. _____

4. I am the emperor who united China. _____

5. I am the second-largest sand desert in the world. _____

6. I am a high desert that divides Mongolia and China. _____

7. I will provide hydroelectric power to parts of China. _____

8. I am the area where China's earliest civilization began. _____

9. I am the routes that brought traders and Buddhism to China. _____

10. I am the location of an important political demonstration for democratic rights. _____

Buddhism
Chang Jiang
Confucianism
Gobi Desert
Great Wall
Himalayas
Huang He
Mao Zedong
Middle Kingdom
North China Plain
Shi Huangdi
Silk Roads
Taklimakan Desert
Three Gorges Dam
Tiananmen Square

Activities

GeoGame

Use this online map to show what you know about China's location, geographic features, and important places. Drag and drop each place name to its location on the map.

Geo GAME

Himalayas

North China Plain

South Korea

Beijing

Shanghai

To play the complete game, go to **Interactive Review @ ClassZone.com**

Physical Geography of China

Himalayas 🖑

13,100 ft. (4,000 m)
6,600 ft. (2,000 m)
3,280 ft. (1,000 m)
650 ft. (200 m)
0 ft. Below sea level

Elevation

▲ Mountain peak

Crossword Puzzle

Complete an online crossword puzzle to test your knowledge of China's road to the present.

ACROSS
1. the first emperor to rule China

VOCABULARY

Explain the significance of each of the following.

1. Three Gorges Dam
2. Taklimakan Desert
3. Chang Jiang
4. Shi Huangdi
5. Confucianism
6. Mao Zedong
7. Daoism
8. Silk Roads
9. Buddhism
10. National People's Congress

Explain how the terms and names in each group are related.

11. Confucianism, Daoism, and Buddhism
12. Shi Huangdi and Mao Zedong

KEY IDEAS

1 Land of Three Rivers

13. How does China depend on its rivers?
14. What crops are grown in eastern China?
15. What natural disasters are most common in China?

2 Middle Kingdom to Communist Power

16. What was the Mandate of Heaven?
17. How did Confucius' teaching help produce order?
18. What was Mao Zedong's goal for China, and how did he try to accomplish it?

3 Changing Chinese Culture

19. What is the role of family in Chinese life?
20. Which of China's three belief systems had the greatest influence on Chinese society and government? Why?
21. Where do the majority of Chinese live?

4 A Rising Power

22. What is the role of the NPC in China's government?
23. What has China done to improve its economy?
24. Why are the Chinese concerned about their environment?

CRITICAL THINKING

25. **Compare and Contrast** Create a chart to compare and contrast the landforms and water, climate, and population density of eastern China and western China.

EASTERN CHINA	WESTERN CHINA

26. **Analyze Causes and Effects** How did China change after Shi Huangdi unified it?
27. **Draw Conclusions** What parts of Chinese culture have changed little since dynastic times?
28. **Connect to Economics** How has the right to own private businesses changed the economy in China?
29. **Five Themes: Human-Environment Interaction** Explain which natural barriers helped to shape Chinese civilization.
30. **Connect Geography & Economics** How will the presence of oil and natural gas in western China influence its economy?

Answer the ESSENTIAL QUESTION

How is China's traditional way of life changing in response to global trends?

Written Response Write a two- or three-paragraph response to the Essential Question. Use the rubric below to guide your thinking.

Response Rubric
A strong response will:
- identify the characteristics of traditional life
- discuss the modern global trends affecting China
- explain ways in which the Chinese culture has adapted to the global trends

STANDARDS-BASED ASSESSMENT

✓ **Test Practice**
- Online Test Practice @ ClassZone.com
- Test-Taking Strategies and Practice
  at the front of this book

THEMATIC MAP

Use the map to answer questions 1 and 2 on your paper.

Energy and Mineral Resources of China

Legend:
- Coal
- Lead
- Copper
- Natural gas
- Hydroelectric power
- Oil
- Iron ore

Yellow Sea
East China Sea
South China Sea

0 500 1,000 miles
0 500 1,000 kilometers

1. Which source of energy is found throughout China?

A. coal
B. hydroelectric power
C. natural gas
D. oil

2. Where is most of China's hydroelectric power found?

A. in the far west
B. in the southeast
C. in central China
D. in the far north

LINE GRAPH

Examine the graph below. Use the information in the graph to write short answers for questions 3 and 4.

China's Iron and Steel Trade *1999–2003*

Sales (in billions of U.S. $)

25
20
15
10
5
0

1999 2000 2001 2002 2003

Year

Imports — Exports

Source: "China's New Heights," *Time Magazine,* June 27, 2005

3. What was the approximate value of China's exports in 2001?

4. Based on the graph, how would you describe China's iron and steel trade between 1999 and 2003?

GeoActivity

1. INTERDISCIPLINARY ACTIVITY–SCIENCE

With a small group, review the Chinese inventions discussed in Section 2. Choose one invention to research further and create a museum-style display. Be sure your display shows how the invention works, and explain how it changed life in China or elsewhere.

2. WRITING FOR SOCIAL STUDIES

Reread the part of Section 3 on Chen's day. Imagine that Chen is coming to visit your town or city. Write a tour schedule describing the places you would take Chen so that he would experience life the way you do.

3. MENTAL MAPPING

Create an outline map of China and label the following:

- Himalayas
- Huang He
- Chang Jiang
- Gobi Desert
- Taklimakan Desert
- East China Sea
- Yellow Sea
- Beijing

The Korean Peninsula

1
GEOGRAPHY

A Rugged Peninsula

2
HISTORY & CULTURE

Strong Traditions, Modern Innovations

3
GOVERNMENT & ECONOMICS

Contrasting Countries

 ESSENTIAL QUESTION

How can North Korea and South Korea overcome their differences and live in peace?

CONNECT ⟶ **Geography & History**

Use the map and the time line to answer the following questions.

1. Which countries are the Koreas' closest neighbors?
2. What major religion spread to the Korean Peninsula from China?

A.D. 300

Culture
◄ **300s** Buddhism is introduced from China.

Government
1392 The Choson Dynasty is established and rules until 1910.

History
660s The kingdom of Silla unifies the Korean Peninsula.
(Silla crown) ►

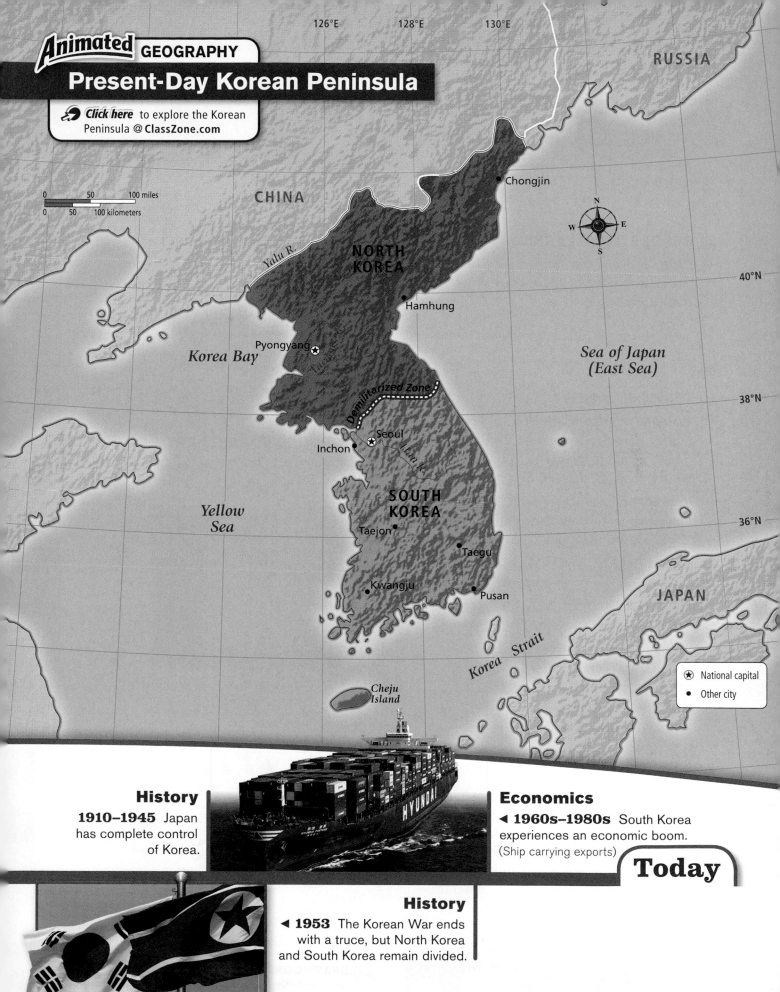

Animated GEOGRAPHY
Present-Day Korean Peninsula

Click here to explore the Korean Peninsula @ ClassZone.com

RUSSIA

CHINA

NORTH KOREA

• Chongjin

• Hamhung

Yalu R.

Pyongyang ⊛

Korea Bay

Demilitarized Zone

Sea of Japan (East Sea)

Inchon • ⊛ Seoul

SOUTH KOREA

Taejon •

• Taegu

Yellow Sea

Kwangju •

• Pusan

JAPAN

Korea Strait

Cheju Island

0   50   100 miles
0   50   100 kilometers

126°E   128°E   130°E

40°N

38°N

36°N

⊛ National capital
• Other city

History

1910–1945 Japan has complete control of Korea.

Economics

◄ **1960s–1980s** South Korea experiences an economic boom. (Ship carrying exports)

Today

History

◄ **1953** The Korean War ends with a truce, but North Korea and South Korea remain divided.

Reading for Understanding

▶ Key Ideas

BEFORE, YOU LEARNED

China is a vast country in East Asia with a variety of landforms, climates, and natural resources.

NOW YOU WILL LEARN

Korea lies on a peninsula, which provides a moderate climate and plentiful resources.

▶ Vocabulary

TERMS & NAMES

Korean Peninsula a body of land bordered by the Yellow Sea to the west, the East Sea (or Sea of Japan) to the east, the Korea Strait to the south, and China and Russia to the north

Yalu River the longest river on the Korean Peninsula; forms part of the border between China and North Korea

Mount Paektu (PAHK•too) the highest mountain (9,003 feet) on the Korean Peninsula

Cheju (CHEH•JOO) **Island** largest island off the southern coast of the Korean Peninsula

monsoon a seasonal wind that usually brings moist air during the summer and dry air during the winter

typhoon a tropical storm that starts in the western Pacific or Indian oceans

BACKGROUND VOCABULARY

peninsula a large mass of land surrounded on three sides by water

Visual Vocabulary satellite image of a typhoon

▶ Reading Strategy

Re-create the web diagram shown at right. As you read and respond to the **KEY QUESTIONS**, use the diagram to record main ideas about the physical geography of North Korea and South Korea. Add ovals or start a new diagram as needed.

 Skillbuilder Handbook, page R4

FIND MAIN IDEAS

Landforms — KOREA'S PHYSICAL GEOGRAPHY — Plants

Climate — Animals

Resources

GRAPHIC ORGANIZERS
Go to **Interactive Review** @ClassZone.com

A Rugged Peninsula

Connecting to Your World

Have you ever seen a photograph of a sunrise over a mountain range, such as the Rockies or Appalachians in the United States? These pictures often convey a sense of calm and peace. Korea is dominated by mountainous terrain. The peaceful sunrises over its mountains have inspired people to call Korea the "Land of the Morning Calm." The peninsula's rocky landscape has played a large part in shaping the history and culture of the Korean people.

An Isolated Land

▼ **KEY QUESTION** What are some of the geographic features of the Korean Peninsula?

Korea is a **peninsula**, which means that it is surrounded on three sides by water: the East Sea (or Sea of Japan) to the east, the Yellow Sea to the west, and the Korea Strait to the south. China and Russia border Korea to the north. The **Korean Peninsula** has both isolated and protected its people. In fact, ancient Korea was called the "hermit kingdom." Today, the Korean Peninsula contains two nations—North Korea and South Korea. The tradition of isolation continues in North Korea, which has little contact with other nations.

Cheju Waterfall
According to legend, heavenly creatures bathed under this fall, which is surrounded by lush vegetation.

Mount Daedunsan
This mountain in South Korea is famous for its rocky cliffs.

The Korean Peninsula The map on the opposite page shows the bodies of water and landforms on the Korean Peninsula. As you have already learned, the Yellow Sea Ⓐ is situated to the west of the peninsula. The Korea Strait lies between the peninsula's southern coast and the west coast of Japan. The eastern side of the Korean Peninsula borders the East Sea (also known as the Sea of Japan). The **Yalu River** Ⓑ—known as the Amnok River in Korean—is the longest river on the peninsula. The Yalu and the Tumen rivers form the border between China and North Korea.

The rugged terrain of the Korean Peninsula consists of several mountain ranges. The Hamgyong (HAHM•GYUHNG) range extends along the peninsula's northern border and contains **Mount Paektu** (PAHK•too) Ⓒ. At 9,003 feet, this peak is the highest on the peninsula. The Nangnim Mountains run from north to south through the center of North Korea. Farther south, the Taebaek (TAY•BACK) Mountains Ⓓ run north to south along the eastern coast. Branching off from this range are the Sobaek Mountains, which extend across the center of South Korea.

More than 3,000 islands lie off the coasts of the Korean Peninsula. Many of them are small and uninhabited. But the largest, **Cheju** (CHEH•JOO) **Island** Ⓔ, has a population of about 530,000. Cheju lies near the southern part of the peninsula and plays an active role in the culture and economy of South Korea.

Impact of Geography on Korea The isolation and protection provided by Korea's geography have allowed the Koreans to develop their own distinct culture. Of course, Chinese culture has had a strong influence. But Koreans have always adapted this culture to fit their own. Koreans even adapted the Chinese language to create their own, as you'll learn at left.

In general, Koreans have been content to remain in their land and follow their own way of life. However, maintaining a peaceful Korean state has not always been easy. Korea's aggressive neighbors, China, Japan, and Russia, have each attempted to control the peninsula. You will learn more about how these superpowers affected Korea's history in Section 2.

▲ **SUMMARIZE** Describe some of the geographic features of the Korean Peninsula.

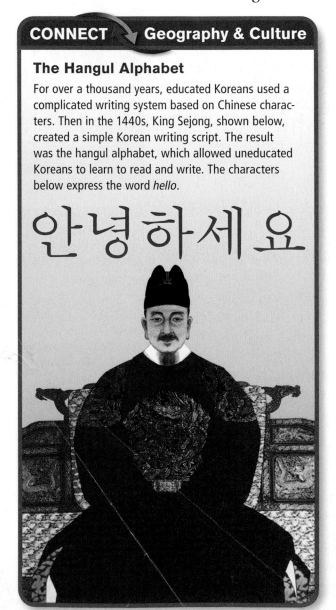

CONNECT > **Geography & Culture**

The Hangul Alphabet

For over a thousand years, educated Koreans used a complicated writing system based on Chinese characters. Then in the 1440s, King Sejong, shown below, created a simple Korean writing script. The result was the hangul alphabet, which allowed uneducated Koreans to learn to read and write. The characters below express the word *hello*.

안녕하세요

Physical Geography of the Korean Peninsula

Click here to see geographic features of the Korean Peninsula @ ClassZone.com

RUSSIA

CHINA

CHANGBAI SHAN

Tumen R.

Mt. Paektu
9,003 ft
(2,744 m)

HAMGYONG MTS.

NANGNIM MTS.

Yalu R.

NORTH KOREA

Korea Bay

Yalu R.

Yesong R.

Sea of Japan
(East Sea)

Demilitarized Zone

TAEBAEK MTS.

Han R.

A Yellow Sea

SOUTH KOREA

SOBAEK MTS.

D

N
W   E
S

B Yalu River, North Korea

D Taebaek Mountains, South Korea

0   50   100 miles
0   50   100 kilometers

Korea Strait

JAPAN

Cheju Island **E**

Elevation

13,100 ft.   (4,000 m)
6,600 ft.   (2,000 m)
1,600 ft.   (1,000 m)
650 ft.   (200 m)
0 ft.   (0 m)
Below sea level

▲ Mountain peak

CONNECT Geography & Culture
READING A PHYSICAL MAP

As you study the map,
- note the Demilitarized Zone, which marks the boundary between North and South Korea
- think about the impact on Korea of its neighbors
- note locations of high and low elevation in Korea

1. **Region** In what ways is the physical geography of North and South Korea similar?

2. **Movement** What impact might this physical geography have on both nations?

124°E   126°E   128°E   130°E   132°E

Climate, Plants, and Animals

▼ **KEY QUESTION** What types of climates, plants, and animals are found on the Korean Peninsula?

The mountains of the Korean Peninsula and the seas that surround it both have a major impact on Korea's climate. This climate, in turn, has played a large role in determining the type of plant and animal life on the peninsula.

A Moderate Climate In general, the climate on the peninsula is moderate. Summer weather differs little throughout Korea, with average July temperatures ranging from 70°F to 80°F. But in the winter, the difference in temperature between North Korea and South Korea can be extreme. For example, the average January temperature in southeast Korea is around 35°F. During the same month, the average temperature in the northern mountains is only about –8°F.

Most of the Korean Peninsula receives around 40 inches of precipitation each year. The majority of this rain arrives during the summer monsoons. A **monsoon** is a seasonal wind that usually brings moist air during the summer and dry air during the winter. At times, summer monsoons help produce **typhoons**, fierce tropical storms that start in the western Pacific or Indian oceans. The Korean Peninsula is usually hit with one or two typhoons a year. Typhoons are similar to hurricanes, which you have probably heard about. Hurricanes are tropical storms that start in the northern Atlantic Ocean, the Caribbean Sea, or the eastern Pacific Ocean.

↖ **COMPARING** ↘ **Climates**

North Korea Winter in North Korea can be long, cold, and dry.
1. How do you think the winters affect the North Korean people?

South Korea Spring temperatures average about 50°F in South Korea. **2. What impact does this climate appear to have on the country's vegetation?**

Plant and Animal Life The Korean Peninsula contains much diverse plant life, but the region's natural vegetation is largely forest. Today, forests cover about two-thirds of the land area of South Korea. Fir, spruce, pine, and elm trees grow in the northern and central parts of the country. Bamboo and evergreens grow along the southern coast.

The Korean Peninsula also has a wide variety of wildlife. Deer, mountain antelope, bears, and leopards make their home in mountainous areas and in the forests. Many types of birdlife also live on the peninsula, including herons, cranes, and wild pigeons. In addition, the peninsula is a popular stopover for ducks, wild geese, and swans migrating to Japan, Southeast Asia, and Australia.

As in much of the world, human activities have threatened the survival of wildlife on the Korean Peninsula, particularly in forested areas. People have cut down many of the trees for construction, heating, and cooking. This deforestation destroyed many of the animals' homes. Since the 1970s, however, strong efforts have been made to reforest the land. As a result, some animals that had been considered endangered are making a comeback. The black bear, for example, has returned to some remote mountain areas.

Some of the animals have been rescued by chance. In Section 2, you will learn about a wildlife preserve that accidentally developed along the border between North Korea and South Korea. This accidental preserve has become the Korean Peninsula's most important wildlife refuge.

Red-Crowned Crane In Korean culture, the red-crowned crane symbolizes happiness, good luck, and long life, and often appears in traditional paintings. **Why might a bird represent such positive attributes?**

▲ **CATEGORIZE** Tell what types of climates, plants, and animals are found on the Korean Peninsula.

Natural Resources

▼ **KEY QUESTION** How are the natural resources of North Korea and South Korea similar and different?

The rainfall and warm temperatures during the summer make Korea's climate ideal for growing rice. But the rocky terrain of the peninsula makes farmland scarce. Koreans have been able to squeeze tiny fields along hillsides by using terraced farming. Even so, the overall lack of good farmland has led Koreans to rely on other resources, including the abundant fish along the coastlines and mineral deposits.

Farmland and Agriculture The largest portion of farmland on the Korean Peninsula is found on the western and southern coastal plains. Because of overuse, however, the soil is not very fertile. To remedy this, farmers have extensively used irrigation and fertilizers.

Since most of the best farmland is located in South Korea, this nation has a much higher crop yield than North Korea. Rice is the most important crop in both North Korea and South Korea. These nations also grow wheat, potatoes, and barley. South Koreans, in addition, grow Chinese cabbage, melons, onions, and soybeans. Cheju Island is famous for its mandarin oranges. In fact, Cheju oranges constitute South Korea's major cash fruit crop.

Fishing The lack of usable land has affected Korea's fishing industry. Since the Korean Peninsula does not have enough land to raise much livestock, Koreans rely on fish as an important source of protein. As a result, the fishing industries of the Koreas have risen to keep up with the nutritional needs of the rising population. Both North Korea and South Korea have taken full advantage of their extensive coastal areas. In fact, South Korea has become one of the major deep-sea fishing countries of the world.

CONNECT ▶ Geography & Culture

Women Divers of Cheju Island

For more than 1,500 years, the women divers, or *haenyo*, of Cheju Island have caught shellfish, squid, and sea urchins, such as the one shown here. This seafood has provided the main source of nourishment for themselves and their families. Their husbands often stay at home and watch the children.

The women divers work until they are well into their 60s—and beyond. They can plunge down to depths of 60 feet and stay underwater for three to five minutes. And all of this is done without the aid of any breathing equipment. This tradition of diving has been handed down from mother to daughter for generations.

CRITICAL THINKING

Make Inferences What inferences can you make about the women divers?

Mineral Resources The vast majority of mineral resources on the Korean Peninsula are in the north. In fact, North Korea has the largest magnesite deposit in the world. Other minerals include iron ore, coal, gold, lead, and zinc. North Koreans have taken advantage of these rich deposits by mining them extensively. Mineral resources in South Korea are few. However, the nation does have some large graphite and tungsten deposits.

Most of North Korea's electric power is produced by coal-burning plants. In contrast, the majority of electricity in South Korea is provided by petroleum-burning plants. However, this nation has to import all of its oil. As a result, the oil crisis of the 1970s hit South Korea hard. To reduce South Korea's dependency on oil, the government had built 20 nuclear power plants by 2006. By 2015, the government hopes to have about 30 such plants.

 COMPARE AND CONTRAST Explain how the natural resources of North Korea and South Korea are similar and different.

Minerals in the Koreas

Minerals	Uses
Graphite	• pencils • applications that involve high heat
Magnesite	• flooring materials • fertilizers • bricks
Tungsten	• filament in light bulbs • heating element in electric furnaces
Zinc	• coating on iron and steel to protect from corrosion • batteries

---

Section 1 Assessment

ONLINE QUIZ
For test practice, go to **Interactive Review** @ ClassZone.com

TERMS & NAMES

1. Explain the importance of
- Korean Peninsula
- Yalu River
- Mount Paektu
- Cheju Island

USE YOUR READING NOTES

2. Find Main Ideas Use your completed web to answer the following question:

What impact have people had on the vegetation on the Korean Peninsula?

KEY IDEAS

3. What are some of the major mountain ranges of the Korean Peninsula?

4. Why did deforestation occur on the Korean Peninsula?

5. What have Korean farmers done to try to make their soil more fertile?

CRITICAL THINKING

6. Draw Conclusions How has the geography of the Korean Peninsula influenced Korea's culture?

7. Compare and Contrast How do the climates of North Korea and South Korea differ?

8. CONNECT to Today How has South Korea recently reduced its dependency on oil?

9. WRITING Compose an Essay Research and write an essay about the deep-sea fishing industry in South Korea. Include information about the types of ships used, the methods used to catch various fish, and the effect of this fishing on the environment.

Reading for Understanding

2

▶ Key Ideas

BEFORE, YOU LEARNED

Korea is surrounded by powerful neighbors, including China, Russia, and Japan.

NOW YOU WILL LEARN

The Korean Peninsula has been invaded by China, Russia, and Japan but has still maintained its cultural identity.

▶ Vocabulary

TERMS & NAMES

Three Kingdoms the three kingdoms that had formed on the Korean Peninsula by A.D. 300

Korean War (1950–1953) a conflict between North Korea and the Soviet Union on one side and South Korea, the United States, and the UN on the other

demilitarized zone a buffer zone between North Korea and South Korea

shamanism (SHAH•muh•NIHZ•uhm) a belief system in which a person called a shaman is believed to be able to communicate with spirits and heal the sick

celadon (SEHL•uh•DAHN) Korean ceramic pottery with a thin blue or green glaze

hanbok a traditional Korean costume

kimchi (KIHM•chee) a Korean dish made of pickled vegetables

REVIEW

Confucianism a belief system based on the teachings of Confucius

Buddhism a religion that began in India and is based on the teachings of Siddhartha Gautama

Visual Vocabulary *hanbok*

▶ Reading Strategy

Re-create the chart shown at right. As you read and respond to the **KEY QUESTIONS**, use the chart to summarize what you have learned about the history and culture of the Korean Peninsula.

📖 **Skillbuilder Handbook, page R5**

SUMMARIZE

KOREAN HISTORY	KOREAN CULTURE
The first state. . .	

 GRAPHIC ORGANIZERS
Go to **Interactive Review** @ClassZone.com

Strong Traditions, Modern Innovations

Connecting to Your World

You have probably learned that the United States was torn apart by a civil war between the North and the South during the 1860s. After four years of fighting, the two sides reunited to form a stronger union. In the 1950s, Korea became a battleground for a war waged by the United States and the Soviet Union. The war pitted North Korea against South Korea. But this conflict had a different ending: North and South Korea remained divided. As you will see, however, the Korean Peninsula has been united for much of its history.

Korean History

▼ **KEY QUESTION** What are the major events in Korean history?

The first state on the Korean Peninsula was established around 2000 B.C. It took the name *Choson*. Around 108 B.C., China conquered the northern part of the peninsula. However, Korean tribes gradually won back the territory. In the northern area of the Korean Peninsula, several tribes united during the A.D. 100s and formed the state of Koguryo (KOH•gur•YOO). By about 300, two other states had been created on the peninsula. Historians refer to these states as the **Three Kingdoms**.

Koguryo Painting
A Korean noble-woman is waited on by her attendants in this fourth-century tomb mural painting.

Three Kingdoms Period The Three Kingdoms were Koguryo in the northeast, Paekche (PAHK•CHAY) in the southwest, and Silla (SIHL•uh) in the southeast. The kingdoms had much in common. For example, they all had a strong military system, which they used to help them expand their territory. In addition, each had powerful kings and aristocracies made up of tribal chiefs.

During the 660s, Silla conquered Paekche and Koguryo and took control of the entire peninsula. Unified Silla was broken apart by rebels in the 800s. But the state reunited around 935 and called itself *Koryo*. *Korea* comes from *Koryo*. In 1392, a general named Yi Song-gye became the ruler of Korea. He gave the country back its ancient name of Choson. The Choson Dynasty lasted until 1910, more than 500 years.

Japanese Conquest Starting in the 1600s, the rulers of the Choson Dynasty closed Korea to all foreigners. In 1876, however, Japan forced Korea to open a few ports to trade. Soon, the United States, Russia, and several European nations signed trade agreements with Korea. In 1904 and 1905, Japan fought Russia for control over Manchuria. Japan won the Russo-Japanese War and then attacked Korea. By 1910, the Japanese had gained complete control of Korea.

ANALYZING Primary Sources

The Proclamation of Korean Independence was published on March 1, 1919, during the Japanese occupation of Korea. It was inspired by the Fourteen Points of U.S. President Woodrow Wilson, which supported returning self-government to some occupied nations following World War I. The painting shown here depicts Japanese soldiers marching into Seoul.

> We have no desire to accuse Japan of breaking many solemn treaties since 1836, nor to single out specially the teachers in the schools or government officials who treat the heritage of our ancestors as a colony of their own, . . . finding delight only in beating us down and bringing us under their heel. . . . Our urgent need today is the settling up of this house of ours and not a discussion of who has broken it down, or what has caused its ruin.
>
> Source: Proclamation of Korean Independence

DOCUMENT–BASED QUESTION

What did the writers of this document probably hope to achieve?

During the Japanese occupation, Japan turned Korea into a colony to benefit its own interests. The Japanese government managed Korean farms and businesses and reduced the Koreans to low-paid workers in their own country. As the Japanese prepared for war during the 1930s, they tried to stamp out Korean culture. They even ordered Koreans to speak only Japanese and to take Japanese names. As World War II raged, Koreans were forced to help Japan's war effort and to endure many hardships. Japan's harsh rule is still a source of bitterness for many Koreans.

The Korean War Korea remained under Japanese rule until Japan was defeated in World War II in 1945. The Koreans wanted independence. But U.S. forces occupied southern Korea, and Soviet troops occupied the northern half. Soon, North Korea established a Communist government, and South Korea set up a republic.

In 1950, North Korean troops invaded South Korea, starting the **Korean War**. The Soviet Union had supplied North Korea with tanks, airplanes, and money in an attempt to take over the peninsula. South Korea fought back with Allied forces consisting of U.S. and UN troops. In time, China entered the war on the side of North Korea. You can follow the course of the war by studying the maps on this page. A cease-fire was declared in 1953, but no peace treaty was ever agreed on. In time, a 2.5-mile-wide buffer zone, called the **demilitarized zone** (DMZ), was set up. It separates North Korea and South Korea to this day.

The Allies lost about 500,000 troops, and the Communists lost around 1,500,000 troops. Civilian deaths were also very high. A total of about two million civilians died in North Korea and South Korea.

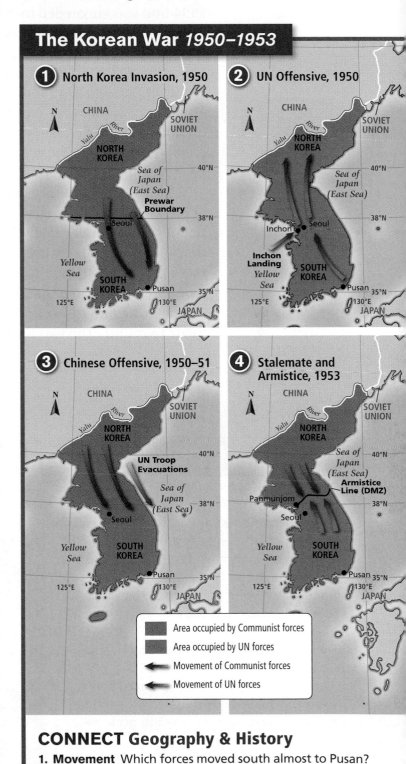

The Korean War 1950–1953

1 North Korea Invasion, 1950

2 UN Offensive, 1950

3 Chinese Offensive, 1950–51

4 Stalemate and Armistice, 1953

Area occupied by Communist forces
Area occupied by UN forces
Movement of Communist forces
Movement of UN forces

CONNECT Geography & History

1. **Movement** Which forces moved south almost to Pusan?
2. **Region** Compare maps 1 and 4. Which side, if any, gained more territory?

Two Koreas In 1948, Kim Il Sung became North Korea's leader and continued to rule after the Korean War. Kim strove to make North Korea as self-sufficient as possible by emphasizing the development of heavy industry. He established a strict dictatorship. Kim died in 1994 and was succeeded by his son, Kim Jong Il. In the 2000s, North Korea started a nuclear weapons program, despite opposition from the United States, South Korea, and many other countries. North Korea has also been charged with numerous human rights violations.

Since the 1960s, South Korea has enjoyed an economic boom. The boom was due, in part, to financial aid from the United States and other countries. Also, South Korea began to produce goods that could be exported. The country used the resulting income to increase production of these goods.

However, democracy in South Korea has faced a rockier road. Several rulers violated the 1948 constitution and used the military to retain power. Finally, in 1987, South Korea adopted a new constitution that allowed for almost unlimited political freedom and granted greater individual rights. The constitution declared South Korea a democratic republic. It also stated that the country would seek reunification based on the principles of freedom and democracy. Some efforts have been made to reunify the two Koreas, as you will learn in Section 3.

▲ **SEQUENCE EVENTS** Discuss the major events in Korean history.

CONNECT History & Geography

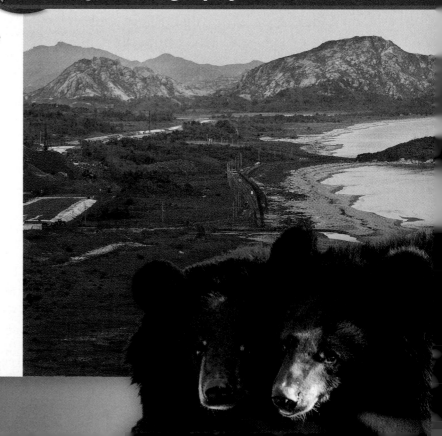

Wildlife Preserve in the DMZ Since the end of the Korean War, the DMZ has been a no-man's-land. As a result, plants, birds, and animals have flourished in this region. In fact, the DMZ has developed into an important wildlife refuge. Extending about 150 miles from coast to coast, the zone has become home to many endangered animals, including the Asiatic black bears shown here. Some people have proposed turning the DMZ into a peace park. The park would honor those who died during the war and save the wildlife preserve.

CRITICAL THINKING

Make Predictions What might happen to the preserve if the two Koreas reunite?

To learn more about Yumi and her world, go to the **Activity Center @ ClassZone.com**

In Korean, Yumi's name looks like this:

유미

Hi! My name is Yumi. I am 14 years old and live in Seoul, the capital and largest city in South Korea. Seoul is a combination of old and new. For example, I live in a modern apartment complex, but nearby is Kyongbok, a medieval palace. My daily life also combines the old and new. Let me show you by describing a typical day.

6 A.M. Today, I am preparing for exams, so I get up early to study. Then I eat a traditional breakfast of rice, soup, kimchi, and fish. After breakfast, I ride my bike to school.

8 A.M.–3 P.M. At school, I study about new discoveries in science class and about my country's past in history class. Other courses include math and English. I eat a light lunch, which is provided by the school.

5 P.M. Sometimes, I spend a couple of hours after school with my friends. We go to shopping malls and play video games. But usually I have after-school classes in violin and English conversation.

7 P.M. I eat a traditional dinner with my family that includes rice and many *banchan* (side dishes). Then I study some more. When I can, I make time to watch my favorite TV show.

CONNECT to Your Life

Journal Entry Make a list of the recreational activities that you do on a regular basis. Then compare your activities with Yumi's. How are they different? How are they the same?

Haein-sa Temple This 8th-century temple houses the Tripitaka Koreana: woodblocks containing the most complete collection of Buddhist texts. **What do the woodblocks suggest about Buddhism in Korean culture?**

Preserving Korean Culture

▼ **KEY QUESTION** How have Koreans tried to preserve their distinct culture?

Over the past century, Korea has faced much adversity. But the Korean people are united by a common ethnicity and language—and the determination to preserve their culture.

Religious Beliefs The original belief system practiced on the Korean Peninsula is **shamanism**. A shaman is a person who is believed to be able to communicate with the spirit world and heal the sick. Another belief system, **Confucianism**, entered the peninsula around 100 B.C. from China. Confucianism stresses social order and good government and influences Korean society today.

Buddhism, an Indian religion that seeks to put an end to suffering, arrived during the A.D. 300s. It was the dominant religion in Korea for several hundred years. Today, many South Koreans still practice Buddhism. Christianity was introduced around 1784 and is South Korea's fastest-growing religion.

Many Koreans practice aspects of several religions. Because of this, South Korea has strong religious tolerance. North Korea, on the other hand, discourages any religious practice.

Korean Arts Buddhist influence can be seen in the many temples found throughout South Korea, such as the one above. These temples often contain stone towers called pagodas. They also include stone sculptures of Buddha.

Korean pottery has been strongly influenced by the Chinese. During the Koryo Dynasty, Korean artisans used Chinese techniques to develop a unique type of ceramic pottery called **celadon**. This pottery has a thin glaze that usually ranges in color from blue to green.

Celadon The ceramic pottery originated in China, but Korean potters made it their own. Even Chinese visitors remarked on the beauty of Korean celadon. ▶

Daily Life Because North Korea is a closed country, not much is known about the daily life of its people. Much of the following, therefore, describes life in South Korea.

Most Koreans wear modern-style clothing. However, on special occasions, South Koreans often wear traditional clothes, such as the **hanbok**. The woman's *hanbok* is made up of a short jacket and a long skirt. For men, a *hanbok* consists of roomy pants tied at the ankles and a jacket. The basic food for most Koreans is rice. Meals also often include soup and **kimchi**, a side dish made of pickled vegetables. Sports, including the martial art of *tae kwon do*, are popular pastimes.

Life in rural villages centers on farming, especially rice-growing. Many people live in houses with heated floors called *ondols*. These floors are traditionally heated by channels carrying hot air underneath them. Because the floors are so warm, Koreans often prefer to sit and even sleep on them. Many rural houses have modern conveniences, including satellite dishes. In cities, millions of people live in high-rise apartment buildings.

 FIND MAIN IDEAS Discuss how Koreans have tried to preserve their distinct culture.

Fun Facts!

KIMCHI

Kimchi is eaten at almost every meal. There are more than 200 varieties of the pickled vegetable side dish. Traditionally, Koreans get together in the fall to prepare huge batches of kimchi. They then store the kimchi in large earthenware jars, which they bury in their yards. Kimchi is so popular that it is celebrated in its own museum.

Section 2 Assessment

ONLINE QUIZ
For test practice, go to **Interactive Review** @ ClassZone.com

TERMS & NAMES

1. Explain the importance of
- Three Kingdoms
- demilitarized zone
- celadon
- *hanbok*

USE YOUR READING NOTES

2. Summarize Use your completed chart to answer the following question:

Why did the Koreans deeply resent the Japanese occupation?

KOREAN HISTORY	KOREAN CULTURE
The first state. . .	

KEY IDEAS

3. What are some of the traits that the Three Kingdoms had in common?

4. How did Japan gain control over Korea?

5. What does life in rural villages center on?

CRITICAL THINKING

6. Make Inferences Do you think the Korean people benefited from the Korean War? Explain why or why not.

7. Sequence Events In what chronological order did major belief systems enter the Korean Peninsula?

8. (CONNECT to Today) Why do you think North Korea has recently started a nuclear weapons program?

9. (TECHNOLOGY) **Create a Slide Show** Using the Internet and your library, research the various artworks found in Buddhist temples, such as pagodas and sculptures. Then do a slide presentation that shows these works, and provide a brief history about each slide.

Reading for Understanding

▶ Key Ideas

BEFORE, YOU LEARNED

After the Korean War, the peninsula was divided into two countries: North Korea and South Korea.

NOW YOU WILL LEARN

North Korea and South Korea have very different government systems and economic structures.

▶ Vocabulary

TERMS & NAMES

totalitarian a type of government that controls every aspect of public and private life

Korean Workers' Party (KWP) a Communist political group that controls the government of North Korea

dictator a ruler who exercises complete political power

Kim Jong Il the leader of North Korea

chaebol (JEH•buhl) a family-owned conglomerate made up of related businesses

BACKGROUND VOCABULARY

conglomerate an organization made up of several companies in different businesses

Visual Vocabulary Samsung is a major *chaebol* in South Korea.

▶ Reading Strategy

Re-create the Venn diagram shown at right. As you read and respond to the **KEY QUESTIONS**, use the diagram to compare and contrast North Korea and South Korea.

 Skillbuilder Handbook, page R9

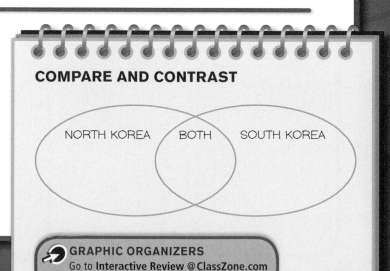

COMPARE AND CONTRAST

NORTH KOREA   BOTH   SOUTH KOREA

GRAPHIC ORGANIZERS
Go to **Interactive Review** @ ClassZone.com

Contrasting Countries

Connecting to Your World

Have you ever visited relatives in a nearby state? In the United States, making such a trip is pretty easy. However, similar visits have not been allowed between North Korea and South Korea for decades. When Korea split into two nations, many families were separated. As a result, Koreans could not visit relatives across the border at all. Recently, some movement between the two nations has been permitted, but only on a limited basis.

Satellite Image This nighttime image contrasts well-lit South Korea with the darkness of North Korea.

North Korea

▼ **KEY QUESTION** How are the government and economy of North Korea structured?

As you have learned, a Communist government was set up in North Korea that isolated its people from the rest of the world. As a result, most North Koreans have no contact with ideas that contradict their government. Also, North Korea became economically isolated, especially from the West. Instead of encouraging interaction with non-Communist economies, the government promotes a policy of *juche* (joo•cheh), or self-reliance.

North Korea May Day People hold colored placards to form a picture of Communist strength and victory in a show of national unity.

1945

Kim Jong Il born 1941

After Kim Il Sung (above left) died in 1994, his son, Kim Jong Il (above right), became the dictator of North Korea. Soon a cult developed within North Korea around the new leader. Official government accounts praised him as a godlike hero and created legends about his birth. To the outside world, however, Kim Jong Il is a secretive and dangerous figure who starves his people into submission. Above all, many regard Kim Jong Il's determination to develop nuclear weapons as a real threat to the United States and its allies.

➜ ONLINE BIOGRAPHY
For more on the life of Kim Jong Il, go to the
Research & Writing Center @ClassZone.com

Government North Korea is ruled by a highly centralized, totalitarian form of government. A **totalitarian** government controls every aspect of public and private life. The country does have a constitution, which, on paper, gives political power to the people. However, in reality, the people have almost no freedom. All of the power lies with a Communist group called the **Korean Workers' Party (KWP)**. This party controls elections and chooses who may run for office. The KWP itself is controlled by the chairman of the National Defense Commission. In effect, the chairman is a **dictator**, or a ruler who has complete political power. Since 1994, **Kim Jong Il** has been the chairman of the National Defense Commission and the dictator of North Korea. The country does have a law-making body called the Supreme People's Assembly. This legislature, though, has little power.

Since the early 2000s, the North Korean government has been dealing with an international dispute over its program to develop nuclear weapons. Many nations object to the program, but North Korea has refused to halt it. North Korea claims that it needs nuclear weapons to defend its people against possible aggressors.

Economy Like the government, all means of production in North Korea are controlled by the state. In addition, the economy stresses the good of the state over the welfare of the people. For example, the government spends huge amounts on military development. As a result, it has little money to invest in producing goods for its people.

The North Korean economy is also very isolated. True to its policy of self-reliance, the country has generally discouraged foreign investment. However, North Korea did accept economic aid from the former Soviet Union and from China.

North Korea's economic plans have not been a success. Since the late 1990s, the North Korean people have had one of the lowest standards of living in Asia. But hopeful signs have begun to emerge. During the last few years, South Korean businesses have started to move into North Korea. The money that these businesses make may help the North Korean people. The economic partnership may also help improve relations between the two countries.

Industries and Agriculture Throughout its history, North Korea has promoted heavy industry, especially for military production. Because of this, North Korea produces much military equipment, general machinery, steel, cement, textiles, and chemicals. The nation also heavily mines its many mineral deposits.

However, in the 1990s, the development of heavy industry in North Korea began to rapidly decline. One reason for this lies with the state's emphasis on military spending. North Korea spends so much on developing weapons that it does not have enough money to invest in its industrial equipment and infrastructure.

North Korea produces a variety of crops, including rice, barley, corn, wheat, and potatoes. Recently, though, crop production has fallen on hard times. During the mid-1990s, floods and droughts destroyed crops, causing thousands of people to starve to death. North Korean agriculture has never recovered. The lack of good farmland, the failures of state-run farms, and shortages of fertilizer and fuel have all added to the country's agricultural difficulties. In the early 2000s, North Korea has had to rely on aid from around the world to prevent its people from starving.

Fabric The production of textiles is an important industry in North Korea. The sales clerk shown here displays her colorful fabric in a Pyongyang department store.

▲ **EVALUATE** Discuss the structure of North Korea's government and economy.

CONNECT ↘ to Math

In the image below, a North Korean woman makes textiles for the trade market. Study the chart of North Korea's major trading partners, and then use the decimal numbers in it to play a rounding numbers matching game. Remember to round down any number that contains a decimal of 0.4 or less. Round up any number that contains a decimal of 0.5 or more.

North Korea's Major Trading Partners

3.8% 15.2%
6.0%
7.1%
9.3% 19.6% 39.0%

■ China   ■ Russia
■ South Korea ■ India
■ Thailand   ■ Others
■ Japan

Source: *KOTRA*, 2004

Activity
Rounding Numbers

1. Study the numbers in the box below. The numbers with decimals are taken from the trading partners pie chart.

2. Copy the Matching Game box on your paper.

3. Circle each number that contains a decimal. Then draw a line to match it with its rounded number.

Matching Game			
8	15.2	9	16
3	19.6	39.0	4
7	6	10	19
39	3.8	40	20
9.3	15	7.1	6.0

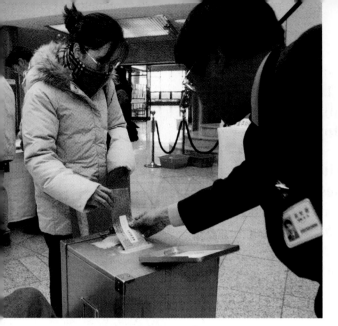

South Korea

▼ **KEY QUESTION** How do the government and economy of South Korea compare with those of North Korea?

In many ways, the government and economy of South Korea are the opposite of North Korea's government and economy. You can compare the two countries' governments in the feature below.

Voting South Koreans cast their ballots during the 2002 presidential election. **Does a similar election take place in North Korea?**

Government Like the United States, the South Korean government is divided into three branches—the executive, the legislative, and the judicial. The president heads the executive branch and serves a five-year term. He or she is chosen by popular election and cannot be reelected. The president appoints a prime minister, who handles the running of the government. South Korea's legislature has a single house called the National Assembly. Citizens elect the members of the assembly to four-year terms.

During the 1980s and 1990s, South Korea began to allow more political freedom. It developed a multiparty system. The country also allowed fairer elections and greater freedom for its people.

◄ COMPARING ► Korean Governments

NORTH KOREA

North Korean citizens elect the members of the Supreme People's Assembly. This body, however, is controlled by the National Defense Commission and the Korean Workers' Party.

CITIZENS
↓ elect ↓
SUPREME PEOPLE'S ASSEMBLY
controls ↗   ↖ controls
CHAIRMAN OF NATIONAL DEFENSE COMMISSION → controls → KOREAN WORKERS' PARTY

SOUTH KOREA

South Korean citizens directly elect the president and the members of the National Assembly.

CITIZENS
↙ elect ↘
PRESIDENT   NATIONAL ASSEMBLY
appoints ↘   ↙ approves
SUPREME COURT

CRITICAL THINKING

1. **Compare and Contrast** How do the roles of chairman in North Korea and president in South Korea differ?

2. **Draw Conclusions** How much power do the people of North Korea have?

Economy After the Korean War, South Korea developed its economy with a series of five-year plans. The goal of these plans was to export goods and use the resulting income to increase production. The government expressed this approach through the slogan "Production, Exports, Construction!"

Soon South Korean businesses began to thrive. In fact, some companies expanded into family-owned conglomerates called **chaebols** (JEH•buhlz). A **conglomerate** is made up of several companies in different businesses. The businesses within a *chaebol* are related. For example, Samsung is one of South Korea's largest *chaebols*. It is made up of companies that produce electronic equipment such as televisions, microwave ovens, and computers.

Eventually, *chaebols* controlled much of South Korea's economy and greatly contributed to its growth. These organizations, though, had drawbacks. For instance, *chaebols* sometimes underpaid their workers, causing many to demand higher wages. Also, some *chaebols* made bad economic decisions that led to an economic downturn in 1997. After the government received foreign loans and closed poorly run businesses, the economy began to rebound. *Chaebols* continue to play a vital role in South Korea's economy today.

Industries and Agriculture South Korea has developed both heavy and light industries. Products include chemicals, steel, shipbuilding, automobiles, electronics, and telecommunications. You can learn about the locations of South Korea's industries by studying the map on this page.

South Korea's economy has shifted away from agriculture. And, as you have learned, South Korea's mountainous terrain does not provide much land for farming. Nevertheless, South Korean farms produce a variety of crops, including rice, root crops, barley, vegetables, and fruit.

▲ **COMPARE AND CONTRAST**
Compare the government and economy of South Korea with those of North Korea.

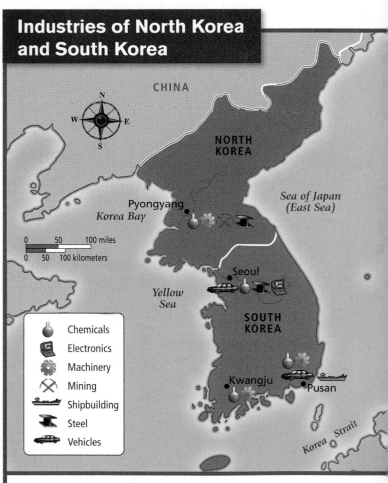

Industries of North Korea and South Korea

Chemicals
Electronics
Machinery
Mining
Shipbuilding
Steel
Vehicles

CONNECT Geography & Economics
1. **Location** Where are most of the industries in North Korea and South Korea located?
2. **Region** What are North Korea's major industries?

Efforts Toward Reunification

🔻 **KEY QUESTION** What steps have been taken toward the reunification of North Korea and South Korea?

Many obstacles remain before North Korea and South Korea can be reunited. For one thing, North Korea considers the South Korean government unlawful. Also, over the past decades, North Korea and South Korea have developed very different cultures.

But gradually, contacts between the two Koreas have increased. For example, more visits between family members have been allowed. Also, as you have already learned, a few South Korean businesses have moved into North Korea. The desire for reunification has even been reflected at the Olympic games. During the 2000, 2004, and 2006 games, North and South Korean athletes marched under the same flag during the opening ceremony. The two Koreas have agreed to compete as a single team in the 2008 Olympics.

🔺 **FIND MAIN IDEAS** Discuss the steps that have been taken toward the reunification of North and South Korea.

Unified Korea Flag Korean athletes carry a flag showing a map of the entire Korean Peninsula in the 2006 Olympics.

ONLINE QUIZ
For test practice, go to
Interactive Review
@ ClassZone.com

Section ③ Assessment

TERMS & NAMES
1. Explain the importance of
- totalitarian
- Korean Workers' Party
- dictator
- *chaebol*

USE YOUR READING NOTES
2. Compare and Contrast Use your completed Venn diagram to answer the following question:

How do North Korea and South Korea differ in their economic relationships with other countries?

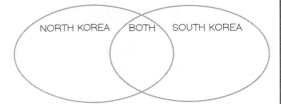

NORTH KOREA   BOTH   SOUTH KOREA

KEY IDEAS
3. What is *juche*?

4. How much power does the chairman of the National Defense Commission have in North Korea?

5. What have been some of the benefits and drawbacks of the *chaebols*?

CRITICAL THINKING
6. Recognize Bias and Propaganda Reread the History Makers on Kim Jong Il. How do official accounts of the leader reflect bias and propaganda?

7. Evaluate What might result from allowing the Korean people to travel freely within North and South Korea?

8. CONNECT to Today What message would North Korea and South Korea convey by competing in the Olympics as a single team?

9. ECONOMICS Research a *Chaebol* Choose a *chaebol* and research the type of products it makes and how well they sell in the United States. Summarize your findings in a one-paragraph report.

Click here to complete these and other activities online @ ClassZone.com

CHAPTER SUMMARY

Key Idea 1
Korea lies on a peninsula, which provides a moderate climate and plentiful resources.

Key Idea 2
The Korean Peninsula has been invaded by China, Russia, and Japan but has still maintained its cultural identity.

Key Idea 3
North Korea and South Korea have very different government systems and economic structures.

For **Review and Study Notes**, go to **Interactive Review @ ClassZone.com**

NAME GAME

Use the Terms & Names list to complete each sentence on paper or online.

1. I am the highest mountain on the Korean Peninsula. **Mount Paektu**

2. I am the largest island off the coast of the Korean Peninsula. _____

3. I am the dictator of North Korea. _____

4. I am made up of the states of Koguryo, Paekche, and Silla. _____

5. I am the buffer zone between North Korea and South Korea. _____

6. I am the original belief system practiced on the Korean Peninsula. _____

7. I am a traditional Korean costume. _____

8. I am a Korean side dish. _____

9. I am the political group that controls the North Korean government. _____

10. I am a family-owned conglomerate of businesses. _____

Buddhism
chaebol
Cheju
conglomerate
demilitarized zone
hanbok
kimchi
Kim Jong Il
Korean Workers' Party
Mount Paektu
shamanism
Three Kingdoms

Activities

GeoGame

Use this online map to show what you know about the location, geographic features, and important places of the Korean Peninsula. Drag and drop each place name to its location on the map.

Geo GAME

North Korea

South Korea

demilitarized zone

Yalu River

Cheju Island

To play the complete game, go to **Interactive Review @ ClassZone.com**

Physical Geography of Korea

North Korea

Crossword Puzzle

Complete an online crossword puzzle to test your knowledge of Korean history and culture.

ACROSS
1. traditional Korean clothing

VOCABULARY

Explain the significance of each of the following.

1. Korean Peninsula
2. Mount Paektu
3. Cheju Island
4. Korean War
5. demilitarized zone
6. shamanism
7. *hanbok*
8. celadon
9. Three Kingdoms
10. *chaebol*

Explain how the terms and names in each group are related.

11. shamanism, Confucianism, and Buddhism
12. Korean Workers' Party, Kim Jong Il, and dictator

KEY IDEAS

1 A Rugged Peninsula

13. What bodies of water surround the Korean Peninsula?
14. What do the Yalu and Tumen rivers form?
15. How do summer monsoons affect the Korean Peninsula's climate?
16. How is the majority of the electricity produced in South Korea?

2 Strong Traditions, Modern Innovations

17. How did the Choson Dynasty isolate Korea?
18. How did the Korean War start?
19. What belief systems influence Korean society today?
20. What influences have inspired Korean arts?

3 Contrasting Countries

21. What is the role of the Korean Workers' Party in North Korea?
22. How is South Korea's government similar to the U.S. government?
23. What was the goal of South Korea's five-year economic plans?
24. How has the desire for the reunification of North and South Korea been reflected in the Olympics?

CRITICAL THINKING

25. **Compare and Contrast** Create a chart to compare and contrast the natural resources of North Korea and South Korea.

NORTH KOREA'S RESOURCES	SOUTH KOREA'S RESOURCES

26. **Evaluate** What steps has South Korea taken to overcome some of its problems?
27. **Make Inferences** Why do you think many South Koreans practice aspects of several religions?
28. **Identify Problems** What are some of the problems faced by North Korea?
29. **Connect Geography & Economics** How has North Korea's farmland affected its economy?
30. **Five Themes: Human-Environment Interaction** How have the geographic features of the Korean Peninsula affected this region's history?

Answer the ESSENTIAL QUESTION

How can North Korea and South Korea overcome their differences and live in peace?

Written Response Write a two- or three-paragraph response to the Essential Question. Use the rubric below to guide your thinking.

Response Rubric
A strong response will:
- identify the countries' differences and conflicts
- discuss the steps the two Koreas have taken toward overcoming these differences
- offer solutions about what more the two countries could do

STANDARDS-BASED ASSESSMENT

✓ Test Practice
• Online Test Practice @ ClassZone.com
• Test-Taking Strategies and Practice
  at the front of this book

LINE GRAPH

Use the graph to answer questions 1 and 2 on your paper.

Stock Market in South Korea

*KOSPI—Korea's Stock Price Index

Source: Republic of Korea, Ministry of Finance and Economy

1. In what year did the stock market in South Korea reach its lowest level?

A. 1997
B. 1998
C. 2001
D. 2003

2. When did the stock market reach 850 points?

A. 1999
B. 2000
C. 2002
D. 2004

CHART

Examine the chart below. Use the information in the chart to answer questions 3 and 4 on your paper.

Spread of Chinese Influence A.D. 600–1400		
Korea	**Japan**	**Southeast Asia**
Buddhism	Buddhism	Buddhism
Writing system	Writing system	Ideas
Civil service	Printing	
Printing		
Porcelain		

3. Which aspect of Chinese culture was most widely spread?

A. writing system
B. printing
C. Buddhism
D. porcelain

4. Which region was most influenced by China?

A. Korea
B. Japan
C. Southeast Asia
D. They were all equally influenced by China.

GeoActivity

1. INTERDISCIPLINARY ACTIVITY–SCIENCE

With a small group, use appropriate resources to research the causes and effects of typhoons on the Korean Peninsula. Display your findings on a poster. Include pictures, charts, and captions that explain the causes and effects.

2. WRITING FOR SOCIAL STUDIES

Do you think North Korea should be allowed to develop a nuclear weapons program? Examine the conflicting viewpoints of North Korea and of the United States and others who oppose it. Write your opinion in a brief essay.

3. MENTAL MAPPING

Create an outline map of the Korean Peninsula and label the following:

• Yellow Sea
• East Sea
• Korea Strait
• Yalu River
• Cheju Island
• Mount Paektu
• Nangnim Mountains
• Taebaek Mountains

27

Japan

ESSENTIAL QUESTION

How has Japan balanced its ancient traditions with its modern economy?

CONNECT   Geography & History

Use the map and the time line to answer the following questions.

1. When did Heian become Japan's capital?

2. What is the capital of Japan today?

History
◄ **300s** The Yamato clan gains control of Japan. (Seventh-century ruler Shotoku Taishi)

A.D. 300

History
1100s Shogun rule is established. (Japan's first shogun, Minamoto no Yoritomo) ►

Government
◄ **794** Heian period begins, and the capital moves from Nara to Heian, modern Kyoto. (Phoenix Hall)

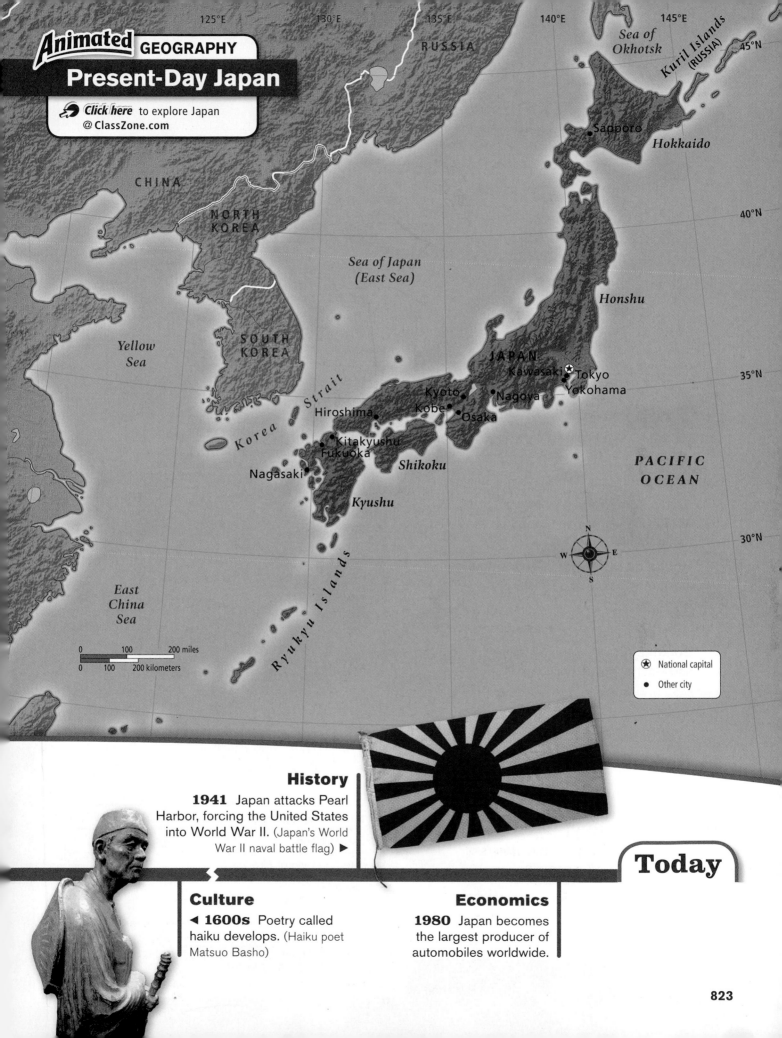

125°E
130°E
135°E
140°E
145°E

45°N

RUSSIA

Sea of Okhotsk

Kuril Islands (RUSSIA)

CHINA

NORTH KOREA

Sapporo

Hokkaido

40°N

Sea of Japan (East Sea)

Honshu

SOUTH KOREA

Yellow Sea

JAPAN

35°N

Korea Strait

Kyoto

Kawasaki Tokyo

Nagoya

Yokohama

Hiroshima

Kobe

Osaka

Kitakyushu

Fukuoka

Shikoku

Nagasaki

PACIFIC OCEAN

Kyushu

East China Sea

30°N

N

W   E

S

Ryukyu Islands

0   100   200 miles
0   100   200 kilometers

⊛ National capital

● Other city

History

1941 Japan attacks Pearl Harbor, forcing the United States into World War II. (Japan's World War II naval battle flag) ▶

Today

Culture

◀ **1600s** Poetry called haiku develops. (Haiku poet Matsuo Basho)

Economics

1980 Japan becomes the largest producer of automobiles worldwide.

Reading for Understanding

▶ Key Ideas

BEFORE, YOU LEARNED

The Korean Peninsula is a ruggedly mountainous landmass in East Asia, bordered by China, Russia, and Japan.

NOW YOU WILL LEARN

The mountainous islands that make up Japan provide the country's people with scant living space, a varied climate, and limited resources.

▶ Vocabulary

TERMS & NAMES

Honshu Japan's largest and most populous island

Mount Fuji Japan's highest mountain peak

Kanto Plain the largest lowland of Japan, which extends from the Japanese Alps east to the Pacific

Hokkaido (hah•KY•doh) Japan's northernmost and second largest island

Kyushu (kee•OO•shoo) Japan's southernmost island and home to several large cities

Shikoku (shee•KAW•koo) Japan's smallest and least populated major island

Ring of Fire a geographic zone that extends along the rim of the Pacific Ocean and has numerous volcanoes and earthquakes

Visual Vocabulary Ring of Fire

▶ Reading Strategy

Re-create the chart shown at right. As you read and respond to the **KEY QUESTIONS**, use the chart to analyze the causes and effects of Japan's physical geography.

 Skillbuilder Handbook, page R8

ANALYZE CAUSES AND EFFECTS

PHYSICAL GEOGRAPHY	CAUSES AND/OR EFFECTS
Crowded Islands	
Located on Ring of Fire	
Varied Climate	
Limited Resources	
Abundant Wildlife	

GRAPHIC ORGANIZERS
Go to **Interactive Review** @ ClassZone.com

Land of the Rising Sun

Connecting to Your World

Think about the most beautiful scenery you've ever seen. You might recall majestic mountains, spectacular sunsets or sunrises, thundering waterfalls, or rapidly flowing rivers cutting through canyons. Japan possesses all of this natural beauty. Perhaps as a result, many of the Japanese people have a strong emotional bond with nature. In fact, the Japanese name for their country, *Nippon*, refers to nature. *Nippon* means "source of the sun" and is often translated as "Land of the Rising Sun."

Mountainous Islands

▼ **KEY QUESTION** What are the main geographic features of Japan's four major islands?

Japan is made up of about 4,000 islands. It lies to the east of the Korean Peninsula, China, and Russia. The island nation is surrounded by the East Sea, or Sea of Japan, to the west and the Pacific Ocean to the south and east. The islands of Japan are actually the tops of a huge, mostly underwater, mountain range.

Cherry Blossoms Cherry trees from Japan blossom in Washington, D.C.

Mount Fuji A high-speed train runs past Mount Fuji.

JAPAN

Mount Fuji

Major Islands Although Japan has thousands of islands, most of its people live on the four largest ones: Honshu, Hokkaido, Kyushu, and Shikoku. Locate the islands on the map on the opposite page.

- **Honshu Ⓐ** is Japan's largest island and is home to about 80 percent of its people. Honshu is a land of extreme elevations. The towering Japanese Alps run down the center of the island. Honshu also contains **Mount Fuji Ⓑ**, Japan's highest peak. The largest lowland of Japan, the **Kanto Plain Ⓒ**, extends from the Japanese Alps east to the Pacific.

- **Hokkaido** (hah•KY•doh) Ⓓ lies to the north and is the second largest of Japan's four major islands. It has many mountains and thick forests. This island is sparsely populated, but its long winters make it ideal for winter sports.

- **Kyushu** (kee•OO•shoo) Ⓔ is the southernmost of the major islands. A steep chain of mountains runs down the center of this island. The heavily populated northwestern plains are home to several large cities.

- **Shikoku** (shee•KAW•koo) Ⓕ is the smallest of Japan's main islands. Because almost all of Shikoku is covered with mountains, only about 3 percent of Japan's population lives there.

CONNECT Geography & History

Japan and the Ring of Fire As you can see on the inset map on the opposite page, Japan is located along the **Ring of Fire**. This zone, which extends along the rim of the Pacific Ocean, has many active volcanoes and is subject to many earthquakes. Japan has about 80 active volcanoes and experiences about 1,500 earthquakes each year. Most of these earthquakes are minor—but not all. In 1923, the Great Kanto earthquake struck the Tokyo area, resulting in the deaths of about 140,000 people. The Kobe earthquake of 1995 killed about 6,000 people in that city. Some of the damage caused by the Kobe earthquake is shown here.

CRITICAL THINKING

Summarize What damage is apparent in this photograph of the Kobe earthquake?

Click here to see geographic features of Japan @ **ClassZone.com**

The Ring of Fire

ASIA

JAPAN

NORTH AMERICA

PACIFIC OCEAN

SOUTH AMERICA

AUSTRALIA

■ Ring of Fire

CHINA

RUSSIA

Sea of Okhotsk

Sakhalin (RUSSIA)

Kuril Islands (RUSSIA)

45°N

Ⓓ Hokkaido

40°N

Honshu Ⓐ

Ou Mts.

Elevation

6,560 ft. (4,000 m)
3,280 ft. (2,000 m)
1,640 ft. (1,000 m)
660 ft.   (200 m)
0 ft.   (0 m)
Below sea level

▲ Mountain peak

Sea of Japan (East Sea)

JAPAN

Ⓒ

35°N

Kanto Plain

SOUTH KOREA

Japanese Alps

Tone R.

Ⓑ Mt. Fuji 12,388 ft. (3,776 m)

PACIFIC OCEAN

Chugoku Mtns.

Korea Strait

Ⓕ Shikoku

Kyushu Mtns.

Ⓔ Kyushu

East China Sea

Ryukyu Islands

N
W E
S

0   100   200 miles
0   100   200 kilometers

CONNECT Geography & History
READING A THEMATIC MAP

The Ring of Fire map shows the location of active volcanoes in the Pacific Rim. As you study the map and key,

• use the color symbol to find the Ring of Fire
• note Japan's position along the Ring of Fire
• think about the impact the Ring of Fire might have on Japan's landforms

1. Region How much of Japan is on the Ring of Fire?

2. Place Compare the two maps. What can you conclude about Mount Fuji?

130°E   135°E   140°E

A Shortage of Space About 70 percent of Japan is covered with mountains and hills. As a result, Japan has only a small amount of land where its people can live. The nation also has a high population density. To give you an idea, Japan is just a little smaller than California, but it has about four times as many people. As you can imagine, Japanese cities are very crowded.

The Japanese have learned to adapt to their limited space. For one thing, Japanese homes tend to be smaller than those in the United States. Also, many people live in apartments. It is not uncommon for a family of four to live in a one-bedroom apartment. Since these dwellings are often noisy and crowded, students usually study at their schools or in public libraries.

▲ **SUMMARIZE** Describe the main geographic features of Japan's four major islands.

Climate and Resources

▼ **KEY QUESTION** What impact do mountains have on Japan's climate, resources, and wildlife?

Since Japan consists of many islands, the sea strongly affects its climate. The mountainous terrain of these islands also influences Japan's climate and its resources.

A Varied Climate The climates on the major islands are influenced by their latitudes and by the currents of the Pacific Ocean. The northern islands of Japan have generally cool weather, while the southern ones have a more tropical climate. The central islands have a moderate climate, with warm summers and mild winters. The mountains throughout the islands have colder temperatures because of their higher elevations. Most of Japan gets at least 40 inches of rain each year.

Resources and Wildlife Japan has deposits of coal, lead, and silver, but many of these are of poor quality. Forests are abundant, but they are located in remote mountain areas and are difficult to harvest. Not surprisingly, given its vast coastal waters, Japan looks to the sea for food. In fact, Japan has one of the largest fishing industries in the world.

Despite its dense human population, Japan has a great deal of wildlife, especially in regions that are thickly forested. Bears, wild boars, raccoon dogs, and deer can be found in these areas. Japan's wilderness also contains a large, shaggy-haired monkey called the Japanese macaque (muh•KAK).

Japanese Macaques
Also called snow monkeys, Japanese macaques live farther north than any other monkeys in the world.

▲ **ANALYZE EFFECTS** Discuss the impact of mountains on Japan's climate, resources, and wildlife.

Section 1 Assessment

⟳ **ONLINE QUIZ**
For test practice, go to
Interactive Review
@ ClassZone.com

TERMS & NAMES

1. Explain the importance of
- Honshu
- Mount Fuji
- Kanto Plain
- Ring of Fire

USE YOUR READING NOTES

2. Analyze Causes and Effects Use your completed chart to answer the following question:

Why does Japan have such limited living space?

PHYSICAL GEOGRAPHY	CAUSES AND/OR EFFECTS
Crowded Islands	
Located on Ring of Fire	
Varied Climate	
Limited Resources	
Abundant Wildlife	

KEY IDEAS

3. On which two islands do most of the Japanese people live?

4. Why does Japan have so many earthquakes?

5. How does latitude affect Japan's climate?

CRITICAL THINKING

6. Evaluate What characteristics do the Japanese reveal in their ability to live on their crowded island nation?

7. Draw Conclusions What do you think is Japan's most important natural resource? Explain.

8. **CONNECT to Today** Subway employees push passengers into Tokyo subways and trains during rush hour. What does this tell you about the city?

9. **WRITING** **Pen a Journal Entry** Imagine that you are on a hike in the Japanese Alps. Write a journal entry about your experiences in these mountains. Record the sights you might see, the type of weather you might deal with, and the vegetation and wildlife you might encounter.

▶ Key Ideas

BEFORE, YOU LEARNED

Japan is a chain of islands that lies off the coast of China and the Korean Peninsula.

NOW YOU WILL LEARN

Over the centuries, Japan has adapted ideas and technologies from other lands and created a unique culture.

▶ Vocabulary

TERMS & NAMES

Heian (hay•ahn) **period** the era in Japanese history from A.D. 794 to 1185; arts and writing flourished during this time

samurai (SAM•uh•RY) professional soldiers of Japan

shogun the leader of the military government of Japan beginning in 1192

daimyo (DY•mee•OH) powerful samurai who became warrior-chieftains

Tokugawa Ieyasu (TOH•koo•GAH•wah EE•yeh•YAH•soo) shogun who unified Japan

Shinto Japan's original religion; involves worshiping gods believed to be found in nature

BACKGROUND VOCABULARY

clan a group of families related through a common ancestor

REVIEW

emperor a man who is the ruler of an empire

Visual Vocabulary statue of daimyo draped with war flag

▶ Reading Strategy

Re-create the time line shown at right. As you read and respond to the **KEY QUESTIONS**, use the time line to keep track of some of Japan's important historical and cultural events.

 See Skillbuilder Handbook, page R6

SEQUENCE EVENTS

```
┌──────┐   ┌──────┐   ┌──────┐   ┌──────┐
│      │   │      │   │      │   │      │
└──────┘   └──────┘   └──────┘   └──────┘
    ↓          ↓          ↓          ↓
┌────────────────────────────────────────┐
│ 300 B.C.                          1945   │
└────────────────────────────────────────┘
```

⟳ **GRAPHIC ORGANIZERS**
Go to **Interactive Review** @ ClassZone.com

Samurai to Animé

Connecting to Your World

Have you ever played a video game or watched an animated film? If so, you have probably used a product from Japan. Japanese culture has strongly influenced culture in the United States and throughout the world. But the reverse has also been true. Hundreds of years ago, several cultures played an important role in shaping Japanese culture. In this section, you will learn what these cultures were and how they affected Japan.

Isolated Nation to World Power

▼ **KEY QUESTION** How did Japan change from an isolated nation to a world power?

The first influences on Japanese culture probably arrived from China and Korea around 300 B.C. At this time, Japanese families were organized into **clans**, who fought over land. Eventually, the Yamato family became the leading clan and established a member of its family as ruler, or **emperor**. The Yamato line of emperors continues to this day.

Video Games Only the United States sells more video games than Japan.

Influence from China Buddhism arrived in Japan from China. This statue of Buddha in Kyoto reflects China's influence.

Heian Period In the late 700s, the emperor moved his court from the capital of Nara to Heian (hay•ahn), which is modern Kyoto (kee•OH•toh). Heian remained the center of Japan's government for about 400 years. This era in Japanese history, which lasted from 794 to 1185, is called the **Heian period**.

Art and writing flourished during this period. Men and women of the nobility filled their days by painting and writing poetry and prose. In fact, one of the best accounts of Heian society was written by Lady Murasaki Shikibu (MOO•rah•SAH•kee SHEE•kee•boo). Her masterpiece, *The Tale of Genji*, is an account of the life of a prince in the emperor's court. The work is considered the world's first novel.

Samurai and Shoguns During the Heian period, the central government was relatively strong. However, by the mid-1000s, this power had begun to decrease. Wealthy clans bought large areas of land and set up private armies. The countryside became lawless and dangerous. As a result, smaller landowners sold parts of their land to strong warlords in exchange for protection. With more land, the lords gained more power. Soon, wars between rival lords became commonplace. To defend himself, each lord surrounded himself with a bodyguard of loyal warriors called **samurai** (SAM•uh•RY).

COMPARING Samurai & Knights

Samurai were similar to knights, a class of warriors that formed in medieval Europe. Here is how the two groups compare.

JAPANESE SAMURAI	EUROPEAN KNIGHTS
Live by code of honor and value bravery and loyalty to their lord above all else	Value bravery and loyalty to heavenly God, earthly lord, and chosen lady
Prefer death to defeat	Show humility
Expect women to live up to same values of honor and courage; women can fight as samurai	Regard women as weak creatures to be idolized and defended
Enter into battle with iron and leather armor, swords, and bows and arrows	Fight battles with chain mail or plate armor, broadsword, and lance

CRITICAL THINKING

Compare and Contrast What are some similarities and differences between Japanese samurai and European knights?

During the 1100s, two powerful clans fought for control—the Taira (TY•rah) and the Minamoto. Each clan had a large samurai army. After about 30 years of war, the Minamoto gained control. This clan set up a military government in Kamakura. In 1192, the leader of this government was given the title of **shogun**, which means "supreme general of the emperor's army." Although the emperor still reigned, the shogun held real power. This pattern of government, in which shoguns ruled through puppet emperors, lasted until 1867.

Unified Japan Between 1192 and 1600, Japan was torn by internal warfare. Peasants had to fight to defend their villages. Sometimes, they hired samurai to protect them. Very powerful samurai arose and became warrior-chieftains called **daimyo** (DY•mee•OH), who became lords in their own right. The daimyo formed armies and fought for military supremacy.

Finally, in 1600, a daimyo named **Tokugawa Ieyasu** (TOH•koo•GAW•wah EE•yeh•YAH•soo) restored order. Three years later, he became shogun and unified Japan. He then moved the capital to his base at Edo, a small fishing village that would later become the city of Tokyo.

The Tokugawa shogunate held power until 1868. During this time, Japan enjoyed a period of stability—and isolation. For more than 200 years, the country was closed to Westerners.

HISTORY MAKERS

Tokugawa Ieyasu 1543–1616

Tokugawa Ieyasu could be merciless in the defense of his clan. In the late 1500s, his wife and eldest son were accused of conspiring against the family. As a result, Ieyasu ordered his son to commit suicide and had his wife executed. He also never forgot a grudge. As an adult, he executed a prisoner who had insulted him in childhood. On the other hand, Ieyasu could also be kind and generous. He rewarded those who were loyal to him and even showed compassion to his enemies.

ONLINE BIOGRAPHY
For more on the life of Tokugawa Ieyasu, go to the
Research & Writing Center @ ClassZone.com

Himeji Castle Tokugawa Ieyasu's son-in-law built the castle after he helped win the battle that brought Ieyasu to power.

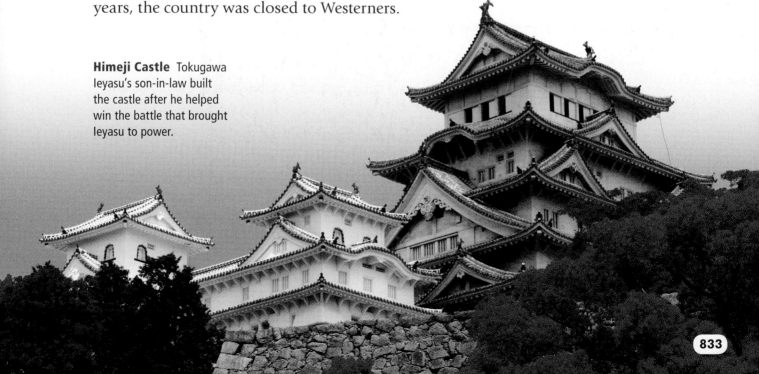

Rise of Modern Japan   In 1853, the United States forced Japan to end its isolation. The government sent Commodore Matthew Perry to Japan with several warships to frighten the Tokugawa shogun. He soon agreed to open several Japanese ports to Western powers.

The Japanese people were angry that the shogun had given in to the foreigners' demands. As a result, the emperor was restored as head of government in 1868. The emperor chose the name *Meiji* (MAY•jee), which means "enlightened rule," for his reign. In an effort to counter Western influence, the emperor began a policy of modernization. Before long, Japan became a powerful nation.

As Japan's power grew, the nation sought to obtain an empire. In the early 1900s, Japan gained control of Korea. By 1937, Japan had invaded China and formed an alliance with Nazi Germany and Fascist Italy. Between 1939 and 1945, Japan joined and fought with these powers during World War II—and lost.

After the United States and the Allies won the war, they occupied Japan for several years and set up a democracy. In time, Japan developed into an economic superpower.

▲ **SUMMARIZE** Explain how Japan changed from an isolated nation to a world power.

Japanese Empire 1942

Map labels: U.S.S.R, MONGOLIA, MANCHURIA, KOREA, JAPAN, CHINA, PACIFIC OCEAN, 30°N, Formosa, Wake Island, BURMA, Hainan, SIAM, FRENCH INDOCHINA, PHILIPPINES, Guam, MALAYA, Borneo, Equator, Gilbert Islands, 0°, DUTCH EAST INDIES, New Guinea, 120°E AUSTRALIA, 150°E

— Areas controlled by Japan

0   500   1,000 miles
0 500 1,000 kilometers

CONNECT Geography & History

1. **Location** What part of mainland China did Japan control?
2. **Region** What body of water borders all of the conquered territories?

Traditional and Modern Japanese Culture

▼ **KEY QUESTION** How does Japanese culture blend traditional and modern influences?

As you have learned, Japan has been isolated for long periods of time throughout its history. Because of this, 99 percent of the people who live there are of Japanese descent. Other groups include Chinese, Koreans, and the Ainu (EYE•noo). Some historians believe that the Ainu were Japan's original people. Most Ainu live on Hokkaido.

Japanese is the country's only official language. The written form reflects the influence of China on Japan. Chinese characters, called *kanji*, are used for nouns. Japanese characters, known as *kana*, can be used for changing nouns into adjectives and verbs.

Religious Traditions Japan's religious traditions also demonstrate China's influence—and Japan's ability to take in new ideas and make them its own. The two major religions of Japan are Shinto and Buddhism. **Shinto** is Japan's original religion and is rarely practiced anywhere else in the world. Followers of this belief worship many gods, called *kami*. These gods are believed to be found in aspects of nature, such as rivers, trees, and rocks.

Buddhism, which originated in India, spread from China to Japan during the 500s. A form of this religion, called Zen Buddhism, became important in Japan. Zen stresses strict discipline of the body and mind as the path to wisdom. Many Japanese use rituals from both religions in their daily lives.

Torii Gate Like all torii gates, this one on Miyajima Island near Hiroshima serves as an entry to a Shinto shrine. **How does the gate reflect the importance of nature in Shinto?**

Japanese Arts The arts in Japan blend traditional and modern influences. Kabuki is a traditional form of Japanese drama that features colorful costumes and an exaggerated acting style. Other traditional Japanese arts include flower arranging and the tea ceremony. Both reflect the importance of traditional Japanese virtues such as simplicity, discipline, and love of nature.

Modern arts are also popular in Japan. These include animated films called *animé*, which often feature characters with large, expressive eyes, and comic books called *manga*. Japan has many manga cafes, where people can read manga over a cup of tea or coffee.

CONNECT to Culture

Origami is an art form that involves folding paper into decorative shapes. Although origami started in China, it has thrived in Japan. One of the most popular origami shapes is the crane, shown here. The crane is considered a sacred bird in Japan. A finished sailboat is also shown.

Activity

Create an Origami Sailboat

Materials
• colored paper

1. With colored side down, fold your paper on line A–C. Open and fold point B to the diagonal crease. Then fold D to the crease.

2. Turn your paper around so that A is nearest to you. Fold A so that it meets points D and B. Then fold G–H up and crease on line E–F.

3. Finally, fold E–F up and crease on line G–H.

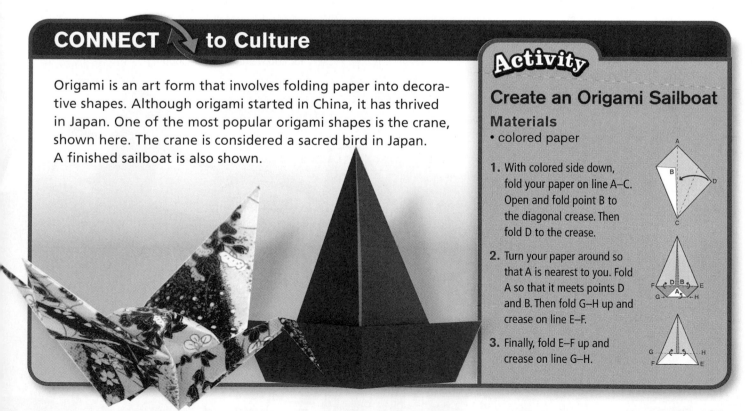

Japanese Literature

The earliest known Japanese poetry, called tanka, was the dominant verse form from the 700s until the 1500s. Tanka means "short songs" and consists of 31 syllables divided among five lines. During the Heian period, aristocrats routinely composed and exchanged tanka with their loved ones. In the 1600s, another type of poetry called haiku (HY•koo) developed. This verse has 17 syllables arranged in three lines. The following haiku is by Matsuo Basho, who is considered a master of the form.

Cool crescent moon

shining faintly high above

Feather Black Mountain

In addition to poetry, Japanese writers have made many contributions to fiction and drama. As you have learned, Lady Murasaki Shikibu is credited with writing the first novel. Zeami Motokiyo, who wrote in the late 1300s, is one of Japan's greatest playwrights.

Life in Japan

Because of Japan's shortage of living space, Japanese cities are very crowded. About three-fourths of the Japanese people live in cities. These urban areas are filled with dazzling, high-rise buildings, elegant department stores, and trendy shops. Even though the people live in small houses and apartments, overcrowding remains a constant problem. During rush hour, for instance, white-gloved employees push as many people into subways and trains as possible. Passengers have suffered broken bones from holding their arms in awkward positions in these cramped conditions.

Woodblock Print Haiku convey images of nature that are often illustrated with landscape prints.

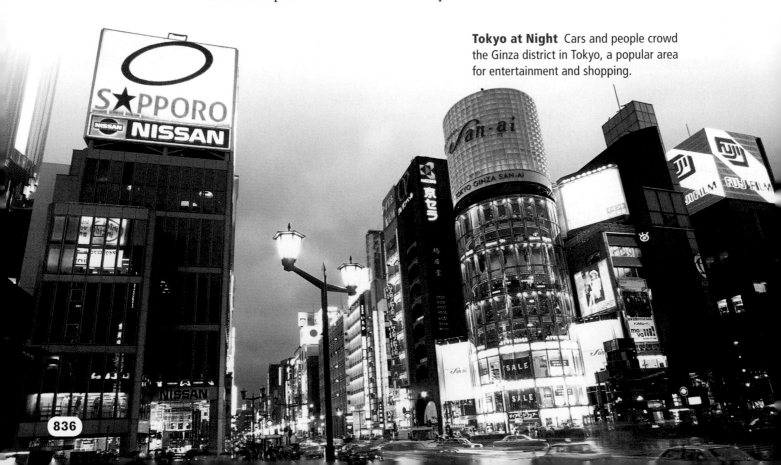

Tokyo at Night Cars and people crowd the Ginza district in Tokyo, a popular area for entertainment and shopping.

In Japan's cities, most Japanese wear clothes that are similar to those worn in the United States. However, for special occasions, Japanese men and women might wear a traditional dress called a kimono. These garments are tied around the waist with a sash and are worn with sandals.

Although Western fast foods are popular in Japan, many Japanese still enjoy traditional fare, including rice with almost every meal. Other traditional foods include tofu (soybean curd cake) and sushi—vinegared rice usually topped with raw fish. Soups made with a soybean paste called *miso* are also popular.

You may be surprised to learn that the number one spectator sport in Japan is baseball. However, traditional sumo wrestling also has a wide following. Other popular traditional sports include *kendo* (fencing with bamboo sticks) and martial arts.

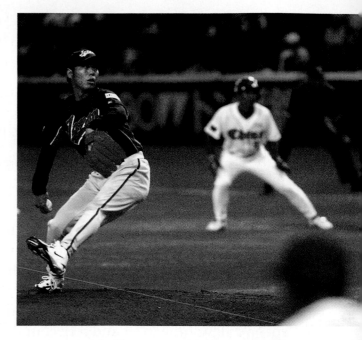

Japanese Baseball Japan won the first World Baseball Classic in 2006. Two of the players on the Japanese team played in the U.S. major leagues during the regular season.

 FIND MAIN IDEAS Describe how Japanese culture blends traditional and modern influences.

Section 2 Assessment

ONLINE QUIZ
For test practice, go to **Interactive Review** @ ClassZone.com

TERMS & NAMES

1. Explain the importance of
- samurai
- shogun
- daimyo
- Shinto

USE YOUR READING NOTES

2. Sequence Events Use your completed time line to answer the following question:

During which period was the haiku developed?

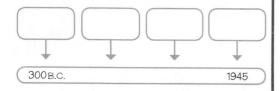

300 B.C.   1945

KEY IDEAS

3. How did the nobility fill their time during the Heian period?

4. Why did Japan begin to modernize during the mid- to late 1800s?

5. What is daily life like in Japanese cities?

CRITICAL THINKING

6. Make Inferences Why do you think the Japanese wanted to live in isolation from the West for so long?

7. Synthesize Reread the haiku in this section. How does the poem reflect the traditional Japanese values of simplicity, discipline, and love of nature?

8. CONNECT to Today What aspects of Japanese culture are popular in the United States today?

9. TECHNOLOGY Give a Kabuki Slide Show Research to learn about kabuki theater. Find pictures of costumes, make-up, and the set designs used. Then give a slide show about the drama form, using authentic kabuki music in the background.

Japan is a land of ancient traditions. But it is also an ultra-modern country, where new styles are set. Today, as you can see from these pictures, the past and present live side by side in Japan.

Traditional Japan

Since the 1600s, the Japanese people have enjoyed kabuki drama, with its colorful costumes and revolving stages. The dramas recall a time when the Japanese wore kimonos and musicians played a three-stringed instrument called the *shamisen*. In this traditional Japan, people have time to sit and reflect in the peaceful calm of a Zen garden.

Dress

Many different types of kimonos can be worn by men, women, and children.

Zen garden in Kyoto ▼

Entertainment

All of the roles in a kabuki drama are played by men.

Music

The sound of the *shamisen* is similar to that of a banjo.

Modern Japan

The worldwide popularity of animé attests to Japan's ability to set cultural trends. Other exports include karaoke and stylish, modern fashions. As you can see, modern life in Japan is also characterized by busy rush hours.

Dress

Today, Japanese fashion designers are copied throughout the world.

Crowded Tokyo subway ▼

Entertainment

Many animé films tell sophisticated stories about love, growing up, and female empowerment.

Music

In Japan, people can sing along with a karaoke player in public bars or in private shops.

CRITICAL THINKING

1. **Compare and Contrast** Select two corresponding images from traditional and modern Japan. How do they differ? What do they have in common?

2. **Analyze Causes** Why do you think animé and karaoke have become so popular in other countries?

Economic Miracle and Setbacks From the early 1950s to the early 1970s, Japan's economy skyrocketed. One reason for this economic boom was trade. Japan imported raw materials at low costs and exported manufactured goods. The nation also switched from producing products such as textiles to products such as electronics, which require fewer raw materials.

The success of the economy brought many social changes to Japan. Many people moved from rural areas to cities to work in factories and service industries. As a result, fewer people earned a living by farming. Some families saw their income doubling or tripling. In cities, the pressure to conform to traditional ways lessened. Because of this, young people often felt freer to develop their individuality.

By the 1990s, though, Japan's economy started to suffer some setbacks. The high price of Japanese products made them difficult to sell overseas. Also, Japanese industry faced stiff competition from low-cost businesses in developing nations. Soon, unemployment rose, and consumer spending declined. Many economists refer to the 1990s as Japan's "lost decade." In 2001, Prime Minister **Junichiro Koizumi** (JU•NEE•chee•roh KOH•EE•zoo•mee) made the economy his top priority. By 2006, many companies were again reporting record profits.

▲ **FIND MAIN IDEAS** Explain how Japan developed its economy.

ANALYZING Primary Sources

Junichiro Koizumi (born 1942) served as prime minister of Japan from 2001 to 2006. At one point, his popularity reached almost rock-star status. In this speech, he tried to inspire confidence in Japan's economic future.

> The top priority that I must address is to rebuild our economy and reconstruct our society into ones full of pride and confidence. . . . We must embrace difficulties ahead . . . and free ourselves of past limitations as we create an economic social structure befitting the 21st century in the spirit of "No fear, no hesitation, and no constraint."
>
> Source: Speech to the Diet, May 7, 2001, Junichiro Koizumi

DOCUMENT-BASED QUESTION
What does Koizumi think the Japanese must do to achieve economic reforms?

What the Economy Produces

▼ **KEY QUESTION** What are the major manufacturing, agricultural, and service industries of Japan?

As you have learned, Japan's economic strategy called for producing many high-quality products that could be made with materials imported for a low cost. As a result, the Japanese focused on making electronic equipment and automobiles.

Manufacturing During the 1950s, the Japanese got a foothold in the electronics industry by producing transistor radios. These small radios became very popular with young people, especially in the United States and Europe. Soon, the Japanese began to manufacture televisions, tape recorders, VCRs, and computers. Innovations in the manufacturing process spurred the development of electronics.

Innovations also helped the growth of Japan's auto industry. For example, as early as 1970, the Japanese used digital technology with assembly lines. The rise of the auto industry in Japan is incredible. In 1962, Japan was sixth in the world in automobile production. By 1967, it had overtaken West Germany to rank second. And then in 1980, Japan surpassed the United States to become the largest producer of automobiles in the world.

Agriculture As you may recall, Japan has little farmland. However, Japanese farmers have been able to make this land as productive as possible. First of all, it has helped that Japan's climate is ideal for growing certain crops, such as rice. In addition, farmers extensively use irrigation and fertilizers.

The primary crop by far is rice. Other products include eggs, potatoes, fruits, and vegetables. Japan, though, does need to import some agricultural products, such as animal feed, wheat, and beans.

Major Industries of Japan

Chemicals
High-tech
Iron and steel
Machinery
Precision instruments
Shipbuilding
Textiles
Vehicles

Sea of Okhotsk

Hokkaido

Sapporo

Sea of Japan (East Sea)

Honshu

Toyama

Tokyo

Nagoya

Kobe

Hiroshima

Osaka

Shikoku

Kyushu

PACIFIC OCEAN

CONNECT Geography & Economics

1. **Region** On which island are most of the industries located?
2. **Human-Environment Interaction** Why do you think shipbuilding is a major industry in Japan?

Tokyo Disneyland Tokyo Disneyland was the first Disney park to be built outside of the United States. It is one of the most visited theme parks in the world, attracting tourists from all over the globe.

Service Industries As manufacturing industries thrived in Japan, so too did the industries that served them. Banks, for example, have a lot of power in Japan. In fact, the Bank of Japan strongly influences the government's economic policies. Also, some of Japan's banks have a major impact on international banking.

In addition, Japan has many service industries that deal with entertainment, such as nightclubs, movie theaters, and restaurants. Although Western fast-food restaurants have become popular, traditional Japanese restaurants continue to attract many customers. Japan has a great variety of traditional eating places, including sushi restaurants. It also has a healthy tourist industry. Tourism was an important part of Junichiro Koizumi's policies. His efforts paid off. In 2005, Japan hosted more than 6 million visitors from overseas.

 SUMMARIZE Identify Japan's major manufacturing, agricultural, and service industries.

Section 3 Assessment

 ONLINE QUIZ
For test practice, go to
Interactive Review
@ ClassZone.com

TERMS & NAMES

1. Explain the importance of
- militarism
- Diet
- *zaibatsu*
- Junichiro Koizumi

USE YOUR READING NOTES

2. Find Main Ideas Use your completed chart to answer the following question:

What economic obstacles did Japan have to overcome after World War II?

JAPAN'S GOVERNMENT	JAPAN'S ECONOMY
1.	1.
2.	2.
3.	3.

KEY IDEAS

3. What does Japan's constitution prohibit?

4. How did the *zaibatsu* influence Japan's businesses after World War II?

5. What are Japan's major manufacturing industries?

CRITICAL THINKING

6. Form and Support Opinions Do you think Japan's constitution should be amended to allow the Japanese to wage war? Explain why or why not.

7. Analyze Effects How do you think families are affected by the long workdays put in by many Japanese employees?

8. CONNECT to Today What impact do Japanese products have on the everyday lives of Americans?

9. ECONOMICS Compare Cars Research a car produced by a Japanese company. Then research a comparable car made by a U.S. company. Compare the two cars and write a report including information on style, price, features, and consumer ratings.

Interactive ◀ Review

CHAPTER SUMMARY

Key Idea 1
The mountainous islands that make up Japan provide the country's people with scant living space, a varied climate, and limited resources.

Key Idea 2
Over the centuries, Japan has adapted ideas and technologies from other lands and created a unique culture.

Key Idea 3
The Japanese have drawn on their culture to create a modern government and become an economic giant.

For **Review and Study Notes**, go to **Interactive Review @ ClassZone.com**

NAME GAME

Use the Terms & Names list to complete each sentence on paper or online.

1. I am Japan's highest mountain. <u>Mount Fuji</u>
2. I am the largest lowland of Japan. _____
3. I am a powerful samurai who became a warrior-chieftain. _____
4. I am the shogun who unified Japan and moved the capital to Edo. _____
5. I am Japan's original religion. _____
6. I am the aggressive use of a government's armed forces. _____
7. I am Japan's law-making body, which consists of two houses._____
8. I am a large family-controlled business group that owned many companies in Japan before World War II._____
9. I am Japan's largest and most populous island.
   _____
10. I am a period in Japanese history in which arts and writing flourished. _____

daimyo
Diet
Heian
Honshu
Kanto Plain
Junichiro Koizumi
militarism
Mount Fuji
Shinto
shogun
Tokugawa Ieyasu
zaibatsu

Activities

GeoGame

Use this online map to show what you know about Japan's location, geographic features, and important places. Drag and drop each place name to its location on the map.

Mount Fuji

Honshu

Hokkaido

Kyushu

Shikoku

To play the complete game, go to **Interactive Review @ ClassZone.com**

Crossword Puzzle

Complete an online crossword puzzle to test your knowledge of Japan.

ACROSS
1. professional soldier of Japan

CHAPTER 27

Assessment

VOCABULARY

Explain the significance of each of the following.

1. Mount Fuji
2. Kanto Plain
3. Heian period
4. samurai
5. shogun
6. daimyo
7. Shinto
8. militarism
9. Diet
10. Junichiro Koizumi

Explain how the terms and names in each group are related.

11. samurai, shogun, and daimyo
12. Honshu, Hokkaido, Kyushu, and Shikoku

KEY IDEAS

1 Land of the Rising Sun

13. What geographic feature forms the islands of Japan?
14. What is the Ring of Fire?
15. How does the climate of Japan's mountains differ from other regions of Japan?
16. Where does Japan get much of its food?

2 Samurai to Animé

17. To which clan have Japanese emperors belonged throughout history?
18. How did the Tokugawa shogunate affect Japan's foreign relations?
19. What are the two major religions of Japan?
20. What is tanka poetry?

3 Economic Giant

21. What is the role of the Japanese emperor today?
22. What were the *zaibatsu*?
23. What social changes did Japan's booming economy bring to the country between the 1950s and the 1970s?
24. Why did Japan focus on producing electronic equipment and automobiles?

CRITICAL THINKING

25. **Compare and Contrast** Use a Venn diagram to compare Japan in the early 1900s before World War II with the country after the war.

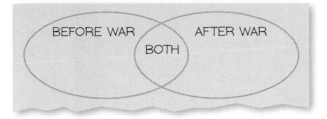

26. **Evaluate** How is the Japanese love of nature reflected in the country's culture?
27. **Form Opinions** Do you think the Tokugawa shogunate did more to help or to hurt Japanese society? Explain your answer.
28. **Make Inferences** Why do you think the Allies dissolved the *zaibatsu* after World War II?
29. **Connect Geography & Economics** How have Japan's natural resources affected its economy?
30. **Five Themes: Human-Environment Interaction** How has Japan's geography affected the way the Japanese live in cities?

Answer the ESSENTIAL QUESTION

How has Japan balanced its ancient traditions with its modern economy?

Written Response Write a two- or three-paragraph response to the Essential Question. Use the rubric below to guide your thinking.

Response Rubric
A strong response will:
- discuss the importance of Japan's cultural traditions
- explain how Japan has built up its strong economy
- emphasize Japan's ability to adapt to new ideas and changing times

STANDARDS-BASED ASSESSMENT

✓ **Test Practice**

• Online Test Practice @ ClassZone.com
• Test-Taking Strategies and Practice
  at the front of this book

THEMATIC MAP

Use the earthquake map to answer questions 1 and 2 on your paper.

Major Earthquakes in Japan *1986–2005*

Earthquake Magnitude
• 6.8 to 7.2
● 7.3 to 7.7
⬤ 7.8 and greater

RUSSIA
Hokkaido
NORTH KOREA
40°N
Honshu
Kobe Jan. 17, 1995
SOUTH KOREA   JAPAN
PACIFIC OCEAN
0 150 300 miles
0 150 300 kilometers
Shikoku
Kyushu
140°E
N

1. What was the magnitude of the 1995 earthquake in Kobe?

A. less than 6.8
B. 6.8 to 7.2
C. 7.3 to 7.7
D. 7.8 and greater

2. Near which island have most of the greatest magnitude earthquakes occurred?

A. Hokkaido
B. Honshu
C. Kyushu
D. Shikoku

PIE GRAPH

Use the pie graph on Japan's exports to answer questions 3 and 4 on your paper.

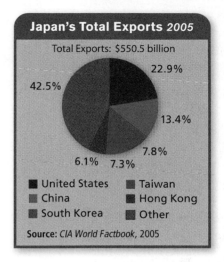

Japan's Total Exports *2005*

Total Exports: $550.5 billion
22.9%
42.5%
13.4%
7.8%
6.1% 7.3%

■ United States ■ Taiwan
■ China   ■ Hong Kong
■ South Korea   ■ Other

Source: *CIA World Factbook*, 2005

3. Which country among those listed below is Japan's biggest export partner?

A. South Korea
B. China
C. United States
D. Taiwan

4. What percentage of Japan's total exports were sent to China?

A. 6.1 percent
B. 7.3 percent
C. 13.4 percent
D. 42.5 percent

GeoActivity

1. INTERDISCIPLINARY ACTIVITY–ART

With a small group, design and create a miniature Japanese Zen garden. Use your library and the Internet to research this art form. Find out about patterns used in gravel and what rocks can represent. Present your Japanese Zen garden to your class.

2. WRITING FOR SOCIAL STUDIES

Imagine that you are a tourist in a Japanese city. Write a diary entry describing a typical day. Discuss the crowds, the sights, the food, and the blend of old and new you witness.

3. MENTAL MAPPING

Create an outline map of Japan and label the following:

• Pacific Ocean
• East Sea
• Honshu
• Hokkaido
• Kyushu
• Shikoku
• Japanese Alps
• Kanto Plain

Southeast Asia

ESSENTIAL QUESTION

How can Southeast Asian nations establish stable governments and economies?

CONNECT Geography & History

Use the map and the time line to answer the following questions.

1. What two island chains are part of Southeast Asia?

2. Which Southeast Asian country was once known as Siam?

Culture
◄ **1300s** Muslim traders bring Islam to Indonesia.
(Mosque in Jakarta)

History
500s A people known as the Khmers establish an empire on the mainland peninsula.

History
1688 Siam, or present-day Thailand, begins to limit relations with Europeans.
(King Chulalongkorn of Siam) ▶

CHINA

INDIA

MYANMAR

Irrawaddy River

Hanoi

LAOS

Red River

Vientiane

Yangon

THAILAND

Mekong River

Bangkok

CAMBODIA

VIETNAM

Phnom Penh

Ho Chi Minh City

TAIWAN

Tropic of Cancer

South China Sea

Philippine Sea

Luzon

PHILIPPINES

Manila

Philippine Islands

PACIFIC OCEAN

20°N

N
W E
S

PALAU

10°N

Banda Aceh

BRUNEI

Bandar Seri Begawan

MALAYSIA

Kuala Lumpur

SINGAPORE

Singapore City

Borneo

Sumatra

I N D O N E S I A

Sulawesi

New Guinea

PAPUA NEW GUINEA

Equator 0°

INDIAN OCEAN

Jakarta

Java

Surabaya

Bali

Dili

Timor

EAST TIMOR

10°S

AUSTRALIA

⊛ National capital
● Other cities

| 0 | 250 | 500 miles |
| 0 | 250 | 500 kilometers |

Geography

2004 Devastating tsunamis hit Southeast Asia.

Today

Government

▲ **1975** Vietnam War ends; in time, north and south unite under Communist rule.

Geography

◀ **1991** Mount Pinatubo in the Philippines erupts.

Reading for Understanding

▶ Key Ideas

BEFORE, YOU LEARNED

East Asia is made up of a vast mainland area and a number of important islands off the eastern coast.

NOW YOU WILL LEARN

Nearby Southeast Asia is a mountainous region with a tropical climate and much volcanic activity on its many islands.

▶ Vocabulary

TERMS & NAMES

Indochinese Peninsula one of two peninsulas on which mainland Southeast Asia lies; the peninsula is located south of China

Malay Peninsula the second peninsula of mainland Southeast Asia; the narrow strip of land serves as a bridge between the mainland and islands

Mekong River a major river that runs south from southern China through Laos, Cambodia, and Vietnam

archipelago (AHR•kuh•PEHL•uh•GOH) a set of closely grouped islands, which sometimes form a curved arc

tsunami (tsu•NAH•mee) one or a series of large ocean waves caused by an underwater earthquake or volcanic eruption

REVIEW

monsoon a seasonal wind that causes wet and dry seasons

Visual Vocabulary Malay Archipelago

▶ Reading Strategy

Re-create the chart shown at right. As you read and respond to the **KEY QUESTIONS**, use the chart to jot down main ideas about Southeast Asia's geographic features, climate, plants, and animals.

 Skillbuilder Handbook, page R4

FIND MAIN IDEAS

	MAINLAND	ISLANDS
Geographic Features		
Climate		
Plants and Animals		

GRAPHIC ORGANIZERS
Go to **Interactive Review @ ClassZone.com**

Physical Geography of Southeast Asia

Connecting to Your World

You may have heard of Mount St. Helens, the volcano that erupted in 1980 in the state of Washington. The blast killed 57 people and sent ash thousands of feet into the air. In 1991, a volcanic eruption that was ten times larger occurred on Mount Pinatubo in the Philippines. More than 300 people died in this eruption, and many thousands more lost their homes. In this section, you will learn why volcanic eruptions and other natural disasters occur frequently in Southeast Asia.

Mainland and Islands

▼ **KEY QUESTION** What are some of the advantages and disadvantages of Southeast Asia's physical geography?

Southeast Asia has two distinct subregions: the southeastern corner of the Asian mainland and a great number of islands. Both regions have many mountains. Most of the mountains on the islands were formed from volcanoes. Southeast Asia is part of the Ring of Fire, a zone of volcanoes around the rim of the Pacific Ocean. As a result, volcanic eruptions and earthquakes are common.

Island Nation A temple built in the 17th century to honor a Hindu water goddess floats on the water in Bali, one of the islands that makes up Indonesia.

Mekong River The Mekong River is the heart and soul of mainland Southeast Asia. Millions of people rely on the river for farming, fishing, water, and transport. **What does this Vietnamese farmer seem to be using the Mekong for?**

Peninsulas As shown on the map on the opposite page, mainland Southeast Asia lies on two peninsulas. The **Indochinese Peninsula** Ⓐ is located south of China. The **Malay Peninsula** Ⓑ is a narrow strip of land about 700 miles long. It serves as a bridge between the mainland and the islands.

The Indochinese Peninsula has a series of north-south mountain ranges separated by river valleys and lowlands. To the west of these mountains flows one of the world's great rivers—the **Mekong** Ⓒ. It runs south for about 2,600 miles from southern China through Laos, Cambodia, and Vietnam. The river opens onto a wide fertile delta on Vietnam's coast.

Island Chains Most of the islands of Southeast Asia are grouped into archipelagoes. An **archipelago** (AHR•kuh•PEHL•uh•GOH) is a set of closely grouped islands. The largest of these island groups is the Malay Archipelago, which includes Indonesia Ⓓ and the Philippines Ⓔ. Indonesia is made up of about 17,500 islands. Java, Sumatra, and Borneo are the most important islands. The Philippines lies to the north of Indonesia. This nation consists of about 7,100 islands. The largest and most important of these islands is Luzon.

Natural Disasters You have already learned about the volcanic eruption of Mount Pinatubo in 1991. An even greater disaster occurred on December 26, 2004, when a series of tsunamis hit many parts of Southeast Asia. A **tsunami** (tsu•NAH•mee) is a very large ocean wave caused by an underwater earthquake or volcanic eruption. The Asian tsunami, as the disaster was called, was one of the deadliest in modern history. The tsunamis were caused by an earthquake that released energy equal to about 23,000 atomic bombs.

▲ **ANALYZE EFFECTS** Describe some of the advantages and disadvantages of Southeast Asia's physical geography.

Physical Geography of Southeast Asia

CHINA

INDIA

Mt. Hkakabo Razi
19,294 ft
(5,881 m)

MYANMAR

LAOS

(A)

Indochinese
Peninsula
THAILAND

(C)

CAMBODIA

VIETNAM

(B)

Malay Peninsula

MALAYSIA

SINGAPORE

BRUNEI

Borneo

Sumatra

(D)

INDONESIA

INDIAN
OCEAN

TAIWAN

South
China
Sea

Luzon

Philippine
Sea

PHILIPPINES

(E)

Philippine
Islands

Mindanao

Celebes
Sea

Sulawesi

Java   Bali   Sumbawa   Flores

Timor

EAST
TIMOR

AUSTRALIA

PACIFIC
OCEAN

10°N

New
Guinea

PAPUA
NEW
GUINEA

Equator   0°

10°S

Elevation

13,100 ft.	(4,000 m)
6,600 ft.	(2,000 m)
3,280 ft.	(1,000 m)
650 ft.	(200 m)
0 ft.	(0 m)
Below sea level	

▲ Mountain peak

N W E S

0   250   500 miles
0 250   500 kilometers

CONNECT ▶ Geography & History

The 2004 Asian Tsunami
On December 26, 2004, a 9.0-magnitude earthquake in the Indian Ocean triggered tsunamis up to 50 feet high. The gigantic waves caused devastating damage in many parts of Indonesia, southern Thailand, Sri Lanka, southern India, and elsewhere. The inset map shows the worst-affected areas. Besides taking more than 200,000 lives, the tsunamis also destroyed thousands of miles of coastline. The image here shows the devastation in Banda Aceh, a city in Sumatra.

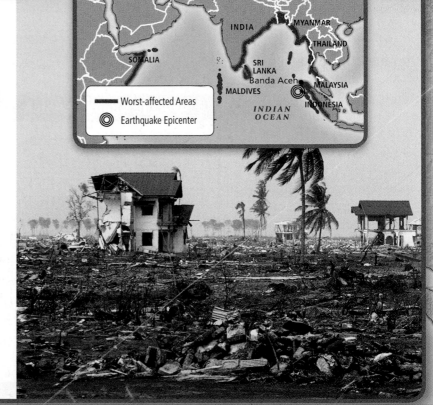

INDIA
MYANMAR
THAILAND
SOMALIA
SRI
LANKA
Banda Aceh
MALDIVES
MALAYSIA
INDIAN
OCEAN
INDONESIA

━━━ Worst-affected Areas
◎ Earthquake Epicenter

CRITICAL THINKING
Draw Conclusions Study the large map above. Why do you think Sumatra and southern Thailand were especially affected by the tsunamis?

90°E   100°E   110°E   120°E   130°E

Climate, Vegetation, and Wildlife

▼ **KEY QUESTION** How does Southeast Asia's climate affect its vegetation and wildlife?

Most of Southeast Asia has a tropical climate characterized by heavy rainfall and generally warm temperatures. Tropical climates fall into two categories: a tropical wet climate and a tropical wet and dry climate.

Rain and Monsoons The coastal areas of Myanmar, Thailand, and Vietnam and most of Malaysia, Indonesia, and the Philippines have a tropical wet climate. These areas receive abundant rainfall. Parts of Malaysia get an average of about 100 inches of rain per year. In addition, temperatures are very warm, with an average annual temperature of 80°F. However, areas with higher elevation have cooler temperatures.

Much of mainland Southeast Asia has a tropical wet and dry climate that is shaped by monsoons. Remember that **monsoons** are seasonal winds. Monsoons bring dry air during the winter and moist air during the summer. Rainfall brought by the wet monsoon winds is often very heavy. The winds can also cause typhoons. Vietnam experiences about five typhoons each year.

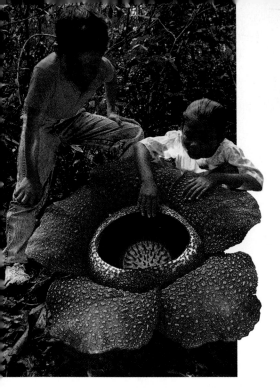

Rafflesia The Rafflesia, which is native to Indonesia, is the world's largest flower. It can grow to be about three feet across.

◀ COMPARING ▶ Regional Rainfall

In the image shown here, Malaysian schoolgirls walk in the rain. As you can see in the graph, Malaysia receives more rain than any other country in Southeast Asia. Compare the amounts of rainfall received by these Southeast Asian cities with that received by Seattle, one of the rainiest cities in the United States.

CRITICAL THINKING
Compare and Contrast
Which three cities receive about the same amount of rainfall?

Average Annual Rainfall

Inches of Rain — Kuala Lumpur, Malaysia; Manila, Philippines; Hanoi, Vietnam; Bangkok, Thailand; Seattle, United States

Source: World Travel Guide Web site

Vegetation and Wildlife Southeast Asia's hot, humid climate supports tropical vegetation. In fact, Southeast Asia has one of the greatest varieties of vegetation on Earth. For example, it has a remarkable number of tree species. Tropical evergreen forests are situated in areas with much rainfall near the equator. Deciduous forests are common in the wet and dry climate zone. Teak, a wood used in shipbuilding and furniture, comes from these forests. Some unusual plants thrive in Southeast Asia. Many of these plants have strong-smelling flowers and fruits.

Sumatran Rhinoceros
This small species of rhino has two horns and a coat of coarse hair. Most of these rhinos live in remote mountain areas of Indonesia.

Southeast Asia also has thousands of varieties of birds and animals, and new species are still being discovered. In 2005, scientists found dozens of new plant and animal species in an isolated forest area of Indonesia. Not even people from nearby villages had ever visited the area. In addition, Southeast Asia is home to such large animals as the rhinoceros, tiger, and elephant. The orangutan is native to Indonesia and Malaysia.

▲ **EVALUATE** Explain how Southeast Asia's climate affects its vegetation and wildlife.

Section 1 Assessment

ONLINE QUIZ
For test practice, go to
Interactive Review
@ ClassZone.com

TERMS & NAMES

1. Explain the importance of
- Indochinese Peninsula
- Malay Peninsula
- Mekong River
- archipelago

USE YOUR READING NOTES

2. Find Main Ideas Use your completed chart to answer the following question:

Which Southeast Asian subregion receives more rainfall, the mainland or the islands?

	MAINLAND	ISLANDS
Geographic Features		
Climate		
Plants and Animals		

KEY IDEAS

3. Why are earthquakes and volcanic eruptions common in Southeast Asia?

4. Why is the Mekong an important river?

5. How do monsoons affect the climate of Southeast Asia?

CRITICAL THINKING

6. Make Inferences Based on the geographic features of Indonesia, what might be some of the major economic activities of this nation?

7. Draw Conclusions Why do you think new species of animals are still being discovered in Southeast Asia?

8. CONNECT to Today What do you think people in Southeast Asia could do to prevent a huge loss of life in the event of another tsunami?

9. TECHNOLOGY Create a Multimedia Presentation Create a multimedia presentation that shows how a volcano in the Ring of Fire forms and erupts. Use library and Internet sources. Include descriptions with your visuals.

▶ Key Ideas

BEFORE, YOU LEARNED

Southeast Asia is made up of mainland countries and island chains.

NOW YOU WILL LEARN

The nations of mainland Southeast Asia have closely connected histories and diverse cultures.

▶ Vocabulary

TERMS & NAMES

Indochina the name for a former French colony in Southeast Asia made up of Cambodia, Laos, and Vietnam

Khmer (kmair) **Empire** an empire that began in the 500s and had gained control of much of mainland Southeast Asia by the 800s

colonialism the control by one power over a dependent area or people

Tet the Vietnamese New Year and most important holiday in Vietnam

Siam the former name of Thailand

constitutional monarchy a government in which the powers of the king or queen are limited by a constitution

Aung San Suu Kyi (awng sahn soo chee) leader of the democracy movement in Myanmar

microstate an independent country that is very small in area and population

Visual Vocabulary celebration of Tet

▶ Reading Strategy

Re-create the web diagram shown at right. As you read and respond to the **KEY QUESTIONS**, use a different copy of the diagram to summarize the history, government, economy, and culture of each mainland country.

 See Skillbuilder Handbook, page R5

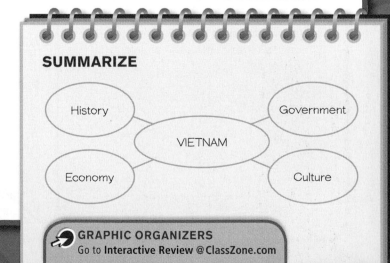

SUMMARIZE

History — VIETNAM — Government
Economy — VIETNAM — Culture

GRAPHIC ORGANIZERS
Go to **Interactive Review** @ ClassZone.com

The Mainland Countries

Connecting to Your World

What have you already learned about the Vietnam War? Maybe you know that the war was fought between Communist and anti-Communist forces in North and South Vietnam. You might also know that the United States got involved in the conflict and that this involvement deeply divided the country. Vietnam is one of the mainland countries of Southeast Asia. In this section, you'll learn about the history and politics of mainland Southeast Asia and some of the causes that led to the Vietnam War.

Cambodia, Laos, and Vietnam

▼ **KEY QUESTION** How are the histories, cultures, and economies of Indochina connected?

Indochina is the name given to a former French colony made up of Cambodia, Laos, and Vietnam. Indochina got its name because of its location east of India and south of China. India and China have also had a strong influence on Indochinese culture. The Mekong River flows through Cambodia, Laos, and Vietnam, forming a highway that connects them. For centuries, this river has been used to transport goods and ideas. Not surprisingly, the histories of these nations are also closely connected.

Angkor Wat This temple in Cambodia was built in the 1100s as a Hindu temple but became a Buddhist temple about 100 years later. **Which two countries probably influenced the temple's religious uses?**

859

Colonies in Southeast Asia 1895

Legend:
- British
- Dutch
- French
- Portuguese
- Spanish
- Independent States

CHINA

Macau • Hong Kong

Tropic of Cancer

40°N

20°N

BURMA

Rangoon •

SIAM

Bangkok •

FRENCH INDOCHINA

Saigon •

South China Sea

Manila •

PACIFIC OCEAN

PHILIPPINES

N

MALAYA

Singapore •

Borneo

Equator

Sumatra

Celebes

Moluccas

0°

INDIAN OCEAN

Batavia •

Java

DUTCH EAST INDIES

DUTCH NEW GUINEA

New Guinea

TIMOR

100°E   120°E   140°E

0   400   800 miles

0   400   800 kilometers

CONNECT Geography & History

1. **Location** What colony was controlled by France?
2. **Region** Which European country could access both the Indian and the Pacific oceans from its colony?

History and Government By the 800s, the **Khmer** (kmair) **Empire** had gained control of much of mainland Southeast Asia. The empire reached its peak around 1200. At different times, the Chinese also exerted political influence over parts of the mainland.

European colonists had been arriving in Southeast Asia since 1509. In the 1850s, France began to take control of Vietnam. The French also seized Laos and Cambodia. They took over the countries' political, economic, and social systems in order to obtain wealth, a policy called **colonialism**. By the 20th century, Europeans had colonized all of Southeast Asia except Siam (now Thailand).

In 1953, Laos and Cambodia gained their independence from France. The following year, a peace agreement ended fighting between Vietnam and France, dividing the country into a Communist north and a non-Communist south. But in 1957, a war between North Vietnam and South Vietnam broke out. In time, the fighting involved the United States and also spilled over into Cambodia and Laos. Finally, in 1975, South Vietnam was taken over by North Vietnam. Both Vietnam and Laos established Communist governments. Cambodia was ruled by a brutal Communist dictator until it became a democracy in 1993.

Culture and Economy More than 80 percent of the people in the three nations of Indochina live in rural areas. The majority of Indochinese practice Buddhism. They celebrate religious holidays as well as other traditional holidays. In Vietnam, the most important holiday is **Tet**, the Vietnamese New Year.

Laos and Cambodia have developing economies made up of small industries, such as clothing and textiles. Most of the people work as rice and peanut farmers. Vietnam, on the other hand, has one of the fastest-growing economies in the world. It is developing its oil industry and exports more coffee than any other country except Brazil.

▲ **EVALUATE** Explain how the histories, cultures, and economies of Indochina are connected.

Thailand

▼ **KEY QUESTION** What events in Thailand's past have helped the country prosper?

Thailand is one of the most prosperous countries in Southeast Asia. For most of its history, it was known as **Siam**. Some scholars believe that the word *Siam* means "golden." The nation changed its name to Thailand in 1949.

History and Government The first people to live in the region of Thailand called themselves the Thai, which means "free." The Thai remained free, even after the Europeans began to arrive in Southeast Asia in the 1500s.

In the mid-1800s, Thai leader King Mongkut began to modernize his country. He and his son, King Chulalongkorn, started schools, built railroads, and abolished slavery in Siam. Through their leaders' guidance, the Siamese people escaped the harsh treatment that many other Southeast Asians experienced under foreign control.

Thailand has been a **constitutional monarchy** since 1932, a government in which the powers of the king or queen are limited by a constitution. Thailand came under the control of Japan in 1941. After World War II, a series of military dictators ruled the country. In the mid-1970s, Thailand began to develop a more democratic government. This process was halted in 2006, however, when the military overthrew the prime minister.

Culture and Economy Most of Thailand's people live in rural areas. In the early 1960s, though, large numbers of Thai began to move to cities in search of work. By 2006, the capital city of Bangkok had over 9 million people.

Thai food, including a noodle dish called pad thai, has become very popular in the United States and other countries. In fact, Thai cuisine ranks as the fourth most popular in the world.

Nearly 50 percent of the workers in Thailand earn a living by farming or fishing. Rice, corn, and sugar cane are some of the crops grown. Thailand's industries produce automobiles, electronic equipment, clothing, and plastics. Tourism is also a booming industry.

▲ **DRAW CONCLUSIONS** Identify the events in Thailand's history that have helped the country prosper.

CONNECT **Geography & History**

Neutral Zone

Siam lay between British-controlled Burma (now Myanmar) and French Indochina. Siamese kings skillfully promoted their country as a neutral zone between the two powers. However, King Chulalongkorn was influenced by European architecture. He had the palace shown here decorated with marble imported from Italy.

Myanmar and Malaysia

▼ **KEY QUESTION** How do Myanmar and Malaysia compare?

Thailand's neighbors, Myanmar and Malaysia, present contrasting pictures. Malaysia has a thriving market economy and freely elected officials. However, Myanmar has widespread poverty and suffers under a military dictatorship.

History and Government In 1044, the Myanmar region united into a kingdom. Its people adopted Buddhism, which arrived from India. Since the main ethnic group of the kingdom was Burman, the region came to be called Burma. During the 1800s, Great Britain colonized Burma. Although Burma won its independence in 1948, it soon came under the control of a military dictator. In 1989, a new military government changed the country's name to Myanmar. A pro-democracy movement led by **Aung San Suu Kyi** (awng sahn soo chee) has struggled against this government ever since.

For hundreds of years, much of Malaysia was known as Melaka. This country was founded around 1400 and was strongly influenced by Arab Muslim traders. In the 1500s, Melaka came under the control of European colonizers and other rulers. Finally, in 1963, the states of Malay, Sabah, Sarawak, and Singapore united to form the Federation of Malaysia. Singapore left this group in 1965. Today, Malaysia is governed by a constitutional monarchy.

Culture and Economy Most of the people of Myanmar live in rural areas, while more than half the population of Malaysia lives in cities. About two-thirds of Myanmar's population are Burmese who practice Buddhism. Malaysia is ethnically much more diverse. About 60 percent of the people are Muslim.

Myanmar's economy is based on agriculture. Rice and teak are important crops. Malaysia, on the other hand, has an industrialized economy. The country produces a wide range of goods, including electronics and automobiles, which it trades on the international market.

▲ **COMPARE AND CONTRAST** Compare and contrast Myanmar and Malaysia.

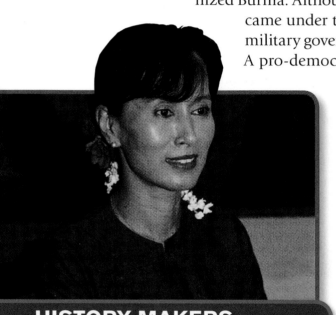

HISTORY MAKERS

Aung San Suu Kyi born 1945

Suu Kyi and other peace activists traveled throughout Myanmar, calling for democratic reforms and free elections. In 1989, after thousands of peaceful demonstrators had been shot and killed, Suu Kyi herself came face to face with an army unit that had been ordered to shoot her. At the last minute, however, an army major stepped in and withdrew the order. In 1991, while under house arrest, Suu Kyi's efforts to establish democracy in her country earned her the Nobel Peace Prize.

ONLINE BIOGRAPHY
For more on the life of Aung San Suu Kyi, go to the
Research & Writing Center @ ClassZone.com

Singapore

▲ **KEY QUESTION** What type of economy and government does Singapore have?

Singapore is a densely populated island nation located at the southern tip of the Malay Peninsula. It is sometimes called a **microstate** because of its very small area—about 225 square miles. Singapore is a wealthy and powerful country. Its industrialized economy depends heavily on its exported goods, including electronics, chemicals, and clothing. In addition, the nation is a major financial center and has many banks and a stock exchange.

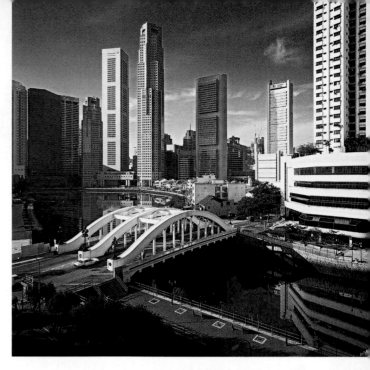

Singapore The Central Area district is the hub of economic activity in Singapore.

Officially, Singapore is a republic, but the government is dominated by one political party. This party limits freedom of speech and controls economic activities. Because Singapore favors order over liberty, the government enforces strict rules on its people. As a result, the country has a clean, corruption-free image throughout the world.

▲ **SUMMARIZE** Describe Singapore's economy and government.

ONLINE QUIZ
For test practice, go to
Interactive Review
@ ClassZone.com

Section ②2 Assessment

TERMS & NAMES

1. Explain the importance of
- Indochina
- Khmer Empire
- Siam
- Aung San Suu Kyi

USE YOUR READING NOTES

2. Summarize Use your completed web diagrams to answer the following question:

Which mainland countries appear to have the strongest economies?

KEY IDEAS

3. How did the war between North Vietnam and South Vietnam affect Indochina?

4. How did Siam avoid colonization?

5. What is the Federation of Malaysia?

CRITICAL THINKING

6. Identify Problems In your opinion, what are the most difficult problems facing the mainland countries of Southeast Asia?

7. Make Inferences What influences might account for the fact that about 60 percent of the population of Malaysia is Muslim?

8. CONNECT to Today How might colonialism have affected the ability of some Southeast Asian countries to establish stable governments and economies?

9. WRITING Write a Feature Article Imagine that you have been assigned to write a feature on the Vietnamese holiday of Tet. Research to find images and information on the holiday's history and traditions.

Reading for Understanding

▶ Key Ideas

BEFORE, YOU LEARNED

The mainland countries of Southeast Asia are a mix of rural and urban cultures and wealthy and poor economies.

NOW YOU WILL LEARN

Indonesia and the Philippines both have rich cultural traditions and long histories as centers of trade.

▶ Vocabulary

TERMS & NAMES

Bahasa Indonesia (bah•HAH•suh in•duh•NEE•zhuh) the language of Indonesia

shadow puppet traditional Indonesian art, in which puppets are handled from behind a screen lit by a bright light

Filipino an inhabitant of the Philippines

Ferdinand Marcos dictatorial president of the Philippines between 1965 and 1986

Corazon Aquino (uh•KEE•noh) politician who opposed Marcos and was president of the Philippines between 1986 and 1992

REVIEW

archipelago a set of closely grouped islands, which sometimes form a curved arc

Visual Vocabulary Ferdinand Marcos

▶ Reading Strategy

Re-create the chart shown at right. As you read and respond to the **KEY QUESTIONS**, use the chart to categorize facts about the history, government, culture, and economy of Indonesia and the Philippines.

 See Skillbuilder Handbook, page R7

CATEGORIZE

	INDONESIA	THE PHILIPPINES
History		
Government		
Culture		
Economy		

GRAPHIC ORGANIZERS
Go to **Interactive Review @ ClassZone.com**

Indonesia and the Philippines

Connecting to Your World

If you wanted to travel to a friend's house, would you try to get there by boat? Probably not. Most Americans journey from one place to another by car, bus, or train. However, on the islands of Southeast Asia, people often travel by boat. As a result, the surrounding seas serve as a sort of highway connecting the islands in this region. The seas, though, have also made it difficult to unify the island nations of Southeast Asia.

Indonesia

▼ **KEY QUESTION** What unites and divides the people of Indonesia?

Indonesia is an **archipelago** that stretches for about 3,200 miles and consists of more than 17,500 islands. As you have already learned, the main islands are Java, Sumatra, and Borneo. Some of the smaller islands are uninhabited, but others are densely populated. Java, for instance, contains about 60 percent of Indonesia's population. Many cities in Indonesia are huge. For example, Jakarta, the country's capital, has more than 8 million people. Indonesia is the fourth most populous country in the world.

Jakarta Jakarta has broad boulevards, but traffic is a problem. To reduce congestion, some roads are only open to vehicles carrying three or more passengers.

History and Government As early as 1000 B.C., the region of Indonesia had become a crossroads for trade. Over the years, many goods and ideas arrived from distant lands. Indian traders brought Hinduism, and traders from both India and China carried Buddhism. By the 1300s, Muslim traders from Arabia had introduced Islam.

During the 1500s, Portugal gained control of present-day Indonesia and set up trade. The Dutch took over in 1641. They established the Dutch East India Company, a group that dominated trade on most of the islands. Indonesia gained independence from the Dutch in 1949 but was controlled by a military regime for many years. Today, Indonesia is a republic. In 2004, it held its first direct presidential elections. The new president pledged to promote democratic reforms.

Culture and Economy Most of the people of Indonesia live in rural areas. The population of the country is one of the most ethnically diverse in the world. About 300 ethnic groups make this island nation their home and speak about 250 different languages. For years, Indonesia lacked a common language. Then in the late 1920s, the nation created a language called **Bahasa Indonesia** that helped unify the people. Cultural traditions also unite Indonesians. Traditional arts include **shadow puppets**, in which puppets, such as those below, are worked from behind a screen lit by a bright light **A**. On the other side of the screen, the audience sees the puppets as shadows **B**.

From 1987 to 1997, Indonesia's economy grew rapidly. Then the nation suffered a financial slump when its money became devalued and its stock market fell. Indonesia's economy is still recovering. Today, oil and natural gas produce the greatest wealth in Indonesia. In fact, it is the world's largest exporter of liquefied natural gas. Manufacturing is also a major activity. Nonetheless, fishing and farming are a huge part of the economy, employing about half of all Indonesians.

🔺 **DRAW CONCLUSIONS** Identify some of the factors that unite and divide Indonesians.

Fun Facts!

SHADOW PUPPETS

The ancient art of shadow puppets is over 1,000 years old and probably originated in India and Egypt. Tiny holes are punched in the flat puppets to cast interesting shadow patterns. In the first image below, a handler works the puppets behind a screen under a bright light. The second image shows what the audience sees on the other side of the screen.

The Philippines

▼ **KEY QUESTION** How has the Philippines improved its government and economy?

The Philippines is made up of around 7,100 islands, but only about 1,000 of them are inhabited. The nation is named for King Philip II of Spain, who sent explorers to the region during the 1500s. The people who live in the Philippines are called **Filipinos**.

History and Government Since ancient times, traders from China and the Malay region have had a strong influence on the culture of the Philippines. By the late 1500s, the Spanish Empire had colonized the Philippines. The Spanish controlled the area until 1898. After being defeated in the Spanish-American War, Spain handed control of the Philippines over to the United States. U.S. rule of the region lasted until 1946, when the Philippines gained its independence.

After independence, however, the country faced many economic problems. In 1965, **Ferdinand Marcos** became president and improved the economy. But in 1973, Marcos seized complete control of the government. **Corazon Aquino** (uh•KEE•noh) opposed Marcos during the 1986 election. Although the government declared that Marcos had won, many people suspected fraud. After much protest, Marcos left the country and Aquino took over as president. Today, the Philippines has a democratic government headed by a president.

ONLINE PRIMARY SOURCE To read more of Aquino's speeches, go to the **Research & Writing Center** @ ClassZone.com

ANALYZING Primary Sources

Corazon Aquino (born 1933) was married to Benigno Aquino, Jr., a political rival of Ferdinand Marcos. When her husband was assassinated in 1983, Aquino suspected that Marcos was behind the death. She ran against Marcos in 1986 and became the first woman president of the Philippines. In the following, Aquino describes her political philosophy.

> I don't have any formula for ousting [overthrowing] a dictator or building democracy. . . . All I can suggest is to forget about yourself and just think of your people. It's always the people who make things happen.

Source: *Time Asia*, August 1999, article by Sandra Burton

DOCUMENT–BASED QUESTION
According to Corazon Aquino, who builds a democracy?

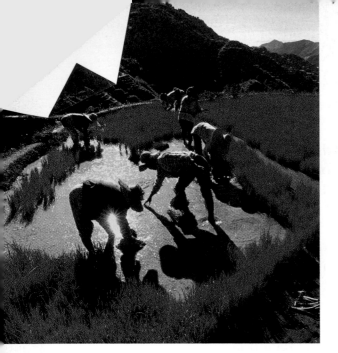

Rice Terraces in Luzon
Farmers first carved rice terraces into the mountains of Luzon about 2,000 years ago. The levels were reinforced with stone walls.

Culture and Economy Filipino culture blends Malay, Chinese, Spanish, and American influences. These influences can be seen in the country's languages and religions. The official languages of the country are Filipino and English. More than 80 percent of the people are Roman Catholic. In fact, the Philippines has more Christians than any other nation in Asia. Christianity was introduced when the Philippines became a Spanish colony. The country also has a large Muslim population. Forty-seven percent of the people live in cities. The largest city is the capital, Manila.

Traditionally, the economy of the Philippines has depended on farming. Over the last few decades, however, manufacturing and mining have developed significantly. Factories produce clothing, electronic goods, and wood products for export. The fertile volcanic soil of the islands helps farmers grow many crops, such as rice, sweet potatoes, bananas, and sugar cane. Kapok trees, which produce a fiber used for insulation and mattresses, are plentiful.

▲ **IDENTIFY SOLUTIONS** Explain how the Philippines has improved its government and economy.

Section **3** Assessment

ONLINE QUIZ
For test practice, go to
Interactive Review
@ ClassZone.com

TERMS & NAMES

1. Explain the importance of
- Bahasa Indonesia
- Filipino
- Ferdinand Marcos
- Corazon Aquino

USE YOUR READING NOTES

2. Categorize Use your completed chart to answer the following question:

What probably accounts for the great ethnic diversity in Indonesia?

	INDONESIA	THE PHILIPPINES
History		
Government		
Culture		
Economy		

KEY IDEAS

3. Why did Indonesia create a new language?

4. What problems did the Philippines face after gaining independence?

5. How did Corazon Aquino come to power?

CRITICAL THINKING

6. Make Inferences How did Corazon Aquino further the development of democracy in the Philippines?

7. Compare and Contrast How are the economies of Indonesia and the Philippines similar and different?

8. CONNECT to Today What do you think the people of Indonesia could do today to become a more united nation?

9. ART Draw a Shadow Puppet Using the Internet and library sources, find pictures of Indonesian shadow puppets. Then draw a shadow puppet of your own. Explain the role the puppet would play in a traditional performance.

Interactive ⟵ Review

Click here to complete these and other activities online @ **ClassZone.com**

CHAPTER SUMMARY

Key Idea 1
Southeast Asia is a mountainous region with a tropical climate and much volcanic activity on its many islands.

Key Idea 2
The nations of mainland Southeast Asia have closely connected histories and diverse cultures.

Key Idea 3
Indonesia and the Philippines both have rich cultural traditions and long histories as centers of trade.

For **Review and Study Notes**, go to Interactive Review @ ClassZone.com

NAME GAME

Use the Terms & Names list to complete each sentence on paper or online.

1. I am a narrow strip of land that serves as a bridge between the mainland and islands.
   Malay Peninsula

2. I was the dictatorial president of the Philippines between 1965 and 1986. _____

3. I am a very large ocean wave caused by an underwater earthquake or volcanic eruption.
   _____

4. I am a region that contains Cambodia, Laos, and Vietnam. _____

5. I had gained control of much of mainland Southeast Asia by the 800s. _____

6. I am the former name of Thailand. _____

7. I am a term for an independent country that is very small in area. _____

8. I am the leader of the pro-democracy movement in Myanmar. _____

9. I am the common language of Indonesia. _____

10. I am a set of closely grouped islands. _____

archipelago
Bahasa Indonesia
Indochina
Indochinese Peninsula
Khmer Empire
Malay Peninsula
Ferdinand Marcos
microstate
Siam
Aung San Suu Kyi
tsunami

Activities

Flip Cards

Use the online flip cards to quiz yourself on the terms and names introduced in this chapter.

Mekong River

Crossword Puzzle

Complete an online crossword puzzle to test your knowledge of the history and culture of Southeast Asia.

ACROSS
1. the most important holiday in Vietnam

VOCABULARY

Explain the significance of each of the following.

1. Indochinese Peninsula
2. Malay Peninsula
3. Mekong River
4. Indochina
5. Khmer Empire
6. Siam
7. Aung San Suu Kyi
8. microstate
9. Bahasa Indonesia
10. Filipino

Explain how the terms and names in each group are related.

11. Indochina, Siam, and colonialism
12. Ferdinand Marcos and Corazon Aquino

KEY IDEAS

1 **Physical Geography of Southeast Asia**

13. Which island nations are located on the Malay Archipelago?
14. What causes a tsunami?
15. Which two types of climate predominate in Southeast Asia?
16. How does the climate in Southeast Asia affect its vegetation?

2 **The Mainland Countries**

17. What historical events have affected all of Indochina?
18. How did King Chulalongkorn modernize Siam?
19. What does Malaysia trade on the international market?
20. In what ways is the government of Singapore powerful?

3 **Indonesia and the Philippines**

21. What religions did traders bring to Indonesia?
22. Where do most of the people of Indonesia live?
23. Why did Ferdinand Marcos leave the Philippines?
24. What cultures have strongly influenced the Philippines?

CRITICAL THINKING

25. **Analyze Causes and Effects** Create a chart to identify the impact in Southeast Asia of colonization, the war between North and South Vietnam, and the Asian tsunami.

CAUSES	EFFECTS
Colonization	
War between North and South Vietnam	
Asian tsunami	

26. **Form Opinions** Why do you think Southeast Asia attracted so many colonists?
27. **Make Inferences** Why do you think Aung San Suu Kyi is considered a hero throughout much of the world?
28. **Draw Conclusions** How are Spanish and American influences reflected in Filipino culture?
29. **Five Themes: Location** How has Singapore's location benefited its economy?
30. **Connect Geography & Culture** Why do you think the tourism industry is booming in Thailand?

Answer the
ESSENTIAL QUESTION

How can Southeast Asian nations establish stable governments and economies?

Written Response Write a two- or three-paragraph response to the Essential Question. Use the rubric below to guide your thinking.

Response Rubric
A strong response will:

- describe the governments and economies of the Southeast Asian nations today
- discuss the problems the nations have faced in the past
- detail the steps the nations are taking to improve their governments and economies

STANDARDS-BASED ASSESSMENT

✓ **Test Practice**
• Online Test Practice @ ClassZone.com
• Test-Taking Strategies and Practice at the front of this book

THEMATIC MAP

Use the map to answer questions 1 and 2 on your paper.

Major Religions of Southeast Asia

Legend:
- Buddhism
- Protestant
- Roman Catholic
- Sunni Muslim
- Traditional

1. What Is the predominant religion of mainland Southeast Asia?

A. Roman Catholic   C. Traditional
B. Buddhism   D. Sunni Muslim

2. Which country has the largest population of Sunni Muslims?

A. the Philippines   C. Indonesia
B. Cambodia   D. Thailand

BAR GRAPH

Examine the bar graph below. Use the graph to answer questions 3 and 4 on your paper.

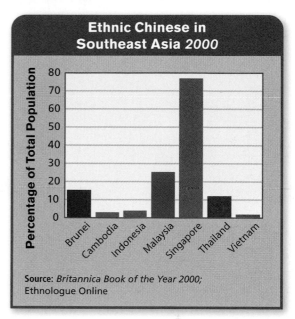

Ethnic Chinese in Southeast Asia 2000

Source: *Britannica Book of the Year 2000;* Ethnologue Online

3. Which Southeast Asian nation has the highest percentage of ethnic Chinese?

A. Singapore   C. Indonesia
B. Malaysia   D. Thailand

4. What percentage of Vietnam's population is made up of ethnic Chinese?

A. 77.0   C. 12.1
B. 15.4   D. 1.5

GeoActivity

1. INTERDISCIPLINARY ACTIVITY–SCIENCE

With a small group, prepare a poster on tsunamis. Research to find information on the size and speed of the waves, how they are formed, and possible warning systems. Use pictures and diagrams to illustrate the information.

2. WRITING FOR SOCIAL STUDIES

Unit Writing Project Revisit your country slide show. To further convince your family to go to the country, write a detailed description of a place that best represents it. For Cambodia, for instance, you might write about Angkor Wat.

3. MENTAL MAPPING

Create an outline map of Southeast Asia and label the following:

- Pacific Ocean
- Mekong River
- Indochinese Peninsula
- Indochina
- Malay Peninsula
- Malay Archipelago
- Indonesia
- the Philippines

UNIT 9

Oceania and Antarctica

Why It Matters:

As modern technology shrinks our world, the people of the lands of Oceania have become much closer neighbors. Their lands include resources important to world trade. Their unique cultures add to the diversity of our world.

Two friends in Western Australia

CHAPTER 29 Australia and New Zealand

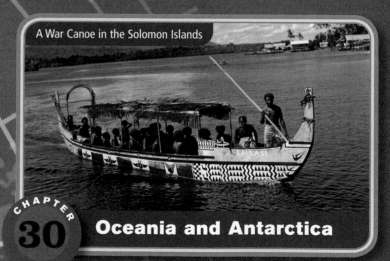

A War Canoe in the Solomon Islands

CHAPTER 30 Oceania and Antarctica

◀ Meet Mick

In this unit, you will meet Mick, a middle-school boy from the Outback in Australia. Learn more about him on **Worldster** @ ClassZone.com

Oceania and Antarctica

Use the Unit Atlas to learn about the geography of Oceania and Antarctica. As you study the maps in the atlas, notice geographic patterns and specific details about the two regions. Answer the questions on each map in your notebook.

As you study the graphs on this page, compare the landmass, population, islands, and volcanoes of Oceania and Antarctica with those of the United States. Then jot down the answers to the following questions in your notebook.

Comparing Data

1. How does the landmass of Oceania compare with that of the United States?

2. How much larger is the population of the United States than that of Oceania?

3. How does the South Island of New Zealand compare with the world's largest island?

4. How does the number of active volcanoes for this entire region compare to the United States?

Comparing Data

Landmass

Oceania
3,275,375 sq. mi.

Continental United States
3,165,630 sq. mi.

Antarctica
5,405,430 sq. mi.

Population

Oceania and Antarctica
31,377,000

United States
296,410,404

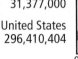

| 0 | 50 | 100 | 150 | 200 | 250 | 300 |

Population (in millions)

Islands

World's Largest
Greenland
839,999 sq. mi.

U.S. Largest
Hawaii
4,021 sq. mi.

New Guinea
341,631 sq. mi.

South Island, New Zealand
58,439 sq. mi.

Tasmania
26,383 sq. mi.

Volcanoes

Oceania   130
United States   156
Antarctica   31
Australia and New Zealand   19

| 0 | 30 | 60 | 90 | 120 | 150 |

Number of Active Volcanoes

Population Density

120°E   140°E   160°E   180°   160°W   140°W

40°N

JAPAN

CHINA

PACIFIC OCEAN

MIDWAY IS. (U.S.)

Tropic of Cancer

20°N

PHILIPPINES

NORTHERN MARIANA IS. (U.S.)

GUAM (U.S.)

WAKE I. (U.S.)

MARSHALL ISLANDS

HAWAII (U.S.)

JOHNSTON ATOLL (U.S.)

PALAU

FEDERATED STATES OF MICRONESIA

Equator   0°

INDONESIA

PAPUA NEW GUINEA

NAURU

SOLOMON ISLANDS

KIRIBATI

TUVALU

TOKELAU (N.Z.)

VANUATU

WALLIS AND FUTUNA (Fr.)

SAMOA

AMERICAN SAMOA (U.S.)

COOK ISLANDS (N.Z.)

FRENCH POLYNESIA (Fr.)

Darwin

NEW CALEDONIA (Fr.)

FIJI

TONGA

NIUE (N.Z.)

20°S

Tropic of Capricorn
AUSTRALIA

PITCAIRN IS. (U.K.)

Perth

Brisbane

Adelaide

Sydney

Melbourne

Canberra

Persons per square mile

Over 520	
260–519	
130–259	
25–129	
1–24	
0	

INDIAN OCEAN

Auckland
NEW ZEALAND

Wellington

Christchurch

40°S

0   500   1,000 miles
0   500   1,000 kilometers

SOUTHERN OCEAN

THINK LIKE A GEOGRAPHER

1. **Place** Which island group is most densely populated?

2. **Human-Environment Interaction** How would you describe the population density pattern of Australia?

PACIFIC OCEAN

Tropic of Cancer

MIDWAY IS. (U.S.)

WAKE I. (U.S.)

HAWAII (U.S.) — 20°N

CHINA

JAPAN

PHILIPPINES

NORTHERN MARIANA IS. (U.S.)

GUAM (U.S.)

JOHNSTON ATOLL (U.S.)

PALAU

MARSHALL ISLANDS

FEDERATED STATES OF MICRONESIA

Equator — 0°

INDONESIA

PAPUA NEW GUINEA

NAURU

SOLOMON ISLANDS

KIRIBATI

TOKELAU (N.Z.)

TUVALU

SAMOA

FRENCH POLYNESIA (Fr.)

WALLIS AND FUTUNA (Fr.)

AMERICAN SAMOA (U.S.)

COOK ISLANDS (N.Z.)

VANUATU

NEW CALEDONIA (Fr.)

FIJI

TONGA

NIUE (N.Z.)

20°S

PITCAIRN IS. (U.K.)

Tropic of Capricorn

AUSTRALIA

INDIAN OCEAN

NEW ZEALAND

0   500   1,000 miles
0   500   1,000 kilometers

Legend

Tropical
- Tropical wet
- Tropical wet and dry

Dry
- Desert
- Semiarid

Mid-Latitude
- Mediterranean
- Marine west coast
- Humid subtropical

High Latitude
- Tundra
- Icecap
- Highland

60°W ATLANTIC OCEAN

30°W   0°   30°E

60°W

60°E

SOUTHERN OCEAN

ANTARCTICA

90°W

90°E

Antarctic Circle

80°S

70°S

60°S

120°E

180°   150°E

SOUTHERN OCEAN

60°S

0   500   1,000 miles
0   500   1,000 kilometers

THINK LIKE A GEOGRAPHER

1. **Region** Which climate do Australia and New Zealand have in common?

2. **Region** What is Australia's smallest climate region?

3. **Region** Which climate region occupies the greatest area of Australia?

Economic Activity

120°E 140°E 160°E 180°

JAPAN

CHINA

PACIFIC OCEAN

MIDWAY IS. (U.S.)

Tropic of Cancer

HAWAII (U.S.) 20°N

PHILIPPINES

NORTHERN MARIANA IS. (U.S.)

WAKE I. (U.S.)

JOHNSTON ATOLL (U.S.)

GUAM (U.S.)

MARSHALL ISLANDS

PALAU

FEDERATED STATES OF MICRONESIA

Equator 0°

PAPUA NEW GUINEA

NAURU

KIRIBATI

INDONESIA

SOLOMON ISLANDS

TUVALU

TOKELAU (N.Z.)

FRENCH POLYNESIA (Fr.)

WALLIS AND FUTUNA (Fr.)

SAMOA

AMERICAN SAMOA (U.S.)

COOK ISLANDS (N.Z.)

VANUATU

NEW CALEDONIA (Fr.)

FIJI

TONGA

NIUE (N.Z.)

20°S

PITCAIRN IS. (U.K.)

Tropic of Capricorn

AUSTRALIA

Sydney

Auckland

NEW ZEALAND

40°S

INDIAN OCEAN

Sn

0 500 1,000 miles
0 500 1,000 kilometers

Land use

	Commercial agriculture
	Livestock raising
	Dairying
	Subsistence agriculture
	Forestland
	Limited agriculture
●	Major manufacturing center

Major resources

	Bauxite		Natural gas
	Coal		Oil
	Copper		Silver
	Diamonds		Timber
	Fish	Sn	Tin
	Gold		Other minerals
	Iron ore		

THINK LIKE A GEOGRAPHER

1. **Human-Environment Interaction**
   Which of the economic activities occupies the most land in Australia and New Zealand?

2. **Place** In which nations is commercial fishing important?

3. **Place** What resources are found in the nation of Papua New Guinea?

Oceania and Antarctica

This region contains two continents and thousands of islands spread across hundreds of thousands of square miles of the Pacific Ocean. Until recently the area was considered distant and remote. But with electronic devices and fast transportation, even remote lands have been integrated into the world at large.

GEOGRAPHY

This region contains a wide range of physical geography. Australia is a vast dry land, while New Zealand has active volcanoes and earthquakes. Antarctica is a frozen desert. Thousands of islands in the Pacific are atolls or parts of volcanic cones.

The isolation from the rest of the world led to the development of unique plants and animals in Australia and New Zealand.

Roald Amundsen
This Norwegian explorer was the first to reach the South Pole.

HISTORY

People migrating from eastern Asia populated the lands of this region. They moved across land bridges or the ocean and settled on the islands. Australia and New Zealand and the islands of Oceania were later colonized mostly by European nations.

CULTURE

The cultures of Australia and New Zealand reflect some of the customs of the United Kingdom, which colonized them. However, their cultures also have many aspects unique to their way of life. The people of the islands of Oceania had little contact with the outside world so they developed their own ways. Only recently have these island cultures begun to connect with the outside world.

GOVERNMENT

Many of the countries of this region were colonies of European nations or the United States. Many of them gained their independence after World War II. The governments of the two largest nations, Australia and New Zealand, are linked to the United Kingdom. The governments of most of the nations are democratic.

ECONOMICS

Australia and New Zealand have well developed economies that focus primarily on producing raw materials such as wool, meat, and minerals. These products are traded in the international marketplace. Both Australia and New Zealand, along with the island nations of Oceania, have begun to expand their tourism industries.

Emperor Penguins
Colonies of many types of penguins are found in the Antarctic region.

Country Almanac

Click here to compare the most recent data on countries @ ClassZone.com

Unit Project

Illustrated Time Line

As you read this unit, look for a description of the migration of people across the region. Do research to find information about people settling the lands. Create an illustrated time line showing the arrival of different groups in the subregions and countries of Oceania.

Think About:

- the first people to arrive in the region
- European colonizers

Oceania and Antarctica

Many of the nations in this region are tiny. The smallest nation is Nauru, which covers only 8.2 square miles with about 13,000 people. The region of Oceania, on the other hand, is gigantic— 3,275,375 square miles and 32 million people.

Water Lily Water Lily on an island in Fiji

Australia

GEOGRAPHY
Capital: Canberra
Total Area: 2,967,909 sq. mi.
Population: 20,155,000

ECONOMY
Imports: machinery; chemicals; fuels; food
Exports: fuels; metals; textiles; food

CULTURE
Language: English
Religion: Catholic 27%; Protestant 37%; Orthodox 3%; no religion 16%

Fiji

GEOGRAPHY
Capital: Suva
Total Area: 7,054 sq. mi.
Population: 848,000

ECONOMY
Imports: fuels; machinery; textiles; animals
Exports: clothing; sugar; fish; gold

CULTURE
Language: English; Fijian; Hindustani
Religion: Christian 57%; Hindu 33%; Muslim 7%; nonreligious 1%

Kiribati

GEOGRAPHY
Capital: Tarawa
Total Area: 313 sq. mi.
Population: 103,092

ECONOMY
Imports: food; machinery; fuels
Exports: seaweed; fish; copra

CULTURE
Language: English
Religion: Catholic 55%; Protestant 37%; Mormon 3%; Baha'i 2%

Marshall Islands

GEOGRAPHY
Capital: Majuro
Total Area: 70 sq. mi.
Population: 59,071

ECONOMY
Imports: fuels; machinery; food
Exports: copra; coconut oil; aquarium fish

CULTURE
Language: Marshallese; English
Religion: Protestant 63%; Catholic 7%; Mormon 3%

Federated States of Micronesia

GEOGRAPHY
Capital: Palikir
Total Area: 271 sq. mi.
Population: 110,000

ECONOMY
Imports: food; fuels; machinery; tobacco
Exports: fish; bananas

CULTURE
Language: English; Trukese
Religion: Catholic 53%; Protestant 42%; Mormon 1%

Nauru

GEOGRAPHY
Capital: Yaren District
Total Area: 8 sq. mi.
Population: 13,048

ECONOMY
Imports: agricultural products
Exports: phosphate

CULTURE
Language: Nauruan; English
Religion: Protestant 54%; Catholic 28%

New Zealand

GEOGRAPHY
Capital: Wellington
Total Area: 103,738 sq. mi.
Population: 4,028,000

ECONOMY
Imports: machinery; petroleum; cars
Exports: beef; dairy products; wood

CULTURE
Language: English; Maori
Religion: Protestant 27%; Catholic 13%; no religion 27%

Palau

GEOGRAPHY
Capital: Koror
Total Area: 177 sq. mi.
Population: 20,303

ECONOMY
Imports: machinery; food; fuels; chemicals
Exports: high-grade tuna; clothing

CULTURE
Language: Palauan; English
Religion: Catholic 42%; Protestant & other Christian 30%; Modekngei 9%

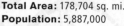

Papua New Guinea

GEOGRAPHY
Capital: Port Moresby
Total Area: 178,704 sq. mi.
Population: 5,887,000

ECONOMY
Imports: petroleum; food; machinery
Exports: gold; petroleum; copper; logs

CULTURE
Language: English; Motu; Tok Pisin
Religion: Protestant 63%; Catholic 30%; traditional beliefs 4%; Baha'i 1%

Samoa

GEOGRAPHY
Capital: Apia
Total Area: 1,137 sq. mi.
Population: 185,000

ECONOMY
Imports: petroleum; machinery
Exports: fish; clothing; coconut products

CULTURE
Language: Samoan; English
Religion: Protestant 57%; Mormon 26%; Catholic 21%

Solomon Islands

GEOGRAPHY
Capital: Honiara
Total Area: 10,985 sq. mi.
Population: 478,000

ECONOMY
Imports: food; petroleum; machinery
Exports: timber; fish; cacao beans

CULTURE
Language: English
Religion: Protestant 74%; Catholic 11%; traditional beliefs 3%

Tonga

GEOGRAPHY
Capital: Nuku'alofa
Total Area: 289 sq. mi.
Population: 102,000

ECONOMY
Imports: food; fuels; machinery
Exports: squash; fish; vanilla beans

CULTURE
Language: Tongan; English
Religion: Free Wesleyan 41%; Catholic 16%; Mormon 14%

Tuvalu

GEOGRAPHY
Capital: Funafuti
Total Area: 10 sq. mi.
Population: 11,636

ECONOMY
Imports: food; fuels; machinery; metals
Exports: copra; stamps; handicrafts

CULTURE
Language: Tuvalan; English; Samoan
Religion: Church of Tuvalu 85%; Seventh-day Adventist 4%; Catholic 1%

Vanuatu

GEOGRAPHY
Capital: Port-Vila
Total Area: 4,710 sq. mi.
Population: 211,000

ECONOMY
Imports: machinery; food; chemicals; fuels
Exports: coconut oil; timber; beef; kava

CULTURE
Language: Bislama; French; English
Religion: Protestant 54%; Catholic 16%; traditional beliefs 4%; Baha'i 3%

Outrigger canoe The lands of Oceania were settled by people who came there in oceangoing outrigger canoes.

Australia and New Zealand

 ESSENTIAL QUESTION

How has the human geography of Australia and New Zealand changed since European settlement?

CONNECT **Geography & History**

Use the map and the time line to answer the following questions.

1. Which body of water did Captain Cook cross to get from Australia to New Zealand?

2. What is the approximate location in latitude and longitude of the 2000 Olympic Games?

Culture

◀ **40,000 B.C.** Australia is gradually settled by aboriginal people. (Aboriginal art—Iguana painted on tree bark)

40,000 B.C.

Geography
1000 A.D. The Maori migrate to New Zealand from Polynesia.

Geography
1769–1770 Captain James Cook explores New Zealand and Australia for Great Britain. ▶

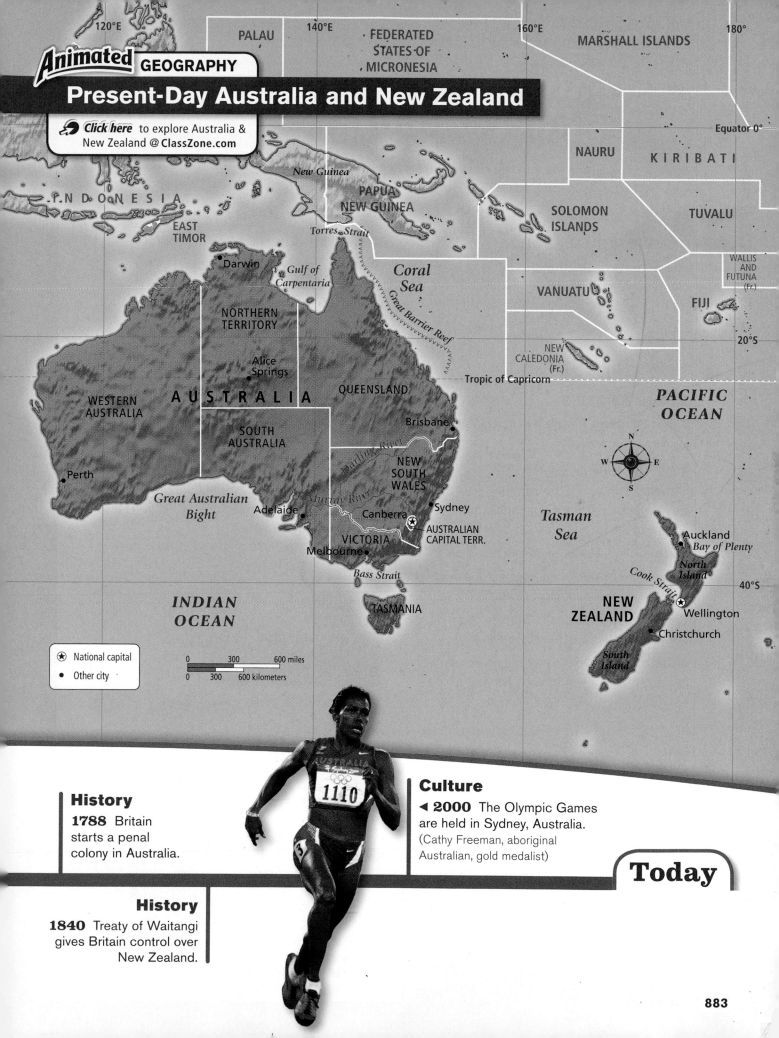

120°E   140°E   160°E   180°

PALAU   FEDERATED STATES OF MICRONESIA   MARSHALL ISLANDS

Equator 0°

New Guinea   NAURU   KIRIBATI

INDONESIA

EAST TIMOR   PAPUA NEW GUINEA   SOLOMON ISLANDS   TUVALU

Torres Strait   WALLIS AND FUTUNA (Fr.)

Darwin   Gulf of Carpentaria   Coral Sea   VANUATU   FIJI   20°S

NORTHERN TERRITORY   Great Barrier Reef   NEW CALEDONIA (Fr.)

Alice Springs   Tropic of Capricorn

WESTERN AUSTRALIA   A U S T R A L I A   QUEENSLAND   PACIFIC OCEAN

SOUTH AUSTRALIA   Brisbane

Perth   Darling River   NEW SOUTH WALES

Great Australian Bight   Adelaide   Murray River   Canberra   Sydney

VICTORIA   AUSTRALIAN CAPITAL TERR.   Tasman Sea   Auckland   Bay of Plenty

Melbourne   North Island

Bass Strait   Cook Strait   40°S

INDIAN OCEAN   TASMANIA   NEW ZEALAND   Wellington

Christchurch

South Island

★ National capital
• Other city

0   300   600 miles
0   300   600 kilometers

History
1788 Britain starts a penal colony in Australia.

History
1840 Treaty of Waitangi gives Britain control over New Zealand.

Culture
◀ **2000** The Olympic Games are held in Sydney, Australia. (Cathy Freeman, aboriginal Australian, gold medalist)

Today

Reading for Understanding

▶ Key Ideas

BEFORE, YOU LEARNED

The nations of Southeast Asia face challenges with diverse cultures and with developing economies.

NOW YOU WILL LEARN

Australia and New Zealand have plant and animal life found nowhere else on Earth.

▶ Vocabulary

TERMS & NAMES

Great Dividing Range a range of low mountains in Australia

Southern Alps a mountain chain in New Zealand

geyser (GY•zuhr) a hot spring that shoots sprays of steam and boiling water into the air

Outback the interior region of Australia

Uluru (oo•LOO•roo) a spectacular rock out-cropping in the Australian Outback

Great Barrier Reef a 1,250-mile chain of coral reefs off the coast of Australia

marsupial (mahr•SOO•pee•uhl) an animal with an abdominal pouch to carry its young

BACKGROUND VOCABULARY

outcropping bedrock that rises above the soil

draft animal an animal used to pull a heavy load

Visual Vocabulary geyser

▶ Reading Strategy

Re-create the web diagram shown at right. As you read and respond to the **KEY QUESTIONS**, use the diagram to categorize important details about the physical geography of Australia and New Zealand.

 See Skillbuilder Handbook, page R7

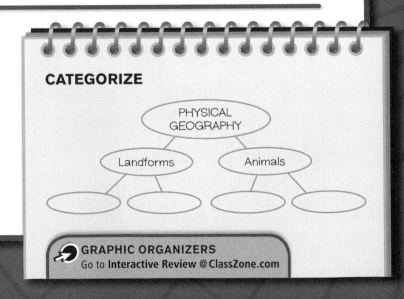

CATEGORIZE

PHYSICAL GEOGRAPHY

Landforms   Animals

GRAPHIC ORGANIZERS
Go to **Interactive Review** @ ClassZone.com

Unique Lands

Connecting to Your World

In some ways, the first explorations of Australia and New Zealand by Europeans were like the first explorations of the moon. The explorers and astronauts had to cross enormous distances to their destinations and knew little about actual conditions in the unknown lands. The early European explorers in Australia found a land very different from their native countries of England and the Netherlands. Australia was a vast, dry region inhabited by many exotic creatures. Think about how strange it would be to encounter kangaroos, if you had never seen one before!

Landforms

A girl and a wallaby

▼ **KEY QUESTION** What are the landscapes of Australia and New Zealand like?

Australia is the world's smallest continent. Geographically, the continent consists of the island of Australia, the islands of New Zealand, Papua New Guinea, and several nearby islands. Australia is located about 7,000 miles southwest of North America. The continent of Australia is completely in the Southern Hemisphere. In fact, the continent is so far away from the other inhabited continents that it has developed some characteristics not found anywhere else in the world.

Uluru This enormous sandstone rock in the middle of the Australian desert is 5 miles around, and more than 1,100 feet high.

AUSTRALIA

● Uluru
(Ayers Rock)

A Geyser Erupts New Zealand's location on the Ring of Fire makes geysers a part of the landscape. **What other physical features are found on the Ring of Fire?**

A Silvertip Shark Patrols the Great Barrier Reef Among many thousands of species of fish and animals found on or around the reef, the shark is one of the largest.

Mountains and Coastlands Australia has few highland areas and only one range of low mountains called the **Great Dividing Range** Ⓐ. This range lies on the eastern side of the continent. The area east of the range is quite hilly. See the map on the opposite page.

New Zealand consists of two main islands—North Island and South Island—and several smaller islands. Located on the volcanic Ring of Fire, much of the country is covered by mountains and hills. A mountain chain, the **Southern Alps** Ⓑ, runs down the middle of South Island. Seventeen peaks in this chain rise higher than 10,000 feet. Hundreds of rivers flow into narrow, deep-sided inlets created by melting glaciers. North Island has dense forests, active volcanoes, and many hot springs. Some hot springs called **geysers** (GY•zuhrz) shoot sprays of steam and boiling water into the air.

Deserts and Flatlands One-third of Australia is a low-lying desert region. The Great Dividing Range blocks moisture-bearing winds, making the interior dry. Australia has four major deserts, which range from sand to gravel and rock. Australians call the entire isolated region the **Outback**. Within the Outback is an immense rock **outcropping** called **Uluru** (oo•LOO•roo) Ⓒ, also called Ayers Rock. This enormous piece of red sandstone is 1.5 miles wide, 2.2 miles long, and rises more that 1,100 feet above the desert floor. Uluru is sacred to Australian native peoples.

The Great Barrier Reef One of Australia's most spectacular physical features is the **Great Barrier Reef** Ⓓ. The reef is located off the northeast coast of Australia and is a 1,250-mile chain of about 2,900 coral reefs formed by about 400 species of coral. Thousands of species of fish, mollusks, and sponges, as well as endangered green and loggerhead turtles, inhabit the reefs. Humpback whales also come to the reef's warm waters to bear their young. You can learn more about the reef in Animated Geography at the end of this section.

▲ **COMPARE AND CONTRAST** Describe the landscapes of Australia and New Zealand.

Physical Geography of Australia & New Zealand

20°N

PALAU

FEDERATED STATES OF MICRONESIA

MARSHALL ISLANDS

Equator 0°

NAURU

KIRIBATI

New Guinea

PAPUA NEW GUINEA

SOLOMON ISLANDS

TUVALU

I N D O N E S I A

EAST TIMOR

Arafura Sea

Torres Strait

Coral Sea

D

VANUATU

FIJI

Timor Sea

Gulf of Carpentaria

Great Barrier Reef

20°S

Kimberly Plateau

NEW CALEDONIA (Fr.)

Tropic of Capricorn

Great Sandy Desert

C

Great Dividing Range

A

PACIFIC OCEAN

Uluru (Ayers Rock)

Simpson Desert

Great

AUSTRALIA

Artesian

Great Victoria Desert

Basin

Darling River

Great Dividing Range

Tasman Sea

Bay of Plenty

North Island

Cook Strait

Great Australian Bight

Murray River

Australian Alps

Mt. Kosciusko 7,310 ft. (2,228 m.)

Bass Strait

Tasmania

NEW ZEALAND

40°S

INDIAN OCEAN

Southern Alps

B

South Island

0   300   600 miles
0   300   600 kilometers

CONNECT Geography & Culture
READING A PHYSICAL MAP

Study the elevation legend on the map. As you study the map,

- find the three desert areas in Australia and look at their elevation
- compare the desert elevations with that of the Great Dividing Range

Place How would you describe the elevation of Australia's deserts?

Elevation

13,100 ft. (4,000 m)
6,600 ft. (2,000 m)
3,280 ft. (1,000 m)
650 ft. (200 m)
0 ft. (0 m)
Below sea level

▲ Mountain peak

Australia is home to marsupials, a unique class of animals that carry their young in pouches. There are about 125 species of these animals. They range in size from a mouse, to an average-sized dog, to kangaroos that can reach a height of five feet.

Koala

Wallaby

Wombat

Kangaroo

Activity

Make an Illustrated Book

Materials
• animal books
• paper
• markers

1. Study the animal books or use the Internet to gather information about marsupials.

2. Plan your booklet to include pictures and information about 3 or 4 animals.

3. Draw pictures and write out the information.

4. Bind the book together.

Australia's Animals

▼ **KEY QUESTION** What types of animals are found only in Australia and New Zealand?

Australia and New Zealand separated from the rest of the Earth's landmasses millions of years ago. Their isolation from other continents allowed plants and animals there to develop differently. For example, Australia has **marsupials** (mahr•SOO•pee•uhlz), animals with abdominal pouches to carry their young. Many of these marsupials, such as the kangaroo, are not found elsewhere.

Native Animals Australia's marsupials are not its only interesting native animals. Two species of mammals that hatch their young from eggs, the platypus (PLAT•ih•puhs) and the echidna (ih•KIHD•nuh), are found there. Two flightless birds—the emu and the cassowary—are also native to Australia. The most famous Australian bird is the kookaburra. An Australian folk song celebrating the kookaburra is known around the world.

Except for two species of bats, New Zealand has no native mammals. Almost all other species were brought there. New Zealand's many native birds include the kiwi, the only bird in the world with nostrils on the tip of its bill. In fact, New Zealanders' slang term for themselves is "kiwi."

Non-Native Animals Over the years, many animals were brought to Australia and New Zealand. Geographers believe that the dingo, a doglike, meat-eating animal, probably came to Australia with the earliest settlers at least 3,500 years ago. More recent imports to both Australia and New Zealand are sheep, goats, cattle, and pigs. They were brought to establish farming and ranching operations.

Perhaps the most dramatic story of non-native animals concerns rabbits in Australia. In 1859, Thomas Austin released 24 rabbits into Australia so that he could hunt them. The rabbit population exploded because rabbits had few natural enemies. By 1900, Australia had more than a billion rabbits! The Australian government built a 2,000-mile fence to keep the rabbits from spreading. Rabbits destroyed crops and competed with grazing animals for grasslands. They are still a problem today, in spite of efforts to keep them under control.

 SUMMARIZE Identify unique animals of Australia and New Zealand.

CONNECT Geography & Culture

Australia's Camels

Camels were introduced into Australia by explorers who used them to travel its deserts. Later, camels became farm animals. They also were used in construction projects as **draft animals**, animals used to pull heavy loads. When machines replaced camels, they were released into Australia's semiarid lands. Today, there are free-range camel herds in the Outback.

ONLINE QUIZ
For test practice, go to **Interactive Review** @ ClassZone.com

Section 1 Assessment

TERMS & NAMES

1. Explain the importance of
- Great Dividing Range
- Southern Alps
- Outback
- Great Barrier Reef

USE YOUR READING NOTES

2. Categorize Use your completed web diagram to answer the following question:

What physical features are found in New Zealand?

PHYSICAL GEOGRAPHY

Landforms   Animals

KEY IDEAS

3. What is the Australian Outback?

4. What are the two main islands of New Zealand?

5. Why did unique animal species develop in Australia and New Zealand?

CRITICAL THINKING

6. Find Main Ideas What is one of the many differences between the physical landscapes of Australia and New Zealand?

7. Analyze Causes and Effects What geographical factor accounted for the early isolation of Australia and New Zealand?

8. CONNECT to Today Why might governments want to limit the importation of non-native animals?

9. SCIENCE Draw a Species Map Research the plants and animals native to your state. Create an illustrated map showing five or six of these native species.

Click here to dive into the Great Barrier Reef
@ ClassZone.com

THE GREAT BARRIER REEF

The Great Barrier Reef is the grand-est of all the coral reefs found in the ocean. Chains of coral reefs stretch 1,250 miles off the coast of Australia. The reef is home to thousands of species of plants and animals.

 Click here to learn about sea life that has been around for 400 million years.

 Click here Learn how the skeletons of millions of tiny animals and plants build a reef.

 Click here to learn why the Great Barrier Reef is a World Heritage Area.

Map of Reef

Great Barrier Reef

Cairns

Townsville

AUSTRALIA

PACIFIC OCEAN

N

GeoActivity

Design a Conservation Poster Research the environmental threats to the Great Barrier Reef. Design a poster that encourages people to take care of the reef and avoid harmful practices.

Reading for Understanding

▶ Key Ideas

BEFORE, YOU LEARNED

Australia is home to unique animals and physical features.

NOW YOU WILL LEARN

Australia's history, culture, and economic life have been shaped by both aborigines and European immigrants.

▶ Vocabulary

TERMS & NAMES

James Cook a British explorer who claimed land in Australia

aborigine (ab•uh•RIHJ•uh•nee) an original inhabitant of Australia

penal colony a settlement that serves as a prison

Charles Perkins an aboriginal rights leader

BACKGROUND VOCABULARY

mechanized equipped with machines

REVIEW

hunter-gatherer a person who hunts animals and gathers plants for food

constitutional monarchy a government in which the powers of the king or queen are limited by a constitution

Visual Vocabulary Charles Perkins and aborigines

▶ Reading Strategy

Re-create the web diagram shown at right. As you read and respond to the **KEY QUESTIONS**, use the diagram to record main ideas and details about the history, culture, and economy of Australia.

 Skillbuilder Handbook, page R4

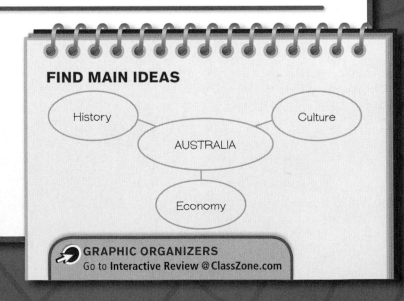

FIND MAIN IDEAS

History

Culture

AUSTRALIA

Economy

⚡ **GRAPHIC ORGANIZERS**
Go to **Interactive Review @ ClassZone.com**

Australia

Connecting to Your World

Did you know that Australia is called "The Land Down Under"? It lies completely in the Southern Hemisphere. Its seasons are reversed from those in the Northern Hemisphere. So, people there go to the beach from December through March and often celebrate New Year's Day with a backyard barbecue. Now you will learn how similar and how different Australia is from North America.

History and Government

▼ **KEY QUESTION** How did the arrival of British settlers change life in Australia?

Early European explorers believed there was a "great southern land" somewhere in the vast area of the Pacific and Indian Oceans. In the 1600s, explorers investigated the west, southwest, and northwest coasts of Australia but found it a dry desert, worth little. Then in 1770, British sea captain **James Cook** claimed the fertile east coast for Britain. The European explorers were not the first people to arrive in this southern land. Peoples from Southeast Asia had migrated there across water and by a land bridge at least 40,000 years before.

Aboriginal Art
This modern wall mural is based on traditional aboriginal styles of painting.

Aborigines: The First Settlers The British called the first settlers of Australia **aborigines** (ab•uh•RIHJ•uh•neez), meaning "original inhabitants." They were **hunter-gatherers**, who spread across the vast island continent to hunt animals and gather plants for food. They lived in distinct groups that had their own languages. When European colonists arrived, over 300,000 aborigines lived on the continent.

British Colony In 1786, Britain established a **penal colony**, or prison settlement, in this remote land. Men and women who had been imprisoned in England were transported by ship to Australia. The first group arrived in 1788, complete with guards and their families. Over the years, a total of about 160,000 came.

In 1790, the British government began to offer land grants to settlers, army officers, and even freed convicts to help populate the land. Four colonies were set up along the coasts and one on the island of Tasmania. In 1851, gold was discovered. Thousands of people from around the world flocked to Australia, and the population tripled. Clashes broke out between aborigines and settlers over the ownership of land. Many aborigines were killed or driven into the Outback. In the later part of the 20th century, **Charles Perkins**, an aborigine himself, led the fight for aboriginal rights. Aborigines continue to struggle to regain lands taken from them by later immigrants.

Independent Nation In 1901, Australia gained independence from Britain. The six colonies merged into a single government. Australia is a **constitutional monarchy**, a government in which the authority of the monarch is limited by a constitution. The monarch of the United Kingdom is Australia's monarch, but the monarch has little to do with running the government. An appointed governor general represents the monarch. The prime minister heads Australia's parliamentary-style government. The political party that wins the most seats in the two-house federal parliament selects the prime minister. All Australians 18 years of age and older are required to vote.

▲ **SUMMARIZE** Explain how the arrival of Europeans changed Australia.

HISTORY MAKERS

Charles Perkins 1936–2000

Charles Perkins, an important aboriginal leader, has been compared to U.S. civil rights leader Dr. Martin Luther King, Jr. Both of them worked for the rights of their people, and both led protests against racial discrimination.

Perkins was born on a reservation in the Outback and was sent away to school at age ten. There, he saw firsthand the unfair treatment of the aborigines. He was one of the first of his ethnic group to graduate from college. In 1984, Perkins became head of the Department of Aboriginal Affairs, the first aborigine to head a government department.

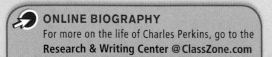

ONLINE BIOGRAPHY
For more on the life of Charles Perkins, go to the
Research & Writing Center @ ClassZone.com

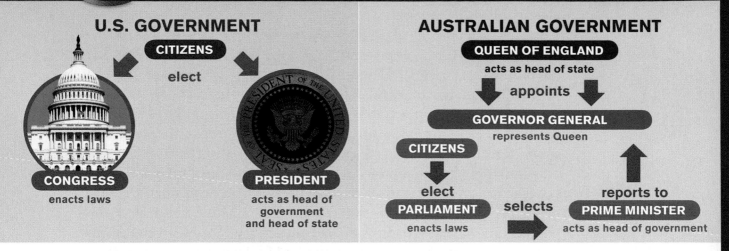

COMPARING Governments

U.S. GOVERNMENT

CITIZENS
elect

CONGRESS
enacts laws

PRESIDENT
acts as head of
government
and head of state

AUSTRALIAN GOVERNMENT

QUEEN OF ENGLAND
acts as head of state
appoints

GOVERNOR GENERAL
represents Queen

CITIZENS
elect

PARLIAMENT
enacts laws

selects

reports to
PRIME MINISTER
acts as head of government

CRITICAL THINKING
Compare and Contrast How does the Prime Minister's role differ from that of the U.S. president?

Aussie Culture

🔻 **KEY QUESTION** What makes Australian culture unique?

Australia's distinctive culture has mainly been influenced by its earliest inhabitants, the aborigines, and its British settlers. Australia's isolation and its unusual plants and animals have also helped to develop a distinctive "Aussie" culture.

Aboriginal Heritage Each aborigine group had traditional lands that were defined by mountains, rivers, or lakes. Aborigines believe there is a close connection between people and the land, plants, and animals. This special relationship with the land forms the basis of their spiritual life. It helps them to understand and care for their environment.

Aboriginal people describe the creation of their land in a series of traditional stories known as "dreamtime" stories. The stories explain the lives of their ancestors and also the aborigines' relationship to the land. Often, the stories are linked to sacred sites, such as Uluru. Today, about 2 percent of the population is aborigine.

Modern Australia Australia is home to immigrants from many parts of the world. Most of these immigrant groups have only come since the end of World War II. About 20 percent of all Australians were born in other countries. However, Australia's early settlement was by immigrants who came from British Isles. Many elements of Australian culture are similar to the cultures of those countries. For example, English is the official language, and about 70 percent of the people are Christians.

About 85 percent of all Australians live in cities located in the southeastern quarter of the country. Sydney, Melbourne, and Brisbane are on the east coast. The capital, Canberra, is further inland. The rest of Australia is lightly populated, with most of the population living in coastal areas. Unlike cities in other countries you have studied, Australian cities have few apartment buildings. Most people live in single-family homes with small gardens.

The language spoken in Australia is English, but it has a unique vocabulary unfamiliar to those who do not live there. The language developed because the settlers had to describe unfamiliar animals and plants and unusual situations. Sometimes the settlers borrowed words from the aborigines, such as *kangaroo* and *koala*. Other words, such as *brumbies* for wild horses and *outback*, were invented by the settlers.

Sports and Entertainment Because of their country's generally sunny, warm climate, Australians enjoy outdoor sports and recreation. Australians like team games such as rugby and cricket, which were introduced by British settlers. A popular spectator game is Australian-rules football, a combination of soccer and rugby played on a cricket field. Australians also enjoy sun and surf activities. They are very proud of their world-class athletes in tennis, swimming, and golf. Australians have also won many Olympic medals in track and field events, swimming, and diving.

The film industry in Australia is more than 100 years old. In the early years, movies tried to create a separate Aussie identity by using themes from the country's history. In recent years, a number of Australian actors and directors have gained international fame for their acting and productions.

Living in the Bush Australians call the lightly populated interior of their country the Outback, or the bush. People in the bush frequently live on huge ranches called "stations." Neighbors may be many miles away. People living on these stations often have a small plane that they use the way most people use a car.

Children in the bush may live 200 miles from a school. These children are educated by correspondence schools and "schools of the air." They listen to instruction broadcast over two-way radio several times a week. At least once a week, most have an on-air private lesson with a teacher. Students receive their assignments by mail, complete them, and return them to the teacher. Today, they use e-mail and the Internet for their lessons as well.

▲ **FIND MAIN IDEAS** Explain why Australian culture is unique.

THE BOOMERANG

Aborigines of Australia created the boomerang. They used the curved, flat wooden stick to hunt animals, as a tool, and as a weapon in warfare. "Returning" boomerangs can be thrown into the wind, go hundreds of feet, and then return to the thrower. Today, the sports-loving Australians hold boomerang competitions.

Worldster
A Day in Mick's Life

 To learn more about Mick and his world, go to the **Activity Center @ ClassZone.com**

To tell you about his day Mick might say:

"G'day, mates! Here's a Captain Cook (a look) at my day."

G'day! My name is Mick. I am 13 years old and live with my family on a sheep station (you probably know it as a ranch) in the Outback of Australia. We Aussies call it "living in the bush." Sometimes I miss not being with other kids. But I play games and sports with my two sisters and my brothers. Let me tell you about my day.

8 A.M. I get up, get dressed, and go have brekkie (breakfast). We usually eat eggs and snags (sausages) and put Vegemite (a yeast and vegetable spread) on our toast.

9 A.M.–3 P.M. Time for school. One room in our home is a school room for me and my brothers and sisters. We use computers and two-way radios to be in contact with our teacher, who is hundreds of miles away. Our mum helps us with our lessons.

4 P.M. I am going with my dad, who is flying our family's small plane over the station to check on our sheep. He lets me sit in the copilot seat and, sometimes, even take the controls.

6 P.M. My mum is grilling on the barbie (barbeque grill) tonight. After dinner, my family and I are going to watch our country's favorite sport, Australian-rules football, on the telly (television).

CONNECT to Your Life

Journal Entry Think about your school day. How is your school experience different from Mick's? What else is different about your life? Record your ideas in your journal.

Australia and New Zealand **897**

A Well-Developed Economy

KEY QUESTION What are Australia's economic activities?

Australia has abundant mineral resources and productive agricultural lands. It also has a well-educated workforce. As a result, it is one of the world's wealthier nations. But unlike many of the developed nations, much of Australia's wealth comes from the processing of raw materials rather than the manufacturing of finished goods.

Opals The stones are valued for their fiery appearance. This photo shows a raw piece at right and a finished piece at left.

Economic Resources Raw materials needed in many different manufacturing processes and as energy sources are easily found in Australia. Coal, natural gas, and oil provide energy for the country. Natural gas is also exported. Minerals, such as copper, nickel, lead, and bauxite (used for producing aluminum), are in great supply. Gold, diamonds, and opals (a gemstone) are also found here.

In addition to its mineral resources, about 65 percent of Australia's land is suitable for agriculture. Most of the agricultural land is dry grazing land that supports large sheep and cattle ranches. Less than 10 percent of the agricultural land is cropland.

Economic Activities Mining and farming are important to Australia's economy. Large quantities of raw materials, such as coal,

COMPARING Economic Activities

Ranching Raising cattle and sheep is a major economic activity.

Opal Mining Australia's mines produce diamonds, lead, zinc, and opals for the world market.

Tourism Millions of people travel to Australia to visit unique parks.

petroleum, wheat, wool, meat, minerals, and gemstones, are exported. Australian exports are sold on the world market, but especially to Japan, China, and South Korea.

Because Australia was so far from other industrialized countries, it had to either make products locally or import them at great cost. So, Australia produces many of the goods that it needs. Such goods include automobiles, food products, iron and steel, textiles, and household appliances. It imports the machines used to make these products and also imports construction equipment and mining machines. Australia's farms are highly **mechanized**, or equipped with machines, so the demand for farm workers is small. In addition to wool and cattle hides, Australians also produce dairy products, sugar cane, and fruits such as bananas, pineapples, and apples.

Many Australians work in the tourism industry. The Great Barrier Reef and Australia's many beaches attract about 5 million visitors a year. The largest numbers of tourists come from Japan, New Zealand, and nations in Southeast Asia.

Australia's Top Export Markets

Country	Exports from Australia
China	wool, iron ore, copper, coal
Japan	coal, iron ore
New Zealand	motor vehicles, chemicals
South Korea	wheat, zinc, wool, beef, sugar
United States	beef, crude petroleum

Source: *Australian Government Bureau of Statistics 2005*

 SUMMARIZE Identify Australia's major economic activities.

Section ② Assessment

ONLINE QUIZ
For test practice, go to
Interactive Review
@ ClassZone.com

TERMS & NAMES

1. Explain the importance of
- James Cook
- aborigine
- penal colony
- Charles Perkins

USE YOUR READING NOTES

2. Find Main Ideas Use your completed web diagram to answer the following question:

How did immigration change the culture of Australia?

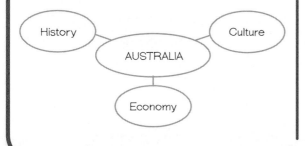

KEY IDEAS

3. What was the original reason for British colonization of Australia?

4. What are the two main cultural influences on Australia?

5. How do people in Australia make their living?

CRITICAL THINKING

6. Make Inferences How did European settlement influence Australia's development?

7. Analyze Cause and Effect What effect did Australia's location far from other inhabited areas have on its economic development?

8. **CONNECT to Today** How does the situation of the aborigines today compare to that of Native Americans?

9. **WRITING** Create an Australian-English Dictionary Use the Internet and library books to research Australian English. List ten unique Australian words and the word in American English that has the same meaning.

Reading for Understanding

▶ Key Ideas

BEFORE, YOU LEARNED

Life in Australia has been shaped by both aboriginal and European influences.

NOW YOU WILL LEARN

New Zealand's history, culture, and economy have been influenced by the Maori and European immigrants.

▶ Vocabulary

TERMS & NAMES

Maori (MOW•ree) a Polynesian people who were the first inhabitants of New Zealand

Polynesia islands of the central and southern Pacific

Treaty of Waitangi (WY•TAHNG•gee) a treaty between the British and the Maori signed in 1840

Pakeha (PAH•kee•HAH) a Maori word that means "white people"

hydroelectric power electricity produced by moving water

geothermal energy power produced by the internal heat of the Earth

REVIEW

geyser an erupting hot spring

Visual Vocabulary Maori in traditional costume

▶ Reading Strategy

Re-create the web diagram shown at right. As you read and respond to the **KEY QUESTIONS**, use the diagram to record important main ideas and details about the history, culture, and economy of New Zealand.

 Skillbuilder Handbook, page R4

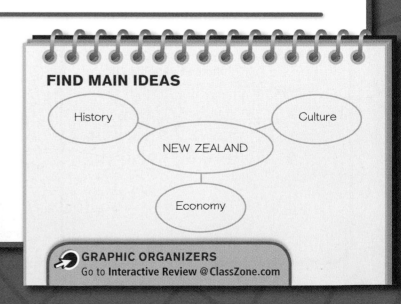

FIND MAIN IDEAS

History

Culture

NEW ZEALAND

Economy

GRAPHIC ORGANIZERS
Go to **Interactive Review** @ClassZone.com

◀ *A Micronesian child in traditional headdress and grass skirt gets ready for a special dance.*

Micronesia

The oceanic islands in this subregion depend on agriculture for their economy. The coral islands have coconuts and fishing industries. The region was mostly under control of the United States as a group of trust territories.

Islands of Palau ▼

Melanesia

Hundreds of languages are spoken in this subregion, and the cultures are quite varied. Many of the people living here are subsistence farmers. The rugged lands are rich in minerals, which attracted European settlement.

MELANESIA

◀ *A Melanesian tribesman wears a traditional headdress and boar's tusks for a ritual ceremony.*

Melanesian Work

New Guinea lumbermen take advantage of the forests on the island.

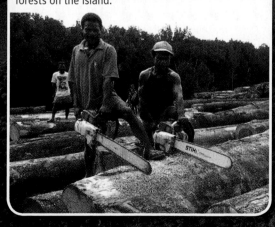

CRITICAL THINKING

1. **Draw Conclusions** How do the islanders of Oceania use their environment to meet their needs?

2. **Form and Support Opinions** What challenges do you think the people of Oceania face?

Reading for Understanding

▶ Key Ideas

BEFORE, YOU LEARNED

Oceania has three distinct subregions, Melanesia, Micronesia, and Polynesia.

NOW YOU WILL LEARN

Antarctica has no permanent residents because it has such a harsh environment.

▶ Vocabulary

TERMS & NAMES

Transantarctic Mountains mountains that divide Antarctica into two parts

geographic South Pole the point where all lines of longitude meet

icecap a glacier that covers a large area

Antarctic Peninsula an S-shaped peninsula that is part of the Andes Mountain chain

ice shelf huge flat sheet of ice extending over the ocean, but attached to the land

iceberg a large piece of floating ice

Robert Scott a British polar explorer

Roald Amundsen Norwegian polar explorer who was the first to reach the South Pole

Antarctic Treaty an agreement signed in 1959 calling for the peaceful use of Antarctica

BACKGROUND VOCABULARY

ozone hole the seasonal thinning of a protective layer of atmospheric gas high above Antarctica

Visual Vocabulary iceberg

▶ Reading Strategy

Re-create the Venn diagram shown at right. As you read and respond to the **KEY QUESTIONS**, use the diagram to organize important details and draw conclusions about the physical geography of Antarctica.

 Skillbuilder Handbook, page R13

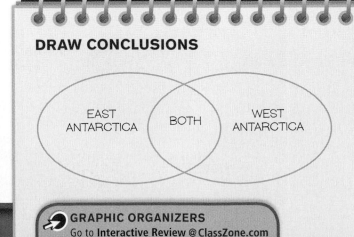

DRAW CONCLUSIONS

EAST ANTARCTICA   BOTH   WEST ANTARCTICA

🔁 **GRAPHIC ORGANIZERS**
Go to **Interactive Review @ ClassZone.com**

Antarctica: A Frozen Desert

Connecting to Your World

You just learned about lands that have a climate many people believe to be ideal. Now try to imagine a place where the summer temperatures range from –30°F to 59°F. In the winter, it is so cold (–40°F to –100°F) that even a short exposure to the elements could mean certain death. This place is Antarctica—the land at the "bottom of the Earth."

An Icy Landscape

🔽 **KEY QUESTION** What are the physical features of East and West Antarctica?

Like Australia, Antarctica is an island continent. It is the world's fifth largest continent. It is the coldest, windiest, and most isolated continent, and one of the driest. Unlike other continents, Antarctica is buried under thousands of feet of ice. At its thickest point, the ice is around two miles deep. This ice-cover holds as much as 70 percent of the Earth's fresh water. Poking up through the ice are mountains. But just 2 percent of the land is ice-free. Even more floating ice surrounds Antarctica. Geographically, it is divided into sections, East Antarctica and West Antarctica.

Leopard Seal
Herds of leopard seals roam the Antarctic waters.

Gentoo Penguins
An adult feeds a baby penguin at an Antarctic seashore.

Antarctica: Physical

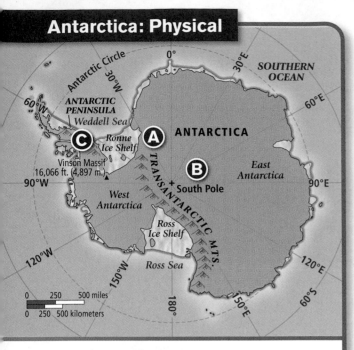

CONNECT Geography & History

1. **Location** At what point do the lines of longitude come together?
2. **Place** Which ocean surrounds the continent of Antarctica?

East Antarctica The **Transantarctic Mountains** Ⓐ run across the continent from the Ross Sea to the Weddell Sea. They divide Antarctica into two sections. Some mountain peaks in East Antarctica are higher than 14,000 feet. Dry, ice-free valleys are located within these mountains where glaciers were once found. What little snow falls is blown out of the valleys by the wind. Some of the valleys have frozen lakes. The eastern side of the continent is covered by a huge plateau, mountains, and the **geographic South Pole** Ⓑ. That is the point where all lines of longitude meet. The entire region is a cold, high, and dry land.

It is hard to believe that Antarctica, with its snow and ice, has a dry climate. However, desert climate is one in which precipitation is under 10 inches per year. Only a little more than six inches of snow falls in Antarctica each year. That makes it a polar desert. The yearly amount of precipitation in Antarctica is somewhat larger than the amount of rain that falls in Africa's Sahara desert. See the graphs below.

COMPARING Climate: Antarctica and Sahara

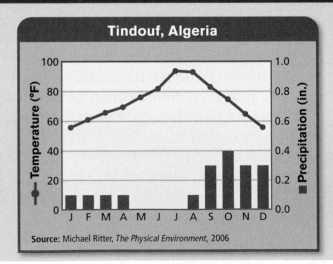

CRITICAL THINKING

Compare and Contrast How do the two regions compare in the amount of precipitation received each year?

West Antarctica The western side of Antarctica has a huge **icecap**, a glacier that covers a large area. The icecap links five off-shore islands into a frozen land of mountains, volcanoes, and the **Antarctic Peninsula ©**. This S-shaped peninsula points toward South America and actually is a part of the Andes Mountain chain. The peninsula is the warmest, most ice-free region of Antarctica.

Ice Shelves and Icebergs The rugged coastline of Antarctica is marked by bays and channels. **Ice shelves** are huge, flat sheets of ice extending over the ocean, but attached to the land. In the summer, parts of these shelves break off and float away. These large floating pieces of ice are called **icebergs**. Antarctic icebergs are enormous, sometimes covering thousands of square miles. Their smooth, flat shape and massive size make them different from the usually smaller, peaked icebergs found in the Arctic.

▲ **COMPARE AND CONTRAST** Describe how West Antarctica differs from East Antarctica.

Exploration of Antarctica

▼ **KEY QUESTION** Why do scientists continue to explore Antarctica?

Geographers had long thought there might be a seventh continent, but it was not until 1820 that a Russian explorer probably made what was the first sighting of Antarctica. Soon, European explorers were trying to map the coastline and to sail completely around the island continent. By 1895, explorers thought about crossing Antarctica to reach the geographic South Pole.

The Race to the South Pole Early expeditions failed to reach the South Pole because of the extremely harsh conditions. Then, in 1911, two explorers—**Robert Scott** of Great Britain and **Roald Amundsen** of Norway—organized polar expeditions. Using dog sleds, Amundsen and his team reached the South Pole on December 14, 1911. Scott's team, which used ponies and motor-powered sleds, arrived on January 17, 1912. Unfortunately, all members of Scott's expedition froze to death on the return journey. An American admiral, Richard Byrd, led five expeditions to the continent between the late 1920s and the 1950s. Later expeditions used aircraft and satellites to photograph the continent's features.

Robert F. Scott The British explorer perished on his return trip from the South Pole.

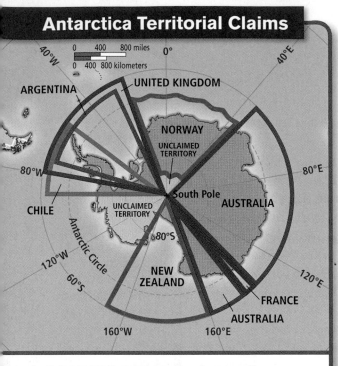

Antarctica Territorial Claims

CONNECT Geography & History

1. **Place** Which three countries have overlapping claims?
2. **Place** Which of the nations making claims are not Antarctica's neighbors?

Scientific Outpost In 1957, a worldwide program of scientific investigation called the International Geophysical Year began. Sixty-seven countries agreed to conduct scientific experiments around the world and at science stations in Antarctica. When it ended, 7 of the 12 countries that had set up research stations in Antarctica claimed a part of the continent. Fearing attempts to use the land for military purposes, the nations later agreed to the **Antarctic Treaty** (1959). The treaty stated that Antarctica should be used for peaceful scientific research and the environment should be protected. Today, more than 25 countries have scientific outposts there. They study climate, animal behavior, earthquakes, solar radiation, and changes in the **ozone hole** (the seasonal thinning of a protective layer of atmospheric gas above Antarctica).

 MAKE INFERENCES Identify reasons why Antarctica continues to be explored.

ONLINE QUIZ For test practice, go to **Interactive Review** @ ClassZone.com

Section 2 Assessment

TERMS & NAMES

1. **Explain the importance of**
   - Transantarctic Mountains
   - geographic South Pole
   - Antarctic Peninsula
   - Antarctic Treaty

USE YOUR READING NOTES

2. **Draw Conclusions** Use your completed Venn diagram to answer the following question:

   Which physical features do both East and West Antarctica share?

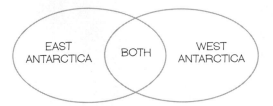

EAST ANTARCTICA — BOTH — WEST ANTARCTICA

KEY IDEAS

3. What physical feature divides Antarctica?
4. What is the warmest, most ice-free region of Antarctica?
5. Which explorer was the first to lead a successful expedition to the South Pole?

CRITICAL THINKING

6. **Find Main Ideas** What was the purpose of the Antarctic Treaty?
7. **Understand Effects** What might happen to Antarctica if global warming increases?
8. **CONNECT to Today** What might Antarctica be like today if the Antarctic Treaty had not prevented more land claims there?
9. **SCIENCE Create a Plant and Animal Life Poster** Use the Internet to research the plants and animals found on Antarctica and collect images. Then label and display them on a poster.

Interactive ◄Review

Click here to complete these and other activities online @ ClassZone.com

CHAPTER SUMMARY

Key Idea 1
Oceania is home to hundreds of cultural groups living on islands spread across thousands of miles of the Pacific Ocean.

Key Idea 2
Antarctica has no permanent residents because it has such a harsh environment.

For **Review and Study Notes**, go to **Interactive Review @ ClassZone.com**

NAME GAME

Use the Terms & Names list to complete each sentence on paper or online.

1. I am the region in the Pacific Ocean with thousands of islands. _____**Oceania**_____

2. I am a ring of reefs around a lagoon. _____

3. I am the point where all lines of longitude meet. _____

4. I am a subregion of Oceania that includes islands of the central and southern Pacific and stretches north. _____

5. I am a glacier that covers a large land area. _____

6. I am a Norwegian polar explorer who was the first to reach the South Pole. _____

7. I am the mountains that divide Antarctica into two parts. _____

8. I am an agreement signed in 1959 calling for the peaceful use of Antarctica. _____

9. I am a subregion of Oceania that includes islands northeast of Australia and south of the equator. _____

10. I am a form of speech that is a mixture of words from two or more languages. _____

atoll
Roald Amundsen
Antarctic Peninsula
Antarctic Treaty
geographic South Pole
icecap
ice shelf
Melanesia
Micronesia
Oceania
pidgin
Polynesia
Robert Scott
Transantarctic Mountains
trust territory

Activities

Flip Cards

Use the online flip cards to quiz yourself on the terms and names introduced in this chapter.

oceanic island

an island created by volcanic action

Crossword Puzzle

Complete an online crossword puzzle to test your knowledge of Oceania and Antarctica.

ACROSS
1. a large piece of floating ice

VOCABULARY

Explain the significance of each of the following.

1. pidgin
2. Transantarctic Mountains
3. Antarctic Peninsula
4. geographic South Pole
5. Antarctic Treaty

Explain how the terms and names in each group are related.

6. oceanic island, coral island, and atoll
7. Melanesia, Micronesia, and Polynesia
8. Oceania and trust territory
9. icecap, ice shelf, and iceberg
10. Roald Amundsen and Robert Scott

KEY IDEAS

1 Oceania: The Pacific World

11. How is Oceania divided?
12. What were the three waves of settlement of the Pacific islands?
13. Why did Europeans come to Oceania?
14. What are the two traditional economic activities of the Pacific Islanders?
15. What is a trust territory?
16. Why did pidgin language develop?

2 Antarctica: A Frozen Desert

17. Why are their no permanent residents in Antarctica?
18. What are the two geographical divisions of Antarctica?
19. How are Antarctic icebergs formed?
20. Which European explorer was the first to reach the geographic South Pole?
21. What is the major activity conducted in Antarctica?
22. What is the purpose of the Antarctic Treaty?

CRITICAL THINKING

23. **Compare and Contrast** Create a table to compare and contrast the physical description, climate, population, and political status of Oceania and Antarctica.

CHARACTERISTICS	OCEANIA	ANTARCTICA
Physical Description		
Climate		
Population		
Political Status		

24. **Five Themes: Movement** Why was Antarctica the last continent to be discovered and explored?
25. **Make Generalizations** How has the world benefited from international cooperation in Antarctica?
26. **Connect to Economics** Why is the growth of the tourist industry important for the economies of the Pacific islands?
27. **Connect Geography & History** What happened to the colonies of Oceania after World War II?
28. **Connect Geography & Culture** What is distinctive about Oceania in terms of its languages?

Answer the ESSENTIAL QUESTION

How do the regions of Oceania demonstrate cultural diffusion?

Written Response Write a two- or three-paragraph response to the Essential Question. Be sure to consider the key ideas of each section as well as basic ideas related to cultural diffusion. Use the rubric below to guide your thinking.

Response Rubric
A strong response will:
- point out the waves of settlers and colonizers in the region
- identify aspects of the culture that show changes

Test Practice
- Online Test Practice @ ClassZone.com
- Test-Taking Strategies and Practice at the front of this book

CHART

Use the chart to answer questions 1 and 2 on your paper.

Countries of Oceania		
Country	Date of Independence	Population (2005 Estimate)
Fiji	1970	905,949
Marshall Islands	1986	60,422
Nauru	1968	13,287
Palau	1994	20,579
Papua New Guinea	1975	5,670,544
Samoa	1962	176,908
Vanuatu	1980	208,754
Source: *CIA World Fact Book*, 2006		

1. Which country was the first to gain independence?

A. Fiji   **C.** Papua New Guinea

B. Nauru   **D.** Samoa

2. Which is the smallest nation to gain independence?

A. Marshall Islands

B. Nauru

C. Palau

D. Vanuatu

CLIMATE GRAPH

Examine the climate graph below. Use the information in the graph to answer questions 3 and 4 on your paper.

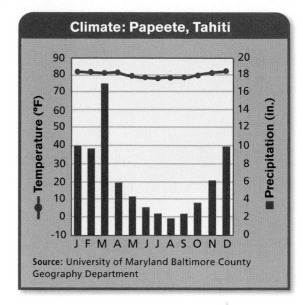

Source: University of Maryland Baltimore County Geography Department

3. In which month does it rain the most?

4. Why would the month of August be a good time to visit Papeete?

GeoActivity

1. INTERDISCIPLINARY ACTIVITY-SCIENCE

With a small group, research the various types of ice formations found in Antarctica. Create a museum-style display of these formations. Be sure your display includes images of the formations, their names, and descriptions.

2. WRITING FOR SOCIAL STUDIES

Unit Writing Project After you have completed your illustrated time line showing the arrival of different groups in the region, add a series of newspaper headlines to the time line that also tell the story of migration in this region.

3. MENTAL MAPPING

Create an outline map of the southern Pacific and label the following:

- Melanesia
- Micronesia
- Polynesia
- Antarctica
- Australia
- New Zealand

World Cultures
and
GEOGRAPHY

Contents

1.1 Taking Notes

Defining the Skill

When you **take notes,** you write down the important ideas and details of a passage. A chart or an outline can help you organize your notes to use in the future.

Applying the Skill

The following passage describes several different types of bodies of water. Use the strategies listed below to help you take notes on the passage.

How to Take and Organize Notes

Strategy 1 Look at the title to find the main topic of the passage.

Strategy 2 Identify the main ideas and details of the passage. Then summarize the main ideas and details in your notes.

Strategy 3 Identify key terms and define them. The term *hydrosphere* is shown in boldface type and highlighted; both techniques signal that it is a key term.

Strategy 4 In your notes, use abbreviations to save time and space. You can abbreviate words such as *gulf (G.)*, *river (R.)*, and *lake (L.)*, as long as you write the proper name of the body of water with the abbreviation.

---

1 BODIES OF WATER

2 All the bodies of water on Earth form what is called **3** the **hydrosphere**. The world's **2** oceans make up the largest part of the hydrosphere. Oceans have smaller regions. **2** Gulfs, such as the Gulf of Tonkin, and seas, such as the Sea of Japan, are extensions of oceans. Land partially encloses these waters.

2 Oceans and seas contain salt water, but most lakes and rivers contain fresh water. The water in rivers, such as the **2** Nile River in Africa, flows down a channel in one direction. This movement is the current. Lake water, such as that found in **2** Lake Victoria in Africa, can have currents too, even though the water is surrounded by land. Some lakes feed into rivers, and some rivers supply water to lakes.

Make a Chart

Making a chart can help you take notes on a passage. The chart below contains notes from the passage you just read.

2 Item	Notes
1. **3** hydrosphere	all water on Earth
a. oceans	salt water; largest part of hydrosphere
b. gulfs and seas	**4** G. of Tonkin; **4** S. of Japan; part of ocean
c. lakes and rivers	usually fresh water; **4** Nile R. flows; **4** L. Victoria surrounded by land

Practicing the Skill

Turn to Chapter 1, Section 2, "Technology Tools for Geographers." Read "The Science of Mapmaking," and use a chart to take notes on the passage.

1.2 Finding Main Ideas

Defining the Skill

A **main idea** is a statement that summarizes the subject of a speech, an article, a section of a book, or a paragraph. Main ideas can be stated or unstated. The main idea of a paragraph is often stated in the first or last sentence. If it is the first sentence, it is followed by sentences that support that main idea. If it is the last sentence, the details build up to the main idea. To find an unstated idea, use the details of the paragraph as clues.

Applying the Skill

The following paragraph provides reasons why Japan and Australia make such good trading partners. Use the strategies listed below to help you identify the main idea.

How to Find the Main Idea

Strategy ❶ Identify what you think may be the stated main idea. Check the first and last sentences of the paragraph to see if either could be the stated main idea.

Strategy ❷ Identify details that support the main idea. Some details explain that idea. Others give examples of what is stated in the main idea.

> **TRADING PARTNERS**
>
> Australia is an island. Japan is also an island, though much smaller than Australia. Australia is not as densely populated as Japan. ❷ In Japan, an average of 881 people live in each square mile. Australia averages 7 people per square mile. ❷ Australia has wide-open lands available for agriculture, ranching, and mining. ❷ Japan buys wool from Australian ranches, wheat from Australian farms, and iron ore from Australian mines. To provide jobs for its many workers, ❷ Japan developed industries. Those industries ❷ sell electronics and cars to Australia. ❶ Australia and Japan are trading partners because each has something the other needs.

Make a Chart

Making a chart can help you identify the main idea and details in a passage or paragraph. The chart below identifies the main idea and details in the paragraph you just read.

Main Idea: Australia and Japan are good trading partners because each supplies something the other needs.

Detail: Japan's population density is 881 people per square mile; Australia's is 7 per square mile.

Detail: Australia has land, natural resources, and agricultural products.

Detail: Japan buys wool, wheat, and iron ore from Australia.

Detail: Japan has many industries.

Detail: Australia buys electronics and cars from Japanese industries.

Practicing the Skill

Turn to Chapter 15, Section 1, "Sweeping Across Eurasia." Read "Human-Environment Interaction." Create a chart that identifies the main idea and the supporting details.

1.3 Summarizing

Defining the Skill

When you **summarize,** you restate a paragraph, passage, or chapter in fewer words. You include only the main ideas and most important details. It is important to use your own words when summarizing.

Applying the Skill

The passage below describes the origins of several state names in the United States. Use the strategies that follow to help you summarize the passage.

How to Summarize

Strategy ❶ Look for topic sentences stating the main idea or ideas. These are often at the beginning of a section or paragraph. Briefly restate each main idea in your own words.

Strategy ❷ Include key facts and any names, dates, numbers, amounts, or percentages from the text.

Strategy ❸ After writing your summary, review it to see that you have included only the most important details.

STATES' NAMES

❶ The name of a state often comes from that state's geography. For example, ❷ the name for Montana comes from a Spanish word that means "mountainous."

❶ Other states are named after people who were in power at the time the area was explored or settled. ❷ A French explorer named Louisiana after the French king at the time, Louis XIV. The state of ❷ Georgia was named after King George II of England, who granted the right to start the colony.

❶ Still other states get their names from Native American tribes living in the area when Europeans arrived. ❷ Arkansas, Alabama, and Massachusetts were named for the Native American tribes living there.

Write a Summary

You should be able to write your summary in a short paragraph. The paragraph at right summarizes the passage you just read.

❸ The names of states in the United States often came from geographical features, the names of people in power, or the names of Native American tribes.

Practicing the Skill

Turn to Chapter 6, Section 1, "Mountains, Prairies, and Coastlands." Read "Climates of Canada," and write a short paragraph summarizing the passage.

1.4 Sequencing Events

Defining the Skill

Sequence is the order in which events occur. Learning to follow the sequence of events through history will help you to better understand how events relate to one another.

Applying the Skill

The following passage explains the sequence of events that led to the U.S. Civil War. Use the strategies listed below to help you follow the sequence of events.

How to Find the Sequence of Events

Strategy 1 Look for specific dates provided in the text. The dates may not always read from earliest to latest, so be sure to match an event with the date.

Strategy 2 Look for clues about time that allow you to order events according to sequence. Words and phrases, such as *day*, *week*, *month*, or *year*, may help to sequence the events.

THE CIVIL WAR BEGINS

On **1** December 20, 1860, South Carolina became the first state to secede, or leave the Union. Many others followed. In **2** February of the next year, these states united to form the Confederate States of America, also called the Confederacy. Soon afterward, Confederate soldiers began seizing federal forts. By the time that Lincoln was sworn in as president on **1** March 4, 1861, few southern forts remained in Union hands. The most important was Fort Sumter.

On the morning of **1** April 12, Confederate cannons began firing on Fort Sumter. The war between North and South had begun.

Make a Time Line

Making a time line can help you sequence events. The time line below shows the sequence of events in the passage you just read.

December 20, 1860: South Carolina leaves the Union.

February 1861: Confederacy forms.

March 4, 1861: Lincoln sworn in as president.

April 12, 1861: Confederacy attacks Fort Sumter. Civil War begins.

Practicing the Skill

Turn to Chapter 7, Section 4, "From Colonization to Independence." Read "Mexico's Path to Independence," and make a time line showing the sequence of events in the passage.

1.5 Categorizing

Defining the Skill

To **categorize** is to sort people, objects, ideas, or other information into groups, called categories. Geographers categorize information to help them identify and understand patterns in geographical data.

Applying the Skill

The following passage discusses the involvement of various countries in World War II. Use the strategies listed below to help you categorize information.

How to Categorize

Strategy ❶ First, decide what kind of information needs to be categorized. Decide what the passage is about and how that information can be sorted into categories. For example, look at the different ways countries reacted to World War II.

Strategy ❷ Then find out what the categories will be. To learn how countries reacted to the war, look for clue words such as *in response*, *some*, *other*, and *both*.

Strategy ❸ Once you have chosen the categories, sort information into them. Which countries were Axis Powers? Which were Allies? What about the ones who were conquered and those who never fought at all?

WORLD WAR II ALLIANCES

❶ During World War II, most countries around the world had to choose which side to take in the conflict. Some countries were conquered so quickly that they could not join either side. ❷ *Others* chose to remain neutral. ❷ Italy and Japan joined with Germany to form the Axis Powers. In 1939, Germany began the war by invading Poland. ❷ *In response*, Great Britain and France (the first two Allied Powers) declared war on Germany. Germany quickly conquered many countries, including Denmark, Norway, the Netherlands, Belgium, and France. ❷ During 1941, *both* the Soviet Union and the United States entered the war on the Allied side. ❷ Sweden and Switzerland remained neutral during the war.

Make a Chart

Making a chart can help you categorize information. The chart below shows how the information from the passage you just read can be categorized.

❸

Name of Alliance	Axis Powers	Allied Powers	Neutral
Countries	• Germany • Japan • Italy	• Great Britain • France • Soviet Union • United States	• Sweden • Switzerland

Practicing the Skill

Turn to Chapter 2, Section 1, "The Earth and Its Forces." Read "External Forces Shaping the Earth." Make a chart in which you categorize the external forces shaping Earth.

1.6 Analyzing Causes and Effects

Defining the Skill

A **cause** is an action that makes something happen. An **effect** is the event that is the result of the cause. A single event may have several causes. It is also possible for one cause to result in several effects. Geographers identify cause-and-effect relationships to help them understand patterns in human movement and interaction.

Applying the Skill

The following paragraph describes events that caused changes in the way of life of the ancient Maya people of Central America. Use the strategies below to help you identify the cause-and-effect relationships.

How to Analyze Causes and Effects

Strategy ❶ Ask why an action took place. Ask yourself a question about the title and topic sentence, such as, "What caused Mayan civilization to decline?"

Strategy ❷ Look for effects. Ask yourself, "What happened?" (the effect). Then ask, "Why did it happen?" (the cause). For example, "What caused the Maya to abandon their cities?"

Strategy ❸ Look for clue words that signal causes, such as *caused*, *contributed to*, and *led to*.

> ❶ DECLINE OF MAYAN CIVILIZATION
>
> ❶ The civilization of the Maya went into a mysterious decline around A.D. 900. ❷ Mayan cities in the southern lowlands were abandoned, trade ceased, and the huge stone pyramids of the Maya fell into ruin. No one really understands what happened to the Maya, but there are many theories.
>
> ❸ Some believe that a change in climate *caused* the decline of Mayan civilization. Three long droughts between 810 and 910 meant that there was not enough water for Mayan crops. ❷ As a result, the Maya abandoned their cities. ❸ Other researchers believe that additional problems *contributed to* the crisis. They include overpopulation and warfare among the Mayan nobility.

Make a Diagram

Making a diagram can help you analyze causes and effects. The diagram below shows two causes and an effect for the passage you just read.

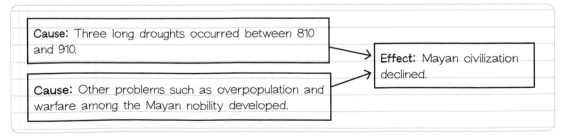

Cause: Three long droughts occurred between 810 and 910. → Effect: Mayan civilization declined.

Cause: Other problems such as overpopulation and warfare among the Mayan nobility developed. →

Practicing the Skill

Turn to Chapter 29, Section 1, "Unique Lands." Read "Non-Native Animals." Then make a diagram about the causes and effects of Australia's rabbit population.

1.7 Comparing and Contrasting

Defining the Skill

Comparing means looking at the similarities and differences between two or more things. **Contrasting** means examining only the differences between them. Geographers compare and contrast physical features, regions, cultures, beliefs, and situations in order to understand them.

Applying the Skill

The following passage describes the Dead Sea, in southwest Asia, and the Red Sea, located between northeast Africa and southwest Asia. Use the strategies below to help you compare and contrast these two bodies of water.

How to Compare and Contrast

Strategy ❶ Look for two aspects of the subject that can be compared and contrasted. This passage compares the Red Sea and the Dead Sea, two salty bodies of water close to one another.

Strategy ❷ To find similarities, look for clue words indicating that two things are alike. Clue words include *both, together,* and *similarly.*

Strategy ❸ To contrast, look for clue words that show how two things differ. Clue words include *however, but, on the other hand,* and *yet.*

SALTY SEAS

❶ According to the Bible, God parted the Red Sea so Moses could lead his people across it. The Bible also mentions the Dead Sea, calling it the Salt Sea. The Dead Sea is one of the saltiest bodies of water in the world. ❷ *Similarly,* the Red Sea also has a high salt content. Many observers argue that the Dead Sea is not really a sea at all. It is more of a lake since it is fed by the Jordan River and is surrounded by land on all four sides. ❸ *On the other hand,* the Indian Ocean feeds the Red Sea. The Red Sea is also the larger of the two seas. It is 170,000 square miles, while the Dead Sea is under 400 square miles. ❷ *Both* bodies of water provide minerals for commercial use, especially salt.

Make a Venn Diagram

Making a Venn diagram can help you identify similarities and differences between two things. In the overlapping area, list characteristics shared by both subjects. Then, in the separate ovals, list the characteristics of each subject not shared by the other. This Venn diagram compares and contrasts the Red Sea and the Dead Sea.

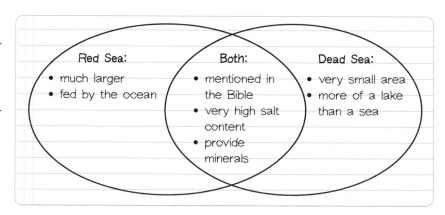

Red Sea:
- much larger
- fed by the ocean

Both:
- mentioned in the Bible
- very high salt content
- provide minerals

Dead Sea:
- very small area
- more of a lake than a sea

Practicing the Skill

Turn to Chapter 3, Section 3, "Resources and Economics." Read "Measuring Economic Development." Then make a Venn diagram showing similarities and differences between developed and developing nations.

1.8 Identifying Problems and Solutions

Defining the Skill

Identifying problems means finding and understanding the difficulties faced by a particular group of people during a certain time. **Identifying solutions** means understanding how people tried to remedy those problems. By studying how people solved problems in the past, you can learn ways to solve problems today.

Applying the Skill

The following passage describes the problems of floods and droughts in early Mesopotamia. Use the strategies listed below to find and understand these problems.

How to Identify Problems and Solutions

Strategy ❶ Look for the difficulties or problems faced by a group of people.

Strategy ❷ Consider how situations that existed at that time and place contributed to these problems.

Strategy ❸ Look for the solutions that people or groups employed to deal with the problems. Think about whether the solutions were good ones.

FLOOD AND DROUGHT IN MESOPOTAMIA

❶ In ancient Mesopotamia, farmers had to deal with both floods and droughts. They often had either too much rain or too little. ❷ If too much rain fell, the rivers might overflow and wash everything away. Too little rain also created difficulties. ❷ During a drought, the river levels dropped, making it hard to water crops.

❸ To combat the lack of rain, farmers in Mesopotamia eventually built canals to carry water from the river to the fields. Such a system is called irrigation. ❸ Farmers also built dams to hold back excess water during floods.

Make a Chart

Making a chart can help you identify information about problems and solutions. The chart below shows the problem, contributing factors, and solutions in the passage you just read.

❶ Problem	❷ Contributing Factors	❸ Solutions
Floods and droughts made farming difficult in Mesopotamia.	Too much rain caused floods that washed everything away.	Farmers built canals to carry water from the river to the fields.
	Droughts caused the river level to drop, making it hard to water crops.	Farmers built dams to hold back excess water during floods.

Practicing the Skill

Turn to Chapter 2, Section 4, "Environmental Challenges." Read "Desertification." Then make a chart that summarizes the problem of desertification faced by many arid and semiarid areas and the solutions that people who live in these areas are applying.

1.9 Making Inferences

Defining the Skill

Inferences are ideas that the author has not directly stated. **Making inferences** involves reading between the lines to interpret the information you read. You can make inferences by studying what is stated and using your common sense and previous knowledge.

Applying the Skill

The passage below examines the great pyramids of ancient Egypt. Use the strategies below to help you make inferences from the passage.

How to Make Inferences

Strategy ❶ Read to find statements of facts and ideas. Knowing the facts will give you a good basis for making inferences.

Strategy ❷ Use your knowledge, logic, and common sense to make inferences that are based on facts. Ask yourself, "What does the author want me to understand?" For example, from the facts about the pyramids' purpose, you can make the inference that the Egyptians believed in life after death. See other inferences in the chart below.

> **THE PYRAMIDS OF EGYPT**
>
> One reason that ancient Egypt is famous is for its giant pyramids. ❶ The Egyptians built these magnificent monuments for their kings, or pharaohs. Each pyramid was a resting place where an Egyptian pharaoh planned to spend the afterlife. ❶ Overseers, who ran the construction of each pyramid for the pharaoh, managed the workers and tracked the supplies. The largest pyramid, built for Khufu, required workers to place 6.5 million tons of stone. ❶ Workers built these long-lasting structures with none of the modern cutting tools and machines that we have today.

Make a Chart

Making a chart can help you organize information and make logical inferences. The chart below organizes information from the passage you just read.

❶ Stated Facts and Ideas	❷ Inferences
Egyptians built their pyramids as resting places for their pharaohs in the afterlife.	Egyptians believed in life after death.
A staff oversaw construction of the project.	Pyramid building was a complicated task that required organization.
The Egyptians built the pyramids without modern equipment.	The Egyptians were skilled engineers and hard workers.

Practicing the Skill

Turn to Chapter 26, Section 3, "Contrasting Countries." Read "Economy" under "North Korea." Then use a chart like the one above to make inferences about the effect of North Korea's economy on its citizens.

1.10 Making Generalizations

Defining the Skill

To **make generalizations** means to make broad judgments based on information. When you make generalizations, you should gather information from several sources.

Applying the Skill

The following three passages contain views on the United States as a melting pot of different cultures. Use the strategies below to make a generalization about these ideas.

How to Make Generalizations

Strategy ❶ Look for information that the sources have in common. These three sources all look at the relationship of immigrants to the United States.

Strategy ❷ Form a generalization that describes this relationship in a way that all three sources would agree with. State your generalization in a sentence.

> **THE MELTING POT**
>
> At the turn of the century, ❶ many native-born Americans thought of their country as a melting pot, a mixture of people of different cultures and races who blended together by abandoning their native languages and customs.
>
> —*The Americans*
>
> ❶ A nation, like a tree, does not thrive well till it is engrafted with a foreign stock.
>
> —*Journals* (Emerson, 1823)
>
> ❶ The United States has often been called a *melting pot.* But in other ways, U.S. society is an example of *cultural pluralism.* . . . That is, large numbers of its people have retained features of the cultures of their ancestors.
>
> —*World Book Encyclopedia*

Make a Diagram

Using a diagram can help you make generalizations. The diagram below shows how the information you just read can be used to generalize about immigrants' contributions.

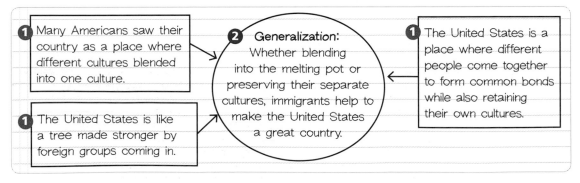

❶ Many Americans saw their country as a place where different cultures blended into one culture.

❶ The United States is like a tree made stronger by foreign groups coming in.

❷ Generalization: Whether blending into the melting pot or preserving their separate cultures, immigrants help to make the United States a great country.

❶ The United States is a place where different people come together to form common bonds while also retaining their own cultures.

Practicing the Skill

Turn to Chapter 19, Section 1, "Three Trading Empires." Read "European Imperialism," and study the chart on page 584. Also examine the map on page 579. Use a diagram to make a generalization about imperialism in Africa.

1.11 Drawing Conclusions

Defining the Skill

Drawing conclusions means analyzing what you have read and forming an opinion about its meaning. To draw conclusions, look at the facts and then use your own common sense and experience to decide what the facts mean.

Applying the Skill

The following passage presents information about Europe's mountain ranges. Use the strategies listed below to help you draw conclusions about their effects.

How to Draw Conclusions

Strategy ❶ Read carefully to identify and understand all the facts.

Strategy ❷ List the facts in a diagram and review them. Use your own experiences and common sense to understand how the facts relate to each other.

Strategy ❸ After reviewing the facts, write down the conclusions you have drawn about them.

EUROPE'S MOUNTAIN RANGES

Mountains are a key landform in Europe. ❶ The Alps stretch across eight countries in southern Europe. The mountain range affects travel within those countries. ❶ The Pyrenees once formed a natural barrier between France and Spain. Europe also has several smaller mountain ranges.

Europe's mountain ranges separated the groups of people who settled the land thousands of years ago. ❶ With the mountains in between them, many different cultures were able to develop in Europe. ❶ Mountain ranges contain natural resources, such as timber. These resources also influenced where people chose to settle.

Make a Diagram

Making a diagram can help you draw conclusions. The diagram below shows how to organize facts to draw a conclusion about the passage you just read.

❷ FACTS

| Mountain ranges, such as the Alps and the Pyrenees, formed natural barriers and affected travel between European nations. | Mountains separated groups of settlers, allowing different cultures to develop. | Mountain ranges contain natural resources that also influenced settlement. |

❸ CONCLUSION

Mountain ranges had a significant impact on the settlement of and the development of cultures in Europe.

Practicing the Skill

Turn to Chapter 10, Section 2, "A Multicultural Society." Read "Africans." Then make a diagram to help you draw conclusions about African influences on Brazilian culture.

1.12 Making Decisions

Defining the Skill

Making decisions involves choosing between two or more options, or courses of action. In most cases, decisions have consequences, or results. Sometimes decisions may lead to new problems. By understanding how historical figures made decisions, you can learn how to improve your own decision-making skills.

Applying the Skill

The passage below explains the decision British Prime Minister Chamberlain faced when Germany threatened aggression in 1938. Use the strategies below to analyze his decision.

How to Make Decisions

Strategy ➊ Identify a decision that needs to be made. Think about what factors make the decision difficult.

Strategy ➋ Identify possible consequences of the decision. Remember that there can be more than one consequence to a decision.

Strategy ➌ Identify the decision that was made.

Strategy ➍ Identify actual consequences that resulted from the decision.

PEACE OR WAR?

In 1938, German leader Adolf Hitler demanded a part of Czechoslovakia. ➊ British Prime Minister Neville Chamberlain had to decide how to respond to that aggression. ➋ He could threaten to go to war, but he feared that Britain was not ready. ➋ If he gave Germany the region, he might avoid war, but he would be setting a bad example by giving in to a dictator. ➌ Chamberlain decided to give Germany what it demanded. In exchange, Hitler promised not to take any more land in Europe. ➍ Six months later, Germany took the rest of Czechoslovakia and later invaded Poland.

Make a Flow Chart

Making a flow chart can help you identify the process of making a decision. The flow chart below shows the decision-making process in the passage you just read.

➊ **Decision to Be Made:** How should Chamberlain handle German aggression? Should he give Hitler what he wants or fight against it?

➋ **Possible Consequence:** Go to war and risk losing because his country is not ready.

➋ **Possible Consequence:** Give Hitler what he wants and risk setting a bad example.

➌ **Decision Made:** Give Hitler and Germany part of Czechoslovakia.

➍ **Actual Consequence:** Hitler broke his word and invaded Czechoslovakia and Poland. Britain had to fight a war with Germany anyway.

Practicing the Skill

Turn to Chapter 15, Section 2, "Governing a Vast Land." Read "Superpower and Collapse." Then make a flow chart to identify Gorbachev's policy decision and its consequences.

1.13 Evaluating

Defining the Skill

To **evaluate** is to make a judgment about something. Geographers evaluate the actions of people in history. One way to do this is to examine both the positives and the negatives of an action, and then decide which is stronger—the positive or the negative.

Applying the Skill

The following passage examines the rule of Mustafa Kemal of Turkey. Use the strategies listed below to evaluate the success of his reforms.

How to Evaluate

Strategy ❶ Before you evaluate a person's actions, first determine what that person was trying to do. In this case, think about what Kemal wanted to accomplish.

Strategy ❷ Look for statements that show the positive, or successful, results of his actions. For example, did he achieve his goals?

Strategy ❸ Also look for statements that show the negative, or unsuccessful, results of his actions. Did he fail to achieve something he tried to do?

Strategy ❹ Write an overall evaluation of the person's actions.

KEMAL RULES TURKEY

In 1923, Turkey became an independent republic. Mustafa Kemal became Turkey's first president. ❶ Kemal wanted his nation to resemble European countries rather than its Islamic neighbors. Kemal quickly replaced Turkey's Islamic government with a nonreligious system. He also replaced the Arabic alphabet and the Islamic calendar with Western versions of each. ❸ Kemal's actions drew protests from traditionalists. ❷ However, Kemal's moves helped to modernize Turkey. ❷ They also benefited women, who had lived with many restrictions under Islamic law. Women now had greater social freedom. They also could vote and run for political office.

Make a Diagram

Making a diagram can help you evaluate. List the positives and negatives of the person's actions and decisions. Then make an overall judgment. The diagram below shows how the information from the passage you just read can be evaluated.

❷ Positive Results:
• Turkey becomes more modern.
• Women attain greater freedoms.

❸ Negative Results:
• Traditionalists oppose and protest Kemal's reforms.

❹ Evaluation:
While traditionalists criticized Kemal's actions, the reforms helped modernize Turkey and improve life for women. Therefore, he succeeded at his goal.

Practicing the Skill

Turn to Chapter 11, Section 3, "The Middle Ages and Renaissance." Read "Forces of Change," and make a diagram to evaluate the decision to take part in the Crusades.

1.14 Distinguishing Fact from Opinion

Defining the Skill

Facts are events, dates, statistics, or statements that can be proved to be true. **Opinions** are judgments, beliefs, and feelings. By identifying facts and opinions, you will be able to think critically when a person is trying to influence your own opinion.

Applying the Skill

The following passage describes the church Hagia Sophia. It was one of the more notable structures in the development of Constantinople as the capital of the Byzantine Empire. Use the strategies listed below to distinguish facts from opinions.

How to Distinguish Fact from Opinion

Strategy ❶ Look for specific information that can be proved or checked for accuracy.

Strategy ❷ Look for assertions, claims, and judgments that express opinions. In this case, one speaker's opinion is addressed in a direct quote.

Strategy ❸ Think about whether statements can be checked for accuracy. Then, identify the facts and opinions in a chart.

> **HAGIA SOPHIA**
>
> ❶ Hagia Sophia was built between A.D. 532 and 537. The Byzantine emperor Justinian ordered that the cathedral be built on the site where an earlier church had burned down. ❶ The church is noted for its large central dome, which rises 185 feet above the ground. With numerous windows, arches, and vaults, the structure is hailed by many as an architectural masterpiece. ❷ Said one observer, "You would declare that the place is not lighted by the sun from without, but that the rays are produced from within."

Make a Chart

Making a chart can help you distinguish fact from opinion. The chart below analyzes the facts and opinions in the passage above.

Statement	❸ Can It Be Proved?	❸ Fact or Opinion
Hagia Sophia was built between A.D. 532 and 537.	Yes. Check historical documents.	fact
Hagia Sophia's dome is 185 feet high.	Yes. Check measurement records.	fact
The inside of Hagia Sophia is so beautiful that it appears to make its own sunlight.	No. This cannot be proved. It is what one speaker believes.	opinion

Practicing the Skill

Turn to Chapter 28, Section 2, "The Mainland Countries." Read "Singapore." Then make a chart like the one above in which you analyze key statements about Singapore to determine whether they are facts or opinions.

1.15 Analyzing Points of View

Defining the Skill

Analyzing points of view means looking closely at a person's arguments to understand the reasons behind that person's beliefs. The goal of analyzing a point of view is to understand different thoughts, opinions, and beliefs about a topic.

Applying the Skill

The following passage describes the difference between Native American and European attitudes about land use. Use the strategies below to help you analyze the points of view.

How to Analyze Points of View

Strategy ❶ Look for statements that show you a particular point of view on an issue. For example, Native Americans believed land should be preserved for the future. European colonists believed land could be owned and changed as desired.

Strategy ❷ Think about why different people or groups held a particular point of view. Ask yourself what they valued. What were they trying to gain or to protect? What were they willing to sacrifice?

Strategy ❸ Write a summary that explains why different groups of people might have taken different positions on this issue.

> **LAND USE**
>
> Native Americans and Europeans had many conflicts because of differing ideas about land use. ❶ Most Native Americans believed that land must be preserved for future generations. They believed the present generation had the right to use land for hunting and farming. However, no one had the right to buy or sell land.
>
> In contrast, Europeans had a long history of taming wilderness and owning land. As a result, ❶ Europeans believed that they could buy land, sell it, and alter it. For example, if they wished to mine for gold underground, they could destroy landscape as they dug the mine. ❶ Europeans used land to make money.

Make a Diagram

Making a diagram can help you analyze points of view. The diagram below analyzes the different points of view of the Native Americans and the European colonists in the passage you just read.

❷ Native Americans:
- preserved land for the future
- used land to provide for present needs
- no one could buy or sell land

❷ Colonists:
- tradition of taming wilderness and owning land
- bought and sold land; changed and sometimes harmed it
- wanted to make money

❸ Native Americans wanted to preserve the land. They did so because they valued their heritage. The colonists bought land, sold it, and changed it. They did so because they valued making money.

Practicing the Skill

Turn to Chapter 22, Section 2, "Israel and the Palestinian Territories." Read "A New Israel" and "The Palestinian Territories." Make a diagram to analyze the different points of view of the Israelis and the Palestinians.

1.16 Recognizing Bias

Defining the Skill

Bias is a prejudiced point of view. Accounts that are biased tend to present only one side of an issue and reflect the opinions of the writer. Recognizing bias will help you understand how much to trust the primary and secondary sources that you find.

Applying the Skill

The following passage is from an 1883 speech in which Jules Ferry supported the French policy of imperialism. Use the strategies listed below to help you recognize bias in the passage.

How to Recognize Bias

Strategy ❶ Identify the author and examine any information about him or her. Does the author belong to a group, social class, or political party that might lead to a one-sided view of the subject?

Strategy ❷ Think about the opinions the author is presenting. Look for words, phrases, statements, or images that might convey a positive or negative slant.

Strategy ❸ Examine the evidence provided to support the author's opinions. Is the opinion correct? Would the same information appear in another account of the same event?

❶ **JULES FERRY ARGUES FOR FRENCH IMPERIALISM**

Nations are great in our times only by means of the activities which they develop; . . . Something else is needed for France: . . . that ❷ she must also be a great country exercising all of her rightful influence over the destiny of Europe, that ❷ she ought to propagate [spread] this influence throughout the world and carry everywhere that she can ❸ her language, her customs, her flag, her arms, and her genius.

—Jules Ferry, Speech Before the French National Assembly, July 28, 1883

Make a Chart

Making a chart can help you recognize bias in primary and secondary sources. The chart below analyzes the bias in the passage you just read.

Author	Jules Ferry
Occasion and Purpose	speech in front of the French National Assembly, arguing for France to practice imperialism
Tone	urging, superior
Slanted Language	"exercising all of her rightful influence;" "ought to propagate [spread] this influence"
Description of Bias	Ferry argues that France had the right and the obligation to practice imperialism and spread French control and culture to colonies around the world.

Practicing the Skill

Look through newspapers and news magazines to find an article related to geography. Then use a chart like the one above to analyze the article for bias.

1.17 Synthesizing

Defining the Skill

Synthesizing involves putting together clues, information, and ideas to form an overall picture. Geographers synthesize information in order to develop interpretations of important facts.

Applying the Skill

The following passage describes the agricultural revolution. The highlighting indicates the different kinds of information that will help you synthesize.

How to Synthesize

Strategy ❶ Look carefully for facts that will help you base your interpretations on evidence.

Strategy ❷ Look for explanations that link the facts together. This statement is based on the evidence of ancient tools mentioned in the next sentence.

Strategy ❸ Consider what you already know that could apply. Your knowledge will probably lead you to accept this statement.

Strategy ❹ Bring together the information you have about the subject. This interpretation brings together different kinds of information to arrive at a new understanding.

> **THE AGRICULTURAL REVOLUTION**
>
> ❶ Flaked arrowheads found with mammoth bones at ancient sites suggest that some early people lived as big game hunters. ❷ After the big game became extinct, people shifted to hunting smaller game. They made tools, such as bows and arrows for hunting small game as well as baskets for collecting nuts.
>
> About 10,000 years ago, people began to farm. ❸ The rise of agriculture brought tremendous change. More people lived in settled villages, and the storage of surplus food became more important. As their surplus increased, people had time to develop specialized skills and think about the world. ❹ From this agricultural base rose larger, more stable, and more complex societies.

Make a Diagram

Making a diagram can help you organize the facts, examples, and interpretations that you need to synthesize. The diagram below synthesizes the passage you just read.

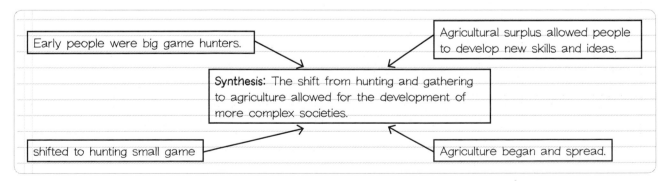

Practicing the Skill

Turn to Chapter 3, Section 2, "Why People Move." Read "Causes of Migration." Then use a diagram like the one above to form a synthesis about why people migrate.

2.1 Reading Maps: Physical

Defining the Skill

Physical maps represent the landforms, or physical features, on Earth's surface, such as mountains or bodies of water. By learning about the different elements of maps, it will be easier for you to read them.

Applying the Skill

A physical map of Peru is shown below. Use the strategies listed below to help you read the map.

How to Read a Physical Map

Strategy ❶ Read the title. This will tell you what place or region is represented by the map.

Strategy ❷ Look for the gridlines that form a pattern of squares over the map. These numbered lines represent latitude (horizontal) and longitude (vertical). They indicate the location of the area on Earth.

Strategy ❸ Read the map legend. On a physical map, the legend often includes a scale to help you determine elevation as well as information about physical features.

Strategy ❹ Use the scale and the pointer or compass rose to determine distance and direction.

Make a Chart

Making a chart can help you organize the information given on a map. The chart below summarizes information about the physical map you just studied.

Title	Peru: Physical
Location	the Pacific coast of South America, near the equator and latitude 70° W
Legend Information	colors = elevation
Scale	1 in. = 500 miles, 5/8 in. = 500 km
Summary	Peru is located on the Pacific Ocean. The Andes run along the west coast, and the Amazon River and Ucayali River flow through the country.

Practicing the Skill

Turn to Chapter 21, Section 2, "Physical Geography of South Asia." Study the physical map of South Asia on page 661. Make a chart to identify the information on the map.

2.2 Reading Maps: Political

Defining the Skill

Political maps represent political features of various places, such as national borders and capital cities. The countries on political maps are often shaded in different colors to make them easier to distinguish from each other.

Applying the Skill

A political map of Peru is shown below. Use the strategies listed below to help you read the map.

How to Read a Political Map

Strategy ❶ Read the title. This identifies the main idea of the map and will tell you what place or region the map represents.

Strategy ❷ Look for the gridlines that form a pattern of squares over the map. These numbered lines represent latitude (horizontal) and longitude (vertical). They indicate the location of the area on Earth.

Strategy ❸ Read the map legend. The legend will help you to interpret the symbols on the map. On a political map, these symbols often include icons for major and capital cities.

Strategy ❹ Use the scale and the pointer or compass rose to determine distance and direction.

Make a Chart

Making a chart can help you organize the information given on a map. The chart below summarizes information about the political map you just studied.

Title	Peru: Political
Location	the Pacific coast of South America, near the equator and latitude 70° W
Legend Information	star icon = national capital; dot = other city
Scale	1 in. = 500 miles, 5/8 in. = 500 km
Summary	Peru, located on the Pacific Ocean, borders Ecuador, Colombia, Brazil, Bolivia, and Chile. Its capital is Lima.

Practicing the Skill

Turn to Chapter 26, "The Korean Peninsula," and study the political map of North and South Korea on page 795. Make a chart to identify the information on the map.

2.3 Reading Maps: Thematic

Defining the Skill

Thematic maps represent specific themes, or ideas. Climate, language, migration, population density, and economic activity maps are all different kinds of thematic maps.

Applying the Skill

The following map shows selected products of Mexico. Use the strategies listed below to help you read the map.

How to Read a Thematic Map

Strategy 1 Read the title. This identifies the theme of the map and will tell you what place or region is represented by the map.

Strategy 2 Some thematic maps have latitude (horizontal) and longitude (vertical) lines. They can help indicate the location of the area on Earth.

Strategy 3 Read the map legend. On a thematic map, the legend is very important because the colors and symbols on the map are specific to the theme. The legend will help you interpret them.

Strategy 4 Use the pointer or compass rose to determine direction. If the map has a scale, it can help you determine distance.

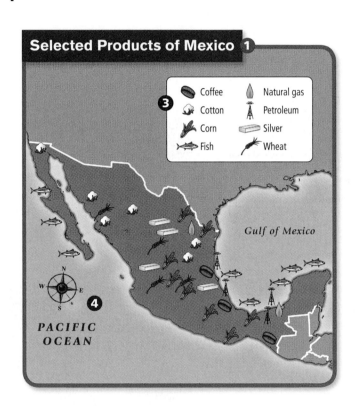

Make a Chart

Making a chart can help you organize the information given on a map. The chart below summarizes information about the thematic map you just studied.

Title	Selected Products of Mexico
Location	Mexico, which borders the Pacific Ocean and the Gulf of Mexico
Legend Information	Icons represent specific products.
Summary	Mexico's different regions produce a variety of goods and crops, including coffee, corn, fish, petroleum, and silver.

Practicing the Skill

Turn to Chapter 12, Section 2, "Spain and Portugal." Study the map of the Iberian Peninsula on page 372, and make a chart to identify the information on the map.

2.4 Reading Maps: Cartograms

Defining the Skill

A **cartogram** takes statistical data and represents it visually in the form of a map. Rather than representing land area, a cartogram shows a different set of data about a country, such as population or gross domestic product. The size of the nations on the cartogram are adjusted to reflect the selected data for each one.

Applying the Skill

The following cartogram shows world population. Use the strategies listed below to help you read the cartogram.

How to Read a Cartogram

Strategy ❶ Read the title. This identifies the data and region represented by the cartogram.

Strategy ❷ Look at the sizes of the countries shown to see how they compare to each other. Cartograms adjust the sizes of countries to convey relative data. Because of this, the countries' shapes are altered.

Strategy ❸ Compare the cartogram to a conventional map such as the world political map on pp. A16–A17. This will help you determine how much more or less of the selected data a particular country has by comparing its relative size on the cartogram to its size on the map.

Make a Chart

Making a chart can help you organize the information given on a cartogram. The chart below summarizes information about the cartogram you just studied.

Title	World Population
Location	the world
Summary	Countries are shown either smaller or larger than their actual area depending on their population. For instance, India and Japan are shown larger than normal because they have high populations. Canada and Russia, which are more sparsely populated, are smaller than normal.

2.5 Reading Graphs and Charts

Defining the Skill

Graphs and charts translate information into a visual form. Graphs take numerical information and present it using pictures and symbols instead of words. Different kinds of graphs include bar graphs, line graphs, and pie graphs. Charts are created by simplifying, summarizing, and organizing information. This information is then presented in a format that is easy to understand. Tables and diagrams are examples of commonly used charts.

Applying the Skill

Use the strategies listed to read the graphs and chart on these pages.

How to Read Graphs

Strategy ❶ Read the title to identify the main idea of the graph. Ask yourself what kind of information the graph shows. Check the graph's source line to make sure the data is reliable.

Strategy ❷ Read the labels on the graph. Bar and line graphs have labels on their vertical axis and horizontal axis. Pie graphs have labels for each wedge of the pie. These labels tell you what data the graph represents.

Strategy ❸ Look at the graph. Try to find patterns, such as similarities and differences or increases and decreases.

Strategy ❹ Summarize the information shown on the graph. Use the title to help you focus on what information the graph is presenting.

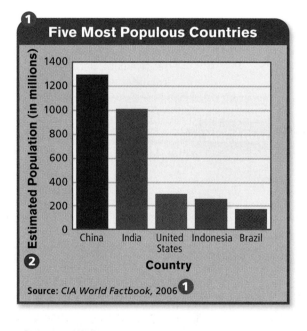

❶ **Five Most Populous Countries**

❷ Country

Source: *CIA World Factbook, 2006* ❶

❶ **China's Iron and Steel Trade** *1999–2003*

❷ ─●─ Imports ─●─ Exports

Source: "China's New Heights," *Time Magazine,* June 27, 2005 ❶

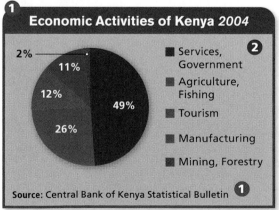

❶ **Economic Activities of Kenya** *2004*

❷
- Services, Government
- Agriculture, Fishing
- Tourism
- Manufacturing
- Mining, Forestry

2% — 11% — 12% — 26% — 49%

Source: Central Bank of Kenya Statistical Bulletin ❶

How to Read Charts

Strategy ❶ Read the title to find out what the chart is about. Ask yourself what kind of information the chart shows.

Strategy ❷ Read the headings to see how the chart is organized.

Strategy ❸ Study the data in the chart to understand the facts that it was designed to show.

Strategy ❹ Summarize the information shown in each part of the chart. Use the title to help you focus on what information the chart is presenting.

❶ World Economic Development

❷ Country	Status	GDP in US Dollars*	GDP/ Person in US Dollars*	Infant Mortality per 1,000 Live Births	Life Expectancy at Birth	Literacy Rate (Percent)
❸ Burkina Faso	developing	5.4 billion	1,300	91.35	48.9	26.6
India	developing	719.8 billion	3,400	54.63	64.7	59.5
Uruguay	developing	13.2 billion	9,600	11.61	76.3	98.0
Germany	developed	2.8 trillion	30,400	4.12	78.8	99.0
Japan	developed	4.9 trillion	31,500	3.24	81.3	99.0
United States	developed	12.5 trillion	42,000	6.43	77.9	99.0

Source: *CIA World Factbook,* 2006   * official exchange rate

Write a Summary

Writing a summary can help you understand the information contained in graphs and charts. The paragraph below summarizes information from the chart above.

❹ The chart compares several indicators of economic development for three developing and three developed nations: Burkina Faso, India, Uruguay, Germany, Japan, and the United States. The developed nations have higher GDPs and literacy rates, longer life expectancies, and lower infant mortality than the developing nations. Of the countries shown, the United States has the highest GDP per person, Burkina Faso the lowest.

Practicing the Skill

Turn to Chapter 5, Section 3, "A Diverse Culture." Look at "Comparing Languages, Religion, and Ethnicity," and study the language chart and religion pie graph. Then write a paragraph each summarizing what you learned from the chart and the graph.

2.6 Interpreting Political Cartoons

Defining the Skill

Political cartoons express an opinion about a serious subject. A political cartoonist uses symbols, familiar objects, and people to make his or her point quickly and visually. Sometimes words used in the cartoon will help to clarify its meaning.

Applying the Skill

The cartoon below is about the competition between the Russian Empire and Great Britain over territory in Central Asia. Use the strategies listed below to help you interpret this and other political cartoons.

How to Interpret Political Cartoons

Strategy ❶ Identify the subject of the cartoon. Look at the cartoon as a whole. If the cartoon has them, read the title and caption.

Strategy ❷ Look for symbols that the cartoonist used to communicate ideas. The bear in this cartoon represents Russia. The lion is a symbol of Great Britain.

Strategy ❸ Analyze the other visual details of the cartoon. The man in the middle, wearing Central Asian dress, is crouching in fear as the bear and lion stare at him hungrily. This suggests that the Russian Empire and Great Britain are interested in devouring Central Asian territory.

PUNCH, OR THE LONDON CHARIVARI.—November 30, 1878.

❷ ❸

❶ "SAVE ME FROM MY FRIENDS!"

Make a Chart

Making a chart can help you interpret a political cartoon. The chart below summarizes the information from the cartoon above.

Subject	competition between Russia and Great Britain over Central Asia
Symbols and Details	The bear, representing the Russian Empire, and the lion, symbolizing Great Britain, are circling their prey, a man representing Central Asia.
Message	Central Asia is afraid that its "friends," the Russian Empire and Great Britain, are going to take control of its territory.

Practicing the Skill

Turn to Chapter 20, "East, Central, and Southern Africa." Study the political cartoon on page 639. Use a chart like the one above to summarize information from the cartoon to help you interpret its meaning.

2.7 Creating a Map

Defining the Skill

When you **create a map,** you can choose what geographical information to include. You can show political information, such as the area covered by empires or countries. Your map can also be a thematic map, showing data on climates, population, or resources.

Applying the Skill

Below is a map that a student created that shows the vegetation zones of Africa. Use the strategies listed below to learn how to create your own map.

How to Create a Map

Strategy ❶ Select a title that identifies the map's geographical area and purpose.

Strategy ❷ Use dashes to draw latitude and longitude lines. Using these as a guide, draw the area you are representing.

Strategy ❸ Create a legend that identifies the map's colors or icons.

Strategy ❹ Draw the colors or icons on the map to show information.

Strategy ❺ Draw a compass rose and scale.

Practicing the Skill

Turn to Chapter 14, Section 2, "Hungary and the Czech Republic." Read "Government and Economics" under "Hungary." Using the map on page 325 as a guide, create a map of Europe showing Hungary's trading partners.

2.8 Creating a Model

Defining the Skill

When you **create a model,** you use information and ideas to show an event, situation, or place in a visual way. A model might be a poster or diagram that explains something. Or, it might be a three-dimensional model, such as a diorama, that depicts an important scene or situation.

Applying the Skill

The following sketch shows the early stages of a model of a feudal manor in Europe. Use the strategies listed below to help you create your own model.

How to Create a Model

Strategy ❶ Gather the information you need to understand the situation or event. In this case, you need to be able to show the parts of a manor and their uses.

Strategy ❷ Visualize an idea for your model. Once you have created a picture in your mind, make an actual sketch to plan how it might look.

Strategy ❸ Think of symbols you may want to use. Since the model should give information in a visual way, think about ways you can use color, pictures, or other visuals to tell the story.

Strategy ❹ Gather the supplies you will need. Then create the model. For example, you would need pictures of manors and art supplies to make this model.

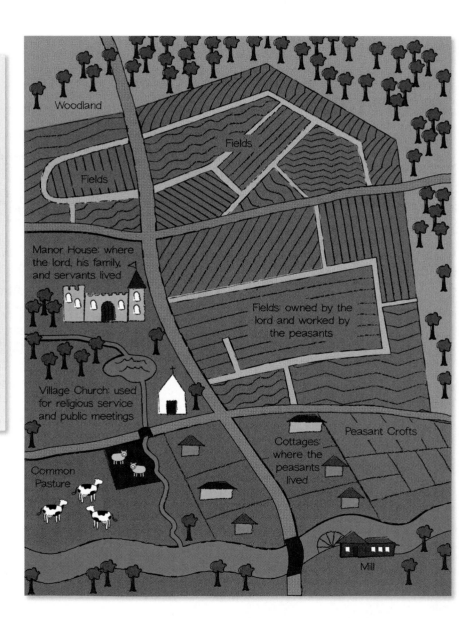

Woodland

Fields

Fields

Manor House: where the lord, his family, and servants lived

Fields: owned by the lord and worked by the peasants

Village Church: used for religious service and public meetings

Peasant Crofts

Cottages: where the peasants lived

Common Pasture

Mill

Practicing the Skill

Turn to Chapter 28, Section 3, "Indonesia and the Philippines." Read "Culture and Economy" under "Indonesia" and the text about shadow puppets in the "Fun Facts," and look at the images on page 866. Then create a model of a shadow puppet theater.

3.1 Outlining

Defining the Skill

Outlining is a method of organizing information. Once you have settled on a topic for a report or paper, you must do research. When you have all the information you need, then you have to organize it. An outline lists your report's main ideas in the order in which they will appear. It also organizes main ideas and supporting details according to their importance.

Applying the Skill

The outline at right is for a research report about the causes and effects of earthquakes. Use the strategies listed below to help you make an outline.

How to Outline

Strategy ❶ Read the main ideas of this report. They are listed on the left and labeled with capital Roman numerals. Each main idea will need at least one paragraph in your report.

Strategy ❷ Read the supporting ideas for each main idea. These are indented and labeled with capital letters. Notice that some main ideas require more supporting ideas than others.

Strategy ❸ Read the supporting details in the outline. They are indented farther and labeled with numerals. Some supporting ideas will not have supporting details. It is not necessary to include every piece of information that you have. An outline is merely a guide to follow as you write your report.

Strategy ❹ Reports can be organized in different ways. This report is arranged to show the causes and effects of earthquakes. The outline should clearly reflect the way the report is organized.

❶ I. Causes of Earthquakes
    A. Shifting tectonic plates
❷   B. Volcanoes
    C. Human activities
      ❸ 1. Large underground nuclear explosions, deep mine excavations, and filling large reservoirs can all cause earthquakes.
II. Effects of Earthquakes
    A. Earthquakes usually do not kill people directly.
    B. Damage to natural features
      1. shifting of large blocks of Earth's crust
        a. can cause landslides
        b. can break down the banks of rivers and lakes and cause flooding
    C. Damage to man-made structures
      1. Ground shaking causes structures to sway, bounce, and possibly collapse.
    D. Cause other catastrophic events
      1. Fires
        a. San Francisco, 1906
      2. Tsunamis
        a. Indian Ocean, 2004

Practicing the Skill

Turn to Chapter 17, Section 2, "Human Beginnings in Africa." Read the section and gather information from it about hominid finds in Africa. Write an outline for a report about the topic using the correct outline form.

3.2 Writing for Social Studies

Defining the Skill

Writing is an important skill to learn. It allows you to communicate your thoughts and ideas. There are many different kinds of writing used in social studies.

Narrative Writing

Narrative writing tells a story. Some narratives are fictional, but historians and geographers write narratives about events that really happened. A narrative has three basic parts. The beginning sets the scene. The body presents a conflict. The resolution settles the conflict and ends the narrative. The sample below describes the volcano Krakatoa.

> One of the most destructive volcanic eruptions in recorded history happened in 1883, when two-thirds of the Indonesian island of Krakatoa was blown apart. The explosion sent volcanic ash 50 miles into the air. The surrounding area was plunged into darkness for two days. Krakatoa was uninhabited by humans, but the eruption buried all life on the island under a layer of ash. It took five years for plants and animals to thrive again on Krakatoa.

Persuasive Writing

Persuasive writing is writing whose purpose is to convince another person to adopt your opinion or position. People use persuasive writing for many reasons, such as convincing a government to adopt a proposal. Geographers and historians use persuasive writing to propose interpretations of facts. The sample below presents arguments for establishing a tsunami warning system in the Indian Ocean. The system began operations in 2006.

> In December 2004, a catastrophic tsunami struck Southeast Asia. Massive losses underline the need for a tsunami early warning system in the Indian Ocean. Such a system would predict and detect tsunamis and communicate warnings to the region's inhabitants. It will cost millions of dollars and require the cooperation of nations already monitoring seismic activity. However, many feel it is worth the effort to reduce destruction from tsunamis.

Expository Writing

Expository writing is meant to explain. It might examine a process or event, compare and contrast two different regions or civilizations, explain causes and effects, or explore problems and solutions. Expository writing has three main parts. The introduction states the main idea. The body supports the main idea with facts and examples. The conclusion summarizes the information and restates the main idea. In the sample below, the author explains some of the major causes of earthquakes.

> Earthquakes, the sudden movement of Earth's crust followed by a series of vibrations, have several causes. Most are caused by shifts in tectonic plates. Stress builds up along fault lines until it is finally released, making the ground shake. Earthquakes can also be triggered by the explosive action of a volcano. Human activities, such as deep mining, can prompt earthquakes as well. No matter the cause, earthquakes can have dramatic effects.

Applying the Skill

No matter what kind of writing you are doing—whether it is narrative, persuasive, or expository writing or something more complicated such as a research report—it needs to be clear, concise, and factually accurate. The strategies listed below will help you achieve your goal. The following passage is part of a larger research report about earthquakes. Notice how using these strategies helped the author convey information about the effects of earthquakes.

How to Write for Social Studies

Strategy ❶ Focus on your topic. Be sure that you clearly state the main idea of your piece so that your readers know what you intend to say.

Strategy ❷ Collect and organize facts and supporting details. Gather accurate information about your topic to support the narrative you are crafting or the point you are trying to make. Creating an outline can help you organize your thoughts and information.

Strategy ❸ Write a first draft, using standard grammar, spelling, sentence structure, and punctuation. Proofread your writing. Make sure it is well organized and grammatically correct. Make any necessary revisions in your final draft.

EFFECTS OF EARTHQUAKES

❶ Earthquakes usually do not kill people directly. Instead, most deaths and injuries occur as a result of damage to natural features and man-made structures. Earthquakes can also cause other catastrophes that harm people.

❷ During an earthquake, large blocks of Earth's crust shift. These shifts can cause landslides or break down the banks of rivers and lakes and cause flooding. ❷ The ground shaking that occurs during an earthquake can make buildings sway and bounce. The stress causes some buildings to collapse. All of these situations are dangerous for people.

Sometimes, earthquakes can cause other disasters, such as tsunamis or fires. ❷ A 1906 quake in San Francisco started a fire that burned for three days. About 3,000 people died in this event. ❷ An undersea earthquake caused the Indian Ocean tsunami in 2004, which claimed at least 280,000 lives.

Practicing the Skill

Turn to Chapter 11, Section 1, "Europe's Dramatic Landscape." Read "Europe's Resources." Then write a persuasive paragraph convincing European government leaders about the importance of developing renewable energy sources. Use the strategies listed above to help you make your paragraph clear and informative.

3.3 Forming and Supporting Opinions

Defining the Skill

When you **form opinions,** you interpret and judge the importance of events and people in history. You should always **support your opinions** with facts, examples, and quotations.

Applying the Skill

The following passage describes the impact of the policy of apartheid on South Africa. Use the strategies listed below to form and support an opinion about the policy.

How to Form and Support Opinions

Strategy 1 Look for important information about the subject. Information can include facts, quotations, and examples.

Strategy 2 Form an opinion about the subject by asking yourself questions about the information. For example, how important was the subject? How does it relate to similar subjects in your own experience?

Strategy 3 Support your opinions with facts, quotations, and examples. If the facts do not support the opinion, then rewrite your opinion so that it is supported by the facts.

THE POLICY OF APARTHEID

From the mid- to late-twentieth century, South Africa had a policy called apartheid, which separated whites and nonwhites. **1** Nonwhites faced discrimination concerning where they could live, what jobs they could hold, and what they were taught in school. Many were forced to leave their homes and relocate in less desirable areas. Nonwhites' protests of these policies led to years of conflict. A number of nations also criticized apartheid. **1** In 1985, the United States and Great Britain restricted trade with South Africa. In 1989, Frederik Willem de Klerk became president of South Africa. He opposed apartheid. His efforts helped to end the country's policy of segregation.

Make a Chart

Making a chart can help you organize your opinions and supporting facts. The following chart summarizes one possible opinion about the policy of apartheid in South Africa.

2 Opinion	The policy of apartheid oppressed many South Africans and hurt the nation's economy.
3 Facts	Nonwhites faced discrimination concerning where they could live, what jobs they could hold, and what they were taught in school.
	Many nonwhites were forced to relocate in less desirable regions.
	Nations opposed to apartheid restricted trade with South Africa.

Practicing the Skill

Turn to Chapter 16, Section 1, "Center of a Landmass." Read "Human-Environment Interaction," and form your own opinion about Soviet projects in Central Asia. Make a chart like the one above to summarize your opinion and the supporting facts and examples.

3.4 Using Primary and Secondary Sources

Defining the Skill

Primary sources are materials written or created by people who lived during historical events. The writers might have been participants or witnesses. Primary sources include letters, journals, articles, and artwork. **Secondary sources** are materials that teach about an event, such as textbooks. When you research, you will use both kinds of sources.

Applying the Skill

The following passage uses primary and secondary sources to describe Kublai Khan's lifestyle. Use the strategies listed below to help you learn how to use these sources.

How to Use Primary and Secondary Sources

Strategy ❶ Distinguish secondary sources from primary sources. Most of the paragraph is a secondary source. The observation by Marco Polo is a primary source. The primary source supports the point the secondary source is making.

Strategy ❷ Determine the main idea of the secondary source. Look for details that support it.

Strategy ❸ Identify the author of the primary source and consider why the author produced it. Consider what the document was supposed to achieve. Is it credible? Is it promoting a particular viewpoint? In this case, Polo seems to be an objective observer.

LIFESTYLE OF KUBLAI KHAN

❶ Unlike his Mongol ancestors, Kublai Khan spent almost his entire life in China. ❷ He enjoyed living in the luxurious manner of a Chinese emperor. He maintained a beautiful summer palace at Shangdu, on the border between Mongolia and China. He also built a new square-walled capital at the site of modern Beijing. The size of Kublai's palace in Beijing greatly impressed the European traveler ❸ Marco Polo. "The whole building is at once so immense and so well constructed that no man in the world . . . could imagine any improvement in design or execution," Polo observed.

Make a Chart

Making a chart can help you assess information from primary and secondary sources. The chart below summarizes information from the passage above.

Questions	Answers
What is the main idea?	Kublai Khan enjoyed a life of luxury.
What are the supporting details?	He had a beautiful summer palace. He built a new capital in Beijing.
Who wrote the primary source?	Marco Polo
What can you tell about the primary source?	Polo appears to be an objective observer. The source seems credible.

Practicing the Skill

Turn to Chapter 21, Section 2, "Physical Geography of South Asia." Read "Monsoons" and the primary source on page 662. Make a diagram to summarize the information found in the sources and to help you read them.

3.5 Using a Database

Defining the Skill

A **database** is a collection of data, or information, that is organized so that you can find and retrieve information on a specific topic quickly and easily. Once a computerized database is set up, you can search it to find specific information without going through the entire database. The database will provide a list of all information in the database related to your topic. Learning how to use a database will help you learn how to create one.

Applying the Skill

The chart below is a database for famous mountains in the Eastern Hemisphere. Use the strategies listed below to help you understand and use the database.

How to Use a Database

Strategy ❶ Identify the topic of the database. The most important words in this title are *Mountains* and *Eastern Hemisphere*. These words were used to begin the research for this database.

Strategy ❷ Identify the kinds of data you need to enter in your database. These will be the column headings of your database. The keywords *Mountain, Location, Height,* and *Interesting Facts* were chosen to focus the research.

Strategy ❸ Identify the entries included under each heading.

Strategy ❹ Use the database to help you find information quickly. For example, in this database, you could search for "Mountains over 28,000 feet" to find a list of famous mountains that are more than 28,000 feet tall.

❶ FAMOUS MOUNTAINS OF THE EASTERN HEMISPHERE

❷ MOUNTAIN	LOCATION	HEIGHT ABOVE SEA LEVEL (FEET)	INTERESTING FACTS
❸ Dhaulagiri	Nepal	26,810	name means "White Mountain"
Everest	border of Nepal and China	❹ 29,035	tallest mountain in the world
Fuji	Japan	12,388	considered sacred by many Japanese
K2	Pakistan	❹ 28,250	second tallest mountain in the world
Khan-Tengri	border of China, Kazakhstan, and Kyrgyzstan	22,949	pyramid-shaped mountain is highest point in Kazakhstan
Xixabangma Feng (formerly Gosainthan)	China	26,291	Gosainthan means "place of God" in Sanskrit.

Practicing the Skill

Create a database of countries in Oceania that shows the name of each country, its capital, its land area, and its population. Use the information on pages 880 and 881 in the Unit 9 Atlas "Country Almanac" to provide the data. Use a format like the one above for your database.

3.6 Creating a Multimedia Presentation

Defining the Skill

Audio and video recordings, photographs, CD-ROMs, television, and computer software are all different kinds of media. To **create a multimedia presentation,** you need to collect information in different media and organize them into one presentation so that your audience watches, listens, and learns.

Applying the Skill

The photographs below show students using computers to create multimedia presentations. A multimedia presentation can incorporate computers, but it does not have to. Use the strategies listed below to help you create your own multimedia presentation.

How to Create a Multimedia Presentation

Strategy ❶ Identify the topic of your presentation and decide which media are best for an effective presentation. For example, you may want to use video or photographic images to show the dry character of a desert. Or, you may want to use CDs or audio tapes to provide music or to make sounds that go with your presentation, such as the sounds of a camel.

Strategy ❷ Research the topic in a variety of sources. Images, text, props, and background music should reflect the region and the historical period of your topic.

Strategy ❸ Write the script for the presentation. You could use a narrator and characters' voices to tell the story. Primary sources are an excellent source for script material.

Strategy ❹ Put together your presentation. Supplement your script with the images, props, music, and other media that you selected from your research. If you create your presentation on your computer, you can save the file for future viewing.

Practicing the Skill

Create a multimedia presentation about Red Square in Moscow, Russia. Turn to Chapter 15, Section 3, "Blending Europe and Asia," and look at the images on page 479 for ideas about what your presentation might include.

4.1 Using a Search Engine

Defining the Skill

Using a **search engine** can be a useful way to do research on the Internet. A search engine is a tool designed to find information on the Internet. There are billions of Web sites and documents available on the Internet. Using a search engine properly can help you sort through the vast amount of information.

Applying the Skill

The screen below shows a popular search engine. Use the strategies listed below to help you search the Internet.

How to Use a Search Engine

Strategy ❶ Brainstorm keywords to enter into the search engine. Make a list of possible search terms. It often helps to try to be specific. If your research topic is what careers geographers can have, try entering *careers in geography* instead of just *geography*. This will narrow the results to relevant information.

Strategy ❷ Many search engines will provide an excerpt of a Web site below the link to the site. Read these to help you determine if the Web site is relevant to your topic and worth visiting.

Strategy ❸ Click on the link to go to the Web site you are interested in exploring in depth. If you can, open the new Web site in a separate window, so that it is easier to come back to your original search.

Practicing the Skill

Choose a topic from Unit 1 that you would like to learn more about. Develop a list of keywords to help you search the Internet for information about that topic. Visit a search engine, and enter your keywords. Take a look at your search results, and consider which keywords were the most useful and why.

4.2 Evaluating Internet Sources

Defining the Skill

By **evaluating Internet sources** for credibility, you can make sure that you are only using the most accurate, reliable information as a resource.

Applying the Skill

The screen below shows a Web site about geography. Use the strategies listed below to learn how to assess its credibility.

How to Evaluate Internet Sources

Strategy ❶ Look at the Web site's Internet address. The three-letter code in it will help you determine who created the site. Almost anyone can set up a Web site with a ".com," or commercial, address. School Web sites use ".edu," or education, addresses. Addresses that end with ".org" are used by nonprofit organizations. Official government Web sites end in ".gov." These last three will often be more reliable than commercial Web sites.

Strategy ❷ Try to identify the author of the Web site and when it was last updated. This information does not always appear. Some sites are anonymous, or created by an unidentified author. You should not use these as sources because the information could be outdated, or the author might not know much about the Web site's topic.

Strategy ❸ Use another source to verify the information you find on the Internet. Online encyclopedias contain accurate information. Sources with .gov and .edu addresses are usually reliable. So is information from newspaper, magazine, and television news channel Web sites. Search several sites, and try to find two or three sources with the same information.

Practicing the Skill

Choose one of the Web sites that you found in your search from "Practicing the Skill" for "Using a Search Engine" on page R36 of this handbook. Evaluate the Web site to assess its credibility and its usefulness as a resource. Use the strategies listed above to help you.

World Religions and Ethical Systems

A Global View

A religion is an organized system of beliefs and practices, often centered on one or more gods. In this book, you have learned about many different religions and their impact on the world. Religions have guided people's beliefs and actions for thousands of years. They have brought people together. But they have also torn them apart.

Religions are powerful forces today as well. They affect everything from what people wear to how they behave. There are thousands of religions in the world. In the following pages, you will learn about five major religions: Buddhism, Christianity, Hinduism, Islam, and Judaism. You will also learn about Confucianism, an ethical system. Like a religion, an ethical system provides guidance on how to live your life. However, unlike religions, ethical systems do not center on the worship of gods. The chart on the opposite page shows what percentages of the world population practice the five major religions. The map shows where these religions are predominant or where they are practiced by significant numbers.

Christianity
Islam
Hinduism
Buddhism
Judaism
Other

NORTH AMERICA

Tropic of Cancer

ATLANTIC OCEAN

Equator

PACIFIC OCEAN

SOUTH AMERICA

150°W   120°W   90°W   60°W

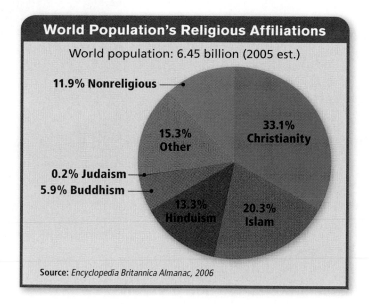

World Population's Religious Affiliations

World population: 6.45 billion (2005 est.)

- 11.9% Nonreligious
- 15.3% Other
- 33.1% Christianity
- 0.2% Judaism
- 5.9% Buddhism
- 13.3% Hinduism
- 20.3% Islam

Source: *Encyclopedia Britannica Almanac, 2006*

Buddhism

Buddhism began in India in the sixth century B.C. The religion was founded by Siddhartha Gautama (sihd•DAHR•tuh GOW•tuh•muh), who came to be known as the Buddha. *Buddha* means "enlightened one." He was born into a noble family but left home to search for enlightenment, or wisdom. The Buddha is said to have achieved enlightenment after long study. According to Buddhist tradition, he taught his followers that the way to end suffering was by practicing the Noble Eightfold Path. This path involved observing the following: right opinions, right desires, right speech, right action, right job, right effort, right concentration, and right meditation.

After the Buddha's death, Buddhism spread in India, Ceylon, and Central Asia. Missionaries spread the faith. Buddhist ideas also traveled along trade routes. The religion, however, did not survive on Indian soil. Today, most Buddhists live in Sri Lanka (formerly Ceylon), East Asia, Southeast Asia, and Japan.

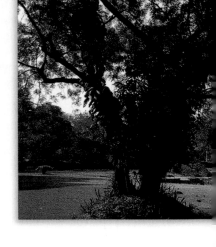

▼ Monks

Buddhist monks dedicate their entire lives to the teachings of the Buddha. They live together in religious communities called monasteries. There, the monks lead lives of poverty, meditation, and study. In this photograph, Buddhist monks in Myanmar hold their begging bowls.

▼ Buddha

Statues of the Buddha, such as this one in Japan, appear in shrines throughout Asia. Buddhists try to follow the Buddha's teachings by meditating, a way of emptying the mind of thought. They also make offerings at shrines, temples, and monasteries.

New Zealand

Connecting to Your World

Imagine a place so far away that it would take you 17 hours to fly there from New York or 12 hours from Los Angeles. That place is New Zealand, about a thousand miles southeast of Australia and about 30 times smaller than Australia. Now imagine trying to find that small bit of land by ship in a vast ocean without good maps. That is what the earliest explorers had to do in their search for the southern islands. Their voyages took years to complete. But their discoveries expanded the knowledge of the planet and its people.

History and Government

▼ **KEY QUESTION** How did the Maori lose control of New Zealand?

Earlier you read that two large islands—North Island and South Island—and several smaller outlying islands make up the country of New Zealand. The islands were inhabited mostly by birds until the **Maori** (MOW•ree) people migrated there some time between A.D. 950 and 1150. The Maori people came by canoes from other islands of **Polynesia**, which are in the central and southern Pacific Ocean.

Waiting for a Flight Flight times to New Zealand from the United States are more than 12 hours.

Marlborough Sounds South Island, New Zealand

NEW ZEALAND

North Island

Marlborough Sounds

South Island

PACIFIC OCEAN

Maori Settlement The Maori called the land Aotearoa (ow•tay•ah•ROH•ah). It means "land of the long white cloud" and refers to the thick clouds and snow-capped mountains. The Maori, like the aborigines of Australia, were hunter-gatherers and fishers. They settled mainly on North Island and hunted a large flightless bird called the moa. By the 1500s, they had killed almost all of these birds. Over the years, the Maori learned to be farmers. They lived in separate tribes of about 500 members. Their culture was rich and included skilled woodcarvers who created wood sculptures using stone tools.

Maori Wood Sculpture
Wood sculptures tell stories to the viewer. The surface carvings have specific meaning to those who can read them. The carvings tell the history of the Maori people.

Europeans began to arrive in the mid-1600s. A Dutch sea captain, Abel Tasman, stopped in the islands in 1642. Cartographers named the area *Nieuw Zeeland* after a territory in the Netherlands. English Captain James Cook came to the islands more than a hundred years later, in 1769. He was the first European to explore New Zealand and claimed it for Great Britain.

A British Colony Soon, other Europeans—sailors, explorers, and traders—stopped at the islands. In the late 1700s, about 100,000 Maori lived there. In 1814, British Protestant missionaries established the first European settlement on North Island. Because there was no official government, there was much lawlessness in New Zealand. The Maori and the settlers fought each other. The British colonists asked their government to come and establish law and order.

In 1840, Maori chiefs signed the **Treaty of Waitangi** (WY•TAHNG•gee) with Britain. It stated that the Maori accepted the British queen as their ruler in exchange for British protection. The British believed the treaty allowed them to control the land while protecting Maori rights. But the Maori thought that they still had control of the land and that the British were only minor officials. The difference in the understanding of the treaty terms caused problems. British settlers began buying land without Maori permission. Between 1845 and 1872, land wars broke out. When they were over, the British had control of the islands, and the Maori had suffered great losses. Today, Maoris make up about 15 percent of the population.

After gold was discovered in 1861, more settlers arrived. Like the Australian gold rush, many unsuccessful gold seekers did not have the funds to return home. So, they settled on the land and began farming or raising sheep or cattle.

Even though they were a British colony, the New Zealanders thought of themselves as a separate group. In 1907, they asked Britain to allow them to be a self-governing country.

Self-Government Today, New Zealand has a government similar to that of Australia. New Zealand is a constitutional monarchy. The monarch of the United Kingdom is head of state, but has little control. The monarch appoints a governor general, who also has little power. A parliamentary-style government is in place. The one-house parliament has 120 members. Seven seats in parliament are reserved for Maori members, but Maori may also be elected to other seats.

New Zealanders have always been concerned about equal rights for all citizens. The country was one of the first to guarantee women the vote, in 1893. (The United States did not guarantee this right to women until 1920.) The Maori continued to make efforts to get provisions of the Treaty of Waitangi to be enforced. In the 1990s, the Maori finally gained a settlement that provided land and money to the Maori people. New Zealand also provides many social services and old-age pensions for all its people.

▲ **ANALYZE CAUSE AND EFFECT** Explain how the British gained control of New Zealand.

ANALYZING Primary Sources

◀ *Present-day rally for Maori rights*

The Treaty of Waitangi was signed by Maori leaders and the British government on February 6, 1840. Under the treaty, Britain annexed New Zealand. Because the treaty was written in both Maori and English, each party interpreted the treaty terms differently. Below is a part of the treaty.

> Her Majesty the Queen of England confirms and guarantees to the Chiefs and Tribes of New Zealand and to the respective families and individuals thereof the full exclusive and undisturbed possession of their Lands and Estates Forests Fisheries and other properties which they may collectively or individually possess so long as it is their wish and desire to retain the same in their possession.
>
> Source: Government of New Zealand

DOCUMENT–BASED QUESTION

What right does the British government appear to be granting to the Maori?

Culture

▼ **KEY QUESTION** What have been the main influences on New Zealand's culture?

Most New Zealanders are descendants of early British colonists. All New Zealanders of European ancestry are called **Pakehas** (PAH•kee•HAHS), or white people, by the Maori. New Zealand's culture reflects both British and Maori influences. For example, English and Maori are official languages. New Zealand has an urban culture. Almost 85 percent of the people live in coastal cities, mainly on the North Island. In rural areas, most people live in small villages or on farms or ranches.

Traditional Maori Costumes and Tattoos Facial tattoos are common for both men and women.

Maori Culture The Maori have worked hard to preserve their culture. They also have a good relationship with the *Pakehas*. But Maori leaders would like more opportunities for their people. The Maori have set up Web sites, cultural schools, and newspapers to help retain their culture. In recent years, they have filed claims in court to try to recover their traditional lands. One of the most distinctive aspects of Maori culture is body tattooing. The tattoos are signs of power and prestige. Most Maori follow traditional religious beliefs that honor ancestors and the natural environment.

Sports and Recreation Since most New Zealanders live no more than 80 miles from the sea, water sports such as swimming, sailing, surfing, and fishing are popular. Many families own a small beach house where they go on weekends. New Zealand's mild climate and its mountains, especially those on the South Island, make hiking, climbing, and camping year-round activities. Skiing and snowboarding are also popular. Team sports like rugby and cricket, borrowed from the British, are enjoyed by many.

Wellywood New Zealand's scenic mountains, beaches, forests, and pasturelands have become popular locations for international movie productions, as well as the country's own. In fact, the New Zealand film industry has become big business. It is called Wellywood because it has its headquarters in the capital city of Wellington, and also because it is compared to America's Hollywood. Large studios and technical-effects companies work together to produce a variety of films. One of the biggest projects in motion-picture history, the *Lord of the Rings* trilogy, was filmed in New Zealand.

▲ **SUMMARIZE** Explain the influence of geography on life in New Zealand.

CONNECT ⟩ Geography & Culture

Film Production in New Zealand

You probably know that J.R.R. Tolkien's *Lord of the Rings* takes place in Middle Earth. But did you know that Middle Earth was New Zealand? Director Peter Jackson selected 150 locations in his native country of New Zealand for the three films. New Zealand also supplied about 2,000 production people and thousands of minor performers.

CRITICAL THINKING

Make Inferences Why did the *Lord of the Rings* director choose to film in New Zealand?

a scene from Lord of the Rings ▶

An Economy Based on Land Resources

🔻 **KEY QUESTION** What are New Zealand's major economic activities?

New Zealand has a few mineral resources, and it also has good cropland and pastureland, abundant forests, and beautiful scenery. These land resources are the basis for New Zealand's economy. Many of New Zealand's goods are exported to Asia, Australia, Great Britain, and the United States.

Agriculture, Forestry, and Fishing Did you know that New Zealand has about 25 times as many sheep and cattle as people? Raised on rich pasturelands, these animals produce wool, meat, and dairy products in great quantities that are exported around the world. North Island forests provide timber for export. The fishing industry also supplies huge catches of fish and rock lobster.

Sheep New Zealand's economy relies heavily on the raising of sheep. **Why is New Zealand suited for sheep raising?**

905

Hydroelectric Plant
New Zealand relies heavily on this form of power. **What aspect of New Zealand's geography makes this possible?**

Manufacturing There has been a growing emphasis on manufacturing in New Zealand since the end of World War II. Since that time New Zealand has worked hard to build businesses in the country so that they would not need to import so many products. Today food products and manufactured goods, including automobiles, electronics, furniture, and metal products, are produced in New Zealand. Some textiles are produced because of the great quantities of wool available here. About 40 percent of the workforce is employed in manufacturing. Auckland, New Zealand's largest city, is the country's largest manufacturing center.

New Zealand has a very limited supply of petroleum. Its industrial production depends on the use of **hydroelectric power**, electricity produced by moving water. The many waterfalls in mountainous areas are some of the sources of hydroelectric power. About three-fourths of all power in New Zealand is created by moving water.

Geothermal energy, power produced by the internal heat of the Earth, is another source of power. Geothermal energy is generated by harnessing the steam or hot water in New Zealand's **geysers**. In some areas, engineers have drilled deep holes to release the underground steam that is then piped to stations to be converted to electricity.

 SUMMARIZE Identify the major economic activities of New Zealand.

Section ❸ Assessment

 ONLINE QUIZ
For test practice, go to
Interactive Review
@ ClassZone.com

TERMS & NAMES

1. Explain the importance of
- Maori
- Treaty of Waitangi
- *Pakeha*

USE YOUR READING NOTES

2. Find Main Ideas Use your completed web diagram to answer the following question:

In what ways have the Maori preserved their culture?

KEY IDEAS

3. Who were the first settlers of New Zealand and when did they arrive?

4. What was the purpose of the Treaty of Waitangi?

5. What are New Zealand's three major agricultural products?

CRITICAL THINKING

6. Analyze Cause and Effect What type of government developed in New Zealand? Why?

7. Evaluate How did New Zealand's physical geography contribute to its economic development?

8. CONNECT to Today Why might the government of New Zealand want to encourage the New Zealand film industry?

9. TECHNOLOGY Plan a Power Presentation Plan a power presentation about the cultural life of New Zealand. Include pictures and descriptions in your presentation.

Interactive ← Review

CHAPTER SUMMARY

Key Idea 1
The nations of Australia and New Zealand have plant and animal life found nowhere else on earth.

Key Idea 2
Australia's history, culture, and economic life have been shaped by both aborigines and European immigrants.

Key Idea 3
New Zealand's history, culture, and economy have been influenced by the Maori and European immigrants.

 For **Review and Study Notes**, go to **Interactive Review @ ClassZone.com**

NAME GAME

Use the Terms & Names list to complete each sentence on paper or online.

1. I am the interior desert region of Australia.
   _____ Outback 🖑 _____

2. I am an animal with an abdominal pouch.
   _____

3. I am descended from a Polynesian people that settled New Zealand._____

4. I worked to ensure that aborigines gained the rights they deserve._____

5. I am a mountain chain in New Zealand.
   _____

6. I am a British explorer who was one of the first Europeans to explore Australia. _____

7. I am the islands of the central and southern Pacific. _____

8. I am an agreement between the British and the Maori. _____

9. I am an original inhabitant of Australia.
   _____

10. I am a settlement that serves as a prison.
    _____

aborigine
James Cook
geyser
Great Barrier Reef
Great Dividing Range
Maori
marsupial
Outback
Pakeha
penal colony
Polynesia
Charles Perkins
Polynesia
Southern Alps
Treaty of Waitangi

Activities

GeoGame

Use this online map to reinforce your understanding of the geography of Australia and New Zealand. Click and drag each place name to its location on the map.

Geo GAME

Australia

North Island

South Island

Tasmania

Southern Ocean

🖑 To play the complete game, go to **Interactive Review** @ ClassZone.com

Australia and New Zealand

Australia

Crossword Puzzle

Complete an online crossword puzzle to test your knowledge of Australia and New Zealand.

Across
1. an animal with an abdominal pouch to carry its young

VOCABULARY

Explain the significance of each of the following.

1. geyser
2. marsupial
3. James Cook
4. penal colony
5. constitutional monarchy

Explain how the terms and names in each group are related.

6. Outback, Uluru, and Great Barrier Reef
7. Great Dividing Range and Southern Alps
8. aborigine and Maori
9. Maori, Treaty of Waitangi, and *Pakeha*
10. aborigine and Charles Perkins

KEY IDEAS

① Unique Lands

11. Why did Australia and New Zealand develop unique plant and animal life?
12. What are the three distinct landforms of Australia?
13. What are the two main islands of New Zealand?
14. Why does New Zealand have so many mountains, geysers, and volcanoes?

② Australia

15. When did the aborigines arrive in Australia and from what locations did they come?
16. What mineral drew Europeans to Australia in the 1800s?
17. What two peoples influenced Australia's culture?
18. What are five of Australia's major exports?

③ New Zealand

19. Who were the first settlers of New Zealand and from what locations did they come?
20. Why did the Treaty of Waitangi cause problems between the British and the Maori?
21. What are three elements of Maori culture?
22. What are New Zealand's most important natural resources?

CRITICAL THINKING

23. **Compare and Contrast** Create a table to compare and contrast Australia with New Zealand.

FEATURE	AUSTRALIA	NEW ZEALAND
geography		
first settlers		
European colonizer		

24. **Draw Conclusions** How do the landforms of Australia and New Zealand affect where people live?
25. **Connect to Economics** How important is trade to Australia and New Zealand?
26. **Five Themes: Movement** Why did it take so long for Europeans to settle Australia and New Zealand?
27. **Connect Geography & Culture** How did the arrival of British settlers affect the native peoples of Australia and New Zealand?

Answer the
ESSENTIAL QUESTION

How has the human geography of Australia and New Zealand changed since European settlement?

Written Response Write a two- or three-paragraph response to the Essential Question. Be sure to consider the key ideas of each section as well as specific ideas about how life in Australia and New Zealand has changed from their earliest settlement. Use the rubric below to guide your thinking.

Response Rubric
A strong response will:
- discuss the first settlers in the region
- identify changes that occurred in culture and economics because of European settlement

STANDARDS-BASED ASSESSMENT

TABLES

Use the chart to answer questions 1 and 2 on your paper.

| World Production of Wool ||
Country	Metric Tons
Australia	395,000
New Zealand	199,000
China	152,000
United Kingdom	42,000
South Africa	32,000
United States	10,000

Source: Commodity Research Bureau, *CRB Commodity Yearbook 2004*

1. Which country is the largest producer of wool in the world?

A. Australia   **C.** New Zealand

B. China   **D.** South Africa

2. How does U.S. wool production compare to the wool production of New Zealand and Australia?

A. They are about the same.

B. The United States produces more than New Zealand.

C. Australia produces less than the United States.

D. Australian and New Zealand produce more than the United States.

PRIMARY SOURCE

Read the primary source below and use context clues to answer questions 3 and 4 on your paper.

> In 1812, the schooner *Parramatta* put into the Bay of Islands . . . for provisions and water. She was supplied by the natives [Maori] with potatoes, pork, and fish . . . and when they [Maori] required payment they were thrown overboard, fired at, and wounded. The schooner immediately [left] but was . . . driven on shore in a storm and the islanders revenged themselves by putting the crew to death.
>
> Source: Committee of the Church of England Missionary Society, *Memorandum to the Earl of Bathurst, Secretary of State of the Colonies,* 1817

3. The subject of this primary source is

A. a list of typical foods eaten by the Maori

B. a story about an early explorer of New Zealand

C. the relationship between European sailors and the Maori

D. missionaries in New Zealand converting Maoris

4. Does this quotation show evidence of a bias? Explain your answer.

GeoActivity

1. INTERDISCIPLINARY ACTIVITY–SCIENCE

With a small group, review New Zealand's energy sources. Choose either hydroelectric power or geothermal energy to research and create a museum-style display. Be sure that your display shows where the energy sources are located in New Zealand and how they work.

2. WRITING FOR SOCIAL STUDIES

Review information on the Maori attempts to regain their traditional lands. Form an opinion on the issue. Then write a paragraph supporting your opinion that could be posted on a Web log (blog).

3. MENTAL MAPPING

Create an outline map of Australia and New Zealand and label the following:

Australia
- Great Dividing Range
- Outback
- Tasmania

New Zealand
- North Island
- South Island
- Southern Alps

CHAPTER 30

Oceania and Antarctica

 ESSENTIAL QUESTION

How do the regions of Oceania demonstrate cultural diffusion?

CONNECT Geography & History

Use the map and the time line to answer the following questions.

1. Which state of the United States is found in Oceania?

2. Which European nations who staked claims to islands in the Pacific still control them?

Geography

1521 Sailing under the Spanish flag, explorer Ferdinand Magellan reaches Guam. ▶

40,000 B.C.

History

c. 40,000 B.C. Settlers of Oceania come from Southeast Asia in outrigger canoes like the one above.

Culture

1800s European colonies are established on larger islands of Oceania.

PACIFIC OCEAN

UNITED STATES

160°E · 180° · 160°W · 140°W · 120°W

40°N

20°N

Tropic of Cancer

MIDWAY I. (U.S.)

Hawaiian Islands
Honolulu

WAKE I. (U.S.)

JOHNSTON ATOLL (U.S.)

NORTHERN MARIANA IS. (U.S.)

GUAM (U.S.)

MARSHALL ISLANDS

Koror
PALAU

Palikir

Majuro

FEDERATED STATES OF MICRONESIA

Tarawa

Equator · 0°

NAURU

Fongafale

KIRIBATI

PAPUA NEW GUINEA

Port Moresby

Honiara

SOLOMON ISLANDS

TUVALU

TOKELAU (N.Z.)

SAMOA
Apia

AMERICAN SAMOA (U.S.)

COOK ISLANDS (N.Z.)

FRENCH POLYNESIA (Fr.)

Papeete

VANUATU

Port-Vila

WALLIS AND FUTUNA (Fr.)

NEW CALEDONIA (Fr.)

FIJI
Suva

TONGA

NIUE (N.Z.)

20°S

PITCAIRN I. (U.K.)

Easter Island

Tropic of Capricorn

AUSTRALIA

NEW ZEALAND

★ National capital
● Other city

0 — 500 — 1,000 miles
0 — 500 — 1,000 kilometers

ATLANTIC OCEAN

Antarctic Circle

60°W · 30°W · 0° · 30°E

SOUTHERN OCEAN

SOUTH AMERICA

Antarctic Peninsula

Weddell Sea

Queen Maud Land

Enderby Land

60°E

ANTARCTICA

Ronne Ice Shelf
Palmer Island

90°W

South Pole

90°E

40°S

SOUTHERN OCEAN

Marie Byrd Land

Ross Ice Shelf

Wilkes Land

PACIFIC OCEAN

120°W

Ross Sea

Victoria Land

70°S

120°E

0 — 250 — 500 miles
0 — 250 — 500 kilometers

150°W · 180° · 150°E · 60°S

Geography

◄ **1911** Norwegian explorer Roald Amundsen is the first to reach the South Pole.

History

1941–1945 Islands of the Pacific are battlegrounds during World War II.

Culture

▼ **1959** Antarctic Treaty opens Antarctica to international scientific research.

Today

Reading for Understanding

1

▶ Key Ideas

BEFORE, YOU LEARNED
Australia and New Zealand were influenced by the cultures of their native peoples and by European settlers.

NOW YOU WILL LEARN
Oceania is home to hundreds of cultural groups living on islands spread across thousands of miles of the Pacific Ocean.

▶ Vocabulary

TERMS & NAMES

Oceania the region of the Pacific Ocean with thousands of islands

Melanesia a subregion of Oceania that includes islands northeast of Australia and south of the equator

Micronesia a subregion of Oceania that includes islands east of the Philippines and north of the equator

Polynesia a subregion of Oceania that includes islands of the central and southern Pacific

oceanic island an island rising from the deep sea floor on a volcanic foundation

coral island a type of oceanic island that is a coral reef

atoll a ring-shaped coral reef encircling a central lagoon with no inner island

trust territory a territory placed under the control of a country by the United Nations

pidgin a simple form of speech that is a mixture of words from two or more languages

Visual Vocabulary atoll

▶ Reading Strategy

Re-create the chart shown at right. As you read and respond to the **KEY QUESTIONS**, use the chart to compare and contrast details about the subregions of Oceania.

 Skillbuilder Handbook, page R9

COMPARE AND CONTRAST

MELANESIA	MICRONESIA	POLYNESIA
1.	1.	1.
2.	2.	2.
3.	3.	3.

 GRAPHIC ORGANIZERS
Go to **Interactive Review** @ClassZone.com

Oceania: The Pacific World

Connecting to Your World

What do you think is the ideal climate? Many people believe that the climate and weather of the Pacific islands are ideal. The Pacific islands have a mild tropical climate with warm, but not too hot, temperatures. Gentle ocean breezes cool off the evenings, and sandy beaches are everywhere. In this section, you will study life in the Pacific islands and decide for yourself if they are your idea of a perfect place.

Three Subregions of Oceania

▼ **KEY QUESTION** What are the three subregions of Oceania?

Oceania is a region of the Pacific Ocean with thousands of islands. It stretches from Hawaii on the northeast, to Easter Island on the east, south to New Zealand, and west to the island of New Guinea. Geographers estimate there are between 20,000 and 30,000 islands in the Pacific Ocean. Some are just tiny specks in the vast ocean. Others are very large, such as Australia, a continent; New Zealand; and New Guinea, the second largest island in the world. Islands located close to Asia, such as the Philippines, Indonesia, and Japan, are not considered part of the region.

Easter Island Statues Hundreds of carved stone heads on this island look out over the Pacific Ocean.

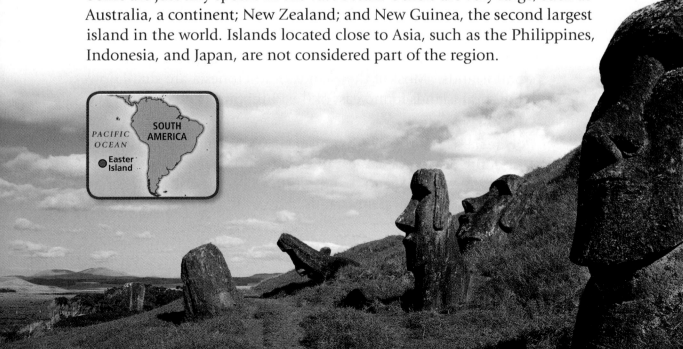

PACIFIC
OCEAN

SOUTH
AMERICA

Easter
Island

Subregions of Oceania

Click here to view the three subregions of Oceania @ ClassZone.com

MIDWAY I. (U.S.)

Tropic of Cancer

MEXICO

20°N

NORTHERN MARIANA IS. (U.S.)

WAKE I. (U.S.)

Hawaiin Is.

HAWAII (U.S.)

GUAM (U.S.)

Ⓑ MARSHALL ISLANDS

JOHNSTON ATOLL (U.S.)

PACIFIC OCEAN

M i c r o n e s i a

PALAU

FEDERATED STATES OF MICRONESIA

Line Is.

Ⓒ

Equator   0°

NAURU

INDONESIA

M e l a n e s i a

PAPUA NEW GUINEA

Ⓐ

SOLOMON ISLANDS

Coral Sea

VANUATU

NEW CALEDONIA (Fr.)

KIRIBATI

TUVALU   TOKELAU (N.Z.)

WALLIS AND FUTUNA (Fr.)   SAMOA   AMERICAN SAMOA (U.S.)   COOK ISLANDS (N.Z.)

TONGA

FIJI   NIUE (N.Z.)

P o l y n e s i a

Marquesas Is.

FRENCH POLYNESIA (Fr.)

Tuamotu Archipelago

20°S

PITCAIRN IS. (U.K.)

EASTER I. (Chile)

Tropic of Capricorn

AUSTRALIA

Tasman Sea

NEW ZEALAND

0   500   1,000 miles
0   500   1,000 kilometers

120°E   140°E   160°E   180°

CONNECT Geography & History

Movement Which of the three subregions was most likely first settled by people from the mainland of Asia?

Geographers divide Oceania into three subregions. These divisions are based on the physical geography of the islands and the culture and ethnic backgrounds of the peoples living there. The subregions are Melanesia, Micronesia, and Polynesia.

Melanesia The islands of **Melanesia** Ⓐ are close to Southeast Asia, northeast of Australia, and south of the equator. The world's second largest island—New Guinea—is located here.

Micronesia As you might have guessed, **Micronesia** Ⓑ means "small islands." Most of the islands of Micronesia are small, low-lying coral islands found east of the Philippines and north of the equator.

Polynesia The third region, **Polynesia** Ⓒ, means "many islands." This subregion is the largest in Oceania. It covers thousands of square miles of the central and southern Pacific and stretches as far north as the Hawaiian Islands.

▲ **SUMMARIZE** Describe the subregions of Oceania.

In Oceania, islands are constantly building and eroding. Islands can be created by natural forces. They are also subject to erosion and, thus, might disappear.

There are three types of islands in Oceania—continental islands, **oceanic islands** rising from the deep sea floor on a volcanic foundation, and **coral islands**, which are coral reefs. An **atoll** is a ring-shaped coral reef encircling a lagoon with no inner island. Below, see oceanic and coral islands.

Activity

Make a Model

Materials
- modeling materials
- colored pencils or markers, paper

1. Study the diagrams below. Choose one of the two types of islands to create in three dimensions.

2. Using the illustrations below as a guide, create a series of 3–5 small models showing in more detail how the type of island you selected is formed.

3. Write a caption for each model.

Modeling Clay

Oceanic Islands

Oceanic Islands

1. Magma sometimes erupts through cracks in the ocean floor.

2. Over time, layers of lava can build up to form a volcanic cone.

3. Some volcanic cones rise above sea level and become islands.

Coral Islands

1. Some corals form reefs on the sides of volcanic islands.

2. As the island erodes, the reef continues to grow upward.

3. In time, only the low islands of the reef remain.

History and Government

▼ **KEY QUESTION** Who settled the islands of Oceania?

The islands of Oceania were settled in three waves. The first peoples settled around 40,000 years ago on the islands of Melanesia and, later, those of Micronesia. Thousands of years later, groups from the settled islands moved east as far as Polynesia. In the 1800s, Europeans arrived in Oceania to establish colonies.

Oceania's First Settlers The earliest settlers of Oceania probably moved across land bridges or came by large canoes from the mainland of Asia and from Indonesia. These people may have left crowded conditions where they lived to look for more land. As they moved, they took animals and plants with them to start their new lives. In this way, the environment of the Pacific islands was changed to accommodate the culture of the newcomers.

Navigation Chart Pacific Islanders used charts like this to record the patterns of waves and ocean currents. **How would these charts aid the migrations across the Pacific?**

Colonization and Independence The first European contact with Oceania was made by explorer Ferdinand Magellan, who reached Guam in 1521. Later, British and French explorers came to the islands, bringing traders and Christian missionaries and colonists. In time, the United States, Germany, and Japan also set up colonies. The colonizers brought their language and religions with them.

Shells mark the location of islands.

Diagonal sticks mark the ocean currents and swells.

During World War II, the Allies fought the Japanese across the region of Oceania for control of the Pacific. After the war, people living on islands that were European colonies began to pressure the colonizers for self-rule. Some islands became trust territories administered by larger nations, such as the United States, New Zealand, Australia, and Britain. A **trust territory** is a territory placed under the control of another country by the United Nations. The countries prepared the territories to achieve self-government.

From 1962 to 1994, 12 islands or island groups were given independence. Some islands, such as French Polynesia, are still controlled by the original colonizers.

▲ **FIND MAIN IDEAS** Identify the groups that settled the islands of Oceania.

Culture

▼ **KEY QUESTION** What are the cultures of Oceania like?

The many peoples of Oceania's small islands live a traditional way of life. Family and village are the focus of their lives. Most live in small farming or fishing villages, just as their ancestors did. Households include parents, grandparents, uncles, aunts, and cousins. They may occupy one house or a cluster of houses. A chief heads each village.

About one-third of the world's languages are spoken in Oceania. Scholars estimate about 1,000 languages are found there. About 740 are spoken in Papua New Guinea alone. With so many languages, communication between peoples in Oceania was difficult. So, a form of speech called pidgin developed. **Pidgin** is a mixture of two or more languages and is spoken by people with different native languages.

▲ **MAKE GENERALIZATIONS** Describe the cultures of Oceania.

CONNECT ↘ **Geography & Culture**

Pidgin

Melanesian pidgin is spoken widely in Oceania. Pidgin languages often are a combination of a Western language, such as English, French, or German, and the local language.

The language is quite colorful. Here is how a piano is described in Melanesian pidgin: "bigfala bokis garem plande tit, iu hitim hemi kraeout" (a big box with many teeth, when you hit it, it cries).

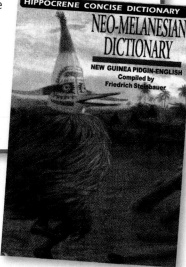

HIPPOCRENE CONCISE DICTIONARY

NEO-MELANESIAN DICTIONARY

NEW GUINEA PIDGIN-ENGLISH
Compiled by
Friedrich Steinbauer

 Section 1 Assessment

⊙ **ONLINE QUIZ**
For test practice, go to
Interactive Review
@ ClassZone.com

TERMS & NAMES

1. Explain the importance of
- Oceania
- Melanesia
- Micronesia
- Polynesia

USE YOUR READING NOTES

2. Compare and Contrast Use your completed chart to answer the following question:

In which of the subregions of Oceania would you find people who had traveled the farthest from Southeast Asia?

MELANESIA	MICRONESIA	POLYNESIA
1.	1.	1.
2.	2.	2.
3.	3.	3.

KEY IDEAS

3. What are the three subregions of Oceania?

4. How were the Pacific islands first settled?

5. What is the traditional way of life for Pacific Islanders?

CRITICAL THINKING

6. Draw Conclusions How did contact with Europeans and Americans affect the peoples of Oceania?

7. Understand Causes Why was it necessary to set up trust territories in Oceania?

8. CONNECT to Today Why might tourism be an important industry for the islands of Oceania to develop?

9. WRITING Prepare a Travel Brochure Select one of the nations of Oceania and prepare a travel brochure for tourists. Describe the nation's physical setting, climate, and attractions, and include pictures.

The entire population of Oceania, excluding Australia and New Zealand, is over 12 million. The population is spread out over thousands of square miles of the Pacific Ocean. Geographers divide the areas into three regions based on ethnic groups and on language.

Polynesia

Ancestors of Polynesians sailed across thousands of miles of the Pacific to settle these islands. Although the lands are widespread, the cultures of the subregion are similar in language, housing, and art forms. Tourism forms the basis of some economies.

POLYNESIA

▲ *A Polynesian man displays traditional tattoos from head to toe.*

French Polynesia ▼

Polynesian Work

A Polynesian works with an oyster to create a pearl for the pearl industry.

Micronesian Work

Ifalik Island fishermen bring in a catch. Many in Micronesia work in the fishing industry.

▲ Pilgrimage

For centuries, Buddhists have come to visit places in India and Nepal associated with the Buddha's life. These sites include the Buddha's birthplace and the fig tree where he achieved his enlightenment. Worshipers also visit the Dhamekha Stupa in Sarnath, India, the site of the Buddha's first sermon, shown here.

Symbol The Buddha's teaching, known as the dharma, is often symbolized by a wheel because his teaching was intended to end the cycle of births and deaths. The Buddha is said to have "set in motion the wheel of the dharma" during his first sermon.

Primary Source

The Buddha called his insight into the nature of suffering the Four Noble Truths. In the following selection, the Buddha tells his followers how they can end suffering and find enlightenment. The path involves understanding that life on Earth is brief and full of sadness. It also involves giving up selfish desire.

All created things are transitory [short-lived]; those who realize this are freed from suffering. This is the path that leads to pure wisdom.

All created beings are involved in sorrow; those who realize this are freed from suffering. This is the path that leads to pure wisdom.

All states are without self; those who realize this are freed from suffering. This is the path that leads to pure wisdom.

> from the Dhammapada
> Translated by Eknath Easwaran

Christianity

Christianity is the largest religion in the world, with about 2 billion followers. It is based on the life and teachings of Jesus, as described in the Bible's New Testament. Jesus, a Jew, taught many ideas from the Jewish tradition. Some biblical prophets had spoken of a day when a promised figure would come to save all of humankind. By the end of the first century A.D., many Jews and non-Jews had come to believe that Jesus was the one who would make this happen. Now called "Christians," they spread their faith throughout the Roman Empire.

Christians regard Jesus as the Son of God. They believe that Jesus entered the world and died to save humanity.

▼ Easter and Palm Sunday

On Easter, Christians celebrate their belief in Jesus' resurrection, or his being raised to heavenly life after he was put to death. The Sunday before Easter, Christians observe Palm Sunday. This day celebrates Jesus' triumphal entry into Jerusalem. Palm branches, like those carried in this procession in El Salvador, were spread before him.

▲ **Jesus and the Disciples**
Jesus' followers included 12 disciples, or pupils. Jesus passed on his teachings to his disciples. This painting from the 1400s shows Jesus with his disciples.

▼ **St. Paul's Cathedral**
Paul was a missionary who spread Christian beliefs throughout the Roman Empire. He started churches almost everywhere he went. Many churches today, such as this great cathedral in London, are named for Paul.

Symbol According to the New Testament, Jesus was crucified, or put to death on a cross. As a result, the cross became an important symbol of Christianity. It represents the belief that Jesus died to save humanity.

Primary Source

One of Jesus' most famous sermons is the Sermon on the Mount. In this talk, Jesus provided guidance to his followers. His words were written down in the New Testament, the part of the Bible that describes the teachings of Jesus. In the following verses, Jesus explains that people can be saved by opening their hearts to God and by treating others as they would like to be treated.

Ask, and it will be given you; seek, and you will find; knock, and it will be opened to you. For every one who asks receives, and he who seeks finds, and to him who knocks it will be opened. Or what man of you, if his son asks him for a loaf, will give him a stone? Or if he asks for a fish, will give him a serpent? If you then, who are evil, know how to give good gifts to your children, how much more will your Father who is in heaven give good things to those who ask him? So whatever you wish that men would do to you, do so to them; for this is the law and the prophets.

Matthew 7:7–12

Hinduism

Hinduism is a way of life guided by religious beliefs and practices that developed over thousands of years. Hindus believe that a supreme being called Brahman is the soul of the universe. The same presence, they believe, can also be found within each person. People can be freed from suffering and desires once they understand the nature of Brahman. The religious practices of Hindus include prayer, meditation, selfless acts, and worship of the various Hindu deities.

Today, Hinduism is the major religion of India and Nepal. It also has followers in Indonesia, Africa, Europe, and the Western Hemisphere.

▼ Festival of Diwali

Diwali, the Festival of Lights, is the most important festival in India. Diwali may have begun as a harvest festival in ancient India. Today, it marks the beginning of the year for many Hindus. They celebrate the festival by lighting candles and lamps, as shown in this photograph.

▲ Deities
Brahman often takes the form of three deities in Hinduism. Brahma is the creator of the universe. Vishnu is its protector. Shiva is its destroyer. All three deities are represented in this sculpture.

▼ Brahmin Priest
Brahmin priests, like the one shown here, are among Hinduism's religious leaders. These priests take care of the holy images in temples and read from the religion's sacred books.

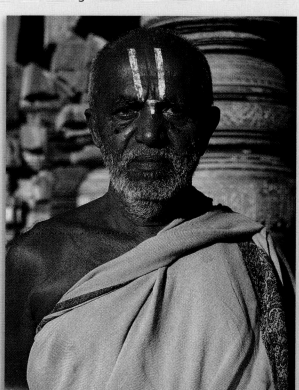

Symbol The syllable *Om* (or *Aum*) is often recited at the beginning of Hindu prayers. *Om* is the most sacred sound in Hinduism because it is believed to contain all other sounds. The syllable is represented by the symbol shown below.

Primary Source

Hinduism has many sacred texts. The Vedas, four collections of prayers, rituals, and other sacred texts, are the oldest Hindu scriptures. They are believed to contain all knowledge, past and future.

The *Bhagavad-Gita* is another sacred Hindu text. In this work, Vishnu takes on the personality of a chariot driver named Krishna. Krishna and the warrior Arjuna discuss the meaning of life and religious faith. In this selection, Krishna explains that Brahman cannot be destroyed.

> Weapons do not cut it,
> fire does not burn it,
> waters do not wet it,
> wind does not wither it.
>
> It cannot be cut or burned;
> it cannot be wet or withered;
> it is enduring, all-pervasive,
> fixed, immovable, and timeless.
>
> *Bhagavad-Gita* 2:23–24

Islam

Islam is a religion based on the teachings of the Qur'an, the religion's holy book. Followers of Islam, known as Muslims, believe that God revealed these teachings to the prophet Muhammad through the angel Gabriel around A.D. 610. Islam teaches that there is only one God—the same God that is worshiped in Christianity and Judaism. In Arabic, God is called Allah. Muslims also believe in the prophets of Judaism and Christianity. In fact, Muslims traditionally refer to Christians and Jews as "people of the book." That is because Christians and Jews have received divine revelations from scriptures in the Bible.

Today, most Muslims live in southwestern and central Asia and parts of Africa. Islam also has many followers in Southeast Asia. Muslims show their devotion by performing acts of worship known as the Five Pillars of Islam. These include faith, prayer, charity, fasting, and a pilgrimage to Mecca.

▲ Muslim Prayer
Five times a day—dawn, noon, mid-afternoon, sunset, and evening—Muslims face toward Mecca to pray. Like the people in this photograph, Muslims stop what they are doing when they hear the call to prayer. Everything comes to a halt—even traffic.

▼ The Dome of the Rock
The Dome of the Rock in Jerusalem is one of Islam's holiest sites. The rock on the site is the spot from which Muslims say Muhammad rose to heaven to learn Allah's will. With Allah's blessing, Muhammad returned to Earth to bring God's message to all people.

▼ Ramadan

During the holy month of Ramadan, Muslims fast, or do not eat or drink, from dawn to sunset. The family shown here is ending their fast. The most important night of Ramadan is called the Night of Power. This is believed to be the night the angel Gabriel first spoke to Muhammad.

Symbol The crescent moon has become a symbol of Islam. The symbol may be related to the new moon that begins each month in the Islamic lunar calendar.

Primary Source

The Qur'an is the spiritual guide for Muslims. It also contains teachings for Muslim daily life. The following chapter is called the Exordium (introduction). It is also called Al-Fatihah. Muslims recite this short chapter, as well as other passages from the Qur'an, when they pray.

In the Name of God, the Compassionate, the Merciful

Praise be to God, Lord of the Universe,
The Compassionate, the Merciful,
Sovereign of the Day of Judgment!
You alone we worship, and to You alone
  we turn for help.
Guide us to the straight path,
The path of those whom You have favored,
Not of those who have incurred Your wrath,
Nor of those who have gone astray.

Qur'an 1:1–6

Judaism

Judaism was the first major monotheistic religion—that is, based on the concept of one God. The basic teachings of Judaism come from the Torah, the first five books of the Hebrew Bible. Judaism teaches that a person serves God by studying the Torah and living by its teachings. The Torah became the basis for the civil and religious laws of Judaism. The followers of Judaism, or Jews, also believe that God set down many moral laws for all of humanity with the Ten Commandments.

Today, there are more than 15 million Jews throughout the world. Many live in Israel, where a Jewish state was created in 1948.

▼ Abraham

According to the Torah, God chose a Hebrew shepherd named Abraham to be the "father" of the Hebrew people. In the 19th century B.C., Abraham led his family to a land that he believed God had promised them. This painting illustrates their journey.

▲ Rabbi
Rabbis are the Jewish people's spiritual leaders and teachers. A rabbi often conducts the services in a synagogue, or Jewish house of worship. Like the rabbi shown here, he or she may also conduct the ceremony that marks Jewish children's entrance into the religious community.

▼ Western Wall
Many Jews make the pilgrimage to the Western Wall, shown here. The sacred wall formed the western wall of the courtyard of the Second Temple of Jerusalem. The temple was built in the second century B.C. The Romans destroyed it in A.D. 70.

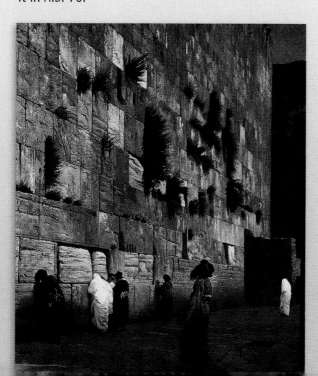

Learn More About Judaism

Symbol The Star of David, also called the Shield of David, is a very important symbol of Judaism. The symbol honors King David, who ruled the kingdom of Israel about 1000–962 B.C.

Primary Source

The Book of Genesis is the first book of the Hebrew Bible and of the Torah. Genesis tells the history of the Hebrew people. It focuses on the individuals with whom God had a special relationship. In the following verses, God speaks to Abraham. His words express a promise of land and a special pledge to the Hebrew people.

Now the Lord said to Abram [Abraham], "Go from your country and your kindred and your father's house to the land that I will show you. And I will make of you a great nation, and I will bless you, and make your name great, so that you will be a blessing. I will bless those who bless you, and him who curses you I will curse; and by you all the families of the earth will bless themselves."

Genesis 12:1–3

Confucianism

Confucianism is an ethical system based on the teachings of the Chinese scholar Confucius. It stresses social and civic responsibility. Confucius was born in 551 B.C., during a time of crisis in China. He hoped his ideas and teachings would restore the order of earlier times to his society. But although Confucius was active in politics, he never had enough political power to put his ideas into practice. After his death, Confucius' students spread his teachings. As a result, his ideas became the foundation of Chinese thought for more than 2,000 years.

Today, Confucianism guides the actions of millions of Chinese people and other peoples of the East. It has also greatly influenced people's spiritual beliefs. While East Asians declare themselves to follow a number of religions, many also claim to be Confucians.

▼ Temple
Although Confucianism has no clergy or gods to worship, temples, like this one in Taiwan, have been built to honor Confucius. In ancient times, the temples provided schools of higher education. Today, many have been turned into museums.

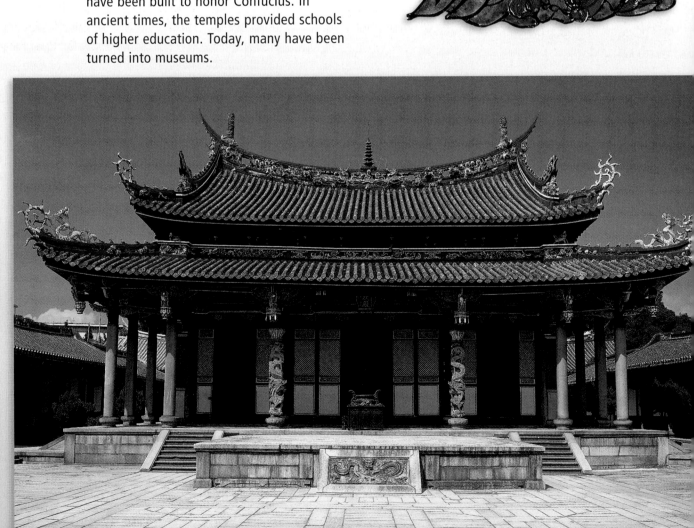

◄ Confucius

Confucius believed that society should be organized around five basic relationships. These are the relationships between (1) ruler and subject, (2) father and son, (3) husband and wife, (4) elder brother and junior brother, and (5) friend and friend.

Symbol The yin-and-yang symbol represents opposite forces in the world working together. Yin represents all that is cold, dark, soft, and mysterious. Yang represents everything that is warm, bright, hard, and clear. The yin-and-yang symbol represents the harmony that Confucius hoped to restore to society.

▲ Confucius' Birthday

Historians do not know for certain the day when Confucius was born, but people in East Asia celebrate his birthday on September 28. In Taiwan and China, it is an official holiday known as Teachers' Day. The holiday pays tribute to teachers because Confucius himself was a teacher. Here, students in Beijing take part in a ceremony honoring their teachers.

Primary Source

Confucius' teachings were collected by his students in a book called the *Analects*. In the following selections from the *Analects*, Confucius (called the Master) instructs his students about living a moral and thoughtful life.

The Master said: "Even in the midst of eating coarse rice and drinking water and using a bent arm for a pillow happiness is surely to be found; riches and honors acquired by unrighteous means are to me like the floating clouds." (7.16)

The Master said: "When I walk with two others, I always receive instruction from them. I select their good qualities and copy them, and improve on their bad qualities." (7.22)

The Master said: "The people may be made to follow something, but may not be made to understand it." (8.9)

from the *Analects*
Translated by Raymond Dawson

Other Important Religions

You have learned about the five major world religions. Now find out about some other important religions: Bahaism, Shinto, Sikhism, and Zoroastrianism. These religions are important both historically and because they have many followers today.

▼ Shinto

Shinto, meaning "way of the gods," is Japan's oldest and only native religion. Shintoists worship many gods, called *kami*. They believe that kami are spirits found in mountains, rivers, rocks, trees, and other parts of nature. Shintoists often worship the kami at shrines in their homes. They also celebrate the gods during special festivals, such as the one shown here. Today, there are about 3 million Shintoists, mostly in Japan.

▲ Bahaism

Bahaism (buh•HAH•ihz•uhm) is a young religion, with more than 7 million followers throughout the world. It was founded in 1863 in Persia (modern-day Iran) by a man known as Bahaullah, which means "splendor of God" in Arabic. Followers believe that, in time, God will break down barriers of race, class, and nation. When this happens, people will form a single, united society. All of the Baha'i houses of worship have nine sides and a central dome, symbolizing this unity. The Baha'i house of worship shown here is located in Illinois.

◀ Sikhism

Sikhism was founded in India over 500 years ago by Guru Nanak. The religion's 24 million followers, called Sikhs, believe in one God. Like Buddhists and Hindus, Sikhs believe that the soul goes through repeated cycles of life and death. However, Sikhs do not believe that they have to live outside the world to end the cycle. Rather, they can achieve salvation by living a good and simple life. Uncut hair symbolizes this simple life. Many Sikh men cover their long hair with a turban, like the one worn by this man.

▲ Zoroastrianism

Zoroastrianism (ZAWR•oh•AS•tree•uh•NIHZ•uhm) was founded in ancient Persia around 600 B.C. by a prophet named Zoroaster. This prophet taught that Earth is a battleground where a great struggle is fought between the forces of good and the forces of evil. Each person is expected to take part in this struggle. At death, the Zoroastrian god, called Ahura Mazda (ah•HUR•uh MAZ•duh), will judge the person on how well he or she fought. This stone relief shows Ahura Mazda (*right*) giving the crown to a Persian king. Today, there are about 2.5 million Zoroastrians throughout the world.

World Religions and Ethical Systems **R53**

Comparing World Religions and Ethical Systems

	Buddhism	Christianity	Hinduism	Islam	Judaism	Confucianism
Followers worldwide (estimated 2005 figures)	379 million	2.1 billion	860 million	1.3 billion	15.1 million	6.5 million
Name of god	no god	God	Brahman	Allah	God	no god
Founder	the Buddha	Jesus	no founder	no founder but spread by Muhammad	Abraham	Confucius
Holy book	many sacred books, including the Dhammapada	Bible, including Old Testament and New Testament	many sacred texts, including the Upanishads	Qur'an	Hebrew Bible, including the Torah	*Analects*
Clergy	Buddhist monks	priests, ministers, monks, and nuns	Brahmin priests, monks, and gurus	no clergy but a scholar class, called the ulama, and imams, who may lead prayers	rabbis	no clergy
Basic beliefs	• Followers can achieve enlightenment by understanding the Four Noble Truths and by following the Noble Eightfold Path of right opinions, right desires, right speech, right action, right jobs, right effort, right concentration, and right meditation.	• There is only one God, who watches over and cares for his people. • Jesus is the Son of God. He died to save humanity. His death and resurrection made eternal life possible for others.	• The soul never dies but is continually reborn until it becomes divinely enlightened. • Persons achieve happiness and divine enlightenment after they free themselves from their earthly desires. • Freedom from earthly desires comes from many lifetimes of worship, knowledge, and virtuous acts.	• There is only one God, who watches over and cares for his people. • Persons achieve salvation by following the Five Pillars of Islam and living a just life. The pillars are faith, prayer, charity, fasting, and pilgrimage to Mecca.	• There is only one God, who watches over and cares for his people. • God loves and protects his people but also holds people accountable for their sins and shortcomings. • Persons serve God by studying the Torah and living by its teachings.	• Social order, harmony, and good government should be based on strong family relationships. • Respect for parents and elders is important to a well-ordered society. • Education is important for the welfare of both the individual and society.

Source: *Encyclopedia Britannica Almanac, 2006*

Review

KEY IDEAS

Buddhism (pages R40–R41)

1. How did the Buddha believe that his followers could end their suffering?

2. How did Buddhism spread?

Christianity (pages R42–R43)

3. Why is Jesus important to the Christian religion?

4. What are some Christian beliefs?

Hinduism (pages R44–R45)

5. What is the importance of Brahman in Hinduism?

6. What three deities does Brahman often take the form of?

Islam (pages R46–R47)

7. How do Muslims believe the teachings of the Qur'an were revealed?

8. Why do Muslims traditionally refer to Christians and Jews as "people of the book"?

Judaism (pages R48–R49)

9. What does it mean to say that Judaism is a monotheistic religion?

10. What are the Ten Commandments?

Confucianism (pages R50–R51)

11. What did Confucius hope to restore?

12. What five relationships are important in Confucianism?

Other Important Religions (pages R52–R53)

13. How does Shinto differ from Bahaism, Sikhism, and Zoroastrianism?

14. How is Sikhism similar to Buddhism and Hinduism?

CRITICAL THINKING

15. **Compare and Contrast** What goal do Buddhists and Hindus share?

16. **Draw Conclusions** How does Islam affect the everyday lives of its followers?

STANDARDS-BASED ASSESSMENT

INTERPRETING A PIE CHART

The pie chart below shows what percentages of the population of India practice the major religions. Use the pie chart to answer the following questions.

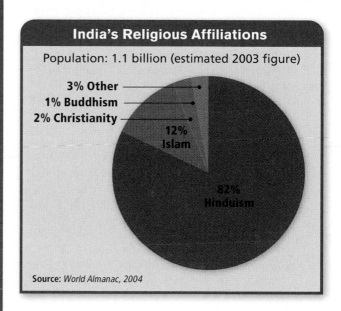

India's Religious Affiliations

Population: 1.1 billion (estimated 2003 figure)

3% Other
1% Buddhism
2% Christianity
12% Islam
82% Hinduism

Source: *World Almanac, 2004*

1. **What percentage of the people in India practice Hinduism?**

   A. 1 percent

   B. 2 percent

   C. 12 percent

   D. 82 percent

2. **Which religion is practiced by 12 percent of the population?**

   A. Buddhism

   B. Christianity

   C. Hinduism

   D. Islam

Glossary

A

aborigine (AB•uh•RIHJ•uh•nee) *n.* an original inhabitant of Australia (p. 892)

African National Congress (ANC) *n.* South African political party opposing apartheid (p. 624)

Afrikaner *n.* a South African of European ancestry who speaks a language called Afrikaans (p. 624)

agricultural revolution *n.* the shift from gathering food to raising food (p. 96)

Aksum *n.* an empire that controlled much of northern Ethiopia from the first to the eighth century A.D. (p. 606)

alpaca *n.* a South American mammal related to the llama (p. 272)

Alpine *adj.* having to do with the Alps mountain range (p. 382)

Alps *n.* Europe's tallest mountain range, stretching across southern Europe (p. 326)

altiplano *n.* a high plateau (pp. 204, 272)

Amazon River *n.* South America's longest river (about 4,000 miles, or 6,400 kilometers) and the second-longest river in the world (p. 204)

amendment *n.* a written change to the U.S. Constitution that must go through an approval process (p. 146)

Amundsen, Roald *n.* Norwegian polar explorer first to reach the South Pole (p. 920)

Anatolian peninsula *n.* in Southwest Asia between the Black Sea and Mediterranean Sea (p. 652)

ancestor *n.* an early relative (p. 544)

Andes Mountains *n.* a mountain range located on South America's west coast and extending the full length of the continent (p. 204)

animism *n.* the belief that spirits exist in animals, plants, natural forces, and ancestors (p. 544)

annex *v.* to add to an existing territory (p. 230)

Antarctic Peninsula *n.* an S-shaped peninsula that is part of the Andes Mountain chain (p. 920)

Antarctic Treaty *n.* an agreement signed in 1959 calling for the peaceful use of Antarctica (p. 920)

anthropologist (AN•thruh•PAHL•uh•jihst) *n.* a scientist who studies culture (p. 88)

apartheid (uh•PAHRT•hyt) *n.* the official policy of racial segregation practiced in South Africa from 1950 to 1991 (p. 624)

Appalachian (AP•uh•LAY•chee•uhn) **Mountains** *n.* a mountain chain in the Eastern United States, running parallel to the Atlantic Ocean (p. 122)

Aquino (uh•KEE•noh), **Corazon** *n.* politician who opposed Marcos and was president of the Philippines between 1986 and 1992 (p. 864)

Arabian Peninsula *n.* peninsula of Southwest Asia between the Red Sea and Persian Gulf (p. 652)

Aral Sea *n.* an inland body of water in Central Asia that has been steadily shrinking (p. 496)

archipelago (AHR•kuh•PEHL•uh•GOH) *n.* a set of closely grouped islands, which sometimes form a curved arc (pp. 198, 736, 852, 864)

artisan *n.* a worker skilled in making products or art with his or her hands (p. 254)

Aryan *n.* one of a group of Indo-European nomadic herders who are believed to have migrated to the Indian subcontinent (p. 698)

Ashanti (uh•SHAN•tee) *n.* a people of Ghana (pp. 580, 586)

Aswan High Dam *n.* a structure to control the floodwaters of the Nile River and provide electricity (p. 554)

Atlas Mountains *n.* series of mountain ranges stretching from Morocco to Tunisia (p. 568)

atmosphere *n.* the layer of gases that surround the Earth (p. 34)

atoll *n.* a ring-shaped coral reef encircling a central lagoon with no inner island (p. 912)

Aung San Suu Kyi (awng sahn soo chee) *n.* leader of the democracy movement in Myanmar (p. 858)

autonomy *n.* self-governance or independence (p. 376)

Aztec *n.* an early civilization in the Valley of Mexico (p. 212)

B

Bahasa Indonesia (bah•HAH•suh in•duh•NEE•zhuh) *n.* the common language of Indonesia (p. 864)

Baltic States *n.* Latvia, Lithuania, and Estonia, three countries that border the Baltic Sea (p. 424)

Bangalore *n.* south-central Indian city that is home to many high-tech industries (p. 716)

basin *n.* a region drained by a river system (p. 536)

Basque (bask) *n.* an ethnic group living in the western Pyrenees and along the Bay of Biscay in Spain and France; also the name of their language (p. 370)

Bechuanaland (bech•WAH•nuh•LAND) *n.* colonial name for Botswana (p. 630)

Bedouin *n.* an Arabic-speaking, traditionally nomadic people of Southwest Asia (p. 676)

Beirut *n.* capital of Lebanon and a center of banking and finance (p. 688)

Benelux (BEHN•uh•LUHKS) *n.* name for the economic union formed by Belgium, the Netherlands, and Luxembourg to ensure the fast and efficient movement of people, goods, and services within these nations (p. 376)

Berbers (BUR•buhrz) *n.* the original inhabitants of North Africa and the Sahara (p. 568)

Berlin Wall *n.* a wall built by East Germany's Communist government to close off East Berlin from West Berlin; torn down in 1991 (p. 382)

Bhagavad-Gita *n.* one of the sacred writings of Hinduism (p. 706)

Biafra (bee•AF•ruh) *n.* a largely Igbo region of Nigeria that declared its independence in 1967, but surrendered after losing a civil war with Nigeria in 1970 (p. 586)

bilingual *adj.* using or able to use two languages equally well (p. 164)

bipedal *adj.* walking on two feet (p. 544)

birth rate *n.* the number of births per 1,000 people per year (p. 58)

blues *n.* a type of music with lyrics that express sorrow, usually about problems in love or the hardships of life (p. 138)

Boer *n.* a Dutch colonist or descendant in South Africa (p. 624)

Bogotá *n.* capital city of Colombia (p. 266)

Bolívar, Simón (boh•LEE•vahr, see•MOHN) *n.* leader for independence in northern South America (pp. 220, 266)

Bolsheviks (BOHL•shuh•VIHKS) *n.* a group of revolutionaries who took control of the Russian government in 1917 (p. 468)

Bosniac *n.* an ethnic Muslim from Bosnia and Herzegovnia (p. 440)

bossa nova (BAHS•uh NOH•vuh) *n.* a jazz version of the samba, a Brazilian dance (p. 296)

Botero, Fernando *n.* Colombian artist known for portraits of people with exaggerated forms (p. 266)

boycott *v.* to stop buying and using products from certain sources as a way of protest (p. 304)

brain drain *n.* the loss of skilled workers who move in search of better opportunities (p. 424)

Brasília *n.* Brazil's current capital city (p. 290)

bread basket *n.* an abundant grain-producing region (p. 424)

Briton *n.* a British person (p. 408)

Buddha *n.* a name, meaning the "enlightened one," used for Siddhartha Gautama, the founder of Buddhism (pp. 698, 706, 774)

Buddhism *n.* a major world religion that began in India and is based on the teachings of Siddhartha Gautama (pp. 476, 698, 706, 774, 804)

Byzantine Empire *n.* the eastern half of the Roman Empire that survived for a thousand years after the fall of Rome (p. 362)

C

cabinet system *n.* a system of government that links the executive and legislative branches by choosing the prime minister and major department heads from the legislature (p. 176)

Cabral, Pedro Álvares *n.* Portuguese explorer who in 1500 claimed land that is now part of Brazil for Portugal (p. 290)

camel *n.* a humped mammal used in the desert as a pack animal and provider of meat, milk, and wool (p. 580)

Camp David Accords *n.* peace treaty negotiated by U.S. President Jimmy Carter, Egyptian President Anwar el-Sadat, and Israeli Prime Minister Menachem Begin between Egypt and Israel, signed at the U.S. presidential retreat in Maryland in 1979 (p. 562)

Canadian Shield *n.* a horseshoe-shaped, rocky plateau that covers much of eastern central Canada (p. 156)

Candomblé (kahn•duhm•BLEH) *n.* African religious practices that are mixed with Roman Catholic beliefs to produce a unique belief system (p. 296)

canopy *n.* the highest layer in a forest, formed by the treetops (p. 536)

Cape Colony *n.* South African land settled by Dutch colonists called Boers in the 1600s and 1700s (p. 624)

capoeira (KAP•oh•AY•ruh) *n.* a Brazilian dance combined with martial arts (p. 296)

Caracas *n.* capital city of Venezuela (p. 266)

carbon dioxide *n.* a gas composed of carbon and oxygen (p. 48)

Caribbean Community and Common Market (CARICOM) *n.* a trade organization of several Caribbean nations (p. 260)

Carthage (KAR•thihj) *n.* an ancient North African city-state (p. 568)

cartographer (kahr•TAHG•ruh•fur) *n.* a geographer who creates maps (p. 10)

Caspian Sea *n.* a large body of water bordering Russia to the south and situated between Transcaucasia and Central Asia (pp. 460, 496)

caste *n.* in India, a social class that a person belongs to by birth (p. 698)

cataract *n.* a high waterfall or rapids (p. 554)

Caucasus (KAW•kuh•suhs) **Mountains** *n.* a mountain range that runs between the Black Sea and the Caspian Sea (p. 496)

celadon (SEHL•uh•DAHN) *n.* Korean ceramic pottery with a thin blue or green glaze (p. 804)

Central America Free Trade Agreement (CAFTA) *n.* an agreement to promote trade between the United States and countries of Central America (pp. 254, 260)

Central Asia *n.* a region that contains the republics of Kazakhstan (KAH•zahk•STAN), Kyrgyzstan (KEER•gee•STAN), Tajikistan (tah•JIHK•ih•STAN), Turkmenistan (TURK•mehn•ih•STAN), and Uzbekistan (uz•BEHK•ih•STAN) (p. 496)

cession *n.* surrendered territory (p. 230)

chaebol (JEH•buhl) *n.* in Korea, a family-owned conglomerate made up of related businesses (p. 812)

Chang Jiang (chahng jyahng) *n.* the longest river in Asia, flowing through eastern China (p. 756)

Channel Tunnel *n.* the underwater railroad tunnel between France and England under the English Channel (p. 414)

Chechnya (CHEHCH•nee•uh) *n.* a largely Islamic republic in southwestern Russia that continues to fight for its independence (p. 486)

Cheju (CHEH•JOO) **Island** *n.* largest island off the southern coast of the Korean Peninsula (p. 796)

chinampas *n.* in Mexico, artificial islands used for farming (p. 212)

Christianity *n.* a monotheistic religion based on the life and teachings of Jesus of Nazareth and on the writings of the Christian Bible (p. 682)

Church of England *n.* the official church of England headed by the Archbishop of Canterbury (p. 408)

citizen *n.* a person who owes loyalty to a country and receives its protection (p. 78)

city-state *n.* a political unit made up of a city and its surrounding lands (pp. 334, 666)

Civil War (1861–1865) *n.* a conflict between the U.S. North and South over the issues of states' rights and slavery (p. 130)

civilization *n.* an advanced form of culture that developed in cities (p. 666)

clan *n.* a group of families related through a common ancestor (p. 830)

climate *n.* the typical weather conditions of a region over a long period of time (p. 40)

climatologist *n.* a geographer who studies climates (p. 16)

coalition *n.* an alliance or partnership, often a temporary one (p. 362)

Cold War *n.* a conflict between the United States and the Soviet Union after World War II that never developed into open warfare (p. 468)

colonia *n.* a neighborhood in Mexico (p. 236)

colonialism *n.* the control by one power over a dependent area or people (p. 858)

colony *n.* a group of people who settle a distant land but are ruled by their homeland, such as the United States; overseas territory ruled by a nation, such as Mexico from the 1500s to 1821 (pp. 130, 220)

Columbian Exchange *n.* the movement of plants and animals between Latin America and Europe after Columbus' voyage to the Americas in A.D. 1492 (p. 220)

Columbus, Christopher *n.* Italian navigator and explorer who sailed for Spain and explored the Caribbean and the coast of Central and South America (p. 370)

command economy *n.* an economic system in which the production of goods and services is decided by a central government (pp. 72, 424, 486, 512, 784)

commonwealth *n.* a self-governing political unit that is associated with another country (p. 260)

Commonwealth of Nations *n.* an association made up of the United Kingdom and many former British colonies (pp. 164, 400, 624)

communal *adj.* referring to shared ownership of property (p. 774)

communism *n.* a type of government in which the Communist Party holds all political power and controls the economy (pp. 78, 260, 424, 468, 764)

compulsory *adj.* required (p. 362)

Confucianism (kuhn•FYOO•shuh•nihz•uhm) *n.* a belief system based on the teachings of Confucius, a Chinese scholar (pp. 764, 774, 804)

conglomerate *n.* an organization made up of several companies in different businesses (p. 812)

Congo River *n.* Africa's second-longest river (p. 618)

conquistador (kahn•KWIHS•tuh•DAWR) *n.* Spanish word for "conqueror" (p. 220)

Constitution *n.* the document that is the basis for the U.S. government (p. 130)

constitution *n.* the set of laws and principles that defines the nature of a government (pp. 176, 230)

Constitution of 1917 *n.* Mexican constitution written during the revolution that is still in effect today (p. 230)

constitutional monarchy *n.* a government in which the powers of the king or queen are limited by the constitution (pp. 176, 414, 736, 858, 892)

continent *n.* one of seven large landmasses on the Earth's surface (pp. 26, 122)

Continental Divide *n.* a high ridgeline in the Rocky Mountains that divides east-flowing from west-flowing rivers (p. 122)

continental shelf *n.* the submerged land at the edge of a continent (p. 34)

Cook, James *n.* a British explorer who claimed land in Australia (p. 892)

coral island *n.* a type of oceanic island that is a coral reef (p. 912)

cottage industry *n.* a small business in which the workers manufacture items in their homes (pp. 716, 728)

coup (koo) *n.* military takeover (p. 586)

cuíca (KWEE•kuh) *n.* a friction drum used in the samba, a Brazilian dance (p. 296)

cultural blending *n.* something new created from combining the elements of two or more cultures (p. 138)

cultural hearth *n.* the heartland of a major culture; an area where a culture originated and spread to other areas (pp. 96, 212)

culture *n.* the shared attitudes, knowledge, and behaviors of a group (pp. 66, 88, 138, 212, 544)

cuneiform (KYOO•nee•uh•form) *n.* the first known writing system, which used wedge-shaped symbols and was developed in Sumer (p. 666)

cyclone *n.* a violent storm with fierce winds that rotate in a circular pattern like a hurricane (p. 658)

Cyrillic (suh•RIHL•ihk) **alphabet** *n.* the official writing system of Russia (p. 476)

czar (zahr) *n.* title for the rulers of Russia from the mid-1500s to the early 1900s (p. 468)

Czechoslovakia (CHEHK•uh•sluh•VAH•kee•uh) *n.* former country in Eastern Europe that existed from 1918 until 1993, when it split into the Czech Republic and Slovakia (p. 432)

D

daimyo (DY•mee•OH) *n.* in Japan, powerful samurai who became warrior-chieftains (p. 830)

Dao (DOW) *n.* according to the belief system of Daoism, a force that guides the whole universe (p. 774)

Daoism (DOW•IHZ•uhm) *n.* a Chinese belief system based on the idea of natural order in the world (p. 774)

database *n.* a collection of information that can be analyzed (p. 10)

Day of the Dead *n.* holiday to remember loved ones who have died (p. 236)

death rate *n.* the number of deaths per 1,000 people per year (p. 58)

debris (duh•BREE) *n.* the scattered remains of something broken or destroyed (p. 10)

Deccan (DEHK•uhn) **Plateau** *n.* a high area of land at the center of the Indian subcontinent (p. 658)

deforestation *n.* the cutting and clearing away of trees (p. 304)

degraded *adj.* of a lower quality than previously existed (p. 48)

delta *n.* the triangle-shaped deposit of rich soil at a river's mouth (p. 554)

demilitarized zone *n.* a buffer zone between North Korea and South Korea (p. 804)

democracy *n.* a government in which the citizens make political decisions, either directly or through elected representatives (p. 334)

demographer *n.* a geographer who studies the characteristics of human populations (p. 58)

demonstration *n.* a public gathering to protest a policy or action (p. 784)

dependency *n.* a place governed by a country that it is not officially a part of (p. 260)

deport *v.* to expel from a country (p. 424)

desert *n.* a region with plants specially adapted to dry conditions (p. 40)

desertification *n.* the change of fertile land to desert; the process in which farmland becomes less productive because the land is degraded (pp. 48, 536)

devolution *n.* the process of shifting some power from national to regional government (p. 414)

dictator *n.* a person with complete control over a country's government (pp. 254, 260, 266, 812)

dictatorship *n.* a state or government ruled by a leader with absolute power (pp. 78, 568)

Diet (DY•iht) *n.* Japan's law-making body, which consists of a House of Representatives and a House of Councillors (p. 840)

diffusion *n.* the spread of ideas, inventions, and patterns of behavior from one group to another (p. 96)

discrimination *n.* actions that might be hurtful to an individual or a group (p. 66)

diversity *n.* having many different ways to think or to do something, or a variety of people (p. 66)

Dom Pedro I *n.* Brazil's first Portuguese emperor; declared Brazil's independence from Portugal in 1822 (p. 290)

Dom Pedro II *n.* second emperor of Brazil, under whose rule slavery was abolished in Brazil in 1888 (p. 290)

domesticate *v.* to adapt or train plants or animals for human use (p. 544)

domestication *n.* the raising and tending of a plant or an animal to be of use to humans (p. 96)

dominion *n.* in the British Empire, a nation that is allowed to govern its domestic affairs (p. 164)

draft animal *n.* an animal used to pull a heavy load (p. 884)

drainage basin *n.* the area drained by a major river (p. 34)

Dravidian (druh•VIHD•ee•uhn) *n.* speakers of a language group found in India since the earliest times; mostly spoken in South India today (p. 698)

drought *n.* a long period of little or no rainfall (p. 594)

duchy (DUHCH•ee) *n.* the territory ruled by a duke or duchess (p. 376)

Dust Bowl *n.* a region of the U.S. Great Plains that suffered drought and suffocating dust storms in the 1930s (p. 130)

dynastic (dy•NAS•tihk) **cycle** *n.* in China, the pattern of the rise and fall of dynasties (p. 764)

dynasty (DY•nuh•stee) *n.* a family or group that rules for several generations, such as in China (pp. 554, 606, 764)

E

earthquake *n.* a sudden movement of the Earth's crust followed by a series of shocks (p. 26)

eclectic *adj.* made up of parts from a variety of sources (p. 432)

economic system *n.* a way people use resources to make and exchange goods (p. 72)

economy *n.* a system for producing and exchanging goods and services among a group of people (pp. 72, 304)

ecotourism *n.* travel to unique environments by people who take care to preserve them in their natural state (pp. 254, 736)

edible *adj.* fit for eating (p. 272)

emissions *n.* substances discharged into the air (p. 48)

emperor *n.* a ruler of an empire, which is a group of different territories or cultures led by a single all-powerful authority (pp. 764, 830)

empire *n.* a political system in which people or lands are controlled by one ruler (pp. 212, 220)

Enlightenment *n.* a philosophical movement in the 1600s and 1700s that was characterized by the use of reason and scientific methods (p. 350)

environment *n.* the physical surroundings of a location (p. 4)

equinox *n.* one of the two times a year when the sun's rays are over the equator and days and nights around the world are equal in length (p. 40)

Eritrea *n.* a former region of Ethiopia that became an independent country in 1993 (p. 606)

erosion *n.* the wearing away and movement of weathered materials by water, wind, or ice (p. 26)

escarpment *n.* a steep slope separating two flat areas of different heights (p. 536)

estancia (eh•STAHN•see•ah) *n.* large farm or ranch in Argentina (p. 280)

ethanol (EHTH•uh•NAWL) *n.* a liquid made by using a chemical process to convert sugar cane to a kind of alcohol that can be used for fuel (p. 304)

ethnic cleansing *n.* removing an ethnic or religious group from an area by force or the mass killing of members of such a group (p. 440)

ethnic group *n.* a group of people who share language, customs, and a common heritage (pp. 88, 476, 504)

Euphrates (yoo•FRAY•teez) **River** *n.* a river of Southwest Asia that flows from a plateau on the Anatolian peninsula to the Persian Gulf (p. 652)

Eurasia *n.* a term used to refer to a single continent made up of Europe and Asia (pp. 460, 496)

European Union (EU) *n.* an organization of European nations whose members cooperate on economic, social, and political issues (pp. 350, 362, 688)

Everglades *n.* a huge wetlands area of southern Florida (p. 122)

export *n.* a product or resource sold to another country (pp. 72, 304)

export *v.* to send something from one country to another (p. 146)

extended family *n.* the family unit that contains more relatives than just parents and children, including grandparents and other close family (p. 688)

F

famine *n.* a severe shortage of food that causes widespread hunger (pp. 594, 658)

fascism (FASH•IHZ•uhm) *n.* a political philosophy that promotes blind loyalty to the state and a strong central government controlled by a powerful dictator (p. 362)

fast *v.* to avoid eating, often for religious reasons (p. 728)

favelas (fuh•VEH•lahs) *n.* Brazilian name for the poor neighborhoods that surround the cities (p. 290)

federal republic *n.* form of government in which power is divided between a national government and state governments (p. 266)

federal system *n.* a government system in which powers are divided between the national and state or provincial governments (pp. 146, 176)

federation *n.* colonies, states, or countries that have joined together (p. 594)

Fertile Crescent *n.* a region stretching from the Persian Gulf northwest up the Tigris and Euphrates rivers and west over to the Mediterranean Sea (p. 666)

feudalism *n.* a political system in which lords gave land to vassals in exchange for services (p. 342)

fiesta *n.* a holiday celebrated with parades, games, and food (p. 236)

Filipino *n.* an inhabitant of the Philippines (p. 864)

First Nations *n.* organized cultural groups of Canada's native peoples (p. 164)

foreign investment *n.* money put into a business by people from another country (p. 512)

fossil *n.* remains of early life preserved in the ground (p. 544)

fossil fuels *n.* sources of energy from ancient plant and animal remains; includes fuels such as coal, oil, and natural gas (pp. 48, 326)

Fox, Vicente *n.* Mexican president from the National Action Party who was elected in 2000 (p. 230)

free enterprise *n.* an economic system in which businesses are free to operate without much government involvement (pp. 146, 176, 784)

French Revolution *n.* a conflict in France between 1789 and 1799 that ended the monarchy and led to changes in the way France was governed (p. 350)

G

Gaelic *n.* any of the Celtic family of languages spoken in Ireland or Scotland (p. 408)

Gandhi, Mohandas (GAHN•dee, MOH•hehn•DAHS) *n.* a 20th-century Indian who helped lead his country to independence by using nonviolent resistance to colonial rule (p. 698)

Ganges (GAN•JEEZ) **River** *n.* a river of South Asia that flows southeast from the Himalayas to the Bay of Bengal (p. 658)

García Márquez, Gabriel *n.* Colombian author and Nobel Prize winner (p. 266)

gaucho (GAOW•choh) *n.* Argentinian cowboy (p. 280)

Gautama, Siddhartha (GAW•tuh•muh, sihd•DAHR•tuh) *n.* the founder of Buddhism also known as the Buddha, or "enlightened one" (p. 774)

Gaza Strip *n.* a narrow territory along the Mediterranean Sea (p. 682)

Geographic Information Systems (GIS) *n.* a computer- or Internet-based mapping technology (pp. 10, 16)

geographic South Pole *n.* the point where all lines of longitude meet (p. 920)

geography *n.* the study of people, places, and environments (p. 4)

geomorphology (JEE•oh•mawr•FAHL•uh•jee) *n.* the study of how the shape of the Earth changes (p. 16)

geothermal energy *n.* power produced by the internal heat of the Earth (p. 900)

geyser (GY•zuhr) *n.* a hot spring that shoots sprays of steam and boiling water into the air (pp. 884, 900)

Ghana *n.* a West African kingdom between the A.D. 700s and the A.D. 1000s in what is now Mauritania and Mali; a modern country in West Africa (p. 580)

glacier *n.* a large, slow-moving mass of ice (p. 26)

global economy *n.* economy in which buying and selling occurs across national borders (pp. 146, 244)

Global Positioning System (GPS) *n.* a system that uses a network of Earth-orbiting satellites to pinpoint location (p. 10)

global warming *n.* an increase in the average temperature of the Earth's atmosphere (pp. 48, 304)

globe *n.* a model of the Earth in the shape of a sphere (p. 10)

glyph *n.* a carved or engraved symbol that stands for a syllable or a word (p. 212)

Gobi (GOH•bee) **Desert** *n.* a high desert in China and Mongolia (p. 756)

Golan Heights *n.* a region that was formerly part of southwest Syria that Israel has occupied since the 1967 war (p. 688)

golden age *n.* a period during which a society attains prosperity and cultural achievements (p. 698)

Good Friday Agreement *n.* an agreement between Northern Ireland's unionists and nationalists that set up a new government (p. 414)

Gorbachev (GAWR•buh•CHAWF), **Mikhail** *n.* Soviet leader from 1985 to 1991 who increased freedoms for the Russian people (p. 468)

government *n.* an organization set up to make and enforce rules for a society (p. 78)

Grand Canyon *n.* a deep gorge cut through northern Arizona by the Colorado River (p. 122)

Great Barrier Reef *n.* a 1,250-mile chain of coral reefs off the coast of Australia (p. 884)

Great Depression *n.* a period of severe economic decline from 1929 into the early 1940s (p. 130)

Great Dividing Range *n.* a range of low mountains in Australia (p. 884)

Great Lakes *n.* five lakes forming the largest group of freshwater lakes in the world (pp. 122, 156)

Great Plains *n.* a vast grassland in central North America (p. 122)

Great Wall *n.* a long, huge wall built over several centuries to keep nomads out of China (p. 764)

Great Zimbabwe *n.* an empire built by the Shona people from the first to the eighth century A.D. (p. 630)

Greater Antilles *n.* the northern largest Caribbean islands that include Cuba, Jamaica, Hispaniola (which includes Haiti and the Dominican Republic), and Puerto Rico (p. 198)

Green Revolution *n.* the use of special seeds, irrigation, fertilizers, and pesticides to produce high crop yields and food production (pp. 716, 728)

greenhouse effect *n.* the trapping of the sun's heat by gases in the Earth's atmosphere (p. 48)

greenhouse gas *n.* any gas in the atmosphere that contributes to the greenhouse effect (p. 48)

grid *n.* a network of horizontal and vertical lines that create squares or rectangles (p. 666)

griot (gree•OH) *n.* a West African storyteller (p. 544)

Gross Domestic Product (GDP) *n.* the total value of all the goods and services produced in a country in a year (pp. 72, 280)

ground water *n.* water found beneath the Earth's surface (p. 34)

guerrilla *n.* a member of an irregular army that operates in small bands (p. 630)

Gulf of Mexico *n.* an arm of the Atlantic Ocean that lies south of the United States (p. 122)

H

habitable lands *n.* lands suitable for human living (p. 58)

Hammurabi's Code *n.* one of the world's first law codes, compiled by the ruler Hammurabi (p. 666)

hanbok *n.* a traditional Korean costume (p. 804)

Harappan civilization *n.* an ancient civilization that developed along the Indus River (p. 666)

Hausa (HOW•suh) *n.* a people of northern Nigeria and southern Niger (p. 586)

Heian (hay•ahn) **Period** *n.* an era in Japanese history from A.D. 794 to 1185; arts and writing flourished during this time (p. 830)

Hidalgo, Miguel ("Father Hidalgo") *n.* father of Mexican independence (p. 220)

hieroglyphics *n.* an Egyptian writing system in which picture symbols stand for meanings or sounds (p. 554)

highlands *n.* mountainous or hilly sections of a country (pp. 198, 204)

Himalayas (HIHM•uh•LAY•uhz) *n.* the highest mountains in the world, which stretch along northern India, separating India from China and the rest of Asia (pp. 658, 756)

Hinduism *n.* the modern name for the major religion of India, which developed from Brahmanism (pp. 698, 706)

Hitler, Adolf *n.* German head of state from 1933 to 1945 (p. 382)

Hokkaido (hah•KY•doh) *n.* Japan's northernmost and second largest island (p. 824)

Holocaust *n.* the systematic murder of Jews and other minorities by the Nazis during World War II (pp. 350, 382, 682)

hominid *n.* a human primate; an early human (p. 544)

Honshu *n.* Japan's largest and most populous island (p. 824)

Horn of Africa *n.* a horn-shaped extension of land on the east coast of Africa (p. 606)

Huang He (hwahng huh) *n.* a river that flows from the Kunlun Mountains to the Yellow Sea (p. 756)

Hudson Bay *n.* a large inland sea to the north of the Canadian province of Ontario (p. 156)

hunter-gatherer *n.* a person who hunts animals and gathers plants for food (pp. 618, 892)

hydroelectric *adj.* having to do with electricity created by water-powered engines (p. 156)

hydroelectricity *n.* electric power generated by water (p. 304)

hydroelectric power *n.* electricity made by water-powered engines (pp. 326, 756, 900)

hydrologic cycle *n.* the circulation of water between the Earth, the oceans, and the atmosphere (p. 34)

I

ice shelf *n.* huge flat sheet of ice extending over a body of water, but attached to the land (p. 920)

iceberg *n.* a large piece of floating ice (p. 920)

icecap *n.* a glacier that covers a large area (p. 920)

icon *n.* religious image used by Orthodox Christians in their worship (p. 476)

Igbo (IHG•bo) *n.* a people of southeastern Nigeria (p. 586)

igloo *n.* a house made of snow (p. 170)

immigrant *n.* a person who leaves one area to settle in another (pp. 66, 130, 296, 408)

immigration *n.* process of coming to another country to live (p. 244)

imperialism *n.* the practice of one country controlling the government and economy of another country or territory (pp. 350, 400, 580)

import *n.* a product or resource that comes into a country (p. 72)

import *v.* to bring something from one country into another (p. 146)

Inca *n.* an early civilization in the Andes Mountains of Peru (p. 212)

indigenous *n.* native to a region (p. 272)

Indochina *n.* the name for a former French colony in Southeast Asia made up of Cambodia, Laos, and Vietnam (p. 858)

Indochinese Peninsula *n.* one of two peninsulas on which mainland Southeast Asia lies; the peninsula is located south of China (p. 852)

Indus River *n.* a river in South Asia that flows from the Himalayas to the Arabian Sea (p. 658)

Industrial Revolution *n.* the shift that began in Great Britain in the 1760s from making goods by hand to making them by machine (pp. 350, 400)

inflation *n.* a price increase or a fall in the purchasing power of money (p. 594)

infrastructure *n.* basic services a community needs, such as roads, railroads, water and power lines, schools, and post offices (p. 594)

innovation *n.* something new that is introduced for the first time (p. 96)

Interstate Highway System *n.* a network of more than 45,000 miles of roads that links every major U.S. city (p. 146)

Inuit (IHN•yoo•iht) *n.* the native peoples who inhabit the Arctic region of North America (p. 164)

Inuktitut (ih•NOOK•tih•tut) *n.* the language of the Inuit (p. 170)

Islam *n.* a monotheistic religion based on the teachings of Muhammad and the writings of the Qur'an, the Muslim holy book (pp. 476, 504, 562, 676)

isolate *v.* to cut off or set apart from a group (p. 334)

Istanbul *n.* the largest city of Turkey, formerly called Constantinople (capital of the Byzantine, or Eastern Roman, Empire) and originally called Byzantium in ancient times (p. 688)

isthmus *n.* strip of land that connects two landmasses (p. 198)

ivory *n.* the hard white substance that makes up an elephant's tusk (p. 618)

J

jaguar *n.* a large cat mainly found in Central and South America (p. 212)

jazz *n.* a type of music that developed from a blending of African rhythms, American band music, and the musical styles of African Americans and Europeans (p. 138)

jellaba *n.* a traditional Berber garment; a robe with full sleeves (p. 568)

Jerusalem (juh•ROO•suh•luhm) *n.* the current capital of Israel and an ancient city that is holy to Judaism, Christianity, and Islam (p. 682)

joropo (huh•ROH•poh) *n.* Venezuelan national folk dance (p. 266)

Juárez, Benito (1806–1872) *n.* Indian who became president and a Mexican national hero (p. 230)

Judaism (JOO•day•IHZ•uhm) *n.* the monotheistic religion of the Jews, based on the writings of the Hebrew Bible (pp. 476, 682)

K

Kalahari *n.* a desert in southern Africa (p. 630)

Kanto Plain *n.* the largest lowland of Japan, which extends from the Japanese Alps east to the Pacific (p. 824)

Kara Kum *n.* a huge desert that covers most of Turkmenistan (p. 496)

karma *n.* in Hinduism, the consequences of a person's actions in this life, which determine his or her fate in the next life (p. 706)

Kashmir *n.* a region in the northwest part of the Indian subcontinent; India and Pakistan dispute control of Kashmir (p. 716)

Kente cloth *n.* a brightly colored, woven cloth made by the Ashanti and Ewe peoples (p. 586)

Kenyatta, Jomo *n.* independent Kenya's first president (p. 612)

Khmer (kmair) **Empire** *n.* an empire that began in the 500s and had gained control of much of mainland Southeast Asia by the 800s (p. 858)

kibbutz (kih•BOOTS) *n.* a type of settlement in Israel in which the community shares all wealth and property (p. 682)

Kim Jong Il *n.* the Communist leader of North Korea (p. 812)

kimchi (KIHM•chee) *n.* a Korean dish made of pickled vegetables (p. 804)

King, William Lyon Mackenzie *n.* Canadian prime minister who led his country to independence (p. 164)

knight *n.* a vassal trained in combat who fought on behalf of lords (p. 342)

Koizumi, Junichiro (KOH•EE•zoo•mee, JU•NEE•chee•roh) *n.* Japan's prime minister from 2001 to 2006 (p. 840)

Kongo *n.* a member of a people living along the lower Congo River; a Bantu-speaking kingdom of the Congo River region arising in the 1300s (p. 618)

Korean Peninsula *n.* a body of land bordered by the Yellow Sea to the west, the East Sea (or Sea of Japan) to the east, the Korea Strait to the south, and China and Russia to the north (p. 796)

Korean War (1950–1953) *n.* a conflict between North Korea and the Soviet Union on one side and South Korea, the United States, and the UN on the other (p. 804)

Korean Workers' Party (KWP) *n.* a Communist political group that controls the government of North Korea (p. 812)

Kosovo *n.* a self-governing province within Serbia (p. 440)

Kurd *n.* a member of an ethnic group that does not have its own country but whose homeland lies in parts of Turkey, Iraq, and Iran (p. 676)

Kush *n.* an ancient Nubian kingdom in northern Sudan (pp. 554, 606)

Kyushu (kee•OO•shoo) *n.* Japan's southernmost island and home to several large cities (p. 824)

L

lacrosse *n.* a team sport invented by Native Americans (p. 170)

Lake Balkhash *n.* a lake in eastern Kazakhstan (p. 496)

land bridge *n.* dry land that appeared between Asia and Alaska during the Ice Age (p. 130)

land reform *n.* dividing up large plots of land to distribute land more evenly (p. 630)

landform *n.* a feature on the Earth's surface formed by physical force (p. 34)

landlocked *adj.* surrounded by land with no access to an ocean or sea (pp. 272, 280, 496, 728)

Landsat *n.* a series of information-gathering satellites that orbit above Earth (p. 10)

language *n.* human communication, either written, spoken, or signed (p. 88)

language family *n.* a group of languages that have a common origin (p. 88)

Latin America *n.* the region that includes Mexico, Central America, the Caribbean Islands, and South America (p. 198)

legislature *n.* the law-making body of a government (p. 716)

Leopold II *n.* King of Belgium, who was forced to give up his private ownership of the Congo Free State (p. 618)

Lesser Antilles *n.* the smaller Caribbean islands southeast of the Greater Antilles (p. 198)

Lewis and Clark Expedition *n.* a journey made by Lewis and Clark to explore the Louisiana Territory (p. 130)

lineage *n.* descent from an ancestor (p. 544)

literacy *n.* the ability to read and write (p. 138)

llama *n.* a South American mammal related to the camel (p. 272)

llanos (YAH•nohs) *n.* grasslands of South America's Central Plains (pp. 204, 266)

location analyst *n.* a person who studies an area to find the best location for a client (p. 16)

location *n.* an exact position using latitude and longitude, or a description of a place in relation to places around it (p. 4)

lord *n.* a powerful landowner (p. 342)

Louisiana Purchase *n.* the action by which President Thomas Jefferson bought the Louisiana Territory from France in 1803 (p. 130)

Loyalist *n.* a person who supported Great Britain during the American Revolutionary War (p. 164)

M

Maghrib (MUHG•ruhb) *n.* the Arab name for North Africa, which means "the West" (p. 568)

magma *n.* molten rock (p. 26)

Magna Carta *n.* a charter, or document, signed by England's King John in 1215 that limited the power of the monarch and guaranteed nobles basic rights (p. 400)

Magyar *n.* an ethnic Hungarian person or the Hungarian language (p. 432)

mainland *n.* the primary landmass of a continent or territory rather than its islands or peninsulas (p. 400)

Malay Peninsula *n.* the second peninsula of mainland Southeast Asia; the narrow strip of land that serves as a bridge between the mainland and islands (p. 852)

Mali *n.* a West African empire between the A.D. 1200s and the A.D. 1500s; a modern West African country (p. 580)

Mandela, Nelson *n.* South Africa's first African president (p. 624)

manifest destiny *n.* the idea that the United States should own all the land between, and even beyond, the Atlantic and Pacific Oceans (p. 130)

manor *n.* a noble's house and the villages on his land where the peasants lived (p. 342)

Mao Zedong (MOW dzuh•dahng) *n.* Communist leader of China from 1949 to 1976 (p. 764)

Maori (MOW•ree) *n.* a Polynesian people who were the first inhabitants of New Zealand (p. 900)

map *n.* a representation of a part of the Earth (p. 10)

maquiladora (mah•kee•la•DOHR•uh) *n.* factory in which materials are imported and assembled into products for export (pp. 244, 254)

Marcos, Ferdinand *n.* dictatorial president of the Philippines between 1965 and 1986 (p. 864)

market economy *n.* an economic system in which the production of goods and services is decided by supply and the demand of consumers (pp. 72, 146, 382, 424, 486, 512)

marsupial (mahr•SOO•pee•uhl) *n.* an animal with an abdominal pouch to carry its young (p. 884)

Marxist *n.* a person who supports the philosophy behind communism, including government ownership of the land and the means of production (p. 630)

Mau Mau *n.* a Kenyan independence movement that began in the 1940s (p. 612)

Maya *n.* an early civilization located in what is now the Yucatán Peninsula, Guatemala, and northern Belize (p. 212)

mechanized *adj.* equipped with machinery (pp. 304, 892)

medieval *adj.* from the Middle Ages (p. 342)

Mekong River *n.* a major river that runs south from southern China through Laos, Cambodia, and Vietnam (p. 852)

Melanesia *n.* a subregion of Oceania that includes islands northeast of Australia and south of the equator (p. 912)

Mercosur *n.* association of several South American countries to promote trade among the countries (p. 280)

Mesopotamia *n.* the land between the Tigris and Euphrates rivers (p. 666)

mestizo (mehs•TEE•zoh) *n.* person with mixed European and Native American ancestry (pp. 220, 254)

Mexican Revolution *n.* a fight for reforms in Mexico from 1910 to 1920 (p. 230)

Micronesia *n.* a subregion of Oceania that includes islands east of the Philippines and north of the equator (p. 912)

microstate *n.* an independent country that is very small in area and population (p. 858)

Middle Ages *n.* the period between the fall of the Roman Empire and the modern era, from about A.D. 476 to 1453 (p. 342)

Middle Kingdom *n.* an ancient Chinese name for China (p. 764)

migration *n.* the process of relocating to a new region (p. 66)

militarism *n.* a government's aggressive use of its armed forces (p. 840)

millet *n.* a grain raised in West Africa, often made into porridge (p. 594)

Milosevic, Slobodan (muh•LOH•suh•VICH, SLAW•baw•dahn) *n.* president of Serbia from 1989 to 1997 and of Yugoslavia from 1997 to 2000; a key figure in the ethnic conflicts in the Balkans in the 1990s (p. 440)

missionary *n.* a person sent to do religious work in another place (p. 88)

Mississippi River *n.* the largest river and chief waterway of the United States (p. 122)

Mobuto Sese Seko (moh•BOO•too SAY•say SAY•koh) *n.* dictator of the Democratic Republic of the Congo from 1965 to 1997 (p. 618)

modernize *v.* to accept new ways or ideas (pp. 562, 606)

monarch *n.* a king or queen who rules a country or territory (p. 716)

monarchy *n.* a type of government in which a ruling family headed by a king or queen holds political power (pp. 78, 334)

monotheism *n.* a belief in one god (p. 676)

monsoon *n.* a seasonal wind system that produces a wet or dry season in a region, sometimes with heavy rainfall (pp. 612, 658, 796, 852)

Moors *n.* the group of Muslims from North Africa who conquered Spain in the eighth century (p. 370)

mosaic *n.* a picture made by placing small, colored pieces of stone, tile, or glass on a surface (p. 266)

Mount Everest *n.* the world's tallest mountain, located in the Himalayas (p. 658)

Mount Fuji *n.* Japan's highest mountain peak (p. 824)

Mount Kilimanjaro *n.* the highest mountain in Africa, in northeast Tanzania (p. 536)

Mount McKinley (also called Denali) *n.* the tallest mountain of North America, located in Alaska (p. 122)

Mount Paektu (PAHK•too) *n.* the highest mountain (9,003 feet) on the Korean Peninsula (p. 796)

Muhammad (also spelled Mohammed) *n.* the founder and major prophet of Islam (p. 676)

multicultural *adj.* relating to or including many different cultures (p. 408)

multilingual *n.* able to speak many languages (p. 376)

multinational corporation *n.* a company that operates in more than one country (p. 146)

mummy *n.* a body prepared for burial according to ancient Egyptian practice (p. 554)

mural *n.* a wall painting (pp. 236, 296)

Musa, Mansa (moo•SAH, MAHN•sah) *n.* leader of the Mali empire from 1312 to about 1337 (p. 580)

Muslim *n.* a follower of Islam (pp. 504, 562, 676)

N

Nagorno-Karabakh (nuh•GAWR•noh-KARH•uh•BAHK) *n.* a province in Azerbaijan that Armenians believe should be a part of their country (p. 512)

National People's Congress (NPC) *n.* China's national law-making body (p. 784)

nationalism *n.* pride in and loyalty to one's nation (pp. 350, 362)

natural resource *n.* something that is found in nature that is necessary or useful to humans (p. 72)

neutrality *n.* a policy of not taking part in war (p. 382)

Nile River *n.* the longest river in the world, which empties into the Mediterranean Sea in northeast Egypt (pp. 536, 554)

nirvana *n.* in Buddhism, a state of wisdom that breaks the cycle of reincarnation (p. 706)

Nkrumah, Kwame (uhn•KROO•muh, KWAHM•eh) *n.* modern Ghana's first president (p. 586)

nomad *n.* member of a group who makes a living by herding animals and moving from place to place as the seasons change (pp. 96, 504)

nonviolent resistance *n.* a method of protest that draws attention to a problem without using violence (p. 698)

Nordic *adj.* relating to Scandinavia (p. 388)

North American Free Trade Agreement (NAFTA) *n.* agreement that reduced trade barriers among Mexico, Canada, and the United States (pp. 244, 254)

North Atlantic Drift *n.* warm ocean current that helps keep Europe's climate mild (p. 326)

North China Plain *n.* the fertile region between the Huang He and Chang Jiang rivers (p. 764)

Northern European Plain *n.* vast area of flat or gently rolling land from France to Russia (pp. 326, 376)

Nubia *n.* in ancient times, the Nile River valley of southern Egypt and northern Sudan (p. 554)

Nunavut (NOO•nuh•VOOT) *n.* a territory created in 1999 from the eastern part of the Northwest Territories and home to many Inuit (p. 156)

O

oasis *n.* fertile or green spot in a desert created by underground water coming to the surface (p. 652)

obelisk *n.* a pillar-shaped stone monument (p. 606)

Oceania *n.* the region of the Pacific Ocean with thousands of islands (p. 912)

oceanic island *n.* an island rising from the deep sea floor on a volcanic foundation (p. 912)

official language *n.* a language that by law must be used for government, business, and education (p. 138)

oligarchy (AHL•ih•GAHR•kee) *n.* a government ruled by a few powerful individuals (pp. 78, 334)

Olmec *n.* an early civilization along the Gulf Coast of what is now southern Mexico (p. 212)

ombudsman *n.* an official who investigates citizens' complaints against the government (p. 388)

one-crop economy *n.* an economy that depends on a single crop for income (pp. 260, 512)

Organization of the Petroleum Exporting Countries (OPEC) *n.* a group of oil-producing countries founded in 1960 (p. 676)

Orthodox Christianity *n.* the Eastern branch of Christianity that spread to Russia in the 900s and became the state religion (p. 476)

Ottoman Empire *n.* a Muslim empire based in Turkey that lasted from the 1300s to 1922 (pp. 676, 688)

Outback *n.* the interior region of Australia (p. 884)

outcropping *n.* bedrock that rises above the soil (p. 884)

ozone hole *n.* the seasonal thinning of a protective layer of atmospheric gas high above Antarctica (p. 920)

P

Pakeha (PAH•kee•HAH) *n.* a Maori word that means "white people" (p. 900)

Palestine Liberation Organization (PLO) *n.* a political group that claims to represent all Palestinians and to be working toward gaining an independent Palestinian nation (pp. 682, 688)

Palestinian territories *n.* the West Bank and Gaza Strip combined (p. 682)

Pampas *n.* grassy plains in south-central South America (pp. 204, 280)

Pan-Africanism *n.* a movement calling for the unity of all people of African descent (p. 580)

papyrus *n.* a paperlike material made from the stems of the papyrus reed (p. 554)

Parliament *n.* the national legislature of the United Kingdom (pp. 176, 400)

parliamentary *adj.* relating to a government with the parliament form of legislature (p. 716)

patrician (puh•TRIHSH•uhn) *n.* a wealthy landowner who held a high government position in ancient Rome (p. 334)

patrilineal *adj.* descent from father to father (p. 544)

patron *n.* a wealthy or powerful person who provides money, support, and encouragement to an artist or a cause (p. 342)

peacekeeping *n.* referring to military forces whose purpose is to prevent or end war (p. 688)

Peloponnesus (PEHL•uh•puh•NEE•suhs) *n.* the peninsula in southern Greece where Sparta was located (p. 334)

penal colony *n.* a settlement that serves as a prison (p. 892)

peninsula *n.* a body of land nearly surrounded by water (pp. 326, 796)

Perkins, Charles *n.* in Australia, an aboriginal rights leader (p. 892)

permafrost *n.* ground that is frozen throughout the year (p. 460)

persecution *n.* cruel treatment on the basis of religion, race, ethnic group, nationality, political views, gender, or class (p. 66)

Persia *n.* a historic region of Southwest Asia located mostly in what is now Iran (p. 676)

perspective *n.* a technique used by artists to give the appearance of depth and distance (p. 342)

Peter the Great *n.* a czar who ruled Russia from 1682 to 1725 and tried to make Russia more European (p. 468)

pharaoh *n.* a ruler of ancient Egypt (p. 554)

pidgin *n.* a simple form of speech that is a mixture of words from two or more languages (p. 912)

Piedmont (PEED•MAHNT) *n.* a hilly, upland region between the Appalachian Mountains and the coastal plain of the South (p. 122)

place *n.* a geographical term that describes the physical and human characteristics of a location (p. 4)

plantation agriculture *n.* the use of large farms to raise cash crops (p. 736)

plateau *n.* a high area of flat land (pp. 34, 198, 652, 756)

Plateau of Iran *n.* a high plateau in central and eastern Iran, surrounded by mountains (p. 652)

Plaza of the Three Cultures *n.* plaza in Mexico City that shows parts of Aztec, Spanish, and modern influences in Mexico (p. 236)

plebeian (plih•BEE•uhn) *n.* a commoner who was allowed to vote but not to hold government office in ancient Rome (p. 334)

polders (POHL•durz) *n.* land reclaimed by draining it of water with the use of a dam and pump (p. 376)

Polynesia *n.* a subregion of Oceania that includes islands of the central and southern Pacific (pp. 900, 912)

polytheistic *adj.* believing in many gods (p. 666)

population *n.* the number of people who live in a specified area (p. 58)

population density *n.* the average number of people who live in a certain area (p. 58)

porridge *n.* a soft food, made by boiling cereal grain in milk or water (p. 612)

precipitation *n.* falling water droplets in the form of rain, snow, sleet, or hail (p. 40)

prime minister *n.* the head of the cabinet and chief executive of government in a parliamentary system; for example, the head of the Canadian government (pp. 176, 716)

privatization (PRY•vuh•tih•ZAY•shuhn) *n.* the process of selling government-owned businesses to private individuals (p. 486)

privatize *v.* to sell government-owned businesses to private individuals (p. 512)

propaganda *n.* distorted or inaccurate information that is deliberately used to influence opinion (p. 476)

protectorate *n.* a weaker country or area controlled by a stronger country (p. 562)

Protestant *n.* a member of a Christian Church founded on the principles of the Reformation (p. 342)

province *n.* a governmental division like a state (pp. 156, 784)

Prussia *n.* the most powerful German state in the Holy Roman Empire (p. 382)

public education *n.* schooling that is paid for by the government (p. 138)

pull factor *n.* a reason that attracts people to another area (p. 66)

Punic (PYOO•nik) **Wars** *n.* wars fought between Rome and Carthage during the third and second centuries B.C. (p. 568)

push factor *n.* a reason that causes people to leave an area (pp. 66, 236)

Putin (POOT•ihn), **Vladimir** *n.* president of Russia who increased executive power in the 2000s (p. 486)

Pygmy *n.* a member of a people with an average height of less than five feet (p. 618)

pyramid *n.* an ancient Egyptian structure, built over or around a tomb (p. 554)

Q

quilombos (kih•LOHM•buhs) *n.* communities created by escaped African slaves (p. 296)

quinoa (kih•NOH•uh) *n.* a kind of weed from the Andean region that produces a small grain (p. 272)

quota *n.* a target amount for production (p. 618)

R

rain forest *n.* a broadleaf tree region in a tropical climate (pp. 204, 304)

Ramadan *n.* the ninth month of the Muslim calendar, during which Muslims fast from sunrise to sunset each day (p. 728)

rate of natural increase *n.* the death rate subtracted from the birth rate (p. 58)

raw material *n.* an unprocessed natural resource that will be converted to a finished product (p. 72)

Reconquista *n.* the successful effort by the Spanish to drive the Moors out of Spain (p. 370)

Red Sea *n.* a narrow sea that divides northeast Africa from the Arabian Peninsula (p. 606)

reform *n.* action to improve social or economic conditions (p. 784)

Reformation *n.* a movement in the 1500s to change practices in the Catholic Church (p. 342)

refugee *n.* a person who flees a place to find safety (pp. 66, 440)

region *n.* an area that has one or more common characteristics that unite or connect it with other areas (p. 4)

reincarnation *n.* the rebirth of a soul in another body (p. 706)

relief *n.* the difference in the elevation of a landform from its lowest point to its highest point (p. 34)

religion *n.* an organized system of beliefs and practices, often centered on one or more gods (p. 88)

remote sensing *n.* obtaining information about a site by using an instrument that is not physically in contact with the site (p. 10)

Renaissance (REHN•ih•SAHNS) *n.* a rebirth of creativlty, literature, and learning in Europe from about 1300 to 1600 (p. 342)

renewable energy sources *n.* sources of energy able to be replaced through ongoing natural processes (p. 326)

representative democracy *n.* a type of government in which citizens hold political power through elected representatives (pp. 78, 146)

representative government *n.* a system of government with a legislature that is at least partly elected by the people (p. 400)

republic *n.* a government in which citizens elect representatives to rule in their name; another term for representative democracy (pp. 146, 334)

Republic of Texas *n.* constitutional government of Texas after independence from Mexico (p. 230)

reunify *v.* to bring something that has been separated back together (p. 382)

revolution *n.* the overthrow of a ruler or government; a major change in ideas (p. 230)

Rhodesia *n.* the colonial name for the countries that are today Zambia and Zimbabwe (p. 630)

rig *v.* to influence or fix the results of an election (p. 594)

Ring of Fire *n.* a geographic zone that extends along the rim of the Pacific Ocean and has numerous volcanoes and earthquakes (pp. 26, 824)

Rio de Janeiro (REE•oh day zhuh•NAYR•OH) *n.* Brazil's capital city from 1763 to 1960 (p. 290)

ritual *n.* a set of regularly followed ceremonies (p. 774)

Rivera, Diego *n.* famous muralist who painted the history of Mexico on the walls of the National Palace (p. 236)

Rocky Mountains *n.* a mountain range that extends about 3,000 miles from New Mexico to Alaska (p. 122)

Romance language *n.* any of the languages that developed from the Roman language, Latin, such as Spanish, Portuguese, French, Italian, and Romanian (p. 362)

Rose Revolution *n.* a peaceful uprising in Soviet Georgia that helped force a corrupt president to resign (p. 512)

Rosetta Stone *n.* an ancient Egyptian stone that provided a key to decipher hieroglyphics (p. 562)

Royal Canadian Mounted Police *n.* an organization of officers who were responsible for law enforcement in the Canadian West (p. 170)

rural *adj.* having to do with the countryside (pp. 58, 236)

Russification *n.* the effort to make countries occupied by the Soviet Union more Russian by replacing local languages and customs (pp. 424, 504)

S

Sadat, Anwar el- *n.* president of Egypt from 1970 to 1981 (p. 562)

safari *n.* an overland expedition for exploring, hunting, or photography (p. 612)

Sahara *n.* the world's largest desert (p. 536)

Sahel (suh•HAYL) *n.* a semiarid region just south of the Sahara (p. 536)

samba (SAM•buh) *n.* music and dance, with roots in African rhythms; the most famous form of Brazilian music worldwide (p. 296)

Sami *n.* people of northern Scandinavia who traditionally herd reindeer; also the name of their language (p. 388)

samurai (SAM•uh•RY) *n.* professional soldiers of Japan (p. 830)

San Martín, José de *n.* leader for independence in southern South America (pp. 220, 280)

sanction *n.* a penalty or pressure applied to a country for not obeying an order or law (p. 624)

Sanskrit *n.* an ancient language of India, first spoken by the Aryans (p. 698)

Santa Anna, Antonio López de (1794–1876) *n.* Mexican general, president, and leader of Mexican independence from Spain (p. 230)

savanna *n.* a vegetation region in the tropics or subtropics with a mix of grassland and scattered trees (pp. 40, 536)

scholar-official *n.* an educated person who worked in China's government (p. 764)

Scientific Revolution *n.* a major change in European thinking in the mid-1500s that led to the questioning of old theories (p. 350)

Scott, Robert *n.* a British polar explorer (p. 920)

seafaring *adj.* using the sea for transportation (p. 326)

secular *adj.* worldly or not related to religion (p. 342)

sediment *n.* pieces of rock in the form of sand, stone, or silt deposited by wind, water, or ice (p. 26)

segregation *n.* the policy of separating people of different races (p. 624)

seismic (SYZ•mihk) *adj.* having to do with earthquakes (p. 756)

Selassie, Haile (suh•LAS•ee, HY•lee) *n.* emperor of Ethiopia from 1930 to 1974 (p. 606)

self-rule *n.* independent government (p. 580)

self-sufficient *adj.* able to provide for one's own needs without outside help (p. 304)

selva *n.* Spanish name for the eastern Peruvian regions that contain rain forests (p. 272)

separatist *n.* a person who wants a region to break away from the nation it is a part of (pp. 164, 370)

serf *n.* in Europe, a person who lived and worked on the manor of a lord or vassal; in Russia, a peasant who is bound to the land (pp. 342, 468)

service industry *n.* an industry that provides services rather than objects (p. 254)

Seven Years' War (1756–1763) *n.* a conflict between Britain and France that was fought in North America, Europe, and India (p. 164)

shadow puppet *n.* traditional Indonesian art, in which puppets are handled from behind a screen lit by a bright light (p. 864)

shah *n.* title for the king of Persia or Iran (p. 676)

Shakespeare, William *n.* English playwright and poet during the late 16th and early 17th centuries (p. 408)

shamanism (SHAH•muh•NIHZ•uhm) *n.* a belief system in which a person called a shaman is believed to be able to communicate with spirits and heal the sick (p. 804)

Shi Huangdi (shee hwahng•dee) *n.* the first emperor to unify much of China (p. 764)

Shikoku (shee•KAW•koo) *n.* Japan's smallest and least populated major island (p. 824)

Shinto *n.* Japan's original religion; involves worshiping gods believed to be found in nature (p. 830)

shock therapy *n.* in Russia, term applied to Yeltsin's economic plan, which called for an abrupt shift from a command economy to a market economy (p. 486)

shogun *n.* the leader of the military government of Japan beginning in 1192 (p. 830)

Siam *n.* the former name of Thailand (p. 858)

Siberia *n.* a huge region in Asian Russia (p. 460)

Sierra Madre Occidental *n.* mountain range that runs from north to south down the western part of Mexico (p. 198)

Sierra Madre Oriental *n.* mountain range that runs from north to south down the eastern part of Mexico (p. 198)

Silk Roads *n.* major trade routes that ran from China to the rest of East Asia, through Central Asia, and into Europe (pp. 504, 774)

silt *n.* the fine, fertile soil carried by rivers and deposited on nearby lands (pp. 554, 666)

Solidarity *n.* Poland's first independent labor union, cofounded by Lech Walesa (p. 424)

solstice *n.* the time during the year when the sun reaches the farthest northern or southern point in the sky (p. 40)

Songhai (sawng•hy) *n.* an ancient West African empire, which was most powerful about A.D. 1500 (p. 580)

souk (sook) *n.* open-air market common in North Africa (p. 568)

Southern Alps *n.* a mountain chain in New Zealand (p. 884)

Southern Cone *n.* South American nations located in the cone-shaped southernmost part of South America (p. 280)

Soviet Union *n.* a Communist nation, consisting of Russia and 14 other states, that existed from 1922 to 1991 (p. 728)

spatial *adj.* referring to where a place is located and its physical relationship to other places, people, or environments (p. 4)

specialization *n.* a focus on producing a limited number of a specific product (p. 72)

squatter *n.* person who settles on unoccupied land without having legal claim to it (p. 236)

St. Lawrence Seaway *n.* a waterway made up of the St. Lawrence River, the Great Lakes, and several canals (p. 156)

stability *n.* durability; resistance to change (p. 586)

Stalin, Joseph *n.* a cruel 20th-century dictator who had millions of his political enemies executed (pp. 468, 512)

standard of living *n.* an economic measure relating to the quality and amount of goods available to a group of people and how those goods are distributed across the group (p. 432)

stateless societies *n.* groups that have no single authority, but make decisions based on compromise (p. 544)

steppe *n.* a grassy plain; in Russia, this area lies south of the taiga (p. 460)

Stone Age *n.* the earliest period of human culture, in which people used stone tools (p. 544)

strategic *adj.* relating to a plan of action designed to achieve a specific goal; in relation to the military, helpful in the fighting of a war (pp. 432, 728)

subcontinent *n.* a large landmass that is part of a continent but is considered a separate region (p. 658)

subsistence farming *n.* farming that produces just enough to feed the farmer's family, with little or nothing left over to sell (pp. 254, 586, 728, 736)

Sudan *n.* a country of northeast Africa, located south of Egypt (p. 562)

Suez Canal *n.* a waterway linking the Red Sea with the Mediterranean Sea (p. 562)

Sumer *n.* a region of city-states in Mesopotamia that was home to the first civilization (p. 666)

surveyor *n.* a person who maps and measures the land (pp. 10, 16)

sustainable *adj.* refers to using natural resources in such a way that they exist for future generations (p. 48)

Swahili *n.* an African language, commonly spoken in East Africa (p. 612)

T

taiga *n.* (TY•guh) a vast forest in Russia that lies south of the tundra (p. 460)

Taino (TY•noh) *n.* Indian group in the Caribbean islands (p. 260)

Taj Mahal *n.* a beautiful tomb in India built by the Mughal ruler Shah Jahan to honor his wife, who died in 1631 (p. 698)

Taklimakan (TAH•kluh•muh•KAHN) **Desert** *n.* the second largest sand desert in the world (p. 756)

Taliban *n.* a conservative Islamic group that took control of Afghanistan in the mid-1990s (p. 728)

technology *n.* people's application of knowledge, tools, and inventions to meet their needs (p. 96)

tectonic plate *n.* a large rigid section of the Earth's crust that is in constant motion (pp. 26, 198, 536)

territory *n.* a Canadian political unit that doesn't have enough people to be a province (p. 156)

Tet *n.* the Vietnamese New Year and most important holiday in Viet Nam (p. 858)

theocracy *n.* a government run by religious leaders (p. 676)

Three Gorges Dam *n.* a barrier built on the Chang Jiang to control floods (p. 756)

Three Kingdoms *n.* the three kingdoms that had formed on the Korean Peninsula by A.D. 300 (p. 804)

three-dimensional *adj.* describing an image in which there is a sense of depth and perspective (p. 4)

Tiananmen (tyahn•ahn•mehn) **Square** *n.* the location in Beijing, China, of a huge demonstration for democratic rights that occurred in 1989 (p. 784)

Tian Shan (TYAHN SHAHN) *n.* a mountain range that runs across Kyrgyzstan and Tajikistan (p. 496)

Tigris River *n.* a river of Southwest Asia that flows from a plateau on the Anatolian peninsula to the Persian Gulf (p. 652)

Tito, Josip Broz *n.* the Communist leader of Yugoslavia from 1953 to 1980 (p. 440)

Tokugawa Ieyasu (TOH•koo•GAH•wah EE•yeh•YAH•soo) *n.* shogun who unified Japan (p. 830)

Tolstoy (TOHL•stoy), **Leo** *n.* a 19th-century writer who is one of Russia's greatest novelists (p. 476)

totalitarian (toh•tal•ih•TAIR•ee•uhn) *adj.* referring to a type of government that controls every aspect of public and private life (pp. 468, 812)

tourism *n.* industry that provides services for travelers (p. 260)

Transantarctic Mountains *n.* mountains that divide Antarctica into two parts (p. 920)

Transcaucasia (TRANS•kaw•KAY•zhuh) *n.* a region between the Black and Caspian seas that contains the republics of Armenia, Azerbaijan (AZ•uhr•by•ZHYAHN), and Georgia (p. 496)

transcontinental railroad *n.* a railroad that crosses a continent (p. 130)

trans-Saharan *adj.* across the Sahara (p. 580)

Treaty of Tordesillas (TAWR•day•SEEL•yahs) *n.* 1494 treaty between Spain and Portugal that gave Portugal control over land that is now Brazil (p. 290)

Treaty of Waitangi (WY•TAHNG•gee) *n.* a treaty between the British and the Maori signed in 1840 (p. 900)

trust territory *n.* a territory placed under the control of a country by the United Nations (p. 912)

tsunami (tsu•NAH•mee) *n.* a series of giant, destructive ocean waves caused by underwater earthquakes, volcanoes, or landslides (pp. 658, 736, 852)

tundra *n.* a cold, dry climate and vegetation adapted to the climate in the Arctic Circle; in Russia, located in the far north (pp. 156, 460)

typhoon *n.* a tropical storm that starts in the western Pacific or Indian oceans (p. 796)

tyrant *n.* someone who takes power illegally (p. 334)

U

Uluru (oo•LOO•roo) *n.* a spectacular rock outcropping in the Australian Outback (p. 884)

Union of Soviet Socialist Republics (USSR), or **Soviet Union** *n.* a nation with a Communist government created by the Bolsheviks in 1922; dissolved in 1991 (p. 468)

unwritten constitution *n.* a framework for government that is not a single written document but includes many different laws, court decisions, and political customs (p. 414)

Ural Mountains *n.* a north-south mountain range that forms the border between European and Asian Russia (p. 460)

urban *adj.* having to do with a city (pp. 16, 58, 236)

urban planner *n.* a person who creates plans for developing and improving parts of a city (p. 16)

urbanization *n.* growth in the number of people living in urban areas; the process of city development (pp. 58, 290)

V

vassal *n.* a less wealthy noble who paid taxes to and served a lord in exchange for land (p. 342)

Vatican *n.* the official residence of the pope in Vatican City, and the political and religious center of the Roman Catholic Church (p. 362)

Vedas *n.* ancient Sanskrit writings that are the earliest sacred texts of Hinduism (p. 698)

vegetation region *n.* an area that has similar plants (p. 40)

Velvet Revolution *n.* the peaceful protest by the Czech people that led to the smooth end of communism in Czechoslovakia (p. 432)

Victoria Falls *n.* a 355-foot waterfall on the Zambezi River in South Central Africa (p. 536)

Vikings *n.* a seafaring Scandinavian people who raided northern and western Europe from the 9th to the 11th century (p. 388)

volcano *n.* an opening in the Earth's crust from which molten rock, ash, and hot gases flow or are thrown out (p. 26)

Volga River *n.* the longest river in Europe, flowing through European Russia (p. 460)

W

Walesa, Lech (wah•LEHN•suh, lehk) *n.* Polish leader who cofounded Solidarity and served as president of Poland from 1990 to 1995 (p. 424)

weather *n.* the condition of the Earth's atmosphere at a given time and place (p. 40)

weathering *n.* the gradual physical and chemical breakdown of rocks on the surface of the Earth (p. 26)

welfare state *n.* a social system in which the government provides for many of its citizens' needs (p. 388)

West Bank *n.* a region west of the Jordan River (p. 682)

wind farm *n.* a power plant that uses windmills to generate electricity (p. 414)

X

Xi Jiang (she jyahng) *n.* a river in southeast China (p. 756)

Y

Yalu River *n.* the longest river on the Korean Peninsula; forms part of the border between China and North Korea; known as the Amnok River in Korean (p. 796)

Yeltsin (YEHLT•sihn), **Boris** *n.* president who abruptly transformed the Russian economy after the Soviet Union collapsed (p. 486)

Yoruba (YAWR•uh•buh) *n.* a people of southwestern Nigeria, parts of Benin, and Togo (p. 586)

Yugoslavia *n.* a country on the Balkan Peninsula from 1918 to 1991 (p. 440)

yurt *n.* a portable, tentlike structure used by the nomads of Central Asia (p. 504)

Z

zaibatsu (ZY•baht•SOO) *n.* large family-controlled banking and industrial groups that owned many companies in Japan before World War II (p. 840)

Zaire *n.* the Democratic Republic of the Congo's name between 1971 and 1997 (p. 618)

ziggurat (ZIG•oo•rat) *n.* a temple built atop a series of increasingly smaller platforms (p. 666)

Spanish Glossary

A

aborigine [aborigen] *s.* habitante originario de Australia (pág. 892)

African National Congress (ANC) [Congreso Nacional Africano] *s.* partido político sudafricano que se oponía al *apartheid* (pág. 624)

Afrikaner [afrikáner] *s.* sudafricano descendiente de europeos que habla un idioma denominado afrikáans (pág. 624)

agricultural revolution [revolución agrícola] *s.* el cambio de recolectar alimentos a cultivarlos (pág. 96)

Aksum *s.* imperio que controló la mayor parte del norte de Etiopía desde el siglo I hasta el siglo VIII a.C. (pág. 606)

alpaca *s.* mamífero suramericano de la misma familia que la llama (pág. 272)

Alpine [alpino] *adj.* relativo a la cadena montañosa de los Alpes (pág. 382)

Alps [Alpes, los] *s.* la cadena montañosa más alta de Europa, que se extiende por el sur de Europa (pág. 326)

altiplano *s.* meseta situada a gran altitud (págs. 204, 272)

Amazon River [río Amazonas] *s.* el río más extenso de Suramérica (aproximadamente 4,000 millas o 6,400 kilómetros) y el segundo más extenso del mundo (pág. 204)

amendment [enmienda] *s.* cambio realizado por escrito a la Constitución de EUA, que debe pasar un proceso de aprobación (pág. 146)

Amundsen, Roald *s.* explorador polar noruego, primero en llegar al Polo Sur (pág. 920)

Anatolian peninsula [península de Anatolia] *s.* en el sudoeste de Asia, entre el mar Negro y el mar Mediterráneo (pág. 652)

ancestor [ancestro] *s.* antepasado (pág. 544)

Andes Mountains [Cordillera de los Andes] *s.* cadena montañosa ubicada en la costa oeste de Suramérica, que se extiende a lo largo de todo el continente (pág. 204)

animism [animismo] *s.* creencia en la existencia de espíritus en los animales, plantas, fuerzas naturales y ancestros (pág. 544)

annex [anexar] *v.* añadir a un territorio existente (pág. 230)

Antarctic Peninsula [Península Antártica] *s.* península en forma de S que forma parte de la cadena de la cordillera de los Andes (pág. 920)

Antarctic Treaty [Tratado Antártico] *s.* acuerdo firmado en 1959 que acordó el uso pacífico de la Antártida (pág. 920)

anthropologist [antropólogo] *s.* científico que estudia la cultura (pág. 88)

apartheid [*apartheid*] *s.* política oficial de segregación racial establecida en Sudáfrica desde 1950 hasta 1991 (pág. 624)

Appalachian Mountains [montes Apalaches] *s.* cadena montañosa en el este de los Estados Unidos, que corre paralela al océano Atlántico (pág. 122)

Aquino, Corazon [Corazón Aquino] *s.* política que se opuso a Marcos y fue presidenta de las Filipinas entre 1986 y 1992 (pág. 864)

Arabian Peninsula [Península Arábiga] *s.* península del sudoeste de Asia, entre el mar Rojo y el golfo Pérsico (pág. 652)

Aral Sea [Mar de Aral] *s.* cuerpo de agua interior ubicado en Asia central que se está reduciendo de manera continua (pág. 496)

archipelago [archipiélago] *s.* conjunto de islas agrupadas, que a veces toma la forma de un arco curvo (págs. 198, 736, 852, 864)

artisan [artesano] *s.* trabajador hábil en fabricar con sus manos productos o arte (pág. 254)

Aryan [ario] *s.* uno de los grupos de pastores nómadas indoeuropeos, que se cree emigraron al subcontinente indio (pág. 698)

Ashanti [asante o ashanti] *s.* un pueblo de Ghana (págs. 580, 586)

Aswan High Dam [presa de Asuán] *s.* estructura para controlar las inundaciones del río Nilo y para proporcionar electricidad (pág. 554)

Atlas Mountains [montes Atlas] *s.* grupo de cadenas montañosas que se extiende desde Marruecos hasta Túnez (pág. 568)

atmosphere [atmósfera] *s.* capa de gases que rodea la Tierra (pág. 34)

atoll [atolón] *s.* arrecife de coral en forma de anillo que contiene una laguna central sin islas en su interior (pág. 912)

Aung, San Suu Kyi *s.* líder del movimiento democrático de Myanmar (pág. 858)

autonomy [autonomía] *s.* gobernabilidad propia o independencia (pág. 376)

Aztec [azteca] *s.* antigua civilización del valle de México (pág. 212)

B

Bahasa Indonesia [indonesio] *s.* lengua común de Indonesia (pág. 864)

Baltic States [Países Bálticos] *s.* Letonia, Lituania y Estonia, tres países cuyas costas dan al mar Báltico (pág. 424)

Bangalore [Bengaluru] *s.* ciudad en el sur de la región central de la India que alberga muchas industrias de tecnología de punta (pág. 716)

basin [cuenca] *s.* región drenada por un sistema fluvial (pág. 536)

Basque [vasco] *s.* grupo étnico que vive en los Pirineos occidentales y a lo largo del golfo de Vizcaya, en España y Francia; también el nombre de su idioma (pág. 370)

Bechuanaland [Bechuanalandia] *s.* nombre colonial de Botsuana (pág. 630)

Bedouin [beduino] *s.* pueblo de habla árabe y tradicionalmente nómada del sudoeste de Asia (pág. 676)

Beirut *s.* capital del Líbano y centro bancario y financiero (pág. 688)

Benelux *s.* nombre de la unión económica formada por Bélgica, los Países Bajos y Luxemburgo para asegurar la rapidez y la eficiencia en el movimiento de personas, bienes y servicios entre los tres países (pág. 376)

Berbers [bereberes] *s.* habitantes originarios del norte de África y el Sahara (pág. 568)

Berlin Wall [Muro de Berlín] *s.* muro construido por el gobierno comunista de Alemania Oriental para separar Berlín Oriental de Berlín Occidental; derribado en 1991 (pág. 382)

Bhagavad-Gita s. uno de los escritos sagrados del hinduismo (pág. 706)

Biafra *s.* región de Nigeria, habitada mayormente por igbos (o ibos), que declaró su independencia en 1967 pero se rindió después de perder una guerra civil con Nigeria en 1970 (pág. 586)

bilingual [bilingüe] *adj.* que usa o es capaz de usar correctamente dos idiomas (pág. 164)

bipedal [bípedo] *adj.* que camina en dos pies (pág. 544)

birth rate [tasa de natalidad] *s.* cantidad de nacimientos por año, por cada 1,000 personas (pág. 58)

blues [*blues*] *s.* tipo de música donde las letras de las canciones expresan congoja, habitualmente debido a problemas amorosos o a las penurias de la vida (pág. 138)

Boer [bóer] *s.* colono o descendiente de colonos holandeses de Sudáfrica (pág. 624)

Bogotá *s.* capital de Colombia (pág. 266)

Bolívar, Simón *s.* líder independentista del norte de Suramérica (págs. 220, 266)

Bolsheviks [bolcheviques] *s.* grupo de revolucionarios que tomó el control del gobierno de Rusia en 1917 (pág. 468)

Bosniac [bosnio] *s.* grupo étnico musulmán de Bosnia-Herzegovina (pág. 440)

bossa nova *s.* versión estilo *jazz* de la samba, un baile brasileño (pág. 296)

Botero, Fernando *s.* artista colombiano famoso por sus retratos de personas con figuras exageradas (pág. 266)

boycott [boicotear] *v.* dejar de comprar y de usar productos de ciertos orígenes, a modo de protesta (pág. 304)

brain drain [fuga de cerebros] *s.* pérdida de trabajadores calificados que emigran en búsqueda de mejores oportunidades laborales (pág. 424)

Brasília [Brasilia] *s.* capital actual de Brasil (pág. 290)

bread basket [granero] *s.* región de producción abundante de granos (pág. 424)

Briton [británico] *s.* natural de Gran Bretaña (pág. 408)

Buddha [Buda] *s.* palabra que significa "el iluminado", usada para denominar a Siddhartha Gautama, el fundador del budismo (págs. 698, 706, 774)

Buddhism [budismo] *s.* una de las principales religiones del mundo, que se inició en la India y se basa en las enseñanzas de Siddhartha Gautama (págs. 476, 698, 706, 774, 804)

Byzantine Empire [Imperio Bizantino] *s.* la mitad oriental del Imperio Romano, que sobrevivió más de mil años después de la caída de Roma (pág. 362)

C

cabinet system [sistema parlamentario] *s.* sistema de gobierno que vincula el poder ejecutivo y el legislativo a través de la elección de un primer ministro y varios ministros de la legislatura (pág. 176)

Cabral, Pedro Álvares *s.* explorador portugués que en el año 1500 reclamó como posesión portuguesa parte del territorio actual de Brasil (pág. 290)

camel [camello] *s.* mamífero con gibas en su dorso utilizado en el desierto como animal de transporte y para la producción de carne, leche y algodón (pág. 580)

Camp David Accords [Acuerdos de Camp David] *s.* tratado de paz entre Egipto e Israel, negociado por el presidente de EUA, Jimmy Carter, el presidente de Egipto, Anwar el-Sadat, y el primer ministro israelí, Menachem Begin, firmado en la residencia presidencial de Maryland, en 1979 (pág. 562)

Canadian Shield [escudo canadiense] *s.* planicie rocosa con forma de herradura que cubre gran parte del este de la región central de Canadá (pág. 156)

candomblé s. prácticas religiosas africanas que se mezclan con creencias católicas para crear un sistema único de creencias (pág. 296)

canopy [cubierta forestal] *s.* la capa superior de un bosque, formada por las copas de los árboles (pág. 536)

Cape Colony [Colonia del Cabo] *s.* territorio sudafricano donde se establecieron los colonos holandeses denominados bóers a fines del siglo XVII y principios del siglo XVIII (pág. 624)

capoeira *s.* danza brasileña combinada con artes marciales (pág. 296)

Caracas *s.* capital de Venezuela (pág. 266)

carbon dioxide [dióxido de carbono] *s.* gas compuesto de carbono y oxígeno (pág. 48)

Caribbean Community and Common Market (CARICOM) [Comunidad del Caribe] *s.* organización comercial de varias naciones del Caribe (pág. 260)

Carthage [Cartago] *s.* antigua ciudad estado del norte de África (pág. 568)

cartographer [cartógrafo] *s.* geógrafo que traza mapas (pág. 10)

Caspian Sea [Mar Caspio] *s.* gran cuerpo de agua en el límite sur de Rusia, ubicado entre Transcaucasia y Asia Central (págs. 460, 496)

caste [casta] *s.* en la India, clase social a la cual se pertenece desde el nacimiento (pág. 698)

cataract [catarata] *s.* salto grande de agua o rápidos (pág. 554)

Caucasus Mountains [cordillera del Cáucaso] *s.* cadena montañosa que se extiende entre el mar Negro y el mar Caspio (pág. 496)

celadon [porcelana *celadón*] *s.* cerámica vidriada de Corea con un barniz de brillo azul tenue o verde (pág. 804)

Central America Free Trade Agreement (CAFTA) [Tratado de Libre Comercio entre Estados Unidos y América Central] *s.* acuerdo para fomentar el comercio entre los Estados Unidos y los países de América Central (págs. 254, 260)

Central Asia [Asia Central] *s.* región que comprende las repúblicas de Kazajistán, Kirguistán, Tayikistán, Turkmenistán y Uzbekistán (pág. 496)

cession [cesión] *s.* territorio entregado (pág. 230)

chaebol [*chaebol*] *s.* en Corea, un conglomerado familiar que se compone de empresas afines (pág. 812)

Chang Jiang [Yangsté] *s.* el río más extenso de Asia, que fluye a través del este de China (pág. 756)

Channel Tunnel [*Eurotúnel*] *s.* túnel ferroviario entre Francia e Inglaterra que corre bajo el Canal de la Mancha (pág. 414)

Chechnya [Chechenia] *s.* república mayormente islámica del sudoeste de Rusia que continúa su lucha por la independencia (pág. 486)

Cheju Island [Isla de Jeju] *s.* la isla más grande de la costa sur de la península de Corea (pág. 796)

chinampas *s.* en México, islas artificiales utilizadas para la agricultura (pág. 212)

Christianity [cristianismo] *s.* religión monoteísta basada en la vida y las enseñanzas de Jesús de Nazaret y en las escrituras de la Biblia cristiana (pág. 682)

Church of England [Iglesia de Inglaterra o Anglicana] *s.* iglesia oficial de Inglaterra, cuya cabeza es el Arzobispo de Canterbury (pág. 408)

citizen [ciudadano] *s.* persona que debe lealtad a un país y recibe su protección (pág. 78)

city-state [ciudad estado] *s.* unidad política compuesta de una ciudad y las tierras a su alrededor (págs. 334, 666)

Civil War [Guerra Civil o de Secesión] (1861–1865) *s.* conflicto entre el Norte y el Sur de EUA sobre las cuestiones de los derechos de los estados y la esclavitud (pág. 130)

civilization [civilización] *s.* una forma de cultura avanzada que se desarrolló en las ciudades (pág. 666)

clan *s.* grupo de familias que tienen en común los mismos ancestros (pág. 830)

climate [clima] *s.* condiciones habituales del tiempo de una región durante un largo período de tiempo (pág. 40)

climatologist [climatólogo] *s.* geógrafo que estudia los climas (pág. 16)

coalition [coalición] *s.* alianza o asociación, habitualmente transitoria (pág. 362)

Cold War [Guerra Fría] *s.* conflicto entre los Estados Unidos y la Unión Soviética tras la Segunda Guerra Mundial, que nunca se desarrolló en forma de combate armado explícito (pág. 468)

colonia *s.* un vecindario de México (pág. 236)

colonialism [colonialismo] *s.* control de una potencia sobre un área o sobre personas que dependen de ella (pág. 858)

colony [colonia] *s.* grupo de personas que se asientan en una tierra lejana pero están gobernadas por su madre patria, como los Estados Unidos; territorio de ultramar gobernado por una nación, como México desde el siglo XVI hasta 1821 (págs. 130, 220)

Columbian Exchange [intercambio colombino] *s.* traslado de plantas y animales entre América Latina y Europa, después del viaje de Colón a América en 1492 d.C. (pág. 220)

Columbus, Christopher [Cristobal Colón] *s.* navegante y explorador italiano que navegaba al servicio de España y exploró el Caribe y las costas de América Central y de Suramérica (pág. 370)

command economy [economía planificada] *s.* sistema económico en donde la producción de bienes y servicios es decidida por un gobierno central (págs. 72, 424, 486, 512, 784)

commonwealth [mancomunidad] *s.* unidad política de gobierno autónomo que está asociada a otro país (pág. 260)

Commonwealth of Nations [Mancomunidad Británica de Naciones] *s.* asociación compuesta por el Reino Unido y muchas antiguas colonias británicas (págs. 164, 400, 624)

communal [comunal] *adj.* relativo a la posesión compartida de los bienes (pág. 774)

communism [comunismo] *s.* tipo de gobierno en donde el Partido Comunista posee la totalidad del poder político y controla la economía (págs. 78, 260, 424, 468, 764)

compulsory [obligatorio] *adj.* exigido (pág. 362)

Confucianism [confucianismo] *s.* sistema de creencias basado en las enseñanzas de Confucio, un sabio chino (págs. 764, 774, 804)

conglomerate [conglomerado] *s.* organización compuesta por varias empresas de diferentes industrias (pág. 812)

Congo River [río Congo] *s.* el segundo río más extenso de África (pág. 618)

conquistador *s.* explorador y guerrero español que llegó al continente americano en el siglo XVI (pág. 220)

Constitution [Constitución] *s.* documento que es la base del gobierno de los EUA (pág. 130)

constitution [constitución] *s.* conjunto de leyes y principios que definen la naturaleza de un gobierno (págs. 176, 230)

Constitution of 1917 [Constitución de 1917] *s.* constitución mexicana redactada durante la revolución que aún está en vigencia (pág. 230)

constitutional monarchy [monarquía constitucional] *s.* gobierno donde los poderes del rey o la reina están limitados por la constitución (págs. 176, 414, 736, 858, 892)

continent [continente] *s.* una de las siete enormes extensiones de tierra de la superficie de la Tierra (págs. 26, 122)

Continental Divide [divisoria continental] *s.* formación lineal a lo largo de las montañas Rocosas que divide las aguas que fluyen hacia el oeste de las que fluyen hacia el este (pág. 122)

continental shelf [plataforma continental] *s.* tierra sumergida al borde de un continente (pág. 34)

Cook, James *s.* explorador británico que reclamó tierras en Australia (pág. 892)

coral island [isla de coral] *s.* tipo de isla oceánica que es un arrecife de coral (pág. 912)

cottage industry [industria artesanal] *s.* pequeña empresa donde los trabajadores fabrican ítems en sus hogares (págs. 716, 728)

coup [golpe de Estado] *s.* toma del poder por parte de los militares (pág. 586)

cuíca *s.* zambomba utilizada en la samba, una danza brasileña (pág. 296)

cultural blending [mezcla cultural] *s.* algo nuevo que se crea al combinar los elementos de dos o más culturas (pág. 138)

cultural hearth [núcleo cultural] *s.* la zona central de una cultura importante; el área en la cual una cultura se originó y se expandió a otras áreas (págs. 96, 212)

culture [cultura] *s.* actitudes, conocimientos y comportamientos compartidos por un grupo de personas (págs. 66, 88, 138, 212, 544)

cuneiform [cuneiforme] *s.* el primer sistema de escritura conocido, que usaba símbolos en forma de cuña y fue desarrollado en Sumeria (pág. 666)

cyclone [ciclón] *s.* tormenta violenta de vientos feroces que rotan en una pauta circular como un huracán (pág. 658)

Cyrillic alphabet [alfabeto cirílico] *s.* el sistema oficial de escritura de Rusia (pág. 476)

czar [zar] *s.* título de los soberanos de Rusia desde mediados del siglo XVI hasta comienzos del siglo XX (pág. 468)

Czechoslovakia [Checoslovaquia] *s.* antiguo país de Europa del Este que existió desde 1918 hasta 1993, cuando se dividió en la República Checa y Eslovaquia (pág. 432)

D

daimyo [daimio] *s.* en Japón, samuráis poderosos que se convirtieron en caciques guerreros (pág. 830)

Dao [Tao] *s.* de acuerdo al sistema de creencias del taoísmo, una fuerza que guía todo el universo (pág. 774)

Daoism [taoísmo] *s.* sistema de creencias chino basado en la idea del orden natural del mundo (pág. 774)

database [base de datos] *s.* recopilación de información que puede analizarse (pág. 10)

Day of the Dead [Día de Muertos] *s.* día feriado para recordar a los seres queridos que han fallecido (pág. 236)

death rate [tasa de mortalidad] *s.* cantidad de muertes por año, por cada 1,000 personas (pág. 58)

debris [escombros] *s.* restos dispersos de algo roto o destruido (pág. 10)

Deccan Plateau [meseta de Decán] *s.* área elevada a gran altura en el centro del subcontinente indio (pág. 658)

deforestation [deforestación] *s.* tala y eliminación de árboles (pág. 304)

degraded [degradado] *adj.* de calidad menor a la que existía previamente (pág. 48)

delta *s.* depósito de tierra de forma triangular en la boca de un río (pág. 554)

demilitarized zone [zona desmilitarizada] *s.* zona de separación entre Corea del Norte y Corea del Sur (pág. 804)

democracy [democracia] *s.* gobierno en el cual los ciudadanos toman decisiones políticas, ya sea de manera directa o a través de los representantes que han elegido (pág. 334)

demographer [demógrafo] *s.* geógrafo que estudia las características de las poblaciones humanas (pág. 58)

demonstration [manifestación] *s.* reunión pública para protestar por una política o una decisión (pág. 784)

dependency [dependencia] *s.* lugar gobernado por un país del cual oficialmente no forma parte (pág. 260)

deport [deportar] *v.* expulsar de un país (pág. 424)

desert [desierto] *s.* región con plantas especialmente adaptadas a condiciones secas (pág. 40)

desertification [desertificación] *s.* transformación de tierra fértil en tierra desértica; proceso por el cual la tierra de cultivo pierde su productividad debido a que la tierra se degrada (págs. 48, 536)

devolution [traspaso] *s.* proceso por el cual se transfiere algo del poder del gobierno nacional al gobierno regional (pág. 414)

dictator [dictador] *s.* persona que tiene el control absoluto sobre el gobierno de un país (págs. 254, 260, 266, 812)

dictatorship [dictadura] *s.* estado o gobierno regido por un líder con poder absoluto (págs. 78, 568)

Diet [Dieta] *s.* organismo legislativo del Japón, que se compone de una Cámara de Representantes y una Cámara de Consejeros (pág. 840)

diffusion [difusión] *s.* propagación de ideas, inventos y pautas de conducta de un grupo a otro (pág. 96)

discrimination [discriminación] *s.* acciones que pueden herir a un individuo o a un grupo (pág. 66)

diversity [diversidad] *s.* tener muchas maneras diferentes de pensar o de hacer algo, o una variedad de personas (pág. 66)

Dom Pedro I [Pedro I] *s.* primer emperador portugués de Brasil; proclamó Brasil independiente de Portugal en 1822 (pág. 290)

Dom Pedro II [Pedro II] *s.* segundo emperador de Brasil; durante su reinado, en 1888, se abolió la esclavitud en Brasil (pág. 290)

domesticate [domesticar] *v.* adaptar o entrenar plantas o animales para uso de los seres humanos (pág. 544)

domestication [domesticación] *s.* cría y cuidado de una planta o un animal para ser de utilidad a los seres humanos (pág. 96)

dominion [dominio] *s.* en el Imperio Británico, nación a la que se le permite administrar sus asuntos internos (pág. 164)

draft animal [animal de carga] *s.* animal usado para jalar una carga pesada (pág. 884)

drainage basin [cuenca de drenaje] *s.* área drenada por un río principal (pág. 34)

Dravidian [lenguas drávidas] *s.* grupo de lenguas que se hablan en la India desde tiempos muy remotos; en la actualidad, se las habla principalmente en el sur de la India (pág. 698)

drought [sequía] *s.* largo período de escasa precipitación o carencia total de lluvia (pág. 594)

duchy [ducado] *s.* territorio regido por un duque o una duquesa (pág. 376)

Dust Bowl [Cuenca de Polvo] *s.* región de las Grandes Planicies de los EUA que padeció sequías y tormentas de polvo sofocantes durante la década de 1930 (pág. 130)

dynastic cycle [ciclo dinástico] *s.* en China, el patrón de caída y ascenso de las dinastías (pág. 764)

dynasty [dinastía] *s.* familia o grupo que gobierna durante varias generaciones, como en China (págs. 554, 606, 764)

E

earthquake [terremoto] *s.* movimiento repentino de la corteza terrestre seguido de una serie de sacudidas (pág. 26)

eclectic [ecléctico] *adj.* compuesto a partir de partes de diversos orígenes (pág. 432)

economic system [sistema económico] *s.* manera en que las personas usan los recursos para fabricar e intercambiar bienes (pág. 72)

economy [economía] *s.* sistema de producción e intercambio de bienes y servicios entre un grupo de personas (págs. 72, 304)

ecotourism [ecoturismo] *s.* viajes que algunas personas realizan a medio ambientes únicos, en los que se preocupan por preservarlos en su estado natural (págs. 254, 736)

edible [comestible] *adj.* apto para ser comido (pág. 272)

emissions [emisiones] *s.* sustancias liberadas en el aire (pág. 48)

emperor [emperador] *s.* líder de un imperio, que es un grupo de territorios o de culturas diferentes regido por una autoridad suprema (págs. 764, 830)

empire [imperio] *s.* sistema político en donde las personas o las tierras son controladas por un soberano único (págs. 212, 220)

Enlightenment [Ilustración] *s.* movimiento filosófico de los siglos XVII y XVIII que se caracterizó por el uso de la razón y los métodos científicos (pág. 350)

environment [medio ambiente] *s.* el entorno físico de una ubicación (pág. 4)

equinox [equinoccio] *s.* una de las dos ocasiones en el año en que los rayos del sol caen directamente sobre el ecuador y los días y las noches tienen la misma duración en todo el mundo (pág. 40)

Eritrea *s.* antigua región de Etiopía, que se convirtió en un país independiente en 1993 (pág. 606)

erosion [erosión] *s.* desgaste y movimiento de materiales desgastados por el agua, el viento o el hielo (pág. 26)

escarpment [escarpa] *s.* pendiente empinada que separa dos áreas llanas de diferente altura (pág. 536)

estancia *s.* hacienda o finca agrícola de gran tamaño de la Argentina (pág. 280)

ethanol [etanol] *s.* líquido que se obtiene mediante un proceso químico que convierte la caña de azúcar en un tipo de alcohol que se puede usar como combustible (pág. 304)

ethnic cleansing [limpieza étnica] *s.* eliminar un grupo étnico o religioso de un área a través de la fuerza o del asesinato en masa de los miembros del grupo (pág. 440)

ethnic group [grupo étnico] *s.* grupo de personas que comparten un idioma, costumbres y un patrimonio cultural común (págs. 88, 476, 504)

Euphrates River [río Éufrates] *s.* río del sudoeste de Asia que fluye desde una planicie de la península de Anatolia hasta el golfo Pérsico (pág. 652)

Eurasia *s.* término usado para designar a un único continente compuesto por Europa y Asia (págs. 460, 496)

European Union (EU) [Unión Europea (UE)] *s.* organización de naciones europeas cuyos miembros cooperan en asuntos económicos, sociales y políticos (págs. 350, 362, 688)

Everglades [los *Everglades*] *s.* área inmensa de terrenos pantanosos al sur de Florida (pág. 122)

export [exportación] *s.* producto o recurso vendido a otro país (págs. 72, 304)

export [exportar] *v.* enviar algo de un país a otro (pág. 146)

extended family [familia ampliada] *s.* unidad familiar que agrupa a otros familiares además de los padres y los hijos, incluyendo a los abuelos y a otros parientes cercanos (pág. 688)

F

famine [hambruna] *s.* escasez severa de alimentos que causa hambre generalizada (págs. 594, 658)

fascism [fascismo] *s.* filosofía política que fomenta la lealtad ciega hacia el estado y un fuerte gobierno central controlado por un dictador poderoso (pág. 362)

fast [ayunar] *v.* no comer, habltualmente por motivos religiosos (pág. 728)

favelas [*favelas*] *s.* término brasileño para designar a los vecindarios pobres que rodean las ciudades (pág. 290)

federal republic [república federal] *s.* forma de gobierno donde el poder está dividido entre un gobierno nacional y los gobiernos estatales (pág. 266)

federal system [sistema federal] *s.* sistema de gobierno donde los poderes están divididos entre el Estado nacional y los gobiernos provinciales o estatales (págs. 146, 176)

federation [federación] *s.* colonias, estados o países que se han unido (pág. 594)

Fertile Crescent [Creciente Fértil] *s.* región que se extiende desde el golfo Pérsico hacia el noroeste, hasta los ríos Tigris y Éufrates, y hacia el oeste, hasta el mar Mediterráneo (pág. 666)

feudalism [feudalismo] *s.* sistema político en el cual los señores feudales daban tierras a sus vasallos a cambio de servicios (pág. 342)

fiesta *s.* día feriado que se celebra con desfiles, juegos y comida (pág. 236)

Filipino [filipino] *s.* habitante de las Filipinas (pág. 864)

First Nations [Primeras Naciones] *s.* pueblos indígenas de Canadá organizados en grupos culturales (pág. 164)

foreign investment [inversión extranjera] *s.* dinero aportado a una empresa por personas de otro país (pág. 512)

fossil [fósil] *s.* restos de vida primitiva preservados bajo tierra (pág. 544)

fossil fuels [combustibles fósiles] *s.* fuentes de energía a partir de restos antiguos de animales y plantas; se incluyen los combustibles como el carbón, el petróleo y el gas natural (págs. 48, 326)

Fox, Vicente *s.* presidente mexicano perteneciente al Partido de Acción Nacional, elegido en 2000 (pág. 230)

free enterprise [libre empresa] *s.* sistema económico en el cual las empresas son libres de operar, con poca interferencia del gobierno (págs. 146, 176, 784)

French Revolution [Revolución Francesa] *s.* conflicto ocurrido en Francia, entre 1789 y 1799, que puso fin a la monarquía y produjo cambios en la manera de gobernar Francia (pág. 350)

G

Gaelic [gaélico] *s.* cualquiera de los dialectos de la familia de lenguas celtas habladas en Irlanda o Escocia (pág. 408)

Gandhi, Mohandas *s.* hindú del siglo XX que ayudó a obtener la independencia de su país usando la resistencia pacífica frente al dominio colonial (pág. 698)

Ganges River [río Ganges] *s.* río de Asia del Sur que fluye al sudeste desde los Himalayas hasta el Golfo de Bengala (pág. 658)

García Márquez, Gabriel *s.* autor colombiano ganador del Premio Nobel (pág. 266)

gaucho s. vaquero argentino (pág. 280)

Gautama, Siddhartha *s.* fundador del budismo, también conocido como Buda, o "el iluminado" (pág. 774)

Gaza Strip [Franja de Gaza] *s.* territorio estrecho que se extiende a lo largo del Mar Mediterráneo (pág. 682)

Geographic Information Systems (GIS) [Sistemas de Información Geográfica] *s.* tecnología de mapeo basada en las computadoras o Internet (págs. 10, 16)

geographic South Pole [Polo Sur geográfico] *s.* punto de encuentro de todas las líneas de longitud (pág. 920)

geography [geografía] *s.* estudio de las personas, los lugares y los medios ambientes (pág. 4)

geomorphology [geomorfología] *s.* estudio de cómo cambia la forma de la Tierra (pág. 16)

geothermal energy [energía geotérmica] *s.* energía producida por el calor interno de la Tierra (pág. 900)

geyser [géiser] *s.* manantial caliente que dispara chorros de vapor y agua hirviendo al aire (págs. 884, 900)

Ghana *s.* reino de África Occidental entre el siglo VIII y XI d.C. ubicado en lo que hoy es Mauritania y Malí; país moderno de África Occidental (pág. 580)

glacier [glaciar] *s.* gran masa de hielo de movimiento lento (pág. 26)

global economy [economía global] *s.* economía en la cual se compra y vende atravesando las fronteras nacionales (págs. 146, 244)

Global Positioning System (GPS) [Sistema de Posicionamiento Global] *s.* sistema que usa una red de satélites que orbitan la Tierra para dar una ubicación exacta (pág. 10)

global warming [calentamiento global] *s.* aumento de la temperatura promedio de la atmósfera terrestre (págs. 48, 304)

globe [globo] *s.* modelo de la Tierra con forma esférica (pág. 10)

glyph [glifo] *s.* símbolo tallado o grabado que representa una sílaba o una palabra (pág. 212)

Gobi Desert [Desierto de Gobi] *s.* desierto elevado en China y Mongolia (pág. 756)

Golan Heights [Altos de Golán] *s.* región que formaba parte del suroeste de Siria y que Israel ha ocupado desde la guerra de 1967 (pág. 688)

golden age [edad dorada] *s.* período durante el cual una sociedad alcanza prosperidad y realiza logros culturales (pág. 698)

Good Friday Agreement [Acuerdo de Viernes Santo] *s.* acuerdo entre los unionistas y nacionalistas de Irlanda del Norte que estableció un nuevo gobierno (pág. 414)

Gorbachev, Mikhail *s.* líder soviético de 1985 a 1991 que incrementó las libertades del pueblo ruso (pág. 468)

government [gobierno] *s.* organización establecida para crear y hacer cumplir las reglas de una sociedad (pág. 78)

Grand Canyon [Gran Cañón] *s.* barranco profundo que atraviesa el norte de Arizona excavado por el río Colorado (pág. 122)

Great Barrier Reef [Gran Arrecife de Coral] *s.* cadena de arrecifes de coral de 1,250 millas, cerca de la costa de Australia (pág. 884)

Great Depression [Gran Depresión] *s.* período de severo declive económico, desde 1929 hasta comienzos de la década de 1940 (pág. 130)

Great Dividing Range [Gran Cordillera Divisoria] *s.* cordillera de montañas bajas en Australia (pág. 884)

Great Lakes [Grandes Lagos] *s.* cinco lagos que forman el mayor grupo de lagos de agua dulce del mundo (págs. 122, 156)

Great Plains [Grandes Llanuras] *s.* grandes prados del centro de América del Norte (pág. 122)

Great Wall [Gran Muralla] *s.* muralla enorme y extensa construida en el transcurso de varios siglos para mantener a los nómadas fuera de China (pág. 764)

Great Zimbabwe [Gran Zimbabue] *s.* imperio erigido por el pueblo shona desde el siglo I hasta el siglo VIII d.C. (pág. 630)

Greater Antilles [Antillas Mayores] *s.* las islas más grandes del norte del Caribe, entre las que se incluyen Cuba, Jamaica, La Española (la cual incluye Haití y la República Dominicana) y Puerto Rico (pág. 198)

Green Revolution [Revolución Verde] *s.* uso de semillas especiales, irrigación, fertilizantes y pesticidas para lograr un elevado rendimiento de los cultivos y una gran producción de alimentos (págs. 716, 728)

greenhouse effect [efecto invernadero] *s.* retención del calor del sol producido por los gases de la atmósfera terrestre (pág. 48)

greenhouse gas [gas invernadero] *s.* cualquier gas de la atmósfera que contribuye al efecto invernadero (pág. 48)

grid [cuadrícula] *s.* red de líneas horizontales y verticales que crean cuadrados o rectángulos (pág. 666)

griot *s.* narrador de África Occidental (pág. 544)

Gross Domestic Product (GDP) [Producto Bruto Interno (PBI)] *s.* valor total de todos los bienes y servicios producidos por un país en un año (págs. 72, 280)

ground water [agua subterránea] *s.* agua que se encuentra debajo de la superficie terrestre (pág. 34)

guerrilla [guerrillero] *s.* miembro de un ejército irregular que opera en unidades militares pequeña (pág. 630)

Gulf of Mexico [Golfo de México] *s.* ensenada del océano Atlántico que se ubica al sur de los Estados Unidos (pág. 122)

H

habitable lands [tierras habitables] *s.* tierras apropiadas para ser habitadas por los seres humanos (pág. 58)

Hammurabi's Code [Código de Hammurabi] *s.* uno de los primeros códigos legales del mundo, compilado por el gobernante Hammurabi (pág. 666)

hanbok [*hanbok*] *s.* traje tradicional coreano (pág. 804)

Harappan civilization [civilización Harappa] *s.* civilización antigua que se desarrolló a lo largo del río Indo (pág. 666)

Hausa [hausa] *s.* un pueblo del norte de Nigeria y sur de Níger (pág. 586)

Heian Period [Período Heian] *s.* era de la historia japonesa desde 794 d.C. hasta 1185 d.C.; las artes y la escritura florecieron durante esta época (pág. 830)

Hidalgo, Miguel ("Padre Hidalgo") *s.* padre de la independencia mexicana (pág. 220)

hieroglyphics [jeroglíficos] *s.* sistema de escritura egipcio en el cual los símbolos pictográficos representan significados o sonidos (pág. 554)

highlands [tierras altas] *s.* regiones montañosas o accidentadas de un país (págs. 198, 204)

Himalayas [Himalayas] *s.* las montañas más altas del mundo, las cuales se extienden a través del norte de India, separando la India de China y del resto de Asia (págs. 658, 756)

Hinduism [Hinduismo] *s.* nombre actual para la religión principal de la India, la cual se desarrolló a partir del bramanismo (págs. 698, 706)

Hitler, Adolf *s.* jefe de estado alemán desde 1933 a 1945 (pág. 382)

Hokkaido *s.* isla más septentrional de Japón y segunda en tamaño (pág. 824)

Holocaust [Holocausto] *s.* asesinato sistemático de judíos y otras minorías por parte de los nazis durante la Segunda Guerra Mundial (págs. 350, 382, 682)

hominid [homínido] *s.* primate humano; ser humano primitivo (pág. 544)

Honshu *s.* la isla más grande y más poblada de Japón (pág. 824)

Horn of Africa [Cuerno de África] *s.* extensión de tierra con forma de cuerno en la costa este de África (pág. 606)

Huang He *s.* río que fluye desde las montañas Kunlun hasta el Mar Amarillo (pág. 756)

Hudson Bay [Bahía de Hudson] *s.* gran mar en el interior al norte de Ontario, provincia canadiense (pág. 156)

hunter-gatherer [cazador-recolector] *s.* persona que caza animales y recolecta plantas para obtener alimento (págs. 618, 892)

hydroelectric [hidroeléctrico] *adj.* relativo a la electricidad generada por motores que funcionan con agua (pág. 156)

hydroelectricity [hidroelectricidad] *s.* energía eléctrica generada por el agua (pág. 304)

hydroelectric power [energía hidroeléctrica] *s.* electricidad generada por motores que funcionan gracias a la fuerza del agua (págs. 326, 756, 900)

hydrologic cycle [ciclo hidrológico] *s.* circulación del agua entre la Tierra, los océanos y la atmósfera (pág. 34)

I

ice shelf [barrera de hielo] *s.* inmensa capa plana de hielo que se extiende sobre un cuerpo de agua, pero permanece unida a la tierra (pág. 920)

iceberg [glaciar] *s.* gran pedazo de hielo flotante (pág. 920)

icecap [casquete glaciar] *s.* glaciar que cubre un área extensa (pág. 920)

icon [ícono] *s.* imagen religiosa usada por los cristianos ortodoxos en su culto (pág. 476)

Igbo [igbo] *s.* pueblo del sureste de Nigeria (pág. 586)

igloo [iglú] *s.* vivienda hecha de nieve (pág. 170)

immigrant [inmigrante] *s.* persona que deja un área para habitar en otra (págs. 66, 130, 296, 408)

immigration [inmigración] *s.* proceso de ir a vivir a otro país (pág. 244)

imperialism [imperialismo] *s.* la práctica de un país de controlar el gobierno y la economía de otro país o territorio (págs. 350, 400, 580)

import [importación] *s.* producto o recurso que llega a un país (pág. 72)

import [importar] *v.* llevar algo de un país a otro (pág. 146)

Inca [inca] *s.* civilización antigua que se desarrolló en la Cordillera de los Andes, en Perú (pág. 212)

indigenous [indígena] *s.* nativo de una región (pág. 272)

Indochina [Indochina] *s.* nombre de una antigua colonia francesa del sureste de Asia constituida por Camboya, Laos y Vietnam (pág. 858)

Indochinese Peninsula [península de Indochina] *s.* una de las dos penínsulas en las que se ubica el sureste de Asia continental; la península está ubicada al sur de China (pág. 852)

Indus River [río Indo] *s.* río de Asia del sur que fluye desde los Himalayas hasta el Mar Arábigo (pág. 658)

Industrial Revolution [Revolución Industrial] *s.* cambio que comenzó en Gran Bretaña en la década de 1760 de producir bienes a mano a hacerlo mediante máquinas (págs. 350, 400)

inflation [inflación] *s.* aumento de los precios o caída del poder adquisitivo del dinero (pág. 594)

infrastructure [infraestructura] *s.* servicios básicos que necesita una comunidad, tales como carreteras, ferrocarriles, agua y líneas eléctricas, escuelas y oficinas de correos (pág. 594)

innovation [innovación] *s.* algo nuevo que es presentado por primera vez (pág. 96)

Interstate Highway System [Sistema de Carreteras Interestatales] *s.* red de más de 45,000 millas de carreteras que une a todas las ciudades principales de EUA (pág. 146)

Inuit [inuit] *s.* pueblos nativos que habitan la región ártica de América del Norte (pág. 164)

Inuktitut [inuktitut] *s.* idioma de los inuit (pág. 170)

Islam [islam] *s.* religión monoteísta basada en las enseñanzas de Mahoma y los escritos del Corán, el libro sagrado de los musulmanes (págs. 476, 504, 562, 676)

isolate [aislar] *v.* separar o apartar de un grupo (pág. 334)

Istanbul [Estambul] *s.* la ciudad más grande de Turquía, anteriormente llamada Constantinopla (capital del Imperio Bizantino, o Imperio Romano Oriental) y originariamente llamada Bizancio en la antigüedad (pág. 688)

isthmus [istmo] *s.* franja de tierra que conecta dos territorios (pág. 198)

ivory [marfil] *s.* sustancia dura y blanca de la que están hechos los colmillos de los elefantes (pág. 618)

J

jaguar *s.* felino de gran tamaño que habita principalmente en América Central y del Sur (pág. 212)

jazz [*jazz*] *s.* tipo de música que se desarrolló a partir de una mezcla de ritmos africanos, música estadounidense de orquesta y estilos musicales afroamericanos y europeos (pág. 138)

jellaba [chilaba] *s.* vestimenta tradicional bereber; túnica de mangas largas (pág. 568)

Jerusalem [Jerusalén] *s.* capital actual de Israel y ciudad antigua considerada sagrada por el judaísmo, el cristianismo y el islam (pág. 682)

joropo *s.* baile folklórico nacional de Venezuela (pág. 266)

Juárez, Benito (1806–1872) *s.* indio que se convirtió en presidente y héroe nacional mexicano (pág. 230)

Judaism [judaísmo] *s.* religión monoteísta de los judíos, basada principalmente en los escritos de la Biblia hebrea (págs. 476, 682)

K

Kalahari *s.* desierto del sur de África (pág. 630)

Kanto Plain [Planicie de Kanto] *s.* la llanura de Japón de mayor extensión, que se extiende desde los Alpes japoneses al este, hasta el Pacífico (pág. 824)

Kara Kum *s.* desierto inmenso que cubre la mayor parte de Turkmenistán (pág. 496)

karma *s.* en el hinduismo, las consecuencias de las acciones de una persona en esta vida, las cuales determinan su destino en la próxima vida (pág. 706)

Kashmir [Cachemira] *s.* región en la parte noroeste del subcontinente indio; India y Pakistán se disputan el control de Cachemira (pág. 716)

Kente cloth [tela *kente*] *s.* tela tejida de colores vivos, hecha por los pueblos ashanti y ewe (pág. 586)

Kenyatta, Jomo *s.* primer presidente después de la independencia de Kenia (pág. 612)

Khmer Empire [Imperio Khmer] *s.* imperio que comenzó en el siglo VI y había ganado el control de gran parte del sureste de Asia continental hacia el siglo IX (pág. 858)

kibbutz [kibutz] *s.* tipo de colonia agrícola de Israel en el que la comunidad comparte la riqueza y todos los bienes (pág. 682)

Kim Jong Il *s.* líder comunista de Corea del Norte (pág. 812)

kimchi [kimchi] *s.* plato coreano hecho de vegetales encurtidos (pág. 804)

King, William Lyon Mackenzie *s.* primer ministro canadiense que llevó a su país a la independencia (pág. 164)

knight [caballero] *s.* vasallo entrenado en el combate que peleaba en nombre de un señor feudal (pág. 342)

Koizumi, Junichiro *s.* primer ministro japonés de 2001 a 2006 (pág. 840)

Kongo [Congo] *s.* pueblo que habitaba a lo largo del río Congo; reino de habla bantú de la región del río Congo surgido en el siglo XIV (pág. 618)

Korean Peninsula [península de Corea] *s.* masa de tierra bordeada por el Mar Amarillo al oeste, el Mar del Este (o Mar del Japón) al este, el Estrecho de Corea al sur y China y Rusia al norte (pág. 796)

Korean War [Guerra de Corea] (1950–1953) *s.* conflicto entre Corea del Norte y la Unión Soviética por un lado, y Corea del Sur, los Estados Unidos y las Naciones Unidas por el otro (pág. 804)

Korean Workers' Party (KWP) [Partido Coreano de los Trabajadores] *s.* grupo político comunista que controla el gobierno de Corea del Norte (pág. 812)

Kosovo *s.* provincia autónoma dentro de Serbia (pág. 440)

Kurd [kurdo] *s.* miembro de un grupo étnico que no tiene su propio país pero cuya tierra natal se ubica en partes de Turquía, Irak e Irán (pág. 676)

Kush *s.* antiguo reino de Nubia ubicado en el norte de Sudán (págs. 554, 606)

Kyushu *s.* isla del extremo sur de Japón donde se hallan muchas ciudades grandes (pág. 824)

L

lacrosse [*lacrosse*] *s.* deporte de equipo inventado por los americanos nativos (pág. 170)

Lake Balkhash [lago Balkhash] *s.* lago del este de Kazakstán (pág. 496)

land bridge [puente terrestre] *s.* tierra firme que surgió entre Asia y Alaska durante la Edad de Hielo (pág. 130)

land reform [reforma agraria] *s.* acción de dividir grandes porciones de terreno para distribuir la tierra más equitativamente (pág. 630)

landform [accidente geográfico] *s.* rasgo de la superficie terrestre formado por la fuerza física (pág. 34)

landlocked [mediterráneo] *adj.* rodeado por tierra sin acceso a un océano o mar (págs. 272, 280, 496, 728)

Landsat [*Landsat*] *s.* serie de satélites que reúnen información y orbitan sobre la Tierra (pág. 10)

language [lenguaje] *s.* comunicación humana ya sea escrita, hablada o por señas (pág. 88)

language family [familia de lenguas] *s.* conjuntos de lenguas que derivan de una misma lengua originaria (pág. 88)

Latin America [Latinoamérica] *s.* región que incluye México, América Central, las islas del Caribe y Suramérica (pág. 198)

legislature [legislatura] *s.* organismo legislativo de un gobierno (pág. 716)

Leopold II [Leopoldo II] *s.* rey de Bélgica, obligado a entregar su propiedad privada del Estado Libre del Congo (pág. 618)

Lesser Antilles [Antillas Menores] *s.* las islas del Caribe más pequeñas ubicadas al sureste de las Antillas Mayores (pág. 198)

Lewis and Clark Expedition [Expedición de Lewis y Clark] *s.* viaje realizado por Lewis y Clark para explorar el Territorio de Luisiana (pág. 130)

lineage [linaje] *s.* descendencia de un ancestro (pág. 544)

literacy [alfabetización] *s.* la capacidad de leer y escribir (pág. 138)

llama *s.* mamífero suramericano emparentado con el camello (pág. 272)

llanos *s.* prados de las planicies centrales de Suramérica (págs. 204, 266)

location analyst [analista de ubicación] *s.* persona que estudia un área para encontrar la mejor ubicación para un cliente (pág. 16)

location [ubicación] *s.* posición exacta según la latitud y longitud, o la descripción de un lugar en relación a los lugares que lo rodean (pág. 4)

lord [señor] *s.* terrateniente poderoso (pág. 342)

Louisiana Purchase [Adquisición de Luisiana] *s.* acción por la cual el presidente Thomas Jefferson compró el Territorio de Luisiana a Francia en 1803 (pág. 130)

Loyalist [Leal] *s.* persona que apoyó a Gran Bretaña durante la Guerra Revolucionaria Norteamericana (pág. 164)

M

Maghrib [Magreb] *s.* nombre árabe de África del norte, que significa "el oeste" (pág. 568)

magma *s.* roca fundida (pág. 26)

Magna Carta [Carta Magna] *s.* carta, o documento, firmado por el rey Juan de Inglaterra en 1215 que limitaba el poder del monarca y le garantizaba derechos básicos a los nobles (pág. 400)

Magyar [magiar] *s.* persona de la etnia húngara o el idioma húngaro (pág. 432)

mainland [continente] *s.* masa terrestre principal de un continente o territorio, excluyendo a sus islas o penínsulas (pág. 400)

Malay Peninsula [península de Malaya] *s.* la segunda península del sureste de Asia continental; la franja estrecha de tierra que sirve como puente entre el continente y las islas (pág. 852)

Mali [Malí] *s.* imperio de África Occidental entre el siglo XIII d.C. y el siglo XVI d.C.; país actual de África Occidental (pág. 580)

Mandela, Nelson *s.* primer presidente africano de Sudáfrica (pág. 624)

manifest destiny [destino manifiesto] *s.* idea de que Estados Unidos debía poseer toda la tierra entre, e inclusive más allá de, los océanos Atlántico y Pacífico (pág. 130)

manor [finca solariega] *s.* casa del noble y las aldeas ubicadas en sus tierras donde vivían los campesinos (pág. 342)

Mao Zedong [Mao Tsé Tung] *s.* líder comunista de China entre 1949 y 1976 (pág. 764)

Maori [maorí] *s.* pueblo de Polinesia compuesto por los primeros habitantes de Nueva Zelanda (pág. 900)

map [mapa] *s.* representación de una parte de la Tierra (pág. 10)

maquiladora *s.* fábrica en la que los materiales son importados y ensamblados para producir bienes de exportación (págs. 244, 254)

Marcos, Ferdinand *s.* presidente dictatorial de las Filipinas entre 1965 y 1986 (pág. 864)

market economy [economía de mercado] *s.* sistema económico en el que la producción de bienes y servicios se determina según la oferta y la demanda de los consumidores (págs. 72, 146, 382, 424, 486, 512)

marsupial *s.* animal provisto de una bolsa abdominal para llevar a sus crías (pág. 884)

Marxist [marxista] *s.* persona que apoya la filosofía subyacente al comunismo, incluyendo la posesión de la tierra y de los medios de producción por parte del gobierno (pág. 630)

Mau Mau *s.* movimiento por la independencia de Kenia que comenzó en la década de 1940 (pág. 612)

Maya [maya] *s.* civilización antigua ubicada en lo que hoy es la Península de Yucatán, Guatemala y el norte de Belice (pág. 212)

mechanized [mecanizado] *adj.* equipado con maquinaria (págs. 304, 892)

medieval *adj.* relativo a la Edad Media (pág. 342)

Mekong River [río Mekong] *s.* río principal que corre hacia el sur, desde el sur de China a través de Laos, Camboya y Vietnam (pág. 852)

Melanesia *s.* subregión de Oceanía que incluye las islas al noreste de Australia y al sur del ecuador (pág. 912)

Mercosur *s.* asociación de varios países de Suramérica con el fin de promover el comercio entre los países (pág. 280)

Mesopotamia *s.* tierra entre los ríos Tigris y Éufrates (pág. 666)

mestizo *s.* persona con mezcla de ancestros europeos y americanos nativos (págs. 220, 254)

Mexican Revolution [Revolución Mexicana] *s.* lucha por lograr reformas en México entre 1910 y 1920 (pág. 230)

Micronesia *s.* subregión de Oceanía que incluye las islas al este de las Filipinas y al norte del ecuador (pág. 912)

microstate [microestado] *s.* país independiente con un área y una población muy pequeñas (pág. 858)

Middle Ages [Edad Media] *s.* período entre la caída del Imperio Romano y la Edad Moderna, desde aproximadamente el 476 d.C. hasta 1453 (pág. 342)

Middle Kingdom [Reino Medio] *s.* antiguo nombre chino de China (pág. 764)

migration [migración] *s.* proceso de trasladarse a una nueva región (pág. 66)

militarism [militarismo] *s.* uso agresivo de las fuerzas armadas por parte de un gobierno (pág. 840)

millet [mijo] *s.* grano cultivado en África Occidental, a menudo convertido en gachas (pág. 594)

Milosevic, Slobodan *s.* presidente de Serbia desde 1989 a 1997, y de Yugoslavia desde 1997 a 2000; una figura clave en los conflictos étnicos de los países balcánicos en la década de 1990 (pág. 440)

missionary [misionero] *s.* persona enviada para realizar trabajo religioso en otro lugar (pág. 88)

Mississippi River [río Misisipi] *s.* río más largo y vía fluvial principal de los Estados Unidos (pág. 122)

Mobuto Sese Seko *s.* dictador de la República Democrática del Congo desde 1965 a 1997 (pág. 618)

modernize [modernizar] *v.* aceptar nuevas costumbres o ideas (págs. 562, 606)

monarch [monarca] *s.* rey o reina que gobierna un país o territorio (pág. 716)

monarchy [monarquía] *s.* tipo de gobierno en el cual una familia gobernante encabezada por un rey o una reina ejerce el poder político (págs. 78, 334)

monotheism [monoteísmo] *s.* creencia en un solo dios (pág. 676)

monsoon [monzón] *s.* sistema de vientos estacionales que produce una estación húmeda o seca en una región, en ocasiones con lluvias intensas (págs. 612, 658, 796, 852)

Moors [moros] *s.* grupo de musulmanes de África del Norte que conquistó España en el siglo VIII (pág. 370)

mosaic [mosaico] *s.* imagen creada al colocar pequeñas piezas coloreadas de piedra, azulejo o vidrio sobre una superficie (pág. 266)

Mount Everest [Monte Everest] *s.* la montaña más alta del mundo, ubicada en los Himalayas (pág. 658)

Mount Fuji [Monte Fuji] *s.* la cumbre más alta de Japón (pág. 824)

Mount Kilimanjaro [Monte Kilimanjaro] *s.* la montaña más alta de África, al noreste de Tanzania (pág. 536)

Mount McKinley [Monte McKinley (también llamado Denali)] *s.* montaña más alta de América del Norte, ubicada en Alaska (pág. 122)

Mount Paektu [Monte Paektu] *s.* la montaña más alta de la Península Coreana (9,003 pies) (pág. 796)

Muhammad (Mohammed) [Mahoma] *s.* fundador y profeta principal del islam (pág. 676)

multicultural [multicultural] *adj.* relativo a muchas culturas diferentes o que las incluye (pág. 408)

multilingual [multilingüe] *s.* capaz de hablar muchos idiomas (pág. 376)

multinational corporation [corporación multinacional] *s.* compañía que opera en más de un país (pág. 146)

mummy [momia] *s.* cuerpo preparado para el entierro de conformidad con la antigua práctica egipcia (pág. 554)

mural *s.* pintura hecha sobre una pared (págs. 236, 296)

Musa, Mansa *s.* líder del Imperio Malí desde 1312 a 1337 aproximadamente (pág. 580)

Muslim [musulmán] *s.* seguidor del islam (págs. 504, 562, 676)

N

Nagorno-Karabakh [Nagorno Karabaj] *s.* provincia de Azerbaiyán sobre la que los armenios tienen reclamos territoriales, pues creen que debe ser parte de su país (pág. 512)

National People's Congress (NPC) [Congreso Nacional del Pueblo] *s.* organismo legislativo nacional de China (pág. 784)

nationalism [nacionalismo] *s.* orgullo por la propia nación y lealtad a ella (págs. 350, 362)

natural resource [recurso natural] *s.* algo que se halla en la naturaleza que es necesario o útil para los seres humanos (pág. 72)

neutrality [neutralidad] *s.* política de no tomar parte en la guerra (pág. 382)

Nile River [río Nilo] *s.* río más largo del mundo, que desemboca en el Mar Mediterráneo al noreste de Egipto (págs. 536, 554)

nirvana *s.* en el budismo, estado de sabiduría que rompe con el ciclo de la reencarnación (pág. 706)

Nkrumah, Kwame *s.* primer presidente de la actual Ghana (pág. 586)

nomad [nómada] *s.* miembro de un grupo que vive del pastoreo de animales y que se desplaza de un lugar a otro con el cambio de estación (págs. 96, 504)

nonviolent resistance [resistencia pacífica] *s.* método de protesta que atrae la atención hacia un problema sin usar la violencia (pág. 698)

Nordic [nórdico] *adj.* relativo a Escandinavia (pág. 388)

North American Free Trade Agreement (NAFTA) [Tratado de Libre Comercio de América del Norte] *s.* acuerdo que redujo las barreras comerciales aduaneras entre México, Canadá y los Estados Unidos (págs. 244, 254)

North Atlantic Drift [Corriente del Atlántico Norte] *s.* corriente oceánica cálida que ayuda a mantener moderado el clima de Europa (pág. 326)

North China Plain [Planicie del Norte de China] *s.* región fértil entre los ríos Huang He y Chang Jiang (pág. 764)

Northern European Plain [Planicie del Norte de Europa] *s.* área vasta de tierras llanas o de relieve leve que se extiende desde Francia hasta Rusia (págs. 326, 376)

Nubia *s.* en la antigüedad, el valle del río Nilo al sur de Egipto y al norte de Sudán (pág. 554)

Nunavut *s.* territorio creado en 1999 con la parte este de los Territorios del Noroeste, hogar de muchos inuit (pág. 156)

O

oasis *s.* sitio verde o fértil de un desierto, creado por aguas subterráneas que llegan a la superficie (pág. 652)

obelisk [obelisco] *s.* monumento de piedra con forma de columna (pág. 606)

Oceania [Oceanía] *s.* región del Océano Pacífico con miles de islas (pág. 912)

oceanic island [isla oceánica] *s.* isla que emerge del fondo del mar sobre una base volcánica (pág. 912)

official language [idioma oficial] *s.* idioma que de acuerdo con la ley debe ser usado en los asuntos del gobierno, los negocios y la educación (pág. 138)

oligarchy [oligarquía] *s.* gobierno regido por unos pocos individuos poderosos (págs. 78, 334)

Olmec [olmeca] *s.* civilización antigua a lo largo de la Costa del Golfo en lo que hoy es el sur de México (pág. 212)

ombudsman [defensor del pueblo] *s.* funcionario que investiga las quejas de los ciudadanos contra el gobierno (pág. 388)

one-crop economy [economía de monocultivo] *s.* economía que depende de un único cultivo para obtener ingresos (págs. 260, 512)

Organization of the Petroleum Exporting Countries (OPEC) [Organización de Países Exportadores de Petróleo (OPEP)] *s.* grupo de países productores de petróleo fundado en 1960 (pág. 676)

Orthodox Christianity [cristianismo ortodoxo] *s.* rama oriental del cristianismo que se difundió en Rusia en el siglo X y se convirtió en su religión oficial (pág. 476)

Ottoman Empire [Imperio Otomano] *s.* imperio musulmán basado en Turquía que duró desde el siglo XIV hasta 1922 (págs. 676, 688)

Outback [*outback*, desierto australiano] *s.* región interior de Australia (pág. 884)

outcropping [filón] *s.* afloramiento de una masa metalífera o pétrea que asoma a la superficie del terreno (pág. 884)

ozone hole [agujero de ozono] *s.* disminución estacional de una capa protectora de gas atmosférico que se encuentra por encima de la Antártida (pág. 920)

P

Pakeha *s.* palabra maorí que significa "gente blanca" (pág. 900)

Palestine Liberation Organization (PLO) [Organización para la Liberación de Palestina (OLP)] *s.* grupo político que dice representar a todos los palestinos y trabajar para la obtención de una nación palestina independiente (págs. 682, 688)

Palestinian territories [territorios palestinos] *s.* Cisjordania y la Franja de Gaza juntas (pág. 682)

Pampas *s.* llanuras cubiertas de pasto en la zona central del sur de Suramérica (págs. 204, 280)

Pan-Africanism [panafricanismo] *s.* movimiento que reclama la unidad de todas las personas de ascendencia africana (pág. 580)

papyrus [papiro] *s.* material semejante al papel hecho de los tallos de la caña de papiro (pág. 554)

Parliament [Parlamento] *s.* legislatura nacional del Reino Unido (págs. 176, 400)

parliamentary [parlamentario] *adj.* relativo a un gobierno que tiene un parlamento como poder legislativo (pág. 716)

patrician [patricio] *s.* terrateniente acaudalado que ocupaba un alto puesto gubernamental en la antigua Roma (pág. 334)

patrilineal *adj.* descendencia de padre a padre, o predominio de la línea paterna en una organización social (pág. 544)

patron [mecenas] *s.* persona acaudalada o poderosa que provee dinero, apoyo y ánimo a un artista o a una causa (pág. 342)

peacekeeping [fuerza de paz] *s.* relativo a las fuerzas armadas cuyo propósito es prevenir, evitar o poner fin a la guerra (pág. 688)

Peloponnesus [Peloponeso] *s.* la península del sur de Grecia donde se encontraba Esparta (pág. 334)

penal colony [colonia penal] *s.* asentamiento que sirve como prisión (pág. 892)

peninsula [península] *s.* una masa de tierra rodeada casi completamente por agua (págs. 326, 796)

Perkins, Charles *s.* en Australia, un líder de los derechos de los aborígenes (pág. 892)

permafrost [permahielo] *s.* suelo que se mantiene congelado a lo largo del año (pág. 460)

persecution [persecución] *s.* trato cruel por motivo de religión, raza, grupo étnico, nacionalidad, opiniones políticas, género o clase (pág. 66)

Persia *s.* región histórica del suroeste de Asia ubicada principalmente en lo que hoy es Irán (pág. 676)

perspective [perspectiva] *s.* técnica usada por los artistas para dar la impresión de profundidad y distancia (pág. 342)

Peter the Great [Pedro el Grande] *s.* zar que gobernó Rusia desde 1682 a 1725 y trató de hacerla más europea (pág. 468)

pharaoh [faraón] *s.* gobernante del antiguo Egipto (pág. 554)

pidgin [pidgin] *s.* forma simple de hablar que es una mezcla de palabras de dos o más idiomas (pág. 912)

Piedmont [piedemonte] *s.* región alta de montaña entre los montes Apalaches y la llanura costera del sur (pág. 122)

place [lugar] *s.* término geográfico que describe las características físicas y humanas de una ubicación (pág. 4)

plantation agriculture [agricultura de plantación] *s.* uso de grandes granjas para obtener cultivos comerciales (pág. 736)

plateau [meseta] *s.* área plana situada a considerable altura (págs. 34, 198, 652, 756)

Plateau of Iran [Meseta de Irán] *s.* meseta de altura ubicada en el este y en el centro de Irán, rodeada por montañas (pág. 652)

Plaza of the Three Cultures [Plaza de las Tres Culturas] *s.* plaza de la Ciudad de México que muestra partes de las influencias azteca, española y moderna en México (pág. 236)

plebeian [plebeyo] *s.* persona humilde a la que se le permitía votar pero no podía ocupar un cargo gubernamental en la antigua Roma (pág. 334)

polders [pólder] *s.* terreno pantanoso ganado al mar drenándole el agua con el uso de una presa y una bomba y que una vez desecado se dedica al cultivo (pág. 376)

Polynesia [Polinesia] *s.* subregión de Oceanía que incluye las islas del centro y del sur del Pacífico (págs. 900, 912)

polytheistic [politeísta] *adj.* que cree en muchos dioses (pág. 666)

population [población] *s.* número promedio de personas que viven en una área determinada (pág. 58)

population density [densidad de población] *s.* número promedio de personas que vive en una determinada área (pág. 58)

porridge [gacha] *s.* comida blanda que se prepara hirviendo granos de cereal en leche o agua (pág. 612)

precipitation [precipitación] *s.* agua que cae en forma de lluvia, nieve, aguanieve o granizo (pág. 40)

prime minister [primer ministro] *s.* jefe del gabinete y el funcionario principal del poder ejecutivo en un gobierno de sistema parlamentario; por ejemplo, el jefe del gobierno canadiense (págs. 176, 716)

privatization [privatización] *s.* el proceso de vender empresas que son propiedad del gobierno a individuos (pág. 486)

privatize [privatizar] *v.* vender empresas que son propiedad del gobierno a individuos (pág. 512)

propaganda *s.* información tergiversada o imprecisa que se usa deliberadamente para influenciar la opinión pública (pág. 476)

protectorate [protectorado] *s.* área o país más débil controlado por un país más fuerte (pág. 562)

Protestant [protestante] *s.* miembro de una iglesia cristiana basada en los principios de la Reforma (pág. 342)

province [provincia] *s.* división gubernamental similar a un estado (págs. 156, 784)

Prussia [Prusia] *s.* el estado alemán más poderoso del Sacro Imperio Romano (pág. 382)

public education [educación pública] *s.* educación que es financiada por el gobierno (pág. 138)

pull factor [factor de atracción] *s.* motivo que atrae a la gente a otra área (pág. 66)

Punic Wars [Guerras Púnicas] *s.* guerras entre Roma y Cartago durante los siglos III y II a.C. (pág. 568)

push factor [factor de exclusión] *s.* motivo que hace que la gente abandone un área (págs. 66, 236)

Putin, Vladimir *s.* presidente de Rusia que incrementó el poder ejecutivo en la década de 2000 (pág. 486)

Pygmy [pigmeo] *s.* miembro de un pueblo con una altura media aproximada de menos de cinco pies (pág. 618)

pyramid [pirámide] *s.* antigua estructura egipcia, construida sobre una tumba o cerca de ella (pág. 554)

Q

quilombos *s.* comunidades creadas por esclavos africanos fugitivos (pág. 296)

quinoa [quinua] *s.* tipo de planta de la región andina que produce semillas pequeñas comestibles (pág. 272)

quota [cupo] *s.* meta de la cantidad de producción (pág. 618)

R

rain forest [bosque tropical] *s.* región poblada de árboles en un clima tropical (págs. 204, 304)

Ramadan [ramadán] *s.* noveno mes del calendario musulmán, durante el cual los musulmanes ayunan todos los días desde el amanecer hasta la puesta del sol (pág. 728)

rate of natural increase [tasa de crecimiento natural] *s.* tasa de muertes restada de la tasa de nacimientos (pág. 58)

raw material [materia prima] *s.* recurso natural no procesado que será convertido en un producto acabado (pág. 72)

Reconquista *s.* esfuerzo exitoso realizado por los españoles para expulsar de España a los moros (pág. 370)

Red Sea [Mar Rojo] *s.* mar estrecho que separa el noreste de África de la Península Arábiga (pág. 606)

reform [reforma] *s.* acción de mejorar las condiciones sociales o económicas (pág. 784)

Reformation [Reforma] *s.* movimiento del siglo XVI que buscó cambiar las prácticas de la Iglesia Católica (pág. 342)

refugee [refugiado] *s.* persona que huye de un lugar para encontrar seguridad (págs. 66, 440)

region [región] *s.* área que tiene una o más características en común que la unen o conectan con otras áreas (pág. 4)

reincarnation [reencarnación] *s.* el renacimiento de un alma en otro cuerpo (pág. 706)

relief [relieve] *s.* diferencia en la elevación de un accidente geográfico desde su punto más bajo a su punto más alto (pág. 34)

religion [religión] *s.* sistema organizado de creencias y prácticas, a menudo centrado en uno o más dioses (pág. 88)

remote sensing [detección remota] *s.* obtención de información sobre un sitio mediante el uso de un instrumento que no está en contacto físico con el mismo (pág. 10)

Renaissance [Renacimiento] *s.* renacimiento de la creatividad, la literatura y el aprendizaje en Europa desde aproximadamente el siglo XIV hasta el siglo XVII (pág. 342)

renewable energy sources [fuentes de energía renovables] *s.* fuentes de energía que pueden ser reemplazadas a través de procesos naturales en curso (pág. 326)

representative democracy [democracia representativa] *s.* sistema de gobierno en el cual los ciudadanos ejercen el poder político a través de representantes elegidos (págs. 78, 146)

representative government [gobierno representativo] *s.* sistema de gobierno con una legislatura que es al menos en parte elegida por el pueblo (pág. 400)

republic [república] *s.* gobierno en el que los ciudadanos eligen representantes para que gobiernen en su nombre; otro término para la democracia representativa (págs. 146, 334)

Republic of Texas [República de Texas] *s.* gobierno constitucional de Texas luego de la independencia de México (pág. 230)

reunify [reunificar] *v.* volver a unir algo que había sido separado (pág. 382)

revolution [revolución] *s.* el derrocamiento de un gobernante o gobierno; un cambio importante en las ideas (pág. 230)

Rhodesia [Rodesia] *s.* nombre colonial de los países que hoy son Zambia y Zimbabwe (pág. 630)

rig [manipular] *v.* influenciar o arreglar los resultados de una elección (pág. 594)

Ring of Fire [Anillo de Fuego] *s.* zona geográfica que se extiende a lo largo del borde del Océano Pacífico y tiene numerosos volcanes y terremotos (págś. 26, 824)

Rio de Janeiro [Río de Janeiro] *s.* capital de Brasil desde 1763 a 1960 (pág. 290)

ritual *s.* conjunto de ceremonias llevadas a cabo regularmente (pág. 774)

Rivera, Diego *s.* muralista famoso que pintó la historia de México sobre las paredes del Palacio Nacional (pág. 236)

Rocky Mountains [Montañas Rocosas] *s.* cordillera que se extiende aproximadamente 3,000 millas desde Nuevo México hasta Alaska (pág. 122)

Romance language [lengua romance] *s.* cualquiera de las lenguas que se desarrollaron a partir de la lengua romana, el latín, tales como el español, el portugués, el francés, el italiano y el rumano (pág. 362)

Rose Revolution [Revolución de las Rosas] *s.* levantamiento pacífico en la Georgia soviética que contribuyó a forzar la renuncia de un presidente corrupto (pág. 512)

Rosetta Stone [Piedra Roseta] *s.* antigua piedra egipcia que proporcionó un código para descifrar los jeroglíficos (pág. 562)

Royal Canadian Mounted Police [Real Policía Montada de Canadá] *s.* organización de oficiales responsables del cumplimiento de la ley en el oeste canadiense (pág. 170)

rural *adj.* relativo al campo (págs. 58, 236)

Russification [rusificación] *s.* esfuerzo en hacer que los países ocupados por la Unión Soviética se volvieran similares a Rusia mediante la sustitución de los idiomas y costumbres locales (págs. 424, 504)

S

Sadat, Anwar el- *s.* presidente de Egipto desde 1970 a 1981 (pág. 562)

safari *s.* una expedición por tierra en la que se practica la exploración, la caza o la fotografía (pág. 612)

Sahara *s.* el desierto más grande del mundo (pág. 536)

Sahel *s.* región semiárida al sur del Sahara (pág. 536)

samba *s.* música y baile, con raíces en los ritmos africanos; el estilo de música brasileña más famosa en el mundo (pág. 296)

Sami [sami] *s.* pueblo del norte de Escandinavia que tradicionalmente arrea renos; también es el nombre de su idioma (pág. 388)

samurai [samuráis] *s.* soldados profesionales de Japón (pág. 830)

San Martín, José de *s.* líder de la independencia en el sur de Suramérica (págs. 220, 280)

sanction [sanción] *s.* castigo o presión aplicados a un país por no obedecer una orden o ley (pág. 624)

Sanskrit [sánscrito] *s.* idioma antiguo de la India, hablado por primera vez por los arios (pág. 698)

Santa Anna, Antonio López de (1794–1876) *s.* general mexicano, presidente y líder de la independencia mexicana de España (pág. 230)

savanna [sabana] *s.* región de vegetación en los trópicos o subtrópicos con una mezcla de pastizales y árboles dispersos (págs. 40, 536)

scholar-official [académico-funcionario] *s.* persona educada que trabajaba en el gobierno chino (pág. 764)

Scientific Revolution [Revolución Científica] *s.* cambio rotundo en el pensamiento europeo a mediados del siglo XVI que llevó al cuestionamiento de viejas teorías (pág. 350)

Scott, Robert *s.* explorador británico que recorrió el polo (pág. 920)

seafaring [marinero] *adj.* que usa el mar para transportarse (pág. 326)

secular *adj.* mundano, no relacionado con la religión (pág. 342)

sediment [sedimento] *s.* pedazos de roca en forma de arena, piedra o cieno depositados por el viento, el agua o el hielo (pág. 26)

segregation [segregación] *s.* política de separar a la gente de razas diferentes (pág. 624)

seismic [sísmico] *adj.* relativo a los terremotos (pág. 756)

Selassie, Haile *s.* emperador de Etiopía de 1930 a 1974 (pág. 606)

self-rule [gobierno autónomo] *s.* gobierno independiente (pág. 580)

self-sufficient [autosuficiente] *adj.* capaz de satisfacer las propias necesidades sin ayuda externa (pág. 304) *selva* s. nombre que se le da en español a la región al este de Perú que contiene bosques tropicales (pág. 272)

separatist [separatista] s. persona que quiere que una región se separe de la nación de la que forma parte (págs. 164, 370)

serf [siervo] s. en Europa, persona que vivía y trabajaba en la finca de un señor feudal o de un vasallo; en Rusia, campesino atado a la tierra (págs. 342, 468)

service industry [industria de servicios] s. industria que provee servicios en lugar de objetos (pág. 254)

Seven Years' War [Guerra de los Siete Años] (1756–1763) s. conflicto entre Gran Bretaña y Francia cuyos combates tuvieron lugar en América del Norte, Europa y la India (pág. 164)

shadow puppet [títeres de sombras] s. arte tradicional indonesio, en el que se manejan títeres desde detrás de una pantalla iluminada por una luz brillante (pág. 864)

shah [sah] s. título del rey de Persia o Irán (pág. 676)

Shakespeare, William s. dramaturgo y poeta inglés de finales del siglo XVI y principios del siglo XVII (pág. 408)

shamanism [chamanismo] s. sistema de creencias en el cual una persona llamada chamán se supone dotada de poderes para comunicarse con los espíritus y sanar a los enfermos (pág. 804)

Shi Huangdi s. primer emperador en unificar gran parte de China (pág. 764)

Shikoku s. isla principal más pequeña y menos poblada de Japón (pág. 824)

Shinto [sintoísmo] s. religión original de Japón; involucra la adoración de dioses que se cree se hallan en la naturaleza (pág. 830)

shock therapy [terapia de choque] s. en Rusia, término dado al plan económico de Yeltsin, el cual exigía un cambio abrupto desde una economía dirigida a una economía de mercado (pág. 486)

shogun [sogún] s. líder del gobierno militar japonés que comenzó en 1192 (pág. 830)

Siam s. antiguo nombre de Tailandia (pág. 858)

Siberia [Siberia] s. inmensa región de Rusia asiática (pág. 460)

Sierra Madre Occidental s. cordillera que se extiende de norte a sur por la parte oeste de México (pág. 198)

Sierra Madre Oriental s. cordillera que se extiende de norte a sur por la parte este de México (pág. 198)

Silk Roads [Rutas de la seda] s. principales rutas de comercio que iban desde China hasta el resto del este de Asia, a través de Asia Central y hasta Europa (págs. 504, 774)

silt [cieno] s. suelo fértil y blando transportado por los ríos y depositado en los terrenos circundantes (págs. 554, 666)

Solidarity [Solidaridad] s. primer sindicato independiente de Polonia, cuyo cofundador fue Lech Walesa (pág. 424)

solstice [solsticio] s. época del año en la que el Sol alcanza en el cielo su punto extremo al norte o al sur (pág. 40)

Songhai s. antiguo imperio de África Occidental, que tuvo su mayor poderío alrededor del siglo XVI d.C. (pág. 580)

souk [zoco] s. mercado al aire libre común en África del Norte (pág. 568)

Southern Alps [Alpes del Sur] s. cadena montañosa de Nueva Zelanda (pág. 884)

Southern Cone [Cono Sur] s. naciones de Suramérica ubicadas en la parte con forma de cono del extremo sur de Suramérica (pág. 280)

Soviet Union [Unión Soviética] s. nación comunista, compuesta por Rusia y otros 14 Estados, que existió entre 1922 y 1991 (pág. 728)

spatial [espacial] adj. relativo a la ubicación de un lugar y a su relación física con otros lugares, personas o ambientes (pág. 4)

specialization [especialización] s. énfasis en producir una cantidad limitada de un producto específico (pág. 72)

squatter [ocupante ilegal] s. persona que se asienta en tierras sin ocupar sin tener un derecho legal sobre ellas (pág. 236)

St. Lawrence Seaway [vía marítima de San Lorenzo] s. vía fluvial compuesta por el río San Lorenzo, los Grandes Lagos y diversos canales (pág. 156)

stability [estabilidad] s. durabilidad; resistencia al cambio (pág. 586)

Stalin, Joseph s. cruel dictador del siglo XX que hizo ejecutar a millones de sus enemigos políticos (págs. 468, 512)

standard of living [estándar de vida] s. medida económica relativa a la calidad y cantidad de bienes disponibles para un grupo de personas y cómo se distribuyen esos bienes en el grupo (pág. 432)

stateless societies [sociedades sin estado] s. grupos que no tienen una autoridad única, sino que toman decisiones basadas en el acuerdo (pág. 544)

steppe [estepa] s. planicie cubierta de hierba; en Rusia, esta área se ubica al sur de la taiga (pág. 460)

Stone Age [Edad de Piedra] s. primer período de la cultura humana, en el que las personas usaban herramientas de piedra (pág. 544)

strategic [estratégico] *adj.* relativo a un plan de acción diseñado para alcanzar una meta específica; con relación a lo militar, de ayuda en la lucha de una guerra (págs. 432, 728)

subcontinent [subcontinenté] *s.* gran masa de tierra que es parte de un continente pero se considera como una región separada (pág. 658)

subsistence farming [agricultura de subsistencia] *s.* agricultura que produce tan sólo lo suficiente para alimentar a la familia del agricultor, quedando poco excedente o nada para vender (págs. 254, 586, 728, 736)

Sudan [Sudán] *s.* país del noreste de África, ubicado al sur de Egipto (pág. 562)

Suez Canal [Canal de Suez] *s.* vía marítima que une el Mar rojo con el Mar Mediterráneo (pág. 562)

Sumer [Sumeria] *s.* región de ciudades-estado de la Mesopotamia que albergó a la primera civilización (pág. 666)

surveyor [agrimensor] *s.* persona que traza un mapa del terreno y lo mide (págs. 10, 16)

sustainable [sostenible] *adj.* relativo al uso de recursos naturales de tal manera que existan para las generaciones futuras (pág. 48)

Swahili [swahili] *s.* idioma africano, comúnmente hablado en África Oriental (pág. 612)

T

taiga *s.* extenso bosque de Rusia que se ubica al sur de la tundra (pág. 460)

Taino [taíno] *s.* pueblo indígena de las islas del Caribe (pág. 260)

Taj Mahal *s.* hermosa tumba que se halla en India, construida por el gobernante mogol Shah Jahan para honrar a su esposa, que murió en 1631 (pág. 698)

Taklimakan Desert [Desierto de Taklimakán] *s.* el segundo desierto de arena más grande del mundo (pág. 756)

Taliban [talibán] *s.* grupo islámico conservador que tomó el control de Afganistán a mediados de la década de 1990 (pág. 728)

technology [tecnología] *s.* aplicación del conocimiento, herramientas e inventos de las personas para satisfacer sus necesidades (pág. 96)

tectonic plate [placa tectónica] *s.* sección rígida de gran tamaño en la corteza terrestre que se encuentra en movimiento constante (págs. 26, 198, 536)

territory [territorio] *s.* unidad política canadiense que no tiene suficientes personas como para ser una provincia (pág. 156)

Tet *s.* año nuevo vietnamita y el feriado más importante en Vietnam (pág. 858)

theocracy [teocracia] *s.* gobierno regido por líderes religiosos (pág. 676)

Three Gorges Dam [Presa de las Tres Gargantas] *s.* barrera construida en el río Chang Jiang para controlar las inundaciones (pág. 756)

Three Kingdoms [Tres Reinos] *s.* los tres reinos que se habían formado en la Península de Corea hacia el año 300 d.C. (pág. 804)

three-dimensional [tridimensional] *adj.* que describe una imagen en la que hay un sentido de profundidad y perspectiva (pág. 4)

Tiananmen Square [Plaza Tiananmen] *s.* la ubicación en Pekín, China, de una inmensa manifestación a favor de los derechos democráticos que se realizó en 1989 (pág. 784)

Tian Shan *s.* cordillera que se extiende a través de Kirguistán y Tayikistán (pág. 496)

Tigris River [río Tigris] *s.* río del suroeste de Asia que fluye desde una meseta en la Península de Anatolia hasta el Golfo Pérsico (pág. 652)

Tito, Josip Broz *s.* líder comunista de Yugoslavia desde 1953 a 1980 (pág. 440)

Tokugawa Ieyasu *s.* sogún que unificó Japón (pág. 830)

Tolstoy, Leo *s.* escritor del siglo XIX que es uno de los más grandes novelistas rusos (pág. 476)

totalitarian [totalitario] *adj.* relativo a un tipo de gobierno que controla todos los aspectos de la vida pública y privada (págs. 468, 812)

tourism [turismo] *s.* industria que provee servicios para los viajeros (pág. 260)

Transantarctic Mountains [Montañas Transantárticas] *s.* montañas que dividen a la Antártida en dos partes (pág. 920)

Transcaucasia *s.* región entre los mares Negro y Caspio que comprende las repúblicas de Armenia, Azerbaiyán y Georgia (pág. 496)

transcontinental railroad [ferrocarril transcontinental] *s.* ferrocarril que cruza un continente (pág. 130)

trans-Saharan [trans-sahariano] *adj.* que atraviesa el Sahara (pág. 580)

Treaty of Tordesillas [Tratado de Tordesillas] *s.* tratado de 1494 entre España y Portugal que le dio a Portugal el control sobre la tierra que hoy es Brasil (pág. 290)

Treaty of Waitangi [Tratado de Waitangi] *s.* tratado entre los británicos y los maoríes firmado en 1840 (pág. 900)

trust territory [territorio en fideicomiso] *s.* territorio puesto bajo el control de un país por las Naciones Unidas (pág. 912)

tsunami [tsunami] *s.* serie de olas oceánicas gigantes y destructivas causadas por terremotos, volcanes o desplazamientos de tierras submarinos (págs. 658, 736, 852)

tundra *s.* clima seco y frío y vegetación adaptada a tal clima que se halla en el Círculo Polar Ártico; en Rusia, ubicada en el extremo norte (págs. 156, 460)

typhoon [tifón] *s.* tormenta tropical que comienza en los océanos Pacífico o Índico (pág. 796)

tyrant [tirano] *s.* alguien que toma el poder ilegalmente (pág. 334)

U

Uluru *s.* espectacular afloramiento rocoso en el desierto interior australiano (pág. 884)

Union of Soviet Socialist Republics (USSR), o Soviet Union [Unión de Repúblicas Socialistas Soviéticas (URSS), o Unión Soviética] *s.* nación con un gobierno comunista creada por los bolcheviques en 1922; disuelta en 1991 (pág. 468)

unwritten constitution [constitución no escrita] *s.* marco de gobierno que no es un único documento escrito sino que incluye muchas leyes diferentes, decisiones judiciales y costumbres políticas (pág. 414)

Ural Mountains [montes Urales] *s.* cordillera que se extiende de norte a sur y forma la frontera entre la Rusia europea y la asiática (pág. 460)

urban [urbano] *adj.* relativo a la ciudad (págs. 16, 58, 236)

urban planner [urbanista] *s.* persona que crea planes para desarrollar y mejorar partes de una ciudad (pág. 16)

urbanization [urbanización] *s.* crecimiento en el número de personas que viven en áreas urbanas; el proceso de desarrollo de las ciudades (págs. 58, 290)

V

vassal [vasallo] *s.* noble menos acaudalado que pagaba impuestos y servía a un señor feudal a cambio de tierras (pág. 342)

Vatican [Vaticano] *s.* la residencia oficial del Papa en la Ciudad de Vaticano y el centro político y religioso de la Iglesia Católica Romana (pág. 362)

Vedas *s.* antiguos escritos en sánscrito que son los primeros textos sagrados del hinduismo (pág. 698)

vegetation region [región de vegetación] *s.* un área que tiene plantas similares (pág. 40)

Velvet Revolution [Revolución de Terciopelo] *s.* protesta pacífica del pueblo checo que condujo al fin paulatino del comunismo en Checoslovaquia (pág. 432)

Victoria Falls [cataratas Victoria] *s.* cataratas de 355 pies de alto en el río Zambezi, en el sur de África Central (pág. 536)

Vikings [vikingos] *s.* pueblo marinero escandinavo que realizó incursiones en Europa occidental y del norte desde el siglo IX al siglo XI (pág. 388)

volcano [volcán] *s.* abertura en la corteza terrestre de la que fluyen o salen expelidos roca fundida, ceniza y gases calientes (pág. 26)

Volga River [río Volga] *s.* río más largo de Europa, que fluye a través de la Rusia europea (pág. 460)

W

Walesa, Lech *s.* líder polaco, cofundador de Solidaridad, que fue presidente de Polonia desde 1990 a 1995 (pág. 424)

weather [tiempo] *s.* la condición de la atmósfera terrestre en un momento y lugar dados (pág. 40)

weathering [desgaste] *s.* erosión física y química gradual de las rocas en la superficie de la Tierra (pág. 26)

welfare state [estado de bienestar] *s.* sistema social en el que el gobierno satisface muchas de las necesidades de sus ciudadanos (pág. 388)

West Bank [Cisjordania] *s.* región al oeste del río Jordán (pág. 682)

wind farm [parque eólico] *s.* central de energía que usa molinos de viento para generar electricidad (pág. 414)

X

Xi Jiang *s.* río en el sureste de China (pág. 756)

Y

Yalu River [río Yalu] *s.* el río más largo de la Península de Corea; forma parte de la frontera entre China y Corea del Norte; conocido como el río Amnok en coreano (pág. 796)

Yeltsin, Boris *s.* presidente que transformó abruptamente la economía rusa después del colapso de la Unión Soviética (pág. 486)

Yoruba [yoruba] *s.* pueblo del suroeste de Nigeria, parte de Benín y Togo (pág. 586)

Yugoslavia *s.* país en la Península de los Balcanes desde 1918 a 1991 (pág. 440)

yurt [yurta] *s.* estructura portátil semejante a una tienda usada por los nómadas de Asia Central (pág. 504)

Z

zaibatsu *s.* grandes grupos financieros e industriales controlados por familias que poseían muchas compañías en Japón antes de la Segunda Guerra Mundial (pág. 840)

Zaire *s.* nombre de la República Democrática del Congo entre 1971 y 1997 (pág. 618)

ziggurat [zigurat] *s.* templo construido encima de una serie de plataformas progresivamente más pequeñas (pág. 666)

Index

Page references in **boldface** indicate Key Terms & Names and Background Vocabulary that are highlighted in the main text.

Page references in *italics* indicate illustrations, charts, and maps.

E

eagle hunting, *511*
Earth, 24–52
  climate and vegetation, 43–45, *44*
  composition of, 27–28, *28*
  desertification, **48, 51**–52
  earthquakes and volcanoes, 8–9, 26, 30–31, *31*
  global warming, **48, 49**–50
  population of, 59–60, *60, 62*
  rotation and revolution of, 41–42, *42*
  satellite views of, *3, 13, 57*
  tectonic plates, **25, 26, 29, 29**–30, 38–39
  water and landforms, 35–39
  weathering and erosion, **26, 32**–33
earthquakes, 9, **26, 30**–31
  in China, 763
  in Japan, *826*
  in South Asia, 663
  in Southwest Asia, 657
  in the United States, **27**
earth scientist, 20
East Africa, 604–617
  Ethiopia, 584, *607, 607*–611
  Kenya, 613–617
  political map of, *605*
  trading cities of, 613–614, *614*
East Asia. *See also* China; Japan; Korean Peninsula.
  almanac, 752–753
  economic activity in, *749*
  political and physical geography of, *747*
  population density, *750*
  regional overview of, 751
Easter Island, *913*
Eastern Europe, 422–444
  Balkan States, 441–444, *443*
  Baltic States, **424, 425,** 430–431
  Czech Republic, 436–439
  Hungary, 433–435
  languages of, *435*
  Poland, *425, 425*–427
  political map of, *423*
  religion in, 426, 434
  Ukraine, 428–429
East Germany, 384
East Sea, 798
East Timor, 752
eclectic, **432, 437**
Economic Community of West African States (ECOWAS), 82
economic system, **72, 75**
economy, **72, 75, 304, 307**. *See also* command economy; market economy.

ecotourism, **254, 255, 736, 738**
Ecuador, 193, *209*, 275–277, *276*
edible, **272, 276**
Edinburgh, *410*
Edo, 833
education
  in Australia, 896
  in Central America, 258
  in China, 779
  culture and, 90, *91*
  public, **138, 140**
  in the United States, 140
Edward I, King, 402
Egypt, 529, 542, 555–566
  ancient history and culture of, 556–559
  Egyptian and Kush kingdoms, *557*
  government and economy, 565–566
  independence, 564
  social roles in, *558*
Eiffel Tower, *379*
Eightfold Path, 708, R40–R41
Eisenstein, Sergei, 483
ejidos, 234
Elburz Mountains, 654
elders, 548
electronics industry, 845
elephants, *613*
Elizabeth II, Queen, *178*, 415, *415*
Ellis Island, *67, 142*
El Salvador, 193
emeralds, 270–271
emissions, **48, 50**
emperor, **764, 765, 830, 831,** 841
empire, **212, 216, 220, 222**
encomienda, 222
England. *See* United Kingdom.
English Bill of Rights, 402, *403*
Enlightenment, **350, 351**–352
environment, **4, 5**. *See also* human-environment interaction.
  migration and, 68
  pollution and, *169*, 247, 789
  protection of, 307–308
  society and, 7
equator, A2, 539
Equatorial Guinea, 529
equinox, **40, 42**
Ericson, Leif, 389, *389*
Eritrea, 530, **606, 608**
erosion, **26, 32**–33
escarpment, **536, 538**
Esquivel, Laura, 239
estancia, **280, 282**
Estonia, 320, 430–431
ethanol, **304, 306**

ethical system, R38. *See also* religion.
  Confucianism, **764, 767, 774, 776, 777, 804, 810,** R50–R51
Ethiopia, 530, 584, *607, 607*–611
  culture of, 610–611
  government and economics, 609
ethnic cleansing, **440, 442**
ethnic groups, **88, 90, 476, 504, 507**
  in Africa, *579*, 588, *588*, 615
  in Canada, 172, *172*
  in Russia and Eurasian republics, 477, 507, *507*
  in Southwest Asia, *679*
  in United States, *141*
Euphrates River, **652, 654,** 667
Eurasia, 28, **460, 496, 497**
Eurasian republics, 494–516
  almanac, 457
  climate, *453,* 500
  culture of, 509–510
  economic activity in, *454*
  ethnic groups in, 507, *507*
  food in, 511
  government and economics, 513–516
  history of, 505–506
  lakes in, *450*
  landmass, *450*
  languages of, 507
  natural resources of, 501–503, 516
  physical geography of, 497–498, *499*
  political map of, *495*
  population density, *452*
  population of, *450*
  regional overview of, *455*
  Soviet Union and, 502–503, 508, 514
euro, 356, *356,* 418
Europe, 324–356. *See also* Eastern Europe; Western Europe.
  Africa and, 583–585
  almanac, 319–323
  ancient Greece and Rome, 335–339
  climate, *316, 330,* 330–331, *331*
  colonial possessions, *353, 579,* 583–584
  economic activity in, *317*
  Enlightenment, **350, 351**–352
  Industrial Revolution in, **350, 353**
  landmass, *314*
  landscape, 327–328
  Middle Ages in, 343–345
  mountains of, *314*, 328
  natural resources of, 332–333
  physical geography of, *329*
  political map of, *325*
  population density, *315*

Chapter 30

910 © Bill Curtsinger/NGSImages.com; *bottom left* Owen Franken/ Corbis; *bottom* The Granger Collection, New York; **911** *bottom left* The Granger Collection, New York; *bottom right* © Danita Delimont/ Alamy; **912** © Paul Chesley/Getty Images; **913** *top left* © Chris Cheadle/Getty Images; *top center* © Peter Scoones/Getty Images; *top right* © David Tipling/Getty Images; *bottom* © Kevin Schafer/Getty Images; **915** © Jodi Cobb/NGSImages.com; **916** © NGSImages.com; **917** © Hippocrene Books; **918** *top right* © Gary Steer/Lonely Planet Images; *bottom left* © Jean-Bernard Carillet/Lonely Planet Images; *bottom right* © Wolfgang Kaehler/Corbis; *center* © Jean-Bernard Carillet/Lonely Planet Images; **919** *top left* © Anders Ryman/Corbis; *center right* © Jodi Cobb/NGSImages.com; *bottom left* © Klaus Nigge/NGSImages.com; *center* © Tim Laman/NGSImages.com; **920** © Photo Researchers, Inc.; **921** *top left* © Chris Cheadle/Getty Images; *top center* © Peter Scoones/Getty Images; *top right* © David Tipling/ Getty Images; *center right* © Getty Images; *bottom* © Maria Stenzel/ NGSImages.com; **923** *center right* © Photo Researchers, Inc.; *bottom right* The Granger Collection, New York; **925** *top left* © Kevin Cooley/ Getty Images; *bottom left* © Jodi Cobb/NGSImages.com; **926** © Paul Chesley/Getty Images.

End Matter

R1 Photograph by Ed-Imaging; **R23** © Mark Newman/University of Michigan; **R26** © HIP-Archive/Topham/The Image Works, Inc.; **R35** *top* © Michael Newman/PhotoEdit; *bottom* © Bob Daemmrich/PhotoEdit; **R36** Screenshot © Google Inc. and is used with permission; **R37** Courtesy of USGS; **R40-R41** *top* © Lindsay Hebberd/Corbis; *bottom* © Dave Bartruff/Corbis; **R40** *bottom left* © Comstock; **R41** *top right* © David Samuel Robbins/Corbis; **R42-R43** *top* The Tribute Money, Masaccio (Maso di San Giovanni). S. Maria del Carmine, Florence, Italy. Photo © Scala/Art Resource, New York; **R42** *bottom left* Luis Romero/AP/Wide World Photos; **R43** *bottom left* © Angelo Hornak/ Corbis; *top right* © Comstock Images/Jupiter Images; **R44** © Reuters/ Corbis; **R45** *top left* Heads of Brahma, Vichnu and Shiva (late 800's). Phnom Bok (Siemreap). Musée des Arts Asiatiques-Guimet, Paris. Photo © Erich Lessing/Art Resource, New York; *bottom left* © Bennett Dean; Eye Ubiquitous/Corbis; *top right* © ArkReligion.com/Alamy; **R46-R47** © Richard T. Nowitz/Corbis; **R46** *bottom left* Muslim men praying in the street. Photo © Arthur Thévenart/Corbis; **R47** *top left* Jassim Mohammed/AP/Wide World Photos; *top right* © Michael S. Yamashita/Corbis; **R48-R49** *top* Photograph by Bill Aron; **R48** *bottom left* © The Art Archive/Corbis; **R49** *bottom left* © Christie's Images/ Corbis; *top right* © Nathan Benn/Corbis; **R50** *bottom* © Yoshio Tomii/ SuperStock Inc.; *top* © SuperStock Inc.; **R51** *left* © ImagineChina; *top right* Chinese ying and yang (200's). Roman. Mosaic. Archaeological Museum, Sousse, Tunisia. Photo © Dagli Orti/Art Archive; **R52-R53** © Bob Krist/Corbis; **R52** © Royalty-Free/Corbis; **R53** *top* © Chris Lisle/ Corbis; *center right* © Paul Almasy/Corbis.

Illustrations

Maps by Rand McNally **A14-A37**

All other maps, locators and globe locators by GeoNova LLC

Illustration by Nick Rotondo/Bizzy Productions **162-163**

Illustration by Peter Bull **218-219, 218** *both*, **474-475, 474, 560-561, 560** *center left*, **664-665, 890-891, 890** *top left*

Illustration by Peter Dennis **348**

Illustration by Ken Goldammer **A8-A9**

Illustration by Martin Hargraves **345**

Illustration by Michael Jaroszko **Graphs, Charts, and Tables, 558**

Illustration by Bob Kayganich **46-47, 46** *top left*

Illustration by Precision Graphics **28, 29, 37, 42, 50, 655, 659, 915** *both*

Illustration by Sebastian Quigley **772-773, 772** *both*

Illustration by Robert Sikora **406-407, 406** *both*

Illustration by Stephen R. Wagner **540**

All other illustrations by McDougal Littell/Houghton Mifflin Co.

The editors have made every effort to trace the ownership of all copyrighted material found in this book and to make full acknowledgment for its use. Omissions brought to our attention will be corrected in a subsequent edition.

Pennsylvania Academic Standards for Geography
Grades 6 and 9

GRADE 6

7.1. Basic Geographic Literacy
7.1.6.

Pennsylvania's public schools shall teach, challenge and support every student to realize his or her maximum potential and to acquire the knowledge and skills needed to . . .

A. Describe geographic tools and their uses.
-   Basis on which maps, graphs and diagrams are created
    -   Aerial and other photographs
    -   Reference works
    -   Field observations
    -   Surveys
-   Geographic representations to display spatial information
    -   Absolute location
    -   Relative location
    -   Flows (e.g., goods, people, traffic)
    -   Topography
    -   Historic events
-   Mental maps to organize an understanding of the human and physical features of Pennsylvania and the home county
-   Basic spatial elements for depicting the patterns of physical and human features
    -   Point, line, area, location, distance, scale
    -   Map grids
    -   Alpha–numeric system
    -   Cardinal and intermediate directions
B. Describe and locate places and regions.
-   Coordinate systems (e.g., latitude and longitude, time zones)
-   Physical features
    -   In the United States (e.g., Great Lakes, Rocky Mountains, Great Plains)
    -   In Pennsylvania (e.g., Coastal Plain, Piedmont, Appalachians)
-   Human features
    -   Countries (e.g., United Kingdom, Argentina, Egypt)
    -   Provinces (e.g., Ontario, Quebec, Nova Scotia)
    -   Major human regions (e.g., Mid Atlantic, New England, Southwest)
    -   States (e.g., California, Massachusetts, Florida)
    -   Major cities (e.g., London, Los Angeles, Tokyo)
    -   Counties (e.g., Lancaster, Lackawanna, Jefferson)
    -   Townships (e.g., Dickinson, Lower Mifflin, Southampton)
-   Ways in which different people view places and regions (e.g., as places to visit or to avoid)
-   Community connections to other places
    -   Dependence and interdependence
    -   Access and movement

7.2 The Physical Characteristics of Places and Regions
7.2.6. Grade 6

Pennsylvania's public schools shall teach, challenge and support every student to realize his or her maximum potential and to acquire the knowledge and skills needed to . . .

A. Describe the physical characteristics of places and regions.

- Components of Earth's physical systems (e.g., clouds, storms, relief and elevation [topography], tides, biomes, tectonic plates)
- Comparison of the physical characteristics of different places and regions (e.g., soil, vegetation, climate, topography)
- Climate types (e.g., marine west coast, humid continental, tropical wet and dry)
B. Describe the physical processes that shape patterns on Earth's surface.
- Earth–sun relationships (i.e., differences between equinoxes and solstices, reasons they occur and their relationship to latitude)
- Climate influences (e.g., elevation, latitude, nearby ocean currents)
- Climate change, (e.g., global warming/cooling, desertification, glaciations)
- Plate tectonics
- Hydrologic cycle

7.3 The Human Characteristics of Places and Regions

7.3.6. Grade 6

Pennsylvania's public schools shall teach, challenge and support every student to realize his or her maximum potential and to acquire the knowledge and skills needed to . . .

A. Describe the human characteristics of places and regions by their population characteristics.
- Spatial distribution, size, density and demographic characteristics of population at the county and state level.
- Causes of human movement
  - Mobility (e.g., shopping, commuting, recreation)
  - Migration models (e.g., push/pull factors, barriers to migration)
B. Describe the human characteristics of places and regions by their cultural characteristics.
- Ethnicity of people at the county and state levels (e.g., customs, celebrations, languages, religions)
- Spatial arrangement of cultures creates distinctive landscapes (e.g., cultural regions based on languages, customs, religion, building styles as in the Pennsylvania German region)
C. Describe the human characteristics of places and regions by their settlement characteristics.
- Current and past settlement patterns in the local area
- Factors that affect the growth and decline of settlements (e.g., immigration, transportation development, depletion of natural resources, site and situation)
D. Describe the human characteristics of places and regions by their economic activities.
- Spatial distribution of economic activities in the local area (e.g., patterns of agriculture, forestry, mining, retailing, manufacturing, services)
- Factors that influence the location and spatial distribution of economic activities (e.g., market size for different types of business, accessibility, modes of transportation used to move people, goods and materials)
- Spatial distribution of resources and their relationship to population distribution
  - Historical settlement patterns and natural resource use (e.g., waterpower sites along the Fall Line)
  - Natural resource–based industries (e.g., agriculture, mining, fishing, forestry)
E. Describe the human characteristics of places and regions by their political activities.
- Spatial pattern of political units in Pennsylvania
- Functions of political units (e.g., counties, municipalities, townships, school districts, PA General Assembly districts [House and Senate], U.S. Congressional districts, states)

7.4 The Interactions Between People and Places

7.4.6. Grade 6

Pennsylvania's public schools shall teach, challenge and support every student to realize his or her maximum potential and to acquire the knowledge and skills needed to . . .

A. Describe the impacts of physical systems on people.
- How people depend on, adjust to and modify physical systems on regional scale (e.g., coastal industries, development of coastal communities, flood control)
- Ways in which people adjust to live in hazard–prone areas (e.g., California and earthquakes, Florida and hurricanes, Oklahoma and tornadoes)
B. Describe the impacts of people on physical systems.
- Changing spatial patterns on Earth's surface that result from human activities (e.g., lake desiccation as in the Aral Sea, construction of dikes, dams and storm surge barriers in the Netherlands, creation of state parks and forests throughout Pennsylvania)
- Ways humans adjust their impact on the habitat (e.g., Endangered Species Act, replacement of wetlands, logging and replanting trees)

GRADE 9

7.1. Basic Geographic Literacy

7.1.9. Grade 9

Pennsylvania's public schools shall teach, challenge and support every student to realize his or her maximum potential and to acquire the knowledge and skills needed to . . .

A. Explain geographic tools and their uses.
- Development and use of geographic tools
  - Geographic information systems [GIS]
  - Population pyramids
  - Cartograms
  - Satellite–produced images
  - Climate graphs
  - Access to computer–based geographic data (e.g., Internet, CD–ROMs)
- Construction of maps
  - Projections
  - Scale
  - Symbol systems
  - Level of generalization
  - Types and sources of data
- Geographic representations to track spatial patterns
  - Weather
  - Migration
  - Environmental change (e.g., tropical forest reduction, sea–level changes)
- Mental maps to organize and understand the human and physical features of the United States

B. Explain and locate places and regions.
- How regions are created to interpret Earth's complexity (i.e., the differences among formal regions, functional regions, perceptual regions)
- How characteristics contribute to regional changes (e.g., economic development, accessibility, demographic change)
- How culture and experience influence perceptions of places and regions
- How structures and alliances impact regions
  - Development (e.g., First vs. Third World, North vs. South)
  - Trade (e.g., NAFTA, the European Union)
  - International treaties (e.g., NATO, OAS)
- How regions are connected (e.g., watersheds and river systems, patterns of world trade, cultural ties, migration)

7.2 The Physical Characteristics of Places and Regions

7.2.9. Grade 9

Pennsylvania's public schools shall teach, challenge and support every student to realize his or her maximum potential and to acquire the knowledge and skills needed to . . .

A. Explain the physical characteristics of places and regions including spatial patterns of Earth's physical systems.
- Climate regions
- Landform regions

B. Explain the dynamics of the fundamental processes that underlie the operation of Earth's physical systems.
- Wind systems
- Water cycle
- Erosion/deposition cycle
- Plate tectonics
- Ocean currents
- Natural hazards

7.3 The Human Characteristics of Places and Regions

7.3.9. Grade 9

Pennsylvania's public schools shall teach, challenge and support every student to realize his or her maximum potential and to acquire the knowledge and skills needed to . . .

A. Explain the human characteristics of places and regions by their population characteristics.
   - Spatial distribution, size, density and demographic characteristics of population at the state and national level
   - Demographic structure of a population (e.g., life expectancy, fertility rate, mortality rate, infant mortality rate, population growth rate, the demographic transition model)
   - Effects of different types and patterns of human movement
     - Mobility (e.g., travel for business)
     - Migration (e.g., rural to urban, short term vs. long term, critical distance)
B. Explain the human characteristics of places and regions by their cultural characteristics.
   - Ethnicity of people at national levels (e.g., customs, celebrations, languages, religions)
   - Culture distribution (e.g., ethnic enclaves and neighborhoods)
   - Cultural diffusion (e.g., acculturation and assimilation, cultural revivals of language)
C. Explain the human characteristics of places and regions by their settlement characteristics.
   - Current and past settlement patterns in Pennsylvania and the United States
   - Forces that have re–shaped modern settlement patterns (e.g., central city decline, suburbanization, the development of transport systems)
   - Internal structure of cities (e.g., manufacturing zones, inner and outer suburbs, the location of infrastructure)
D. Explain the human characteristics of places and regions by their economic activities.
   - Spatial distribution of economic activities in Pennsylvania and the United States (e.g., patterns of agriculture, forestry, mining, retailing, manufacturing, services)
   - Factors that shape spatial patterns of economic activity both nationally and internationally (e.g., comparative advantage in location of economic activities; changes in resource trade; disruption of trade flows)
   - Technological changes that affect the definitions of, access to, and use of natural resources (e.g., the role of exploration, extraction, use and depletion of resources)
E. Explain the human characteristics of places and regions by their political activities.
   - Spatial pattern of political units in the United States
   - Geographic factors that affect decisions made in the United States (e.g., territorial expansion, boundary delineation, allocation of natural resources)
   - Political and public policies that affect geography (e.g., open space, urban development)

7.4 The Interactions Between People and Places

7.4.9. Grade 9

Pennsylvania's public schools shall teach, challenge and support every student to realize his or her maximum potential and to acquire the knowledge and skills needed to . . .

A. Explain the impacts of physical systems on people.
   - How people depend on, adjust to and modify physical systems on a national scale (e.g., soil conservation programs, projects of The Corps of Engineers)
   - Ways in which people in hazard–prone areas adjust their ways of life (e.g., building design in earthquake areas, dry–farming techniques in drought–prone areas)
B. Explain the impacts of people on physical systems.
   - Forces by which people modify the physical environment (e.g., increasing population; new agricultural techniques; industrial processes and pollution)
   - Spatial effects of activities in one region on another region (e.g., scrubbers on power plants to clean air, transportation systems such as Trans–Siberian Railroad, potential effects of fallout from nuclear power plant accidents)